MW01195780

BUSINESS STRUCTURES
Fourth Edition

■ ■ ■

by

David G. Epstein
George E. Allen Chair Professor of Law
University of Richmond

Richard D. Freer
Robert Howell Hall Professor of Law
Emory University School of Law

Michael J. Roberts
Senior Lecturer and
Executive Director of the Arthur Rock Center
for Entrepreneurship
Harvard Business School
(retired)

George B. Shepherd
Professor of Law
Emory University School of Law

AMERICAN CASEBOOK SERIES®

WEST
ACADEMIC
PUBLISHING

American Casebook Series is a trademark registered in the U.S. Patent and Trademark Office.

© West, a Thomson business, 2002, 2007
© 2010 Thomson Reuters
© 2015 LEG, Inc. d/b/a West Academic
    444 Cedar Street, Suite 700
    St. Paul, MN 55101
    1-877-888-1330

West, West Academic Publishing, and West Academic are trademarks of West Publishing Corporation, used under license.

Printed in the United States of America

ISBN: 978-0-314-28703-8

We wrote Business Structures *primarily for students who did not take any "business courses" in college. Two of us did not take any "business courses" in college. And then we took this course in law school, and it was our worst law school experience (until, years later, we attended our first law school faculty meeting). We wrote this book to spare you that fate.*

PREFACE

We understand that many of you are taking this course because your law school requires it or because the last bar exam had both a corporation question and a partnership question or because the class meets at 11 on Tuesdays, Wednesdays and Thursdays. Regardless of the reason, we are glad that you are taking the course.

All law students and lawyers need to understand business structures. For law students, business structures are building blocks in other courses. For lawyers, business structures are building blocks in the lives of their clients, in the lives of their communities.

And, like law students, lawyers, clients and communities, business structures have "lives." This book covers the life cycle of a business, Bubba's Burritos, from birth to death. We will see how Bubba's Burritos' life and legal issues change as the business changes from a sole proprietorship to a partnership, to a corporation, to a limited partnership, to a limited liability company. We will also consider how the life and legal issues of Bubba's Burritos differ from those of a larger, more mature business such as McDonald's.

We will look not only at businesses but also at their owners. Generally, people buy a business or an interest in a business to make money. We will consider how the structure of a business affects the ability of its owners to make money from business operations or from the sale of ownership interests.

DAVID G. EPSTEIN
RICHARD D. FREER
MICHAEL J. ROBERTS
GEORGE B. SHEPHERD

February, 2015

ACKNOWLEDGMENTS

First and foremost we want to acknowledge our thanks to the students and professors who have used the book and made suggestions about improving the book (Freer, Roberts, and Shepherd are especially grateful for the repeated comment—"You can't let Epstein say something like that in a casebook."). A special word of thanks to Scott Ward, an extraordinary teacher and friend.

We are grateful to Claire Jordan, Emory Law class of 2015, and to Steven Lippman, University of Richmond class of 2016, for outstanding research and editorial assistance. We are indebted to Jacqueline Archer of the Harvard Business School Case Services Center for her expert assistance in the production of this text.

We are grateful for permission to use the following copyrighted materials:

Chancellor William T. Allen, "Ambiguity in Corporation Law," 22 Del. J. Corp. L. 894 (1997).

Janet C. Arrowood, "The Buy–Sell Agreement: Alternative Forms," 22 Colo. Law 381 (1993). Reprinted by permission of the Colorado Bar Association.

Adolph A. Berle, Jr., "The Theory of Enterprise Entity," 47 Colum. L. Rev. 343 (1947). Reprinted by permission.

Margaret M. Blair, "A Contractarian Defense of Corporate Philanthropy," 28 Stetson L. Rev. 27 (1998).

Jeffrey Brent Brams, "Franchisor Liability: Drafting Around the Problems with Franchisor Control," 24 Okla. City U.L.Rev. 65 (1999).

James A. Cohen, "Lawyer Role, Agency Law and the Characterization Officer of the Court," 48 Buff. L. Rev. 349 (2000).

James D. Cox, "Private Litigation and the Deterrence of Corporate Misconduct," 60 Law & Contemp. Probs. 1 (1997).

Stuart R. Cohn, "The Impact of Securities Laws on Developing Companies: Would the Wright Brothers Have Gotten Off the Ground?" 3 J. Small & Emerging Bus. L. 315 (1999).

Deborah A. DeMott, "A Revised Prospectus for a Third Restatement of Agency," 31 U.C. Davis L. Rev. 1035 (1998). This work, copyright 1998 by Deborah DeMott, was originally published in 31 U.C.Davis L. Rev.

1035 (1998), copyright 1998 by the Regents of the University of California. Reprinted with permission.

Deborah A. DeMott, "The Lawyer As Agent," 67 Fordham. L. Rev. 301 (1998).

George W. Dent, Jr., "Venture Capital and the Future of Corporate Finance," 70 Wash.U.L.Q. 1029 (1992).

Frank H. Easterbrook & Daniel R. Fischel, "Corporate Control Transactions," 91 Yale L.J. 698 (1982). Reprinted by permission of The Yale Law Journal and Company and William S. Hein Company.

Amy Fantini, "Youthful Indiscretions," reprinted with permission from the May 2001 edition of *The American Lawyer*.

Lawrence J. Fox, "Lawyers' Ethics According to Nader: Let the Corporate Clients Beware," 12 Georgetown Journal of Legal Ethics, 367–376 (1999), Reprinted with the permission of the publisher, Georgetown Journal of Legal Ethics.

Philippe Francq and Jean Van Hamme, "Largo Winch—Hostile Takeover Bid," copyright Dupuis (1991).

Richard D. Freer, "Business Organizations," *Oxford Companion to American Law* (2002).

Roland J. Gilson, "Value Created by Business Lawyers: Legal Skills and Asset Pricing," 94 Yale L. J. 239 (1985). Reprinted by permission of The Yale Law Journal Corporation and William S. Hein Company.

Susan Pace Hamill, "The Origins Behind the Limited Liability Company," 59 Ohio State L. J. 1459 (1998).

Robert Hillman, "Business Partners as Fiduciaries: Reflections on the Limits of Doctrine," 22 Cardozo L. Rev. 51 (2000).

Henry Martin, "money" cartoon, The New Yorker Collection, copyright cartoonbank.com.

Douglas K. Moll, "Shareholder Oppression v. Employment at Will in the Close Corporation: The Investment Model Solution," 1999 U.Ill. L. Rev. 517. Copyright to the University of Illinois Law Review is held by the Board of Trustees of the University of Illinois.

Edward R. Rock & Michael L. Wachter, "Waiting for the Omelet to Set: Match Specific Assets and Minority Oppression in Close Corporations," volume 24, issue 4 (1999) *Journal of Corporation Law*, Reprinted with permission of the *Journal of Corporation Law*.

Gary Roma, Charity Frappe, copyright Iron Frog Productions (1991).

Carolyn Rosenberg & Duane Sigleko, "Yes, D & O Coverage Needs to Be Negotiated," *Business Law Today*, Volume 9, No. 1, September/October 1999, Reprinted by Permission.

Kevin Shelley & Susan Morton, "'Control' in Franchising and the Common Law," *Franchise Law Journal*, Volume 19, No. 3, Winter 2000, Reprinted by Permission.

SUMMARY OF CONTENTS

TABLE OF CONTENTS

———————

TABLE OF CASES

The principal cases are in bold type.

BUSINESS STRUCTURES
Fourth Edition

CHAPTER 1

BASIC BUSINESS PROPOSITIONS
FOR LAW STUDENTS

■ ■ ■

A. BUSINESS IS ABOUT MAKING MONEY

1. THE EPSTEIN-FREER VIEW AND THE ROBERTS-SHEPHERD VIEW

Co-author Epstein believes that most people own a business (or an interest in a business) to make money. He asked all of his relatives who own businesses why they do so, and got the same answer from all: "to make money."

"Remember a few years ago when everything was sex, sex, sex?"

To eliminate the possibility that this empirical research was flawed, co-author Freer went to the exclusive Piedmont Driving Club in Atlanta to inquire of members why they own businesses or interests in businesses. He was able to speak with only two people before being asked to leave. But those two gave him the same answer: "to make money."

Co-authors Roberts and Shepherd, who suffer from more sophisticated economic training than Epstein and Freer, believe that the Epstein/Freer view is basically correct, but incomplete. They say that a business is some form of activity that is organized to "create value" for its owners. This means that the business must create a profit in some sense, but not necessarily in the conventional sense.

First, a business can "make money" without creating value. For instance, suppose an erstwhile entrepreneur used her hard-earned savings to purchase a business for $100,000, which generated a profit of $2,000 per year. While this may seem like it is "making money," no real value has been created. She could have put the $100,000 in a CD (certificate of deposit) at a bank and earned the same 2% interest, without the risks, and work, of starting a business.

Second, a business can create value without "making money." Fast-growing, technology-based businesses often require a long cycle—many years—of continued investment and reinvestment on the part of the owners before the business starts throwing off cash—"making money." Still, if these investments create new products that customers want to buy, and develop a competitive advantage for the company in its marketplace, then ownership in the company will be attractive to potential purchasers, and the company will be able to sell its stock at an increasingly high price. Even if the business is spending profusely and earning nothing, potential purchasers' willingness to pay a higher price demonstrates the creation of value. Whether it is a person selling tomatoes from a table in the front yard or a joint venture between Google and Verizon, the usual defining characteristic of a business is that economic activity transpires for the purpose of earning a profit.

But co-author Shepherd is a more sensitive guy, and thinks that the goals of businesses can be broader than just earning profit. Businesses can be established not only to make money, but also—or even primarily—to help people. Some people who are not the least bit greedy start, invest in, and run corporations and other businesses.

For example, several public-interest lawyers may form a professional corporation the purpose of which is to help low-income victims of domestic abuse. Although the lawyers hope to make a modest living from their corporation, the business form is used to limit liability, not maximize profits. Likewise, the team's owner may run the New York Yankees to win the most games, even if the team loses money.

Finally, of course, there are purely "social enterprises," which may be organized solely for charitable purposes, and these enterprises are organized under different rules and regulations (Sec. 501 of the tax code) and will not be treated in this volume.

The law makes careful distinctions among business structures. These distinctions are based upon who the owners are (a sole proprietor, partners, shareholders, etc.), what rights and obligations the owners have, and whether the business itself is a legal "entity" separate from the owners. We will study these distinctions later. What is important now is to understand that businesses—regardless of their legal structure—are the forum for economic activity, the objective of which is often, but not always, and perhaps not exclusively, to earn an economic return, profit, or—in some other manner—create value for the owners. In other words, make money.

2. VIEWS OF OTHER "GONTSER MACHERS"*

The late Milton Friedman, who won the Nobel Prize in Economics in 1976, is widely regarded as the leader of the so-called "Chicago School" of economics. He described his views on the role of business in a *New York Times Magazine* article:

> In a free-enterprise, private-property system, a corporate executive is an employee of the owners of the business. He has direct responsibility to his employers. That responsibility is to conduct the business in accordance with their desires, which generally will be [to] make as much money as possible while conforming to the basic rules of the society, both those embodied in law and those embodied in ethical custom. * * *
>
> * * * [T]he key point is that, in his capacity as a corporate executive, the manager is the agent of the individuals who own the corporation * * * and his primary responsibility is to them. * * *
>
> Of course, the corporate executive is also a person in his own right. As a person, he may have many other responsibilities that he recognizes or assumes voluntarily—to his family, his conscience, his feelings of charity, his church, his clubs, his city, his country. * * * If we wish, we may refer to some of these responsibilities as "social responsibilities." But in these respects he is acting as a principal, not an agent; he is spending his own money or time or energy, not the money of his employers or the time or energy he has contracted to devote to their purposes. If

---

* You should know that "gontser macher" is a Yiddish expression for "big shot." Yiddish is the lingua franca of business. See generally LEON H GILDIN, YOU CAN'T DO BUSINESS (OR MOST ANYTHING ELSE) WITHOUT YIDDISH (2000).

these are "social responsibilities," they are the social responsibilities of individuals, not of business. * * *

* * * [T]he doctrine of "social responsibility" [is] * * * a "fundamentally subversive doctrine" in a free society, and [I] have said that in such a society there is one and only one social responsibility of business—to use its resources and engage in activities designed to increase its profits so long as it stays within the rules of the game, which is to say, engages in open and free competition without deception or fraud.

Milton Friedman, *The Social Responsibility of Business Is to Increase Its Profits*, NEW YORK TIMES MAGAZINE, September 13, 1970.

QUESTIONS AND NOTE

1.   Would Professor Friedman agree with this part of the "mission statement" set out on the Whole Foods website?*

We Serve and Support Our Local and Global Communities

Our business is intimately tied to the neighborhood and larger community that we serve and in which we live. The unique character of our stores is a direct reflection of the customers who shop with us. Without their support, both financial and philosophical, Whole Foods Market would not be in business. Our interdependence at times goes beyond our mutual interest in quality food and, where appropriate, we will respond. We donate 5% of our after-tax profits to not-for-profit organizations (emphasis added).

2.   Would Anne Stausboll, CEO of the board of the California Public Employees Retirement System ("CALPERS"), which has over $296 billion dollars† to invest to provide for medical care and retirement benefits for California state employees, agree with Friedman or Whole Foods? Should she be permitted to refuse to invest CALPERS' money in companies that manufacture overseas or in non-union companies, even if this might reduce the money CALPERS receives from investing in certain businesses?

3.   In the next Chapter, we will read about agency and principals and reconsider Professor Friedman's statement "acting as a principal, not as an agent."

———————————

———————————

*   http://www.wholefoodsmarket.com/mission-values/core-values/declaration-interdependence.

†   As of December 31, 2013, http://www.calpers.ca.gov/eip-docs/about/facts/facts-at-a-glance.pdf.

Another gontser macher, Warren Buffett, the noted investor,* viewed business philanthropy in zoological terms:

> What many big shots love is what I call elephant bumping. I mean they like to go to the places where other elephants are, because it reaffirms the fact when they look around the room and they see all these other elephants that they must be an elephant too. * * * So my friend [a fundraiser] always takes an elephant with him when he goes to call on another elephant. * * * [A]s long as the visiting elephant is appropriately large, my friend gets his money. * * * And in the process of raising this eight million dollars from 60 corporations from people who nod and say that's a marvelous idea, it's prosocial, etc., not one CEO has reached in his pocket and pulled out ten bucks of his own to give to this marvelous charity.

KNIGHTS, RAIDERS AND TARGETS: THE IMPACT OF HOSTILE TAKEOVERS 14 (John C. Coffee et al. eds. 1988).

3. VIEW OF COURTS

You bought an ownership interest in a business that manufactures fire extinguishers. Do you think that the business's donating money to Princeton University is going to help that business make more money? In our first case an owner of a business that manufactures fire extinguishers is complaining about the business's donating money to Princeton.

In reading the following case, please consider these questions:

1. Who owned the A.P. Smith Mfg. Co.?

2. Who is suing whom for what?

3. Why did the stockholders of A.P. Smith Mfg. Co. buy their stock? Why would stockholders care what A.P. Smith Mfg. Co. did with corporate funds

4. Did Hubert F. O'Brien attend Princeton? Was that relevant? Should it have been?

---

* Roberts and Shepherd objected to our explaining who Warren Buffett is until Epstein and Freer assured them that many students would think Warren Buffett was that "Margaritaville guy" their parents listen to. *Cf. Time Magazine*, July 10, 2000. (Former Secretary of the Treasury Robert Rubin was described as believing that "any normal person would say [Jimmy Buffett is] Warren Buffett's son.") See (and hear) http://www.youtube.com/watch?v=BCb-qRdVSwE.

A.P. SMITH MFG. CO. v. BARLOW

Supreme Court of New Jersey, 1953
98 A.2d 581

JACOBS, J. The Chancery Division, in a well-reasoned opinion by Judge Stein, determined that a donation by the plaintiff The A. P. Smith Manufacturing Company to Princeton University was intra vires. * * *

The company was incorporated in 1896 and is engaged in the manufacture and sale of valves, fire hydrants and special equipment, mainly for water and gas industries.

Its plant is located in East Orange and Bloomfield and it has approximately 300 employees. Over the years the company has contributed regularly to the local community chest and on occasions to Upsala College in East Orange and Newark University, now part of Rutgers, the State University. On July 24, 1951 the board of directors adopted a resolution which set forth that it was in the corporation's best interests to join with others in the 1951 Annual Giving to Princeton University, and appropriated the sum of $1,500 to be transferred by the corporation's treasurer to the university as a contribution towards its maintenance. When this action was questioned by stockholders, the corporation instituted a declaratory judgment action in the Chancery Division and trial was had in due course.

Mr. Hubert F. O'Brien, the president of the company, testified that he considered the contribution to be a sound investment, that the public expects corporations to aid philanthropic and benevolent institutions, that they obtain good will in the community by so doing, and that their charitable donations create [a] favorable environment for their business operations. In addition, he expressed the thought that in contributing to liberal arts institutions, corporations were furthering their self-interest in assuring the free flow of properly trained personnel for administrative and other corporate employment. Mr. Frank W. Abrams, chairman of the board of the Standard Oil Company of New Jersey, testified that corporations are expected to acknowledge their public responsibilities in support of the essential elements of our free enterprise system. He indicated that it was not "good business" to disappoint "this reasonable and justified public expectation," nor was it good business for corporations "to take substantial benefits from their membership in the economic community while avoiding the normally accepted obligations of citizenship in the social community." * * *

The objecting stockholders have not disputed any of the foregoing testimony nor the showing of great need by Princeton and other private institutions of higher learning and the important public service being rendered by them for democratic government and industry alike. Similarly, they have acknowledged that for over two decades there has been state legislation on our books which expresses a strong public policy in favor of corporate contributions such as that being questioned by them. Nevertheless, they have taken the position that (1) the plaintiff's certificate of incorporation does not expressly authorize the contribution and under common-law principles the company does not possess any implied or incidental power to make it, and (2) the New Jersey statutes which expressly authorize the contribution may not constitutionally be applied to the plaintiff, a corporation created long before their enactment.

In his discussion of the early history of business corporations Professor Williston refers to a 1702 publication where the author stated flatly that the general intent and end of all civil incorporations is for better government. And he points out that the early corporate charters, particularly their recitals, furnish additional support for the notion that the corporate object was the public one of managing and ordering the trade as well as the private one of profit for the members. However, with later economic and social developments and the free availability of the corporate device for all trades, the end of private profit became generally accepted as the controlling one in all businesses other than those classed broadly as public utilities. As a concomitant the common-law rule developed that those who managed the corporation could not disburse any corporate funds for philanthropic or other worthy public cause unless the expenditure would benefit the corporation. During the 19th Century when corporations were relatively few and small and did not dominate the country's wealth, the common-law rule did not significantly interfere with the public interest. But the 20th Century has presented a different climate. Control of economic wealth has passed largely from individual entrepreneurs to dominating corporations, and calls upon the corporations for reasonable philanthropic donations have come to be made with increased public support. In many instances such contributions have been sustained by the courts within the common-law doctrine upon liberal findings that the donations tended reasonably to promote the corporate objectives. * * *

When the wealth of the nation was primarily in the hands of individuals they discharged their responsibilities as citizens by donating freely for charitable purposes. With the transfer of most of the wealth to corporate hands and the imposition of heavy burdens of individual taxation, they have been unable to keep pace with increased philanthropic needs. They have therefore, with justification, turned to corporations to assume the modern obligations of good citizenship in the same manner as humans do. Congress and state legislatures have enacted laws which encourage corporate contributions, and much has recently been written to indicate the crying need and adequate legal basis therefore. * * *

It seems to us that just as the conditions prevailing when corporations were originally created required that they serve public as well as private interests, modern conditions require that corporations acknowledge and discharge social as well as private responsibilities as members of the communities within which they operate. Within this broad concept there is no difficulty in sustaining, as incidental to their proper objects and in aid of the public welfare, the power of corporations to contribute corporate funds within reasonable limits in support of academic institutions. * * *

In 1930 a statute was enacted in our State which expressly provided that any corporation could cooperate with other corporations and natural persons in the creation and maintenance of community funds and charitable, philanthropic or benevolent instrumentalities conducive to public welfare, and could for such purposes expend such corporate sums as the directors "deem expedient and as in their judgment will contribute to the protection of the corporate interests." * * *

The appellants contend that the foregoing New Jersey statutes may not be applied to corporations created before their passage. Fifty years before the incorporation of The A. P. Smith Manufacturing Company our Legislature provided that every corporate charter thereafter granted "shall be subject to alteration, suspension and repeal, in the discretion of the legislature." * * *

State legislation adopted in the public interest and applied to pre-existing corporations under the reserved power has repeatedly been sustained by the United States Supreme Court above the contention that it impairs the rights of stockholders and violates constitutional guarantees under the Federal Constitution. * * *

It seems clear to us that the public policy supporting the statutory enactments under consideration is far greater and the alteration of pre-existing rights of stockholders much lesser than in the cited cases sustaining various exercises of the reserve power. In encouraging and expressly authorizing reasonable charitable contributions by corporations, our State has not only joined with other states in advancing the national interest but has also specially furthered the interests of its own people who must bear the burdens of taxation resulting from increased state and federal aid upon default in voluntary giving. It is significant that in its enactments the State has not in any way sought to impose any compulsory obligations or alter the corporate objectives. And since in our view the corporate power to make reasonable charitable contributions exists under modern conditions, even apart from express statutory provision, its enactments simply constitute helpful and confirmatory declarations of such power, accompanied by limiting safeguards.

In the light of all of the foregoing we have no hesitancy in sustaining the validity of the donation by the plaintiff. There is no suggestion that it was made indiscriminately or to a pet charity of the corporate directors in furtherance of personal rather than corporate ends. On the contrary, it was made to a preeminent institution of higher learning, was modest in amount and well within the limitations imposed by the statutory enactments, and was voluntarily made in the reasonable belief that it would aid the public welfare and advance the interests of the plaintiff as a private corporation and as part of the community in which it operates. We find that it was a lawful exercise of the corporation's implied and incidental powers under common-law principles and that it came within the express authority of the pertinent state legislation. * * *

The judgment entered in the Chancery Division is in all respects affirmed.

QUESTIONS AND NOTES

1. **Questions about the facts**

    a)   Who decided to make the gift to Princeton?

    b)   Who decided to bring this declaratory judgment action?

    c)   What is the corporation's "most helpful" fact?

    d)   What is the objecting shareholders' "most helpful" fact?

2. **Questions about vocabulary**

    a)   What does "incorporated" mean?

    b)   Are "stockholders" the same thing as "shareholders"?

    c)   Is a "certificate of incorporation" the same thing as "articles of incorporation"?

    d)   Is "intra vires" the same thing as "ultra vires"?

3. **Questions about the law**

a) What are the possible legal consequences of a court's determination that a corporate transaction is not intra vires but instead ultra vires? What would have been the practical consequences of the court's concluding that the corporation's $1,500 donation was ultra vires? Is the following excerpt from the Model Business Corporations Act helpful to your understanding the consequences of successful ultra vires challenges?

§ 3.04 Ultra Vires

(a) Except as provided in subsection (b), the validity of corporate action may not be challenged on the ground that the corporation lacks or lacked power to act.

(b) A corporation's power to act may be challenged:

(1) in a proceeding by a shareholder against the corporation to enjoin the act. . . .

b) What were the bases for the court's determination that the $1,500 donation to Princeton by a corporation that makes fire hydrants was intra vires?

4. Notes

Note the court's linking corporations to "their responsibilities as citizens" and "members of the communities in which they operate." Other courts have referred to corporations as "persons." Most recently, in Burwell v. Hobby Lobby Stores, Inc., et al S.Ct. (2014).

NOTE ON BURWELL V. HOBBY LOBBY STORES, INC.

We are not asking you to read the Hobby Lobby case. While the case does involve corporations, it is not a case that decided a question of corporate law.

The question in Hobby Lobby was the meaning of a term used in the Religious Freedom Restoration Act ("RFRA")—the term "persons." More specifically, the Court was asked to decide whether the three corporations challenging the contraceptive mandate in the Affordable Care Act were exempted because they qualified for the protection afforded "persons" under RFRA. The majority treated the three corporations as "close corporations" and held that close corporations are "persons" as that term in used in RFRA.

Hobby Lobby does not provide a definition or even a description of what a "close corporation" is. We will consider the questions of (1) which corporations are close corporations and (2) when it matters whether a corporation is a close corporation later. For now, simply consider the following dicta from Hobby Lobby.

Some lower court judges have suggested that RFRA does not protect for-profit corporations because the purpose of such corporations is simply to make money. This argument flies in the face of modern corporate law. . . . While it is certainly true that a central objective of for-profit corporations is to make money, modern corporate law does not require for-profit corporations to pursue profit at the expense of everything else, and many do not do so. For-profit corporations, with ownership approval support a wide variety of charitable causes, and it is not at all uncommon for such corporations to further humanitarian and other altruistic objectives. Many examples come readily to mind. So long as its owners agree, a for-profit corporation may take costly pollution-control and energy-conservation measures that go beyond what the law requires. A for-profit corporation that operates facilities in other countries may exceed the requirements of local law regarding working conditions and benefits. If for-profit corporations may pursue such worthy objectives, there is no apparent reason why they may not further religious objectives as well.

The owners of closely held corporations may—and sometimes do—disagree about the conduct of business. And even if RFRA did not exist, the owners of a company might well have a dispute relating to religion. For example, some might want a company's stores to remain open on the Sabbath in order to make more money, and others might want the stores to close for religious reasons. State corporate law provides a ready means for resolving any conflicts by, for example, dictating how a corporation can establish its governing structure. See, e.g., ibid; id., § 3:2; Del. Code Ann., Tit. 8, § 351 (2011) (providing that certificate of incorporation may provide how "the business of the corporation shall be managed"). Courts will turn to that structure and the underlying state law in resolving disputes.

A corporation is simply a form of organization used by human beings to achieve desired ends. An established body of law specifies the rights and obligations of the people (including shareholders, officers, and employees) who are associated with a corporation in one way or another . . . . . Corporations, separate and apart from the human beings who own, run, and are employed by them, cannot do anything at all.

QUESTION

Do you see any connections between Hobby Lobby and A.P. Smith? Any connections among the Hobby Lobby case, the A.P. Smith case and Danny Devito's "Amen" speech to stockholders in *Other People's Money*, http://www.youtube.com/watch?v=62kxPyNZF3Q.

———

Why did we include the *A.P. Smith* case? Why didn't we simply say: "Corporations have the legal authority to make charitable contributions" and leave it at that? What does this case have to do with business basics??

We have included the *A.P. Smith* case and the questions based on the *A.P. Smith* case to show the following general building-block concepts:

- The law views a business, at least a business in the corporate structure, as a separate entity, a separate legal person;
- A body of law—both statutory law and case law—has developed to control the actions of that separate entity or person;
- Real persons act for that corporation—they are "agents";
- A business with more than one owner, at least a business with more than one owner that is a corporation, can distribute and use its funds in ways that are opposed by at least some of its owners.

Accordingly, owners of businesses who want to make money and persons acting as lawyers for owners of businesses who want to make money (and persons studying the law of business structures) should consider questions such as: (i) who makes decisions for the business? (ii) on whose behalf are they acting as agents? (iii) can an owner profitably dispose of her ownership interest in a business if she does not agree with the decisions others are making? and (iv) how does the legal structure of the business affect the answers to the above questions? We will be considering these questions throughout the book.

The business in the *A.P. Smith* case was a corporation. While we will spend more time on corporations than on any other business structure, we will study other forms of business structures.

B. FINANCIAL STATEMENTS HELP THE OWNER OF A BUSINESS UNDERSTAND ITS PERFORMANCE AND VALUE

As we discussed earlier, the owners of a business are generally trying to "make money" from owning a business. There are generally two ways of making money from the business. First, the owner can receive distributions of all or part of the money the business has earned. Second, she can sell all or part of her ownership interest in the business for more than she paid for it.* But how does the owner of a business (and her lawyer) know how much money the business has made (if indeed it has made any money at all) and how much money the business is worth?

---

* Of course, an owner of a business can also make money from the business by working for the business and receiving a salary for her work. But, one does not have to be an owner of a business to work for and be compensated by, the business. Therefore, we deal here with making money specifically in return for one's role *as an owner*.

The entity's financial statements are the key to understanding the health of the business as well as how much money it is making, and what it might be worth. And, so law students and lawyers need to have some understanding about financial statements. Generally, business entities are required to keep "appropriate accounting records" and to make those records available to the owners of the business. *See, e.g.*, MBCA §§ 16.01(b) and 16.02(b); Delaware § 220(b). *See also* Revised Uniform Partnership Act (RUPA) §§ 403(a) and 403(b). Businesses typically maintain several financial statements, which are provided to investors, the company's managers, and—in the case of large public companies (ones for which the stock is publicly traded)—to the public and to public enforcement authorities. Much as medical instruments measure a patient's vital signs, the financial reports measure the company's financial health. Without accurate reports, the company can sicken or die without managers or the public knowing until too late.

The main financial statements are (1) the income statement, which computes profit (or loss) during a given period (e.g., month or year) based on data about revenues and costs; (2) the cash flow statement, which measures the cash earned, or lost, by a business from its operations during a given period; and, (3) the balance sheet, which shows the company's assets, liabilities and the owners' "equity" in the business at a particular point in time. There are several things you should know about these three statements.[*]

Financial statements are usually prepared according to GAAP—Generally Accepted Accounting Principles. We will not get into intricate accounting rules, but two important generally accepted accounting principles are: (1) *matching*: costs or expenses should be "booked" in the same period as the revenues those expenditures helped generate, and (2) *conservatism*: the data should be conservative—that is, they should present the firm's financial data in an accurate way, but err on the side of understating its revenues and the value of its assets, and on overestimating its costs and liabilities.[†]

---

[*]   An American Lawyer article on the summer work experiences of a Stanford law student [Janar Wasito] supports this view: "Law students throughout the country are clamoring for more training in business as they realize that serving start-ups goes beyond grinding out legal documents * * * 'From what I have seen, the best attorneys are business planners who help chart out the pitfalls and opportunities of a company.' He [Wasito] also plans to take a *second* accounting class this year, noting that if he can't read a balance sheet, 'I'm just a well-spoken guy who has some contacts. Those are fleeting qualities.' " Susan Orenstein, *Golden Boy*, THE AMERICAN LAWYER 80, 82, 84 (October 1999) (emphasis in original).

[†]   Perhaps the most famous example of what can happen when the principle of conservatism is violated is the case of Enron. This large energy firm engaged in a tactic called "off-balance-sheet" financing. The theory of off-balance-sheet financing is that certain activities of the firm may be carried out in other legal entities (e.g., subsidiaries, joint ventures) and that the firm need not show the obligations of those entities on its balance sheet as long as there is no chance that it, the parent company, could be forced to make good on those obligations (this is known as "nonrecourse" debt). When Enron disclosed the existence of the partnerships it had

In reviewing a financial statement, you need to be mindful of not only the principles that underpin the preparation of the statement but also the time period the statement covers. The most frequently published financial statements are annual ones, which cover the company's fiscal year—by definition, the twelve months of economic activity included in an annual financial statement. However, the fiscal year may not always be the natural January 1 to December 31 calendar year. For some enterprises—like a retail store—the holiday season is such an important part of the business that it might be misleading to cut off the fiscal year before the full effects of the holiday sales—and returns—could be accounted for. Thus, many retail businesses have a fiscal year that ends on the last day of March, so they can fully account for the important holiday season in their fiscal year. It is also true that—since most companies have a Dec. 31 fiscal year end—accountants are most busy during this time. Thus, they may give a discount to firms with other fiscal year ends, creating an incentive to do just that.

1. THE INCOME STATEMENT

We begin our analysis with an income statement, also called "profit and loss statement," or "P & L." In its simplest form, an income statement computes the profit of a business for the period in question—usually one year. The computation involved in an income statement is pretty easy: Profit Before Taxes [PBT] equals Revenue minus Costs. Let's take the example of an individual—Bubba—who makes and sells burritos. Let's assume he purchases burritos for $1 each and sells them for $2. If he buys and sells a thousand burritos in 2015, Bubba's income statement looks like this:

---

created as sources of off-balance-sheet financing, it did not disclose the partnership's debt, claiming that the debt in these entities was nonrecourse to Enron.

It turned out, however, that the debt was recourse to Enron under certain conditions after all. That is, the parent could be forced to make good on these obligations. This revelation brought the house of cards tumbling down. Under the principle of conservatism, Enron (and its accountants) should have made worst-case assumptions about what might happen, and should have disclosed these obligations to Enron's shareholders. By the time everyone learned of this, it was too late. Enron's stock, which had reached a high of $84 per share, plummeted to less than $1, taking with it the jobs and pensions of many Enron employees.

Bubba's Burritos Income Statement 2015

	Revenue (from sales)	$2,000	($2 × 1,000)
−	Cost of Goods Sold [COGS]	1,000	($1 × 1,000)
=	Profit Before Taxes [PBT]	$1,000	

Let's suppose Bubba is pleased with his profit and hires two people to work for him in 2016. If he hires two employees at $100 each, and each of them also sells 1,000 burritos (at $2 each), Bubba's 2016 income statement looks like this:

Bubba's Burritos Income Statement 2016

	Revenue (sales)	$6,000	(3 × 1,000 × $2)
−	COGS	3,000	($1 × 3,000)
−	Salaries	200	(2 × $100)
=	PBT	$2,800	

Now suppose in 2017 Bubba bought a $5,000 burrito manufacturing machine, and the machine was expected to last for five years. If we followed the process we've been using, we would add an item to the income statement as "machinery expense" and note a $5,000 expense for this item.

But this would be misleading. Profits would be understated in the first year. We would be charging the business's profits for the entire cost of the machine in only the first year, even though Bubba will use the machine over five years. (Recall the "matching" principle discussed above.) In subsequent years, profits would be overstated because we would be charging the business nothing for the machine, even though we were getting the benefit from its use.

The solution to this problem is to use something called *depreciation.* For example, we could charge the income statement for one-fifth of the machine ($1,000) each year. This one-fifth figure comes from the fact that the machine has a useful life of five years. Thus, at the end of that time we will have charged the business fully for the machine. This $1,000 figure reflects that the machine is getting less valuable each year, since we are "using" part of it up. The portion that we use up is called depreciation.*

---

* The approach we used above is called "straight-line" depreciation. We simply take the value of the equipment, divide it by the number of years of useful life, and then deduct this much each year from the income statement as depreciation. It is called straight-line depreciation because the value of the equipment decreases by the same amount each year in a straight line. Other forms of depreciation, called accelerated methods, deduct proportionally more of the cost of the equipment in the earlier years and less later on. Note also that "useful life" is taken from a table published by the IRS that prescribes the useful life for various kinds of assets, and this figure may bear no relation to the actual useful life of an asset.

Now let us assume that in 2017 Bubba did the following:

- bought the burrito machine;
- depreciated it at $1,000 a year;
- manufactured and sold 5,000 burritos for $2 each;
- paid $500 for the materials for the 5,000 burritos;
- paid someone a salary of $500 to run the machine;
- paid someone a salary of $500 to sell burritos for him; and
- paid $100 for phone calls and other general and administrative (G & A) expenses.

Then Bubba's income statement would look like this:

Bubba's Burritos Income Statement 2017

Revenue (sales)	$10,000
– COGS	500
– Salaries	1,000
– G & A	100
– Depreciation	1,000*
= PBT	$ 7,400

Up to now, we have been ignoring taxes. You simply cannot do that (even if you work for the federal government). For this exercise, we will assume that Bubba's tax rate is 50%. We have to add two more lines to the bottom of Bubba's 2017 income statement:

Bubba's Burritos Income Statement 2017

Revenue (sales)	$10,000
– COGS	500
– Salaries	1,000
– G & A	100
– Depreciation	1,000
= PBT	$ 7,400
– Taxes	3,700
= Profit after Tax	$ 3,700

Note that "Profit After Tax" is often abbreviated as "PAT."

An income statement provides a useful perspective on a business. By looking at an income statement, we can learn a great deal about the operations of a business in a particular year. And looking at income

---

* Consider the effect of depreciation and depreciation methods on PBT and on taxes. If Bubba could choose an accelerated method of depreciation so that he could allocate more of the $5,000 cost of the machine to 2017, his 2017 PBT would be lower, his taxes would be lower, and he could keep more of his 2017 earnings. Of course, in future years, his depreciation would be lower, his PBT would be higher, and his taxes would be higher. But, of course, Bubba would rather have the money now. The sooner he gets the money, the sooner he can invest it and begin earning a return on it. This is why business groups lobby hard for accelerated depreciation.

statements for several years allows us to see how a business's performance changes.

One thing we cannot see from an income statement is how much cash a business may be generating or using up in a given year. This is because some entries in the income statement, such as depreciation, do not represent any actual movement of cash. And, some activities that do impact cash—like selling stock, borrowing money or buying equipment—do not show up on the income statement. To measure the cash, we need to look at a cash flow statement.

2. THE CASH FLOW STATEMENT: A FIRST LOOK

The cash flow statement is a measure of how much more or less cash a business has at the end of the year than it had at the beginning of that year. Cash flow would be easy to measure if all of a business's cash went into the bank; cash flow would simply be the change in the amount in the bank account.

But that is not what happens in the real world, or even in the hypothetical world of Bubba's Burritos. Recall that we saw from Bubba's income statement that Bubba could buy a machine for $5,000 and charge the business only $1,000 on the income statement. (The remaining $4,000 still comes out of the cash at the bank, but it does not show up as an expense on the income statement.) Conversely, in the years after Bubba buys the machine, he will be charging the income statement $1,000 but he will not have to pay this in cash, because he's already paid for the machine. The $1,000 is just a charge for the portion of the machine that was "used up" in that year.

We can readily see how depreciation changes the relationship between the business's income statement and its real cash flow. In our simple model, until we added depreciation, the income statement was also a cash flow statement; whatever the profit after tax was, this amount was also the cash profit the business had made. Now, when we add depreciation, we see this relationship has changed.

In the first year of the machine's use, cash flow is less than profit because we have a cash outflow of $5,000 to buy the machine, but this appears nowhere on the income statement. The only figure we see is a $1,000 charge for depreciation. In future years, cash flow will be more than profit, because we will be charging the income statement $1,000 in depreciation, but there is no real cash outflow for this.

Thus, we can see there are two components to the differences we are talking about. One is the depreciation figure, and we've seen where that comes from. The other figure is called investment. It represents the money spent to purchase equipment. The company's cash declines because it exchanges cash for the equipment. When the business buys something that will be used for more than one year, this is an investment and only the depreciation appears on the income statement. In contrast, if the company buys something that it will use up within the year, it is called an expense, and the total amount appears on the income statement. Salaries, G & A, and COGS are expenses, because they are charges for items that are "used up" as the expense is incurred.

In order to account for depreciation and investment, the general formula that converts an income statement to a cash flow statement is: Cash Flow equals Profit after Tax plus Depreciation minus Investment. We can convert Bubba's income statements for the first and second years of the machine's life to cash flow statements:

Bubba's Burritos Cash Flow Statement

Year	2017	2018*
Revenue (sales)	$10,000	$10,000
COGS	500	500
Salaries	1,000	1,000
G & A	100	100
Depreciation	1,000	1,000
PBT	7,400	7,400
Taxes	3,700	3,700
Profit After Taxes	$ 3,700	$ 3,700
+ Depreciation	1,000	1,000
– Investment	5,000	0
= Cash Flow	$ - 300	$ 4,700

This example shows why both the income and cash flow statements provide valuable information about a business. The income statement indicates the business was just as profitable in 2018 as it was in 2017. From a cash flow perspective, however, the two years are dramatically different. Due to the investment in equipment, there is a severe cash drain on the business in 2017. In 2018, the business is getting the benefit of that piece of equipment, but the business does not have to lay out any additional cash to do so. Although profits are the same in both years, the business might well be able to survive an unexpected crisis better in 2018 than 2017.

To understand the difference between an income statement and a cash flow statement more fully, we need to understand what information is provided by a balance sheet.

---

* This assumes that business operations in 2018 mirror business operations in 2017.

3. THE BALANCE SHEET

The last financial statement we will consider is the balance sheet. The income and cash flow statements capture activity *during a period,* showing how much profit or cash flowed into (or out of) the business during the period. In contrast, the balance sheet is a *snapshot at a particular moment in time.*

A balance sheet has three main sections.

(a) *Assets*: These are the things that the company owns that have value. Assets are the business's "stuff." The typical assets on a balance sheet are cash, land, buildings, accounts receivable (money owed to the company by its customers) and machinery and equipment (such as the burrito machine). When equipment such as the burrito machine is depreciated, the dollar amount of that depreciation charge is deducted as an expense on the income statement; the same amount is deducted from the value of the asset on the balance sheet. Assets like cash are not depreciated because they don't get used up. Similarly, accounts receivable are not depreciated but may be "written off." For example, if one of Bubba's credit customers files for bankruptcy, its accounts payable would likely go unpaid. Bubba would then "write off" the account receivable due from the customers. This would ensure that the overall accounts receivable figure is an accurate reflection of the business's expectations for getting paid.

(b) *Liabilities*: Liabilities are the opposite of assets: they are what the company owes. Typical liability items are accounts payable (what the company owes its suppliers), wages that it owes to its employees, and any debts the company incurs (for example, when it borrows money).

(c) *Owners' Equity*: Owners' equity is what is left over after you subtract the liabilities from the assets. Simply put, owners' equity equals assets minus liabilities.

This is why a balance sheet is called a balance sheet—it balances. When you put the assets on the left-hand side of the balance sheet, and the liabilities and owners' equity on the right hand side, then the balance sheet *will* balance. By definition, it must.*

And it makes sense. If the assets are all of the company's things that have value, and the liabilities are all the "claims" on that value, then the difference between the two is the "book value" of the business to the owners—the owners' equity. Even if a company has $1 billion in assets, the value of the owners' equity is zero if the company also has $1 billion

---

* Note that the principle of conservatism means that assets appear on the balance sheet at the lower of cost or market. So, a piece of land purchased in 1950 would appear on the balance sheet with a value equal to its original purchase price. Thus, the balance sheet may not accurately reflect the current market value of the company's assets and might not tell a prospective buyer how much to pay for the business.

in debt. When liabilities exceed assets, the owners' equity is negative—a condition otherwise known as insolvency.

Let's look at what a balance sheet for Bubba's Burritos might look like. First, assume that on January 15, 2016, Bubba invested $666 of his own money in the business. In that case, the balance sheet would look like this:

Bubba's Burritos Balance Sheet
January 15, 2016

Assets		Liabilities & Equity	
Cash	$666	Liabilities	$0
		Equity	$666
Total	$666	Total	$666

Or, Bubba could have lent the money to the business, in which case the balance sheet would look like:

Bubba's Burritos Balance Sheet
January 15, 2016

Assets		Liabilities & Equity	
Cash	$666	Note due Bubba	$666
		Equity	$0
Total	$666	Total	$666

After the first year of operation, we said that Bubba had a profit of $1,000. Assuming for a minute that this was equal to cash flow, that cash would have built up in the Bubba's Burritos bank account over the course of the year, and thus, at year end, the balance sheet would have looked like:

Bubba's Burritos Balance Sheet
December 31, 2016

Assets		Liabilities & Equity	
Cash	$1,666	Liabilities	$666
		Equity	$1,000
Total	$1,666	Total	$1,666

Note that profits accrue to the equity account. Let's suppose that, just before year-end, Bubba has decided Bubba's Burritos should pay back his loan. He could write himself a check for $666, and then both cash and liabilities would decrease by $666, and the balance sheet would still balance. If Bubba instead decided to have Bubba's Burritos distribute

$100 of the profits to himself—as owner of the business—these would be a deduction from owners' equity.*

After several years of business operation and expansion, a more complete balance sheet for Bubba's business might look like this:

Bubba's Burritos Balance Sheet
December 31, 2020

Assets		
Cash	5,000	
Accounts Receivable	22,000	
Inventory	33,000	
Security Deposits	6,000	
Current Assets		66,000
Equipment—Gross	147,000	
Depreciation	24,000	
Equipment—Net		123,000
Total Assets		**189,000**
Liabilities & Equity		
Accounts Payable	19,000	
Taxes Payable	5,000	
Total short-term liabilities		24,000
Bank Note		85,000
Liabilities		**109,000**
Net Total Equity		80,000
Total Liabilities + Equity		**189,000**

Let's see what we can learn from this balance sheet. For example: Bubba's Burritos is relatively low on cash, having only $5,000 to satisfy $19,000 in "bills" (Accounts Payable) which it must pay to its suppliers; and Bubba's Burritos is a relatively heavy user of debt† (the bank note is for more than 100% of the company's equity; that is, the note is for $85,000, while the equity is $80,000—so the note is for 106% of the equity); and Bubba's Burritos has spent $147,000 on equipment, and charged $24,000 in depreciation against it.

4.   THE CASH FLOW STATEMENT: A SECOND LOOK

In our first view of cash flow statements, we compared the impact of purchasing and depreciating equipment on both the income statement

---

*   This assumes that Bubba lent the business the initial $666.

†   Debt in the business world is just like debt in personal life. When you borrow money, you are in debt. Bubba's Burritos used a lot of borrowed money.

and cash flow statement. Now we need to see the possible impact of changes on balance sheet items on a cash flow statement.

Consider for example the impact of changes in accounts receivable on the cash flow statement. Assume that in 2020 Bubba's credit sales are approximately $22,000 every month and that typically his customers pay within 30 days. If in December of 2020, Bubba's collections from prior credit sales total only $18,000 instead of the anticipated $22,000, Bubba's cash entry on his balance sheet for December 31, 2020, will be $4,000 lower and the accounts receivable entry on his December 31, 2020 balance sheet will be $4,000 higher (than expected). More important, Bubba's cash flow statement for 2020 will show that the business produced $4,000 less cash. In sum, an increase in a balance sheet asset account other than cash results in a decrease in cash flow. The business owns the other asset (here the accounts receivable) instead of cash, so things still balance.

In contrast, an increase in a balance sheet liability account can result in an increase in the cash account on the balance sheet and an increase in cash flow. Suppose Bubba borrows $20,000 in December of 2020. That increases the liability shown on the December 31, 2020 balance sheet by $20,000 but also increases the balance sheet cash account by $20,000. And that increase in liability increases cash flow by $20,000. Obviously (we hope), if Bubba spent the $20,000 he borrowed in December of 2015 to buy inventory in December of 2020, that $20,000 inventory expenditure would increase the inventory account on the balance sheet by $20,000 and reduce the cash account and eliminate the $20,000 from the cash flow statement. Again, everything keeps balancing.

Likewise, suppose that the business sold shares of its stock for $100,000. This would appear on the balance sheet as increase in cash of $100,000, and an increase in shareholder equity of the same amount.

Note that not only do the balance sheet totals balance, but every transaction has two separate components which have a balancing effect: an increase in bank borrowings (a liability) also creates an increase in cash (an asset) when the borrowed money is deposited in the company's bank account. This is why accounting—or bookkeeping—is often called a "double entry" system: every transaction has two effects, which always serve to balance.

Accordingly, the definition of a cash flow statement should be expanded to include the effect of changes in balance sheet accounts:

Cash flow equals profits (from the income statement) plus depreciation minus net change in balance sheet asset accounts other than cash plus net change in liabilities and funds from new issues of stock.

And, accordingly, in reviewing a cash flow statement for a particular year, it is helpful to look at the balance sheets for several years and compare the changes in asset accounts and liabilities.

PROBLEMS

1. Review Bubbas's Dec. 31, 2020 balance sheet on page 21. Suppose Bubba had ordered—and had delivered—$5,000 worth of tortillas on Dec. 30. And suppose he agreed to pay for these on his usual terms, i.e., in 30 days. How would the balance sheet look different? The income statement? The cash flow statement?

2. Now suppose that on Dec 30 Bubba buys $100,000 of equipment on credit. Will that affect the balance sheet? The cash flow statement? The income statement?

3. Same facts as 2 except that Bubba pays cash for the equipment.

4. On Dec. 30, Bubba pays his director of operations a $100,000 cash bonus. Will that affect the balance sheet? The cash flow statement? The income statement?

5. What was the effect, if any, of the donation to Princeton on the balance sheet, cash flow statement and income statement of the A.P. Smith Co. (i.e., compared to a scenario where such a donation had never been made)?

5. DETERMINING THE VALUE OF A BUSINESS

It is relatively easy to determine the value of a public company, i.e., a company whose stock is regularly bought and sold on the New York Stock Exchange or other similar market. You simply take the number of shares outstanding and multiply by the stock price, and that is your value. If, for example, on July 13, 2015, there are one billion shares of McDonald's stock outstanding and McDonald's stock is selling for $100 a share, then one could say that the value of the McDonald's corporation is $100 billion.

Even in these simplest of circumstances, it is unclear how accurate a value that really is. Suppose McDonald's is worth $100 billion on a July 13, 2015 afternoon when the market closes, and then a war in the Middle East breaks out overnight. By the time the markets open, oil prices have spiked, analysts are projecting a 20% increase in gas prices, "knowledgeable observers" are projecting a dramatic decrease in family driving, and McDonald's stock drops by 10%, erasing $10 billion of market value. Was the $10 billion value at July 13th's evening's market close really the true "value"? Is the new $90 billion value "true"?

Of course, anyone who buys or sells a stock is implicitly betting that they have a better handle on the "true" value than does the market, with all its trillions of dollars of capital and thousands of informed buyers. So, the question of how to properly value a stock is one that can be left to another course and book*.

---

*   Try Benjamin Graham's THE INTELLIGENT INVESTOR. This is the text that Warren Buffet swears by, so if it good enough for him. . . http://www.youtube.com/watch?v=HCZMs01W0KM.

Most businesses are private companies, i.e., companies with relatively few owners. Valuing these private companies is more difficult. No one is trading the stock of a company with relatively few owners on the New York Stock Exchange. Indeed, the company or its stock may never be sold.

So, in some sense, the question of value matters less if the business is privately owned. But even in the case of many private enterprises, people like to know what their businesses are worth. Bankers may be trying to lend money against the firm, an owner may be trying to sell all or part of her ownership interest, the IRS may be figuring out how much tax to charge upon inheritance.

The topic of valuing an operating business can and does fill an entire B-School. A law student taking the basic business associations course simply needs to have general understanding of "discounted cash flow."

Discounted cash flow valuation converts (a) the opportunity to receive estimated future payments that are risky (in the sense that they may be paid or may not be paid) into (b) an equivalent number of dollars received, for certain, today. The discount (i.e., the reduction) reflects both (i) the greater value of having money now rather than later and (ii) the risk that the future payments may not be made.

Too abstract? Try this: Roberts Company had a positive cash flow of $100,000 last year, slightly more the year before that, but less two years ago. Think of Roberts Company as a machine that prints real legitimate money. How much would you be willing to pay for a machine that prints $100,000 or more (or less) each year that might at some point break down and stop printing money? The amount that you would be willing to pay is in essence the discounted cash flow value of Roberts Company.

Financial statements, which of course, can only describe *past* financial performance, can nonetheless be a useful guide in valuing a business. This is true to the extent that they provide some basis for evaluating the likely *future* cash flows of the business. As in many things, the past is sometimes prologue, and sometimes not. Moreover, as we have seen, financial statements may not be honestly or properly prepared.

Please consider the following problems.

PROBLEMS

1.   Review Bubba's Burritos balance sheet for December 31, 2020. In January of 2021, would you recommend that a client buy Bubba's business for $189,000? For $80,000? Does the balance sheet help a prospective buyer determine how much she should pay for the entire business? Does the balance sheet help a prospective investor determine how much he should pay for a share of the business? Does the balance sheet help a prospective lender determine how much it can safely lend to the business? How?

2.   Review the Bubba's Burritos cash flow statements for 2017 and 2018. In January of 2019, would you recommend to Bubba that he sell the

business for $3,700? For $4,700? For $20,350? Does the cash flow statement help a prospective buyer determine how much she should pay for the business? Does the cash flow statement help an investor determine how much she should pay for a share of the business? Does the cash flow statement help a prospective lender determine how much it can safely loan the business?

C. SOME BUSINESSES HAVE ONLY ONE OWNER AND NO LEGAL STRUCTURE: SOLE PROPRIETORSHIPS

The most common business structure is the sole proprietorship. A sole proprietorship is a business structure without a legal structure. In a sole proprietorship, the business and its owner are the same actual person and the same legal person. Assume, for example, that Bubba, a 25-year-old recent college graduate, wants to lease a building near a college campus and open what he hopes will be the first of thousands of Bubba's Burritos stores. What does Bubba need to do?

Bubba does not need a lawyer to create the sole proprietorship. He does not need to do anything to create the sole proprietorship. Bubba is the sole proprietorship, and the sole proprietorship is Bubba. There is no need to draft any legal document, and no need to file anything. The sole proprietorship is the "default" structure for a business with one owner. Unless the owner files papers to create some other structure, such as a corporation, his business is automatically a sole proprietorship.

The use of a trade name such as "Bubba's Burritos" can present various legal issues. For example, there are statutory procedures for reserving and obtaining a trade name and there are statutory and case law requirements that the trade name not be deceptively similar to existing trade names. The use of a trade name does not, however, create or require a new legal entity. Bubba is Bubba's Burritos and Bubba's Burritos is Bubba.

Similarly, as a sole proprietor, Bubba will not need a lawyer's help in dealing with the questions that confronted the corporation in the *A.P. Smith* case: (1) who decides what the business does; and, (2) who gets the money the business makes. In a sole proprietorship, there is no legal separation of the business, the people who manage the business, and the people who own the business. Bubba simply is Bubba's Burritos. Bubba makes the business decisions and Bubba gets the profits from the business.

Bubba is also responsible for the debts and obligations of the business. For liability purposes, Bubba is Bubba's Burritos. Bubba reports the business's income on his personal tax return and pays the taxes on that income (at his personal rate). People who extend credit to the business or otherwise have legal claims (including tort claims) against the business can sue Bubba personally and collect those claims from Bubba. To summarize:

> The sole proprietorship is as old as business itself. With it, * * * one person owns the enterprise, is responsible for management decisions, receives all profit and bears all loss. The business is indistinguishable from its proprietor. Business income is part of the proprietor's taxable income for federal and state personal income tax purposes. The law imposes no formalities for forming a sole proprietorship. The proprietor simply owns and operates a business, which is a sole proprietorship even if the proprietor is unaware of that fact.

Richard D. Freer, *Business Organizations,* OXFORD COMPANION TO AMERICAN LAW 77 (2002), edited by Kermit Hall, copyright by Oxford University Press, Inc. Used by permission of Oxford University Press, Inc.

D. MOST BUSINESSES HAVE MORE THAN ONE OWNER AND A MORE FORMAL LEGAL STRUCTURE

All businesses with more than one owner have a legal structure. Such businesses are either corporations, limited liability companies, or some form of partnership.

Many businesses with only one owner also have a legal structure. As we will learn, it is possible to have a corporation or a limited liability company with only one owner.

For the most part, this book is about the various forms of legal structures for businesses. By way of preview, the following is an overview of what co-author Roberts teaches people going to business school (which we call "client school" because many of your clients will have gone there) about the legal structures for businesses.

The decision regarding a business structure is driven chiefly by the objectives of the business's founder and the firm's investors, in terms of tax status, exposure to legal liabilities, and flexibility in the operation and financing of the business. The choices are made difficult by the inherent tradeoffs imposed by the law. To get the most favorable tax treatment, one may sometimes have to give up some protection from liability exposure, flexibility or both.

1. WHAT CHOICES ARE AVAILABLE?

The basic legal forms of business organization include:

- The sole proprietorship
- The partnership

- general partnership
- limited partnership
- The corporation (or "C Corp.")
- The limited liability company (LLC)

For the owner, the two most important differences in these various business structures are (1) tax treatment of the business's profits and (2) liability exposure of the owners for the business's debts and other potential liabilities. These differences can be seen most readily by comparing sole proprietorships and corporations. Other business structures such as partnerships, limited partnerships, and limited liability companies are, in a sense, combinations of features from the corporation and partnership structures.

a.   The Sole Proprietorship

The sole proprietorship is the oldest and simplest form of organization: a person undertakes a business without any of the formalities associated with other forms of organization; the individual and the business are one and the same for tax and legal liability purposes.

The proprietorship does not pay taxes as a separate entity. The individual reports all income and deductible expenses for the business on her personal income tax return. These earnings of the business are taxed to the individual regardless of whether they are *actually* distributed in cash. There is no vehicle for "sheltering" income from tax.

For liability purposes, the individual and the business are also one and the same. Thus, legal claimants can pursue all assets of the owner, not simply the assets used in the business.

b.   The Corporation

The corporation is the most common legal structure for large businesses.* One major advantage of the corporation, compared to the sole proprietorship, is that a corporation's owners (stockholders or shareholders) are generally protected from personal liability.

In exchange for this protection, the corporation is considered a tax-paying entity. A corporation must pay taxes on its income, just like a real person.†

---

*   We refer here to "C" corporations. We briefly discuss "S" corporations a bit later in the book.

†   Mitt Romney famously said, during the campaign for the 2012 presidential election, that ". . . corporations are people too, my friend." While he was largely mocked for it, the fact is that corporations are ultimately "people," for many purposes, including paying federal income tax. *But cf.* Sarah Silverman and Lizz Winstead, http://www.youtube.com/watch?v=fYfJWybKCy0.

And, because the business does not get any deduction for dividends paid, the earnings of a corporation are, in essence, taxed twice. First, the corporation pays a tax on its income. Second, the owners of the corporation pay a tax on the part of the corporation's earnings that is distributed to them as dividends. (Note that the federal dividend tax rate is currently 15% although it rises to 20% for individuals in the top tax bracket. In the example below, we'll assume 20% is a reasonable estimate of state and local taxes on dividends.)

The current maximum income tax rate on corporate income is 35%; the assumed rate on individual dividend income is 20%. Thus, $1.00 of pre-tax corporate income becomes $0.52 when it is taxed at the corporate level, distributed as a dividend, and then taxed at the individual level: $[1.00 \times (1-.35) \times (1-.20)] = .52$.

This double taxation of corporations—taxation first of the corporations on its earnings and then second of its shareholders on their dividends—creates powerful incentives for enterprises that anticipate distributing earnings to use a form of business structure which is *not* taxed on its earnings, such as a partnership or limited liability company. (Such structures are often referred to as "pass-through entities" because the profits simply pass through the legal structure but are not taxed there.)

Other forms of organization can best be understood in relation to the sole proprietorship and the corporation. Do not think of these business forms as hermetically sealed; in fact, there is a great deal of overlap among them, and a lawyer may be able to suggest more than one potential business structure to achieve the client's goals. It is helpful to note that the law continues to evolve, and one reason for the multiple business forms is that states have reached various stages of development. Eventually, some people believe, there will be only two basic business forms, the corporation for large businesses and the limited liability company for small ones. The law is not there yet, though, so the lawyer must be facile with the characteristics of various business structures.

c. The (General) Partnership

Partnerships are businesses that consist of two or more owners. A partnership is treated like a sole proprietorship for tax and liability purposes. Earnings are distributed according to the partnership agreement, and taxes are paid only at the personal level on the partner's share of that income (this is called "pass-through" taxation). For liability purposes, each of the partners is jointly and severally liable. Thus, an injured party may pursue one or more of the partners for any amount.

And when corporate taxes reduce profits, there is less cash available for dividends to the ultimate owners.

The claim need not be proportional to invested capital or to the distribution of earnings.

d. The Limited Partnership

Limited partnerships are a hybrid form of organization. It is like a partnership or sole proprietorship for tax purposes. And, it is somewhat like a corporation for liability purposes. A limited partnership is a partnership that has *both* limited and general partners. The general partner assumes the management responsibility *and* unlimited liability for the business. The limited partner has little voice in management and is not individually liable for the company's debts. The limited partner thus looks a lot like a shareholder in a corporation, but with different tax treatment on the earnings attributable to his ownership stake.

e. The Limited Liability Company (LLC)

The limited liability company is a business structure developed to provide both the protection from liability of a corporation and the protection from double taxation of a partnership. The owners of a limited liability company are not individually liable for the company's debts. The limited liability company is not a tax paying entity. Income taxes are only paid once—by the owners of the limited liability company when a part of the company's earnings is distributed to them.

The existence of an LLC depends on compliance with the state limited liability company law. These laws differ from state to state.*

f. The S Corporation and Not-for-Profit Corporations

Although we won't discuss them further in this book, you should know a little about two additional business forms. Like the LLC, the S Corporation is afforded the tax status of a partnership, but the protection from legal liability of a corporation. This advantageous tax treatment comes at a cost. To qualify for S Corporation tax status, the business must meet a number of rather restrictive conditions in the Internal Revenue Code, including being a domestic corporation, owned wholly by human (not entity) citizens of the United States, with 100 or fewer stockholders.

The IRS and individual states have established that certain corporations that, in narrowly specified ways, operate for the public benefit need not pay corporate income tax. In addition, individuals can deduct gifts to these "non-profit" corporations from their tax returns [per

---

* Similar to an LLC, a Limited Liability Partnership (LLP) is a general partnership that files the documents required by state law to provide partners with limited liability—that is, the partners, who ordinarily would be liable for partnership debts, are not personally liable; they can lose nothing more than their investments in the firm. The law varies from state-to-state on whether this freedom from liability is total or partial, depending on the type of claim asserted.

Internal Revenue Code 501(c)(3)]. Churches and universities are examples. Most normal businesses do not qualify.

2. HOW DO YOU CHOOSE?

The right choice depends upon a balance of factors to be assessed in light of the client's needs:

> Persons setting up any business must address certain core questions, including (1) who will own the business, (2) who will manage it, (3) who will reap any profit, (4) who will bear the risk of any loss, and (5) who will pay income tax on any business profit. * * * The development of [various] forms of business organization in the United States is largely the story of attempting to maximize benefit while reducing risk. One example might be assessing the possibility of whether an owner could limit his liability for business debts while sharing in profits and decision-making.

Richard D. Freer, *Business Organizations*, OXFORD COMPANION TO AMERICAN LAW 77 (2002), edited by Kermit Hall, copyright by Oxford University Press, Inc. Used by permission of Oxford University Press, Inc.

CHAPTER 2

BASIC CONCEPTS OF AGENCY LAW

■ ■ ■

A. AGENTS OWE FIDUCIARY DUTIES AND MAY BE LIABLE FOR BREACHING THEM

You have to know agency law to work with any business structure—whether the business is structured as a sole proprietorship like Bubba's Burritos or structured as a corporation like McDonald's. Agency law is relevant in every business because every business deals with third-parties through agents. As we saw in Chapter 1, a sole proprietorship has no legal structure: there is one owner, for whom business income is treated as personal income and for whom business debts are treated as personal debts. Sometimes, the sole proprietor will be the only person actively involved in the business. It is very common, however, for even a sole proprietor to hire employees to discharge various business functions.

Indeed, a sole proprietorship can have thousands of employees. A business remains a sole proprietorship so long as (i) one person *owns* the business, and (ii) the business does not have a legal structure that requires the imprimatur of a state agency, such as a corporation, partnership, or a limited liability company. Obviously a business that has a legal structure such as a corporation, partnership, or a limited liability company can have multiple owners as well as multiple employees.

Whenever a business—any form of business—has employees, we will encounter questions of agency law. Many of you already know a lot about these topics: maybe you have relatives or friends who are insurance agents, real estate agents, or secret agents. A number of you remember the movie *Jerry Maguire* or the TV series *Million Dollar Listings,* or the song, *Agents of Love.* A number of you (Freer insists a smaller number) remember agency law from first year Contracts and first year Torts courses.

Regardless, at the end of this course you "want to be in that number" who can answer the following five questions about agents and agency law:

(1) Where should I look for answers to questions about agents and agency law, such as the next four questions?

(2) When is a person an agent?

(3) What are an agent's duties?

    (4)   What are the legal consequences of contracts entered by an agent?

    (5)   What are the consequences of torts committed by an agent?

1.   WHERE SHOULD YOU LOOK FOR AGENCY LAW?

First, look to case law. Courts developed the principles of agency as part of common law. In some states, the principles were eventually codified. Also look to the Restatements of Agency, in which the American Law Institute (ALI) distills and clarifies the law. The ALI has addressed agency law in three Restatements. The original effort, promulgated in 1934, is of no current interest. The Restatement (Second), which we call "R–2," was issued in 1958 and has been cited approvingly in thousands of cases. In 2006, the ALI published the Restatement (Third), which we call "R–3." It is gaining a following but has not supplanted R–2 (and might never do so).*

Consider R–2, § 1:

(1) Agency is the fiduciary relation which results from the manifestation of consent by one person to another that the other shall act on his behalf and subject to his control, and consent by the other so to act.

(2) The one for whom action is to be taken is the principal.

(3) The one who is to act is the agent.

Note these three points:

First: agency is a "fiduciary relation"—we will discuss that concept in great detail later. For now, realize it means that the agent owes duties—fiduciary duties—to the principal in discharging the act for the principal.

Second: there must be some "manifestation of consent by one person [the principal] to another [the agent] that the other [the agent] shall act on his [the principal's] behalf and subject to his [the principal's] control."

Third: there also must be "consent by the other [the agent] so to act."

These three points answer our questions (2) and (3) from the beginning of the chapter: when is a person an agent and what duties does she owe to the business? The same points are made in R–3, § 1.01, which is set out in the case you are fixing to read.

---

    *   In general, R–3 is written somewhat more clearly then R–2, and in a couple of areas R–3 has adopted different terminology. In addition, R–3 addresses the application of agency law in organizational contexts, such as corporations, that R–2 did not. Nonetheless, courts readily have applied R–2 in such contexts. In all but one substantive area (inherent agency power, discussed below), however, the answers to our questions will be the same under R–2 and R–3. So, for us, there no appreciable substantive difference between the two.

    Throughout these materials, we will cite the relevant provisions of both R–2 and R–3. This will allow your professor to adopt either one for your class. When we quote the language of a Restatement, it will generally be to R–2 (with a citation to the complementary section in R–3).

2. WHO IS AN AGENT AND WHAT DUTIES DOES AN AGENT OWE TO HER PRINCIPAL?

QUALITY CARDIOVASCULAR CARE, LLC v. CASEY

Connecticut Superior Court, 2013
2013 WL 1494379

ROCHE, J. * * * The plaintiff alleges that defendant owed a duty of loyalty to the plaintiff as the plaintiff's office manager and breached that duty by using the plaintiff's confidential trade secrets to unfairly compete with the plaintiff, causing the plaintiff to suffer damages.

* * *

In the defendant's fifth special defense, she alleges that she owed the plaintiff no duty of loyalty because the "[t]he duty of loyalty arises out of a contractual relationship between the parties" and, "[i]n this case, the contractual obligation between the parties was arrived at based on the [p]laintiff's fraud and false representations to the [d]efendant."

DISCUSSION

* * *

The duty of loyalty extends out of the agency relationship. "Agency is the fiduciary relationship that arises when one person (a 'principal') manifests assent to another person (an 'agent') that the agent shall act on the principal's behalf and subject to the principal's control, and the agent manifests assent or otherwise consents so to act." 1 Restatement (Third), Agency § 1.01 (2006). "The elements of common-law agency are present in the relationships between employer and employee . . ." Id., comment (c). . . . Additionally, although "[a]n agent has a duty to act in accordance with the express and implied terms of any contract between the agent and the principal," 1 Restatement (Third), supra, at § 8.07, "a contract is not necessary to create a relationship of agency." Id., comment (b).

"The law is well settled that knowledge acquired by an employee during his employment cannot be used for his own advantage to the injury of the employer during the employment; and after the employment has ceased the employee remains subject to a duty not to use trade secrets, or other confidential information which he has acquired in the course of his employment, for his own benefit or that of a competitor to the detriment of his former employer . . . It matters not that there is no specific agreement on the part of the employee not to disclose the knowledge he has so acquired . . . Employees are bound by such an implied obligation even though they be not under contract at all." Allen Mfg. Co. v. Loika, 145 Conn. 509, 514, 144 A.2d 306 (1958).

The defendant claims that the plaintiff made fraudulent misrepresentations to induce her to agree to be its employee, that the defendant's employment relationship arose out of that fraudulently induced contractual relationship and, therefore, that no duty of loyalty arose from the defendant's employment relationship with the plaintiff. The duty of loyalty, however, is not based in contract but rather in agency. A contract is not necessary to create a relationship of agency. Because the duty of loyalty is based in the law of agency and actionable in tort, the fraudulent misrepresentations of an employer to induce an employee to take a position with the employer does not absolve the employee of the duty of loyalty and, therefore, does not defeat an employer's tort action against that employee for the breach of her duty of loyalty.* [2]

The defendant also claims that, because she was not given a position of trust but rather a position similar to any non-physician employee, she did not have a duty of loyalty to the plaintiff. The duty of loyalty, however, adheres even where the employee's position is that of "any non-physician employee." Every employee has a duty not to use their [sic] employer's trade secrets and confidential information to the detriment of that employer. * * *

QUESTIONS

1. Do you think that the employment agreement between plaintiff and defendant used the term "agent"? Do you think that the defendant thought of herself as an "agent"? Are the answers to these questions relevant? What creates an agency relationship—if not words?

2. Notice that the plaintiff is an "LLC," a limited liability company. Was that relevant to the court's decision?

3. Was it relevant that the defendant was an employee of the plaintiff? Assume that Rod Tidwell asked Jerry Maguire to represent him in contract negotiations with the Arizona Cardinals. Would Maguire be an agent and owe Tidwell a duty of loyalty? Would Tidwell owe Maguire a duty of loyalty?

4. Can there be an agency relationship without a contract? If so, and if the agent breaches her duty to the principal, does the claim sound in tort or in contract?

---

*   [2] This is not to say that an employee has no right of recovery against an employer who makes fraudulent misrepresentations to induce that employee to take an agency role with regard to the employer or that the fraudulent misrepresentations of an employer in inducing an employee to take a position with the employer could not be a valid special defense to certain contractual obligations of the employee to the employer. It is only to say that such fraudulent misrepresentations do not absolve an employee of his duty of loyalty to his employer or bar the employer's right to recover for the employee's breach of that duty.

3. WHAT ARE THE LEGAL CONSEQUENCES OF CONTRACTS ENTERED BY AN AGENT?

In Question 3 above, an agent was negotiating a contract for a principal. Happens all of the time—not just sports agents negotiating with NFL teams or entertainment agents negotiating with NBC but also lower profile deals like a real estate agent negotiating with a home owner.

Sometimes agents enter into contracts for their principals. Suppose you call a travel agent and ask him to make a reservation for you on Delta's 8:00 PM flight from Atlanta to Paris on July 13. He does so. When you show up two hours before the flight, Delta cannot say "We don't need to let you on that flight because we never made a deal with you." Indeed, the airline *did* make a deal with you—*through* your agent. Think of the chaos that would ensue if we could not enter *binding* deals through agents.

But what about the other way around? Does a deal by your agent with a third party bind you? The answer will be yes *if* your agent had "power" (or, as most courts will say, "authority") to bind the principal. Take the airline example above. The travel agent makes the reservation you requested. Can you refuse to pay for the Delta ticket on the theory that you have never dealt directly with Delta? Of course not. You are bound because your agent had authority to bind you in the purchase of that ticket. More specifically, your travel agent had *actual authority*.

Actual Authority (R–3 §§ 2.01, 3.01; R–2 § 26 (R–2 simply calls this "authority")). This is created by manifestations from the principal (P) to the agent (A) that the agent reasonably believes create authority. P simply tells A that A is empowered to act on P's behalf in accomplishing some task.

> Epstein tells his chauffeur, Freer, to have the car serviced at Roberts Service Station. Freer takes the car to Roberts for servicing. Epstein is obliged to pay for the service. Freer had actual authority to bind Epstein to the deal. Epstein gave that authority to Freer.

Sometimes the manifestation by P to A is not direct.

> Roberts goes to see his stockbroker, Shepherd, to place an order for 500 shares of Coca-Cola stock. When he sees that Shepherd is not at his desk, Roberts jots a note saying "Please purchase 500 sh. Coca-Cola for my account," which he signs. Roberts places it on what he thinks is Shepherd's desk. In fact, though, it is the desk of another broker, Epstein, who fills the order for Roberts. Epstein has actual authority to make the purchase for Roberts. The communication from Roberts can reasonably be interpreted to make Epstein believe that he was authorized. Roberts is bound to pay for the stock.

To be precise (always a good thing), what we have seen is "actual *express* authority," because P expressly gave A the power to undertake the act on her behalf.

There is also "actual *implied* authority," which recognizes that an agent has the authority to do what is reasonably necessary to get the assigned job done, even if P did not spell it out in detail. In other words, there is interstitial authority for the agent to do what needs to be done to accomplish the task assigned.

> Shepherd asks his assistant to make travel arrangements for him to attend a law professor conference. Although he does not say anything specifically about airline reservations, his assistant has the implied actual authority to make such a reservation for him.

R–2 § 35 reflects this idea by providing that an agent's authority "includes authority to do acts which are incidental to it, usually accompany it, or are reasonably necessary to accomplish it." The same notion is found in R–3 § 2.02(1), which provides that the agent may take action "necessary or incidental to achieving the principal's objectives."

An agent can also bind a principal on the basis of "apparent authority."

Apparent Authority (R–2 § 27; R–3 §§ 2.03, 3.03). The term "apparent authority" is somewhat misleading because, in apparent authority fact situations, P does not really authorize A to act on her behalf. Indeed P may have privately forbidden A to act. Instead, apparent authority is created by manifestations by P to a third party (TP). The manifestation (1) must be attributable to P, (2) must get to TP, and (3) must lead TP reasonably to conclude that A is an agent for P. Note that the provision does not require detrimental reliance by TP on P's manifestation.

> Epstein tells Roberts, who runs Roberts Service Station, that Freer is Epstein's agent for having the car serviced. Freer has apparent authority. This is true even if Epstein had privately told Freer that Freer had no authority to get the car fixed.

We will call this "apparent authority" (as R–2 and R–3 do) but you should know that some courts refer to this power as "implied authority."

Inherent Agency Power (R–2 § 8A). This power of A to bind P to deals with TP arises from the agency relationship itself. There is a sense that the power to do so just goes with the territory of the agency created

The best example of inherent agency power arises in corporations. As we will see when we study corporations later in the book, corporate officers are agents of the corporation. One such officer is the corporate president. Generally, the office of corporate president carries with it the power to bind the corporation to contracts entered in the ordinary course of business.

Shepherd is president of XYZ Corporation. In that capacity, he signs a contract that obligates XYZ Corporation to buy ordinary supplies from TP. Shepherd did not have actual authority to do this. Neither (to most courts) did he have apparent authority, because the corporation made no manifestation to TP that Shepherd could bind it. Rather, the corporation is bound on the contract because Shepherd, as president, had inherent agency power to bind it.

It is here that we encounter the only substantive distinction we will address between R–2 and R–3. While R–2 recognizes the concept of inherent agency power in § 8A, R–3 purports to abolish it. This abolition was a subject of substantial debate.

In the big picture, however, it is not clear that the abolition will change the way cases are decided. Instead, R–3 simply expands the notion of what constitutes a "manifestation" by P to TP, and hence broadens the scope of apparent authority. So in the hypothetical above about Shepherd, a court applying R–3 would hold the corporation liable on the contract with TP by concluding that the corporation had essentially manifested to TP—by giving Shepherd the title of president— that Shepherd had authority to bind it to deals in the ordinary course of business. That is, Shepherd had "apparent authority by position."

With this background, how do you answer the following problems?

PROBLEMS

1.   Propp, the proprietor of Bubba's Burritos, hires Agee as cook, and tells her that part of her job will be to order the food for the restaurant. Agee does so by ordering grits and the other essential ingredients for Southern-style burritos for the business from TeePee Distributing Co (TP), telling TP that she is ordering the food for Bubba's Burritos. TP delivers the food to Bubba's Burritos.

  a)   Is Propp legally obligated to pay for the food? *See* R–2 §§ 1, 7, 26, 140. *See* R–3 §§ 1.01, 1.02, 3.01, 3.02.

  b)   Is Agee legally obligated to pay for the food? *See* R–2 §§ 4, 320, 321, 322, 326. *See* R–3 §§ 1.04(2), 6.01, 6.02, 6.03, 6.04.

2.   After several months, it becomes clear that Agee has been ordering too much food. Propp instructs Agee to reduce food purchases from TP from $2,200 a month to no more than a $1,000 a month. Notwithstanding this clear instruction, for the next month Agee orders $2,200 of new food from TP.

  a)   Is Propp legally obligated to pay $2,200 to TP? *See* R–2 §§ 8, 27, 140. *See* R–3 §§ 2.03, 3.03.

    b)   Is Agee legally obligated to pay $2,200 to TP? *See* R–2 § 320. *See* R–3 §§ 6.01, 6.10.

    c)   Is Agee liable to Propp for violating her fiduciary duty to Propp? *See* R–2 § 377. *See* R–3 §§ 8.07, 8.09.

    3.   Agee (the cook) calls the local newspaper and tells the advertising director that she is running Bubba's Burritos for Propp (which is simply not true). She then places a series of four full-page ads for Bubba's Burritos with the newspaper.

    a)   Is Propp liable to the newspaper for the Bubba's Burritos advertisements?

    b)   Is Agee liable? *See* R–2 §§ 8A, 320, 321, 322. *See* R–3 §§ 6.01, 6.02, 6.03, 6.10.

    c)   Same facts as 3(a) except that Propp does not contact the newspaper to complain about Agee's lack of authority until after all four of the advertisements have run in the newspaper (even though he knew about them when the first ad was printed). *See* R–2 §§ 93, 319. *See* R-3 § 4.01 *et seq.*

    4.   Your law firm represents the TBS television network. The Leo Burnett advertising agency has been negotiating with TBS for $4,000,000 of McDonald's television advertisements during the NCAA basketball semi-finals. You have drafted the contract. Who should sign the contract—McDonald's or Leo Burnett? Is a signature line for the Leo Burnett advertising agency sufficient or do you need to provide for McDonald's signature? Can a partner in the law firm representing the Leo Burnett agency in negotiating the contract sign on behalf of the agency?

4.   WHAT ARE THE LEGAL CONSEQUENCES OF TORTS COMMITTED BY AN AGENT?

    Suppose Agent (A) is negligent and injures third party (TP) or damages her property. Is Principal (P) liable for that? You may remember the doctrine of *respondeat superior* from Torts. Or you may not.

    Through *respondeat superior*, P can be liable even though P is not personally negligent. For example, P is careful in hiring A and in training A for the job. If A is negligent and injures TP, however, the doctrine of *respondeat superior* will impose liability on P—even though P was not negligent. P's liability is "vicarious" or "secondary," and does not depend on P being negligent.[*]

    But *respondeat superior* does not apply in all cases of agency. Instead, it applies only to a subset of principal-agent relationships

---

[*]   We are concerned only with vicarious liability of P—that is, P's liability for something A did or failed to do, even though P did nothing wrong. P may commit a separate tort by hiring someone negligently—someone who is inappropriate for the job or by failing to supervise an agent. We are not addressing such separate bases of liability here.

traditionally referred to as "master-and-servant." This is antiquated terminology, which is used in R–2 and still employed by many courts. R–2 defines this relationship at §§ 2 and 220. The more modern terminology, reflected in R–3, is "employer-and-employee." The principles are the same, no matter which terminology is used. Problems will work out the same way under R–2 and R–3.

Under both R–2 and R–3, the vicarious liability of the employer (master) for the torts of the employee (servant) depends on her *right* to control the *details* of how the employee (servant) does the job. We have underscored the word "right" to emphasize that liability does not depend on actual control by the employer (master). We have underscored the word "details" because this requirement goes beyond the basic control inherent in all agency relationships, which we discussed above in connection with R–2 § 1 and R–3 § 1.01. For example, Bubba's Burritos could tell its cook when to show up, how to be attired and groomed, how to cook the burritos, etc.

An employee (servant) is to be distinguished from an *independent contractor*, who is hired to do a job, but is not told specifically how to do it. *See* R–2 § 2(3). The torts of an independent contractor generally are *not* attributable to the person who hires him. So vicarious tort liability comes from the fact that the person engaging someone controls the details of how the job is to be done. The dividing line between an employee (servant) and an independent contractor is often hazy, and is always fact-specific. *See* R–2 §§ 220, 228, 229. *See* R–3 § 7.07.

> Roberts hires Shepherd to build a sunroom. Roberts knows nothing about construction. He doesn't care how Shepherd does the job—just so it gets done to Roberts's satisfaction. Shepherd is an independent contractor, and is not a servant. Roberts would not be liable for Shepherd's torts. For example, Roberts would not be liable when Shepherd accidentally hands someone an operating power saw blade-first.

An independent contractor may be an agent or may not be an agent for contract purposes.

> Suppose that when Roberts hires Shepherd, he gives him actual authority to purchase necessary supplies at Home Depot and charge them to Roberts' account. Shepherd is an "agent independent contractor." Although Roberts would be liable in contract to Home Depot for the supplies that Shepherd purchases on Roberts' behalf (he has actual authority), Roberts would not be liable for any torts that Shepherd commits.

> Suppose instead that when Roberts hires Shepherd, he gives him neither actual nor apparent authority to purchase supplies and charge them to his account. Shepherd is a "non-agent

independent contractor." Roberts would be liable for Shepherd's actions neither in contract nor tort.

Finally, note that the employer (master) is liable for the torts of an employee (servant) *only* if the tort was committed within the scope of employment. *See* R–2 § 219. *See* R–3 § 7.07(1). An employer would not be liable when an employee injures his friends by dropping a blender into the hot tub after work.*

Although it might seem that an intentional tort would never be within the scope of one's employment, circumstances might indicate otherwise.

> Freer hires Epstein as bouncer for a party. Epstein punches a guest in the nose. Although Freer did not instruct Epstein to do this, such a tort may go with the territory. Freer is probably vicariously liable. *See* R–2 § 228(1)(d). *See* R–3 § 7.07.

Sometimes an employee (servant) leaves the appointed job to engage in personal business. Case law would say that such a person was on a "frolic." Torts committed during such periods should not be a basis for vicarious liability. Obviously, though, the dividing line here is hazy, and courts may strain to say that a servant was merely on a "detour" (as opposed to a "frolic"), during which torts committed by the servant would create vicarious liability. For example,

> Freer moonlights as a delivery driver for Bubba's Burritos. On his way to make a delivery, he makes a side trip to the stadium to buy tickets to an upcoming game. He commits a tort in the stadium parking lot. This side trip might well be a "frolic," meaning that the master would not be liable. The side trip was not motivated in any way to serve the master. *See* R–2 § 228(1)(c). *See* R–3 § 7.07.

> On his way to make a delivery, Freer goes slightly out of his way to get lunch at McDonald's. He commits a tort in the McDonald's parking lot. This side trip might well be merely a "detour," meaning that the master would be vicariously liable. Although Freer deviated from the most direct route, he is entitled to lunch, and was on his way to do the master's job.

ALMS V. BAUM

Appellate Court of Illinois, 2003
343 Ill.App.3d 67

[Baum, Berger, and Delanty were volunteer counselors at a children's summer camp run by the Ronald McDonald House. They attended four

---

* Shepherd's hypothetical. Freer and Roberts long for the days when they were in hot tubs with friends. Epstein was old before hot tubs and blenders were invented.

mandatory training sessions, the last of which was held on Friday, June 6, 1997, at the camp. Their attendance was also required the following day, when the campers were to arrive. Although rooms were available for the counselors at the camp for that Friday night, counselors were not required to spend the night there. After the training session, Baum, Berger, and Delanty drove in Baum's two-seater sports car to a local bar, the Keg Room. Delanty took camp documents with her to the Keg Room, and worked on those documents at the bar. Baum and Berger watched a basketball game on television and drank beer.

After two hours at the Keg Room, during which Baum drank five beers, the three got back into Baum's car. Delanty sat on Berger's lap. Baum lost control of the vehicle and crashed. Berger was killed and Delanty suffered personal injuries. Berger's estate, represented by Alms, and Delanty sued Baum and the Ronald McDonald House in tort. Their theory against the Ronald McDonald House was *respondeat superior*— that Baum was acting as its employee in the course of employment at the time of the crash. The trial court entered summary judgment in favor of the Ronald McDonald House. Here, the appellate court affirms that decision.]

REID, J. * * * Under the doctrine of *respondeat superior,* an employer can be held vicariously liable for the tortious acts of its employees, including negligent, wilful, malicious, or even criminal acts of its employees when such acts are committed in the course of employment and in furtherance of the business of the employer [citation omitted].

The status of a negligent person as a volunteer worker for a charitable organization does not necessarily preclude a finding that a master-servant relationship existed between the organization and the volunteer [citation omitted]. " 'One who volunteers services without an agreement for or expectation of reward may be a servant of the one accepting such services.' " [citation omitted].

* * *

"The Restatement defines a servant as a type of agent 'employed by a master to perform service in his affairs whose *physical conduct* in the performance of the service is controlled or is subject to the right to control by the master.' (Emphasis added.) Restatement (Second) of Agency § 2(2), at 12 (1958). Although the right to control the physical conduct of the person giving services most often determines whether the relationship of master and servant exists, the right to control may be attenuated [citation omitted]. In addition, a number of other factors may play a role in establishing the master-servant relationship [citation omitted] ... Ultimately, '[t]he relation of master and servant is one not capable of exact definition', and it is generally left to the trier of fact to determine whether the relationship exists [citation omitted]. These facts include the question of the hiring, the right to discharge, the manner of direction of the servant, the right to terminate the relationship, and the character of the supervision of the work done. Unless these facts clearly appear, the relationship cannot become purely a question of law')" [citation omitted].

* * *

"Although the terms 'principal' and 'agent,' 'master' and 'servant,' 'employer' and 'employee' may have separate connotations for purposes of contract authority, such distinctions are immaterial for tort purposes. In order for a plaintiff to invoke the doctrine of *respondeat superior,* it is sufficient that one of the above relationships be established and that the wrongdoer be either the employee, the agent, or the servant [citation omitted]. Incidentally, in some works, the terms 'employer' and 'employee' and 'master' and 'servant' are used interchangeably." [citation omitted]

* * *

[T]he appellants [plaintiffs] point out that attendance at camp events scheduled from June 6, 1997, to June 8, 1997, was mandatory for camp leaders. The appellants note that attendance at the Friday night meeting was mandatory for camp leaders and that accommodations were provided to camp leaders so that they would be present to greet counselors the following Saturday morning. Consequently, the appellants argue that the weekend as a whole was a mandatory working weekend for the camp leaders.

The appellants also contend that Ronald McDonald House had the right to control Baum's physical conduct at the time of the accident. The appellants remind this court that [the director of the camp] testified that it was his belief that he could prohibit camp leaders from drinking alcohol during the time period after the Friday night meeting adjourned and before the subsequent meeting the following Saturday morning commenced.

The appellants maintain that when the accident occurred, Baum was performing a duty that was within the scope of the master-servant relationship that he held with Ronald McDonald House. It is the appellants' assertion that Baum was acting within the scope of the master-servant relationship because he was transporting two camp leaders back to the camp from a place where they had been conducting camp business.

Consequently, the appellants argue that Ronald McDonald House is vicariously liable under the doctrine of *respondeat superior*. At the very least, the appellants contend the determination of whether there existed an agency relationship between Baum and Ronald McDonald House is a question of fact that should be determined by the jury. We disagree.

* * *

In this matter, the trial court's decision to grant summary judgment was proper. * * * It is true that as a volunteer camp leader, Baum had a master-servant relationship with Ronald McDonald House. However, Baum was not acting within the course and scope of his volunteer relationship with Ronald McDonald House when the accident occurred.

At the conclusion of the mandatory Friday night meeting, all official camp business ended until the following morning. As such, when the Friday night meeting concluded, all camp leaders were on their own free time. There was no policy that prohibited camp leaders from leaving the camp premises after the Friday night meeting concluded. Although [the director of the camp] stated that he believed he could prohibit camp leaders from drinking after the Friday night meeting, he admitted that there were no written rules or prohibitions that prevented the campers from doing so. Thus, after the meeting, Baum was free to go wherever he pleased. Baum was only required to return to the camp the following morning to attend the mandatory two-day orientation weekend.

Some camp leaders, but not all, decided to go to the Keg Room on their own volition. Baum drove to and from the Keg Room in his own leased car. At the Keg Room, Baum, who was not working on camp business, drank beer and watched a basketball game on television. It is true that Delanty brought materials with her and indeed worked on camp business while she was at the Keg Room. However, this fact is immaterial. The relevant question that must be answered is whether Baum was acting as an agent of Ronald McDonald House when the accident occurred.

Baum went to the Keg Room to socialize. He did not go with the intent that his trip benefit Ronald McDonald House. The gathering at the Keg Room was not an extension of the Friday night meeting. Attendance at the Keg Room after the Friday night meeting was not mandatory. A number of camp leaders did not go to the Keg Room after the meeting. Moreover, there is no evidence that anyone from the Ronald McDonald House directed Baum to attend the Keg Room.

The accident did not occur within a time or place where Baum would reasonably be performing his duties as a volunteer camp leader. The Keg Room was not located on the camp's premises and was not a place in which Ronald McDonald House would reasonably expect Baum to conduct his duties as a camp leader. Also, the accident, which happened shortly after midnight, occurred at a time when no official camp business was taking place.

When Baum departed from the Keg Room and attempted to drive the appellants back to the camp, he did not reenter the scope of his employment with Ronald McDonald House. Baum attended the Friday night meeting. Thereafter, he went to the Keg Room where he drank and socialized for approximately two hours. Baum then attempted to drive himself and two other people back to the camp in a vehicle that was only intended to transport two people. Such conduct was not reasonable and was not authorized by Ronald McDonald House. This behavior was not incidental to any conduct that Ronald McDonald House authorized Baum to perform as a camp leader.

Baum's act of stopping at the Keg Room and drinking for two hours severed any connection to Ronald McDonald House. There is no evidence that anyone from Ronald McDonald House directed Baum to drive Berger and Delanty back to the camp. Baum's act of driving Delanty and Berger was gratuitous in nature and not within the scope of his employment.

* * * For the foregoing reasons, the decision of the trial court is affirmed.

QUESTIONS

1.   Would the result have been different if the three counselors were required to spend the night at the camp and were returning to the camp for that purpose when the crash occurred?

2.   What if the three had discussed camp business while drinking beer at the Keg Room?

PROBLEMS

1.   Propp hires Servantes to work as a waiter at Bubba's Burritos. Servantes negligently spills scalding coffee on a customer.

a)   Is Propp liable in tort to the customer?

b)   What if Propp specifically told Servantes, both orally and in writing, that his job description did not include spilling scalding liquids of any kind on customers?

c)   Is Servantes also liable in tort to the customer?

2.   While driving to work, Servantes negligently injures a pedestrian.

a)   Is Propp liable in tort to the pedestrian?

b)   Is Servantes liable in tort to the pedestrian?

3.   Propp hires Agee to work as a cook. When Agee overhears a customer criticizing her cooking, she hits the customer over the head with a skillet.

a)   Is Agee liable in tort to the customer?

b)   Is Propp liable in tort to the customer? What if Propp knew about Agee anger management problems when she hired her?

4.   Why should one person ever be liable for torts committed by someone else?

NOTE ON AGENCY THEORY IN ECONOMICS

A considerable body of literature in the management field addresses "agency theory." Briefly put, managers act as agents of the owners of the company. But, agency theory asserts, we cannot always expect the agent to act in the best interests of the principal—the company's owners. Adam Smith made the point long ago:

> The directors of such [joint-stock] companies, however, being the managers rather of other people's money than of their own, it cannot well be expected, that they should watch over it with the same anxious vigilance with which the partners in a private company frequently watch over their own. Like the stewards of a rich man, they are apt to consider attention to small matters as not for their master's honour, and very easily give themselves a dispensation from having it. Negligence and profusion, therefore, must always prevail, more or less, in the management of the affairs of such a company.*

In this context, "agency costs" are the costs that arise from the divergence in behavior between what the principal would do and what the agent does in his place (and also include the costs that the principal bears to monitor the agent). A classic problem is the corporate jet: The CEO gets the benefit of the jet but bears little or none of the cost. If it were up to the shareholders, would they buy the CEO a jet? Probably not. Yet, as principals, the shareholders' individual power is so diluted and diffuse compared with the power of the CEO that such agency costs are common.

In an influential 1996 paper, Jensen and Meckling concluded that one of the chief causes of such agency problems was the fact that CEOs (and other managers) own so little of the stock in their companies that their incentives as managers (agents) outweigh their incentives as principals (owners). The authors proposed that managers should have much higher equity stakes in companies, through such mechanisms as stock option plans.

Jensen and Meckling (and others) did considerable research on leveraged buyouts—"LBOs"—in which publicly-owned companies were "taken private." When this happens, management owns a far higher ownership stake in the company. Research showed that in many cases, the performance of the companies improved considerably, which created "value" (i.e., wealth) for the owners. Many point to these studies as the beginning of the trend towards far higher compensation for CEOs. After all, if these private equity-backed companies' CEOs are making big bucks, why shouldn't the CEOs of public (not private equity-backed) companies make the same?

You can see that the definitions of principal and agent are not quite the same as the legal definitions in this argument, but clearly the concept is borrowed from the legal framework around principals and agents.

---

* Adam Smith, The Wealth of Nations (1776) (Modern Library edition 1937), p. 700.

B. OTHER AGENCY RELATIONSHIPS YOUR CLIENTS AND YOU WILL ENCOUNTER

The application of agency law is not limited to the employment relationship. Lawyers will encounter agency law issues in many other situations.

1. ATTORNEY-CLIENT

The previous problems suggest that Propp might hire an attorney to defend him in various tort and contract actions arising from the business operations of Bubba's Burritos. Is Propp's attorney an agent? If so, for whom? In reading the following case, consider three questions about its facts:

1. What facts support a conclusion that Hayes's attorney was her agent?

2. What facts support a conclusion that Hayes's attorney had actual authority to settle her lawsuit?

3. What facts support a conclusion that Hayes's attorney had apparent authority to settle her lawsuit?

HAYES v. NATIONAL SERVICE INDUSTRIES, INC.

United States Court of Appeals, Eleventh Circuit, 1999
196 F.3d 1252

HOEVELER, SENIOR DISTRICT JUDGE, sitting by designation. Robin Hayes appeals from the decision below enforcing the settlement agreement negotiated by her attorney as to Hayes' action brought pursuant to Title VII, 42 U.S.C. § 2000e. We must decide whether the nature of the underlying action, i.e., the employment discrimination claim, requires a departure from our general reliance on state law principles in determining whether to enforce a settlement agreement. We conclude that under the specific facts of this case it is proper to apply Georgia law to the construction and enforceability of this settlement agreement. Finding no abuse of discretion in the lower court's conclusion that Hayes' attorney had apparent authority to enter into the settlement on Hayes' behalf and that Hayes therefore was bound by the agreement, we affirm.

Hayes sued National Linen Service and its parent company, National Service Industries, Inc. (collectively, "National"), alleging wrongful discharge from her employment as a sales representative. The attorneys for the two parties settled the case. Hayes rejected the settlement, and National filed a motion to enforce the settlement agreement. The Magistrate Judge to whom the motion was referred issued a report finding that Rogers [Hayes's attorney] had apparent authority, and in fact believed he had actual authority, to settle the case. The report found that "the terms of the settlement are clear; plaintiff only contends that she did not consent," but noted that such issue was "irrelevant so long as her attorney has the apparent authority to settle her case [under Georgia law]." Hayes filed her objections to the report, claiming that she did not give Rogers the authority to settle the case on her behalf.

The district court overruled Hayes' objections, and adopted the report and recommendation [of the Magistrate Judge], specifically agreeing that Rogers had "apparent, if not actual, authority" to settle Hayes' claims. Defendants' motion to enforce was granted and Hayes' complaint was dismissed.

We must determine whether the trial judge abused his discretion in deciding to enforce the settlement agreement. * * *

An attorney of record is the client's agent in pursuing a cause of action and under Georgia law "[a]n act of an agent within the scope of his apparent authority binds the principal." The attorney's authority is determined by the representation agreement between the client and the attorney and any instructions given by the client, and that authority may be considered plenary unless it is limited by the client and that limitation is communicated to opposing parties.

"The client is therefore 'bound by his attorney's agreement to settle a lawsuit, even though the attorney may not have had express authority to settle, if the opposing party was unaware of any limitation on the attorney's apparent authority.'" *Ford v. Citizens and Southern Nat. Bank, Cartersville*, 928 F.2d 1118, 1120 (11th Cir. 1991). While Hayes asserts that her attorney lacked authority to settle this matter, it is undisputed that Hayes' attorney, Andrew Rogers, spoke with counsel for National, Sharon Morgan, and expressly told Morgan that he had authority from Hayes to settle the case for $15,000.00. According to Georgia law, an attorney has the apparent authority to enter into a binding agreement on behalf of a client and such agreement is enforceable against the client. Thus, the agreement is enforceable against Hayes according to Georgia law.

Careful attention to the arguments raised by Hayes reveals that her challenge is simply as to the authority of her attorney to enter into the agreement. Her attack on the formation of the contract is answered conclusively by our discussion above. Hayes' attorney told counsel for National that he had authority to settle this matter. An agreement was reached, and it is enforceable against Hayes. We affirm.

QUESTIONS AND NOTES

1. Questions about the law

a) Did the court conclude that Hayes's attorney had "actual authority" or "apparent authority"? Did the court conclude that the attorney had both types of authority?

b) What is the difference, if any, between actual authority and apparent authority?

c) What is the legal significance of the fact that Hayes's attorney told counsel for National that he had authority to settle this matter?

d) Can an agent create his own authority to bind his principal? Is that what happened in this case?

e) Does Hayes have a basis on which to sue her former attorney?

2. Note

Many courts start from the proposition that the settlement decision is the client's decision and conclude that, as a result of that proposition, the traditional rules of agency cannot apply. Courts agree that a client can expressly bestow authority to settle on an attorney-agent. Some courts, however, seem to state that the only way an attorney can have authority to settle is by express authorization. If courts really mean what they say on this point, such a statement necessarily prevents recognizing implied actual authority and apparent authority. For example, in Reutzel v. Douglas, the Supreme Court of Pennsylvania stated that "a client's attorney may not settle a case without the client's grant of express authority, and such authority can only exist where the principal specifically grants the agent the authority to perform a certain task on the principal's behalf."

Grace M. Giesela, *Client Responsibility for Lawyer Conduct: Examining the Agency Nature of the Lawyer-Client Relationship,* 86 NEB. L. REV. 346 (2007). *See also* Yale University v. Out of the Box, LLC., 990 A.2d 869, 874 (Conn.App. 2010)(attorney representing client in litigation does not automatically have either implied or apparent authority to settle or compromise claims).

2. FRANCHISORS AND FRANCHISEES

The relationship of agency law to the franchisor-franchisee relationship is even less clear:

An agency relationship involves consent and control. The parties must have consented that one is to act as a fiduciary on the behalf, and subject to the direction and control, of the other. Whatever the verbalization by the parties about the nature of their relationship, the external facts govern. Agency will then arise if the franchisor-principal has the requisite degree of control over the franchisee-agent, notwithstanding the customary boilerplate provision in the franchising agreement that the parties do not intend an agency relationship.

When a court concludes that in the franchise relationship in issue, the franchisor has retained such control over the operations of the franchisee and its employees as to make the franchisee (and its employees) an agent (or subagents) of the franchisor, long-established principles of relational law come into play. By virtue of its status as a principal, the franchisor becomes liable to third parties for certain acts of its franchisee in its role as an agent. Finally, the control of the franchisor may be so reduced and the relationship sufficiently distant that the franchisee is not viewed as an agent at all. In such event, by definition, vicarious liability can only arise under those agency principles extending agency liability to non-agents under such doctrines as apparent agency or agency by estoppel.

Phillip L. Blumberg & Kurt Strasser, THE LAW OF CORPORATE GROUPS— ENTERPRISE LIABILITY 340–341 (1998).

What are Professors Blumberg and Strasser saying? If Bubba's Burritos prospers and Propp sells franchises, will he be liable to a customer of the Charlottesville franchisee who finds a snuff can lid in his burrito? Is the following case involving a foreign object in a Big Mac helpful in answering this question?

In reading the case, please consider these questions about the facts:

1.   How did the heart-shaped sapphire stone get into the Big Mac? Was that relevant to the court? Should it have been?

2.   Are the employees of 3K "employees" of 3K as that term is used in R–3? "Servants" as that term is used in R–2? Was that relevant to the court? Should it have been?

3.   Are the employees of 3K "servants" of McDonald's Corporation as that term is used in R–2?

4.   How important is it to the court that McDonald's promulgated a manual laying out various requirements for 3K?

MILLER v. MCDONALD'S CORPORATION
Oregon Court of Appeals, 1997
945 P.2d 1107

WARREN, P.J. Plaintiff seeks damages from defendant McDonald's Corporation for injuries that she suffered when she bit into a heart-shaped sapphire stone while eating a Big Mac sandwich that she had purchased at a McDonald's restaurant in Tigard. The trial court granted summary judgment to defendant on the ground that it did not own or operate the restaurant; rather, the owner and operator was a non-party, 3K Restaurants (3K), that held a franchise from defendant. Plaintiff appeals, and we reverse.

    Most of the relevant facts are not in dispute. To the degree that there are disputes, we read the record most favorably to plaintiff, the non-moving party, and review the evidence to determine whether an objectively reasonable juror could return a verdict in her favor on the subject of the motion. 3K owned and operated the restaurant under a License Agreement (the Agreement) with defendant that required it to operate in a manner consistent with the "McDonald's System." The Agreement described that system as including proprietary rights in trade names, service marks and trade marks, as well as "designs and color schemes for restaurant buildings, signs, equipment layouts, formulas and specifications for certain food products, methods of inventory and operation control, bookkeeping and accounting, and manuals covering business practices and policies."

    The manuals [promulgated by McDonald's for franchisees] contain "detailed information relating to operation of the Restaurant," including food formulas and specifications, methods of inventory control, bookkeeping procedures, business practices, and other management, advertising, and personnel policies. 3K, as the licensee, agreed to adopt and exclusively use the formulas, methods, and policies contained in the manuals, including any subsequent modifications, and to use only advertising and promotional materials that defendant either provided or approved in advance in writing.

The Agreement described the way in which 3K was to operate the restaurant in considerable detail. It expressly required 3K to operate in compliance with defendant's prescribed standards, policies, practices, and procedures, including serving only food and beverage products that defendant designated. 3K had to follow defendant's specifications and blueprints for the equipment and layout of the restaurant, including adopting subsequent reasonable changes that defendant made, and to maintain the restaurant building in compliance with defendant's standards. 3K could not make any changes in the basic design of the building without defendant's approval.

The Agreement required 3K to keep the restaurant open during the hours that defendant prescribed, including maintaining adequate supplies and employing adequate personnel to operate at maximum capacity and efficiency during those hours. 3K also had to keep the restaurant similar in appearance to all other McDonald's restaurants. 3K's employees had to wear McDonald's uniforms, to have a neat and clean appearance, and to provide competent and courteous service. 3K could use only containers and other packaging that bore McDonald's trademarks. The ingredients for the foods and beverages had to meet defendant's standards, and 3K had to use "only those methods of food handling and preparation that [defendant] may designate from time to time." In order to obtain the franchise, 3K had to represent that the franchisee had worked at a McDonald's restaurant; the Agreement did not distinguish in this respect between a company-run or a franchised restaurant. The manuals gave further details that expanded on many of these requirements.

In order to ensure conformity with the standards described in the Agreement, defendant periodically sent field consultants to the restaurant to inspect its operations. 3K trained its employees in accordance with defendant's materials and recommendations and sent some of them to training programs that defendant administered. Failure to comply with the agreed standards could result in loss of the franchise.

Despite these detailed instructions, the Agreement provided that 3K was not an agent of defendant for any purpose. Rather, it was an independent contractor and was responsible for all obligations and liabilities, including claims based on injury, illness, or death, directly or indirectly resulting from the operation of the restaurant.

Plaintiff went to the restaurant under the assumption that defendant owned, controlled, and managed it. So far as she could tell, the restaurant's appearance was similar to that of other McDonald's restaurants that she had patronized. Nothing disclosed to her that any entity other than defendant was involved in its operation. The only signs that were visible and obvious to the public had the name "McDonald's,"* [2] the employees wore uniforms with McDonald's insignia, and the menu was the same that plaintiff had seen in other McDonald's restaurants. The general appearance of the restaurant and the food products that it sold were similar to the restaurants and products that plaintiff had seen in national print and television advertising that defendant had run. To the best of plaintiff's knowledge, only McDonald's sells Big Mac hamburgers.

In short, plaintiff testified, she went to the Tigard McDonald's because she relied on defendant's reputation and because she wanted to obtain the same quality of service, standard of care in food preparation, and general attention to detail that she had previously enjoyed at other McDonald's restaurants.

Under these facts, 3K would be directly liable for any injuries that plaintiff suffered as a result of the restaurant's negligence. The issue on summary judgment is whether there is evidence that would permit a jury to find defendant vicariously liable for those injuries because of its relationship with 3K. Plaintiff asserts two theories of vicarious liability, actual agency and apparent agency. We hold that there is sufficient evidence to raise a jury issue under both theories. We first discuss actual agency.

The kind of actual agency relationship that would make defendant vicariously liable for 3K's negligence requires that defendant have the right to control the method by which 3K performed its obligations under the Agreement. The common context for that test is a normal master-servant (or employer-employee) relationship. The relationship between two business entities is not precisely an employment relationship, but the Oregon Supreme Court, in common with most if not all other courts that have considered the issue, has applied the right to control test for vicarious liability in that context as well. We therefore apply that test to this case. * * *

A number of other courts have applied the right to control test to a franchise relationship. The Delaware Supreme Court, in *Billops v. Magness Const. Co.*, 391 A.2d 196 (Del. 1978), stated the test as it applies to that context:

> If, in practical effect, the franchise agreement goes beyond the stage of setting standards, and allocates to the franchisor the right to exercise control over the daily operations of the franchise, an agency relationship exists.

---

* [2] This is plaintiff's testimony in her affidavit. Representatives of 3K testified in their depositions that there was a sign near the front counter that identified Bob and Karen Bates and 3K Restaurants as the owners. There is no evidence of the size or prominence of the sign, nor is there evidence of any other non-McDonald's identification in the restaurant.

* * *

[I]n *Billops* the franchise agreement for a Hilton Inn hotel incorporated a detailed and, in part, mandatory operating manual that covered identification, advertising, front office procedures, cleaning and inspection service for rooms and public areas, minimum room standards, food purchasing and preparation standards, staff procedures and standards for booking group meetings, function, and room reservations, accounting, insurance, engineering, maintenance and numerous other details. The franchisee had to keep detailed records so that the franchisor could ensure compliance with those guidelines, while the franchisor retained the right to enter the premises to ensure compliance. The franchisor could terminate on 20 days notice for an uncorrected violation. The court held that those facts created a jury issue of whether an actual agency relationship existed.

* * *

The facts of this case are close to those in *Billops*. For that reason, we believe that a jury could find that defendant retained sufficient control over 3K's daily operations that an actual agency relationship existed. The Agreement did not simply set standards that 3K had to meet. Rather, it required 3K to use the precise methods that defendant established, both in the Agreement and in the detailed manuals that the Agreement incorporated. Those methods included the ways in which 3K was to handle and prepare food. Defendant enforced the use of those methods by regularly sending inspectors and by its retained power to cancel the Agreement. That evidence would support a finding that defendant had the right to control the way in which 3K performed at least food handling and preparation. In her complaint, plaintiff alleges that 3K's deficiencies in those functions resulted in the sapphire being in the Big Mac and thereby caused her injuries. Thus, * * * there is evidence that defendant had the right to control 3K in the precise part of its business that allegedly resulted in plaintiff's injuries. That is sufficient to raise an issue of actual agency.

Plaintiff next asserts that defendant is vicariously liable for 3K's alleged negligence because 3K was defendant's apparent agent.* [4] The relevant standard is in Restatement (Second) of Agency, § 267. [That section provides: "One who represents that another is his servant or other agent and thereby causes a third person justifiably to rely upon the care or skill of such apparent agent is subject to liability to the third person for

---

*   [4] Apparent agency is a distinct concept from apparent authority. Apparent agency creates an agency relationship that does not otherwise exist, while apparent authority expands the authority of an actual agent. *See Crinkley v. Holiday Inns, Inc.*, 844 F.2d 156, 166 (4th Cir. 1988). In this case, the precise issue is whether 3K was defendant's apparent agent, not whether 3K had apparent authority. However, because courts in Oregon and elsewhere often use the terms interchangeably, we will treat the parties' arguments as based on apparent agency, whichever term they actually use.

harm caused by the lack of care or skill of the one appearing to be a servant or other agent as if he were such."]

We have not applied § 267 to a franchisor/franchisee situation, but courts in a number of other jurisdictions have done so in ways that we find instructive. In most cases the courts have found that there was a jury issue of apparent agency. The crucial issues are whether the putative principal held the third party out as an agent and whether the plaintiff relied on that holding out.

We look first at what may constitute a franchisor's holding a franchisee out as its agent. In the leading case of *Gizzi v. Texaco, Inc.*, 437 F.2d 308 (5th Cir. 1971), the plaintiff purchased a used Volkswagen van from a Texaco service station. He was injured when the brakes failed shortly thereafter. The franchisee had worked on the brakes before selling the car. The station prominently displayed Texaco insignia, including the slogan "Trust your car to the man who wears the star." Texaco engaged in considerable national advertising to convey the impression that its dealers were skilled in automotive servicing. About 30 percent of Texaco dealers sold used cars. There was a Texaco regional office across the street from the station, and those working in that office knew that the franchisee was selling cars from the station. Based on this evidence, the court concluded, under New Jersey law, that the question of apparent agency was for the jury. * * *

In [such] cases, the franchise agreement required the franchisee to act in ways that identified it with the franchisor. The franchisor imposed those requirements as part of maintaining an image of uniformity of operations and appearance for the franchisor's entire system. Its purpose was to attract the patronage of the public to that entire system. The centrally imposed uniformity is the fundamental basis for the courts' conclusion that there was an issue of fact whether the franchisors held the franchisees out as the franchisors' agents.

In this case, for similar reasons, there is an issue of fact about whether defendant held 3K out as its agent. Everything about the appearance and operation of the Tigard McDonald's identified it with defendant and with the common image for all McDonald's restaurants that defendant has worked to create through national advertising, common signs and uniforms, common menus, common appearance, and common standards. The possible existence of a sign identifying 3K as the operator does not alter the conclusion that there is an issue of apparent agency for the jury. There are issues of fact of whether that sign was sufficiently visible to the public, in light of plaintiff's apparent failure to see it, and of whether one sign by itself is sufficient to remove the impression that defendant created through all of the other indicia of its control that it, and 3K under the requirements that defendant imposed, presented to the public.* [7]

Defendant does not seriously dispute that a jury could find that it held 3K out as its agent. Rather, it argues that there is insufficient evidence that plaintiff justifiably relied on that holding out. It argues that it is not sufficient for her to prove that she went to the Tigard McDonald's because it was a McDonald's restaurant. Rather, she also had to prove that she went to it because she believed that McDonald's Corporation operated both it and the other McDonald's restaurants that she had previously patronized. It states: * * * her affidavit does nothing to link her experiences with ownership of those restaurants by McDonald's Corporation."

Defendant's argument both demands a higher level of sophistication about the nature of franchising than the general public can be expected to have and ignores the effect of its own efforts to lead the public to believe that McDonald's restaurants are part of a uniform national system of restaurants with common products and common standards of quality. A jury could find from plaintiff's affidavit that she believed that all McDonald's restaurants were the same because she believed that one entity owned and operated all of them or, at the least, exercised sufficient control that the standards that she experienced at one would be the same as she experienced at others.

Plaintiff testified in her affidavit that her reliance on defendant for the quality of service and food at the Tigard McDonald's came in part from her experience at other McDonald's restaurants. Defendant's argument that she must show that it, rather than a franchisee, operated those restaurants is, at best, disingenuous. A jury could find that it was defendant's very insistence on uniformity of appearance and standards, designed to cause the public to think of every McDonald's, franchised or unfranchised, as part of the same system, that makes it difficult or impossible for plaintiff to tell whether her previous experiences were at restaurants that defendant owned or franchised.

* * *

In this case plaintiff testified that she relied on the general reputation of McDonald's in patronizing the Tigard restaurant and in her expectation of the quality of the food and service that she would receive. Especially in light of defendant's efforts to create a public perception of a common McDonald's system at all McDonald's restaurants, whoever operated them, a jury could find that plaintiff's reliance was objectively

---

   *   **[7]** In addition, operation of the restaurant by a franchisee is not inconsistent as a matter of law with a finding of agency. An agency relationship necessarily requires that the principal and the agent be separate entities.

reasonable. The trial court erred in granting summary judgment on the apparent agency theory.

Reversed and remanded.

QUESTIONS AND NOTES

1. Questions about the law

a) Would 3K be liable for the negligence of its employee? If so, why did Miller sue McDonald's?

b) The Court noted that the agreement between 3K and McDonald's provided that 3K was not an agent of McDonald's. Was that important to the court? Should it have been?

c) How is "apparent agency" (discussed by the court in footnote 4 in *Miller*) different from "apparent authority"? Is apparent agency a basis for imposing contract liability, tort liability, or both?

d) The court in Miller relied upon § 267 of the Restatement (Second) of Agency:

> § 267   Reliance upon Care or Skill or Apparent Servant or Other Agent
>
> One who represents that another is his servant or other agent and thereby causes a third person justifiably to rely upon the care or skill or such apparent agent is subject to liability to the third person for harm caused by the lack of care or skill of the one appearing to be a servant or other agent as if he were such.

The Restatement (Third) of Agency R–3 does not contain a similar section. Instead, a Reporter's Note to § 7.07 of R–3 states: "This section is a consolidated treatment of topics covered in several separate sections of Restatement Second, Agency, including * * * § 267." Section 7.07 of R–3 is entitled "Employee Acting Within Scope of Employment." Is a franchisee an employee of the franchisor?

e) Could the plaintiffs in *Miller* avoid summary judgment by invoking R–2 § 8B or R–3 § 2.05, which deal with estoppel? By the way, how does estoppel compare with apparent authority?

f) Can you see now why a franchisee's stationary and advertising often state, "This company is independently owned and operated"?

2. Notes

a) In granting summary judgments favorable to franchisors, courts in franchisor liability cases sometimes engage in questionable judicial fact finding. Some courts have made unconvincing assumptions and assessments about franchisor control that need to be considered more carefully and realistically.

Moreover, mere clever labeling and drafting in documents should not preclude inquiry by counsel and courts into the fundamental issue of the reality of control in the franchisor-franchisee relationship. Where plaintiffs pursue apparent agency or estoppel claims, dismissing their cases because of premises signs, web site notices, or the like may be inappropriate in the face of the other manifestations to which they have been subjected. After all, customers patronizing franchised businesses lack the sophistication, time or information to negate the powerful impression made by franchisor publicity before they buy their sandwich or register at a hotel. Injured plaintiffs and franchisor defendants should expect realism and not generalized, arbitrary rules in the factual assessment of their positions. Nor is the exclusion of relevant evidence of franchisor manifestations, such as national advertising, appropriate. Obviously, respect for courts is undermined by improper fact finding.

Guidance by analogy or otherwise from agency or tort principles and the underlying policies they serve is reasonable in franchisor liability cases. As courts settle upon applicable legal doctrines for franchisor liability, a vitally important policy consideration is the extent to which tort responsibility will encourage franchisors to emphasize health and safety considerations that would prevent injuries, thereby benefiting individuals and society.

Harvey Gelb, *A Rush to (Summary) Judgment in Franchisor Liability Cases?* 13 WYO. L. REV. 215, 261 (2013).

b) One of Miller's arguments was that McDonald's, a corporation, was liable for the acts of 3K, another corporation, because McDonald's control over 3K's performance made 3K McDonald's agent. While the relationship between the two corporations in this case was franchisor-franchisee, the concept that a corporation can be liable under agency law principles for the acts of another corporation if it controls that corporation's performance of the acts is not limited to franchises. *Cf.* R–2 § 14M. We will talk more about this when we know enough about corporations that we can compare "piercing the corporate veil" and apparent agency.

3. DOCTORS AND HOSPITALS

RAMIREZ V. LONG BEACH MEMORIAL MEDICAL CENTER

California Court of Appeal, 2013
2013 WL 1144257 (not certified for official publication)

BIGELOW, P.J. This appeal challenges a summary judgment in a wrongful death action based on alleged medical malpractice in treating a gunshot victim at Long Beach Memorial Medical Center ("the hospital"). The trial court found the hospital immunized itself against *respondeat superior* liability for any malpractice by the treating physicians by having the patient's mother sign a printed admission form which included an express acknowledgement that the medical providers were independent contractors and not employees or agents of the hospital. * * *

The trial court granted the hospital's motion for summary judgment and entered judgment accordingly. Though the trial court properly found no triable issue of fact as to the emergency room nurse, we find there are unresolved factual issues in determining whether the admission form was binding so that it terminates the hospital's liability. For that reason, we reverse the grant of summary judgment.*

FACTS

Background

An assailant shot Julio Ramirez in the left thigh and lower leg. After the shooting, paramedics transported Ramirez to the hospital. Ramirez arrived at the emergency room at about 11:45 p.m. Ramirez was agitated, suffering a large amount of blood loss, and in extreme pain. Atul Gupta, M.D., the primary emergency room doctor, and Frederick Stafford, M.D., a trauma surgeon, initially examined Ramirez. Dr. Stafford then went into surgery with another gunshot victim. Ramirez remained in Dr. Gupta's care in the emergency room. Based on a lack of pulse in Ramirez's lower leg and severe bleeding, Dr. Gupta ordered an on-call vascular surgeon to be summoned to the hospital.

---

*   Note from your authors:

Celebrating over 100 years, Long Beach Memorial Medical Center has been recognized as a major regional provider of medical and surgical services. Long Beach Memorial consistently achieves national accolades for its quality care, including being named as one of the U.S. top 125 hospitals by Consumers' CHECKBOOK; named Top 100 Hospitals Cardiovascular by Thomson Reuters; and named one of "America's Best Hospitals" for Orthopedics by U.S. News & World Report magazine. Our state-of-the-art electronic medical records system ensures our patients receive the best, safest possible care. http://www.memorialcare.org/long-beach-memorial.

After Ramirez arrived at the hospital, Ramirez's mother, Herminia Ramirez, was presented with a three-page, printed form entitled "CONDITIONS OF ADMISSION." The Conditions of Admission form included a consent to medical and surgical procedures during hospitalization. Paragraph 4 of form stated "LEGAL RELATIONSHIP BETWEEN HOSPITAL AND PHYSICIAN." It reads:

> "All physicians and surgeons furnishing services to the patient, including the * * * emergency department physician, and other hospital-based physicians and the like, are independent contractors with the patient and are not employees or agents of the hospital. The patient is under the care and supervision of his/her attending physician and it is the responsibility of the hospital and its nursing staff to carry out the instructions of such physician. It is the responsibility of the patient's physician or surgeon to obtain the patient's consent or informed consent, when required, to medical or surgical treatment, special diagnostic or therapeutic procedures, or hospital services rendered to the patient under general and special instructions of the physician. The hospital-based physicians fees are billed separately and independently of hospital charges, which means you will receive multiple bills."

Paragraph 14 of the Conditions of Admission form reads: "If any provision of this agreement is finally determined by a court to be unenforceable, the remainder of this agreement shall remain in full force and effect. [¶] This hospital admission agreement shall bind the parties herein, including . . . the heirs, representatives, executors, administrators, successors, and assigns of such parties. . . ." Ms. Ramirez signed the Conditions of Admission form, with a notation that she was Ramirez's "mom."

Meanwhile, there was a significant delay in the arrival of the on-call vascular surgeon to the hospital. Ramirez was not taken from the emergency room to an operating room until about 2:45 a.m., roughly three hours after he arrived at the emergency room. Ramirez died during surgery at about 7:00 a.m. the following morning.

The Litigation

Ms. Ramirez and Ramirez's minor children (collectively Plaintiffs) filed a wrongful death action. The operative pleading is their second amended complaint. It alleges Ramirez "unnecessarily bled to death" as a result of a negligent delay in getting him into surgery. Dr. Gupta, Dr. Stafford, Nurse Lynn Witte, the hospital, and others are listed as defendants.

The hospital filed a motion for summary judgment supported by evidence showing that Herminia Ramirez signed the printed Conditions of Admission form with the language acknowledging that the doctors at the hospital were independent contractors, and not employees, and by an expert's declaration stating that the hospital's nursing staff did not act below the standard of care. * * *

In *Mejia,* Division Two of the Fourth District Court of Appeal traced the history, principles, and law of *respondeat superior* liability and ostensible agency as it involves hospitals and medical professionals. The court reviewed authorities in both California and in other states, and then applied its understanding of the law as it exists today in reversing a judgment of nonsuit in favor of a hospital based on the lack of ostensible agency. We find the following discussion instructive:

> Although the cases discussing ostensible agency use various linguistic formulations to describe the elements of the doctrine, in essence, they require the same two elements: (1) conduct by the hospital that would cause a reasonable person to believe that the physician was an agent of the hospital, and (2) reliance on that apparent agency relationship by the plaintiff.

> Regarding the first element, courts generally conclude that it is satisfied when the hospital 'holds itself out' to the public as a provider of care. In order to prove this element, it is not necessary to show an express representation by the hospital. Instead, a hospital is generally deemed to have held itself out as the provider of care, unless it gave the patient contrary notice. Many courts have even concluded that prior notice may not be sufficient to avoid liability in an emergency room context, where an injured patient in need of immediate medical care cannot be expected to understand or act upon that information.

> The second element, reliance, is established when the plaintiff "looks to" the hospital for services, rather than to an individual physician. . . .

> As should be apparent to an astute observer, there is really only one relevant factual issue: *whether the patient had reason to know that the physician was not an agent of the hospital.* As noted above, hospitals are generally deemed to have held themselves out as the provider of services unless they gave the patient contrary notice, and the patient is generally presumed to have looked to the hospital for care unless he or she was treated by his or her personal physician. *Thus, unless the patient had some reason to know of the true relationship between the hospital and the physician—[e.g.], because the hospital gave the patient actual notice or because the patient* was treated by his or her personal physician—ostensible agency is readily inferred."

Mejia v. Comm. Hosp. of San Bernardino, 99 Cal.App.4th 1448, 1453–55 (Cal. App. 2002) (emphases added) (footnote omitted).

Analysis

If the decedent, Ramirez, had gone to the hospital for *pre-planned* surgery, and, if *he* had signed the Conditions of Admission form acknowledging that the physician doing the surgery was not an agent or employee of the hospital, and if *he* were suing the hospital, then we might find that applied, immunizing the hospital against *respondeat superior* liability based upon Ramirez's own express acknowledgement of the absence of agency. If undisputed evidence shows a patient in a non-emergency treatment situation expressly acknowledged a lack of agency between a physician and hospital, we might conclude the patient was bound by the acknowledgement. However, the scenario we described is not what happened between Ramirez and the hospital.

Here, Ramirez was the *patient* and he was undisputedly an adult. He did not sign the Conditions of Admission form acknowledging that there was no agency relationship between the hospital and the treating physicians. On the contrary, the *patient's mother* signed the form. In the absence of evidence showing that Ramirez authorized his mother to act on his behalf, it cannot definitively be found that the patient acknowledged the non-agent status of the doctors. We see two agency issues in the current case—the ostensible agency between the hospital and the doctors in the emergency room, and the possible agency relationship between Ramirez and his mother. We do not believe this is a proper case for summary judgment under *Mejia* in the absence of evidence showing that the patient, personally or by an authorized agent, acknowledged a non-agency relationship between hospital and doctor. Even if Ramirez had survived, we think his mother's acknowledgement of non-agency might not prevent Ramirez from seeking to impose liability on the hospital. At least not until evidence showed Ms. Ramirez had authority to bind her son to the acknowledgement of non-agency.

It also makes a difference that this is a wrongful death action brought by Ms. Ramirez and Ramirez's children, rather than a malpractice claim by Ramirez himself. In the context of summary judgment, for the reasons stated above, we find there are factual questions about Ms. Ramirez's authority to bind her grandchildren to the acknowledgement of non-agency to defeat the hospital's motion for summary judgment.

We also find the motion for summary judgment should not have been granted as to Ms. Ramirez. She did not, as a matter of law, bind herself to the express acknowledgment of non-agency. Where the evidence shows an acknowledgement of non-agency was signed in a stressful situation, with overtones of duress, it is a question of fact whether the acknowledgement is enforceable against the signator. * * * A jury reasonably could infer that Ms. Ramirez did not understand, or freely accept, the acknowledgement that the doctors in the emergency room were not the hospital's agents or employees.

The existence of a non-agency acknowledgement form, standing on its own as it largely does here, not signed by the patient receiving treatment or shown to be signed by a person who was an authorized agent for medical decisions, is insufficient to establish as a matter of law that the hospital is immune from *respondeat superior* liability via a *Mejia* defense.

DISPOSITION

The summary judgment entered in favor of the hospital is reversed. Appellants to recover their costs on appeal.

QUESTIONS

1.   Before reading this case, did you believe that the doctors working in a hospital's emergency room (ER) were employees of the hospital?

2.   Would *Ramirez* have been decided differently if Julio had told his mother Herminia, "would you please handle all hospital forms for me? I am kind of stressed out and I trust your judgment"?

3.   In this case, what was the "proof of reliance on the apparent agency relationship by the plaintiff"?

4.   Do you agree with the following?

> I concur because precedent requires me to do so. I believe, however, that our twenty-year experiment with the use of apparent agency as a doctrine to determine a hospital's vicarious liability for the acts of various independent contractors has been a failure. Patients, hospitals, doctors, nurses, other licensed professionals, risk managers for governmental agencies, and insurance companies all need to have predictable general rules establishing the parameters of vicarious liability in this situation. Utilizing case-specific decisions by individually selected juries to determine whether a hospital is or is not vicariously liable for the mistakes of a radiology department, an emergency room, or some other corporate entity that has been created as an independent contractor to provide necessary services within the hospital is inefficient, unpredictable and, perhaps most important, a source of avoidable litigation. Our society can undoubtedly function well and provide insurance coverage to protect the risks of malpractice if there is either broad liability upon the hospital for these services as nondelegable duties or if liability is restricted to the independent contractor. The uncertainty of the current system, however, does not work. The supreme court or the legislature needs to simplify the rules of liability in this are.

Roessler v. Novak, 858 So.2d 1158, 1163 (Fla. Dist. Ct. App. 2003) (Altenbernd, J., concurring).

CHAPTER 3

WHAT IS A PARTNERSHIP AND HOW DOES IT WORK?

■ ■ ■

Propp does not know what a partnership is but he knows that he needs some help running Bubba's Burritos. He also knows that he needs to keep Agee as a cook and a manager of Bubba's Burritos, and Agee has said that she will leave unless she shares in the profits and has a "say" in business decisions. And Propp knows that he needs money to expand Bubba's Burritos, money that is available from Capel, who also wants to share in the profits and to participate in business decisions.

Propp also knows that if he brings Capel or anyone else into the business there will be questions about (1) how the profits and losses from the business should be divided, and (2) who makes the various business decisions that affect profitability. This chapter (and the rest of the book) will focus on these questions of who gets the money and who makes the decisions. This chapter will consider what else Propp's attorney (and Agee and Capel's attorneys) should know about starting, operating, growing, profiting from and selling a business as a partnership.

A. WHAT IS A PARTNERSHIP?

Of course, a partnership is a form of business. The two primary differences between a sole proprietorship and a partnership are (i) the number of owners and (ii) the number of legal entities.

Obviously, as we saw in Chapter 1, a *sole* proprietorship is a business with only one owner. A partnership, in contrast, is a business with more than one owner. All of the statutory and common law definitions of a partnership refer to "co-owners", plural. The operative language of all statutory definitions is the same: a partnership is "an association of two or more persons to carry on as co-owners a business for profit." *See* Uniform Partnership Act (UPA) § 6(1) and Revised Uniform Partnership Act (RUPA) §§ 101(6), 202(a).

We will see below that UPA and RUPA are the two leading models of partnership statutes. Most states have partnership statutes based on RUPA. Throughout the chapter, we will compare and contrast UPA and RUPA provisions. We will be referring primarily to RUPA but will provide parallel citations to UPA.

Not only is a sole proprietorship a business with only one owner, but that business and its one owner are treated as a single legal entity. That means that the assets of the business are also the assets of its owner; the obligations of the business are also the obligations of its owner.

Partnerships are different—sort of. While the obligations of a business operated as a partnership are also the obligations of its owners, we will see that a partnership is, in some other respects, treated as a separate legal entity from its owners.

RUPA § 201 provides that a partnership is "an entity distinct from its partners." In contrast, UPA generally embraces an "aggregate theory," i.e., it considers a partnership not as a separate legal person but rather as merely the aggregate of its partners. However, there are provisions in RUPA that are more consistent with the aggregate theory than the entity theory, and there are provisions in UPA that are more consistent with the entity theory than the aggregate theory.

For some purposes, the partnership is routinely seen as an entity and for some it is not. In the area of taxation, which (happily) is beyond the scope of this book and course, the partnership is seen as an aggregate of partners. Thus, the partnership itself does not pay tax on its profits. Instead, only the partners pay tax on the business's profits. This is called "flow-through" taxation, and is a distinct advantage over the corporation, which is universally regarded as an entity separate from those who run and own it. Thus, the corporation itself pays taxes on its profits *and* its shareholders pay taxes on distributions they receive, so-called "double taxation." But enough about tax.

As a bottom line, your answers to specific questions posed by your professors or by clients or by judges will not be based upon whether you embrace an aggregate or entity status, but rather on the language of the relevant statutory provisions. Or as Paul McCartney and Stevie Wonder might have put it:

> *Aggregate and entity, live together in perfect harmony;*
> *Side by side in RUPA and UPA;*
> *Oh Lord, why don't we?*

QUESTIONS

1.   Can a business be both a sole proprietorship and a partnership? Can I start a partnership by myself?

2.   Can a business be both a corporation and a partnership? *See* RUPA § 202(b). *See also* the Official Comments to RUPA § 202.

3.   Can a corporation serve as a partner in a partnership? *See* UPA §§ 2 and 6(1); RUPA §§ 101(10) and 202(a).

B. WHAT IS PARTNERSHIP LAW?

Partnership law deals with the rights and obligations of partnerships and the rights and obligations of partners. For centuries, this law was common law.

Although every state now has some form of general partnership statute, case law remains an important part of partnership law. Case law is important not only in interpreting the provisions in partnership statutes, but also in filling gaps in such statutes. State partnership laws usually contain a provision similar to UPA § 5 and RUPA § 104, which state that "the principles of law and equity" govern to the extent not provided for by statute.

At first blush, this combination of state partnership statutes and case law would seem to be the place to look for answers to all questions about the rights and obligations of partnerships and partners. Blush again. So long as the question involves only the rights and obligations of the partnership and its partners, the primary source of partnership "law" will not be a statute or case law at all. It will be the *partnership agreement*.

As RUPA § 103 states, in part:

SECTION 103. EFFECT OF PARTNERSHIP AGREEMENT;

(a) Except as otherwise provided in subsection (b), relations among the partners and between the partners and the partnership are governed by the partnership agreement. To the extent the partnership agreement does not otherwise provide, this [Act] governs relations among the partners and between the partners and the partnership. See also UPA § 18.

As co-author Freer points out

The resultant flexibility is important, and reflects the clear policy choice that the businesspeople should be left to structure their relationship as best suits them. For example, suppose three people form a partnership. Alpha contributes 70 percent of the capital to start the business, while Beta and Omega each contribute 15 percent. Because of her larger investment and risk, Alpha may naturally expect that she should have the authority to make major business decisions. Similarly, Alpha may naturally expect to receive 70 percent of any profits. Unless such understandings are reflected in a partnership agreement, however, Alpha is subject to the default rules of UPA and RUPA, which provide that management decisions are to be made by majority vote of the partners and that profits will be shared equally.

Richard D. Freer, *Business Organizations*, OXFORD COMPANION TO AMERICAN LAW 78 (2001).

Note that Freer's examples involve disputes among partners or disputes between one or more partners and the partnership. Not a legal problem involving the partnership and someone who is not a partner, i.e., a third party. The partnership agreement may not "restrict the rights of third parties under this Act," RUPA § 103(b)(10).

C. WHAT ARE THE LEGAL ISSUES IN STARTING A BUSINESS AS A PARTNERSHIP?

Starting a business as a partnership, like starting a business as a sole proprietorship, requires no formal legal steps. Both sole proprietorships and partnerships can be viewed as "residual" or "default" business structures. If one person owns a business and she does not take any action to qualify it as a corporation or some other particular form of business structure, it will be a sole proprietorship. If two or more people own a business and they do not take any action to qualify it as a corporation or some other particular form of business structure, it will be a partnership.

Creating a partnership does not require that papers be filed in the public records. As the next case, *In re Estate of Fenimore*, illustrates, if two or more persons are operating a business as co-owners, that business will be a partnership—even if there is no formal partnership agreement, and even if the partners do not realize that they have formed a partnership.

In reading the *Fenimore* case, please consider the following questions:

1.   Who owes money to whom? Were the creditors referred to as "Villabona" owed money by the car business? Was that important to the court?

2.   Who is contending that the agreement between Mrs. Audrey Serge and her brother, Donald Fenimore, was a partnership agreement? Who is arguing instead that the agreement between Mrs. Serge and her brother is a loan? Why?

3.   Did the agreement between sister Audrey and brother Donald use the word "partnership"?

4.   Was Audrey involved in the operation of the car business?

5.   Is anyone contending that Donald did not receive at least $15,000 from Audrey which has not been repaid?

6.   The agreement is reproduced below. Did a lawyer prepare this agreement? If so, was she a good lawyer?

This Agreement between Donald R. Fenimore, Sr. and Audrey F. Watt made this Sixth day of November Nineteen Hundred Eighty-nine sets forth our understanding of our business arrangements.

Audrey F. Watt has advanced Twenty-five Hundred Dollars ($2,500.00) and Ten Thousand Dollars ($10,000.00) to Donald R. Fenimore in order for him to conduct the business of buying and selling of motor vehicles.

Donald R. Fenimore hereby agrees to divide the profits from each vehicle bought and sold with Audrey F. Watt immediately upon the sale of each or as soon as feasible thereafter. Donald R. Fenimore will pay the expenses incident to his conducting the business and Audrey F. Watt will pay the costs incident to her borrowing the said sums of money.

Donald R. Fenimore agrees to execute this document and a Last Will and Testament which will make Audrey F. Watt his sole heir and sole beneficiary of all his assets upon his demise and this shall be in force until his death unless Audrey F. Watt executes a release contrary to this.

Should Donald R. Fenimore die or become incapacitated prior to the settling of the estate of his mother, Annie F. Fenimore, he hereby gives and bequeaths all his rights and interests therein to his sister, Audrey F. Watt, and gives her sole control over his share of his mother's estate.

Donald R. Fenimore appoints his sister, Audrey F. Watt, as his executrix without giving Bond for his Last Will and Testament. However, should he die prior to executing a Will, this will serve as his Last Will and Testament.

Donald R. Fenimore appoints Audrey F. Watt to be the sole individual to make all the arrangements for his funeral and burial. His wish is to be buried in the cemetery plot where his father, Harvey C. Fenimore, and his mother, Annie F. Fenimore, are buried in Silverbrook Cemetery, of which he is an equal owner together with his nine brothers and sisters. His five children or any other person(s) are not to interfere with any arrangements that she makes. His five children will be adequately taken care of by their mother in life and in death. They have no recourse as to their father's estate. This provision is solely the Will of Donald R. Fenimore and Audrey F. Watt has no influence as to his decision and desire.

Should Donald R. Fenimore still have a live-in relationship with Joyce D. Middleton at the time of his death, she shall be given adequate time to move the mobile home and the household furnishings in which they reside and it will be hers solely. However, the time to remove said mobile home will not exceed 60 days unless agreed to in writing by Audrey F. Watt. The personal effects of Donald R. Fenimore in the mobile home shall be turned over immediately to Audrey F. Watt at the time of his death.

This Agreement shall be subject to any additional amount(s) of money that Audrey F. Watt may advance to Donald R. Fenimore. All monies advanced will be due upon the dissolution of this Agreement or upon Donald R. Fenimore's death or incapacitation wherein Audrey F. Watt is appointed Power of Attorney for the protection of Donald R. Fenimore and for her rights and investments under his domain.

If Audrey F. Watt should predecease Donald R. Fenimore, this Agreement will bind Donald R. Fenimore to her heirs, successors and assigns. However, if she should predecease him, Donald R, Fenimore shall be given reasonable and adequate time of at least 90 days to make arrangements to reimburse her estate for any and all debts that may be then due.

This Agreement shall become null and void should a subsequent Agreement be entered into between Donald R. Fenimore and Audrey F. Watt to nullify this Agreement.

Willard H. Middleton Jr.	**Donald R. Fenimore 11/6/89**
Witness	Donald R. Fenimore
Billy Middleton	**Audrey F. Watt 11/6/89**
Witness	Audrey F. Watt

IN RE ESTATE OF FENIMORE

Delaware Court of Chancery, 1999
1999 WL 959204

CHANDLER, CHANCELLOR (adopting the report of the master). [Donald Fenimore is insolvent. Creditors collectively referred to as Villabona have a judgment against Fenimore for $32,000. These creditors are seeking to recover a part of that judgment from approximately $20,000 of property Fenimore recently inherited. Mrs. Serge is also seeking to recover that $20,000 from Fenimore, contending that she is also a creditor of Donald Fenimore and that Fenimore's debt to her should be paid first.]

* * * Mrs. Serge's story is a very sad one. She testified that after the death of her first husband, whose last name was Watt . . . Donald Fenimore asked her for money to get him out of a variety of scrapes, . . . About ten days after Mrs. Serge gave the $10,000.00 to her brother, she and he made an agreement that appears to address this money and another $2,500.00 that she gave him about the same time. Mrs. Serge testified that she has given her brother much more than that over the years, . . . [I]t comes as no surprise that, loving her brother but knowing better than to trust him too much, she had him sign an agreement, dated November 6, 1989, memorializing their understanding. The mortgage came about a year later. Mrs. Serge testified that she believes her brother owes her vastly more than the $15,000.00 she testified about with some detail. She also testified that when the mortgage was given as security for

the previous loans on October 31, 1990, she did not know about the Villabona judgment.

A judgment binds lands from the time it is entered by the Prothonotary,* and a properly recorded mortgage has priority over a judgment subsequently obtained. Because the mortgage was recorded before the judgment was entered on the records of the Prothonotary for the county in which the real estate is located, Villabona must somehow invalidate the effect of the mortgage in order to prevail. * * *

Villabona addresses the financial relationship between Mrs. Serge and her brother. It argues that if the 1989 agreement is indicative of anything, it is a partnership between Mrs. Serge and Donald Fenimore. Villabona notes that the agreement gives their "understanding of [their] business arrangements." It specifically does not characterize the $12,500.00 as a loan, but states that Mrs. Serge "advanced" this money to her brother "for him to conduct the business of buying and selling of motor vehicles." Note that the word used before "business" is a definite article, it is not a possessive. In other words, she is not described as lending him money to operate his business, she is "advancing" money for him to conduct a specific business, the owner(s) of which is not identified. This distinction takes on significance when one reads the next paragraph, in which they agree that Mrs. Serge will pay the costs of her borrowing money for this venture, and Donald Fenimore will pay the ordinary operating expenses of the business, and they will "divide the profits from each vehicle bought and sold. . . ." The balance of the agreement is concerned with securing Mrs. Serge's interests in the event of her brother's death and stating terms of dissolution of the partnership.

The partnership argument is based on 6 Del. Code Ann. § 1507 [which is modeled on § 7 of the Uniform Partnership Act]: "In determining whether a partnership exists, the following rules shall apply: . . . (4) The receipt by a person of a share of the profits of a business is prima facie evidence that he is a partner in the business, but no such inference shall be drawn if such profits were received in payment: (a) As a debt by installments or otherwise; (b) As wages of an employee or rent to a landlord; (c) As an annuity to a widow or representative of a deceased partner; (d) As interest on a loan, though the amount of payment vary with the profits of the business; (e) As the consideration for the sale of a goodwill of a business or other property by installments or otherwise." The November, 1989 document clearly provides for a division of profits and a division of responsibility for debts. The right to receive a share of the profits is nowhere indicated as falling into any of the five exceptions to evidence of a partnership just quoted. Therefore, the language of the

---

* Editors' note: This statement simply refers to the traditional rule that a judgment against someone operates as a lien against that person's real property from the moment the judgment is recorded with the proper officer, here the Prothonotary.

1989 agreement, as evaluated in light of the statute, would seem to be enough to conclude that the relationship between Mrs. Serge and her brother so far as the agreement is concerned is that of partners.

Our courts have taken the view that it is not essential to the existence of a partnership that all partners have the right to make decisions and a duty to share liabilities on dissolution, but at least one of these factors must be present, and there must also be an intent to share profits. The standard of proof necessary to prove the existence of a partnership is stricter when the action is between two partners than if it is between the alleged partners and a third party claiming that a partnership exists as to his opponents. Nonetheless, one must show the existence of the partnership by a preponderance of the evidence, and to do so one may demonstrate an intention to share profits and losses, and may use acts, the dealings and conduct of the parties, and admissions of the parties to do so.

When one examines the November, 1989 agreement in terms of the principles just stated, it is easy to conclude that at the very least the arrangement looks like a partnership. There is a written declaration of the intent of the parties, and it specifically calls for the sharing of profits and the allocation of expenses, that is, liabilities. There is even a plan of dissolution should things not work out. Based on this, and noting that the standard of proof is less strict when between two non-partners (in this case, Villabona and Mrs. Serge) than it would be between the partners themselves, I conclude that a partnership existed in fact between Audrey Serge and Donald Fenimore as of November 6, 1989. One may conclude that the partnership continues to exist because the record is silent as to the occurrence of any of the events that the agreement states will trigger dissolution of the partnership: a decision to dissolve, or the death of either Mrs. Serge or her brother. More importantly, there is no evidence that any of these factors had come about in 1990 when Villabona received its judgment, or in 1991 when the judgment was recorded in New Castle County.

The real thrust of this discussion is the consequence of a finding that a partnership existed. The money referred to in the 1989 agreement amounts to an investment in the partnership. It is part of a "business arrangement," but nowhere in that document or elsewhere is it characterized as a loan. If Mrs. Serge is to claim priority status as a creditor because of the agreement, she must show that she was not a partner and thereby convert the investment to a loan to her brother. Once a determination has been made that she is a partner, the provisions of 6 Del. Code § 1540 [modeled on § 40 of the Uniform Partnership Act] come into play.

The key part of § 1540 is subsection (9) [modeled on § 40(i) of the Uniform Partnership Act]: "Where a partner has become bankrupt or his

SEC. C

WHAT ARE THE LEGAL ISSUES IN STARTING A
BUSINESS AS A PARTNERSHIP?

71

estate is insolvent the claims against his separate property shall rank in the following order: a. Those owing to separate creditors; b. Those owing to partnership creditors; c. Those owing to partners by way of contribution." What this means for the present case is, that once Mrs. Serge is determined to have been her brother's partner, her right to collect under the agreement from him as to his inheritance, which is not partnership property, is subordinate to the claims of his "separate creditors", that is, Villabona. If they are creditors of the partnership, even then her interests would be subordinate to theirs. * * *

QUESTIONS AND NOTE

1. Why is Villabona arguing that the 1989 agreement is "indicative of" a partnership between Audrey and her brother Donald? Why does the court (or, more accurately, the master) wait until the end of the opinion (master's report) to tell us "the consequence of finding that a partnership exists"?

2. What is the basis for the court's conclusion that a partnership exists?

    a) Would the court have reached a different result if the agreement had used the word "lends" instead of the word "advances" or "his business" instead of "the business"?

    b) We noted in the opinion that the applicable Delaware statute was modeled on UPA. Suppose instead that the applicable statute was § 202(c) of RUPA (which is now the law in Delaware). Would the result be the same?

    c) How could a lawyer for Mrs. Serge have drafted the agreement to avoid a finding of partnership?

3. Suppose Capel loaned Propp $250,000 on June 4, 2015 and the loan agreement provided that the loan was to be repaid not later than April 15, 2017 and that until the loan was repaid:

- Capel was to receive 40% of the profits of the firm, not exceeding $50,000 and not less than $10,000;

- Propp was to consult Capel as to important matters in the conduct of Bubba's Burritos;

- Capel could veto any business that she thinks highly speculative or injurious;

Under the *Fenimore* decision, would Capel be Propp's partner? How about under RUPA § 202?

4. The facts in Question 3 were adapted from *Martin v. Peyton*, 158 N.E. 77 (N.Y. 1927), which is the classic case concerning whether a lender has become a partner by having power essentially to call the shots in the business. In that case, Peyton made a loan of $2,500,000 to Martin under terms similar to those outlined in Question 3. Martin became insolvent.

Martin's creditors argued that (i) Peyton's sharing in profits coupled with Peyton's power to veto certain business decisions made Peyton a partner with Martin and (ii) Peyton, as a partner, was liable for the partnership's debts. In finding that Peyton was not a partner, the court distinguished between active control and reactive control. Specifically, the court emphasized that Peyton "may not initiate any transactions as a partner may do." Is *Fenimore* consistent with *Martin v. Peyton*?

5.   Reconsider the *Miller* case on page 49, in which the court found that McDonald's might be liable under a theory of apparent agency. Can you now think of another theory for holding McDonald's liable?

Although partnership agreements are not legally required, in the real world, these documents are *extremely* important. First, a partnership agreement is a contract and is enforceable to the same extent as contracts generally. Second, always remember that partnership agreements can change much of the statutory law that otherwise would govern.

One more time:

RUPA § 103. EFFECT OF PARTNERSHIP AGREEMENT:

(a) Except as otherwise provided in subsection (b), relations among the partners and between the partners and the partnership are governed by the partnership agreement. To the extent the partnership agreement does not otherwise provide, this [Act] governs relations among the partners and between the partners and the partnership.

But not all businesses that are partnerships bother, or can afford, to create a comprehensive partnership agreement. Many partnerships do not have a comprehensive partnership agreement. For these, UPA and RUPA provide reasonable rules that most people would put in a partnership agreement, if they had thought about it. Although these standard rules might be fine for a two-person lawn-mowing business, they would be a disaster for a 400-lawyer law firm or even a four doctor medical practice.

PROBLEMS

1.   To operate Bubba's Burritos as a partnership, do Propp, Agee and Capel need a written partnership agreement?

2.   Do Propp, Agee, and Capel need a lawyer? Do they need more than one lawyer?

3.   Consider the following provisions from a form partnership agreement provided in continuing legal education materials. Are the

SEC. C

WHAT ARE THE LEGAL ISSUES IN STARTING A
BUSINESS AS A PARTNERSHIP?

73

provisions effective under RUPA § 103(a)? Do you think the doctors had a lawyer prepare these provisions? More than one lawyer? Good lawyers?

a.   The net profits of the partnership shall be divided among, and any net losses of the partnership shall be borne by, the partners in the following percentages during the periods indicated:

Partner	August 1, 2014 through July 31, 2016	Effective August 1, 2016 and thereafter
Dr. Alpha	27.67%	25%
Dr. Bravo	27.67%	25%
Dr. Charlie	27.67%	25%
Dr. Motherlover	17.00%	25%

The foregoing agreements as to distribution of net profits are subject, however, to the special provisions hereinafter set out.

b.   Withdrawals of net profits by the partners shall be in such amounts and at such times as the partners shall determine by mutual agreement.

c.   The partnership shall maintain a bank account or bank accounts in such bank or banks as may be agreed upon by the partners. Checks on such account or accounts shall be drawn only for partnership purposes, including distributions of profits agreed upon by the partners, and may be signed by any partner, except that any check for an amount in excess of $6,000 must be signed by two partners.

d.   No partner may, without the written consent of the other partners, assign, encumber or in any manner dispose of all or any part of the interest of such partner in the partnership.

e.   No partner may, on behalf of the partnership, without the express consent of the other partners, borrow or lend money, or make, deliver or accept any commercial paper, or execute any mortgage, deed or bill of sale to secure debt, bond, lease, contract to sell any property of the partnership, or contract to purchase any property for the partnership other than ordinary medical and office supplies.*

a)   Note that paragraph b provides for withdrawals by "mutual agreement." What does that mean? Is the phrase "express consent of the partners" in paragraph e different from "mutual agreement" as used in paragraph b? Which requires unanimity?

---

*   William R. Patterson, Drafting the Partnership Agreement, May 26,. 1996, SB85 ALI-ABA 193. Mr. Patterson, not any of your favorite authors, chose the name "Dr. Motherlover." We are responsible for most of the tacky stuff in this book but not "Motherlover."

      b)   Dr. Motherlover would like the partnership to open a bank account at Delta Bank, a new bank. How many other partners would have to agree on the partnership's opening such a bank account?

4.   Suppose the partnership agreement also provided: "Neither the partners nor the partnership will be liable for injuries to the public." Would the provision be enforceable? Note that RUPA § 103(b) lists certain topics in which the partners lack power to contract. Particularly, for the question asked here, note § 103(b)(10) which, according to the Official Comment: "stating the obvious, subsection(b)(10) provides expressly that the rights of a third party under the Act may not be restricted by an agreement among the partners to which the third party has not agreed."

5.   Acme, Baker, and Carr are partners. Can the three of them enter into more than one partnership agreement? Is the definition of "partnership agreement" in RUPA § 101(7) helpful: " 'Partnership agreement' means the agreement, whether written, oral, or implied, among the partners concerning the partnership, including amendments to the partnership agreement." to answering this question?

D. WHAT ARE THE LEGAL ISSUES IN OPERATING A BUSINESS AS A PARTNERSHIP?

1.   WHO OWNS WHAT?

Under both UPA and RUPA, partnerships can and do own property. In other words, both Acts envision the partnership as an entity for this purpose. *See* UPA §§ 8 and 25 and RUPA §§ 201, 203, and 204. The individual partners do *not* own partnership property. *See* UPA §§ 24 and 26 and RUPA §§ 501 and 502. Apply these sections to the following problems.

PROBLEMS

1.   Propp, Agee and Capel decide to operate Bubba's Burritos as a partnership. How can the partnership acquire property?

2.   Does the intellectual property that will be used in the partnership's online sales developed by Propp before formation of the partnership automatically become partnership property?

3.   Are the cash and credit card receipts from the operation of Bubba's Burritos after the partnership's formation partnership property?

4.   After formation of the partnership, Bubba's Burritos acquires new tables and chairs. Are these partnership property?

5.   After formation of the partnership, Bubba's Burritos uses funds provided by Capel to buy Blackacre. Is Blackacre partnership property? What if the seller deeds Blackacre to Capel?

6.   Is the following partnership agreement provision helpful in answering the preceding questions?

(a) *Partnership property.* Subject to the provisions of Article VII (b) and (c), all property originally paid or brought into, or transferred to, the partnership as contributions to capital by the partners, or subsequently acquired by purchase or otherwise, on account of the partnership, is partnership property.

(b) *Title to Property to Remain in Partner.* It is agreed that the following described property: [description], is being made available to the partnership by ___ solely for the use of the partnership and is to remain the property of ___ and is to be returned to him on [date], or when the partnership is dissolved, if prior to that date.

(c) *Property to be in Partnership Name.* The title to all partnership property shall be held in the name of the partnership.

(d) *Rights in Specific Partnership Property.* It is agreed that [name of partner] has the right at any time during the existence of this partnership to [assign or describe other right] the following specific partnership property: [describe property]. 7A NEW YORK FORMS LEGAL & BUS. § 18.10.

2.   WHO DECIDES WHAT THE PARTNERSHIP WILL DO?

Questions regarding who makes decisions for a partnership arise in two ways: (1) disputes between the partnership and some outside, third party and (2) disputes among the partners. Assume, for example, that Bubba's Burritos is structured as a partnership with Agee, Propp and Capel as the partners. Capel enters into an agreement with Roberts for Bubba's Burritos to lease a building that Roberts owns. This can result in:

(1)   A dispute between Bubba's Burritos and Roberts over whether Capel had the power to make this decision for Bubba's Burritos—i.e., a dispute over whether Bubba's Burritos is legally obligated to Roberts; and,

(2)   A dispute among Agee, Capel and Propp over whether Capel had the right to make this decision for Bubba's Burritos—i.e., a dispute over whether Capel is legally obligated to Agee and Propp for acting beyond his authority.

In situations such as (1)—in which the issue is whether a partner had the power to obligate the partnership to some third party—courts look to agency principles such as actual and apparent authority, with the possible sources of actual authority being (i) the partnership agreement and (ii) partnership statute provisions such as RUPA § 301(1) "Each partner is an agent of the partnership for the purpose of its business An act of a partner . . . for apparently carrying on in the ordinary course, the partnership business . . . binds the partnership, unless the partner had no authority to act for the partnership in the particular matter and the person with whom the partner was dealing knew or had received a notification that the partner lacked authority" as possible sources of authority.

In situations such as (2)—in which the issue is whether a partner had the right to act on behalf of the partnership—courts look first to the provisions of the partnership agreement first, and then to provisions of the relevant partnership statute If the partnership agreement does not clearly or completely delineate a partner's authority to act on behalf of the partnership, courts look to statutory provisions such as RUPA § 401(f) and (j):

> (f) Each partner has equal rights in the management and conduct of the partnership business . . .

> (j) An act outside the ordinary course of the business of a partnership . . . may be undertaken only with the consent of all partners."

Consider the following problems.

PROBLEMS

1.   Bubba's Burritos is a partnership. Agee, Propp and Capel are the partners. Agee and Capel want the partnership to lease a building from Roberts. Propp disagrees. Propp comes to you with the question of whether the partnership can lease the building even though he is opposed. How do you answer his question? Please assume that there is no partnership agreement provision concerning this issue. *See* UPA § 18(e) and RUPA §§ 103 and 401(f).

2.   What if the partners wanted to do something "extraordinary" (BTW, what does that mean?)? What vote would be required? *See* UPA § 18(h) and RUPA § 401(j).

3.   Bubba's Burritos is a partnership. Agee, Propp and Capel are the partners. The partnership agreement provides that "Capel shall serve as managing partner, and, as such, shall have the authority to lease property on behalf of the partnership without consulting any other partner." Capel, without consulting Agee or Propp, rents a building for the partnership from Roberts for ten years at $10,000 a year. Is the partnership legally obligated to pay Roberts? *See* UPA § 18(e) & (h) and RUPA §§ 103 and 401(f) & (j).

4.   Same facts as Question 3 except that the partnership agreement does not make Capel a managing partner. Instead, the partnership agreement provides "No partner may, without the express consent of the other partners, lease property on behalf of the partnership." Notwithstanding this provision, Capel, without consulting Agee or Propp, rents a building for the partnership from Roberts for ten years at $10,000 a year. Is the partnership legally obligated to pay Roberts on this lease? *See* UPA §§ 5, and

9 and RUPA §§ 103(b)(10), 104, and 301. Is Capel legally obligated to the partnership?

3. WHAT ARE THE DUTIES THAT A PARTNER OWES TO THE PARTNERSHIP AND/OR HER FELLOW PARTNERS?

These problems illustrate possible questions relating to *who* makes decisions for a partnership. A lawyer for such a business (or for one of the partners) will also encounter questions about *how* such decisions are to be made. In particular, a lawyer will have to consider whether these decisions are affected by any duties a partner may owe to the partnership or to her fellow partners.

For example, suppose Capel, as managing partner with express authority to rent buildings for the partnership, rents a building for the partnership from his brother-in-law Epstein at a rate significantly above the market rate. Or suppose Capel, as managing partner, learns of an opportunity to rent a building significantly below market rate, but rents the building for himself rather than for the partnership. Common sense (and, as it turns out, common law) tells us there are problems with these examples.

The next case involves somewhat analogous facts. It is the most-cited case on (i) what things a partner has the right to do and (ii) what are the right things for a partner to do.

MEINHARD V. SALMON
Court of Appeals of New York, 1928
164 N.E. 545

CARDOZO, C.J. [Walter Salmon was a real estate developer. He had the opportunity to rent a seven-story building on the corner of Fifth Avenue and Forty-second Street in New York and the lease was for a term of 20 years. The building needed improvements, however, which Salmon could not afford. So Salmon leased the building from the building's owner, Elbridge Gerry. Salmon also entered a separate agreement with Morton Meinhard, a wool merchant. Under this agreement, Meinhard provided the money for renovations to the building in exchange for a share of the profits from the building over the course of the 20-year lease. Their agreement also provided that Salmon and Meinhard were to share any losses equally but that Salmon had the sole power to manage the building.

After more than nineteen years, shortly before the 20-year lease was to expire, Gerry, the building's owner, approached Salmon with a proposal. Gerry, who also owned five adjacent buildings, wanted someone to lease all of these properties, to destroy the existing buildings, and to put up a new, single, larger building. This was valuable real estate. It was three blocks from the site of the Chrysler building, which was being planned at approximately the same time.

Salmon accepted Gerry's proposal and entered into a lease and development agreement with Gerry. Meinhard was not a party to this new agreement. Indeed, Meinhard did not even know of this agreement. When Meinhard learned of the deal, he initiated this litigation, suing for an interest in the new, expanded development.]

[Meinhard and Salmon] were coadventurers, subject to fiduciary duties akin to those of partners. As to this we are all agreed. The heavier weight of duty rested, however, upon Salmon. He was a coadventurer with Meinhard, but he was manager as well. * * *

When the lease was near its end, Elbridge T. Gerry had become the owner of the reversion. He owned much other property in the neighborhood, one lot adjoining the Bristol building on Fifth Avenue and four lots on Forty-Second Street. He had a plan to lease the entire tract for a long term to someone who would destroy the buildings then existing and put up another in their place. In the latter part of 1921, he submitted such a project to several capitalists and dealers. He was unable to carry it through with any of them. Then, in January 1922, with less than four months of the lease to run, he approached the defendant Salmon. The result was a new lease to the Midpoint Realty Company, which is owned

5th Ave and 42d St looking north, 1920*

and controlled by Salmon, a lease covering the whole tract, and involving a huge outlay. * * * The existing buildings may remain unchanged for

---

    *   From the New York Historical Society Library. http://cdm128401.cdmhost.com/cdm/ref/collection/p16124coll2/id/1206.

seven years. They are then to be torn down, and a new building to cost $3,000,000 is to be placed upon the site. The rental, which under the Bristol lease was only $55,000, is to be from $350,000 to $475,000 for the properties so combined. Salmon personally guaranteed the performance by the lessee of the covenants of the new lease until such time as the new building had been completed and fully paid for.

The lease between Gerry and the Midpoint Realty Company was signed and delivered on January 25, 1922. Salmon had not told Meinhard anything about it. Whatever his motive may have been, he had kept the negotiations to himself. Meinhard was not informed even of the bare existence of a project. The first that he knew of it was in February, when the lease was an accomplished fact. He then made demand on the defendants that the lease be held in trust as an asset of the venture, making offer upon the trial to share the personal obligations incidental to the guaranty. The demand was followed by refusal, and later by this suit. * * *

Joint adventurers, like copartners, owe to one another, while the enterprise continues, the duty of the finest loyalty. Many forms of conduct permissible in a workaday world for those acting at arm's length are forbidden to those bound by fiduciary ties. A trustee is held to something stricter than the morals of the market place. Not honesty alone, but the punctilio of an honor the most sensitive, is then the standard of behavior. As to this there has developed a tradition that is unbending and inveterate. Uncompromising rigidity has been the attitude of courts of equity when petitioned to undermine the rule of undivided loyalty by the "disintegrating erosion" of particular exceptions. Only thus has the level of conduct for fiduciaries been kept at a level higher than that trodden by the crowd. It will not consciously be lowered by any judgment of this court.

The owner of the reversion, Mr. Gerry, had vainly striven to find a tenant who would favor his ambitious scheme of demolition and construction. Baffled in the search, he turned to the defendant Salmon in possession of the Bristol, the keystone of the project. He figured to himself beyond a doubt that the man in possession would prove a likely customer. To the eye of an observer, Salmon held the lease as owner in his own right, for himself and no one else. In fact he held it as a fiduciary, for himself and another, sharers in a common venture. If this fact had been proclaimed, if the lease by its terms had run in favor of a partnership, Mr. Gerry, we may fairly assume, would have laid before the partners, and not merely before one of them, his plan of reconstruction. The pre-emptive privilege, or, better, the pre-emptive opportunity, that was thus an incident of the enterprise, Salmon appropriated to himself in secrecy and silence. He might have warned Meinhard that the plan had been submitted, and that either would be free to compete for the award. If he had done this, we do not need to say whether he would have been under a duty, if successful in the competition, to hold the lease so acquired for the benefit of a venture then about to end, and thus prolong by indirection its responsibilities and duties. The trouble about his conduct is that he excluded his coadventurer from any chance to compete, from any chance to enjoy the opportunity for benefit that had come to him alone by virtue of his agency. This chance, if nothing more, he was under a duty to concede. The price of its denial is an extension of the trust at the option and for the benefit of the one whom he excluded.

No answer is it to say that the chance would have been of little value even if seasonably offered. Such a calculus of probabilities is beyond the science of the chancery. Salmon, the real estate operator, might have been preferred to Meinhard, the woolen merchant. On the other hand, Meinhard might have offered better terms, or reinforced his offer by alliance with the wealth of others. * * *

The very fact that Salmon was in control with exclusive powers of direction charged him the more obviously with the duty of disclosure, since only through disclosure could opportunity be equalized. If he might cut off renewal by a purchase for his own benefit when four months were to pass before the lease would have an end, he might do so with equal right while there remained as many years. He might steal a march on his comrade under cover of the darkness, and then hold the captured ground. Loyalty and comradeship are not so easily abjured.

Little profit will come from a dissection of the precedents. None precisely similar is cited in the briefs of counsel. What is similar in many, or so it seems to us, is the animating principle. Authority is, of course, abundant that one partner may not appropriate to his own use a renewal of a lease, though its term is to begin at the expiration of the partnership. The lease at hand with its many changes is not strictly a renewal. Even so, the standard of loyalty for those in trust relations is without the fixed divisions of a graduated scale. * * *

Salmon had put himself in a position in which thought of self was to be renounced, however hard the abnegation. He was much more than a coadventurer. He was a managing coadventurer. For him and for those like him the rule of undivided loyalty is relentless and supreme. A different question would be here if there were lacking any nexus of relation between the business conducted by the manager and the opportunity brought to him as an incident of management. For this problem, as for most, there are distinctions of degree. If Salmon had received from Gerry a proposition to lease a building at a location far removed, he might have held for himself the privilege thus acquired, or so we shall assume. Here the subject-matter of the new lease was an extension and enlargement of the subject-matter of the old one. A managing coadventurer appropriating the benefit of such a lease without warning to his partner might fairly expect to be reproached with conduct that was underhand, or lacking, to say the least, in reasonable candor, if the partner were to surprise him in the act of signing the new instrument. Conduct subject to that reproach does not receive from equity a healing benediction.

A question remains as to the form and extent of the equitable interest to be allotted to the plaintiff. * * *

ANDREWS, J. (dissenting). * * * I am of the opinion that the issue here is simple. Was the transaction, in view of all the circumstances surrounding it, unfair and inequitable? I reach this conclusion for two reasons. There was no general partnership, merely a joint venture for a limited object, to end at a fixed time. The new lease, covering additional property, containing many new and unusual terms and conditions, with a possible duration of 80 years, was more nearly the purchase of the reversion than the ordinary renewal with which the authorities are concerned. * * *

Under these circumstances the referee has found and the Appellate Division agrees with him, that Mr. Meinhard is entitled to an interest in the second lease, he having promptly elected to assume his share of the liabilities imposed thereby. This conclusion is based upon the proposition that under the original contract between the two men "the enterprise was a joint venture, the relation between the parties was fiduciary and governed by principles applicable to partnerships," therefore, as the new lease is a graft upon the old, Mr. Salmon might not acquire its benefits for himself alone.

Were this a general partnership between Mr. Salmon and Mr. Meinhard, I should have little doubt as to the correctness of this result, assuming the new lease to be an offshoot of the old. Such a situation involves questions of trust and confidence to a high degree; it involves questions of good will; many other considerations. * * *

We have here a different situation governed by less drastic principles. I assume that where parties engage in a joint enterprise each owes to the other the duty of the utmost good faith in all that relates to their common venture. Within its scope they stand in a fiduciary relationship. * * *

It seems to me that the venture so inaugurated had in view a limited object and was to end at a limited time. There was no intent to expand it into a far greater undertaking lasting for many years. The design was to exploit a particular lease. Doubtless in it Mr. Meinhard had an equitable interest, but in it alone. * * *

What Mr. Salmon obtained was not a graft springing from the Bristol lease, but something distinct and different—as distinct as if for a building across Fifth Avenue. I think also that in the absence of some fraudulent or unfair act the secret purchase of the reversion even by one partner is rightful. Substantially this is such a purchase. Because of the mere label of a transaction we do not place it on one side of the line or the other. Here is involved the possession of a large and most valuable unit of property for 80 years, the destruction of all existing structures and the erection of a new and expensive building covering the whole. No fraud, no deceit, no calculated secrecy is found. Simply that the arrangement was made without the knowledge of Mr. Meinhard. I think this not enough.

The judgment of the courts below should be reversed and a new trial ordered, with costs in all courts to abide the event.

QUESTIONS AND NOTES

1.   Questions about the law

a)   What is a "joint venture"? Is the following RUPA comment helpful: "Relationships that are called 'joint ventures' are partnerships if they otherwise fit the definition of a partnership." RUPA § 202. Is Judge Andrews use of the term "general partnership" helpful in answering the question "what is a 'joint venture' "?

b)   What did Salmon do wrong? What should he have done differently?

c)   Assume that Gerry approached Salmon about a new expanded lease and development agreement because he had married Salmon's sister. Would Judge (later Justice) Cardozo have reached the same result?

d)   Assume that Gerry had approached and contracted with Meinhard rather than Salmon. If Salmon then sued Meinhard when he learned of the new expanded lease, would Judge Cardozo have reached the same result?

e)   Would Salmon and Meinhard have been partners under UPA or RUPA? *See* UPA § 7 and RUPA § 202.

f)   What did Cardozo mean by the phrase "punctilio of an honor the most sensitive", by the phrase "thought of self was to be renounced, however hard the abnegation"?

2.   Notes

a)   One Cardozo scholar describes the *Meinhard* case as "a culmination of Cardozo's efforts to implant a sense of honorable conduct into law." Andrew L. Kaufman, CARDOZO 241 (1998). In an earlier book about Justice Cardozo, Judge Posner refers to *Meinhard* as the most famous of Cardozo's "moralistic opinions" and praises Cardozo's language as "memorable words and [that] set a tone. They make the difference between an arm's length relationship and a fiduciary relationship vivid, unforgettable." Richard A. Posner, CARDOZO: A STUDY IN REPUTATION 105 (1990).

b)   *Meinhard* involved a joint venture. Indeed, the dissent is based on the fact that "there was no general partnership, merely a joint venture." Nonetheless, as the language in *Meinhard* indicates, the principles applied in the case are not limited to joint ventures. The fiduciary principles espoused in the case transcend the business structure involved. We will reconsider not only the language of *Meinhard* but the *Meinhard* fact pattern of taking an "opportunity" that was "an incident of the enterprise" in later chapters on corporations, limited partnerships and limited liability companies. When you reconsider *Meinhard*, consider also Professor Hillman's comments:

Meinhard has aged well. No case of its period is of comparable contemporary influence in the business law area. *Meinhard* is cited today for the power and vitality of the idea it expresses rather than as a window to an era the values of which have long since been abandoned. The "punctilio of an honor" precept is as enduring as any expression of partnership or corporate law and continues to guide courts in determining the duties business partners owe one another. * * *

To be sure, care must be taken to distinguish how standards are stated from how they are applied * * *. As a matter of common sense, we may know that the *Meinhard* statement is too extreme and inflexible to represent a workable standard for those fiduciary relationships that are business partnerships. At the same time, to dismiss the case as nothing more than a vehicle of exaggerated rhetoric is to ignore the proven staying power of this landmark opinion.

Robert W. Hillman, *Business Partners as Fiduciaries: Reflections on the Limits of Doctrine,* 22 CARDOZO L. REV. 51, 53 (2000).

c)   "Must Salmon love Meinhard? Despite Cardozo's inspiring rhetoric, the law clearly has said 'no.' * * * Should Salmon love Meinhard? Yes and vice versa * * *, Partners who love one another can trust one another. In turn, partners who trust one another will expend considerably less time and effort—and thus incur much lower costs—monitoring one another. Agape thus should not be the law, but the law should promote agape as best practice"

Stephen M. Bainbridge. *Must Salmon Love Meinard?* 17 GREEN BAG2D 257, 270 (2014).

———————

Fiduciary duties were developed by judges, as part of the common law. RUPA attempts to codify these fiduciary duties in RUPA § 404.

Professor Edwin Hecker provides a helpful explanation of RUPA § 404: "When Kansas adopted the Revised Uniform Partnership Act in

1998, it codified partners' fiduciary duties, exclusively and preemptively, as follows: 'The only fiduciary duties a partner owes to the partnership and the other partners are the duty of loyalty and the duty of care set forth in subsections (b) and (c).' Unfortunately, subsection (e) of the same section muddies the water by providing that '[a] partner does not violate a duty or obligation . . . merely because the partner's conduct furthers the partner's own interest.' The drafters of the Revised Uniform Partnership Act explained that subsection (e) embodies the notion that a partner is not literally a trustee and is not held to the same standards as a true trustee. Rather, subsection (e) attempts to strike a balance between a partner's rights as an owner and principal and the partner's duties as an agent and fiduciary."[*]

Use the following questions to see whether Professor Hecker's explanation was "helpful" to you.

QUESTIONS

1.   What duties do partners owe under § 404? To whom do they owe these duties?

2.   What language in § 404 would have been most helpful to Meinhard?

3.   What language in § 404 would have been most helpful to Salmon?

––––––––––––––

RUPA not only codifies the duties that a partner owes to the partnership and her fellow partner, but also expressly empowers the partners to modify the duties in the partnership agreement. Please read RUPA section 103 (b)(3)–(5), which states:

(b) The partnership agreement may not:

(3) eliminate the duty of loyalty under Section 404(b) or 603(b)(3), but:

(i) the partnership agreement may identify specific types or categories of activities that do not violate the duty of loyalty, if not manifestly unreasonable; or

(ii) all of the partners or a number or percentage specified in the partnership agreement may authorize or ratify, after full disclosure of all material facts, a specific act or transaction that otherwise would violate the duty of loyalty;

(4) unreasonably reduce the duty of care under Section 404(c) or 603(b)(3);

––––––––––––––––––––––––

[*]   Edwin W. Hecker, Jr., *Fiduciary Duties in Business Entities Revisited*, 61 U. KAN. L. REV. 923, 930 (2013).

(5) eliminate the obligation of good faith and fair dealing under Section 404(d), but the partnership agreement may prescribe the standards by which the performance of the obligation is to be measured, if the standards are not manifestly unreasonable;

QUESTIONS

1.   How would a court applying RUPA § 103 rule in *Meinhard v. Salmon* if the agreement between Meinhard and Salmon had contained this language:

> *Other Business Activities of Partners.* Any partner may have other business interests or may engage in other business ventures of any nature or description whatsoever, whether presently existing or hereafter created, including, without limitation, the ownership, leasing, management, operation, franchising, syndication and/or development of real estate and may compete, directly or indirectly, with the business of the Partnership. No partner shall incur any liability to the Partnership as the result of such Partner's pursuit of such other business interests and ventures and competitive activity, and neither the Partnership nor any of the partners of Record Holders shall have any right to participate in such other business interests or ventures or to receive or share in any income derived therefrom."[*]

2.   Professor Hynes argues that "The restrictions on waivability in [RUPA] sections 103(b)(2)–(4) should be deleted because they interfere with the right of partners to define their relationship as they wish. Persons entering into a partnership relationship ordinarily bargain from an approximately equal position, an equality created by the fact that each party typically has something of near-equal value to offer the other. * * * This should give presumptive validity to the bargain of the parties." J. Dennis Hynes, *Fiduciary Duties and RUPA: An Inquiry Into Freedom of Contract,* 58 LAW & CONTEMP. PROBS. 29, 39–40 (1995). Do you agree? By the way, why does Professor Hynes *not* include § 103(b)(5) in his proposed deletions?

Professor Hynes's views reflect the "contractarian school" of economic thought. This school holds that people in business with each other ought to be free to agree to the terms of their relationship, with minimal statutory imposition. The provision in RUPA for modification or waiver of fiduciary duties reflects the degree to which this school has affected modern thought on business formation.

---

[*]   We have "borrowed" this provision from Richard A. Booth, *Fiduciary Duty, Contract and Waiver in Partnerships and Limited Liability Companies,* 1 J. SMALL & EMERGING BUS. L. 55 (1998).

4.   WHO IS LIABLE TO CREDITORS OF THE PARTNERSHIP?

To illustrate, Dr. Freer and Dr. Shepherd practice medicine together in the Emory Family Practice Partnership. Patient Roberts is injured through the professional negligence of Dr. Freer. Who is liable, i.e., from whom can Roberts recover?

a.   Liability of the Partnership

Recall that under RUPA § 201, a partnership is a legal person—an entity. As such, a partnership can be held liable and can sue or be sued. The same is also true under UPA, even though UPA does not expressly adopt the entity theory. *See* UPA §§ 13 and 14 and RUPA §§ 305 and 307.

A third party can sue the *partnership* for the contracts entered into by its agents and for the torts committed by its agents. A partner is an agent of the partnership. *See* UPA § 9; RUPA § 301.20. Roberts can sue the Emory Family Practice Partnership for Freer's negligence.

b.   Liability of the Partners

Under RUPA, partners are jointly and severally liable for all obligations of the partnership. In contrast, under UPA § 15, partners are jointly (but not severally) liable in contract but jointly and severally liable in tort.

The difference is significant. With joint liability, the plaintiff must sue *all* of the partners together in a single suit. With joint and several liability, however, the plaintiff is free to sue one or more of the partners. For example, the plaintiff could recover the partnership's entire liability to him from just one partner.

Apply RUPA §§ 305, 306, and 307, set out below, to the problems that follow. (Stay focused; these get tough).

§ 305.   Partnership Liable for Partner's Actionable Conduct

(a) A partnership is liable for loss or injury caused to a person, or for a penalty incurred, as a result of a wrongful act or omission, or other actionable conduct, of a partner acting in the ordinary course of business of the partnership or with authority of the partnership. . . .

§ 306.   Partner's Liability

(a) Except as otherwise provided in subsections (b) and (c), all partners are liable jointly and severally for all obligations of the partnership unless otherwise agreed by the claimant or provided by law. . . .

SEC. D

WHAT ARE THE LEGAL ISSUES IN OPERATING A
BUSINESS AS A PARTNERSHIP?

87

§ 307. Actions by and Against Partnership and Partners

(b) An action may be brought against the partnership and, to the extent not inconsistent with Section 306, any or all of the partners in the same action or in separate actions.

(c) A judgment against a partnership is not by I itself a judgment against a partner. A judgment against a partnership may not be satisfied from a partner's assets unless there is also a judgment against the partner.

(d) A judgment creditor of a partner may not levy execution against the assets of the partner to satisfy a judgment based on a claim against the partnership unless the partner is personally liable for the claim under Section 306 and:

> (1) a judgment based on the same claim has been obtained against the partnership and a writ of execution on the judgment has been returned unsatisfied in whole or in part;

PROBLEMS

1.   Doctors Freer and Shepherd practice medicine together in the Emory Family Practice Partnership. Patient Roberts is injured through the professional negligence of Dr. Freer. We have already seen that Roberts can recover from the Emory Family Practice Partnership.

> a)   Can Roberts also sue and recover from Freer (who is, after all, the tortfeasor)?

> b)   Instead, can Roberts sue and recover from Shepherd, who was not involved in Roberts' care?

2.   Suppose Roberts sues the Emory Family Practice Partnership and obtains a judgment against the partnership. How can he enforce (collect on) that judgment? (In other words, whose assets are available from which to collect the judgment?)

3.   If Roberts successfully sues Freer and collects from Freer does Freer have any right of contribution or indemnity? If so, from whom? Is RUPA § 40(c)—"A partnership shall reimburse a partner for payments made and indemnify a partner for liabilities incurred by the partner in the ordinary course of the business of the partnership or for the preservation of its business or property" helpful? Is any other RUPA provision helpful?

4.   Your client, First Bank, is making a loan to the Emory Family Practice Partnership. Is there any reason to require Doctors Freer and Shepherd to sign personal guarantees?

c. Note About Limited Partnerships (LPs) and Limited Liability Partnerships (LLPs)

One of the drawbacks of the partnership, as we have seen, is that the partners are generally liable for the partnership debts. In a later chapter, we will consider later forms of partnerships in which some or all of the partners are not generally liable for some or all of the debts of the partnership.

E. WHAT ARE THE POSSIBLE LEGAL ISSUES IN A PARTNERSHIP'S ADDING NEW PARTNERS?

First, in adding new partners, a partnership often confronts difficult business questions such as (1) is anyone interested in investing in the partnership, (2) are the people interested in investing in the partnership people that the existing partners want to include as partners, and (3) how much should the new partner be required to invest and in return for such an investment what percentage of the partnership will the new partner receive.

The two legal questions raised by adding new partners are comparatively easy, First, do all existing partners have to approve any new partner? RUPA § 401(i) requires the consent of all existing partners—unless the partnership agreement provides otherwise. (Remember UPA § 18 and RUPA § 103.)

Second, is the new partner personally liable for all of the partnership's existing debts? Under RUPA § 306(b), a new partner is not personally liable for partnership obligations "incurred before the person's admission as a partner." The following problems illustrate these two legal issues.

PROBLEMS

1. The Bubba's Burritos partnership agreement is silent as to admitting new partners. Shepherd has offered to invest $100,000 in Bubba's Burritos. Agee and Propp favor taking Shepherd's money and making him a partner. Capel is opposed. Agee and Propp come to you with the question of whether they can amend the partnership agreement to provide that admission of new partners requires the approval of a simple majority of the partners. How do you answer their question? *See* RUPA §§ 401(j); 103.

2. Shepherd has some questions about becoming a partner in Bubba's Burritos. He wants to know whether he will be personally liable on:

    a) Bubba's Burritos' existing ten-year lease of its Atlanta location;

    b) Bubba's Burritos' anticipated construction mortgage on its new Boston location.

How do you answer his questions?

F. HOW DO THE OWNERS OF A PARTNERSHIP MAKE MONEY?

Recall that all of Epstein's relatives said that they owned businesses to make money. Generally an owner of a business makes money by (1) being paid a salary by the business, (2) receiving all or part of the profits from the business or (3) selling her interest in the business.

1. SALARY

RUPA provisions with respect to partnership salaries are easy to understand and easy to apply. And once you understand these RUPA provisions, you will understand why they are rarely applicable. Nonetheless, apply the cited RUPA provisions in the following problems.

PROBLEMS

1.   Propp, Agee and Capel are the partners in the Bubba's Burritos partnership. Agee and Propp work at the partnership, but Capel does not. Can Agee and Propp receive a salary from the partnership? *See* RUPA §§ 401(h), 401(j), 103(a).

2.   Assume the partnership agreement provides that Agee shall receive an annual salary of $60,000 and that Propp shall receive an annual salary of $55,000. Can Capel prevent Agee and Propp from increasing their salaries?

3.   Can Capel compel the partnership to employ him and pay him a salary?

4.   Can the partnership pay Capel a salary even though he does not do any work for the partnership? Do the other partners care? (Is RUPA § 404(d) relevant?) Why would they agree to this? Do the partnership's creditors care? Does the Internal Revenue Service care?

2. PROFITS

The law with respect to partnership profits, like the law with respect to partnership salaries, is found primarily in the partnership agreement and other contracts and laws—not in the partnership statute or partnership case law. The only provision in RUPA that expressly deals with partners' rights to partnership profits is § 401(b): "Each partner is entitled to an equal share of the partnership profits and is chargeable with a share of the partnership losses in proportion to the partner's share of the profits." And, RUPA § 401(b) needs to be read together with RUPA § 103(a).

PROBLEMS

1.   Who gets what if there is no partnership agreement provision on allocation of profits? Bubba's Burritos is a partnership. Agee, Capel and

Propp are the partners. Capel invests $1,000,000 in the partnership. Propp invests $20,000. Agee does not make a contribution of capital; she works for the partnership and draws a salary. The partnership makes a profit of $99,000 in 2015. How will that profit be shared among Agee, Capel and Propp?

2. Who gets what if there is a partnership provision? Would your answer to (1) be different if the partnership agreement provided that 2/3 of the profits shall be allocated to Capel, 1/6 of the profits shall be allocated to Agee and 1/6 of the profits shall be allocated to Propp?

3. Who decides when the partners receive a distribution in a good year? Again assume that the partnership earned $99,000 in 2015 and that the partnership agreement provides that 2/3 of the profits are to be allocated to Capel. Agee and Propp take the position that the partnership should not make any distribution to partners but rather should use the $99,000 for advertising. Capel comes to you with the question of whether she can compel the partnership to distribute her share of the profits to her. How do you answer her question? *Cf.* RUPA §§ 401(f) & (j).

4. Who decides whether the partners receive a distribution in a bad year? Now assume that 2015 was a bad year for Bubba's Burritos. It had to use earnings retained from prior years' operations to pay its bills. That same year was also a bad one for Agee and Propp personally. They come to you with the question of whether the partnership can make a distribution to partners notwithstanding the bad year. How do you answer their question? *Cf.* RUPA § 807.

Often the answers to questions such as these can be found in the partnership's loan agreements. It is common for a lender to require a business borrower to agree that it will not make any distributions to its owners until the loan is repaid.

3. PARTNER'S SALE OF HER "TRANSFERABLE" INTEREST TO A THIRD PARTY

Assume again that Bubba's Burritos is a partnership and that the partners are Agee, Capel and Propp. Propp wants to make money by selling his part of the partnership to a non-partner—he wants to sell his ownership interest and use that money to go to law school.

Recall the business and legal problems that a partnership encountered when it tried to sell new partnership interests to new investors:

- finding a buyer;
- gaining any necessary approval from existing partners; and,
- dealing with the question of preexisting obligations.

Propp, a partner, will encounter all of these problems when he tries to sell his existing partnership interest to some new investor. And Propp will encounter an additional, unavoidable, statutory problem, RUPA § 502 provides: "The only transferable interest of a partner in the partnership is the partner's share of profits and losses of the partnership and the partner's right to receive distributions." And, RUPA § 503(a)(3) clarifies: "A transfer, in whole or in part, of a partner's transferable interest in the partnership: . . . (3) does not, as against the other partners or the partnership, entitle the transferee, during the continuance of the partnership, to participate in the management or conduct of the partnership business, to require access to information concerning partnership transactions, or to inspect or copy the partnership books or records." *See also* UPA §§ 26 and 27.

PROBLEMS

1.   If Roberts buys Propp's transferable partnership interest, will Roberts have a right to participate in partnership decisions? What is the policy reason for this?

2.   If Roberts buys Propp's transferable partnership interest, will Propp retain the right to participate in the management of the partnership? *See* RUPA § 503(d) ("Upon transfer, the transferor retains the rights and duties of a partner other than the interest in distributions transferred.") What incentive does Propp have to participate actively in partnership management at this point?

3.   If Roberts buys Propp's transferable partnership interest, does Propp remain liable for partnership obligations?

4.   Would your answers to problems 1–3 change if the other partners, Agee and Capel, agree that Roberts can fully participate in the management of the partnership agreement?

5.   Instead of buying Propp's partnership interest, suppose Roberts buys a partnership interest from the partnership itself. Will Roberts have a right to participate in partnership decisions?

4.   PARTNER'S SALE OF HER OWNERSHIP INTEREST BACK TO THE PARTNERSHIP

The partner might also make money by selling her share of the partnership back to the partnership itself. Because of the business and legal problems in an existing partner's selling her partnership interest to an outsider, it is common for the partnership agreement, or some separate agreement among partners, to provide for sale of partnership interests back to the partnership or to other partners. Such agreements are commonly referred to as "buy-sell agreements."

Any buy-sell agreement should answer the following questions:

(1)   Are the other partners or the partnership obligated to buy, or do they instead have the option to buy?

(2)   What events trigger this obligation or option?

(3)   How is the selling partner's interest to be valued?

(4)   What is the method of funding the payment?

Special attention should also be given to the tax effects of the payout (but not in these materials).

Even if there is no buy-sell agreement, a partner has the power to compel the partnership to pay for her partnership interest by withdrawing from the partnership. How much and when a withdrawing partner is paid by the partnership is covered by (i) partnership agreements, (ii) partnership statutes, and (iii) the next part of this chapter.

G. WHAT IS THE "END GAME"?

Under both UPA and RUPA, a partner always has the power to leave the partnership and compel the partnership to buy her out. Our favorite student text tells us that the relevant "provisions of UPA and RUPA differ significantly from each other and were a principal area of controversy in the drafting of RUPA."[*]

The vocabulary is different. The term "dissociation" is unique to RUPA. For example, under RUPA a partner's "express will to withdraw" and a partner's death are among the events described as "Events Causing a Partner's Dissociation." RUPA § 601(1), (7). Under UPA § 31(1)(b) and (4) a partner's "express will" and a partner's death are among the events described as "Causes of Dissolution [of the Partnership]." We will simply use the term "withdrawal" to describe the events listed in RUPA § 601 and causes listed in UPA § 31.

More important, RUPA's rules for withdrawal (dissociation) differ in some significant respects from UPA's rules for withdrawal (dissolution).

Let's now consider the four most important withdraw questions to understand how the rules in RUPA and UPA differ and how the partnership agreement can (and should) displace the RUPA or UPA rules. The four most important withdrawal questions are:

(1)   When can a partner withdraw from the partnership?

(2)   Can the partnership continue regular business operations after a partner withdraws?

(3)   If the partnership continues to operate what are the payment rights of the withdrawing partner?

(4)   Who gets what if the partnership terminates business operations?

---

[*]   Richard D. Freer & Douglas K. Moll, Principles of Business Organizations 119 (2013).

1. WHEN CAN A PARTNER WITHDRAW FROM THE PARTNERSHIP?

Always. Under both UPA and RUPA, a partner always has the power to withdraw. (Under the vocabulary of RUPA, it would be more precise to say that a partner always has the power to "dissociate.")

While a partner's withdrawal is always a possibility, both UPA and RUPA treat some withdrawals as wrongful.

If the withdrawal violates the partnership agreement, or occurs before the expiration of the partnership term, it is "wrongful." And as we will see, whether the withdrawal is wrongful, affects the answer to question 3 what are the payment rights of the withdrawing partner.

An important point in determining whether the withdrawal is wrongful: unless the partnership agreement says otherwise, a partner in a "partnership at will" (a partnership with neither a specified end date nor a specific undertaking to complete) can quit at any time without its being wrongful.

PROBLEMS

1. Bubba's Burritos is a partnership. Agee, Capel and Propp are the partners. The 2015 partnership agreement provides no partner can dissociate until 2020. Can Agee dissociate in 2016? See RUPA § 103(b)(6).

2. Same facts as 1 except that the partnership agreement has no provision with respect to withdrawal or dissociation of a partner, but does provide that the partnership is to have a ten-year term. Can Agee withdraw from the partnership in the partnership's third year? Will such withdrawal be "wrongful"?

3. Same facts as 1 except that the partnership agreement has no provision with respect to withdrawal and no provisions with respect to term. Will Agee's withdrawal be "wrongful"?

––––––––––

The next case tells us that a partner's decision to withdraw can be wrongful even though the partnership agreement has no provision with respect to withdrawal and no provision with respect to the term of the partnership.

PAGE V. PAGE

Supreme Court of California, 1961
359 P.2d 41

TRAYNOR, JUSTICE. Plaintiff and defendant are partners in a linen supply business in Santa Maria, California. Plaintiff appeals from a judgment declaring the partnership to be for a term rather than at-will.

The partners entered into an oral partnership agreement in 1949. Within the first two years each partner contributed approximately $43,000 for the purchase of land, machinery, and linen needed to begin the business. From 1949 to 1957 the enterprise was unprofitable, losing approximately $62,000. The partnership's major creditor is a corporation, wholly owned by plaintiff, that supplies the linen and machinery necessary for the day-to-day operation of the business. This corporation holds a $47,000 demand note of the partnership. The partnership operations began to improve in 1958. The partnership earned $3,824.41 in that year and $2,282.30 in the first three months of 1959. Despite this improvement plaintiff wishes to terminate the partnership. * * *

Defendant testified that the terms of the partnership were to be similar to former partnerships of plaintiff and defendant, and that the understanding of these partnerships was that "we went into partnership to start the business and let the business operation pay for itself, put in so much money, and let the business pay itself out." * * *

In the instant case defendant failed to prove any facts from which an agreement to continue the partnership for a term may be implied. The understanding to which defendant testified was no more than a common hope that the partnership earnings would pay for all the necessary expenses. Such a hope does not establish even by implication a "definite term or particular undertaking" as required by section 15031, subdivision (1)(b) of the Corporations Code. All partnerships are ordinarily entered into with the hope that they will be profitable, but that alone does not make them all partnerships for a term and obligate the partners to continue in the partnerships until all of the losses over a period of many years have been recovered.

Defendant contends that plaintiff is acting in bad faith and is attempting to use his superior financial position to appropriate the now profitable business of the partnership. Defendant has invested $43,000 in the firm, and owing to the long period of losses his interest in the partnership assets is very small. The fact that plaintiff's wholly-owned corporation holds a $47,000 demand note of the partnership may make it difficult to sell the business as a going concern. Defendant fears that upon dissolution he will receive very little and that plaintiff, who is the managing partner and knows how to conduct the operations of the partnership, will receive a business that has become very profitable because of the establishment of Vandenberg Air Force Base in its vicinity. Defendant charges that plaintiff has been content to share the losses but now that the business has become profitable he wishes to keep all the gains.

There is no showing in the record of bad faith or that the improved profit situation is more than temporary. In any event these contentions are irrelevant to the issue whether the partnership is for a term or at-will. Since, however, this action is for a declaratory judgment and will be the basis for future action by the parties, it is appropriate to point out that defendant is amply protected by the fiduciary duties of co-partners.

Even though the Uniform Partnership Act provides that a partnership at will may be dissolved by the express will of any partner, this power, like any other power held by a fiduciary, must be exercised in good faith.

We have often stated that "partners are trustees for each other, and in all proceedings connected with the conduct of the partnership every partner is bound to act in the highest good faith to his copartner, and may not obtain any advantage over him in the partnership affairs by the slightest misrepresentation, concealment, threat, or adverse pressure of any kind."

A partner at will is not bound to remain in a partnership, regardless of whether the business is profitable or unprofitable. A partner may not, however, by use of adverse pressure "freeze out" a co-partner and appropriate the business to his own use. A partner may not dissolve a partnership to gain the benefits of the business for himself, unless he fully compensates his co-partner for his share of the prospective business opportunity. * * *

[P]laintiff has the power to dissolve the partnership by express notice to defendant. If, however, it is proved that plaintiff acted in bad faith and violated his fiduciary duties by attempting to appropriate to his own use the new prosperity of the partnership without adequate compensation to his co-partner, the dissolution would be wrongful and the plaintiff would be liable. * * *

The judgment is reversed.

QUESTIONS

1.   Why did the plaintiff seek a declaratory judgment that the partnership is a partnership at-will?

2.   In this case, who won (other than the attorneys)? Will the party who "won" get more money than he would have received had he not won?

In the preceding problems and in *Page v Page*, the partner's leaving the partnership was voluntary. As the next two cases illustrate, involuntary dissociation can raise more challenging legal issues.

GILES V. GILES LAND COMPANY, L.P.

Court of Appeals of Kansas, 2012
279 P.3d 139

GREEN, J.

Kelly Giles (Kelly), a general partner in a family farming partnership, filed suit against the partnership and his partners, arguing that he had not been provided access to partnership books and records. The remaining members of the partnership then filed a counterclaim requesting that Kelly be dissociated from the partnership. The trial court held that Kelly was not denied access to the partnership books and records. Kelly does not appeal from this decision. Moreover, the trial court held that Kelly should be dissociated from the partnership. Kelly, however, contends that the trial court's ruling regarding his dissociation from the partnership was improper. We disagree. Accordingly, we affirm.

The dispute in this case centers on a family owned and operated limited partnership. * * * The partnership owns both ranchland and farmland. * * *On March 26, 2007, the partnership held a meeting to discuss converting the partnership into a limited liability company. Kelly was unable to attend the meeting, but he later received a letter explaining the family's interest in converting the partnership to a limited liability company. Kelly did not sign the articles of organization for the proposed conversion and instead had his attorney request production of all of the partnership's books and records for his review. Kelly was not satisfied with the records that the partnership had provided, so he filed suit asking the court to force the partnership to turn over all of the documents he was requesting. In response, the defendants filed an answer and a counterclaim seeking to dissociate Kelly from the partnership.

Kelly Giles*

---

* http://www.cliftlandbrokers.com/agent/kelly-giles/ Doesn't Kelly look like the kind of guy you would trust, would want to have as your partner?

After a 2-day trial, the trial court determined that the partnership had properly complied with the document requests. The trial court also held that Kelly should be dissociated from the partnership under K.S.A. 56a–601(e)(3) or, in the alternative, K.S.A. 56a–601(e)(1). The trial court found that due to Kelly's threats and the total distrust between Kelly and his family, it was not practicable to carry on the business of the partnership so long as Kelly was a partner.

Did the Trial Court Err in Finding that Kelly Should Be Dissociated from the Partnership?

On appeal, Kelly argues that the trial court erred in finding that he should be dissociated from the partnership under K.S.A. 56a–601(e)(3) or, alternatively, K.S.A. 56a–601(e)(1). * * *

K.S.A. 56a–601 [same as RUPA 601] states the following: "A partner is dissociated from a partnership upon the occurrence of any of the following events: * * *

"(e) on application by the partnership or another partner, the partner's expulsion by judicial determination because:

(1) The partner engaged in wrongful conduct that adversely and materially affected the partnership business;

* * *

(3) the partner engaged in conduct relating to the partnership business which makes it not reasonably practicable to carry on the business in partnership with the partner."

The trial court relied primarily on K.S.A. 56a–601(e)(3) to dissociate Kelly; therefore, the record must demonstrate that (1) Kelly engaged in conduct relating to the partnership business and (2) such conduct makes it not reasonably practicable to carry on the business in partnership with Kelly. See K.S.A. 56a–601(e)(3). * * *

First, the trial court found that Kelly did not trust the other general partners and that he did not trust some of his sisters who are limited partners in the partnership. The trial court also found that the general partners as well as all of the other partners did not trust Kelly.

The trial court further found that the relationship between Kelly and the other family members was irreparably broken. In reaching that conclusion, the trial court focused on a meeting between the partners in 2006. Kelly turned to each of the general partners and said that they would each die, in turn, and that he would be the last man standing and that he would then get to control the partnership. Although Kelly testified that this was not a threat and that he was simply trying to explain the right of survivorship, the trial court believed the testimony of the rest of the family that it was taken as a threat. The trial court also relied on evidence that Kelly had said that "paybacks are hell" and that he intended to get even with his partners. The trial court also found this to be a threat. Another fact that the trial court relied on in finding that the family relationship was irreparably broken was that it was impossible for any of the family members to communicate with Kelly regarding the partnership. Each family member testified that he or she believed that it was in the best interest of the partnership to not have Kelly remain a partner. * * *

In light of the animosity that Kelly harbors toward his partners and his distrust of them (which distrust is mutual), it is clear that Kelly can no longer do business with his partners and vice-versa. Indeed, the partnership has reached an impasse regarding important business because of a lack of communication between Kelly and his partners. The evidence indicated that most communications with Kelly had to be conducted through his attorney. Moreover, Kelly's statement predicting the deaths of his general partners, his statement that "paybacks are hell," and his statement that he would get even showed a naked ambition on his part to control the partnership, contrary to the interests of the other partners. * * *

Alternative Theory for Dissociation

The trial court also found that there was enough evidence to dissociate Kelly under K.S.A. 56a–601(e)(1). This alternative ground also supports the trial court's decision. * * *

Under this alternative theory of dissociation, the record must demonstrate (1) that Kelly engaged in wrongful conduct and (2) that the wrongful conduct adversely and materially affected the partnership business. See K.S.A. 56a–601(e)(1).

* * *

In applying the alternative theory of dissociation, the trial court held the following: "In addition, Kelly Giles' conduct toward the General Partners who own the largest General Partnership interests by far, his parents, would also constitute wrongful conduct that materially affected the partnership business under 56a–601(e)(1), and the Court so finds."

* * *

Kelly is clearly not cooperating with the other partners and the distrust between Kelly and his partners runs both ways. Thus, even though there is no evidence that Kelly has been dishonest, and even though the partnership has continued to be successful, this does not mean that the other partners should be forced to remain in partnership with an uncooperative and distrustful partner.

Because this is a family partnership, the evidence of Kelly making threats or berating his parents to get them to give him what he wants qualifies as wrongful conduct. None of the partners were able to interact or communicate with Kelly. Additionally, Norman clearly testified that the partnership was at a standstill because of the disputes between Kelly and the rest of the partners. This is evidence that Kelly was materially or adversely affecting the partnership. Moreover, this evidence is clearly enough to support dissolution based on the caselaw listed earlier; therefore, it is also sufficient for dissociation. Based on this evidence, we determine that the trial court properly held that Kelly could also be dissociated under K.S.A. 56a–601(e)(1).

Affirmed.

QUESTIONS

1. Does RUPA distinguish between family partnerships and other partnerships? Does the Kansas Supreme Court?

2. Is Kelly's dissociation wrongful under RUPA § 602(b)(2) which provides in pertinent part: "A partner's dissociation is wrongful only if . . . (2) in the case of a partnership for a definite term or particular undertaking, before the expiration of the term or completion of the undertaking: . . . (ii) the partner is expelled by judicial determination under Section 601(5)."? Is that important?

3. How did Kelly "materially affect [the partnership business]" or "make it not reasonably practicable to carry on the business in partnership with the partner"?

––––––––––––––

Expulsion is among the listed "Events Causing Partner's Dissociation" in RUPA and among the listed "Causes of Dissolution" in UPA. The next case involves a lawyers' partnership agreement that provided expulsion procedures but not the substantive grounds for expulsion. In the case, a partner was expelled from her law firm because she (in good faith, but in error) accused another partner of unethical conduct. She sued the partnership, alleging a breach of fiduciary duty and a breach of the duty of good faith and fair dealing.

BOHATCH v. BUTLER & BINION
Supreme Court of Texas, 1998
977 S.W.2d 543

ENOCH, JUSTICE. Partnerships exist by the agreement of the partners; partners have no duty to remain partners. The issue in this case is whether we should create an exception to this rule by holding that a partnership has a duty not to expel a partner for reporting suspected overbilling by another partner. The trial court rendered judgment for Colette Bohatch on her breach of fiduciary duty claim against Butler & Binion and several of its partners (collectively, "the firm"). The court of appeals held that there was no evidence that the firm breached a fiduciary duty and reversed the trial court's tort judgment; however, the court of appeals found evidence of a breach of the partnership agreement and rendered judgment for Bohatch on this ground. We affirm the court of appeals' judgment.

Bohatch became an associate in the Washington, D.C., office of Butler & Binion in 1986 after working for several years as Deputy Assistant General Counsel at the Federal Energy Regulatory Commission.*

John McDonald, the managing partner of the office, and Richard Powers, a partner, were the only other attorneys in the Washington office. The office did work for Pennzoil almost exclusively.

Bohatch was made partner in February 1990. She then began receiving internal firm reports showing the number of hours each attorney worked, billed, and collected. From her review of these reports, Bohatch became concerned that McDonald was overbilling Pennzoil. * * *

On July 15, 1990, Bohatch met with Louis Paine, the firm's managing partner, to report her concern that McDonald was overbilling Pennzoil. Paine said he would investigate. * * *

In August, Paine met with Bohatch and told her that the firm's investigation revealed no basis for her contentions. He added that she should begin looking for other employment, but that the firm would continue to provide her a monthly draw, insurance coverage, office space, and a secretary. After this meeting, Bohatch received no further work assignments from the firm.

In January 1991, the firm denied Bohatch a year-end partnership distribution for 1990 and reduced her tentative distribution share for 1991 to zero. In June, the firm paid Bohatch her monthly draw and told

---

* http://hagemannfamily8.blogspot.com/2011_11_01_archive.html.   Subsequently, Ms. Bohatch married Roger Mehle, http://www.usna63.org/classmates/roster/cur-bio/316730.html with whom SHE is pictured above.

her that this draw would be her last. Finally, in August, the firm gave Bohatch until November to vacate her office.

By September, Bohatch had found new employment. She filed this suit on October 18, 1991, and the firm voted formally to expel her from the partnership three days later, October 21, 1991. * * *

The jury found that the firm breached the partnership agreement and its fiduciary duty. It awarded Bohatch $57,000 for past lost wages, $250,000 for past mental anguish, $4,000,000 total in punitive damages (this amount was apportioned against several defendants), and attorneys' fees. The trial court rendered judgment for Bohatch in the amounts found by the jury, except it disallowed attorneys' fees because the judgment was based in tort. After suggesting remittitur, which Bohatch accepted, the trial court reduced the punitive damages to around $237,000.

All parties appealed. The court of appeals held that the firm's only duty to Bohatch was not to expel her in bad faith. The court of appeals stated that " '[b]ad faith' in this context means only that partners cannot expel another partner for self-gain." Finding no evidence that the firm expelled Bohatch for self-gain, the court concluded that Bohatch could not recover for breach of fiduciary duty. However, the court concluded that the firm breached the partnership agreement when it reduced Bohatch's tentative partnership distribution for 1991 to zero without notice, and when it terminated her draw three months before she left. The court concluded that Bohatch was entitled to recover $35,000 in lost earnings for 1991 but none for 1990, and no mental anguish damages. Accordingly, the court rendered judgment for Bohatch for $35,000 plus $225,000 in attorneys' fees.

We have long recognized as a matter of common law that "[t]he relationship between * * * partners * * * is fiduciary in character, and imposes upon all the participants the obligation of loyalty to the joint concern and of the utmost good faith, fairness, and honesty in their dealings with each other with respect to matters pertaining to the enterprise." Yet, partners have no obligation to remain partners; "at the heart of the partnership concept is the principle that partners may choose with whom they wish to be associated." The issue presented, one of first impression, is whether the fiduciary relationship between and among partners creates an exception to the at-will nature of partnerships; that is, in this case, whether it gives rise to a duty not to expel a partner who reports suspected overbilling by another partner.

At the outset, we note that no party questions that the obligations of lawyers licensed to practice in the District of Columbia—including McDonald and Bohatch—were prescribed by the District of Columbia Code of Professional Responsibility in effect in 1990, and that in all other respects Texas law applies. Further, neither statutory nor contract law principles answer the question of whether the firm owed Bohatch a duty not to expel her. The Texas Uniform Partnership Act, Tex.Rev.Civ. Stat. Ann. art. 6701b, addresses expulsion of a partner only in the context of dissolution of the partnership. In this case, as provided by the partnership agreement, Bohatch's expulsion did not dissolve the partnership. Finally, the partnership agreement contemplates expulsion of a partner and prescribes procedures to be followed, but it does not specify or limit the grounds for expulsion. Thus, while Bohatch's claim that she was expelled in an improper way is governed by the partnership agreement, her claim that she was expelled for an improper reason is not. Therefore, we look to the common law to find the principles governing Bohatch's claim that the firm breached a duty when it expelled her. * * *

The fiduciary duty that partners owe one another does not encompass a duty to remain partners or else answer in tort damages. Nonetheless, Bohatch and several distinguished legal scholars urge this Court to recognize that public policy requires a limited duty to remain partners—i.e., a partnership must retain a whistleblower partner. They argue that such an extension of a partner's fiduciary duty is necessary because permitting a law firm to retaliate against a partner who in good faith reports suspected overbilling would discourage compliance with rules of professional conduct and thereby hurt clients.

While this argument is not without some force, we must reject it. A partnership exists solely because the partners choose to place personal confidence and trust in one another. Just as a partner can be expelled, without a breach of any common law duty, over disagreements about firm policy or to resolve some other "fundamental schism," a partner can be expelled for accusing another partner of overbilling without subjecting the partnership to tort damages. Such charges, whether true or not, may have a profound effect on the personal confidence and trust essential to the partner relationship. Once such charges are made, partners may find it impossible to continue to work together to their mutual benefit and the benefit of their clients.

We are sensitive to the concern expressed by the dissenting Justices [in this case] that "retaliation against a partner who tries in good faith to correct or report perceived misconduct virtually assures that others will not take these appropriate steps in the future." However, the dissenting Justices do not explain how the trust relationship necessary both for the firm's existence and for representing clients can survive such serious accusations by one partner against another. The threat of tort liability for expulsion would tend to force partners to remain in untenable circumstance—suspicious of and angry with each other—to their own detriment and that of their clients whose matters are neglected by lawyers distracted with intra-firm frictions.

* * *

We emphasize that our refusal to create an exception to the at-will nature of partnerships in no way obviates the ethical duties of lawyers. Such duties sometimes necessitate difficult decisions, as when a lawyer suspects overbilling by a colleague. The fact that the ethical duty to report may create an irreparable schism between partners neither excuses failure to report nor transforms expulsion as a means of resolving that schism into a tort.

We hold that the firm did not owe Bohatch a duty not to expel her for reporting suspected overbilling by another partner. * * *

[The court did affirm the lower courts' rulings, however, that the firm had breached its contract with Ms. Bohatch, which permitted her to recover contract damages and attorneys' fees. The court's rejection of the fiduciary duty claim deprived Ms. Bohatch of her claims for mental anguish and punitive damages.]

QUESTIONS AND NOTES

1. Questions about the law

a) In this case, Bohatch's suggestion of unethical billing conduct by another lawyer, though made in good faith, was incorrect. Would the Texas Supreme Court have reached a different result if she had been correct and was nonetheless expelled?

b) The Texas Supreme Court quotes the Texas Court of Civil Appeals for the proposition that "partners can not expel another partner for self-gain." Can a law firm expel a partner because her practice is no longer profitable? Because other partners find the partner annoying?

c) Should the Texas Supreme Court have quoted from *Meinhard v. Salmon*?

d) When Bohatch was expelled, did she have a right to be paid her share of the value of the Butler & Binion partnership? *See* RUPA §§ 601(3), 701(b).

2. Note

"There have been several recent cases involving expulsions of law partners. * * *

It may seem appropriate in such cases to apply strong fiduciary and good faith duties to protect the helpless fired partner from the firm's career-threatening and possibly opportunistic action. Thus, one recent commentator would strongly qualify a law firm's ability to expel partners, applying a good faith requirement that implicates a cause requirement (unless explicitly disclaimed in writing) and implementation of a common purpose. * * *

In general, * * * there is little to be gained and much to be lost by close judicial scrutiny of law firm expulsions. The firm itself has strong incentives to avoid abusing the expulsion power, and it is very hard for courts to determine when these abuses occur. At the same time, placing judicial constraints on the expulsion power weakens the effectiveness of this remedy. Expulsion is an important complement to other disciplinary mechanisms within the firm because it does not require the firm to prove wrongdoing or precisely calibrate the penalty and the harm done. Requiring a showing of cause or that the penalty fits the harm would significantly weaken the deterrent effect of expulsion and thereby make it harder for firms to protect their reputations. The losers would include not only law firms, but also their clients, who rely on the firm's ability to maintain its reputation.

Larry E. Ribstein, *Law Partner Expulsion,* 55 BUS. LAW. 845, 852 (2000).

2. CAN A PARTNERSHIP CONTINUE REGULAR BUSINESS OPERATIONS AFTER A PARTNER WITHDRAWS?

Consistent with the aggregate theory of partnership, UPA's answer to this question is that generally, after a partner withdraws, the partnership can only do "what may be necessary to wind up partnership affairs or to complete transactions begun, but not then finished." UPA § 33. If, however, the partner's withdrawal was wrongful, the remaining partners can continue regular business operations "if the all desire to." UPA § 38.

Consistent with the entity theory of partnership, RUPA's answer to this question is that, subject to limited exceptions set out in RUPA § 801, a partnership continues regular business operations after a partner dissociates.

Try applying these UPA and RUPA rules and exceptions to the following problems:

PROBLEMS

1.   Drs. A, B, C and D are in a partnership. The partnership agreement has a ten-year term. In year three of the partnership, Dr. A. withdraws. Can Drs. B, C and D continue the partnership?

2.   Does your answer to Question 1 change if Dr. B wants to dissolve the partnership?

3.   Propp, Agee and Capel are partners in Bubba's Burritos. The partnership agreement contains no provision relating to dissolution or to the duration of the partnership. Capel withdraws. Can Propp and Agee continue to operate the partnership?

4.   Same facts as Question 3 except that Capel dies and her widower, Mr. Capel, wants the partnership to dissolve. Again, Agee and Propp do not want the partnership to dissolve. What result? (Reconsider your answer after reading the next case.)

The next case suggest a possible third place to look—instead of either the general rule and exceptions in UPA or the general rule and exceptions in RUPA—for an answer to the question can a partnership continues regular business operations after a partner dies or otherwise leaves the partnership.

CREEL V. LILLY
Court of Appeals of Maryland, 1999
729 A.2d 385

CHASANOW, JUDGE. The primary issue presented in this appeal is whether Maryland's Uniform Partnership Act (UPA) permits the estate of a deceased partner to demand liquidation of partnership assets in order to arrive at the true value of the business. Specifically, Petitioner (Anne Creel) maintains that the surviving partners have a duty to liquidate all partnership assets because (1) there is no provision in the partnership agreement providing for the continuation of the partnership upon a partner's death and (2) the estate has not consented to the continuation of the business. Respondents (Arnold Lilly and Roy Altizer) contend that because the surviving partners wound up the partnership in good faith, in that they conducted a full inventory, provided an accurate accounting to the estate for the value of the business as of the date of dissolution, and paid the estate its proportionate share of the surplus proceeds, they are under no duty to liquidate the partnership's assets upon demand of the deceased partner's estate. * * *

I.   Background

On approximately June 1, 1993, Joseph Creel began a retail business selling NASCAR racing memorabilia. His business was originally located in a section of his wife Anne's florist shop, but after about a year and a half he decided to raise capital from partners so that he could expand and move into his own space. On September 20, 1994, Mr. Creel entered into a partnership agreement—apparently prepared without the assistance of counsel—with Arnold Lilly and Roy Altizer to form a general partnership called "Joe's Racing." * * *

II.   Discussion and Analysis

We begin our analysis by reviewing the law of partnership as it pertains to the issues in this case. Maryland enacted UPA in 1916. * * *

Under UPA, partners may avoid the automatic dissolution of the business upon the death of a partner by providing for its continuation in their partnership agreement. Sophisticated partnerships virtually always use carefully drafted partnership agreements to protect the various partners' interests by providing for the continuation of the business, the distribution of partnership assets, etc., in the face of various contingencies such as death. * * *

Over time, the UPA rule requiring automatic dissolution of the partnership upon the death of a partner, in the absence of consent by the estate to continue the business or an agreement providing for continuation, with the possible result of a forced sale of all partnership assets was viewed as outmoded by many jurisdictions including Maryland. The development and adoption of RUPA by the National Conference of Commissioners on Uniform State Laws (NCCUSL) mitigated this harsh UPA provision of automatic dissolution and compelled liquidation.

RUPA's underlying philosophy differs radically from UPA's, thus laying the foundation for many of its innovative measures. RUPA adopts the "entity" theory of partnership as opposed to the "aggregate" theory that the UPA espouses. Under the aggregate theory, a partnership is characterized by the collection of its individual members, with the result being that if one of the partners dies or withdraws, the partnership ceases to exist. On the other hand, RUPA's entity theory allows for the partnership to continue even with the departure of a member because it views the partnership as "an entity distinct from its partners."

This adoption of the entity theory, which permits continuity of the partnership upon changes in partner identity, allows for several significant changes in RUPA. Of particular importance to the instant case is that under RUPA "a partnership no longer automatically dissolves due to a change in its membership, but rather the existing partnership may be continued if the remaining partners elect to buy out the dissociating partner." In contrast to UPA, RUPA's "buy-out" option does not have to be expressly included in a written partnership agreement in order for it to be exercised; however, the surviving partners must still actively choose to exercise the option, as "continuation is not automatic as with a corporation." This major RUPA innovation therefore delineates two possible paths for a partnership to follow when a partner dies or withdraws: "[o]ne leads to the winding up and termination of the partnership and the other to continuation of the partnership and purchase of the departing partner's share." Critically, under RUPA the estate of the deceased partner no longer has to consent in order for the business to be continued nor does the estate have the right to compel liquidation.

Like UPA, RUPA is a "gap filler" in that it only governs partnership affairs to the extent not otherwise agreed to by the partners in the partnership agreement. See § 9A–103(a), which states: "[R]elations among the partners and between the partners and the partnership are governed by the partnership agreement. To the extent the partnership agreement does not otherwise provide, this title governs relations among the partners and between the partners and the partnership." There are certain RUPA provisions, however, that partners cannot waive, such as unreasonably restricting the right of access to partnership books and records, eliminating the duty of loyalty, unreasonably reducing the duty of care, and eliminating the obligation of good faith and fair dealing. See § 9A–103(b). * * *

In adopting RUPA, the Maryland legislature was clearly seeking to eliminate some of UPA's harsh provisions, such as the automatic dissolution of a viable partnership upon the death of a partner and the subsequent right of the estate of the deceased partner to compel liquidation. * * *

In this appeal, however, we would arrive at the same holding regardless of whether UPA or RUPA governs. Although our holding departs from the general UPA rule that the representative of the deceased partner's estate has a right to demand liquidation of the partnership, our position of "no forced sale" hardly represents a radical departure from traditional partnership law. * * * Because a partnership is governed by any agreement between or among the partners, we must begin our analysis of the compelled liquidation issue by examining the Joe's Racing partnership agreement. We reiterate that both UPA and RUPA only apply when there is either no partnership agreement governing the partnership's affairs, the agreement is silent on a particular point, or the agreement contains provisions contrary to law. * * * Thus, when conflicts between partners arise, courts must first look to the partnership agreement to resolve the issue.

The agreement, whatever its form, is the heart of the partnership. One of the salient characteristics of partnership law is the extent to which partners may write their own ticket. Relations among them are governed by common law and statute, but almost invariably can be overridden by the parties themselves. * * *

The pertinent paragraph and subsections of the Joe's Racing partnership agreement are as follows:

7. TERMINATION

(a) That, at the termination of this partnership a full and accurate inventory shall be prepared, and the assets, liabilities, and income, both in gross and net, shall be ascertained: the remaining debts or profits will be distributed according to the percentages shown above in the 6(e).

(d) Upon the death or illness of a partner, his share will go to his estate.

If his estate wishes to sell his interest, they must offer it to the remaining partners first.

We only turn to UPA and its liquidation rule if there is no other option, and such is clearly not the case here. While this partnership agreement was drafted without the assistance of counsel and is not a sophisticated document that provides for every contingency, if it states the intention of the parties it is controlling. * * *

Particularly in light of Maryland's recent adoption of RUPA, paragraph 7(d) of the partnership agreement can be interpreted to mean that because Mrs. Creel did not wish to remain in business with Lilly and Altizer, they had the option to buy out her deceased husband's interest.

In short, when subsections (a) and (d) of paragraph 7 are read in conjunction, it is apparent that the partners did not intend for there to be a liquidation of all partnership assets upon the death of a partner. * * *

Our goal in this case, and in cases of a similar nature, is to prevent the disruption and loss that are attendant on a forced sale, while at the same time preserving the right of the deceased partner's estate to be paid his or her fair share of the partnership. With our holding, we believe this delicate balance has been achieved. For the reasons stated, we hold that paragraph 7, subsections (a) and (d), of the partnership agreement should be interpreted as outlining an alternative method of winding-up Joe's Racing and arriving at its true value other than a "fire sale" of all its assets. Even if there were no partnership agreement governing this case, however, we hold that Maryland's UPA-particularly in light of the legislature's recent adoption of RUPA-does not grant the estate of a deceased partner the right to demand liquidation of a partnership where the partnership agreement does not expressly provide for continuation of the partnership and where the estate does not consent to continuation. To hold otherwise vests excessive power and control in the estate of the deceased partner, to the extreme disadvantage of the surviving partners. We further hold that where the surviving partners have in good faith wound up the business and the deceased partner's estate is provided with an accurate accounting allowing for payment of a proportionate share of the business, then a forced sale of all partnership assets is unwarranted. * * *

QUESTIONS AND NOTES

1.   Why is Mrs. Creel arguing that the only way to determine the value of her deceased husband's interest in the partnership is to liquidate all of the

assets? Why did Altizer and Lilly reject her demand that they liquidate the partnership's assets?

2. Surely, at least one of your favorite co-authors agrees with this statement from the Freer and Moll student guide: "The problem with allowing alternatives to a forced liquidation of the partnership's business, however, is that the language of § 38(1) [of UPA] seems to require such a forced liquidation regardless of the equities."[*] Do you agree?

3. In *Creel,* the court notes that the partnership agreement was prepared "without the assistance of counsel." Could a competent lawyer have drafted the partnership agreement to avoid this litigation? What would she have provided?

One more time: UPA or RUPA is a gap filler. Don't leave gaps in the partnership agreements you draft.

3. IF THE PARTNERSHIP CONTINUES REGULAR BUSINESS OPERATIONS, WHAT ARE THE PAYMENT RIGHTS OF THE WITHDRAWING PARTNER

Again, UPA and RUPA provides different answers. And both the UPA and the RUPA answers differ depending on whether the withdrawal was wrongful.

Section 38(c) is the relevant UPA provision:

II. If the business is continued . . . the right . . . to have the value of his interest in the partnership, less any damages caused to his co-partners by the dissolution, ascertained and paid to him in cash, or the payment secured by bond approved by the court, and to be released from all existing liabilities of the partnership; but in ascertaining the value of the partner's interest the value of the good will of the business shall not be considered.

A couple of questions that you should have asked in reading this UPA provision: (1) How is "the value of his interest" to be "ascertained"? and (2) What is the relevance of not considering "the value of the good will?"

Sections 602(c) and 701(b) and (h) are the relevant RUPA provisions:

§ 602. Partner's Power to Dissociate; Wrongful Dissociation

* * *

---

* Richard D. Freer & Douglas K. Moll, Principles of Business Organization s 134–35 (2013).

(c) A partner who wrongfully dissociates is liable to the partnership and to the other partners for damages caused by the dissociation.

701. Purchase of Dissociated Partner's Interest

(a) If a partner is dissociated from a partnership without resulting in a dissolution and winding up of the partnership business under Section 801, the partnership shall cause the dissociated partner's interest in the partnership to be purchased for a buyout price determined pursuant to subsection (b).

(b) The buyout price of a dissociated partner's interest is the amount that would have been distributable to the dissociating partner under Section 807(b) if, on the date of dissociation, the assets of the partnership were sold at a price equal to the greater of the liquidation value or the value based on a sale of the entire business as a going concern without the dissociated partner and the partnership were wound up as of that date. Interest must be paid from the date of dissociation to the date of payment.

(c) Damages for wrongful dissociation under Section 602(b), and all other amounts owing, whether or not presently due, from the dissociated partner to the partnership, must be offset against the buyout price. Interest must be paid from the date the amount owed becomes due to the date of payment. * * *

(h) A partner who wrongfully dissociates before the expiration of a definite term or the completion of a particular undertaking is not entitled to payment of any portion of the buyout price until the expiration of the term or completion of the undertaking, unless the partner establishes to the satisfaction of the court that earlier payment will not cause undue hardship to the business of the partnership. A deferred payment must be adequately secured and bear interest.

Are the RUPA provisions easier to apply than the UPA provision?

———————

Easier still is to provide detailed directions for the determination of the buyout price in the partnership agreement. Consider, for example, this provision for a medical partnership:

21. Upon the withdrawal or expulsion of a partner, such partner shall be entitled to the following payments by the partnership in liquidation of the interest of such partner in the partnership:

(a) The amount of the interest of such partner in the capital of the partnership, which shall equal the capital account of such partner as shown on the partnership books as of the date of withdrawal or expulsion, including any undrawn share of profits but not including accounts receivable, and adjusted to reflect the appraised value of the partnership x-ray equipment as provided in paragraph 18 (a)(3).

(b) A portion of the following amounts, which portion in each case shall be the percentage interest of such withdrawn or expelled partner in the accounts receivable of the partnership immediately prior to withdrawal or expulsion:

(1) the amount of collections of accounts receivable on the partnership books as of the date of withdrawal or expulsion which are made by the partnership, under established practices as to billings and use of collection agencies, within three months after such date, less 20 percent of all such collections for costs of collection; and

(2) an amount equal to 70 percent of the uncollected balances at the end of the aforesaid three-month period of accounts receivable which were on the partnership books as of the date of such withdrawn or expelled partner's withdrawal or expulsion. The portion of the amounts of collections specified in clause (1) above to which a withdrawn or expelled partner is entitled shall be paid to such partner, without interest, in three monthly installments, each of which shall be computed on the basis of collections during one of the three months specified in clause (1) and shall be made as soon as reasonably possible after the end of such month. The portion of the amount specified in clause (2) above to which a withdrawn or expelled partner is entitled shall be paid to such partner, without interest, within six months after withdrawal or expulsion.

The partners intend that payments under subparagraph (a) above, except to the extent that they represent the undrawn portion of the withdrawn or expelled partner's share of partnership net profit for the calendar year in which withdrawal or expulsion occurs, shall be distributions under Section 736 (b) of the Internal Revenue Code, and that payments under subparagraph (b) above shall be a distributive share of partnership income or a guaranteed payment under Section 736 (a) of the Internal Revenue Code. When the withdrawn or expelled partner has received the payments provided in this paragraph, such partner shall have no further interest in the partnership or in its assets, records, or property. However, the withdrawn or expelled partner shall have the right, exercisable by written notice to the continuing partners within one month after withdrawal or expulsion, to purchase from the partnership any insurance policy or policies on the life of such partner owned by the partnership for the cash value of such policy or policies on the date of purchase, which date shall be determined by the continuing partners but shall not be later than 10 days after completion of all payments by the partnership to the withdrawn or expelled partner under this paragraph.

William R. Paterson, *Drafting the Partnership Agreement*, SB85 ALI-ABA 193 (May 1, 1997).

Let's stop and review what you should know and what you don't yet know about a partner's getting paid by the partnership for her partnership interest. You should know that:

- Under UPA or RUPA, a partner always has the power to dissociate (withdraw) which triggers an obligation of the partnership to pay the partner for her partnership interest.*
- Under UPA or RUPA, the amount and time of such payment depend in part on whether the withdrawal/dissociation was wrongful and on what the partnership agreement provides.

4.   IF THE PARTNERSHIP CONTINUES REGULAR BUSINESS OPERATIONS, WHAT ARE THE PAYMENT OBLIGATIONS OF THE WITHDRAWING PARTNER

There is also a lot you don't yet (but soon will) know about dissociation. For example, until reading RUPA §§ 702 and 703 and working through the easy problems set out below, you did not know about the effect of dissociation on the possible liability of the partnership and the possible liability of the dissociated partner.

PROBLEMS

1.   Partnership's liability. You represent T Travel Agency (TA). Regency Capital Partners (RC), one of TA's regular customers, refuses to pay for a $4000 ticket charged to RC's account by Dismas Perdue (DP), a partner who dissociated from the firm two days before buying the ticket and asking that it be charged to RC's account. What additional information do you need in order to advise TA of its legal rights? What if the TA partnership

---

*   UPA does not use the term "dissociate", but UPA in essence provides for the same opportunity to withdraw and be paid by the partnership.

agreement provided that it has no liability for post-dissociation actions of dissociated partners?

2.   *Dissociating partner's liability.* Assume that Capel, a partner in the Bubba's Burritos partnership, dissociates from the partnership on April 5 (All dates given are in the same year). Is Capel liable:

a)   To Roberts on the ten-year real property lease that Bubba's Burritos and Roberts executed on January 15?

b)   To Shepherd on his slip and fall claim against Bubba's Burritos based on an alleged July 13 accident there?

c)   To TeePee Distributors, Inc., a long-time supplier of Bubba's Burritos, for food ordered and delivered on April 11?

d)   Would any of your answers change if the Bubba's Burritos partnership agreement provided that a partner's liability ends upon dissociation? *See* RUPA § 103(b)(10).

3.   Assume that Sterling, Cooper, Draper and Pryce is a partnership and tenant of the Time/Life building. The twenty year lease was entered into in 1963. If Draper is expelled from the partnership in 1973, what is his liability exposure, if any, on the lease?

———————

And, we don't yet know about who gets what when a partnership terminates.

5.   WHO GETS WHAT IF THE PARTNERSHIP TERMINATES BUSINESS OPERATIONS?

The "end game" for a business structured as a partnership is generally referred to as winding up. A partnership winds up by (1) dissolving, (2) terminating its business and (3) making payments to creditors and distributions to the partners,

Dissolution then is not the end of the partnership. At most, it is the beginning of the end. As Comment 2 to RUPA § 801 explains:

Under RUPA, "dissolution" is merely the commencement of the winding up process. The partnership continues for the limited purpose of winding up the business. In effect, that means the scope of the partnership business contracts to completing work in process and taking such other actions necessary to wind up the business. Winding up the partnership business entails selling its assets, paying its debts, and distributing the net balance, if any, to the partners in cash according to their interests. The partnership entity continues, and the partners are associated in the winding up of the business until winding up is completed. When the winding up is completed, the partnership entity terminates.

Consider the following problems about the "paying its debts" part of winding up a partnership:

PROBLEMS

1.   On dissolution, Bubba's Burritos owes $100,000 to its creditors, including $20,000 lent to the partnership by one of its partners, Capel. Should the debt owed to Capel be treated differently from the debt owed to the other creditors? *See* RUPA § 807(a) and Comment 2 of Official Comments to § 807.

2.   Suppose that the partnership has no assets. Can the inside and outside creditors collect the unpaid balance of their claims from the partners individually? Recall RUPA §§ 306, 807(b).

If the partnership agreement does not address the issue effectively, the parties can encounter significant problems in trying to distribute assets to the partners "according to their interests." RUPA provides default rules in this area in §§ 401 and 807. These provisions establish four basic concepts:

Unless partners agree to the contrary:

1.   They share responsibility not only for the losses from operation of the partnership business, but also for any partners' losses from investments in the partnership. *See* RUPA § 401(b);

2.   The amount of each partner's loss from her investment in the partnership is determined from her partnership account, a bookkeeping device which keeps track of how much a partner puts into the partnership, how much she has taken out of the partnership, and her share of the partnership's profits and losses. *See* RUPA §§ 401(a), 807(a)–(b);

3.   When the partnership is dissolved, the partnership is legally obligated to pay each partner an amount measured by the balance in her partnership account. *See* RUPA § 807(b). Summarizing and distilling the calculations in § 401, the amount in each partner's account will be:

- The value of each partner's investment in the partnership of money or property, but no credit for the value of a partner's labor (we'll discuss in a bit whether this is fair);

- Minus any distributions to the partner—remember, profits can be either retained or disbursed;

- Plus an equal share of whatever of value remains in the partnership, after paying both creditors and the above amounts. If there are insufficient partnership funds to cover the amounts above, the loss will be divided equally among the partners' accounts.

4.   It is possible that, at the time of dissolution, a partner will have a negative balance in his account. For example, this could occur if a partner, relative to the other partners, has contributed little property or money, but has received relatively large distributions. And, if the partnership has suffered large losses, such a partner may have to contribute additional funds to the partnership in the amount of the negative balance. RUPA § 807(b). This will ensure that the other partners—such as those who received less or no distributions—are dealt with fairly.

Apply these concepts in the following problems.

PROBLEMS

1.   At the start of the Bubba's Burritos partnership, Capel invests $250,000 in the partnership. Propp deeds land to the partnership she believes is worth $150,000. Agee contributes cookware that he purchased for $2,000 and agrees to work for the partnership as manager. They agree to share profits from the partnership equally. Do they also need to agree as to the initial amounts in the three partnership accounts? What are the possible disagreements? Cf. RUPA § 401(a)(1) If any such disagreement arises, can you represent all three of them?

2.   Suppose that, at the dissolution of the Bubba's Burritos partnership described in Question 1, the partnership has cash and property worth $200,000 after paying all of its creditors. As a result of distributions, Capel's partnership account balance is $100,000; Propp's partnership account balance is $8,000; and Agee's partnership account balance is $2,000. How should the $200,000 be distributed?

3.   Same facts as Question 2 except that after paying its creditors, the partnership has only $20,000. (This may have happened, for instance, because the value of the assets that the partners contributed has declined). How is the $20,000 distributed? This one is tougher because there is not enough money to compensate everyone for her contributions. To jump-start these calculations, here are some helpful questions. How much money is owed to compensate each partner for what she has contributed, but that has not yet been distributed to her? How much money does the partnership have to cover that amount? (The hypo says $20,000.) How much is that short? That amount is a loss, to be shared equally. Now do the numbers.

———————

Were your answers for Question 2: Capel gets $130,000, Propp gets $38,000, and Agee gets $32,000? Were your answers for Question 3: Propp pays $22,000, Agee pays $28,000, and Capel receives $70,000?

In answering Question 1, did you actually "see" RUPA § 401(a)(1) Do you think it's fair to Agee? If so, you will probably disagree with the next case.

As you read the next case, please consider the following:

1.   Were the creditors of the partnership paid? Do the creditors of the partnership "have a dog in this fight"?

2.   If the facts of this case had been an exam question and your answer was the last three paragraphs of Justice Schauer's opinion, what grade would your prof have "given" you?

KOVACIK V. REED

Supreme Court of California, 1957
315 P.2d 314

SCHAUER, J. In this suit for dissolution of a joint venture and for an accounting, defendant appeals from a judgment that plaintiff recover from defendant one half the losses of the venture. We have concluded that inasmuch as the parties agreed that plaintiff was to supply the money and defendant the labor to carry on the venture, defendant is correct in his contention that the trial court erred in holding him liable for one half the monetary losses, and that the judgment should therefore be reversed. * * *

Plaintiff, a licensed building contractor in San Francisco, operated his contracting business as a sole proprietorship under the fictitious name of "Asbestos Siding Company." Defendant had for a number of years worked for various building contractors in that city as a job superintendent and estimator.

Early in November, 1952, Kovacik [plaintiff] told Reed [defendant] that Kovacik had an opportunity to do kitchen remodeling work for Sears Roebuck Company in San Francisco and asked Reed to become his job superintendent and estimator in this venture. Kovacik said that he had about $10,000.00 to invest in the venture and that, if Reed would superintend and estimate the jobs, Kovacik would share the profits with Reed on a 50-50 basis. Kovacik did not ask Reed to agree to share any loss that might result and Reed did not offer to share any such loss. The subject of a possible loss was not discussed in the inception of this venture. Reed accepted Kovacik's proposal and commenced work for the venture shortly after November 1, 1952. * * * Reed's only contribution was his own labor. Kovacik provided all of the venture's financing through the credit of Asbestos Siding Company, although at times Reed purchased materials for the jobs in his own name or on his account for which he was reimbursed. * * *

The venture bid on and was awarded a number of remodeling jobs in San Francisco. Reed worked on all of the jobs as job superintendent.

During August, 1953, Kovacik, who at that time had all of the financial records of the venture in his possession, informed Reed that the venture had been unprofitable and demanded contribution from Reed as to amounts which Kovacik claimed to have advanced in excess of the income received from the venture. Reed at no time promised, represented or agreed that he was liable for any of the venture's losses, and he consistently and without exception refused to contribute to or pay any of the loss resulting from the venture. The venture was terminated on August 31, 1953.

Kovacik thereafter instituted this proceeding, seeking an accounting of the affairs of the venture and to recover from Reed one half of the losses. Despite the evidence above set forth from the statement of the oral proceedings, showing that at no time had defendant agreed to be liable for any of the losses, the trial court "found"—more accurately, we think, concluded as a matter of law—that "plaintiff and defendant were to share equally all their joint venture profits and losses between them," and that defendant "agreed to share equally in the profits and losses of said joint venture." Following an accounting taken by a referee appointed by the court, judgment was rendered awarding plaintiff recovery against defendant of some $4,340, as one half the monetary losses* [1] found by the referee to have been sustained by the joint venture.

It is the general rule that in the absence of an agreement to the contrary the law presumes that partners and joint adventurers intended to participate equally in the profits and losses of the common enterprise, irrespective of any inequality in the amounts each contributed to the capital employed in the venture, with the losses being shared by them in the same proportions as they share the profits.

However, it appears that in the cases in which the above stated general rule has been applied, each of the parties had contributed capital consisting of either money or land or other tangible property, or else was to receive compensation for services rendered to the common undertaking which was to be paid before computation of the profits or losses. Where, however, as in the present case, one partner or joint adventurer contributes the money capital as against the other's skill and labor, all the cases cited, and which our research has discovered, hold that neither party is liable to the other for contribution for any loss sustained. Thus, upon loss of the money the party who contributed it is not entitled to

---

* [1] The record is silent as to the factors taken into account by the referee in determining the 'loss' suffered by the venture. However, there is no contention that defendant's services were ascribed any value whatsoever. It may also be noted that the trial court 'found' that 'neither plaintiff nor defendant was to receive compensation for their services rendered to said joint venture, but plaintiff and defendant were to share equally all their joint venture profits and losses between them.' Neither party suggests that plaintiff actually rendered services to the venture in the same sense that defendant did. And, as is clear from the settled statement, plaintiff's proposition to defendant was that plaintiff would provide the money as against defendant's contribution of services as estimator and superintendent.

recover any part of it from the party who contributed only services. The rationale of this rule is that where one party contributes money and the other contributes services, then in the event of a loss each would lose his own capital—the one his money and the other his labor. Another view would be that in such a situation the parties have, by their agreement to share equally in profits, agreed that the values of their contributions—the money on the one hand and the labor on the other—were likewise equal; it would follow that upon the loss, as here, of both money and labor, the parties have shared equally in the losses. Actually, of course, plaintiff here lost only some $8,680—or somewhat less than the $10,000 which he originally proposed and agreed to invest. * * *

It follows that the conclusion of law upon which the judgment in favor of plaintiff for recovery from defendant of one half the monetary losses depends is untenable, and that the judgment should be reversed. * * *

The judgment is reversed.

QUESTIONS AND NOTES

1.   Questions about the law

a).   Does the court regard the business in this case as a partnership? Should the court regard the business in this case as a partnership?

b)   Would the result in this case have been different if the court had applied RUPA? See RUPA §§ 401(a), 401(b), 807(b) and 807(d).

2.   Note

It is important to understand the difference between the questions of (i) who is liable to third parties for unpaid obligations of the partnership and (ii) who must bear the partnership's losses. The questions arise at different times and have different answers.

The question of liability to third parties for unpaid obligations of the partnership can arise at any time during the existence of a partnership. Assume, for example, that Freer and Roberts form a partnership (FR) to do kitchen remodeling. FR buys sinks and disposals on credit from Epstein Sales, Inc. (ES). If FR does not pay, can ES collect from Freer or Roberts personally? That question is answered by RUPA § 306: "all partners are liable jointly and severally for all obligations of the partnership." That question is different from the question in *Kovacik.*

In *Kovacik,* the partnership had already paid its obligations to creditors; it had paid these third-parties with partnership funds that had been invested in the partnership by Kovacik. The partnership had ended. It had no more debts. The question in *Kovacik* was not whether creditors of the partnership would recover on their claims, but whether Kovacik would recover anything on his investment in the partnership (which lost the money he invested). Unless it is answered in the partnership agreement, that question will be answered by RUPA § 807.

―――――――

Thus far we have seen only one way for a partnership to end: dissolution, followed by winding up, followed by termination. Another possible endgame for a partnership is the sale of the entire partnership. The legal issues in such a sale are primarily contracts issues or tax issues.

Partnerships can also end when they are converted from a partnership to some other business structure, or when the partnership is merged into or otherwise combined with another business. These possibilities can be addressed by default provisions of RUPA, by the partnership agreement, or by the next chapters of this book.

Before we move to these next chapters, consider two review questions about partnerships:

1.   Assume that your client owns an interest in a partnership because she wants to make money. What law-related issues should most concern her about her interest? In other words, what are the downsides of being a partner?

2.   And what, if anything, can you do in negotiating and writing the partnership agreement to address those concerns?

CHAPTER 4

WHAT IS A CORPORATION AND HOW DOES A BUSINESS BECOME A CORPORATION?

■ ■ ■

Remember our friends Propp, Agee and Capel? Assume again that Propp wants to start a southern-style burrito restaurant near a college campus. Agee will work as cook and day-to-day manager of the restaurant and Capel will provide needed funds. Now assume that they want to use the corporation structure for the business.

Their questions are familiar: What is a corporation? How do we set up the business as a corporation? Who owns what? Who decides what? Who is liable for what to whom? How can the business grow? How do we make money from the business? And how can the business end? Not surprisingly, some of the answers to these corporation questions are similar to the answers to the partnership questions and some are different. To answer the first of their questions, please read Model Business Corporation Act (MBCA) §§ 2.02 and 2.03,* Delaware §§ 102 and 106,† and the following.

Most people tend to think of corporations as huge businesses. Indeed, most of the billion-dollar multinational businesses are corporations. But there is nothing in the corporate form that requires the business to be big. Most corporations are not big; many are owned and run by one person. Perhaps surprisingly, though, most statutes concerning the formation and running of corporations do not distinguish between large and small businesses. Courts sometimes do make the distinction, however, as we have seen in the *Hobby Lobby* case on pages 10–12 and will see at various points in our chapters dealing with the corporation.

As a matter of terminology, small corporations are often called "close" or "closely-held." They have relatively few shareholders (there is no magic number, usually) and there is no public market for buying or selling interests in them. On the other hand, large corporations are often called "public," for the simple reason that they have many shareholders and the

---

* The Model Business Corporation Act is the work product of an American Bar Association Committee. Over the years, there have been several versions. The first MBCA was prepared in 1969; the current version was completed in 1984 (and has been regularly revised since then). The most recent version is sometimes referred to as the Revised Model Business Corporation Act, or RMBCA. We use "MBCA" to refer to that.

† Throughout the book, we refer to sections of the Delaware General Corporation Law simply as "Delaware."

interests in them are publicly traded (for instance, on stock exchanges). There are many corporations somewhere in the middle, but lawyers tend to group corporations into these two categories—close and public. Keep these two categories in the back of your mind as we delve into the world of the corporate form of doing business.

A. WHAT IS A CORPORATION AND WHAT IS CORPORATION LAW?

Some familiarity with the history of corporations and corporate law in the United States is helpful—you know, understanding where we have been should help us understand where we are. As Professor Susan Hamill explains:

> For as long as America has existed, the primary authority over the creation of business organizations has resided with the individual states. At America's beginnings, only two business forms existed [in addition to the sole proprietorship]: the general partnership, which requires no formal sovereign recognition, and the corporation, which has always required formal recognition by a sovereign person or government.
>
> * * * During America's colonial period and for a few years thereafter, the vast majority of the people in America's agriculturally based society labored on family farms producing the goods necessary for their own survival and occasional surplus to be bartered. The manufacture of goods produced by artisans in small shops and the business of merchants engaged in importing and exporting grew steadily around the cities clustered at the seaboard, with the sole proprietorship and the partnership serving as the legal forms for conducting these businesses. The crude and undeveloped state of transportation made any large-scale movement of goods from the cities prohibitively expensive and kept business at small levels. Business discrepancy had not yet evolved to a point where the legal benefits of forming a corporation proved useful. The colonial assemblies and the early state legislatures granted corporate charters primarily for public purposes, including the establishment of towns, churches, cemeteries, colleges, and charities.
>
> Especially after 1790, state-issued corporate charters for banks proliferated in order to supply credit to the nation's rapidly growing business economy. State-chartered banks, which numbered over two hundred by 1815, played a prominent role in the nation's economy through the circulation of bank notes that served as a medium of exchange within the nation's currency. During the decades leading up to and just after the War of 1812,

the number of state-issued corporate charters increased rapidly because canals and turnpikes increased rapidly, representing the first step in America's transportation revolution. Unlike the majority of purely private business enterprises, which still operated in the partnership form, banks and transportation projects needed the legal advantages offered by the corporate form, specifically the ability to pool large amounts of capital and to exist beyond the natural life of the owners. * * *

During the 1820s, undoubtedly fueled by protective tariffs adopted a few years earlier, state-issued corporate charters for manufacturing companies grew rapidly. Although America's real Industrial Revolution remained several decades away, for most of the 1820s business and commerce steadily grew and the business corporation experienced little overt controversy. However, within the shadows of businesses' progress, the seeds of discontent were present. America's transformation from an agricultural and mercantile economy to a market economy displaced and negatively affected many individuals. The rhetoric surrounding Andrew Jackson's election in 1828 as the sixth President of the United States denounced federal powers and harshly criticized banks, business corporations, and other instruments of power oppressing the large majority of farmers and workers. * * *

Jacksonians did not oppose corporations *per se*. Rather, they objected to the special privileges obtained in the special legislative charters. Prominent Jacksonians, wanting to cure the evils of special privileges conferred by the special corporate charters, advocated the creation of general incorporation laws that would allow equal access to the corporate form to all those meeting the statutory requirements. After President Jackson left office in 1836, state law general incorporation statutes appeared in two states. During the 1840s the idea caught on as six additional states passed general incorporation statutes. By the eve of the Civil War, sixteen additional states enacted statutes, bringing the total to well over fifty percent of the existing states.[*]

The nineteenth-century general incorporation statutes of which Professor Hamill speaks were designed for large businesses.

Businesses have changed. Again, most corporations in the twenty-first century are not large. Take a look at the yellow pages in your local phone book. You'll see entries such as Freer Floor and Tile Co. and Roberts Roto-Rooter Plumbing and Drain Services, Inc. Or take a look at

---

[*] Susan Pace Hamill, *The Origins Behind the Limited Liability Company*, 59 OHIO ST. L.J. 1459, 1484 (1998).

government statistics.* In 2008, more than 5.8 million corporations filed federal tax returns. More than 80% had less than $500,000 of taxable earnings. A corporation is not only the business structure used by most large businesses with thousands of owners, but it is also the business structure used by many small businesses, some with just one owner.

While most twenty-first century corporations are small with relatively few owners, twenty-first century general incorporation law in many ways still reflects the original large-corporation model. And, in most states, there is a single, general corporation law that applies to all corporations. We are going to learn about both small and large corporations. Part of this course will be aimed at understanding how the courts have adapted general corporate statutes based on a large business model to small businesses.

1. A CORPORATION IS . . .

A corporation is whatever the relevant state law says it is.† As Professor Hamill has pointed out, corporations always have been and still are creations of state legislatures. Today every state has a general corporation statute. And every state's corporation statute provides that (i) a corporation is a separate legal entity and (ii) its owners, usually called shareholders (or stockholders), are generally not personally liable for the debts of the corporation. This means that while there is no statutory limit on how much money an owner of a corporation can make from her investment in a corporation, the most that she risks is the amount that she paid for the shares of stock. That is the limit of her liability. This is the concept of "limited liability."

Almost a hundred years ago, Nicholas Murray Butler, who was the President of Columbia University, said: "I weigh my words when I say that . . . the limited liability corporation is the greatest single discovery of modern times."‡ (Of course, he said this before the Walt Disney Company invented *Frozen*.)

More recently, William T. Allen (then a judge in Delaware) offered only slightly moderated praise of corporations and corporate law:

> Stated broadly, but I think accurately, the elemental purpose of corporation law is the facilitation of cooperative activity that produces wealth. A net increase in total wealth, other things remaining unchanged, is an absolute good. With

---

*   U.S. CENSUS BUREAU, STATISTICAL ABSTRACT OF THE UNITED STATES: 2012, 491 (2012), *available at* https://www.census.gov/compendia/statab/2012/tables/12s0744.pdf.

†   As the Supreme Court stated in *The Trustees of Dartmouth College v. Woodward*, 17 U.S. 518, 636 (1819): "A corporation is an artificial being, invisible, intangible and existing only in contemplation of law. Being a mere creature of law, it possesses only those properties which the charter of its creation confers upon it."

‡   Quoted in James Willard Hurst, The Legitimacy of the Business Corporation in the Law of the United States 1780–1970 at p. 9 (1970).

increased wealth, all other things remaining the same, there is a greater ability to relieve human suffering and enhance life. That is an unqualified good. While we no longer take much notice of the fact, the corporate form is a powerful engine for wealth production. * * *

Corporation law facilitates wealth creation principally by creating a legal structure that makes it substantially cheaper for investors to commit their capital to risky ventures. It does this through the innovation of tradable share interests, centralized management, limited liability, and the entity concept itself. The interaction of these legal characteristics facilitates diversification of investments and centralization of management. This allows capital to subject itself to greater risk. It is the ability to increase the degree of risk that can be rationally accepted that provides the greatest source of the efficiency of the corporate form. Much of this utility depends upon investors allowing themselves to be safely passive.

William T. Allen, *Ambiguity in Corporation Law,* 22 DEL. J. CORP. L. 894, 895–96 (1997).

Professor Gabaldon offers a different view of corporations (and other limited liability business structures):

A significant part of the story of American enterprise has been written by state legislators hoping to stimulate entrepreneurship and investment. As a result, there are several forms of business organizations that at least ostensibly will permit an economic actor to limit the amount that she puts at risk. The most popular of these forms is the corporation.

If it was ever true that limited liability was necessary to encourage economic development, it is arguably even more necessary today. The litigious society * * * does exist. Moreover, the statistics indicating the chance of success for any new business are frightening: the majority of start-up enterprises fail, leaving debts in excess of assets. Even traditional bastions of investment security seem to be collapsing in record numbers. Since these facts logically compel a perception that the "upside" potential of entrepreneurship and investment is limited, it may make sense to assure that "downside" possibilities are limited as well.

Limited liability, of course, cannot be regarded as an unmitigated good. * * * Even brief retrospection reveals quite an interesting picture of the historically perceived risks of limited liability. This historical perception may be described in terms of a morality play featuring two important characters. One of these characters is a hapless public, completely unaware that the smiling individual handing out cups of lemonade is not personally and completely on the line for the contents of those cups. The other is Dr. Frankenstein.

According to this Frankensteinian view, irresponsible corporate impresarios regularly dispatch inhuman corporate entities to roam the countryside in search of profits. Lacking both conscience and capital, these entities will inflict injuries for which they cannot, and their heedless inventors need not, pay. In an uncharitable, but not necessarily unrealistic, permutation, the corporate scientist quite deliberately may design the creature to generate short-run gains for the creator, while surreptitiously imposing tremendous costs on third parties.

Theresa A. Gabaldon, *The Lemonade Stand: Feminist and Other Reflections on the Limited Liability of Corporate Shareholders,* 45 VAND. L. REV. 1387, 1390–92 (1992).

QUESTIONS

1.   According to Chancellor Allen, creating a business as a corporation "makes it substantially cheaper for investors to commit their capital to risky ventures." Why?

2.   What is the "Frankenstenian view"? Why is a corporation more likely to do "tacky things" than a partnership?

2.   CORPORATION LAW IS . . .*

There are four primary sources of "corporate law": (1) state statutes, (2) articles of incorporation,† bylaws and other agreements, (3) case law, and (4) federal statutes.

As noted, each state has its own general corporation statute. While no two state statutes are identical, more than half of the states have modeled their statutes in some measure on the Model Business Corporation Act (MBCA).

In addition to the MBCA, Delaware corporation law is centrally important. Far more businesses have incorporated in this small state than in any other.

---

*   In a sense, "corporation law" could be defined as all laws that apply to corporations. Almost all laws apply to corporations—antitrust laws, bankruptcy laws, environmental laws, etc. In this book, we limit coverage of "corporate law" to laws that address the creation and operation of the corporate business structure.

†   In some states, notably Delaware and New York, the articles are called the certificate of incorporation. In other states, such as Maryland, the same document is often referred to as the charter.

Some of the provisions in any state's statutes are mandatory. Others are default rules that apply only if the articles of incorporation or bylaws of the corporation do not contain a different provision. (We saw default provisions with UPA and RUPA.)

Thus a corporation's articles or bylaws, like a partnership's partnership agreement, can be an important source of corporate law. On some matters, the articles and bylaws will be the most important source of law.

Case law serves two separate corporate law functions. First, cases interpret and apply the provisions in corporate statutes and in a corporation's articles and bylaws. Second, cases fill gaps in the law—they resolve problems not covered or not fully covered by statutes, articles or bylaws. Perhaps the most important judicial gap-filling involves the fiduciary duties of directors, officers, and shareholders. Just as cases such as *Meinhard v. Salmon* on page 77 are instrumental in establishing the fiduciary duties of partners, they are also instrumental in establishing the fiduciary duties of directors, officers, and shareholders.

There is no general federal corporation statute. There are, however, important federal statutes that govern certain corporate activities. Later chapters will discuss briefly some of the federal statutes that apply to sales of stock and other corporate securities, and to tender offers and other forms of corporate acquisitions.

B. WHAT ARE THE LEGAL PROBLEMS IN STARTING A BUSINESS AS A CORPORATION?

1. PREPARING THE NECESSARY PAPERS

The "necessary papers" are the articles of incorporation. A corporation does not exist until the articles of incorporation are properly executed and filed with the appropriate state agent or agency (usually the Secretary of State). MBCA § 2.03 sets out where the articles are to be filed, and MBCA § 2.02(a) sets out what the articles of incorporation must contain. Compare this latter provision to the older provision in Delaware § 102.

We have set out below sample articles of incorporation available on the Delaware Division of Corporations Web site.* This form satisfies the Delaware requirements. Assess, however, whether these articles would satisfy the requirements of MBCA § 2.02(a). We will later discuss whether these articles meet the needs of Bubba's Burritos, Inc.

---

* Delaware Division of Corporations, *Stock Certificate of Incorporation*, STATE OF DELAWARE, http://corp.delaware.gov/incstk09.pdf.

STATE OF DELAWARE CERTIFICATE OF INCORPORATION A STOCK CORPORATION

First: *The name of this Corporation is* _____
_____

Second: *Its registered office in the State of Delaware is to be located at* _____ *Street, in the City of* _____ *County of* _____ *Zip Code* _____. *The registered agent in charge thereof is* _____.

Third: *The purpose of the corporation is to engage in any lawful act or activity for which corporations may be organized under the General Corporation Law of Delaware.*

Fourth: *The amount of the total stock this corporation is authorized to issue is* _____ *shares (number of authorized shares) with a par value of* _____ *per share.*

Fifth: *The name and mailing address of the incorporator are as follows:*

Name _____

Mailing Address _____

Zip Code _____.

I, The Undersigned, *for the purpose of forming a corporation under the laws of the State of Delaware, do make, file and record this Certificate, and do certify that the facts herein stated are true, and I have accordingly hereunto set my hand this*

_____ *day of* _____, *A.D.* 20 _____.

BY: _____
(INCORPORATOR)

NAME: _____
(TYPE OR PRINT)

The MBCA provides that a corporation comes into existence as soon as the articles are properly filed. It also permits the corporation to adopt bylaws. MBCA § 2.06(a); *see also* Delaware § 109. Traditionally, nothing has required corporations to have bylaws; adoption of bylaws is not a condition precedent to forming a corporation. Nonetheless, in the real world, almost every corporation does have bylaws.

Just as MBCA §§ 2.02(a) and (b) govern the contents of a corporation's articles, MBCA § 2.06(b) provides for the contents of a corporation's bylaws: "The bylaws may contain any provision for managing the business and regulating the affairs of the corporation that is not inconsistent with laws or the articles of incorporation." *See also* Delaware § 109.

Notice that neither the MBCA nor Delaware requires that bylaws be filed with any state agent or agency. Indeed, no state requires filing of bylaws. In other words, bylaws (unlike articles) are an internal document. Sample bylaws are available on the Internet.

PROBLEMS

1.   How do you decide what goes in the articles of incorporation and what goes in the bylaws? What are the differences between articles of incorporation and bylaws? *Compare* MBCA § 7.07(a) ("The *bylaws* may fix . . . the record date) *with* MBCA § 7.21(a) ("unless the articles of incorporation provide otherwise, each outstanding share . . . is entitled to one vote").

2.   One common statement is that "articles are a contract between the corporation and its shareholders and a corporation and the state, but bylaws are simply a contract between the corporation and its shareholders." If the articles and the bylaws were to conflict on some provision, which one should prevail?

3.   How much should a lawyer charge for preparing articles of incorporation and bylaws and filing the articles? *Incorporate USA* charges only $99.95. *See* http://www.inc123.com/.

2.   CONTRACTING BEFORE INCORPORATING

In the vocabulary of corporations, the word "promoter" has a different and less pejorative meaning than it seems to in the real world. In corporate law, a promoter is not some guy with big hair who sets up boxing matches. Instead, a promoter is someone acting on behalf of a corporation that is not yet formed.

Assume, for example, that Propp, Agee and Capel are still negotiating the provisions that will be in the articles of incorporation when Propp and Agee find the perfect site for a restaurant. Propp and Agee want to lease the building from L & L Properties Corp. ("L & L") before someone else gets it. This means they will sign the lease before they have a chance to file the articles of incorporation to form the corporation. Doing this will raise the following problems about who is liable on a contract entered by the promoters on behalf of a corporation not yet formed.

PROBLEMS

1.   What is the liability of the promoter if the corporation is never formed? Specifically:

a)   Propp negotiates and executes a lease with L & L Properties Corp. (L & L). Propp simply signs the lease "Propp for Bubba's Burritos, Inc." No articles of incorporation are ever filed for

Bubba's Burritos, Inc. Can L & L enforce the lease against Propp?
See MBCA § 2.04.

b)   Same facts as a., except that Propp signs the lease
"Bubba's Burritos, Inc., a corporation to be formed"?

c)   Is there any legal basis for L & L to enforce the lease
against Agee or Capel in either of the two preceding questions?

2.   What is the liability of the corporation if it is formed? Assume that
articles of incorporation are filed forming Bubba's Burritos, Inc. after Propp
had signed the lease with L & L. Is the corporation liable on the lease?

The answer is no—at least not yet. The corporation did not exist when
the lease was entered, and does not become liable on the lease automatically
simply by coming into existence. When we think about it, this is clear from
agency law, which we studied in Chapter 2. Propp was trying to act as an
agent for the corporation (which would be the principal). But there was no
principal when Propp entered the contract, for the simple reason that the
corporation had not been formed then. Propp acted for a non-existent
principal, and thus is liable as a party to the contract.

Does the corporation become liable as soon as it is created? No. The
corporation will be liable on the lease only if it takes some action to *adopt* it.
It might do so in one of two ways. First, the corporation itself might *expressly*
adopt the contract. As we will see later in this book, a corporation generally
acts through its board of directors. So if the board of directors of Bubba's
Burritos, Inc. passes a resolution formally adopting the lease, the corporation
will be liable on the lease from that moment. Second, the corporation might
impliedly adopt the lease. Suppose, for instance, the board of directors does
not take such a formal action, but a corporate official causes the corporation
to use the premises that are subject to the lease. By using the premises, the
corporation has adopted the lease, and is liable from that point.

3.   By adopting the lease in Question 2, the corporation has *ratified*
what its "agent" did. Ratification, in the words of the Restatement (Second) of
Agency (R–2), § 82, is the "affirmance by a person of a prior act which did not
bind him but which was done or professedly done on his account." In the
words of the Restatement (Third) of Agency (R–3), § 4.01, it is the "affirmance
of a prior act done by another, whereby the act is given effect as if done by an
agent acting with actual authority." These mean the same thing—ratification
is the *ex post facto* adoption of something an "agent" purportedly did for a
"principal."

4.   What is the liability of the promoter after incorporation? Assume
that articles of incorporation are filed forming Bubba's Burritos, Inc. after
Propp had signed the lease with L & L. Now—regardless of whether the
corporation adopts the lease—can L & L enforce the lease against Propp?

The answer is yes. And, again, the answer comes from agency law. As a
matter of agency law, why is Propp personally liable on the lease? *See* R–2

§ 326. *See* R–3 § 6.04. Note that this is true *even if Bubba's Burritos adopted the* lease.

The only way for Propp to get off the hook for personal liability at this point is for the parties—meaning Bubba's Burritos, L & L, and Propp—to enter a "novation." As you may recall from Contracts, a novation here would be an agreement that Bubba's Burritos would replace Propp under the lease with L & L.

3.   DE FACTO CORPORATION AND CORPORATION BY ESTOPPEL

In the preceding section, we dealt with a promoter who acted on behalf of a corporation that she knew did not exist (yet). Here, we deal with persons acting on behalf of (or with) a business that they think is a corporation—but, as it turns out, the corporation was not actually formed!

As we saw earlier in this chapter, it is pretty easy to form a corporation. The magic moment at which the corporation comes into being is usually the point at which the state agency accepts the articles for filing. At that point, the corporation (sometimes referred to as "de jure corporation") is formed and the corporation is liable for its own debts going forward.

But what if a de jure corporation was not formed?

PROBLEMS

1.   Propp, Agee and Capel want to incorporate their business as Bubba's Burritos, Inc. They go to Freer, an attorney, who prepares all the necessary documents. Propp, Agee and Capel execute the documents and give Freer the check for the filing fee. Freer tells them that he will deliver the documents and filing fee to the appropriate state agency on March 1 and that they can start doing business as a corporation on that day. Instead, however, Freer moves to Italy and never delivers the documents to the state agency.

On March 2, Propp, Agee, and Capel meet as the directors of Bubba's Burritos, Inc. and elect Propp as president. On March 3, Propp, thinking he is president of Bubba's Burritos, Inc., acting on behalf of the corporation, signs a lease between Bubba's and L & L. Propp and the people at L & L all think that Bubba's Burritos, Inc. is a corporation. When they discover that no corporation was formed, the people at L & L seek to enforce the lease against Propp personally.

   a)   Is Propp liable on the lease?

   b)   Are Agee and Capel liable on the lease? (After all, if they did not form a corporation, what type of business structure did the three have?)

Obviously, the proprietors did not form a de jure corporation (because the state agency never filed the articles). The starting point, then, is that they are personally liable for the acts purportedly taken by the corporation. Over time, however, courts developed the doctrine of "de facto corporation." They concluded that if the proprietors were acting in good faith and came very close to forming a de jure corporation (usually said to have reached "colorable" compliance with the formation requirements), there was a de facto corporation. As a result, the proprietors would not be personally liable.

As it developed, de facto corporation was a broad doctrine—it applied in contract and tort. Indeed, it applied in all cases except an action brought by the state against the proprietors. De facto corporation is an equitable doctrine, so one seeking to use it must act in good faith. That means she must be unaware of the failure to form a de jure corporation.

Because it is now so easy to form a de jure corporation, many states have abolished the de facto corporation doctrine. In such states, if you fail to form a de jure corporation, the proprietors are liable for whatever they purported to do on the "corporation's" behalf.

    c)   How does MBCA § 2.04 deal with the de facto corporation doctrine?

2.   A related but narrower doctrine is "corporation by estoppel." It is narrower because it generally applies only in contract cases, not tort. The name says it all—it is basically just estoppel.

Continuing the fact pattern from Problem 1, suppose on March 3, after Bubba's Burritos, Inc. was thought to have been formed, Epstein enters a contract with the corporation, by which Epstein will sell supplies to the business. Epstein treats the business as though it is a corporation, and deals with Propp as though he were president of a corporation. When he discovers that there is no corporation, can Epstein sue the proprietors individually to recover on the contract?

The starting point, again, is that there is no de jure corporation, so the proprietors will be liable personally. Again, Propp, Agee, and Capel may be able to argue de facto corporation.

They might also argue corporation by estoppel. The corporation by estoppel argument is that Epstein dealt with the business as a corporation and treated it as such, and thus should be estopped from denying that it is. The reason the doctrine is limited to contract cases is clear—Epstein, before entering the deal, could have insisted on seeing the books of the corporation to determine whether it had assets from which to pay.

4. ISSUING STOCK*

Shares of stock are the units of ownership in a corporation. If Agee, Capel, and Propp are going to be the owners of Bubba's Burritos, Inc., they will need to own shares of Bubba's Burritos, Inc. stock. Where does this stock come from? MBCA § 6.03(a) provides "A corporation may issue

---

   *   The MBCA uses the terms "share" and "shareholder" rather than the terms "stock" and "stockholder." The terms are interchangeable.

the number of shares of each class or series authorized by the articles of incorporation. Shares that are issued are outstanding shares until they are reacquired, converted or canceled." There is a lot of information in those two sentences:

- a corporation can sell its own stock;

- a corporation's sale of its own stock is called an "issuance";

- the articles of incorporation determine the number of shares a corporation may issue;

- this number is the number of "authorized shares";

- a corporation is not required to issue all of its authorized shares;

- shares that the corporation actually does issue are called "issued shares";

- "outstanding shares" consist of issued shares that the corporation has not reacquired (the corporation can buy stock back from shareholders, and those shares that have been issued and not reacquired are "outstanding"); and,

- a corporation can have more than one type ("class or series") of stock.

To review, you need to make the following terms a part of your working vocabulary:

- issuance;

- authorized shares;

- issued shares;

- outstanding shares; and

- classes of stock.

While there is a good bit of important legal information about "issuing stock" in the two sentences of MBCA § 6.03, there is also a lot of important legal and business information about issuing stock that is not there. There are three other terms that are not important to MBCA § 6.03 (or any other MBCA provision) but are important to a law practice and (more immediately) to a law school course that includes corporations: (1) preferred stock, (2) common stock, and (3) par value.

Preferred stock is a creature of the articles of incorporation. Recall from the MBCA that the articles of incorporation can authorize more than one type or class of stock. *See* MBCA § 6.01 et seq. If the articles provide that a class of stock is to be treated more favorably than the other class of stock, then it is preferred stock. The other class of stock that does not enjoy special treatment is the common stock.

Generally, the more favorable treatment relates to one or more of the following financial attributes of ownership: (1) dividend rights, (2) liquidation rights, or (3) redemption rights. Assume for example that the articles of Bubba's Burritos, Inc. authorize 1,000 shares of Class 1 stock and 200 shares of Class 2 stock and provides that each share of Class 2 stock shall receive a dividend that is three times greater than any dividend paid to Class 1 stock. Class 2 stock would then be described as preferred stock. More precisely, it would have a dividend preference.

A more typical type of dividend preference would be a dollar amount—like $1 per preferred share. The corporation would be obligated to pay each preferred share a dividend of a $1 before it could pay even one cent of dividends to the common shareholders.

A common type of preference utilized in venture capital (VC) financings is a liquidation preference. The preference amount is often the original purchase price per share. The preference is designed as a form of "downside protection" so that if the company is ultimately sold for a relatively low value, the VCs will get all their money back (assuming there are sufficient proceeds) before the founders (and other holders of common stock) get any proceeds at all.

In this example, Class 1 would be the common stock, i.e., the class of stock that is not preferred. In the event that Bubba's Burritos, Inc. only has one class of stock, then all of its stock would be common stock.

Why would a corporation have two classes of stock? Why would some owners settle for common stock if other owners have preferred stock?

In the following example, Silicon Gaming, Inc. was unable to pay its debts and so gave its creditors 39,750 shares of $.001 par Class D preferred stock in satisfaction of $39,750,000 of debt. The following excerpt from the directors' resolution sets out some of the points of preference:

CERTIFICATION OF DETERMINATION, PREFERENCES AND RELATIVE, PARTICIPATING, OPTIONAL AND OTHER SPECIAL RIGHTS OF PREFERRED STOCK AND QUALIFICATIONS, LIMITATIONS AND RESTRICTIONS OF SERIES D CONVERTIBLE REDEEMABLE PREFERRED STOCK OF SILICON GAMING, INC.

Pursuant to Section 401 of the General Corporation Law of the State of California

Silicon Gaming, Inc. (the "Company"), a Company organized and existing under the laws of the State of California, by execution of this certificate (this "Certificate of Determination") does hereby certify and affirm, that pursuant to the authority contained in Article III of its Amended and Restated Articles of Incorporation (the "Articles of Incorporation") and in accordance with the provisions of Section 401 of the

*General Corporation Law of the State of California, the Board of Directors
of the Company on [date], duly adopted the following resolution which
resolution remains in full force and effect on the date hereof:*

(a) Dividends.

*(1) The holders of outstanding Series D Preferred Stock shall be
entitled to receive in any fiscal year, when, as and if declared by the Board
of Directors, out of any assets at the time legally available therefor, non-
cumulative dividends in cash at a rate per share as declared by the Board
of Directors. No cash dividends shall be paid on any share of Common
Stock unless a cash dividend is paid with respect to all outstanding shares
of Series D Preferred Stock in an amount for each such share of Series D
Preferred Stock equal to or greater than the aggregate amount of such cash
dividends for all shares of Common Stock into which each such share of
Series D Preferred Stock could then be converted. The right to dividends
on Series D Preferred Stock shall not be cumulative and no right shall
accrue to holders of Series D Preferred Stock by reason of the fact that
distributions on said shares are not declared in any prior year, nor shall
any undeclared or unpaid distribution bear or accrue interest.*

(b) Preference on Liquidation.

*(1) In the event of any voluntary or involuntary liquidation,
dissolution, or winding up, of the Company (a "Liquidation Event"), each
holder of shares of the Series D Preferred Stock shall be entitled to
payment out of the assets of the Company available for distribution of an
amount equal to the greater of (A) $1,000 per share of Series D Preferred
Stock held by such holder before any distribution is made to the holders of
Common Stock of the Company, and any other class of capital stock of the
Company ranking junior to the Series D Preferred Stock and (B) the
amount per share that the holders of the Series D Preferred Stock would
receive if the Series D Preferred Stock held by such holder were converted
as of the liquidation date and the holder were to receive assets and funds
of the Company available for distribution to the holders of Common Stock.*

(c) Redemption.

*In the event of a Change of Control the holders of at least a majority of
the shares of Series D Preferred Stock then outstanding taken together as a
series may require the Company to redeem the outstanding shares of Series
D Preferred Stock by delivering a Redemption Notice (as defined in Section
2(c)(4)) within the ninety (90) day period following the Change of Control.
The shares of Series D Preferred Stock will be redeemed at an amount (the
"Series D Redemption Amount") equal to the greater of (A) the Series D
Liquidation Preference and (B) the Fair Market Value of the Common
Stock into which the Series D Preferred Stock held by such holders could
be converted as of the date of such Change of Control, and no payment
shall be made to the holders of the Common Stock or any Capital Stock*

ranking junior to the Series D Preferred Stock unless such amount is paid in full.

Recall that Silicon Gaming, Inc. Class D stock has a "par value" of $.001. What is "par"? "Par value" is the *minimum* price for which a corporation can issue its shares. If, for example, the articles of incorporation of Bubba's Burritos, Inc. provide for a single class of stock with a par value of $1,000 a share, then the corporation must receive at least $1,000 for each share it issues. If the corporation issues seven shares to Propp, then the corporation must receive consideration from Propp with a value of at least $7,000.

Par value is just a minimum issuance price, not a fixed price. *See* Delaware § 153(a). Bubba's Burritos could issue $1,000-par-value stock for more than $1,000 a share; it will certainly try to sell the stock for as high a price as it can. It just could not issue $1,000-par-value stock for less than $1,000 per share. And par value affects only the *issuance* price. It would have no effect on the price for which Propp could later *resell* his $1,000-par Bubba's Burritos stock—for example, on a stock exchange such as the New York Stock Exchange or NASDAQ. Such later sale, because it is not made by the corporation, is simply not an "issuance," and issuance rules, such as par value, therefore do not apply.

In a diminishing number of states, the corporation statutes require that the articles of incorporation state whether the stock, common or preferred, is to have a "par value," and, if so, what the par value amount is. In some states, including Delaware, the corporation may have par stock, but is not required to do so. *See* Delaware § 102(a)(4) and MBCA § 2.02(b)(2)(iv).

State corporation statutes that provide for par value stock also generally provide for the corporation's keeping two separate funds or accounts—"stated capital" and "capital surplus." "Stated capital" includes the aggregate par value of all issued shares of par value stock. If, for example, Bubba's Burritos had issued 50 shares of $1,000-par-value stock, then its stated capital would be $50,000. This is the figure that would appear on the balance sheet as one of the items in the account for "shareholders' equity" or "owners' equity." The stated capital account cannot be distributed to shareholders. It is, in theory, a cushion to protect creditors, to ensure that the company retains at least some money to pay its bills.

Suppose Bubba's Burritos had received funds for its issuance *in excess of par*. Such excess goes into an account called "capital surplus" or "additional paid-in capital" and may be distributed back to shareholders in dividends. If, for example, Bubba's Burritos had received $99,000 from its issuance of 50 shares of $1,000-par-value stock, then its stated capital would still be $50,000 and its capital surplus / additional paid-in capital would be $49,000.

Two developments have significantly limited the practical impact of "par value," "stated capital," and "capital surplus." First, the MBCA and the corporation statutes of the majority of states have eliminated the requirements that articles of incorporation provide a "par value" for stock and that corporations maintain a "stated capital" account. Second, even in the states that require "par value" and "stated capital" (or just "capital") (*see* Delaware § 154 and New York § 510),* corporations have reduced the importance of the concepts by setting par value at a penny or even a fraction of a cent.

PROBLEMS

1. Read Delaware §§ 152 and 153 and MBCA § 6.21(b) and (c).

   a) Can a corporation issue stock in exchange for land?

   b) How about for a promise of future services to the corporation?

   c) How about for a promissory note?

   d) How about for goodwill?

   e) How about for a release of a claim against the corporation?

2. The articles of incorporation for C Inc., a Delaware corporation, provide that Class A stock shall have a $2 par value. Can C Inc. issue 2000 shares of Class A stock to S for $1 a share?

3. Same facts as Question 2. Can C Inc. issue 3,000 shares of Class A stock to S for $5 a share? BTW, why would a corporation issue par value stock for more than par? What about in a state in which the MBCA applies?

4. Under the facts of Question 2, what portion of the issuance price would be allocated to stated capital?

5. Can S sell her $5 par C Inc. Class A stock to T for $3 a share? Why would a shareholder sell her stock for less than its par value? Recall that when S sells the C Inc. stock, it is not an issuance. An issuance occurs only when the corporation sells its own stock. And because par is an issuance concept, it does not apply when S, rather than the corporation, sells the stock. Note that almost everyone who owns stock bought that stock on an exchange—that is, they bought it from other shareholders, and not as part of an issuance.

6. Can C Inc. issue 100,000 shares of its $2 par value Class A stock to B in exchange for Blackacre?

---

* Throughout the book, we refer to sections of the New York Business Corporation Law simply as "New York."

7.   Capel invests $100,000 in Bubba's Burritos, Inc. and receives stock. Does she care what the par value of the stock is? Does she care whether the stock has a par value? Does par have any necessary relationship to the actual value of the stock?

8.   Suppose that Capel owns half of the stock in Bubba's Burritos. Does she care whether Bubba's sells stock to others, or for what price?

5.   CHOOSING THE STATE OF INCORPORATION AND QUALIFYING AS A "FOREIGN CORPORATION"

Bubba's Burritos, Inc. can choose to incorporate in any state, even a state in which it has no business activity. The laws of that state will then become the default rules that govern the "internal affairs" of Bubba's Burritos, Inc. *See* Restatement (Second) of Conflicts of Laws §§ 296–310 (1971). "Internal affairs" include procedures for corporate actions and the rights and duties of directors, shareholders and officers with respect to each other. For example, if Bubba's Burritos, Inc. incorporates in Hawaii, Hawaiian law will govern issues such as shareholders' right to vote and the procedures by which the board of directors acts. This is true even though none of Bubba's Burritos' shareholders, directors, officers, customers, or greasy burritos has ever been to Hawaii.

The company's internal affairs would not include the rights of third parties with respect to Bubba's Burritos. If a Bubba's customer is injured by a falling XXL Grilled Stuft burrito, the law that governs her personal injury suit against Bubba's would be chosen by the general rules for conflicts of laws. For example, even if Bubba's were incorporated in Hawaii, Alabama law would probably govern the suit, if the burrito struck the plaintiff in Alabama.

LIDOW V. THE SUPERIOR COURT OF LOS ANGELES COUNTY
California Court of Appeal, 2012
206 Cal.App.4th 351, 141 Cal.Rptr.3d 729

BOREN, P. J. The novel question presented in this case is whether, under a conflict of laws principle known as the internal affairs doctrine, California law or foreign law applies to a claim brought by an officer of a foreign corporation for wrongful termination in violation of public policy. We hold that under the circumstances alleged here, specifically where a foreign corporation has removed or constructively discharged a corporate officer in retaliation for that person's complaints of possible harmful or unethical activity, California law applies.

BACKGROUND

* * *

Petitioner, Alexander Lidow,* has a Ph.D. in applied physics.

Real party in interest, International Rectifier Corporation (IR) is incorporated in Delaware and based in El Segundo, California. IR is a semiconductor company founded by petitioner's father. Petitioner began working for IR in 1977 after graduating from Stanford University. Petitioner became a member of IR's Board of Directors (Board) in 1994, Co-Chief Executive Officer (CEO) in 1995, and sole CEO in 1999. At no point in time did petitioner have a written employment contract with IR. IR's bylaws provided at all relevant times that the corporation's officers (including the CEO) "shall be chosen annually by, and shall serve at the pleasure of, the Board, and shall hold their respective offices until their resignation, removal, or other disqualification from service[.]" Removal of an officer, according to IR's bylaws, may be "with or without cause, by the Board at any time[.]"

---

*   John Soat, *Meet Alexander Lidow, CEO of International Rectifier*, INFORMATION WEEK, http://www.informationweek.com/meet-alexander-lidow-ceo-of-international-rectifier/d/d-id/ 1052068?

In early 2007, IR commenced an internal investigation after accounting irregularities surfaced at IR's subsidiary in Japan. In late August 2007, the Board placed petitioner on paid administrative leave. * * * Petitioner stepped down as CEO and Board member in October 2007 pursuant to a negotiated separation agreement entered into by petitioner and IR. * * *

Approximately 18 months later, petitioner sued IR in superior court, alleging * * * wrongful termination in violation of public policy.* * *

IR moved for summary adjudication of petitioner's cause of action [asserting that] pursuant to the "internal affairs doctrine," Delaware law governed petitioner's wrongful termination claim. Under Delaware law, a CEO serves at the pleasure of the corporation's Board of Directors and is barred from bringing a wrongful termination claim (unless authorized by specific statutory enactments) as a matter of law. * * *

The superior court granted IR's motion for summary adjudication. * * * It reasoned that pursuant to the internal affairs doctrine, Delaware law applied to petitioner's wrongful termination claim, and under Delaware law, petitioner "could be removed without the threat of litigation arising from a wrongful termination claim (except a claim based upon a subsequent statutory enactment such as one relating to discrimination of which there is no allegation or proof before this Court)." * * *

Based on our de novo review, we conclude the superior court erred by granting summary adjudication in favor of IR. Accordingly, we direct the superior court to vacate the order in question, and to enter a new order denying IR's motion for summary adjudication of petitioner's cause of action for wrongful termination in violation of public policy.

* * *

II. Internal Affairs Doctrine

A. Allegations

As related to the claim for wrongful termination in violation of public policy, petitioner alleged the following events took place:

In October 2006, IR's internal finance department raised concerns that possible accounting improprieties were taking place at the corporation's subsidiary in Japan. In response, the Board's Audit Committee, which was comprised of all the Board members except for petitioner and his father, and IR's general counsel hired the law firm of Sheppard Mullin Richter & Hampton LLP (Sheppard Mullin) to conduct an investigation into the possible accounting improprieties. Sheppard Mullin had a longstanding relationship with the general counsel . . .

As a result of the investigators' aggressive and coercive tactics, employees at the Japanese subsidiary filed multiple complaints and threatened to resign in mass numbers. Productivity at the Japanese subsidiary came to a halt.

Concerned about the deteriorating situation, petitioner travelled to Japan in order to convince the remaining employees to cooperate with the investigation, and to ensure, that going forward, the employees were treated with fairness and respect. * * * At the same time, petitioner spoke out against the tactics used by the investigators, and criticized how Sheppard Mullin, the general counsel, and the Audit Committee were overseeing the investigation. Additionally, petitioner criticized the Audit Committee for failing to control the mounting legal and accounting fees associated with the investigation, which were already in the millions of dollars.

When news broke that IR was investigating possible accounting improprieties at its Japanese subsidiary, a class action securities lawsuit was filed against IR. IR's general counsel decided to retain Sheppard Mullin to defend the lawsuit. Petitioner protested Sheppard Mullin's retention, complaining that it would be a conflict of interest for Sheppard Mullin to defend a lawsuit based on accounting irregularities and to conduct a purportedly independent investigation into the irregularities at the same time.

Because of petitioner's complaints about the manner in which employees were being treated in Japan, his critical remarks about how the investigation was progressing, and his protestations over Sheppard Mullin's retention to defend the securities lawsuit, petitioner became a target of Sheppard Mullin, the general counsel, and the Audit Committee. Approximately 10 months after the investigation commenced, Sheppard Mullin issued a report to the Audit Committee implicating petitioner in the alleged accounting irregularities. According to the report, which petitioner claims is pure conjecture, petitioner either ordered employees at the Japanese subsidiary to create false accounting documents, or knew that the employees were creating false accounting documents and turned a blind eye to the fraud.

Based on the report, the Audit Committee, which was now acting as the *de facto* Board, placed petitioner on administrative leave without giving him an opportunity to respond to the charges. Shortly after the Audit Committee placed petitioner on administrative leave, it informed him that if he did not resign as CEO in seven days, he would be removed. Petitioner entered in a separation agreement with IR wherein he agreed to step down as CEO and Board member at IR's request.

B.   Legal Framework

The internal affairs doctrine is a conflict of laws principle which recognizes that only one State should have the authority to regulate a corporation's internal affairs—matters peculiar to the relationships among or between the corporation and its current officers, directors, and shareholders—because otherwise a corporation could be faced with conflicting demands.

Matters falling within the scope of the [internal affairs doctrine] and which involve primarily a corporation's relationship to its shareholders include steps taken in the course of the original incorporation, the election or appointment of directors and officers, the adoption of by-laws, the issuance of corporate shares, preemptive rights, the holding of directors' and shareholders' meetings, methods of voting including any requirement for cumulative voting, shareholders' rights to examine corporate records, charter and by-law amendments, mergers, consolidations and reorganizations and the reclassification of shares. (Rest.2d Conf. of Laws, § 302, com. a, p. 307b. * * *

There is, however, a vital limitation to the internal affairs doctrine:

The local law of the state of incorporation will be applied . . . *except where, with respect to the particular issue, some other state has a more significant relationship . . . to the parties and the transaction* [.]" (Rest.2d Conf. of Laws, § 309, p. 332; italics added.) Indeed, "[t]here is no reason why corporate acts" involving "the making of contracts, the commission of torts and the transfer of property" "should not be governed by the local law of different states. (*Id.* at § 302, com. e, p. 309.)

The issue of whether the termination of a corporate officer for reasons that allegedly violate public policy falls within the scope of a corporation's internal affairs is one of first impression. * * *

Certainly, the removal of a CEO for any number of reasons (e.g., the corporation is not performing well, the CEO did not meet certain financial expectations set by the Board) falls within the scope of a corporation's internal governance, thus triggering the application of the internal affairs doctrine. This case, however, presents an entirely different set of allegations. Removing an officer in retaliation for his complaints about possible illegal or harmful activity (e.g., witness intimidation, physical threats to employees, etc.) and breaches of ethical conduct (e.g., defending a client against allegations of accounting irregularities and conducting an independent investigation in the same irregularities) goes beyond internal governance and touches upon broader public interest concerns that California has a vital interest in protecting . . .

[U]nder the circumstances presented here, i.e., where there are allegations made by a corporate officer that he was removed for complaining about possible illegal or harmful activity, the internal affairs doctrine is inapplicable and California law governs the claim.

QUESTIONS

1.   Note the court's heading, "Allegations." If the court concludes that petitioner's allegations that he was fired because of his complaints about harmful or unethical activities of others are found to be false, will California law still govern petitioner's claim?

2.   The tort law of some states is viewed as more favorable to plaintiffs than the tort law of other states. For example, business leaders have described Alabama as "torts hell."* Can Bubba's Burritos, Inc. avoid the application of Alabama torts law to accidents in its Alabama stores by incorporating in Delaware?

3.   California has a statute that purports to apply California law to the internal affairs of a foreign corporation on terms far broader than those recognized in *Lidow*. California Corporation Code § 2115 provides that the articles of foreign corporation are deemed amended to comply with California law and are subject to California law governing internal affairs if, inter alia, more than half of the outstanding stock is owned by California residents. You have constitutional law more recently than any of us—especially Roberts who has never been to law school. Is § 2115 constitutional?

4.   We are told in a footnote that IR's "securities are listed on the New York Stock Exchange." What does that mean? Was that important to the court?

———————

Most companies whose stock is listed on the New York Stock Exchange are incorporated in Delaware. For example, General Motors is incorporated in Delaware. To paraphrase a former Secretary of Defense (and President of General Motors), what is good for General Motors is good for the rest of the country. Since General Motors incorporated in Delaware, why shouldn't Bubba's Burritos incorporate in Delaware?

Unless Delaware is where Bubba's will be doing business, though, we need to be aware that incorporating there will impose additional costs. First, consider attorneys' fees. Recall that incorporation requires the preparation and filing of articles of incorporation. And corporations also have bylaws. Will a Delaware lawyer charge more than a lawyer in the state where you intend to sell burritos? Can a lawyer from that state handle a Delaware incorporation? If so, will she charge more for Delaware incorporation than for a local incorporation?

———————

*   *Cf.* David Greising, *Huge Verdicts? Maybe There is a Place for Them*, CHICAGO TRIBUNE, May 12, 1999, 1999 WL 2872434.

Second, consider the fees that have to be paid to Delaware. Businesses incorporated in Delaware must each year pay the State of Delaware an annual report filing of $75 and an annual franchise tax, So we need to ask whether the Delaware fee and tax structure is more burdensome than that in the state where we will be selling burritos or other states.*

Third, if Bubba's Burritos incorporates in Delaware but operates in another state, it will have to make filings in and make payments to *both* states. It will be incorporated in Delaware but will have to qualify to do business as a "foreign corporation" in the other states. *See* MBCA §§ 1.40(10); 15.01. In corporate law, "foreign" does not refer to another country—it applies to another state. So, in Colorado, a Colorado corporation is "domestic" and a corporation formed *anywhere other than Colorado* (even Wyoming) is "foreign."

Every state requires foreign corporations transacting business there to "qualify." Qualification usually includes (1) obtaining authorization from the appropriate state agency, (2) appointing a registered agent in the state, (3) filing annual statements in the state, and (4) paying fees and franchise taxes to the state. So it can be quite expensive to incorporate in one state and qualify to do business in another.

What, then, are the benefits of Delaware incorporation? Here's what Delaware says in the frequently asked questions (FAQ) section on the Delaware Division of Corporations website:

> Why do so many companies incorporate in Delaware?
>
> Businesses choose Delaware not for one single reason, but because we provide a complete package of incorporation services. The Delaware General Corporation Law is the most advanced and flexible business formation statute in the nation. The Delaware Court of Chancery is a unique 215 year old business court that has written most of the modern U.S. corporation case law. Delaware's State Government is business-friendly and accessible. Our Division of Corporations is a model of state-of-the-art efficiency and our staff provides prompt, friendly and professional service to clients, attorneys, registered agents and others. These factors have all contributed to making Delaware a premier legal home to companies around the world.

---

* The most common method of determining the amount of franchise tax a Delaware corporation pays annually looks to the corporation's authorized shares. "If the corporation has 5,000 [authorized] shares or less, it pays the minimum tax of $75. For corporations with 5,001 to 10,000 [authorized] shares the tax is $150. For corporations with over 10,000 [authorized] shares the tax is $150 plus $75 for each additional 10,000 [authorized] shares or portion thereof. The maximum annual tax is $180,000. Go to http://www.state.de.us/corp/frtaxcalc.shtml for additional information on calculating the tax due." John Morrissey, *Frequently Asked Questions About Delaware Corporation Annual Reports and Franchise Tax Payments,* NATIONAL CORPORATE RESEARCH, LTD., http://www.nationalcorp.com/ncr/file?filename=DE_Annual_Report_QA_Nov_2011.pdf.

SEC. B

WHAT ARE THE LEGAL PROBLEMS IN STARTING A
BUSINESS AS A CORPORATION?

145

Do I have to live in Delaware to have a Delaware corporation?

No. Delaware law requires every corporation to have and maintain a Registered Agent in the State who may be either an individual resident, a domestic corporation, or a foreign corporation authorized to transact business in Delaware whose business office is identical with the corporation's registered office.

Must I use an Attorney to incorporate?

No, but you should contact an attorney concerning legal matters. The Delaware Division of Corporations acts solely in an administrative capacity and does not provide legal advice.

If I am incorporated in another state or jurisdiction, do I need to qualify to do business in the State of Delaware?

Yes, Delaware law requires every corporation that is doing business in this state but is formed in another state or jurisdiction to submit a completed "Foreign Qualification" form with the Division of Corporations along with a Certificate of Existence issued by that state or jurisdiction.

How quickly can I incorporate or receive back my request?

The Division of Corporations offers a variety of services including "1-Hour," "2-Hour," "Same Day," and "Next Day" Expedited Services which are designed to meet your business needs.

Moreover, the Hotel du Pont in Wilmington, Delaware, is a much more elegant place to stay than the Motel 6 in other state capitals such as Montgomery, Alabama, or Augusta, Maine, or Belle Fourche in Pierre, South Dakota*, or . . .

---

*   We (or at least Epstein and Freer) know that Pierre is the capital of South Dakota. We have lectured in South Dakota. We also know that there is no Motel 6 in Pierre. Belle Fourche is the closest Motel 6.

QUESTIONS

1.   If Bubba's Burritos incorporates in Delaware instead of Alabama, is Bubba's attorney more likely to be able to stay at the Hotel du Pont?

2.   Why does the Delaware Division of Corporations tout the expertise of the Delaware courts? If Bubba's Burritos, Inc. is incorporated in Delaware but operates only in Alabama, will an Alabama shareholder have to go to Delaware to sue Bubba's Burritos, Inc.? Is the expertise of the Delaware courts only relevant if the lawsuit is tried in Delaware?

3.   We noted that a foreign corporation must qualify to transact business in another state. And we noted that qualifying can be expensive. But the foreign corporation must qualify *only* if it is "transacting business" in the state. What level of activity is required to constitute "transacting business" under these statutes?

Delaware § 373 is typical of other statutes in which state legislatures make clear what activity does *not* constitute transacting business by a foreign corporation. These statutes are based upon the principle that the Commerce Clause of the Constitution prohibits states from excluding a corporation that is engaged in *interstate* commerce. Thus, the foreign corporation provisions apply to foreign corporations engaged in *intrastate* activities within another state.

CHAPTER 5

HOW DOES A CORPORATION OPERATE?

■ ■ ■

In this chapter, we address two aspects of a corporation's operation: (1) liability for business debts and obligations and (2) who makes decisions for the corporation. For both topics, we will start with the general rule prescribed by corporate law, and explore some exceptions to those general rules. As we will see, some of these exceptions apply only in what most people call a "close" or "closely-held" corporation. This is a corporation like Bubba's Burritos, Inc., which has few shareholders and the stock of which is not publicly traded. These are contrasted with "publicly-held" corporations like McDonald's, for which there is a public market in the stock. Many corporations fall between the two extremes, but all corporate lawyers and students need to know the basic bifurcation between close and publicly-traded corporations. In Chapter 7 we will address more topics related to the close corporation and in Chapters 6 and 9 we will see other topics that come up with publicly-held corporations.

A. WHO IS LIABLE TO THE CORPORATION'S CREDITORS?

1. FIRST GENERAL RULE: CREDITORS OF A CORPORATION CAN RECOVER FROM THE CORPORATION'S ASSETS

Recall that a corporation is an "entity" and a "person." As such, a corporation can own property and can sue and be sued for the actions of its employees and other agents. The corporation can be held liable to third parties for contracts, torts, violations of statutes, etc.

If Bubba's Burritos, Inc. fails to pay rent to its landlord, L & L Real Estate, the landlord can sue Bubba's Burritos, Inc. and collect on any judgment by garnishing Bubba's Burritos, Inc.'s bank account or levying on other corporate assets. Similarly, if Vic Timm comes down with food poisoning because of what he ate at Bubba's Burritos, Inc., he can sue and collect from the corporation itself.

2. SECOND GENERAL RULE: SHAREHOLDERS ARE NOT PERSONALLY LIABLE TO THE CORPORATION'S CREDITORS

Recall also that a shareholder's protection from personal responsibility for the corporation's liability is basic to the corporate structure and to corporate law. Please read MBCA § 6.22(b) and Delaware § 162. Neither L & L Real Estate nor Vic Timm can sue and collect from Capel or any of the other Bubba's Burritos, Inc. shareholders. This is the general rule in every state.

3. FIRST EXCEPTION: SHAREHOLDERS CAN BE LIABLE TO THE CORPORATION'S CREDITORS BECAUSE OF PERSONAL GUARANTEES

But there are contractual and judicial exceptions to the rule that shareholders are not personally liable for the acts or debts of the corporation. The contractual exception is easy and obvious. Third parties often refuse to extend credit to a corporation with limited assets unless that corporation's shareholders agree to be personally responsible, i.e., personally guarantee payment. For example, L & L Real Estate may refuse to rent the building to Bubba's Burritos, Inc. unless Capel or the other shareholders personally guarantee the rent payments.

4. SECOND EXCEPTION: SHAREHOLDERS CAN BE PERSONALLY LIABLE TO THE CORPORATION'S CREDITORS THROUGH PIERCING THE CORPORATE VEIL

In the next case, an unpaid supplier of services to a corporation is permitted to collect its claim from the corporation's principal *shareholder*, W. Ray Flemming, because of the judicially created concept of "piercing the corporate veil." As you read the case, consider the following questions:

1. Did the W. Ray Flemming Fruit Company satisfy the requirements of South Carolina law for the creation of a corporation?

2. Did either the corporation or W. Ray Flemming individually violate any provision of the South Carolina corporate code or any other law?

3. Is W. Ray Flemming now personally liable for all of the debts of the corporation?

4. Are the other stockholders of W. Ray Fleming Fruit Company also personally liable to the plaintiff Dewitt Truck Brokers, Inc.?

DEWITT TRUCK BROKERS, INC. v. W. RAY FLEMMING FRUIT COMPANY

United States Court of Appeals, Fourth Circuit, 1976
540 F.2d 681

[W. Ray Flemming Fruit Company ("corporation") sold fruit for growers on commission. When the fruit was sold, the corporation would pay the growers the sales price less (i) the corporation's commissions and (ii) the corporation's transportation costs. The corporation contracted with Dewitt Truck Brokers, Inc., ("plaintiff") to transport the fruit. The corporation owes plaintiff approximately $15,000. W. Ray Flemming, the corporation's principal shareholder, orally assured plaintiff that he would personally pay for the fruit transportation if the corporation did not. This oral promise to answer for the debts of another was not legally enforceable because of the statute of frauds. Accordingly, in this litigation, plaintiff asks the court to "pierce the corporate veil."]

DONALD RUSSELL, CIRCUIT JUDGE. In this action on debt, the plaintiff seeks, by piercing the corporate veil under the law of South Carolina, to impose individual liability on the president of the indebted corporation. The District Court, making findings of fact which may be overturned only if clearly erroneous, pierced the corporate veil and imposed individual liability. The individual defendant appeals. We affirm.

At the outset, it is recognized that a corporation is an entity, separate and distinct from its officers and stockholders, and that its debts are not the individual indebtedness of its stockholders. This is expressed in the presumption that the corporation and its stockholders are separate and distinct. And this oft-stated principle is equally applicable, whether the corporation has many or only one stockholder. But this concept of separate entity is merely a legal theory, "introduced for purposes of convenience and to subserve the ends of justice," and the courts "decline to recognize (it) whenever recognition of the corporate form would extend the principle of incorporation 'beyond its legitimate purposes and (would) produce injustices or inequitable consequences.'" Krivo Industrial Supp. Co. v. National Distill. & Chem. Corp. (5th Cir. 1973), 483 F.2d 1098, 1106. Accordingly, "in an appropriate case and in furtherance of the ends of justice," the corporate veil will be pierced and the corporation and its stockholders "will be treated as identical."

This power to pierce the corporate veil, though, is to be exercised "reluctantly" and "cautiously" and the burden of establishing a basis for the disregard of the corporate fiction rests on the party asserting such claim.

The circumstances which have been considered significant by the courts in actions to disregard the corporate fiction have been "rarely articulated with any clarity." Perhaps this is true because the circumstances "necessarily vary according to the circumstances of each case," and every case where the issue is raised is to be regarded as "sui generis (to) * * * be decided in accordance with its own underlying facts." Since the issue is thus one of fact, its resolution "is particularly within the province of the trial court" and such resolution will be regarded as "presumptively correct and (will) be left undisturbed on appeal unless it is clearly erroneous."

Contrary to the basic contention of the defendant, however, proof of plain fraud is not a necessary element in a finding to disregard the corporate entity. This was made clear in Anderson v. Abbott (1944), 321 U.S. 349, 362, where the Court, after stating that "fraud" has often been found to be a ground for disregarding the principle of limited liability based on the corporate fiction, declared:

* * * The cases of fraud make up part of that exception [which allow the corporate veil to be pierced]. But they do not exhaust it. An obvious inadequacy of capital, measured by the nature and magnitude of the corporate undertaking, has frequently been an important factor in cases denying stockholders their defense of limited liability. * * *

On the other hand, equally * * * as well settled as the principle that plain fraud is not a necessary prerequisite for piercing the corporate veil is the rule that the mere fact that all or almost all of the corporate stock is owned by one individual or a few individuals, will not afford sufficient grounds for disregarding corporateness. But when substantial ownership of all the stock of a corporation in a single individual is combined with other factors clearly supporting disregard of the corporate fiction on grounds of fundamental equity and fairness, courts have experienced "little difficulty" and have shown no hesitancy in applying what is described as the "alter ego" or "instrumentality" theory in order to cast aside the corporate shield and to fasten liability on the individual stockholder.

But, in applying the "instrumentality" or "alter ego" doctrine, the courts are concerned with reality and not form, with how the corporation operated and the individual defendant's relationship to that operation. One court has suggested that courts should abjure "the mere incantation of the term 'instrumentality'" in this context and, since the issue is one of fact, should take pains to spell out the specific factual basis for [their] conclusions. And the authorities have indicated certain facts which are to be given substantial weight in this connection. One fact which all the authorities consider significant in the inquiry, and particularly so in the case of the one-man or closely-held corporation, is whether the corporation was grossly undercapitalized for the purposes of the corporate undertaking. And, "[t]he obligation to provide adequate capital begins with incorporation and is a continuing obligation thereafter * * * during the corporation's operations." Other factors that are emphasized in the application of the doctrine are failure to observe corporate formalities, non-payment of dividends, the insolvency of the debtor corporation at the time, siphoning of funds of the corporation by the dominant stockholder, non-functioning of other officers or directors, absence of corporate records, and the fact that the corporation is merely a facade for the operations of the dominant stockholder or stockholders. The conclusion to disregard the corporate entity may not, however, rest on a single factor, whether undercapitalization, disregard of corporation's formalities, or what-not, but must involve a number of such factors; in addition, it must present an element of injustice or fundamental unfairness. But undercapitalization, coupled with disregard of corporate formalities, lack of participation on the part of the other stockholders, and the failure to pay dividends while paying substantial sums, whether by way of salary or otherwise, to the dominant stockholder, all fitting into a picture of basic unfairness, has been regarded fairly uniformly to constitute a basis for an imposition of individual liability under the doctrine. * * *

If these factors, which were deemed significant in other cases concerned with this same issue, are given consideration here, the finding of the District Court that the corporate entity should be disregarded was not clearly erroneous. Certainly the corporation was, in practice at least, a close, one-man corporation from the very beginning. Its incorporators were the defendant Flemming, his wife and his attorney. It began in 1962 with a capitalization of 5,000 shares, issued for a consideration of one dollar each. At the times involved here Flemming owned approximately 90% of the corporation's outstanding stock, according to his own testimony, though this was not verified by any stock records. Flemming was obscure on who the other stockholders were and how much stock these other stockholders owned, giving at different times conflicting statements as to who owned stock and how much. His testimony on who were the officers and directors was hardly more direct. * * *

The District Court found, also, that the corporation never had a stockholders' meeting. * * * It is thus clear that corporate formalities, even rudimentary formalities, were not observed by the defendant.

Beyond the absence of any observance of corporate formalities is the purely personal manner in which the corporation was operated. No stockholder or officer of the corporation other than Flemming ever received any salary, dividend, or fee from the corporation, or, for that matter, apparently exercised any voice in its operation or decisions. In all the years of the corporation's existence, Flemming was the sole beneficiary of its operations and its continued existence was for his exclusive benefit. During these years he was receiving from $15,000 to $25,000 each year from a corporation, which, during most of the time, was showing no profit and apparently had no working capital. Moreover, the payments to Flemming were authorized under no resolution of the board of directors of the corporation, as recorded in any minutes of a board meeting. Actually, it would seem that Flemming's withdrawals varied with what could be taken out of the corporation at the moment: If this amount were $15,000, that was Flemming's withdrawal; if it were $25,000, that was his withdrawal.

To summarize: The District Court found, and there was evidence to sustain the findings, that there was here a complete disregard of "corporate formalities" in the operation of the corporation, which functioned, not for the benefit of all stockholders, but only for the financial advantage of Flemming, who was the sole stockholder to receive one penny of profit from the corporation in the decade or more that it operated, and who made during that period all the corporate decisions and dominated the corporation's operations.

That the corporation was undercapitalized, if indeed it were not without any real capital, seems obvious. In fact, the defendant Flemming makes no effort to refute the evidence of want of any capital reserves on the part of the corporation. It appears patent that the corporation was actually operating at all times involved here on someone else's capital. This conclusion follows from a consideration of the manner in which Flemming operated in the name of the corporation during the year when plaintiff's indebtedness was incurred. * * *

Were the opinion of the District Court herein to be reversed, Flemming would be permitted to retain substantial sums from the operations of the corporation without having any real capital in the undertaking, risking nothing of his own and using as operating capital what he had collected as due the plaintiff. Certainly, equity and fundamental justice support individual liability of Flemming for plaintiff's charges, payment for which he asserted in his accounting with the growers that he had paid and for which he took credit on such accounting. This case patently presents a blending of the very factors which courts have regarded as justifying a disregard of the corporate entity in furtherance of basic and fundamental fairness.

Finally, it should not be overlooked that at some point during the period when this indebtedness was being incurred, whether at the beginning or at a short time later is not clear in the record, the plaintiff became concerned about former delays in receipt of payment for its charges and, to allay that concern, Flemming stated to the plaintiff, according to the latter's testimony as credited by the District Court, that "he (i. e., Flemming) would take care of (the charges) personally, if the corporation failed to do so * * *." On this assurance, the plaintiff contended that it continued to haul for the defendant. The existence of this promise by Flemming is not disputed. When one, who is the sole beneficiary of a corporation's operations and who dominates it, as did Flemming in this case, induces a creditor to extend credit to the corporation on such an assurance as given here, that fact has been considered by many authorities sufficient basis for piercing the corporate veil. The only argument against this view is bottomed on the statute of frauds. * * *

QUESTIONS AND NOTES

1. Questions about the law

a) Can a corporation have only one shareholder? If so, is that shareholder personally liable for the corporation's debts since he is the "sole beneficiary of its obligations?"

b) What is "undercapitalization?" Was the corporation in this case undercapitalized? If the debtor corporation was adequately capitalized would its creditors need to invoke the piercing doctrine?

c) At what point is undercapitalization determined? If a corporation is adequately capitalized when it is formed but later loses money, is it then undercapitalized for piercing the corporate veil purposes? Assume, for example, that Propp, Agee and Capel organize Bubba's Burritos, Inc. and that the amount they pay for their stock is sufficient to ensure that the corporation is adequately capitalized initially. Bubba's Burritos, Inc., however, suffers operating losses that exhaust virtually all of this initial capital. Does this mean that Propp, Agee and Capel are now at a risk of personal liability for Bubba's Burritos, Inc.'s debts through piercing the corporate veil unless they provide additional capital to the corporation?

d) The Fourth Circuit also mentions "disregard of corporate formalities"? What corporate formalities did the corporation disregard? How was the plaintiff harmed by any such disregard of corporate formalities?

e) Are there any other factors mentioned by the Fourth Circuit that seem to have nothing at all to do with whether a shareholder should be held liable for corporate obligations? Specifically, the court noted that the corporation had not paid dividends. Wouldn't a creditor like Dewitt be *delighted* that the corporation did not pay dividends? After all, if the corporation had paid dividends to its shareholders, there would have been even less money in the corporation's bank account from which creditors could recover. So it seems nonpayment of dividends is actually a *good* thing from the creditors' viewpoint. Might there be valid tax reasons for a corporation not to pay dividends?

f) If you were the lawyer for Flemming or his corporation, could you have offered advice that might have helped him avoid personal liability?

g) If the trial court had ruled for Flemming—had refused to pierce the corporate veil—would the Fourth Circuit have reversed?

2. More questions

a) The court in *Dewitt* mentions that one basis for piercing is to avoid fraud. Suppose Capel leaves her job at Bubba's Burritos. She and Bubba's enter an agreement by which Capel agrees that she will not go into competition with Bubba's in the Tuscaloosa area for at least two years. (Such agreements are called "covenants not to compete" and are usually upheld if reasonable as to temporal and geographic limitations.) The next week she forms Capel's Quesadillas, Inc., which goes into direct competition with Bubba's in Tuscaloosa. Should she be able to say that she is not violating the covenant not to compete because it is Capel's Quesadillas, Inc. (and not she) who is competing with Bubba's? No. Her use of the corporate form to avoid her personal covenant was fraudulent. The court would pierce the corporate veil and put Capel's Quesadillas, Inc. out of business.

b) In *Dewitt,* the plaintiff was invoking the piercing the corporate veil doctrine to hold an individual shareholder liable for his or her corporation's contracts or torts. What if the shareholder is itself a corporation?

A corporation can be a shareholder of another corporation. Indeed, a corporation is often the only shareholder of another corporation. A corporation whose stock is owned by another corporation is commonly referred to as a "subsidiary." More precisely, a subsidiary is a corporation, a majority or all of the outstanding stock of which is owned by another corporation, called the parent corporation.

Remember that every corporation is an entity—a legal person, with its own assets separate from those who own and run it. Accordingly, a parent corporation is not liable for the contracts, torts, and other obligations of its subsidiary corporation unless there is a contractual or judicial exception to the rule that a shareholder is not liable for the acts or debts of the corporation.

The next case involves the issue of piercing the corporate veil to hold a parent corporation liable for torts of its subsidiary.

Bristol-Myers Squibb Co. (Bristol), was the sole shareholder of Medical Engineering Corp. (MEC). MEC was a breast implant maker; Bristol was not. Both MEC and Bristol were defendants in the multidistrict litigation over silicone breast implants. One of the plaintiffs' legal theories was piercing the corporate veil. In reading the court's decision on Bristol's motion for summary judgment, please consider the following:

1. What did Bristol do wrong?

2.   Were the plaintiffs harmed by any of Bristol's actions or inactions? Is that relevant to piercing the corporate veil?

3.   Was MEC undercapitalized?

IN RE SILICONE GEL BREAST IMPLANTS
LIABILITY LITIGATION

United States District Court, Northern District of Alabama, 1995
887 F.Supp. 1447

POINTER, CHIEF JUDGE. Under submission after appropriate discovery, extensive briefing, and oral argument is the motion for summary judgment filed by defendant Bristol-Myers Squibb Co. Bristol is the sole shareholder of Medical Engineering Corporation, a major supplier of breast implants, but has never itself manufactured or distributed breast implants. Bristol asserts that the evidence is insufficient for the plaintiffs' claims to proceed against it, whether through piercing the corporate veil or under a theory of direct liability. The parties agree that, with discovery substantially complete, this motion is ripe for decision. For the reasons stated below, the court concludes that Bristol is not entitled to summary judgment.* * *

Documents reflect that MEC has had, at least in form, a board of three directors, generally consisting of the Bristol Vice President then serving as President of Bristol's Health Care Group, another Bristol executive, and MEC's president. Bristol's Health Care Group President, who reported to Bristol's president or chairman, could not be outvoted by the other two MEC board members. Several of the former MEC presidents did not recall that MEC had a board, let alone that they were members; and one of these stated that he did not attend, call, or receive notice of board meetings in his five years of service because he had a designated Bristol officer to contact. The few resolutions that were adopted by MEC's board were apparently prepared by Bristol officials.

MEC prepared "significant event" reports for Bristol's Corporate Policy Committee. These reports included information on breast implant production, such as publicity, testing, expenses, lawsuit settlements, and backorders caused by sterilization difficulties. Neither Bristol managers nor MEC Presidents recall any orders or recommendations being issued by Bristol as a result of these reviews. Bristol also required MEC to prepare and submit a five-year plan for its review.

MEC submitted budgets for approval by Bristol's senior management. For this submission, MEC filled out a series of standard Bristol forms that included information on projected sales, profits and losses, cash flow, balance sheets, and capital requirements. Bristol had the authority to modify this budget, though it rarely, if ever, actually did so.

Cash received by MEC was transferred to an account maintained by Bristol. This money was credited to MEC, but the interest earned was credited to Bristol. Bristol was MEC's banker, providing such loans as it determined MEC needed. Bristol required MEC to obtain its approval for capital appropriations, though most, if not all, of these requests were approved.

Bristol set the employment policies and wage scales that applied to MEC's employees. Before hiring a top executive or negotiating the salary, MEC was required to seek Bristol's approval. Before hiring a vice president of MEC, MEC's president and his superior at Bristol interviewed the candidate. Key executive employees were rated on the Bristol schedule. Bristol set a target for salary increases below the key executive level and approved those for employees above that level. Key executives of MEC received stock options for Bristol stock. MEC employees could participate in Bristol's pension and savings plans.

Bristol provided various services to MEC. Zimmer International, another Bristol subsidiary, distributed MEC breast implants but did not receive any benefit for doing so. Bristol's corporate development group assisted MEC in seeking out new product lines. Bristol's scientific experts researched the hazards of breast implants and polyurethane foam. Bristol provided funds for MEC to conduct sales contests. Bristol funded tests on breast implants. Another Bristol subsidiary, ConvaTec, assisted MEC in developing its premarket approval application (PMAA) regarding breast implants for the FDA. In addition to this assistance, Bristol hired an outside laboratory to verify ConvaTec's analysis. Bristol also conducted post-market surveillance at the request of the FDA. * * *

Bristol's name and logo were contained in the package inserts and promotional products regarding breast implants, apparently as a marketing tool to increase confidence in the product. Bristol's name was used in all sales and promotional communications with physicians.

MEC posted a profit every year between 1983 and 1990. Total sales increased from approximately $14 million in 1983 to $65 million in 1990. Bristol never received dividends from MEC. Bristol prepared consolidated federal income tax returns but MEC prepared its own Wisconsin tax forms. Bristol also purchased insurance for MEC under its policy. This insurance has a face value of over $2 billion.

Bristol's executive vice president suspended MEC's sales of polyurethane coated breast implants on April 17, 1991, and determined not to submit a PMAA for the implants to the FDA. MEC ceased its breast implant business in 1991 and later that year MEC ceased all operations by selling its urology division. This sale could not have occurred without Bristol's approval, and proceeds from the sale were turned over to Bristol, which then executed a low-interest demand note for $57,518,888 payable to MEC. MEC's only assets at this time are this demand note and its indemnity insurance.

The various theories of recovery made by plaintiffs against Bristol can be generally divided between those involving "corporate control" and those asserting direct liability. The corporate control claims deal with piercing the corporate veil to abrogate limited liability and hold Bristol responsible for actions of MEC. The direct liability theories include strict products liability, negligence, negligent failure to warn, negligence per se for not complying with FDA regulations, misrepresentation, fraud, and participation.

The potential for abuse of the corporate form is greatest when, as here, the corporation is owned by a single shareholder. The evaluation of corporate control claims cannot, however, disregard the fact that, no different from other stockholders, a parent corporation is expected—indeed, required—to exert some control over its subsidiary. Limited liability is the rule, not the exception. However, when a corporation is so controlled as to be the alter ego or mere instrumentality of its stockholder, the corporate form may be disregarded in the interests of justice. So far as this court has been able to determine, some variation of this theory of liability is recognized in all jurisdictions.

An initial question is whether veil-piercing may ever be resolved by summary judgment. Ordinarily the fact-intensive nature of the issue will require that it be resolved only through a trial. Summary judgment, however, can be proper if, as occurred earlier in this litigation with respect to claims against Dow Chemical and Corning, the evidence presented could lead to but one result. Because the court concludes that a jury (or in some jurisdictions, the judge acting in equity) could—and, under the laws of many states, probably should—find that MEC was but the alter ego of Bristol, summary judgment must be denied.

The totality of circumstances must be evaluated in determining whether a subsidiary may be found to be the alter ego or mere instrumentality of the parent corporation. Although the standards are not identical in each state, all jurisdictions require a showing of substantial domination. Among the factors to be considered are whether:

- the parent and the subsidiary have common directors or officers

- the parent and the subsidiary have common business departments

- the parent and the subsidiary file consolidated financial statements and tax returns

- the parent finances the subsidiary

- the parent caused the incorporation of the subsidiary

- the subsidiary operates with grossly inadequate capital

- the parent pays the salaries and other expenses of the subsidiary

- the subsidiary receives no business except that given to it by the parent

- the parent uses the subsidiary's property as its own

- the daily operations of the two corporations are not kept separate

- the subsidiary does not observe the basic corporate formalities, such as keeping separate books and records and holding shareholder and board meetings.

The fact-finder at a trial could find that the evidence supports the conclusion that many of these factors have been proven: two of MEC's three directors were Bristol directors; MEC was part of Bristol's Health Care group and used Bristol's legal, auditing, and communications departments; MEC and Bristol filed consolidated federal tax returns and Bristol prepared consolidated financial reports; Bristol operated as MEC's finance company, providing loans for the purchase of Aesthetech and Natural Y, receiving interest on MEC's funds, and requiring MEC to make requests for capital appropriations; Bristol effectively used MEC's resources as its own by obtaining interest on MEC's money and requiring MEC to make requests for capital appropriations to obtain its own funds; some members of MEC's board were not aware that MEC had a board of directors, let alone that they were members; and the senior Bristol member of MEC's board could not be outvoted by the other two directors. These facts, even apart from evidence that might establish some of the other factors listed above, would provide significant support for a finding at trial that MEC is Bristol's alter ego.

Bristol contends that a finding of fraud or like misconduct is necessary to pierce the corporate veil. Despite Bristol's contentions to the contrary, Delaware courts—to which Bristol would have this court look—do not necessarily require a showing of fraud if a subsidiary is found to be the mere instrumentality or alter ego of its sole stockholder. In addition, many jurisdictions that require a showing of fraud, injustice, or inequity in a contract case do not in a tort situation. A rational distinction can be drawn between tort and contract cases. In actions based on contract, "the creditor has willingly transacted business with the subsidiary" although it could have insisted on assurances that would make the parent also responsible. In a tort situation, however, the injured party had no such choice; the limitations on corporate liability were, from its standpoint, fortuitous and non-consensual.

There is, however, evidence precluding summary judgment even in jurisdictions that require a finding of fraud, inequity, or injustice. This conclusion is not based merely on the evidence that, even accepting Bristol's contentions regarding the amount of insurance available to MEC, MEC may have insufficient funds to satisfy the potential risks of responding to, and defending against, the numerous existing and potential claims of the plaintiffs. Equally significant is the fact that Bristol permitted its name to appear on breast implant advertisements, packages, and product inserts to improve sales by giving the product additional credibility. Combined with the evidence of potentially insufficient assets, this fact would support a finding that it would be inequitable and unjust to allow Bristol now to avoid liability to those induced to believe Bristol was vouching for this product.

Because the evidence available at a trial could support—if not, under some state laws, perhaps mandate—a finding that the corporate veil should be pierced, Bristol is not entitled through summary judgment to dismissal of the claims against it.

QUESTIONS AND NOTES

1.   **Questions on piercing the corporate veil**

a)   Again, what did Bristol do wrong? How did it harm the plaintiffs? Are these questions relevant to the issue of piercing the corporate veil?

b)   Do you agree with Judge Pointer that it should be easier to pierce the corporate veil in cases involving tort claims than in cases involving contract claims? Do you agree with Judge Pointer that the plaintiffs in this case, women who bought implants from MEC, were asserting tort claims?

2.   **Notes on piercing the corporate veil**

a)   In the same multidistrict silicone gel breast implant litigation, Judge Pointer earlier granted a motion by Dow Chemical Co. and Corning, Inc., sole shareholders of Dow Corning Corp., to dismiss a corporate veil piercing count against them, stating:

There is no evidence of intermingling or commingling of funds or of any improper loans between the parents and the subsidiary * * *. There is no evidence that [the parent companies] drained Dow Corning of its assets, even after they had knowledge of the potential liability for silicone gel breast implants * * *. Although Dow and Corning have had significant contacts with their subsidiary, these contacts do not * * * rise to the level of manipulation and control that would support a piercing of the corporate veil * * *. The various business dealings between the three companies appear to have been carried out with due regard for the separate existence and interests of each, with all necessary corporate formalities being observed.

In re Silicone Gel Breast Implants Products Liability Litigation, 837 F.Supp. 1128, 1138 (N.D. Ala. 1993).

b)   Our favorite student text provides this summary on piercing the corporate veil in the parent/subsidiary context: "In general, courts look to the same sorts of factors here as they do in 'regular' piercing cases."[*]

3.   Questions about holding a parent corporation liable for the subsidiary corporation's actions under agency concepts

a)   In the portion of the opinion dealing with piercing the corporate veil, Judge Pointer states "Equally significant is the fact that Bristol permitted its name to appear on the breast implant advertisements, packages, and product inserts to improve sales by giving the product additional credibility." Why is that relevant to piercing the corporate veil? Isn't that more relevant to holding Bristol liable under some theory of apparent agency as in the *McDonald's* case in Chapter 1?

b)   Is the following statement by Judge Learned Hand on holding a parent corporation liable for the subsidiary corporation's actions under agency concepts helpful?

"Control through the ownership of shares does not fuse the corporations, even when the directors are common to each. One corporation may, however, become an actor in a given transaction, or in part of a business, or in a whole business, and, when it has, will be legally responsible. To become so it must take immediate direction of the transaction through its officers, by whom alone it can act at all. At times this is put as though the subsidiary then became an agent of the parent. That may no doubt be true, but only in quite other situations; that is, when both intend that relation to arise, for agency is consensual. [*Kingston Dry Dock v. Lake Champlain Transp. Co.*, 31 F.2d 265, 267 (2d. Cir. 1929).]

c)   If, as Judge Hand suggested in *Kingston Dock* above, "liability normally must depend upon the parent's direct intervention in the transaction," is such liability the derivative liability of a parent/principal for its subsidiary/agent's acts? Or is it, instead, direct liability of the parent for its own acts?

5.   THIRD EXCEPTION: A CORPORATION CAN BE LIABLE FOR THE DEBTS OF ANOTHER CORPORATION BECAUSE OF ENTERPRISE LIABILITY

For more than seven decades, some professors and lawyers have argued for "enterprise liability." This is a theory under which corporations that (although technically separate) are commonly-owned and engage in one enterprise should be treated as a single legal entity for purposes of liability. As you read the following classic explanation of

---

[*]   Richard D, Freer & Douglas K, Moll, PRINCIPLES OF BUSINESS ORGANIZATIONS 336 (2013).

enterprise liability, consider how it differs from (1) piercing the veil liability or (2) agency liability or (3) direct liability.

Classically, a corporation was conceived as an artificial person, coming into existence through creation by a sovereign power.

Its primary business advantage, of course, was insulation of individual stockholders composing the corporation from liability for the debts of the corporate enterprise.

As the scale of business enterprises enlarged, the process of sub-division began; hence subsidiary corporations wholly-owned or partly-owned; or holding companies combined into a series of corporations constituting a combined economic enterprise; and so forth. More often than not, a single large-scale business is conducted, not by a single corporation, but by a constellation of corporations controlled by a central holding company, the various sectors being separately incorporated, either because they were once independent and have been acquired, or because the central concern, entering new fields, created new corporations to develop them, or for tax reasons. In some instances, departments of the business are separately incorporated and operated as separate legal units. Since under modern corporation statutes any three persons can in effect request and get a corporate charter, writing their own grant of powers (with very few limitations) and thus constituting themselves an artificial person, the process has been easy to carry on, and has been a decided business convenience.

This is far from the original conception of a corporation. The legal doctrine of corporate personality was built around the idea of a sovereign grant of certain attributes of personality to a definable group, engaged in an enterprise. The so-called "artificial personality" was designed to be the enterpriser of a project. Multiplicity of artificial personalities within an enterprise unit would probably have been impossible under most early corporation laws.

The divergence between corporate theory and the underlying economic facts has occasioned a variety of problems (dealt with *ad hoc* by the courts) in which the theory of "artificial personality" simply did not work, and was consequently extended, disregarded, sometimes buttressed by further fiction, at others manipulated to get a convenient result.

All this suggests that a review of the classic conception is in order. It has seemed to the writer that one of the pressing needs in the field of corporation law is its systematization. A series of rules has been adopted in varying groups of cases as wrongs appeared and remedies were worked out. These emerged as isolated doctrines applicable to specific situations. This essay is designed to suggest the possibility that a number of rules which are regarded as separate in fact are applications of a single dominant principle.

It is the thesis of this essay:

That the entity commonly known as "corporate entity" takes its being from the reality of the underlying enterprise, formed or in formation;

That the state's approval of the corporate form sets up a prima facie case that the assets, liabilities and operations of the corporation are those of the enterprise;

But that where the corporate entity is defective, or otherwise challenged, its existence, extent and consequences may be determined by the actual existence and extent and operations of the underlying enterprise, which by these very qualities acquires an entity of its own, recognized by law.

For brevity, this hypothesis is hereafter referred to as the theory of "enterprise liability."

Adolph A. Berle, *The Theory of Enterprise Liability*, 47 COLUM. L. REV. 343, 343–44 (1943).

––––––––––

Walkovszky v. Carlton, 223 N.E.2d 6 (N.Y. 1966) is the most frequently mentioned "enterprise liability" case even though its holding is not completely clear. We note the facts simply because they may exemplify the theory of enterprise liability. In *Walkovszky*, the plaintiff was injured when hit by a taxicab. The cab was operated by a corporation owned by Carlton. That corporation's assets consisted of two cabs (not fully paid for), the "medallion" allowing it to operate in New York, and the minimum amount of insurance required by law for each cab. It turns out that Carlton also owned nine other corporations, each of which was set up the same way. All ten taxicab companies were operated out of a single garage, with a single dispatching system. In other words, the ten were operated as a single business. The plaintiff alleged that Carlton continually drained all profits out of the companies, leaving them with little in the way of assets.

If the plaintiff's theory of piercing the corporate veil had been successful, he would have pierced through the one corporation that operated the cab that hit him, and recovered from Carlton. On the other hand, if the plaintiff's theory of enterprise liability had been successful, the court would have treated all ten companies as one. The plaintiff thus would have been able to recover from the combined assets of all ten companies. So, enterprise liability pierces the walls of one corporation *not* to go after the assets of a shareholder, but to go after the assets of related companies.

QUESTIONS

1.   If you represented the plaintiff in the *Walkovszky*, which would you have asserted—piercing the corporate veil or enterprise liability? What, if any, additional facts do you need to answer this question?

2.   *Walkovszky* was a torts case. Is a court more likely to impose enterprise liability in a torts case than a contracts case?

B. WHO MAKES DECISIONS FOR THE CORPORATION?

There was no serious legal question about who gets to make the decisions in a sole proprietorship or in a partnership. After all, in a sole proprietorship, there is only the sole proprietor (and perhaps some employees). And in a partnership, there are only the partners (and perhaps some employees). In the corporation, however, we may have various players: promoter(s), incorporator(s), shareholder(s), director(s) and officer(s). Who decides what?

As we will see, the answer to this question of "who decides what" varies with the type of corporation. The answer will be different in large corporations, the stock of which is traded publicly, and in small, closely-held corporations. The distinction was observed by Adolph A. Berle and Gardiner C. Means in their famous book THE MODERN CORPORATION AND PRIVATE PROPERTY. What they saw in 1932 was that:

- ownership of large corporations was widely dispersed;

- no single shareholder owned sufficient stock in companies such as U.S. Steel or the Pennsylvania Railroad to control the corporation's agenda; and,

- the larger the corporation, the smaller the proportion of stock held by management.

Berle and Means also described this division of ownership and decision-making:

> * * * [T]he position of ownership has changed from that of active to passive agent. In place of the actual physical properties over which the owner could exercise direction and for which he was responsible, the owner now holds a piece of paper representing a set of rights and expectations with respect to an enterprise. But over the enterprise and over the physical property—the instruments of production—in which he has an interest, the owner has little control. * * *. The owner is practically powerless through his own efforts to affect the underlying property * * * in the corporate system, the 'owner' of industrial wealth is left with a mere symbol of ownership while the power, the responsibility and the substance which have been an integral part of ownership in the past are being transferred to a separate group [management] in whose hands lie control.

Adolph A. Berle & Gardiner C. Means, THE MODERN CORPORATION AND PRIVATE PROPERTY 64–65 (1932).

What can we see today in McDonald's, Bubba's Burritos, and other corporations?

———

1. IN A PUBLICLY-HELD CORPORATION, THE BOARD OF DIRECTORS AND ITS DELEGATES DECIDE VIRTUALLY EVERYTHING

a. Directors and Officers

Even though McDonald's Corporation is an entity, a person for all legal purposes, there is no Mr. or Ms. McDonald—as one person—to make decisions for the business. That is not even the role of Ronald McDonald.

It is also not the role of the person who owns one or one hundred or even one thousand of the approximately one billion shares of McDonald's stock now outstanding. Generally, if a corporation has more than four or five shareholders, most shareholders play virtually no role in making decisions regarding the operation of the business. (For most shareholders of corporations with more than four or five shareholders, their only important decision is when to sell their shares—a decision we will consider later.)

Under the corporation statutes of all states, the board of directors is empowered to make the corporation's most important decisions. MBCA § 8.01 is typical of provisions embodying this principle:

8.01.   REQUIREMENT FOR AND DUTIES OF BOARD OF DIRECTORS

(a) Except as provided in section 7.32, each corporation must have a board of directors.

(b) All corporate powers shall be exercised by or under the authority of, and the business and affairs of the corporation managed under the direction of, its board of directors, subject to any limitation set forth in the articles of incorporation or in an agreement authorized under section 7.32.

Note that § 8.01(b) refers to corporate powers exercised "by or under the authority of" the board of directors. What is the difference?

In some states, the initial directors are named in the articles. In others, the incorporators elect the initial directors. Thereafter, in all states, the shareholders (who are the owners) elect the directors. They do so at the annual meeting. So, unlike in a sole proprietorship and partnership, the owners of the corporation do not manage the business. Instead, they elect the people who manage the corporation. As explained by one text, this "traditional pattern of corporate governance" works as follows:

> The traditional corporate pattern is triangular, with the shareholders at the base. The shareholders, who are generally viewed as the ultimate or residual owners of the business, select the personnel at the next level—namely, the board of directors. According to accepted wisdom, the board of directors appoints the chief executive officer and other corporate officers, determines corporate policies, oversees the officers' work, and in general manages the corporation or supervises the management of its affairs. In legal theory the directors are supreme during their term of office (usually one year).[*]

Or, for those of you who were political science majors:

> This corporate model of organization reflects the American embrace of the republican form of government. In it, the owners elect those who make the management decisions, the directors, and may remove them with or without cause. The directors hire and monitor the officers, who implement the directors' management decisions. In turn, the officers, who hire and monitor lower-level employees, are agents of the corporation. Their actions, if made within the scope of their authority, will bind the entity, just as an employee's act might bind a sole proprietor or a partner's act might bind other partners.

Richard D. Freer, *Business Organizations,* OXFORD COMPANION TO AMERICAN LAW 79 (2002).

Are these statements by our own Richie Freer consistent with MBCA §§ 8.01 and 7.32? Are they consistent with the *A.P. Smith Mfg. Co. v. Barlow* case in Chapter 1?

In actual practice, is the board of directors the decisionmaker for a large, publicly-held corporation like McDonald's? Lots of decisions are being made at McDonald's. Can the board of directors make all the decisions? (Remember that corporate power is exercised "by or under the authority of" the board of directors.)

QUESTIONS AND NOTES

1.   How many directors can serve on the board? Where is the number of directors set? See Delaware § 1.41(b) and MBCA § 8.03(a).

---

[*]   James D. Cox, Thomas Lee Hazen, & F. Hodge O'Neal, CORPORATIONS 146 (1997).

2.   Who serves as the directors of a large, publicly-held corporation? For McDonald's, the answer in 2014 was:

Andrew   J.   McKenna: Non-Executive   Chairman   of McDonald's Corporation since April 2004 and also non-executive Chairman of Schwarz Supply Source, a printer, converter, producer and distributor of packaging and promotional materials. Mr. McKenna serves as a director of Ryan Specialty Group and Skyline Corporation. He has served over the years on many civic, community and philanthropic boards and currently serves as a trustee of Ronald McDonald House Charities, Museum of Science and Industry (Chairman Emeritus) and University of Notre Dame (Chairman Emeritus), and as a director of Big Shoulders Fund of the Archdiocese of Chicago, Ann and Robert H. Lurie Children's Hospital of Chicago, Ireland Economic Advisory Board, Lyric Opera of Chicago and United Way of Metropolitan Chicago among others. Mr. McKenna is also the Founding Chairman of Metropolis Strategies. Director since 1991. Class of 2015.

Susan E. Arnold: Operating Executive, Global Consumer & Retail Group of The Carlyle Group, a global alternative asset manager, since 2013. Former President—Global Business Units of The Procter & Gamble Company from 2007 until 2009 when she retired from that post. Prior to that time, she was Vice Chair of P & G Beauty and Health since 2006; and Vice Chair of P & G Beauty since 2004. Director of NBTY, Inc. and The Walt Disney Company. Director since 2008. Class of 2014.

Robert A. Eckert: Former non-executive Chairman of Mattel, Inc., a designer, manufacturer and marketer of toy products during 2012. From 2000 to 2011, he was Chief Executive Officer and Chairman of the Board of Mattel, Inc. Director of Amgen Inc. and Levi Strauss & Co. Director since 2003. Class of 2015.

Enrique Hernandez, Jr.: President and Chief Executive Officer of Inter-Con Security Systems, Inc., a privately owned provider of high-end security and facility support services to government, utilities and industrial customers. Non-executive Chairman of Nordstrom, Inc., and Director of Chevron Corporation and Wells Fargo & Company. Director since 1996. Class of 2015.

Jeanne P. Jackson: President, Product and Merchandising for NIKE, Inc., a designer, marketer and distributor of athletic footwear, equipment and accessories, since 2013. From 2009 to 2013, she was President of Direct to Consumer for NIKE, Inc. Between 2002 and 2009, she was Chief Executive Officer of MSP Capital, a private investment company. Director of Kraft Foods Group, Inc. Director since 1999. Class of 2015.

Richard H. Lenny: Operating Partner of Friedman, Fleischer & Lowe, LLC, a private equity firm, since 2011. Former Chairman,

President and Chief Executive Officer of The Hershey Company, a manufacturer, distributor and marketer of candy, snacks and candy-related grocery products, from 2001 until his retirement in 2007. Director of ConAgra Foods, Inc. and Discover Financial Services. Director since 2005. Class of 2014.

Walter E. Massey: President of the School of the Art Institute of Chicago, since 2010. Also, President Emeritus of Morehouse College having served as its President from 1995 to 2007. Director since 1998. Class of 2014.

Cary D. McMillan: Chief Executive Officer of True Partners Consulting LLC, a professional services firm providing tax and other financial services, since 2005. From 2001 to 2004, he was the Chief Executive Officer of Sara Lee Branded Apparel and from 2000 to 2004, Executive Vice President of Sara Lee Corporation, a branded packaged goods company. Director of American Eagle Outfitters, Inc. and Hyatt Hotels Corporation. Director since 2003. Class of 2014.

Sheila A. Penrose: Non-executive Chairman of Jones Lang LaSalle Incorporated, a global real estate services and money management firm, since 2005. From 2000 to 2007, she was President of the Penrose Group, a provider of strategic advisory services on financial and organization strategies. Director since 2006. Class of 2014.

John W. Rogers, Jr.: Chairman and Chief Executive Officer of Ariel Investments, LLC, a privately held institutional money management firm, which he founded in 1983. Director of Exelon Corporation and a trustee of Ariel Investment Trust. Director since 2003. Class of 2014.

Roger W. Stone: Chairman and Chief Executive Officer of KapStone Paper and Packaging Corporation, formerly Stone Arcade Acquisition Corporation, since 2005. Mr. Stone was Manager of Stone-Kaplan Investments, LLC from 2004 until 2008. Chairman of Stone Tan China Holding Corporation and Stone Tan China Acquisition (Hong Kong) Company Limited. Director since 1989. Class of 2014.

Donald Thompson: President and Chief Executive Officer since July 2012. President and Chief Operating Officer from 2010 to June 2012, and has also served as a Director since 2011. President, McDonald's USA from 2006 to 2010, Executive Vice President and Chief Operations Officer, McDonald's USA from 2005 to August 2006. Mr. Thompson has been with the Company for 23 years and has held various management positions during that time. Class of 2015.

Miles D. White: Chairman and Chief Executive Officer of Abbott Laboratories, a pharmaceuticals and biotechnology company, since 1999. Director of Caterpillar, Inc. Director since 2009. Class of 2015.*

You can see from the list that a director can also be an officer. McDonald's "inside" directors are those who are also officers of McDonald's. The "outside" directors are those who are not.

3.   How much should McDonald's pay an outside director such as Susan Arnold for serving as director? A 2013 study of the 200 largest publicly-held corporations based in the United States found that the median total compensation paid to outside directors was $261,333. Steven Hall & Partners, 2013 DIRECTOR COMPENSATION STUDY 1 (2014).

4.   Section 3.02 of the American Law Institute's Principles of Corporate Governance lists mandatory and permissive functions of the board of directors of a publicly-held corporation:

§ 3.02.   Functions and Powers of the Board of Directors

Except as otherwise provided by statute:

(a) The board of directors of a publicly-held corporation should perform the following functions:

(1) Select, regularly evaluate, fix the compensation of, and, where appropriate, replace the principal senior executives;

(2) Oversee the conduct of the corporation's business to evaluate whether the business is being properly managed;

(3) Review and, where appropriate, approve the corporation's financial objectives and major corporate plans and actions;

(4) Review and, where appropriate, approve major changes in, and determinations of other major questions of choice respecting the appropriate auditing and accounting principles and practices to be used in the preparation of the corporation's financial statements;

(5) Perform such other functions as are prescribed by law, or assigned to the board under a standard of the corporation.

(b) A board of directors also has power to:

(1) Initiate and adopt corporate plans, commitments, and actions;

(2) Initiate and adopt changes in accounting principles and practices;

(3) Provide advice and counsel to the principal senior executives;

---

*   http://www.aboutmcdonalds.com/mcd/investors/corporate_governance/board_of_directors. html.

(4) Instruct any committee, principal senior executive, or other officer and review the actions of any committee, principal senior executive, or other officer;

(5) Make recommendations to shareholders;

(6) Manage the business of the corporation;

(7) Act as to all other corporate matters not requiring shareholder approval.

Why is § 3.02 limited to publicly-held corporations? *See also* MBCA § 8.01(c).

In practice, "outside directors" (those who are not employed full-time by the corporation) have a very difficult job. On one hand, the board holds the ultimate decision-making authority. On the other hand, outside directors simply cannot understand the business as well as officers and others who work there day-to-day. The CEO (often the chairperson of the board) controls the agenda for board meetings. If she decides not to put an item on the agenda for discussion, the directors are unlikely even to know that there might be an issue. And when she does put an item on the agenda for discussion, the board members are unlikely to reply in unison, "you know a lot more about this than we do, so do what you think is right." Directors are smart, motivated people, who are being paid a nice sum for their board service, so they want to "add value." Accordingly, they will ask a lot of questions (often good ones, but ones that may seem naïve to the CEO (who has lived with these issues every day and knows a lot more about them than the outside directors). Directors often suggest areas for further research and more study, which creates more work for the CEO and her team. Thus, CEOs often "manage" their boards, offering them a sanitized look at the workings of the business, and constraining the board's input to a narrow range of issues.

Co-author Roberts once asked a famous venture capital investor, who had served on the boards of many companies that are household names, how he thought about the role of a corporate board. He replied, "Show up every quarter and decide whether to fire the CEO." In practice, there's much truth in this. A board either has confidence in its CEO or it does not. It is impossible for a board to do enough work to make up for a CEO in whom it lacks confidence.

QUESTIONS AND NOTES

1.   The law of every state provides that a corporation has not only a board of directors but officers as well. MBCA §§ 8.40 and 8.41 is typical in permitting the corporation to designate in its bylaws what officers it will have and what their duties will be. Because corporate power is exercised "by

or under the authority" of the board, the board may appoint officers to make management decisions. The degree of engagement by the board in day-to-day activities of the corporation will depend on the size of the corporation. In huge companies like McDonalds, there is no way the board of directors can address directly anything but the largest, general policy matters. The board must oversee and monitor the officers and other employees who are closer to the day-to-day activity of the business.

2. What decisions do you think the McDonald's board of directors actually makes? Consider whether the McDonald's board of directors would have a role in the following corporate decisions (or whether they would be made by an officer or other employee):

a) Personnel: (i) Whether to hire Bill Clinton as president and chief executive officer of McDonald's? (ii) Whom to hire as interns in the executive office?

b) Operations: (i) Whether to close all McDonald's outlets to observe the Sabbath? (ii) Whether to close the McDonald's store near Shepherd's house in Atlanta?

c) Acquisitions: (i) Whether to diversify by acquiring WWE*? (ii) Whether to acquire Bubba's Burritos?

3. Remember that directors are not agents of the corporation. Individual directors have no authority to do anything on behalf of the corporation (unless the authority is delegated to them under agency law). So Roberts, who is one of five directors of Bubba's Burritos, Inc., cannot bind the corporation to a contract or require it to hire someone in the sales department.

4. Because directors are not agents, they take action only as a group: It is not directors who make a decision, but the *board of directors*. In other words, directorial power is held jointly. Study MBCA §§ 8.20 through 8.24 and answer the following:

a) In what two ways may the board of directors take a valid act? Why do you suppose the board cannot make a decision informally—say, as by a series of conversations between various directors?

b) Before any group (including a board of directors) can act at a meeting, there must be a quorum. If there is no quorum, the group cannot act at that meeting. Assume there are nine directors on the board of XYZ, Inc. At a meeting, four of the nine directors show up. Why can the board take no action at that meeting?

c) Again assume there are nine directors on the board of XYZ, Inc. Six of the nine attend the meeting. A proposal is made and the directors vote on it. How many must vote "yes" for the proposal to pass?

---

* http://www.wwe.com.

d)   This time five of the nine directors attend the meeting. On a proposal, two vote "yes," two vote "no," and one abstains. Does the proposal pass?

e)   Same facts as Question 4.4, but this time three vote "yes" and two vote "no." Does the proposal pass? Does it matter that it was approved by only one-third of the total number of directors?

f)   Every meeting of the board will either be a "regular" meeting or a "special" meeting. Must directors be given notice of either type of meeting? What happens if the corporation fails to give required notice to each director?

The general principle in every state is that the board of directors hires and fires officers. It also monitors officer performance and sets officer compensation. (See again MBCA §§ 8.40 and 8.41). Boards generally have several key committees. One is the audit committee, which hires and fires the company's auditors and also holds confidential (i.e., without management present) meetings with the audit team. This allows the auditors to voice any concerns they have about the way in which the company is performing its accounting. Another is the compensation committee, which sets the compensation for the senior management team and approves grants of stock options. The compensation committee is usually made up of solely "outside" directors, i.e., it includes no members of the company's management.

While a member of the board of directors of a corporation is not an agent of the corporation, an officer is. And, other employees are. The agency principles discussed in Chapter 2 apply here: the corporation is the principal and the officer is the agent.

PROBLEMS

1.   You receive a letter from V, a Vice President-Legal of McDonald's Corporation, offering you a position as staff attorney. Does that letter obligate McDonald's to hire you? What if the letter is signed by S, who identifies himself as "Senior Attorney"?

2.   Your client is selling land to McDonald's. How do you determine whether the person signing the contract for McDonald's is authorized to sign such a contract?

b. Role of Shareholders in Electing and Removing Directors

In every state, shareholders elect directors at the annual meeting. *See* Delaware § 211(b) and MBCA § 8.03(c). In addition, shareholders have the right to remove directors before their terms expire. *See* Delaware § 141(k) and MBCA § 8.08.

In a large, publicly-held corporation like McDonald's, the vote of most shareholders in electing and removing directors is of little practical consequence. Most of McDonald's shareholders own too few shares to have any impact. There are almost one billion outstanding shares of McDonald's stock.* The shareholders who are in a position to call the shots will usually not be individuals, but other corporations or institutional investors, such as mutual funds or pension funds.

Shareholders, like individual directors, are not agents of the corporation, and have no authority to bind the corporation to do anything. Shareholders, like the board of directors, must act as a group. And, like the board, shareholders may act either by entering a "written consent" to do something (which generally must be unanimous—see MBCA § 7.04(a)) or by having a meeting that satisfies the quorum and voting rules.

In every publicly-held corporation, shareholder action will be taken at a meeting (and not by unanimous written consent). For a shareholder meeting to result in a valid act, there must be a quorum represented at the meeting of shareholders. Remember from above that a quorum of the board of directors constituted a majority of the directors. With shareholder voting, in contrast, the focus is not on the number of shareholders, but on the number of shares. Unless the articles say otherwise, a quorum is a majority of the outstanding shares.

XYZ, Inc. has 1,000,000 outstanding shares. XYZ, Inc. has 10,000 shareholders, but that latter fact is relevant only to the caterer. With shareholder voting, a quorum consists of a majority of the 1,000,000 shares. So unless at least 500,001 shares are represented at the meeting, there will be no quorum and the shareholders cannot do anything at the meeting.

Once we have a quorum, the shareholders will vote. Unless the articles provide otherwise, each shareholder gets one vote for each share that she owns. So if Epstein owns 10,000 shares and Shepherd owns 50 shares, Epstein gets 10,000 votes and Shepherd gets 50 votes.

In any corporation, it is important for lawyers (and law students) to understand the mechanics of shareholder voting. Specifically, we need to know who votes, where they vote, and how they vote. This understanding requires mastery of the following terms: (1) annual and special meetings, (2) record owner and record date, and (3) proxy.†

---

* http://finance.yahoo.com/q/ks?s=MCD+Key+Statistics.

† There are two other shareholder voting terms—cumulative voting and shareholder voting agreements—that are important in electing directors of small, closely held companies like Bubba's Burritos. We will consider these terms when we consider who gets to make the decisions for small, closely held companies like Bubba's Burritos.

(i) Annual Meetings and Special Meetings

An "annual meeting" is a meeting that is held annually. (Some corporate law concepts are easier than others.) *See, e.g.,* Delaware § 211(b); MBCA § 7.01. Any other meeting of shareholders is a "special meeting." *See, e.g.,* Delaware § 211(d); MBCA § 7.02.

(ii) Record Owner and Record Date

The person who has the legal right to vote at an annual or special meeting of shareholders is the "record owner." The meaning of the phrase "record owner" is almost as obvious as the meaning of the phrases "annual meeting" and "special meeting." A corporation keeps records showing who owns its stock, i.e., the "record owners." The corporation is required to send notice of annual meetings and special meetings to its record shareholders. *See* Delaware § 213(a) and MBCA §§ 7.05 and 7.20(a).

This presents obvious practical questions for a corporation whose stock is regularly resold by its shareholders. Who gets the notice of the meeting? Who gets to vote at the meeting? "The record owner at the record date" is the answer to these questions: the corporation fixes a "record date" before the meeting, and only the record owners *as of that date* are entitled to notice of and a vote at the meeting. *See* Delaware § 213(a) and MBCA § 7.07(a) and (b).

Often the person listed as owner on the corporation's records (the record owner) is not the real owner (the "beneficial owner"). An investor buying shares of a publicly-traded corporation usually buys her shares through a broker, not from the issuing corporation.* She does not receive a stock certificate; she is not shown as the owner in the corporation's records. Instead, a depository company, maintained by a group of brokerage firms, holds the certificate and is shown as the owner in the corporation's records. The investor is shown as the owner in the *brokerage firm's* records. This is commonly referred to as "street name ownership."

A combination of stock exchange rules and Securities and Exchange Commission (SEC) rules ensures that when stock is held in street name, the beneficial owner is informed about shareholder votes, and the shares are voted as instructed by the beneficial shareholder. You will consider these rules in great detail if you take an advanced course in securities regulation. For present purposes, consider the following problems:

PROBLEMS

1. Delaware § 213(a) and MBCA § 7.07(b) introduce the concept of the "record date," which is an administrative convenience for determining who

---

* Accordingly, such a purchase is not an "issuance," and the various issuance rules (including par value) that we see at pages 134–137 do not apply.

gets to vote at an upcoming meeting. Read those statutes and address these hypotheticals:

a)   McDonald's will hold its annual shareholder meeting on June 30. What is the latest date the corporation can use as its record date under the two statutes? What is the earliest date?

b)   McDonald's sets a record date of June 8. Guy Fieri,* who owns 120 shares of McDonald's sells his stock to Shepherd on June 10. Who votes the stock at the annual meeting?

c)   Same facts as Question 1.2 except Fieri transfers his stock to Shepherd on June 5. Who votes the stock at the annual meeting?

2.   The board of directors of McDonald's decides that the Bubba's Burritos' restaurants will sell Gefilte Fish Parmesan† instead of burritos. Do the shareholders have to approve this change? Is remembering the *A.P. Smith* case helpful in answering this question?

———————

A shareholder does not have to be present at the annual or special meeting to vote her shares. State corporation statutes provide for shareholder voting by "proxy."‡ Voting by proxy simply means that the person who is entitled to vote authorizes another person to vote for her. A proxy is a form of agency: the owner is the principal and authorizes the proxy-holder to be her agent for voting.

You will note that we did not mention proxies when we discussed voting by the board of directors earlier in this section. Why? Directors are managers, and thus owe non-delegable fiduciary duties to the corporation. We will discuss these duties in Chapter 6. Their fiduciary position means that directors are required to exercise their independent judgment. Accordingly, they cannot appoint an agent (proxy) for voting at a meeting of the board of directors. And, as we will see below, though shareholders may enter agreements binding how they will vote on particular matters, directors may not do so. Again, they owe non-delegable fiduciary duties to the corporation and must bring their independent judgment to the task at hand. Shareholders, in contrast, are not fiduciaries to the corporation and thus may appoint an agent to vote for them.

———————

*   http://www.guyfieri.com/. [Roberts did not know who Guy Fieri is and insisted that you would not know either.]

†   Cf. Matt A.V. Chaban, Gefilte Fish Is Scarce This Passover: Taste Buds Are Ambivalent, New York Times, April 14, 2014 http://www.nytimes.com/2014/04/15/nyregion/gefilte-fish-is-scarce-this-passover-taste-buds-are-ambivalent.html?_r=.

‡   When McDonald's or some other public corporation holds a shareholders' meeting, few of the shareholders attend the meeting in person. Instead, most of the shareholders of a public corporation who vote use proxies. Because the use of proxies is so important to shareholder participation in public corporations, the SEC has promulgated a series of rules to regulate the proxy process. More specifically, the SEC has regulated the proxy solicitation process. These regulations will be covered in your school's Securities Regulation course.

These rules raise an important fact: one person may wear different hats at the same time. So, for example, Roberts might be both a shareholder and a director of McDonald's. When Roberts is wearing his director's hat—as in going to a board meeting to vote as a director—we apply the director voting rules we saw above. These include the prohibition of voting by proxy. But when Roberts is wearing his shareholder's hat—as in going to a shareholder meeting to vote as a shareholder—we apply the shareholder voting rules, including the fact that he may appoint an agent to vote for him.

Assume that Roberts owns 100 shares of McDonald's stock. He gives Shepherd a proxy to vote his shares at the upcoming annual shareholder meeting. If the proxy is silent as to duration, how long is the proxy effective under Delaware law? Under the MBCA? *See* Delaware § 212(b); MBCA § 7.22.

An example of a proxy is set out below:

PROXY

The undersigned, as record owner of the shares of _____ Corporation described below, hereby appoints_____, as the proxy of the undersigned, to attend and vote at the (annual/special) meeting of the shareholders of _____ Corporation, to be held at _____, on _____, at _____, and to represent, vote, execute, consent, waive and otherwise act for the undersigned in the same manner and with the same effect as if the undersigned were personally present at said meeting. This proxy may be revoked at any time.

The shares represented by this proxy shall be voted in the following manner:

ACTIONS PROPOSED TO BE TAKEN

	FOR	AGAINST	WITHHOLD
Proposal No. *(Describe Proposal)*	[ ]	[ ]	[ ]
Proposal No. 2 *(Describe Proposal)*	[ ]	[ ]	[ ]

FOR ELECTION AS DIRECTOR(S)

	FOR	AGAINST	WITHHOLD
_____ *(Name)*	[ ]	[ ]	[ ]

_____　[　]　[　]　　[　]

(Name)

_____　[　]　[　]　　[　]

(Name)

IF NO INDICATION IS MADE ON HOW YOU DESIRE YOUR SHARES TO BE VOTED, THE PROXY HOLDER WILL HAVE COMPLETE DISCRETION IN VOTING THE SHARES ON ANY MATTER VOTED ON AT THE MEETING.

Number and Class of Shares Owned:　_____

DATED: _____　　_____

　　　　　　　　　　　　　　　　　　Signature(s)

_____

Name(s) (typed or printed)

_____

Address(es)

　　　　　　　　　　_____

Note that the proxy above provides that it can be revoked. What if it were silent on revocability? Remember that we said a proxy is a form of agency: the owner of the shares consents to the proxy holder's voting the shares for her. *See* Restatement (Second) of Agency (R–2) § 1. Because agency law allows a principal to terminate an agent's authority at any time, *see* R–2 § 118, a proxy that does not address revocability will be revocable.

In fact, under case law and corporate codes, a proxy can be revoked even if the proxy states that it is *irrevocable*. Drawing again on agency principles, courts hold that a proxy is irrevocable only if it both (1) states that it is irrevocable and (2) is "coupled with some interest in the stock." *See* R–2 §§ 138 and 139.

MBCA § 7.22(d) provides five non-exclusive examples of a proxy coupled with an interest:

(d) An appointment of a proxy is revocable unless the appointment form or electronic transmission states that it is irrevocable and the appointment is coupled with an interest. Appointments coupled with an interest include the appointment of:

(1) A pledgee;

(2) A person who purchased or agreed to purchase the shares;

(3) A creditor of the corporation who extended it credit under terms requiring the appointment;

(4) An employee of the corporation whose employment contract requires the appointment; or

(5) A party to a voting agreement created under section 7.31.

PROBLEMS

1.   Do you recall the Guy Fieri hypo? Assume now that McDonald's sets a record date of June 8. Guy Fieri, who owns 120 shares of the outstanding stock of McDonald's, sells his stock to Shepherd on June 10. What is the possible relevance of MBCA § 7.22(d)?

2.   In 2015, Shepherd borrows $100,000 from First Bank and pledges his McDonald's stock as collateral for the loan. First Bank wants to be able to vote the shares and thus requires that Shepherd execute an "irrevocable proxy." Can Shepherd revoke the proxy in 2017?

2.   IN A "CLOSE CORPORATION," DECISIONS ARE GENERALLY MADE BY SHAREHOLDERS (OR BY ONE SHAREHOLDER)

We have considered decision-making in large, publicly held corporations like McDonald's—how directors are elected and what directors decide. Close corporations like Bubba's Burritos are different from publicly held corporations. As noted before, a close (or "closely held") corporation has few shareholders and its stock is not publicly traded. In the first half of this Chapter we saw one difference between close and public corporations: a court might pierce the corporate veil in close corporations. Here we focus on another difference: how decisions are made. Chapter 7 will address other characteristics of the close corporation.

a.   How Do the Shareholders of a Closely Held Corporation Like Bubba's Burritos Elect Directors?

The MBCA and other corporate codes contemplate that shareholders will elect directors in closely held corporations as well as publicly-held corporations. And concepts that you learned in connection with the election of shareholders in large, publicly-held corporations like McDonald's—(1) annual meeting and special meeting, (2) record date and record shareholders and (3) proxies—are as applicable to shareholders' election of directors in closely-held corporations like Bubba's Burritos. In addition, though, we now need to learn about (1) cumulative voting and

(2) shareholder voting agreements, which apply almost exclusively to small corporations.

(i) Cumulative Voting

Corporate lawyers (and corporate law students) need to understand the difference between "cumulative voting" and "straight voting." At a meeting to elect directors under straight voting, there is a separate election for each seat on the board. Each shareholder gets to cast her number of shares in any way she desires for each of these separate elections. Unless the articles provide otherwise, she gets one vote for each share she holds.

Assume Bubba's Burritos, Inc. has five directors and three shareholders—Capel (who owns 50 shares), Propp (who owns 30 shares), and Agee (who owns the other 10 shares). In electing the director for Seat 1 on the board, Capel has 50 votes, Propp has 30 votes and Agee has 10 votes. The candidate who receives more votes than any other is elected. As political science majors would say, then, directors are elected by plurality—the winner just needs to have more votes than anyone else, even if that is fewer than a majority of the votes cast.

In our fact pattern, Capel can elect her candidate for Seat 1—her 50 votes for that candidate will be more than Propp and Agee can muster for another candidate. In electing the director for Seat 2 on the board, the same thing will happen—Capel has 50 votes, Propp has 30, and Agee has 10. And so on for the remaining seats. A shareholder owning a majority of the stock will be able to elect every director.

With cumulative voting, however, directors are not elected seat-by-seat. There is one at-large election in which the shareholders cast votes and the top five finishers would be elected to the board (because Bubba's has five directors in this hypo). In voting, however, here the shareholders get to "cumulate." This means that each gets to multiply the number of shares she owns times the number of directors to be elected.

Under this scheme, Capel has 250 votes (50 shares multiplied by five directors to be elected at the meeting). Propp has 150 votes (30 shares multiplied by five directors to be elected at the meeting). Agee has 50 votes (10 shares multiplied by five directors to be elected at the meeting). Each shareholder can allocate her votes as she sees fit, and the top five recipients of votes are elected. If Propp and Agee vote intelligently,* cumulative voting will enable them to elect two of the five directors.

Cumulative voting applies *only* to shareholders' election of or removal of directors. Shareholders do get to vote on some matters other than electing directors. Because these other matters mainly involve

---

* Using cumulative voting "intelligently" can be complicated. *See generally* Lewis R. Mills, *The Mathematics of Cumulative Voting,* 1968 DUKE L.J. 28.

whether the corporation should undertake a fundamental corporate change, however, we will discuss the mechanics of these other votes in Chapter 9.

Moreover, not all corporations use cumulative voting even for election and removal of directors. In some states, cumulative voting is required for all corporations, sometimes by statute and sometimes, as in Arizona, by state constitution. However, in most states, by statute the corporation can choose whether to have cumulative voting.

These states split into two camps, however, over what the "default" provision should be. In other words, if the articles say nothing about cumulative voting, does it exist? In some states, cumulative voting exists unless the articles take it away. In others, cumulative voting does not exist unless the articles affirmatively grant it.

Compare MBCA § 7.28(b) with Delaware § 214.

Many corporations choose not to employ cumulative voting. Why would a corporation make this choice?

PROBLEMS

1.   Propp, Agee, and Capel come to you to incorporate Bubba's Burritos, Inc. You explain cumulative voting to them. They ask you whether you recommend cumulative voting. How do you answer their question? Would this question be easier to answer if Agee were to own 24 shares, Propp 25 shares, and Capel 51 shares?

2.   If cumulative voting is in effect, this formula calculates the number of shares needed for a shareholder to elect various numbers of directors:

$[(N{\times}S) / (D{+}1)] + 1$

N = number of directors the shareholder wants to elect

S = total number of shares voting

D = total number of directors to be chosen at the election

a)   Assume there are nine directors to be elected to the board of Bubba's Burritos, Inc., and that the corporation has 1000 outstanding shares (all of which will be voted at the meeting). Cumulative voting is in effect. You are a shareholder and want to elect Epstein to the board. How many shares do you need to ensure that Epstein will be elected to the board? How many shares do you need to elect two directors, rather than just one?

b)   Suppose now that the board consists of only three directors. How many shares would be needed to elect Epstein?

c)   What do the answers to these two hypotheticals tell you about the effect of a "staggered" board, in which only a fraction (usually one-third) of the entire board is elected each year? If you were interested in continuity on the board, why would you prefer a staggered board?

3.   Questions about removal of directors.

a)   On what basis or bases can shareholders vote to remove a director from office before her term expires? Compare Delaware § 141(k) with MBCA § 8.08. Can you see how the provisions protect cumulative voting? They provide identical bases for removal except if there is a staggered board. What is the difference if there is a staggered board?

b)   Assume that cumulative voting is *not* in effect. The corporation has 1000 outstanding shares. Suppose 600 shares are represented a meeting called to remove one of the board's three directors. (Why does that matter? Remember, we always need a quorum, and 600 would give us a quorum for this meeting because it is a majority of the 1000 entitled to vote.) Those 600 shares are then cast—400 in favor of removing the director and 200 opposed to removing the director. Is the director removed under Delaware law? Is the director removed under the MBCA?

c)   Assume that Bubba's Burritos has three directors and 3000 shares entitled to vote, and it uses cumulative voting. Two thousand shares are represented at a meeting called for the purpose of removing a director. How many of the 2000 shares represented at the meeting would have to vote for removal to effect removal under Delaware law? Under the MBCA?

d)   Some states have oddly restrictive provisions about removal of directors. In New York, for instance, a director can be removed only for cause. She can be removed without cause only if the articles (which New York calls the "certificate") provide. *See* New York § 706.

(ii) Voting Trusts and Voting Agreements

In a small, closely-held corporation, shareholders may try to "pool" their voting power so they can have more influence in the business. Historically, they could do this only through a voting trust. This is cumbersome, because it requires the shareholders to establish a true trust—to transfer the legal title of their stock to the voting trustee. Though they would no longer own legal title, they were the beneficial owners of the stock and hold all rights except the right to vote. The trustee then has a fiduciary duty to vote as instructed in the trust agreement. Voting trusts are recognized in all states. See, e.g., MBCA § 7.30, Delaware § 218(a).

Over time, shareholders tried to pool their votes in an easier way—by entering voting agreements, which are simply contracts requiring them to vote in a particular way. The next case shows how these agreements work (and also shows why they are not terribly effective in some states). In reading the case, consider the following questions:

1. Why did Mrs. Ringling and Mrs. Haley enter into the shareholder voting agreement?

2. Was anyone harmed by their agreement?

3. Who breached the agreement? Why?

4. Who won the lawsuit? What did she win? When did the shareholders' meeting occur? When did compliance with the voting agreement occur?

RINGLING BROS.-BARNUM & BAILEY COMBINED SHOWS, INC. V. RINGLING

Supreme Court of Delaware, 1947

53 A.2d 441

PEARSON, JUDGE. The Court of Chancery was called upon to review an attempted election of directors at the 1946 annual stockholders meeting of the corporate defendant. The pivotal questions concern an agreement between two of the three present stockholders, and particularly the effect of this agreement with relation to the exercise of voting rights by these two stockholders. At the time of the meeting, the corporation had outstanding 1000 shares of capital stock held as follows: 315 by petitioner Edith Conway Ringling; 315 by defendant Aubrey B. Ringling Haley (individually or as executrix and legatee of a deceased husband); and 370 by defendant John Ringling North. The purpose of the meeting was to elect the entire board of seven directors. The shares could be voted cumulatively. Mrs. Ringling asserts that by virtue of the operation of an agreement between her and Mrs. Haley, the latter was bound to vote her shares for a certain slate of directors. Mrs. Haley contends that she was not so bound for reason that the agreement was invalid, or at least revocable. * * *

The agreement then provides:

2. In exercising any voting rights to which either party may be entitled by virtue of ownership of stock, each party will consult and confer with the other and the parties will act jointly in exercising such voting rights in accordance with such agreement as they may reach with respect to any matter calling for the exercise of such voting rights.

3. In the event the parties fail to agree with respect to any matter covered by paragraph 2 above, the question in disagreement shall be submitted for arbitration to Karl D. Loos, of Washington, D. C. as arbitrator and his decision thereon shall be binding upon the parties hereto. Such arbitration shall be

exercised to the end of assuring for the respective corporation's good management and such participation therein by the members of the Ringling family as the experience, capacity and ability of each may warrant.

4.   Each of the parties hereto will enter into and execute such voting trust agreement or agreements and such other instruments as, from time to time they may deem advisable and as they may be advised by counsel are appropriate to effectuate the purposes and objects of this agreement.

5.   This agreement shall be in effect from the date hereof and shall continue in effect for a period of ten years unless sooner terminated by mutual agreement in writing by the parties hereto.

6.   The agreement of April 1934 is hereby terminated.

7.   This agreement shall be binding upon and inure to the benefit of the heirs, executors, administrators and assigns of the parties hereto respectively.

The Mr. Loos mentioned in the agreement is an attorney and has represented both parties. At the annual meetings in 1943 and the two following years, the parties voted their shares in accordance with mutual understandings arrived at as a result of discussions. In each of these years, they elected five of the seven directors. Mrs. Ringling and Mrs. Haley each had sufficient votes, independently of the other, to elect two of the seven directors. By both voting for an additional candidate, they could be sure of his election regardless of how Mr. North, the remaining stockholder, might vote.* [1]

Some weeks before the 1946 meeting, they discussed with Mr. Loos the matter of voting for directors. They were in accord that Mrs. Ringling should cast sufficient votes to elect herself and her son; and that Mrs. Haley should elect herself and her husband; but they did not agree upon a fifth director. * * * Mrs. Ringling made a demand upon Mr. Loos to act under the third paragraph of the agreement 'to arbitrate the disagreement' between her and Mrs. Haley in connection with the manner in which the stock of the two ladies should be voted. * * * Mr. Loos directed Mrs. Ringling to cast her votes:

---

*   [1] Each lady was entitled to cast 2,205 votes (since each had the cumulative voting rights of 315 shares, and there were 7 vacancies in the directorate). The sum of the votes of both is 4,410, which is sufficient to allow 882 votes for each of 5 persons. Mr. North, holding 370 shares, was entitled to cast 2,590 votes, which obviously cannot be divided so as to give to more than two candidates as many as 882 votes each. It will be observed that in order for Mrs. Ringling and Mrs. Haley to be sure to elect five directors (regardless of how Mr. North might vote) they must act together in the sense that their combined votes must be divided among five different candidates and at least one of the five must be voted for by both Mrs. Ringling and Mrs. Haley.

882 for Mrs. Ringling,

882 for her son, Robert, and

441 for a Mr. Dunn, who had been a member of the board for several years. She complied.

Mr. Loos directed that Mrs. Haley's votes be cast:

882 for Mrs. Haley,

882 for Mr. Haley, and

441 for Mr. Dunn.

Instead of complying, Mr. Haley attempted to vote his wife's shares:

1103 for Mrs. Haley, and

1102 for Mr. Haley.

Mr. North voted his shares:

864 for a Mr. Woods,

863 for a Mr. Griffin, and

863 for Mr. North.

The chairman ruled that the five candidates proposed by Mr. Loos, together with Messrs. Woods and North, were elected. The Haley-North group disputed this ruling insofar as it declared the election of Mr. Dunn; and insisted that Mr. Griffin, instead, had been elected. A director's meeting followed in which Mrs. Ringling participated after stating that she would do so 'without prejudice to her position that the directors' meeting was not properly held.' Mr. Dunn and Mr. Griffin, although each was challenged by an opposing faction, attempted to join in voting as directors for different slates of officers. Soon after the meeting, Mrs. Ringling instituted this proceeding.

The Vice Chancellor determined that the agreement to vote in accordance with the direction of Mr. Loos was valid as a "stock pooling agreement" with lawful objects and purposes, and that it was not in violation of any public policy of this state. He held that where the arbitrator acts under the agreement and one party refuses to comply with his direction, "the Agreement constitutes the willing party * * * an implied agent possessing the irrevocable proxy of the recalcitrant party for the purpose of casting the particular vote." It was ordered that a new election be held before a master, with the direction that the master should recognize and give effect to the agreement if its terms were properly invoked. * * *

We come now to defendants' contention that the voting provisions are illegal and revocable. They say that the courts of this state have definitely established the doctrine 'that there can be no agreement, or any device whatsoever, by which the voting power of stock of a Delaware corporation may be irrevocably separated from the ownership of the stock, except by an agreement which complies with Section 18' of the Corporation Law, Rev.Code 1935, and except by a proxy coupled with an interest. * * * The statute reads, in part, as follows:

> Sec. 18. Fiduciary Stockholders; Voting Power of; Voting Trusts:—Persons holding stock in a fiduciary capacity shall be entitled to vote the shares so held, and persons whose stock is pledged shall be entitled to vote, unless in the transfer by the pledgor on the books of the corporation he shall have expressly empowered the pledgee to vote thereon, in which case only the pledgee, or his proxy may represent said stock and vote thereon.
>
> One or more stockholders may by agreement in writing deposit capital stock of an original issue with or transfer capital stock to any person or persons, or corporation or corporations authorized to act as trustee, for the purpose of vesting in said person or persons, corporation or corporations, who may be designated Voting Trustee or Voting Trustees, the right to vote thereon for any period of time determined by such agreement, not exceeding ten years, upon the terms and conditions stated in such agreement. Such agreement may contain any other lawful provisions not inconsistent with said purpose. Said Voting Trustees may vote upon the stock so issued or transferred during the period in such agreement specified; stock standing in the names of such Voting Trustees may be voted either in person or by proxy, and in voting said stock, such Voting Trustees shall incur no responsibility as stockholder, trustee or otherwise, except for their own individual malfeasance.

In our view, neither the cases nor the statute sustain the rule for which the defendants contend. Their sweeping formulation would impugn well-recognized means by which a shareholder may effectively confer his voting rights upon others while retaining various other rights. For example, defendants' rule would apparently not permit holders of voting stock to confer upon stockholders of another class, by the device of an amendment of the certificate of incorporation, the exclusive right to vote during periods when dividends are not paid on stock of the latter class. The broad prohibitory meaning which defendants find in Section 18 seems inconsistent with their concession that proxies coupled with an interest may be irrevocable, for the statute contains nothing about such proxies. The statute authorizes, among other things, the deposit or transfer of stock in trust for a specified purpose, namely, "vesting" in the transferee "the right to vote thereon" for a limited period; and prescribes numerous requirements in this connection. Accordingly, it seems reasonable to infer that to establish the relationship and accomplish the purpose which the statute authorizes, its requirements must be complied with. But the statute does not purport to deal with agreements whereby shareholders attempt to bind each other as to how they shall vote their shares. Various forms of such pooling agreements, as they are sometimes called, have been held valid and have been distinguished from voting trusts. Generally speaking, a shareholder may exercise wide liberality of judgment in the matter of voting, and it is not objectionable that his motives may be for personal profit, or determined by whims or caprice, so long as he violates no duty owed his fellow shareholders. The ownership of voting stock imposes no legal duty to vote at all. A group of shareholders may, without impropriety, vote their respective shares so as to obtain advantages of concerted action. They may lawfully contract with each other to vote in the future in such way as they, or a majority of their group, from time to time determine. Reasonable provisions for cases of failure of the group to reach a determination because of an even division in their ranks seem unobjectionable. The provision here for submission to the arbitrator is plainly designed as a deadlock-breaking measure, and the arbitrator's decision cannot be enforced unless at least one of the parties (entitled to cast one-half of their combined votes) is willing that it be enforced. We find the provision reasonable. It does not appear that the agreement enables the parties to take any unlawful advantage of the outside shareholder, or of any other person. It offends no rule of law or public policy of this state of which we are aware. * * *

The Court of Chancery may, in a review of an election, reject votes of a registered shareholder. The votes representing Mrs. Haley's shares should not be counted. Since no infirmity in Mr. North's voting has been demonstrated, his right to recognition of what he did at the meeting should be considered in granting any relief to Mrs. Ringling; for her rights arose under a contract to which Mr. North was not a party. With this in mind, we have concluded that the election should not be declared invalid, but that effect should be given to a rejection of the votes representing Mrs. Haley's shares. No other relief seems appropriate in this proceeding. With respect to the election of directors, the return of the inspectors should be corrected to show a rejection of Mrs. Haley's votes, and to declare the election of the six persons for whom Mr. North and Mrs. Ringling voted.

This leaves one vacancy in the directorate. The question of what to do about such a vacancy was not considered by the court below and has not been argued here. For this reason, and because an election of directors at the 1947 annual meeting (which presumably will be held in the near future) may make a determination of the question unimportant, we shall not decide it on this appeal. If a decision of the point appears important to the parties, any of them may apply to raise it in the Court of Chancery, after the mandate of this court is received there.

An order should be entered directing a modification of the order of the Court of Chancery in accordance with this opinion.

QUESTIONS

1.   Did all of the shareholders of the circus enter into the voting agreement? Why did the shareholders enter into the voting agreement in *Ringling*?

2.   Who was the real winner at the end of this litigation (other than the lawyers)?

3.   Who would have been the real winner at the end of this litigation if the MBCA had governed? *Compare* Delaware § 218(c) *with* MBCA § 7.31.

4.   The *Ringling* decision mentions the "voting trust"? Was the agreement in the *Ringling* case a "voting trust"? Would the result in *Ringling* have been different if the parties had established a voting trust with Loos as the trustee? In answering, see Delaware § 218(a) and MBCA § 7.30. Can you articulate the differences between a shareholders' voting trust and a shareholders' voting agreement?

_____

Remember proxies? We saw above that a shareholder can appoint someone to be her proxy for shareholder voting. But we also said that a director could not appoint someone to be her proxy for director voting. The reason: directors owe non-delegable fiduciary duties to the corporation, which require them to use their individual judgment in considering board matters. For the same reason, directors cannot enter into voting agreement or voting trusts tying their hands on directorial matters. The next case considers the difference between a shareholders' voting agreement that crossed the line and became an improper directors' voting agreement. In reading the case, consider the following:

1.   Who were the contracting parties?

2.   What were the terms of their deal?

3.   What the important differences are between the enforceable voting agreement in Ringling and the unenforceable agreement in this next case?

MCQUADE V. STONEHAM

New York Court of Appeals, 1934
189 N.E. 234

POUND, CHIEF JUDGE. The action is brought to compel specific performance of an agreement between the parties, entered into to secure the control of National Exhibition Company, also called the Baseball Club (New York Nationals or "Giants"). This was one of Stoneham's enterprises which used the New York polo grounds for its home games. McGraw was manager of the Giants. McQuade was at the time the contract was entered into a city magistrate. * * *

Defendant Stoneham became the owner of 1,306 shares, or a majority of the stock of National Exhibition Company. Plaintiff and defendant McGraw each purchased 70 shares of his stock. Plaintiff paid Stoneham $50,338.10 for the stock he purchased. As a part of the transaction, the agreement in question was entered into. It was dated May 21, 1919. Some of its pertinent provisions are:

VIII. The parties hereto will use their best endeavors for the purpose of continuing as directors of said Company and as officers thereof the following:

Directors:

Charles A. Stoneham,

John J. McGraw,

Francis X. McQuade

—with the right to the party of the first part [Stoneham] to name all additional directors as he sees fit:

Officers:

Charles A. Stoneham, President,

John J. McGraw, Vice-President,

Francis X. McQuade, Treasurer.

IX. No salaries are to be paid to any of the above officers or directors, except as follows:

President $45,000
Vice-President 7,500
Treasurer 7,500

X. There shall be no change in said salaries, no change in the amount of capital, or the number of shares, no change or amendment of the by-laws of the corporation or any matters regarding the policy of the business of the corporation or any matters which may in anywise affect, endanger or interfere with the rights of minority stockholders, excepting upon the mutual and unanimous consent of all of the parties hereto. * * *

XIV. This agreement shall continue and remain in force so long as the parties or any of them or the representative of any, own the stock referred to in this agreement, to wit, the party of the first part, 1,166 shares, the party of the second part 70 shares and the party of the third part 70 shares, except as may otherwise appear by this agreement. * * *

In pursuance of this contract Stoneham became president and McGraw vice president of the corporation. McQuade became treasurer. In June 1925, his salary was increased to $10,000 a year. He continued to act until May 2, 1928, when Leo J. Bondy was elected to succeed him. The board of directors consisted of seven men. The four outside of the parties hereto were selected by Stoneham and he had complete control over them. At the meeting of May 2, 1928, Stoneham and McGraw refrained from voting, McQuade voted for himself, and the other four voted for Bondy. Defendants did not keep their agreement with McQuade to use their best efforts to continue him as treasurer. On the contrary, he was dropped with their entire acquiescence. At the next stockholders' meeting he was dropped as a director although they might have elected him.

The courts below have refused to order the reinstatement of McQuade, but have given him damages for wrongful discharge, with a right to sue for future damages.

The cause for dropping McQuade was due to the falling out of friends. McQuade and Stoneham had disagreed. The trial court has found in substance that their numerous quarrels and disputes did not affect the orderly and efficient administration of the business of the corporation; that plaintiff was removed because he had antagonized the dominant Stoneham by persisting in challenging his power over the corporate treasury and for no misconduct on his part. The court also finds that plaintiff was removed by Stoneham for protecting the corporation and its minority stockholders. We will assume that Stoneham put him out when he might have retained him, merely in order to get rid of him.

Defendants say that the contract in suit was void because the directors held their office charged with the duty to act for the corporation according to their best judgment and that any contract which compels a director to vote to keep any particular person in office and at a stated salary is illegal. Directors are the exclusive executive representatives of the corporation, charged with administration of its internal affairs and the management and use of its assets. They manage the business of the corporation. * * *

Although it has been held that an agreement among stockholders whereby it is attempted to divest the directors of their power to discharge an unfaithful employee of the corporation is illegal as against public policy, it must be equally true that the stockholders may not, by agreement among themselves, control the directors in the exercise of the judgment vested in them by virtue of their office to elect officers and fix salaries. Their motives may not be questioned so long as their acts are legal. The bad faith or the improper motives of the parties does not change the rule. Directors may not by agreements entered into as stockholders abrogate their independent judgment.

Stockholders may, of course, combine to elect directors. That rule is well settled. As Holmes, C. J., pointedly said (Brightman v. Bates, 55 N. E. 809, 811 [1900]): "If stockholders want to make their power felt, they must unite. There is no reason why a majority should not agree to keep together." The power to unite is, however, limited to the election of directors and is not extended to contracts whereby limitations are placed on the power of directors to manage the business of the corporation by the selection of agents at defined salaries.

The minority shareholders whose interests McQuade says he has been punished for protecting, are not, aside from himself, complaining about his discharge. He is not acting for the corporation or for them in this action. It is impossible to see how the corporation has been injured by the substitution of Bondy as treasurer in place of McQuade. * * *

It is urged that we should pay heed to the morals and manners of the market place to sustain this agreement and that we should hold that its violation gives rise to a cause of action for damages rather than base our decision on any outworn notions of public policy. Public policy is a dangerous guide in determining the validity of a contract and courts should not interfere lightly with the freedom of competent parties to make their own contracts. We do not close our eyes to the fact that such agreements, tacitly or openly arrived at, are not uncommon, especially in close corporations where the stockholders are doing business for convenience under a corporate organization. We know that majority stockholders, united in voting trusts, effectively manage the business of a corporation by choosing trustworthy directors to reflect their policies in the corporate management. Nor are we unmindful that McQuade has, so the court has found, been shabbily treated as a purchaser of stock from Stoneham. We have said: "A trustee is held to something stricter than the morals of the market place" (Meinhard v. Salmon, 249 N. Y. 458, 464 [1928]), but Stoneham and McGraw were not trustees for McQuade as an individual. Their duty was to the corporation and its stockholders, to be exercised according to their unrestricted lawful judgment. They were under no legal obligation to deal righteously with McQuade if it was against public policy to do so.

The courts do not enforce mere moral obligations, nor legal ones either, unless someone seeks to establish rights which may be waived by custom and for convenience. We are constrained by authority to hold that a contract is illegal and void so far as it precludes the board of directors, at the risk of incurring legal liability, from changing officers, salaries, or policies or retaining individuals in office, except by consent of the contracting parties. On the whole, such a holding is probably preferable to one which would open the courts to pass on the motives of directors in the lawful exercise of their trust.

A further reason for reversal exists. At the time the contract was made the plaintiff was a city magistrate. * * *

The Inferior Criminal Courts Act (Laws of 1910, c. 659, as amended) provides that no "city magistrate shall engage in any other business." * * *

The judgment of the Appellate Division and that of the Trial Term should be reversed and the complaint dismissed, with costs in all courts.

QUESTIONS AND NOTE

1.   *McQuade* sets out the traditional model of corporate governance: the board of directors is the locus of management power and shareholders cannot intrude upon that power. Would the court have decided this case differently if the contract had been between McQuade and the National Exhibition Company, and that contract had provided that McQuade would serve as treasurer of the company for five years?

2.   Would the court have decided this case differently if McQuade, Stoneham, and McGraw were the only stockholders of the corporation and the agreement provided that McQuade would be re-elected as treasurer so long as he "was faithful, efficient and competent"?

3.   The New York Court of Appeals had misgivings about some of the language it used in *McQuade*. Just two years later, in *Clark v. Dodge*, 199 N.E. 641 (N.Y. 1936), that court upheld an agreement and stated: "The broad statements in the *McQuade* opinion, applicable to the facts there, should be confined to the facts there." Such statements reflected uneasiness with the traditional corporate governance model, at least as applied to close corporations.

Today, the limitations of *McQuade* can be avoided completely. Many states, including New York, have passed statutes that allow shareholders in small, closely-held corporations to set up management as they see fit. These statutes constitute one of the most profound developments in business law over recent decades. They are so important that they deserve their own section in this book, which is next.

b.   Statutes Allowing Direct Shareholder Management in Close Corporations

Close corporations—those with few shareholders and no public market for the stock—are true corporations. They are formed in accordance with corporation statutes and are governed, in general, by the corporate law we learn in this book. In some ways, though, close corporations are treated differently from "ordinary" corporations. Some of these distinctions are the result of case law—such as piercing the corporate veil, which we discussed in Part A of this chapter. Some distinctions are statutory.

In most states today, legislation allows great flexibility in setting up the management of a close corporation. They permit what we will call "shareholder management agreements" (SMA). These are to be distinguished from shareholder voting agreements, which we saw in *Ringling*. Shareholder voting agreements address how shareholders will vote their shares on particular matters. In contrast, shareholder management agreements determine how the corporation will be run.

QUESTIONS

MBCA § 7.32 and similar statutes permit what we will call SMAs. People steeped in the tradition of *McQuade v. Stoneham* will find statutes like MBCA stunning. Why? Because they permit *direct control of a corporation by shareholders (or others)!* Study the portions of MBCA § 7.32 set forth below and answer the following questions.

MBCA § 7.32

(a) An agreement among the shareholders that complies with this section is effective among the shareholders and the corporation even though it is inconsistent with one or more other provisions of this Act in that it:

(1) eliminates the board of directors or restricts the discretion or powers of the board of directors;

(2) governs the authorization or making of distributions whether or not in proportion to ownership of shares, subject to the limitations in section 6.40;

(3) establishes who shall be directors or officers of the corporation, or their terms of office or manner of selection or removal;

* * *

(6) transfers to one or more shareholders or other persons all or part of the authority to exercise the corporate powers or to manage the business and affairs of the corporation * * *

* * *

(b) An agreement authorized by this section shall be:

(1) set forth (A) in the articles of incorporation or bylaws and approved by all persons who are shareholders at the time of the agreement or (B) in a written agreement that is signed by all persons who are shareholders at the time of the agreement and is made known to the corporation;

(2) subject to amendment only by all persons who are shareholders at the time of the amendment, unless that agreement provides otherwise; and

(3) valid for 10 years, unless the agreement provides otherwise.

(c) The existence of an agreement authorized by this section shall be noted conspicuously on the front or back of each certificate for outstanding shares or on the information statement required by section 6.26(b). * * * The failure to note the existence of the agreement on the certificate or information statement shall not affect the validity of the agreement or any action taken pursuant to it. * * *

(d) An agreement authorized by this section shall cease to be effective when the corporation becomes a public corporation. * * *

1.   What part of § 7.32 ensures that SMAs can be entered only in close corporations?

2.   Can a SMA provide for elimination of a board of directors, with managerial power to be vested in shareholders? Can managerial power be vested in a third-party manager to be hired by shareholders?

3.   Can a SMA provide that the corporation's managers will owe no fiduciary duties to the corporation? We discuss these important fiduciary duties (typically owed by directors to the corporation) in Chapter 6.

4.   If a SMA can eliminate the board of directors and vest management power in shareholders, who will owe fiduciary duties to the corporation?

5.   In what two ways can a SMA be set up under MBCA § 7.32?

6.   As you just saw, either of the two routes for setting up an SMA under the MBCA requires the unanimous consent of the existing shareholders. Delaware has a similar provision at Delaware § 351. But read Delaware § 350. How is it even more remarkable than MBCA § 7.32 or Delaware § 351?

7.   Could a SMA have changed the result in *McQuade*?

———————

The next case considers the effect of the Maine statute on an agreement between two shareholders that the corporation could not pay either of them a salary. In reading it, please consider the following questions:

1.   Was there an oral agreement that the corporation would not pay a salary to either Villar or Kernan?

2.   Was that agreement breached? By whom: Kernan? The corporation? Both? Whom is Villar suing?

3.   Were Villar and Kernan directors of the corporation when they made that agreement? Is that relevant?

VILLAR V. KERNAN

Supreme Court of Maine, 1997
695 A.2d 1221

DANA, JUSTICE. The United States District Court for the District of Maine has certified the following questions of state law to this Court:

(1) Does Maine law preclude an action for breach of an oral contract between two shareholders of a closely held corporation prohibiting their receipt of salaries from the corporation?

(2) If the answer to the first question is "no," what factors are to be considered in determining whether specific performance is available to take an oral contract outside the statute of frauds provision for contracts not to be performed within one year?

The United States District Court has prepared a statement of findings of facts. These facts disclose that in 1988 Frederick Villar and Peter Kernan agreed to go into the brick oven pizza business. Villar was responsible for operating the new business and Kernan assumed responsibility for the business's finances. When Villar and Kernan incorporated their business as Ricetta's, Inc., Villar received 49 percent of the shares and Kernan received 51 percent. According to Kernan, the parties agreed that "there would never be salaries. In other words, as owners [they] would never get salaries, just distribution." At some point Ronald Stephan, the manager of the restaurant, became a two percent shareholder of Ricetta's, Inc., obtaining one percent from both Kernan and Villar.

The parties' pizza restaurant succeeded as a business but their relationship deteriorated. Villar and Stephan attempted to buy Kernan out, but the buyout was unsuccessful and ultimately Stephan became allied with Kernan.

In March 1994 Kernan entered into a "so-called consulting agreement" with Ricetta's. The agreement provided for automatic payments to him of $2,000 per week. The agreement was ratified at a shareholders' and board of directors' meeting at which Villar was not present. Kernan's obligations pursuant to the agreement were not specified, but the corporation's rights were restricted. For example, Kernan's compensation could be increased but not decreased by a majority vote of the board of directors, and his services could be terminated only for criminal violation involving dishonesty, fraud, breach of trust, or for willful engagement in misconduct in the performance of his duties. Pursuant to the agreement Kernan received $90,000 in consulting fees in 1994 and $24,000 in early 1995.

In May 1995 Villar filed a complaint in the United States District Court asserting six counts against four defendants. On Kernan's motion for a judgment on the pleadings or for a summary judgment, the court dismissed all of Villar's claims except the breach of contract claim against Kernan. A nonjury trial on Villar's breach of contract claim was held in August 1996. The court concluded that there was an oral agreement between Villar and Kernan that prohibited Kernan from receiving a salary from Ricetta's. The court determined that unless 13–A M.R.S.A. § 618 (1981)* **[1]** precluded the enforcement of an oral shareholder

---

    *   **[1]** 13–A M.R.S.A. § 618 provides:

Agreements among shareholders respecting management of corporation and relations of shareholders

1. No written agreement, whether contained in the articles of incorporation or bylaws or in a written side agreement, and which relates to any phase of the affairs of the corporation, including, but not limited to, the following:

A. Management of the business of the corporation; or

B. Declaration and payment of dividends or division of profits; or

C. Who shall be officers or directors, or both, of the corporation; or

D. Voting requirements, including requirements for unanimous voting of shareholders or directors; or

E. Employment of shareholders by the corporation; or

F. Arbitration of issues as to which the stockholders are deadlocked in voting power or as to which the directors are deadlocked and the shareholders are unable to break the deadlock; or

G. Which purports to treat the affairs of the corporation as if it were a partnership and the shareholders as if they were partners,

shall be deemed invalid because the agreement contains any such provision,

or because it limits or restricts the powers or discretion of the directors of the corporation, or because it transfers to one or more shareholders or to one or more persons or corporations to be selected by him or them all or part of the management of the corporation, if the following conditions are satisfied:

A. Either the agreement is set forth, or its existence is clearly referred to, in the articles of incorporation, and if in an amendment of the articles, such amendment was adopted by the unanimous vote of all outstanding shares, whether or not entitled to vote by the provisions of the articles; or the agreement has been expressly assented to in writing by all shareholders of the corporation, whether or not entitled to vote; and

B. Subsequent to the making of the agreement or its adoption in the articles or bylaws, shares are transferred or issued only to persons who have notice or actual knowledge thereof, or assent in writing thereto.

2. Notwithstanding a failure to satisfy the conditions set out in subsection 1, paragraphs A and B, such an agreement shall be valid and enforceable between the parties thereto, and their assignees and successors who have notice thereof, unless it is affirmatively shown that its enforcement would be prejudicial to the rights of third parties who intervene in objection to its enforcement.

3. To the extent that it contains provisions which would not be valid but for subsection 1, an agreement authorized by subsection 1 shall be valid only so long as no shares of the corporation are traded on any national securities exchange or regularly quoted in any over-the-counter market by one or more members of a national or affiliated securities association.

4. The text of any agreement authorized by subsection 1 shall be set forth in full, or a conspicuous reference shall be made to the agreement, upon the face or back of each certificate for shares issued by the corporation.

5. A transferee of shares in a corporation whose shareholders have entered into an agreement authorized by subsection 1 shall be deemed to have notice thereof if the text of the agreement was set forth, or if the agreement was conspicuously noted, on the face or back of the certificate for such shares when he took them.

6. The effect of an agreement authorized by subsection 1 shall be to relieve the director or directors of, and to impose upon the shareholders consenting to the agreement, the liability for managerial acts or omissions that is imposed by law upon directors to the extent that and so long as the discretion or powers of the directors in their management of corporate affairs is controlled by any such provision.

agreement, the agreement could be enforceable in equity despite the statute of frauds. Finding no controlling precedent in Maine regarding section 618 or the factors the court should consider when determining whether enforcement of an oral agreement within the statute of frauds is appropriate, the court certified the two questions. We answer the first question in the affirmative and, therefore, do not address the second question. * * *

Section 618 operates to validate agreements that would be unenforceable under traditional notions of acceptable corporate practice.* [2] In short, the statute provides that written agreements between shareholders are enforceable even if they (1) relate to a phase of affairs of the corporation, such as the management of the corporation, payment of dividends, or employment of shareholders, (2) restrict director discretion, or (3) transfer management duties to shareholders, as long as such agreements satisfy certain conditions. 13–A M.R.S.A. S 618(1). Specifically, the agreement must be included in the articles of incorporation or expressly assented to by all shareholders, and after the agreement is made anyone who acquires shares must have notice or actual knowledge of the agreement. § 618(1)(A),(B). Even if those specific requirements are not met, however, the agreement may still be enforceable between the parties to the agreement if the rights of any third parties who intervene and object to the enforcement of the agreement are not prejudiced. § 618(2).

Kernan contends that the language in the first sentence of section 618(1) implies that shareholder agreements validated by section 618 must be in writing. We agree. Because the language of subsection (1) refers to written agreements between shareholders, stating that "[n]o written agreement will be invalid . . .", it is logical to conclude that the Legislature intended to validate only written agreements that meet the requirements of the statute. To conclude otherwise would nullify the word "written" in the opening sentence of that subsection.

Villar argues that the parties' agreement is simply an agreement between shareholders that does not affect the corporation and that it need not rely on section 618's validation provision for its validity. We disagree. Their agreement affects the corporation's affairs because it effectively prohibits the corporation from hiring Kernan as a consultant. We are not persuaded by Villar's characterization of the agreement, asserted at oral argument, as one that would allow the corporation to hire Kernan but

---

*   [2] * * * Section 618 was enacted at a time when shareholder agreements were viewed by courts as unenforceable infringements on traditional corporate structure and control. Other states were also enacting laws that ensured such agreements would be enforced by the courts. See also Model Business Corporation Act § 7.32, 2 Model Business Corporation Act Annotated 7–245 (1996) ("In the past, various types of shareholder agreements were invalidated by courts for a variety of reasons. . . . Rather than relying on further uncertain and sporadic development of the law in the courts, [the validation provision of] section 7.32 . . . adds an important element of predictability. . . .").

then require him to pay Villar half of the salary that he received from the corporation. Such an interpretation would effectively rewrite the parties' agreement.

Kernan contends that the agreement at issue falls within the reach of section 618's validation provision because it relates to the affairs of the corporation by affecting the employment of shareholders. We agree. The potential scope of the validation provision of section 618 is broad. It states that an agreement is not invalid because it "relates to any phase of affairs of the corporation, including, but not limited to . . . [e]mployment of shareholders by the corporation. . . ." § 618(1)(E). The agreement between Villar and Kernan relates to the corporation's affairs because it prohibits Kernan from receiving a salary and effectively precludes his employment by the corporation. In addition, the agreement may affect the declaration and payment of dividends because money that is not distributed to Kernan in a salary may be distributed as dividends among the three shareholders. § 618(1)(B). Because the agreement must rely on section 618 for its validity and falls within the validating provision of section 618(1), it must meet the section's specifications and therefore must be in writing to be enforceable.* **[3]**

Subsection (2) of section 618 does not allow enforcement of the agreement at issue here because that subsection does not excuse the requirement in subsection (1) that the agreement be in writing to be validated. Subsection (2) provides that "[n]otwithstanding a failure to satisfy the conditions set out in subsection 1, paragraphs A and B, such an agreement shall be valid and enforceable between the parties thereto . . . unless it is affirmatively shown that its enforcement would be prejudicial to the rights of third parties. . . ." Although subsection (2) reflects an intent to allow enforcement of shareholder agreements despite their failure to comply with the formalities of subsection (1), the language of the subsection does not excuse the writing requirement specified in the first sentence of that subsection. Thus, only written agreements that fail to meet the requirements of subsection (1) may be enforceable among the parties to the agreement by virtue of subsection (2).

Because we conclude that to be enforceable section 618 requires a shareholder agreement prohibiting the shareholders' receipt of salaries from the corporation to be in writing, we answer the first certified question in the affirmative and do not answer the second question.

---

* **[3]** We do not interpret section 618 to provide only a safe harbor for certain agreements that would be invalid pursuant to other provisions of the Maine Business Corporation Act or the common law. Rather, we conclude that an agreement that affects the corporation in a way addressed by section 618(1) must meet the specifications of 618 to be valid, and we need not first determine whether the agreement would be invalid pursuant to the Act or the common law.* * *

QUESTIONS AND NOTES

1.   What was the agreement "that would be unenforceable under traditional notions of acceptable corporate practice"? Why did it violate traditional notions?

2.   Would the court have decided this case differently if the agreement between Villar and Kernan had been in writing?

3.   What can Villar do now? He is a shareholder in a corporation that has only a few shareholders, and he has no control over that corporation's decisions. And he has to watch while his erstwhile friend gets paid over $100,000 per year, in violation of their agreement. He might try to have the corporation dissolved, but, as we will see in Chapter 9, that is tough to do if the corporation is operating at a profit.

4.   Suppose the pizza business in *Villar* had been a partnership instead of a corporation. What could Villar do now? When Villar and Kernan went to a lawyer to set up their business, what should the lawyer have discussed with them about the pros and cons of setting up as a partnership versus a corporation?

5.   Remember cumulative voting? There were only three shareholders in the pizza business in *Villar*. There were three directors, and Mr. Villar was not one. Why can we deduce from these facts that cumulative voting was not in effect?

6.   How are SMAs under MBCA § 7.32 different from shareholder "voting agreements" under MBCA § 7.31?

CHAPTER 6

WHAT DUTIES DO CORPORATE DECISIONMAKERS OWE TO THE CORPORATION?

■ ■ ■

A. WHAT ARE THE DECISIONMAKERS' BUSINESS RESPONSIBILITIES TO THE CORPORATION?

The pressures on publicly-held companies—and the executives who run them—are quite different from those experienced by the management of privately-held businesses, such as close corporations.

As we have discussed before, it is management's job to create value for the owners. The owners of a corporation are of course its shareholders. In privately-held companies, owners and managers are often the same people; most, if not all, shares are usually held by the firm's senior management. In the less common situations in which privately-held companies have outside professional managers running the business, shareholders usually constitute a majority of the board. In all these situations, the owners of the company know intimately what is going on in the business, and they are usually responsible for making and executing the important decisions that influence the enterprise's success or failure. Thus, managers of privately held companies are worried little about the short-term implications of their actions, or about the way in which outsiders perceive those decisions. Indeed, it is doubtful that many outsiders know—or care—about what the company or its management is up to.

Publicly-held companies, however, are different for a variety of reasons. First, their financial results are public. Federal securities laws and the rules of the various stock exchanges require public companies to announce and explain any material actions or issues as they occur. They also require companies to issue annual and quarterly reports on their financial performance. Second, because tremendous amounts of money can be made (or lost) by trading stocks, there is an entire industry devoted to analyzing and opining on the attractiveness of the stock of every publicly traded company—it is worth a lot of money to be right just a little bit more than average. Most stockholders and analysts do not really know—the way management or a board member knows—what is actually going on inside a company. Thus, they rely on what is measurable and observable—such as patterns in the company's short-term earnings—to make their judgments and pronouncements about the relative merit of the stock. Third, most of the shares are owned by financial investors and mutual funds.

As of December 31, 2013, financial institutions and mutual funds owned 65% of the outstanding stock of McDonald's.* The largest "owner" of McDonald's stock was Vanguard Group, Inc. (57,759,625 shares, which comprised 5.84% of the outstanding stock.)†

The word "owner" appears in quotes because, of course, Vanguard doesn't really own the stock. It controlled it, and made the decisions to buy and sell, but the millions of people who own Vanguard's mutual funds were really the shares' ultimate owners. Still, Vanguard—which attracts investors based upon the performance of its mutual funds relative to others—has a strong incentive to make good decisions about if, and when, to sell Vanguard's McDonald's stock. Each difference of $1 per share is worth almost $58 million. Pretty soon, those millions add up to real money.

Because McDonald's has so much outstanding stock, large investment banks that trade stock for clients employ equity research analysts to follow McDonald's business activities and make regular reports about whether to buy or sell McDonald's stock. The investment banks then make these research analysts' reports available—for free to big investors like Vanguard—in the hope that these investors will recognize the value of this research by using their investment bank to buy and sell the stock, thus earning trading commissions for the investment bank. In addition, Vanguard and the other mutual fund firms have their own analysts who follow the industry, visit the company, talk to management, and generally try to figure out what is happening before anyone else. These private analysts don't publish their work, because their firms are the only ones who benefit from it.

Do the billions of dollars that are spent on investment research and analysis do any good? Do people who use research and analysis to pick stocks earn higher returns? Surprisingly, many financial economists, citing the "Efficient Capital Market Hypothesis," think that the answer is generally no. Often, a diversified group of stocks picked at random produces as good a return as the stocks picked by the experts. That is, picking stocks by throwing darts at the stock page of a newspaper often produces as much success as the experts' choices. The substantial fees that experts charge can tip the balance further against the experts. Indeed, this is a major reason that index funds, which have low costs

---

* http://finance.yahoo.com/q/mh?s=MCD+Major+Holders.
† Id.

because they employ no expert stock-choosers, have been so successful over the past decade.

B. WHAT ARE THE DECISIONMAKERS' LEGAL RESPONSIBILITIES TO THE CORPORATION?

Directors and other business decisionmakers are fiduciaries. A fiduciary is someone who is acting in the interest of someone else. For example, a trustee acts on behalf of beneficiaries. Similarly, directors act on behalf of the corporation.

In managing a business, managers owe (1) a duty of care, (2) a duty of loyalty, and (3) a duty of good faith. (We will see that some courts speak of good faith not as a separate duty but as a component of the duty of loyalty.) Courts developed these duties through the common law. Increasingly, states are codifying the duties in general and as applied to specific factual situations. For example, MBCA § 8.30(a) and (b) contain general statements of the classic fiduciary obligations owed by directors to their corporation.

MBCA § 8.30   Standards of Conduct for Directors

(a) Each member of the board of directors, when discharging the duties of a director, shall act: (1) in good faith, and (2) in a manner the director reasonably believes to be in the best interests of the corporation.

(b) The members of the board of directors or a committee of the board, when becoming informed in connection with their decision-making function or devoting attention to their oversight function, shall discharge their duties with the care that a person in a like position would reasonably believe appropriate under similar circumstances.

Which subsection reflects the duty of care? Which reflects the duty of loyalty?

Before looking at the obligations in detail, we emphasize that the directors owe these duties *to the corporation*. Some courts occasionally say that the duties are owed as well to the corporation's shareholders. Such statements should be understood, however, to refer to the shareholders collectively, and not individually. This is another way of saying that the duties run to the corporation. Because the duties are owed to the corporation, breach of duty causes harm to the corporation. The entity may then sue the breaching director for breach of duty. In § D, we will see that shareholders may be able to vindicate this corporate claim if the corporation does not assert its claim.

1. DUTY OF CARE

Roberts becomes a director of Bubba's Burritos, Inc. He convinces Shepherd and the other directors that Bubba's Burritos should sell fragels* as well as burritos. It turns out to be a really bad idea. The corporation loses big bucks because of it. Can Roberts, Shepherd, and the other directors be held liable for their bad decision? If so, to whom?

The next case considered a similar question. In addressing the case, please consider the following:

1.   Who is Shlensky and why does he care whether the Cubs play baseball at night?

2.   Was the Cubs' decision not to play baseball at night a bad decision?

3.   The last time the Cubs won the World Series, was electric lighting of the playing field an option?

SHLENSKY V. WRIGLEY
Illinois Court of Appeals, 1968
237 N.E.2d 776

SULLIVAN, JUSTICE. This is an appeal from a dismissal of plaintiff's amended complaint on motion of the defendants. The action was a stockholders' derivative suit against the directors for negligence and mismanagement. The corporation was also made a defendant. Plaintiff [Shlensky] sought damages and an order that defendants cause the installation of lights in Wrigley Field and the scheduling of night baseball games.

Plaintiff is a minority stockholder of defendant corporation, Chicago National League Ball Club, (Inc.), a Delaware corporation with its principal place of business in Chicago, Illinois. Defendant corporation owns and operates the major league professional baseball team known as the Chicago Cubs. The corporation also engages in the operation of Wrigley Field, the Cubs' home park, the concessionaire sales during Cubs' home games, television and radio broadcasts of Cubs' home games, the leasing of the field for football games and other events and receives its share, as visiting team, of admission moneys from games played in other National League stadia. The individual defendants are directors of the Cubs and have served for varying periods of years. Defendant Philip K. Wrigley is also president of the corporation and owner of approximately 80% of the stock therein.

Plaintiff alleges that since night baseball was first played in 1935 nineteen of the twenty major league teams have scheduled night games.

---

* http://www.examiner.com/review/md-bagel-fragel-what-is-a-fragel-let-s-find-out.

In 1966, out of a total of 1620 games in the major leagues, 932 were played at night. Plaintiff alleges that every member of the major leagues, other than the Cubs, scheduled substantially all of its home games in 1966 at night, exclusive of opening days, Saturdays, Sundays, holidays and days prohibited by league rules. Allegedly this has been done for the specific purpose of maximizing attendance and thereby maximizing revenue and income.

The Cubs, in the years 1961–65, sustained operating losses from its direct baseball operations. Plaintiff attributes those losses to inadequate attendance at Cubs' home games. He concludes that if the directors continue to refuse to install lights at Wrigley Field and schedule night baseball games, the Cubs will continue to sustain comparable losses and its financial condition will continue to deteriorate. * * *

Plaintiff alleges that, except for the year 1963, attendance at Cubs' home games has been substantially below that at their road games, many of which were played at night.

Plaintiff compares attendance at Cubs' games with that of the Chicago White Sox, an American League club, whose weekday games were generally played at night. The weekend attendance figures for the two teams was similar; however, the White Sox week-night games drew many more patrons than did the Cubs' weekday games.

Plaintiff alleges that the funds for the installation of lights can be readily obtained through financing and the cost of installation would be far more than offset and recaptured by increased revenues and incomes resulting from the increased attendance.

Plaintiff further alleges that defendant Wrigley has refused to install lights, not because of interest in the welfare of the corporation but because of his personal opinions "that baseball is a 'daytime sport' and that the installation of lights and night baseball games will have a deteriorating effect upon the surrounding neighborhood." It is alleged that he has admitted that he is not interested in whether the Cubs would benefit financially from such action because of his concern for the neighborhood, and that he would be willing for the team to play night games if a new stadium were built in Chicago.

Plaintiff alleges that the other defendant directors, with full knowledge of the foregoing matters, have acquiesced in the policy laid down by Wrigley and have permitted him to dominate the board of directors in matters involving the installation of lights and scheduling of night games, even though they knew he was not motivated by a good faith concern as to the best interests of defendant corporation, but solely by his personal views set forth above. It is charged that the directors are acting for a reason or reasons contrary and wholly unrelated to the business interests of the corporation; that such arbitrary and capricious acts constitute mismanagement and waste of corporate assets, and that the directors have been negligent in failing to exercise reasonable care and prudence in the management of the corporate affairs.

The question on appeal is whether plaintiff's amended complaint states a cause of action. It is plaintiff's position that fraud, illegality and conflict of interest are not the only bases for a stockholder's derivative action against the directors. Contrariwise, defendants argue that the courts will not step in and interfere with honest business judgment of the directors unless there is a showing of fraud, illegality or conflict of interest.

The cases in this area are numerous and each differs from the others on a factual basis. However, the courts have pronounced certain ground rules which appear in all cases and which are then applied to the given factual situation. * * *

In *Davis v. Louisville Gas & Electric Co.*, 16 Del.Ch. 157 [1928], a minority shareholder sought to have the directors enjoined from amending the certificate of incorporation. The court said:

> We have then a conflict in view between the responsible managers of a corporation and an overwhelming majority of its stockholders on the one hand and a dissenting minority on the other—a conflict touching matters of business policy, such as has occasioned innumerable applications to courts to intervene and determine which of the two conflicting views should prevail. The response which courts make to such applications is that it is not their function to resolve for corporations questions of policy and business management. The directors are chosen to pass upon such questions and their judgment unless shown to be tainted with fraud is accepted as final. The judgment of the directors of corporations enjoys the benefit of a presumption that it was formed in good faith and was designed to promote the best interests of the corporation they serve. * * *

Plaintiff in the instant case argues that the directors are acting for reasons unrelated to the financial interest and welfare of the Cubs. However, we are not satisfied that the motives assigned to Philip K. Wrigley, and through him to the other directors, are contrary to the best interests of the corporation and the stockholders. For example, it appears to us that the effect on the surrounding neighborhood might well be considered by a director who was considering the patrons who would or would not attend the games if the park were in a poor neighborhood. Furthermore, the long run interest of the corporation in its property value at Wrigley Field might demand all efforts to keep the neighborhood from deteriorating. By these thoughts we do not mean to say that we have decided that the decision of the directors was a correct one. That is beyond our jurisdiction and ability. We are merely saying that the decision is one properly before directors and the motives alleged in the amended complaint showed no fraud, illegality or conflict of interest in their making of that decision.

While all the courts do not insist that one or more of the three elements must be present for a stockholder's derivative action to lie, nevertheless we feel that unless the conduct of the defendants at least borders on one of the elements, the courts should not interfere. The trial court in the instant case acted properly in dismissing plaintiff's amended complaint. * * *

Finally, we do not agree with plaintiff's contention that failure to follow the example of the other major league clubs in scheduling night games constituted negligence. Plaintiff made no allegation that these teams' night schedules were profitable or that the purpose for which night baseball had been undertaken was fulfilled. Furthermore, it cannot be said that directors, even those of corporations that are losing money, must follow the lead of the other corporations in the field. Directors are elected for their business capabilities and judgment and the courts cannot require them to forego their judgment because of the decisions of directors of other companies. Courts may not decide these questions in the absence of a clear showing of dereliction of duty on the part of the specific directors and mere failure to "follow the crowd" is not such a dereliction.

For the foregoing reasons the order of dismissal entered by the trial court is affirmed.

Affirmed.

QUESTIONS

1.   Did the trial court conclude that it was a dumb decision for the Cubs to play only day games? Did the trial court care whether it was a dumb decision? Did the appellate court?

2.   What can Shlensky do now?

3.   Why did an Illinois court quote from and rely on a decision of the Delaware Chancery Court? Though the Cubs are based in Chicago, note that the corporation was formed in Delaware. Recall from page 138 that the law of the state of incorporation governs the internal affairs of the corporation. So Delaware law governs the internal affairs of a corporation that runs a baseball team in Chicago!

————————

One of the most quoted modern cases on a director's duty of care is *Joy v. North*, a Second Circuit decision applying Connecticut law. The lawsuit against the officers and directors of a Connecticut bank alleged that they had breached the duty of care in making a series of loans to a real estate developer referred to in the portion of the opinion set out below as "Katz."

The following part of the majority opinion includes a discussion of both (i) the directors' duty of care and (ii) shareholder derivative suits. We will consider shareholder derivative suits in more detail later. Accordingly, much of the detail of Judge Winter's consideration of shareholder derivative suits has been edited. Nonetheless, a general understanding of shareholder derivative suits is necessary to see how the directors' duty of care and other duties are judicially enforced.

JOY V. NORTH
United States Court of Appeals, Second Circuit, 1982
692 F.2d 880

[A shareholder brought a shareholder derivative suit against the corporation's directors and officers. The corporation's board of directors then appointed a "special litigation committee," which issued a report recommending that the suit be dismissed as to "outside" directors. The corporation filed a motion for summary judgment, based on the special litigation committee's report. The trial court granted the motion, holding that "the business judgment rule limits judicial scrutiny of its recommendations to the good faith, independence and thoroughness of the Committee." 692 F.2d 882. A divided Second Circuit here reverses and remands.]

WINTER, J. * * * Our opinion first addresses the nature and function of the business judgment rule, which played a large role in persuading the District Court to dismiss this action. It turns then to the legal oddity known as the derivative action, thought by many to be an endangered species as a consequence of the evolution of special litigation committees. * * *

A.   The Liability of Corporate Directors and Officers and the Business Judgment Rule

While it is often stated that corporate directors and officers will be liable for negligence in carrying out their corporate duties, all seem agreed that such a statement is misleading. Whereas an automobile driver who makes a mistake in judgment as to speed or distance injuring a pedestrian will likely be called upon to respond in damages, a corporate officer who makes a mistake in judgment as to economic conditions, consumer tastes or production line efficiency will rarely, if ever, be found liable for damages suffered by the corporation. Whatever the terminology, the fact is that liability is rarely imposed upon corporate directors or officers simply for bad judgment and this reluctance to impose liability for unsuccessful business decisions has been doctrinally labeled the business judgment rule. Although the rule has suffered under academic criticism, it is not without rational basis.

First, shareholders to a very real degree voluntarily undertake the risk of bad business judgment. Investors need not buy stock, for investment markets offer an array of opportunities less vulnerable to mistakes in judgment by corporate officers. Nor need investors buy stock in particular corporations. In the exercise of what is genuinely a free choice, the quality of a firm's management is often decisive and information is available from professional advisors. Since shareholders can and do select among investments partly on the basis of management, the business judgment rule merely recognizes a certain voluntariness in undertaking the risk of bad business decisions.

Second, courts recognize that after-the-fact litigation is a most imperfect device to evaluate corporate business decisions. The circumstances surrounding a corporate decision are not easily reconstructed in a courtroom years later, since business imperatives often call for quick decisions, inevitably based on less than perfect information. The entrepreneur's function is to encounter risks and to confront uncertainty, and a reasoned decision at the time made may seem a wild hunch viewed years later against a background of perfect knowledge.

Third, because potential profit often corresponds to the potential risk, it is very much in the interest of shareholders that the law not create incentives for overly cautious corporate decisions. Some opportunities offer great profits at the risk of very substantial losses, while the alternatives offer less risk of loss but also less potential profit. Shareholders can reduce the volatility of risk by diversifying their holdings. In the case of the diversified shareholder, the seemingly more risky alternatives may well be the best choice since great losses in some stocks will over time be offset by even greater gains in others. Given mutual funds and similar forms of diversified investment, courts need not bend over backwards to give special protection to shareholders who refuse to reduce the volatility of risk by not diversifying. A rule which penalizes the choice of seemingly riskier alternatives thus may not be in the interest of shareholders generally.

Whatever its merit, however, the business judgment rule extends only as far as the reasons which justify its existence. Thus, it does not apply in cases, e.g., in which the corporate decision lacks a business purpose, is tainted by a conflict of interest, is so egregious as to amount to a no-win decision, *Litwin v. Allen*, 25 N.Y.S.2d 667 (N.Y.Co.Sup.Ct.1940), or results from an obvious and prolonged failure to exercise oversight or supervision. Other examples may occur.

B.   Shareholder Derivative Actions

Whereas ordinary lenders may and will sue directly to enforce their rights and debentureholders look to indenture trustees to enforce obligations to them, direct actions by individual shareholders for injuries to the value of their investment would be an inefficient and wasteful method of enforcing management obligations. The stake of each shareholder in the likely return is usually too small to justify bringing a lawsuit and a multiplicity of such actions would result in corporate and judicial waste. Moreover, the costs of organizing a large number of geographically diverse shareholders to bring an action are usually prohibitively high. If an alternative remedy were not available, therefore, the fiduciary obligations of corporate management, however limited, might well be unenforceable. * * *

The derivative action is the common law's inventive solution to the problem of actions to protect shareholder interests. In its classic form, a derivative suit involves two actions brought by an individual shareholder: (i) an action against the corporation for failing to bring a specified suit and (ii) an action on behalf of the corporation for harm to it identical to the one which the corporation failed to bring. The technical structure of the derivative suit is thus quite unusual. Moreover, the shareholder plaintiffs are quite often little more than a formality for purposes of the caption rather than parties with a real interest in the outcome. Since any judgment runs to the corporation, shareholder plaintiffs at best realize an appreciation in the value of their shares. The real incentive to bring derivative actions is usually not the hope of return to the corporation but the hope of handsome fees to be recovered by plaintiffs' counsel. * * *

C.   Termination of Derivative Suits by Special Litigation Committees

In the normal course of events a decision whether to bring a lawsuit is a corporate economic decision subject to the business judgment rule. Thus, shareholders upset at a corporate failure to bring actions for, say, non-payment of a debt for goods sold and delivered, may not initiate a derivative suit without first making a demand upon the directors to bring the action. Where the directors refuse, and the derivative action challenges that refusal, courts apply the business judgment rule to the action of the directors.

[Judge Winter (who used to teach corporation law at Yale Law School) then acknowledged that situations in which "there is a conflict of interest in the directors' decision not to sue because the directors themselves . . . are named defendants" are treated differently. He rejected the argument that the business judgment rule applies to the recommendations by a special litigation committee composed of directors who are not defendants. We will discuss the use of such committees in derivative litigation in § D of this chapter.]

* * *

E.   The Present Case * * *

We turn now to the contents of the Special Litigation Committee's Report. We emphasize that this recitation is the Committee's version of the facts. The record suggests that a trial might reveal sharply differing versions of the same events from various witnesses as well as sharply differing inferences drawn from that testimony.

According to the Report, Nelson L. North was Citytrust's Chief Executive Officer and Norman Schaff, Jr. was its Chief Lending Officer during the period in question. The management of Citytrust was completely dominated by North. North also exercised strong control over the activities of the Board of Directors. Board members were given neither materials nor agendas prior to meetings and requests for long range planning documents were left unanswered. * * *

We look first to potential liability generally without regard to which defendants are responsible. As to that liability, we find that plaintiff's chances of success are rather high. The loss to Citytrust resulted from decisions which put the bank in a classic "no win" situation. The Katz venture was risky and increasingly so. By continuing extensions of substantial amounts of credit the bank subjected the principal to those risks although its potential gain was no more than the interest it could have earned in less risky, more diversified loans. In a real sense, there was a low ceiling on profits but only a distant floor for losses. It is so similar to the classic case of *Litwin v. Allen*, *supra* (bank purchase of bonds with an option in the seller to repurchase at the original price, the bank thus bearing the entire risk of a drop in price with no hope of gain beyond the stipulated interest) that we cannot agree with the Committee's conclusion that only a "possibility of a finding of negligence" exists.

The issue as to which defendants are responsible is less clear. The Committee concluded that there is "no reasonable possibility" of the outside defendants being found liable because they had neither information nor reasonable notice of the problems raised by the Katz transactions. We note first that members of the inside defendants may contradict that version and, if so, a possibility of liability in the outside group exists. Moreover, lack of knowledge is not necessarily a defense, if it is the result of an abdication of directional responsibility. Directors who willingly allow others to make major decisions affecting the future of the corporation wholly without supervision or oversight may not defend on their lack of knowledge, for that ignorance itself is a breach of fiduciary duty. The issue turns in large part upon how and why these defendants were left in the dark. An individual analysis of each outside defendant's role may show that some are blameless or even that they all were justified in not acting before they did, but neither is an inexorable conclusion on the basis of the present record.

The Report concluded as to the inside defendants that there was a "possibility" of liability. This conclusion is a considerable understatement and not entirely consistent with the Report's finding as to the outside defendants. The outsiders' best defense may well be that the inside group actively concealed the Katz problem. Given the fact that exoneration of the outside defendants may show culpability of the insiders and our conclusion that the probability of liability somewhere is high, we think the exposure of the inside group is considerably more than a "possibility." * * *

The grant of summary judgment is reversed, the protective order is vacated, and the case is remanded. * * *

QUESTIONS AND NOTES

1.   There was no liability exposure for the directors in *Shlensky*. There was liability exposure for the directors in *Joy v. North*. Are the two cases reconcilable?

2.   In *Joy v. North*, the Second Circuit repeatedly refers to the "business judgment rule." Courts, not legislatures, created the business judgment rule. This rule reflects the oft-stated judicial policy that courts will not interfere with business decisions by corporate directors as long as the directors are acting with disinterest, good faith, and due diligence. While courts created the business judgment rule, the MBCA and other corporate codes now contain "guidance as to its application in dealing with director liability claims." Official Comment to § 8.31. *Joy v. North* would have been decided differently under § 8.31. (Note MBCA § 8.31 is limited to directors. *Joy v. North* involved claims against both directors and officers. Should the business judgment rule be limited to directors? *See* MBCA § 8.42, Official Comment.)

3.   *Joy v. North* makes clear (as did *Litwin*, which it discussed) that some business decisions are so absurd that they cannot be saved by the business judgment rule. Such "galactically stupid" acts are rare, but obviously can happen. David Rosenberg, *Galactic Stupidity and the Business Judgment Rule*, 32 J. CORP. LAW 301, 322 (2007).

4.   Professor Booth describes *Joy v. North* as "one of those rare cases in which the plaintiff overcomes the business judgment rule. In fact, the plaintiff does it twice." Richard A. Booth, *A Minimalist Approach to Corporate Law*, 34 GA. L. REV. 431, 439 (2000). Do you agree?

5.   In an earlier article, Professor Booth summarized *Joy v. North* with the following parenthetical: ("bank directors may be held liable for making loan at inadequate interest rate given risk of project being financed"). Richard A. Booth, *Federalism and the Market for Corporate Control*, 69

WASH. U. L. Q. 411, 443 n. 121 (1991). That footnote ends with a *"See also"* reference to a case we will see below, *Smith v. Van Gorkom*.

———————

The duty of care cases we have read so far involved decisions by the board of directors—the decision not to install lights at a ballpark and the decision to continue lending money to someone who was unlikely to pay it back. In other words, the board acted, and the action it took clearly hurt the corporation. The next case involves *inaction*—essentially, laziness by a director.

Assume that Capel is one of the three directors of Bubba's Burritos, Inc. Capel misses all board meetings and otherwise totally ignores what is happening at the corporation. Propp and Agee, the other two directors, make a series of incredibly dumb and costly decisions. Bubba's Burritos, Inc., files for bankruptcy, and the bankruptcy trustee sues Capel.

Barnes v. Andrews is an early, somewhat subtler version of this story. Consider whether Capel would be held liable under the *Barnes* decision.

BARNES V. ANDREWS

United States District Court, Southern District of New York, 1924
298 F. 614

In Equity. Suit by Earl B. Barnes, as receiver of the Liberty Starters Corporation, against Charles Lee Andrews [who was a director of the corporation]. Decree for defendant.

Final hearing on a bill in equity, under section 91–a of the General Corporation Law of New York (Consol. Laws, c. 23), to hold liable the defendant as director for misprision of office. The corporation was organized under the laws of that state to manufacture starters for Ford motors and aeroplanes. On October 9, 1919, about a year after its organization, the defendant took office as a director, and served until he resigned on June 21, 1920. During that period over $500,000 was raised by the sales of stock of the company, made through an agent working on commission. A force of officers and employees was hired at substantial salaries, and the factory, already erected when the defendant took office, was equipped with machinery. Starter parts were made in quantity, but delays were experienced in the production of starters as a whole, and the funds of the company were steadily depleted by the running charges.

After the defendant resigned, the company continued business until the spring of 1921, when the plaintiff was appointed receiver, found the company without funds, and realized only a small amount on the sale of its assets. During the incumbency of the defendant there had been only two meetings of directors, one of which (i.e., that of October 9, 1919) he attended; the other happening at a day when he was forced to be absent because of his mother's death. He was a friend of the president, who had induced him as the largest stockholder to become a director, and his only attention to the affairs of the company consisted of talks with the president as they met from time to time.

The theory of the bill was that the defendant had failed to give adequate attention to the affairs of the company, which had been conducted incompetently and without regard to the waste in salaries during the period before production was possible. This period was unduly prolonged by the incompetence of the factory manager, and disagreements between him and the engineer, upon whose patents the company depended. The officers were unable to induce these men to compose their differences, and the work languished from incompetence and extravagance. More money was paid the engineer than his royalty contracts justified, and money was spent upon fraudulent circulars to induce the purchase of stock.

* * *

LEARNED HAND, DISTRICT JUDGE (after stating the facts as above). * * * The first liability must rest upon the defendant's general inattention to his duties as a director. He cannot be charged with neglect in attending directors' meetings, because there were only two during his incumbency, and of these he was present at one and had an adequate excuse for his absence from the other. His liability must therefore depend upon his failure in general to keep advised of the conduct of the corporate affairs. The measure of a director's duties in this regard is uncertain; the courts contenting themselves with vague declarations, such as that a director must give reasonable attention to the corporate business. While directors are collectively the managers of the company, they are not expected to interfere individually in the actual conduct of its affairs. To do so would disturb the authority of the officers and destroy their individual responsibility, without which no proper discipline is possible. To them must be left the initiative and the immediate direction of the business; the directors can act individually only by counsel and advice to them. Yet they have an individual duty to keep themselves informed in some detail, and it is this duty which the defendant in my judgment failed adequately to perform.

All he did was to talk with Maynard [who was the president of the corporation and a friend of Andrews] as they met, while commuting from Flushing, or at their homes. That, indeed, might be enough, because Andrews had no reason to suspect Maynard's candor, nor has any reason to question it been yet disclosed. But it is plain that he did not press him for details, as he should. It is not enough to content oneself with general answers that the business looks promising and that all seems prosperous. Andrews was bound, certainly as the months wore on, to inform himself of what was going on with some particularity, and, if he had done so, he would have learned that there were delays in getting into production which were putting the enterprise in most serious peril. It is entirely clear from his letters of April 14, 1920, and June 21, 1920, that he had made no effort to keep advised of the actual conduct of the corporate affairs, but had allowed himself to be carried along as a figurehead, in complete reliance upon Maynard. In spite of his own substantial investment in the company, which I must assume was as dear to him as it would be to other men, his position required of him more than this. Having accepted a post of confidence, he was charged with an active duty to learn whether the company was moving to production, and why it was not, and to consider, as best he might, what could be done to avoid the conflicts among the personnel, or their incompetence, which was slowly bleeding it to death.

Therefore I cannot acquit Andrews of misprision in his office, though his integrity is unquestioned. The plaintiff must, however, go further than to show that he should have been more active in his duties. This cause of action rests upon a tort, as much though it be a tort of omission as though it had rested upon a positive act. The plaintiff must accept the burden of showing that the performance of the defendant's duties would have avoided loss, and what loss it would have avoided. I pressed Mr. Alger to show me a case in which the courts have held that a director could be charged generally with the collapse of a business in respect of which he had been inattentive, and I am not aware that he has found one. * * *

The defendant is not subject to the burden of proving that the loss would have happened, whether he had done his duty or not. If he were, it would come to this: That, if a director were once shown slack in his duties, he would stand charged prima facie with the difference between the corporate treasury as it was, and as it would be, judged by a hypothetical standard of success. How could such a standard be determined? How could anyone guess how far a director's skill and judgment would have prevailed upon his fellows, and what would have been the ultimate fate of the business, if they had? How is it possible to set any measure of liability, or to tell what he would have contributed to the event? Men's fortunes may not be subjected to such uncertain and speculative conjectures. It is hard to see how there can be any remedy, except one can put one's finger on a definite loss and say with reasonable assurance that protest would have deterred, or counsel persuaded, the managers who caused it. No men of sense would take the office, if the law imposed upon them a guaranty of the general success of their companies as a penalty for any negligence.

It is, indeed, hard to determine just what went wrong in the management of this company. Any conclusion is little better than a guess. * * *

Suppose I charge Andrews with a complete knowledge of all that we have now learned. What action should he have taken, and how can I say that it would have stopped the losses? The plaintiff gives no definite answer to that question. It is easy to say that he should have done something, but that will not serve to harness upon him the whole loss, nor is it the equivalent of saying that, had he acted, the company would now flourish.

True, he was not very well suited by experience for the job he had undertaken, but I cannot hold him on that account. After all, it is the same corporation that chose him which now seeks to charge him. Directors are not specialists, like lawyers or doctors. They must have good sense, perhaps they must have acquaintance with affairs; but they need not—indeed, perhaps they should not—have any technical talent. They are the general advisers of the business, and if they faithfully give such ability as they have to their charge, it would not be lawful to hold them liable. Must a director guarantee that his judgment is good? Can shareholders call him to account for deficiencies which their votes assured him did not disqualify him for his office? While he may not have been the Cromwell for that Civil War, Andrews did not engage to play any such role.

I conclude, therefore, as to this first claim that there is no evidence that the defendant's neglect caused any losses to the company, and that, if there were, that loss cannot be ascertained. * * *

QUESTIONS AND NOTES

1.   Andrews attended one of the two board of directors meetings held while he was a director. Can a director satisfy her duty of care by attending all meetings of the board of directors?

2.   Do you agree with Judge Hand's statement that "directors are not specialists, like lawyers or doctors"? Would the judge who decided the *Wrigley* case agree? What if a director happens to have special expertise relevant to a matter before the board?

3.   Is the *Barnes* decision consistent with the MBCA? Please read MBCA §§ 8.30(b), and 8.31(a) and (b)(1).

4.   Is the *Barnes* decision consistent with *Meinhard v. Salmon*?

5.   In *Francis v. United Jersey Bank*, 432 A.2d 814 (N.J. 1981), Lillian Pritchard inherited 48 percent of the stock in the family reinsurance brokerage business from her husband. The husband had founded and run the corporation, which also employed the couple's sons, Charles, Jr. and William. When the husband died, the two boys (who owned the rest of the stock) took

over, and allegedly helped themselves to vast sums of the company's clients' money. Lillian and her two sons were the directors. Lillian knew nothing about the reinsurance business and did nothing to inform herself even of its rudiments. She never read corporate documents. She went to the office only once. Even though her husband had warned her that the sons "would take the shirt off my back," Mrs. Pritchard simply did nothing to fulfill the duties of being a director. To make matters worse, after her husband's death Mrs. Pritchard starting drinking heavily.

The sons allegedly misappropriated so much money that the company filed a bankruptcy petition. The trustee in bankruptcy sued Mrs. Pritchard (actually, her estate, since she had died by then).

The New Jersey Supreme Court held her estate liable for her breach of the duty of care. In finding causation, the courts said:

> Her sons knew that she, the only other director, was not reviewing their conduct; they spawned their fraud in the backwater of neglect. Her neglect of duty contributed to the climate of corruption; her failure to act contributed to the continuation of the corruption. Consequently, her conduct was a substantial factor contributing to the loss. Analysis of proximate cause is especially difficult in a corporate context where the allegation is that nonfeasance of a director is a proximate cause of damage to a third party. Where a case involves nonfeasance, no one can say with absolute certainty what would have occurred if the defendant had acted otherwise. Nonetheless, where it is reasonable to conclude that the failure to act would produce a particular result and that result has followed, causation may be inferred. We conclude that even if Mrs. Pritchard's mere objection had not stopped the depredations of her sons, her consultation with an attorney and the threat of suit would have deterred them. That conclusion flows as a matter of common sense and logic from the record. Whether in other situations a director has a duty to do more than protest and resign is best left to case-by-case determinations. In this case, we are satisfied that there was a duty to do more than object and resign. Consequently, we find that Mrs. Pritchard's negligence was a proximate cause of the misappropriations.

6.   The court in *Barnes v. Andrews* places the burden of proof on the plaintiff to show causation. In other words, the plaintiff must show not only that the defendant breached the duty of care, but that this breach caused a loss to the corporation. The court discusses the practical difficulty of placing the burden regarding causation on the defendant (in the paragraph starting "The defendant is not subject to the burden . . .").

While *Barnes* reflects the majority view on this point, Delaware courts do not make the plaintiff show causation. Rather, in *Cede & Co. v. Technicolor*, 634 A.2d 345, 361 (Del. 1993), the Delaware Supreme Court set up a system of shifting burdens. First, the plaintiff must show that the defendant breached the duty of care. Second, the burden shifts to the defendant to show that her actions satisfy the "entire fairness test." This requires the defendant to show both that the process used to approve the deal was fair and that the terms of the deal were fair.

We will discuss the entire fairness test in detail in *HMG Courtland* on page 251 and in *Weinberger* on page 462. As we will see, defendants have a tough time satisfying the entire fairness test, which means that Delaware law on burden of proof regarding causation in duty of care cases seems much more "pro-plaintiff" than the majority view.

7.   *Barnes v. Andrews* is another of the cases on Professor Elson's top ten list:

> This famed 1924 case, decided by the eminent American jurist, Judge Learned Hand, established the now critical corporate law principle that in an action against an inattentive director, a complaining shareholder must establish some linkage between the director's bad behavior and corporate loss—or in legal terms, "causation."

> An inattentive director or directors cannot be held liable for a corporate loss if it is shown that proper attentiveness to corporate affairs by all the directors would still not have prevented the loss complained of. In other words, it must be demonstrated that the accused director's slothfulness was a cause of the company's loss. This notion of causation is thus a critical element in any action brought against a poorly performing board of directors and has had a tremendous impact on the course of modern corporate governance.

Charles M. Elson, *Courts and the Boards: The Top Ten Cases*, SD ALI-ABA 743 (1998).

8.   Section 404 of the Sarbanes-Oxley Act adds to the duty of care that a public corporation's management owes the corporation. All of a corporation's annual financial reports must now include a statement that the corporation has implemented an "adequate internal control structure and procedures for financial reporting."

Smith v. Van Gorkom involves a sale ("cash merger") of a large, publicly-held company, Trans Union Corporation ("Trans Union"). Van Gorkom, Chief Executive Officer (CEO) of Trans Union and a member of its board of directors, negotiated a deal to sell Trans Union to Pritzker for $55 a share (a total of almost $700,000,000). Only one of the other directors, Trans Union's Chief Operating Officer (COO) Chelberg, was involved in the negotiations; the other directors were not even aware of the negotiations until they attended a special meeting of the board of directors and were asked to approve the sale.

The edited portion of the Delaware Supreme Court opinion set out below involves a duty of care challenge to the Trans Union board of directors' approval of the sale at a two-hour meeting, with no prior notice of the purpose of the meeting.* The trial court granted judgment for the defendant directors, holding that they were protected by the business judgment rule. A divided Delaware Supreme Court reversed.

SMITH V. VAN GORKOM

Supreme Court of Delaware, 1985
488 A.2d 858

HORSEY, JUSTICE (for the majority). * * * A class action was brought by shareholders of a corporation, originally seeking rescission of a merger of the corporation into a new corporation. Alternate relief in the form of damages was sought against members of the board of directors, the new corporation, and the owners of the parent of the new corporation. Following trial, the Court of Chancery granted judgment for the directors by an unreported letter opinion. * * *

The Court of Chancery made but one finding; i.e., that the Board's conduct over the entire period from September 20 through January 26, 1981 was not reckless or improvident, but informed. * * *

We conclude that the Court's ultimate finding that the Board's conduct was not "reckless or imprudent" is contrary to the record and not the product of a logical and deductive reasoning process. * * *

Under Delaware law, the business judgment rule is the offspring of the fundamental principle, codified in 8 Del.C. § 141(a), that the business and affairs of a Delaware corporation are managed by or under its board of directors.* **[11]** Aronson v. Lewis, Del.Supr., 473 A.2d 805, 811 (1984). In carrying out their managerial roles, directors are charged with an unyielding fiduciary duty to the corporation and its shareholders. The business judgment rule exists to protect and promote the full and free exercise of the managerial power granted to Delaware directors. The rule itself "is a presumption that in making a business decision, the directors of a corporation acted on an informed basis, in good faith and in the honest belief that the action taken was in the best interests of the company." *Aronson, supra* at 812. Thus, the party attacking a board

---

* If we had not severely edited the facts, you would spend more time trying to understand the deal than the directors of Trans Union did.

* **[11]** 8 Del.C. § 141 provides, in pertinent part:

(a) The business and affairs of every corporation organized under this chapter shall be managed by or under the direction of a board of directors, except as may be otherwise provided in this chapter or in its certificate of incorporation. If any such provision is made in the certificate of incorporation, the powers and duties conferred or imposed upon the board of directors by this chapter shall be exercised or performed to such extent and by such person or persons as shall be provided in the certificate of incorporation.

decision as uninformed must rebut the presumption that its business judgment was an informed one.

The determination of whether a business judgment is an informed one turns on whether the directors have informed themselves "prior to making a business decision, of all material information reasonably available to them." * * *

A director's duty to inform himself in preparation for a decision derives from the fiduciary capacity in which he serves the corporation and its stockholders. Since a director is vested with the responsibility for the management of the affairs of the corporation, he must execute that duty with the recognition that he acts on behalf of others. Such obligation does not tolerate faithlessness or self-dealing. But fulfillment of the fiduciary function requires more than the mere absence of bad faith or fraud. Representation of the financial interests of others imposes on a director an affirmative duty to protect those interests and to proceed with a critical eye in assessing information of the type and under the circumstances present here.

Thus, a director's duty to exercise an informed business judgment is in the nature of a duty of care, as distinguished from a duty of loyalty. * * *

The standard of care applicable to a director's duty of care has also been recently restated by this Court. In *Aronson, supra*, we stated:

> While the Delaware cases use a variety of terms to describe the applicable standard of care, our analysis satisfies us that under the business judgment rule director liability is predicated upon concepts of gross negligence. (footnote omitted) * * *

We again confirm that view. We think the concept of gross negligence is also the proper standard for determining whether a business judgment reached by a board of directors was an informed one. * * *

On the record before us, we must conclude that the Board of Directors did not reach an informed business judgment on September 20, 1980 in voting to "sell" the Company for $55 per share pursuant to the Pritzker cash-out merger proposal. * * *

The Board based its September 20 decision to approve the cash-out merger primarily on Van Gorkom's representations. None of the directors, other than Van Gorkom and Chelberg, had any prior knowledge that the purpose of the meeting was to propose a cash-out merger of Trans Union. No members of Senior Management were present, other than Chelberg, Romans [the Chief Financial Officer] and Peterson; and the latter two had only learned of the proposed sale an hour earlier. Both general counsel Moore and former general counsel Browder attended the meeting, but were equally uninformed as to the purpose of the meeting and the documents to be acted upon.

Without any documents before them concerning the proposed transaction, the members of the Board were required to rely entirely upon Van Gorkom's 20-minute oral presentation of the proposal. No written summary of the terms of the merger was presented; the directors were given no documentation to support the adequacy of $55 price per share for sale of the Company; and the Board had before it nothing more than Van Gorkom's statement of his understanding of the substance of an agreement which he admittedly had never read, nor which any member of the Board had ever seen.

Under 8 Del.C. § 141(e),* [15] "directors are fully protected in relying in good faith on reports made by officers." The term "report" has been liberally construed to include reports of informal personal investigations by corporate officers. However, there is no evidence that any "report," as defined under § 141(e), concerning the Pritzker proposal, was presented to the Board on September 20. Van Gorkom's oral presentation of his understanding of the terms of the proposed Merger Agreement, which he had not seen, and Romans' brief oral statement of his preliminary study regarding the feasibility of a leveraged buy-out of Trans Union do not qualify as § 141(e) "reports" for these reasons: The former lacked substance because Van Gorkom was basically uninformed as to the essential provisions of the very document about which he was talking. At a minimum for a report to enjoy the status conferred by § 141(e), it must be pertinent to the subject matter upon which a board is called to act, and otherwise be entitled to good faith, not blind, reliance. * * *

We do not say that the Board of Directors was not entitled to give some credence to Van Gorkom's representation that $55 was an adequate or fair price. Under § 141(e), the directors were entitled to rely upon their chairman's opinion of value and adequacy, provided that such opinion was reached on a sound basis. Here, the issue is whether the directors informed themselves as to all information that was reasonably available to them. Had they done so, they would have learned of the source and derivation of the $55 price and could not reasonably have relied thereupon in good faith.

None of the directors, management or outside, were investment bankers or financial analysts. Yet the Board did not consider recessing the meeting until a later hour that day (or requesting an extension of Pritzker's Sunday evening deadline) to give it time to elicit more

---

* [15] Section 141(e) provides in pertinent part:

A member of the board of directors . . . shall, in the performance of his duties, be fully protected in relying in good faith upon the books of accounts or reports made to the corporation by any of its officers, or by an independent certified public accountant, or by an appraiser selected with reasonable care by the board of directors . . ., or in relying in good faith upon other records of the corporation.

information as to the sufficiency of the offer, either from inside Management (in particular Romans) or from Trans Union's own investment banker, Salomon Brothers, whose Chicago specialist in merger and acquisitions was known to the Board and familiar with Trans Union's affairs.

Thus, the record compels the conclusion that on September 20 the Board lacked valuation information adequate to reach an informed business judgment as to the fairness of $55 per share for sale of the Company. * * *

We hold, therefore, that the Trial Court committed reversible error in applying the business judgment rule in favor of the director defendants in this case.

On remand, the Court of Chancery shall conduct an evidentiary hearing to determine the fair value of the shares represented by the plaintiffs' class, based on the intrinsic value of Trans Union on September 20, 1980. * * *

Thereafter, an award of damages may be entered to the extent that the fair value of Trans Union exceeds $55 per share.

* * *

REVERSED and REMANDED for proceedings consistent herewith.

* * *

MCNEILLY, JUSTICE, dissenting. The majority opinion reads like an advocate's closing address to a hostile jury. And I say that not lightly. Throughout the opinion great emphasis is directed only to the negative, with nothing more than lip service granted the positive aspects of this case. In my opinion Chancellor Marvel (retired) should have been affirmed. * * *

The majority has spoken and has effectively said that Trans Union's Directors have been the victims of a "fast shuffle" by Van Gorkom and Pritzker. That is the beginning of the majority's comedy of errors. The first and most important error made is the majority's assessment of the directors' knowledge of the affairs of Trans Union and their combined ability to act in this situation under the protection of the business judgment rule.

Trans Union's Board of Directors consisted of ten men, five of whom were "inside" directors and five of whom were "outside" directors. The "inside" directors were Van Gorkom, Chelberg, Bonser, William B. Browder, Senior Vice-President—Law, and Thomas P. O'Boyle, Senior Vice-President—Administration. At the time the merger was proposed the inside five directors had collectively been employed by the Company for 116 years and had 68 years of combined experience as directors. The "outside" directors were A.W. Wallis, William B. Johnson, Joseph B. Lanterman, Graham J. Morgan and Robert W. Reneker. With the exception of Wallis, these were all chief executive officers of Chicago based corporations that were at least as large as Trans Union. The five "outside" directors had 78 years of combined experience as chief executive officers, and 53 years cumulative service as Trans Union directors.

The inside directors wear their badge of expertise in the corporate affairs of Trans Union on their sleeves. But what about the outsiders? Dr. Wallis is or was an economist and math statistician, a professor of economics at Yale University, dean of the graduate school of business at the University of Chicago, and Chancellor of the University of Rochester. Dr. Wallis had been on the Board of Trans Union since 1962. He also was on the Board of Bausch & Lomb, Kodak, Metropolitan Life Insurance Company, Standard Oil and others.

William B. Johnson is a University of Pennsylvania law graduate, President of Railway Express until 1966, Chairman and Chief Executive of I.C. Industries Holding Company, and member of Trans Union's Board since 1968.

Joseph Lanterman, a Certified Public Accountant, is or was President and Chief Executive of American Steel, on the Board of International Harvester, Peoples Energy, Illinois Bell Telephone, Harris Bank and Trust Company, Kemper Insurance Company and a director of Trans Union for four years.

Graham Morgan is a chemist, was Chairman and Chief Executive Officer of U.S. Gypsum, and in the 17 and 18 years prior to the Trans Union transaction had been involved in 31 or 32 corporate takeovers.

Robert Reneker attended University of Chicago and Harvard Business Schools. He was President and Chief Executive of Swift and Company, director of Trans Union since 1971, and member of the Boards of seven other corporations including U.S. Gypsum and the Chicago Tribune.

Directors of this caliber are not ordinarily taken in by a "fast shuffle." I submit they were not taken into this multi-million dollar corporate transaction without being fully informed and aware of the state of the art as it pertained to the entire corporate panorama of Trans Union. True, even directors such as these, with their business acumen, interest and expertise, can go astray. I do not believe that to be the case here. These men knew Trans Union like the back of their hands and were more than well qualified to make on the spot informed business judgments concerning the affairs of Trans Union including a 100% sale of the corporation. Lest we forget, the corporate world of then and now operates on what is so aptly referred to as "the fast track." These men were at the time an integral part of that world, all professional businessmen, not intellectual figureheads. * * *

QUESTIONS AND NOTES

1.   Looking back, is *Smith v. Van Gorkom* consistent with *Joy v. North*?

2.   Looking back further, is *Smith v. Van Gorkom* consistent with *Shlensky*? Is the court in *Van Gorkom* as deferential to the board of directors as the court was in the *Shlensky* case? Did the court in *Shlensky* review the merits of the board's decision? Did the court in *Van Gorkom* review the merits of the board's decision or merely the process by which the decision was reached?

3.   Is *Smith v. Van Gorkom* consistent with the requirement, discussed in *Barnes v. Andrews*, that breach of the duty of care is not actionable unless it caused harm to the corporation? In Note 6 after *Barnes*, we mentioned that the Delaware Supreme Court, in *Cede & Co. v. Technicolor*, concluded that the plaintiff need not show causation to prevail in a duty of care case. One professor makes this connection between *Van Gorkom* and *Cede & Co.*:

> Still another shortcoming in *Van Gorkom*'s legal analysis is its failure to address the concept of causation. Students reading the opinion might be left with the impression that once a breach of the duty of care is established, an award of damages is mandated, without regard to whether the plaintiff establishes that the breach in any way caused the action or injury. Indeed, it may be that the court's lack of focus on the causation issue laid the groundwork for its subsequent and widely criticized determination in *Cede & Co. v. Technicolor* that a plaintiff in a duty-of-care case need not establish a causal relation between the failure to exercise care and the injury. This lack of a need for causal proof is not a matter that should go unexplored, yet nothing in *Van Gorkom* itself addresses the question and gives the student any notice of the issue.

Lawrence Hamermesh, *Why I Do Not Teach* Van Gorkom, 34 GA. L. REV. 477, 487–488 (2000).

Is Professor Hamermesh right? Or did *Barnes v. Andrews* impose a burden to establish causation only in cases involving director *inaction*? After all, *Barnes* involved a claim against one director for a failing to do anything. In cases like *Joy v. North* and *Smith v. Van Gorkom*, the board as a whole has taken some action and the action has harmed the corporation—specifically, by lending money that will not be repaid or by selling the company for less than could be commanded. In such cases, isn't causation clear?

4.   First the court states: "The determination of whether a business judgment is an informed one turns on whether the directors have informed themselves on all material information reasonably available to them." Later in the opinion the court states, "We think the concept of gross negligence is the proper standard for determining whether a business judgment was an informed one." Are these two statements consistent?

5.   Would the directors still be grossly negligent if:

a)   the $55 a share offer price was almost $18 a share more than what a share of Trans Union was selling for; and

b)   under the terms of the deal, the offer would be rescinded if not approved by the board by the end of the next day; and

c)   a Trans Union attorney advised the directors that "they might be sued if they failed to accept the deal"; and

d)   69.9% of the outstanding shares of Trans Union were voted in favor of the merger; and only 7.25% were voted against the merger?

6.   What if Epstein was a shareholder of Trans Union and did not want to sell his three shares of Trans Union common stock for $55 a share? Reconsider this question when we consider mergers and other corporate combinations in Chapter 9.

7.   Why didn't Delaware § 141(e) protect the directors? What if Van Gorkom had provided the directors with a written report summarizing the terms of the deals and his reasons for supporting the deal?

8.   How would *Smith v. Van Gorkom* have been decided under MBCA §§ 8.30 and 8.31? What language in those statutes is most helpful to the defendants?

9.   Professor Fischel has described *Smith v. Van Gorkom* as "one of the worst decisions in the history of corporate law." Daniel R. Fischel, *The Business Judgment Rule and the Trans-Union Case,* 40 BUS. LAW. 1437, 1455 (1985).

10.   Professor Elson puts *Smith v. Van Gorkom* on his list of top ten cases having an impact on corporate law and governance and describes it as having a "major impact on board behavior. It was responsible for the now common use of third-party advisers to provide expert opinions to boards. And it has led to far more elaborate decisionmaking procedures, involving lengthy meetings, voluminous documentation and the like." Charles M. Elson, *Courts and Boards: The Top Ten Cases,* SD 39 ALI-ABA 743 (1998).

11. *Smith v. Van Gorkom* also had an effect on the Delaware legislature. Less than a year after the Delaware Supreme Court's decision in *Smith v. Van Gorkom*, the Delaware legislature decided to permit corporations to limit their directors' liability for money damages for breach of fiduciary duty. Delaware § 102(b)(7) provides in part:

> A provision eliminating or limiting the personal liability of a director to the corporation or its stockholders for monetary damages for breach of fiduciary duty as a director, provided that such provision shall not eliminate or limit the liability of a director (i) for any breach of the director's duty of loyalty to the corporation or its stockholders, (ii) for acts or omissions not in good faith or which involve intentional misconduct or a knowing violation of law, (iii) under section 174 of this Title [concerning proper distributions], or (iv) for any transaction from which the director derived an improper personal benefit.

If Trans Union had had an "exculpation provision" under this statute, would the result in *Smith v. Van Gorkom* have been different?

Compare MBCA § 2.02(b)(4), which provides that articles of incorporation may include:

> a provision eliminating or limiting the liability of a director to the corporation or its shareholders for money damages for any action taken, or any failure to take any action, as a director, except liability for (A) the amount of a financial benefit received by a director to which he is not entitle; (B) an intentional infliction of harm on the corporation or the shareholders; (C) a violation of section 8.33 [concerning proper distributions]; or (D) an intentional violation of criminal law.

Do Delaware § 102(b)(7) and MBCA § 2.02(b)(4) allow exculpation to the same extent—or is one broader than the other?

12. Exculpation provisions under Delaware § 102(b)(7) and similar statutes (like MBCA § 2.02(b)(4)) cannot protect directors from all liability. Such corporate articles can limit directors' liability to the corporation and its shareholders, but not to outside third parties. In addition, the provisions can eliminate liability only for violations of the duty of care, not for violations of the duty of loyalty or conduct that was in bad faith.

The 1996 Delaware Chancery Court decision in *In re Caremark International, Inc., Derivative Litigation* is widely regarded as the seminal modern case on directors' liability for failure to act. As background, we should know about *Graham v. Allis-Chalmers Mfg. Co.*, 188 A.2d 125 (Del. 1963). In that case, several mid-level employees of a large corporation were indicted and pleaded guilty to violating federal antitrust laws by engaging in price fixing. In a derivative suit, a shareholder argued that the directors of the corporation breached the duty of care by failing to monitor the employees sufficiently to uncover the problem.

The Delaware Supreme Court held that the directors had not breached their duty. According to the court, the fact that the corporation had over 30,000 employees in several states meant that the board could be responsible only for very broad policy issues, and not for the immediate supervision of employees. The plaintiff countered by arguing that the board had a duty to establish some sort of monitoring system to uncover pricing problems. The court, in overly sweeping language, said that the directors were not required to set up a monitoring system until they had some reason to suspect that the employees were not being honest.

No one doubts that the board has the right to rely on subordinates. But such reliance must be reasonable. In *Graham*, the plaintiffs simply failed to produce enough evidence to raise the suspicion of price-fixing by employees (even though the company had engaged in such activity previously). In the *Caremark* case, the Delaware Chancery Court revisits the question of when monitoring systems might be required.

IN RE CAREMARK INTERNATIONAL, INC., DERIVATIVE LITIGATION

Delaware Chancery Court, 1996
698 A.2d 959

[Caremark is a health care provider. Caremark's settlement of various governmental and private claims of violations of Medicare and Medicaid rules cost the corporation over $250,000,000. A shareholder derivative action was filed (i) alleging that the directors violated their duty of care by failing to supervise the conduct of Caremark employees and (ii) seeking the recovery from the directors of the $250,000,000 paid by Caremark. The following is an edited version of the opinion approving a settlement of the shareholder derivative suit. Under the settlement, "plaintiffs have been given express assurances that Caremark will have a more centralized, active supervisory system in the future." The court awarded the plaintiffs' attorneys "a fee of $816,000 plus $53,000 of expenses."]

ALLEN, CHANCELLOR. * * * The complaint charges the director defendants with breach of their duty of attention or care in connection with the on-going operation of the corporation's business. The claim is that the directors allowed a situation to develop and continue which exposed the corporation to enormous legal liability and that in so doing they violated a duty to be active monitors of corporate performance. * * *

The theory here advanced is possibly the most difficult theory in corporation law upon which a plaintiff might hope to win a judgment.

1.   Potential liability for directoral decisions. Director liability for a breach of the duty to exercise appropriate attention may, in theory, arise in two distinct contexts. First, such liability may be said to follow from a board decision that results in a loss because that decision was ill advised or "negligent." Second, liability to the corporation for a loss may be said to arise from an unconsidered failure of the board to act in circumstances in which due attention would, arguably, have prevented the loss. * * *

What should be understood, but may not widely be understood by courts or commentators who are not often required to face such questions, is that compliance with a director's duty of care can never appropriately be judicially determined by reference to the content of the board decision that leads to a corporate loss, apart from consideration of the good faith or rationality of the process employed. That is, whether a judge or jury considering the matter after the fact, believes a decision substantively wrong, or degrees of wrong extending through "stupid" to "egregious" or "irrational," provides no ground for director liability, so long as the court determines that the process employed was either rational or employed in a good faith effort to advance corporate interests. To employ a different rule—one that permitted an "objective" evaluation of the decision—would expose directors to substantive second guessing by ill-equipped judges or juries, which would, in the long-run, be injurious to investor interests. Thus, the business judgment rule is process oriented and informed by a deep respect for all good faith board decisions.

Indeed, one wonders on what moral basis might shareholders attack a good faith business decision of a director as "unreasonable" or "irrational." Where a director in fact exercises a good faith effort to be informed and to exercise appropriate judgment, he or she should be deemed to satisfy fully the duty of attention. If the shareholders thought themselves entitled to some other quality of judgment than such a director produces in the good faith exercise of the powers of office, then the shareholders should have elected other directors. Judge Learned Hand made the point rather better than can I. In speaking of the passive director defendant Mr. Andrews in *Barnes v. Andrews*, 298 F. 614 (S.D. N.Y. 1924), Judge Hand said:

> True, he was not very suited by experience for the job he had undertaken, but I cannot hold him on that account. After all it is the same corporation that chose him that now seeks to charge him. . . . Directors are not specialists like lawyers or doctors. . . . They are the general advisors of the business and if they faithfully give such ability as they have to their charge, it would not be lawful to hold them liable. Must a director guarantee that his judgment is good? Can a shareholder call him to account for deficiencies that their votes assured him did not disqualify him

for his office? While he may not have been the Cromwell for that Civil War, Andrews did not engage to play any such role.

In this formulation Learned Hand correctly identifies, in my opinion, the core element of any corporate law duty of care inquiry: whether there was good faith effort to be informed and exercise judgment.

2.   Liability for failure to monitor. The second class of cases in which director liability for inattention is theoretically possible entail circumstances in which a loss eventuates not from a decision but, from unconsidered inaction. Most of the decisions that a corporation, acting through its human agents, makes are, of course, not the subject of director attention. Legally, the board itself will be required only to authorize the most significant corporate acts or transactions: mergers, changes in capital structure, fundamental changes in business, appointment and compensation of the CEO, etc. As the facts of this case graphically demonstrate, ordinary business decisions that are made by officers and employees deeper in the interior of the organization can, however, vitally affect the welfare of the corporation and its ability to achieve its various strategic and financial goals. * * *

In 1963, the Delaware Supreme Court in *Graham v. Allis-Chalmers Mfg. Co.*, 188 A.2d 125 (Del. 1963), addressed the question of potential liability of board members for losses experienced by the corporation as a result of the corporation having violated the anti-trust laws of the United States. There was no claim in that case that the directors knew about the behavior of subordinate employees of the corporation that had resulted in the liability. Rather, as in this case, the claim asserted was that the directors ought to have known of it and if they had known they would have been under a duty to bring the corporation into compliance with the law and thus save the corporation from the loss. The Delaware Supreme Court concluded that, under the facts as they appeared, there was no basis to find that the directors had breached a duty to be informed of the ongoing operations of the firm. In notably colorful terms, the court stated that "absent cause for suspicion there is no duty upon the directors to install and operate a corporate system of espionage to ferret out wrongdoing which they have no reason to suspect exists." The Court found that there were no grounds for suspicion in that case and, thus, concluded that the directors were blamelessly unaware of the conduct leading to the corporate liability.

How does one generalize this holding today? Can it be said today that, absent some ground giving rise to suspicion of violation of law, that corporate directors have no duty to assure that a corporate information gathering and reporting systems exists which represents a good faith attempt to provide senior management and the Board with information respecting material acts, events or conditions within the corporation, including compliance with applicable statutes and regulations? I certainly do not believe so. I doubt that such a broad generalization of the *Graham* holding would have been accepted by the Supreme Court in 1963. The case can be more narrowly interpreted as standing for the proposition that, absent grounds to suspect deception, neither corporate boards nor senior officers can be charged with wrongdoing simply for assuming the integrity of employees and the honesty of their dealings on the company's behalf.

A broader interpretation of *Graham v. Allis-Chalmers*—that it means that a corporate board has no responsibility to assure that appropriate information and reporting systems are established by management— would not, in any event, be accepted by the Delaware Supreme Court in 1996, in my opinion. In stating the basis for this view, I start with the recognition that in recent years the Delaware Supreme Court has made it clear—especially in its jurisprudence concerning takeovers, from *Smith v. Van Gorkom* through *Paramount Communications v. QVC*, 637 A.2d 34 (Del. 1994)—the seriousness with which the corporation law views the role of the corporate board. Secondly, I note the elementary fact that relevant and timely information is an essential predicate for satisfaction of the board's supervisory and monitoring role under Section 141 of the Delaware General Corporation Law. Thirdly, I note the potential impact of the federal organizational sentencing guidelines on any business organization. Any rational person attempting in good faith to meet an organizational governance responsibility would be bound to take into account this development and the enhanced penalties and the opportunities for reduced sanctions that it offers.

* * * [I]t would, in my opinion, be a mistake to conclude that our Supreme Court's statement in *Graham* concerning "espionage" means that corporate boards may satisfy their obligation to be reasonably informed concerning the corporation, without assuring themselves that information and reporting systems exist in the organization that are reasonably designed to provide to senior management and to the board itself timely, accurate information sufficient to allow management and the board, each within its scope, to reach informed judgments concerning both the corporation's compliance with law and its business performance.

Obviously the level of detail that is appropriate for such an information system is a question of business judgment. And obviously too, no rationally designed information and reporting system will remove the possibility that the corporation will violate laws or regulations, or that senior officers or directors may nevertheless sometimes be misled or otherwise fail reasonably to detect acts material to the corporation's compliance with the law. But it is important that the board exercise a good faith judgment that the corporation's information and reporting system is in concept and design adequate to assure the board that appropriate information will come to its attention in a timely manner as a matter of ordinary operations, so that it may satisfy its responsibility.

Thus, I am of the view that a director's obligation includes a duty to attempt in good faith to assure that a corporate information and reporting system, which the board concludes is adequate, exists, and that failure to do so under some circumstances may, in theory at least, render a director liable for losses caused by non-compliance with applicable legal standards. I now turn to an analysis of the claims asserted with this concept of the directors duty of care, as a duty satisfied in part by assurance of adequate information flows to the board, in mind.

* * * Generally where a claim of directorial liability for corporate loss is predicated upon ignorance of liability-creating activities within the corporation in my opinion only a sustained or systematic failure of the board to exercise oversight—such as an utter failure to attempt to assure a reasonable information and reporting system exists—will establish the lack of good faith that is a necessary condition to liability.

Here the record supplies essentially no evidence that the director defendants were guilty of a sustained failure to exercise their oversight function. To the contrary, insofar as I am able to tell on this record, the corporation's information systems appear to have represented a good faith attempt to be informed of relevant facts. If the directors did not know the specifics of the activities that lead to the indictments, they cannot be faulted.

The liability that eventuated in this instance was huge. But the fact that it resulted from a violation of criminal law alone does not create a breach of fiduciary duty by directors. The record at this stage does not support the conclusion that the defendants either lacked good faith in the exercise of their monitoring responsibilities or conscientiously permitted a known violation of law by the corporation to occur. The claims asserted against them must be viewed at this stage as extremely weak.

The proposed settlement provides very modest benefits. Under the settlement agreement, plaintiffs have been given express assurances that Caremark will have a more centralized, active supervisory system in the future. Specifically, the settlement mandates duties to be performed by the newly named Compliance and Ethics Committee on an ongoing basis and increases the responsibility for monitoring compliance with the law at the lower levels of management. In adopting the resolutions required under the settlement, Caremark has further clarified its policies concerning the prohibition of providing remuneration for referrals. These appear to be positive consequences of the settlement of the claims brought by the plaintiffs, even if they are not highly significant. Nonetheless, given the weakness of the plaintiffs' claims the proposed settlement appears to be an adequate, reasonable, and beneficial outcome for all of the parties. Thus, the proposed settlement will be approved. * * *

QUESTIONS

1.   What did the directors do wrong?

2.   Is the duty of care as expressed in *Caremark* consistent with the duty of care in MBCA §§ 8.30 and 8.31? Is it consistent with the earlier statement of Delaware law in the *Graham* case discussed by the *Caremark* court?

3.   *Caremark* was decided by a Delaware trial court. The high court of that state later adopted its reasoning, however, in *Stone v. Ritter*, 911 A.2d 362, 370 (Del. 2006). There, the court explained:

> We hold that *Caremark* articulates the necessary conditions predicate for director oversight liability: (a) the directors utterly failed to implement any reporting or information system or controls; or (b) having implemented such a system or controls, consciously failed to monitor or oversee its operations thus disabling themselves from being informed of risks or problems requiring their attention. In either case, imposition of liability requires a showing that the directors knew that they were not discharging their fiduciary obligations. Where directors fail to act in the face of a known duty to act, thereby demonstrating a conscious disregard for their responsibilities, they breach their duty of loyalty by failing to discharge that fiduciary obligation in good faith.

Wait a minute! Is that last line a typo? This section of the book is about the duty of care. *Graham* and *Caremark* were duty of care cases. In neither case did the court refer to the duty of loyalty. Somehow, by the time the Delaware Supreme Court got to *Stone v. Ritter*, the obligation to monitor corporate activities had morphed into a problem involving the duty of loyalty and the obligation of good faith! Let's study those responsibilities and then we will try to figure out why the court shifted from duty of care to duty of loyalty in *Stone v. Ritter*.

2.   DUTY OF LOYALTY

One great corporations hornbook provides this overview and comparison of the duty of care and the duty of loyalty: "We depart now from cases in which the complaint is that directors and officers breached their duty of care—in other words, they were lazy or dumb." FRANKLIN A. GEVURTZ, CORPORATION LAW 257 (2d ed. 2010). In this section, we consider complaints that directors or officers breached their duty of loyalty—in other words, they were greedy and put their own financial interests ahead of the interests of the corporations and its shareholders. Questions of a director's duty of loyalty generally arise when the director (1) competes with the company, (2) takes for herself a "corporate opportunity," or (3) has some personal pecuniary interest in a corporation's decision. In dealing with the following cases, remember the

Delaware and MBCA provisions regarding a corporation's waiver of directors' duties.

a.   Competing with the Corporation

DUANE JONES CO., INC. V. BURKE
New York Court of Appeals, 1954
117 N.E.2d 237

[An advertising agency, Duane Jones Co., Inc., began to suffer hard times because of "behavior lapses" by its founder Duane Jones. Several of the company's officers, while still in its employ, began a new competing agency, Scheideler, Beck & Werner, Inc. They lured to the new agency both Jones Co.'s key employees and many of its clients. Once the new agency got on its feet, the disloyal officers resigned from Jones Co. Jones Co. sued the disloyal officers and won a jury verdict based upon its finding that the former officers breached their duty of loyalty to Jones Co.]

LEWIS, CHIEF JUDGE. In 1942, Duane Jones, a man of experience in the field of advertising, organized the plaintiff corporation. From the date of its formation, Jones has continued to be the dominating personality and the policy maker of plaintiff corporation, which by 1951 had acquired accounts in such number and quality as produced a gross billing of $9,000,000. Plaintiff's income was derived from commissions paid to it in the amount of 15% of the sum spent by plaintiff's customers with advertising media. Plaintiff's service consisted of originating advertising ideas and campaigns satisfactory to its customers, and of arranging for the execution of such campaigns through various media. * * * In July, 1951, plaintiff serviced approximately twenty-five customers or accounts, including the following which the amended complaint alleges were diverted to the defendant Scheideler, Beck & Werner, Inc.: Manhattan Soap Co., Inc., G.F. Heublein & Bro., Inc., International Salt Co., Inc., Wesson Oil & Snowdrift Sales Co., C.F. Mueller Co., The Borden Company, The Marlin Fire Arms Co. and McIlhenny Corp. * * *

During the preceding six months plaintiff had lost three of its accounts—total gross billings of which approximated $6,500,000—and had received resignations from three executives as well as from certain staff members of the organization. It also appears that Duane Jones, the president of plaintiff corporation, had been guilty of certain behavior lapses at his office, at business functions and during interviews with actual and prospective customers. As a result of those occasions of misbehavior, several of plaintiff's officers and directors expressed dissatisfaction with conditions—described as "intolerable"—which existed at the plaintiff agency in the spring and summer of 1951.

On June 28, 1951, a meeting took place at the Park Lane Hotel in Manhattan, which was attended by a number of the plaintiff's officers, directors and employees, including all the individual defendants named in this action except the defendant Burke. * * * There was substantial evidence of record that at the meeting of June 28th, the defendant Scheideler informed the group that he had spoken to several of plaintiff's customers whose accounts he serviced from whom he gained favorable reaction to a proposal that the group either buy out Duane Jones' interest in the plaintiff corporation or that they form a new corporation. It also appears that Scheideler suggested to the others present that they inquire whether the accounts being serviced by them for the plaintiff would favor such a project. Defendants Scheideler and Hayes each admitted that at the June 28th meeting it was decided that Hayes should speak to Duane Jones concerning a possible purchase by the defendants of Jones' interest in the plaintiff corporation.

According to Hayes, he informed Duane Jones on July 3, 1951, that the nine defendants associated with plaintiff were interested in purchasing Jones' stock in the plaintiff agency. Mr. Jones' recital of that conversation was that Hayes told him of the group's intention either to buy him out or to start their own agency, and that if he did not agree to a sale they would resign en masse within forty-eight hours. Duane Jones further testified that Hayes indicated to him that the agency's customers had been "already presold" on the alternative plan and that the group would notify him on July 5th of the price they would pay for the business. According to Jones he said to Hayes: "In other words, you are standing there with a Colt .45, holding it at my forehead, and there is not much I can do except to give up?", to which Hayes replied: "Well, you can call it anything you want, but that is what we are going to do." * * *

However, despite frequent meetings between representatives of Duane Jones and the individual defendants the proposed sale was never consummated. Negotiations terminated on or about August 6, 1951, the claim of both Duane Jones and the defendants being that the failure to agree was the result of the other's increased demands. * * *

On August 22, 1951, the defendants Scheideler, Werner and Beck signed a certificate of incorporation of the defendant Scheideler, Beck & Werner, Inc., which certificate was filed with the Secretary of State on August 23, 1951. A few days later, on August 30th, the corporate defendant executed a lease of office space at 487 Park Avenue, where it opened for business as an advertising agency on September 10, 1951. [The officers of Jones Co. who had started the Scheideler, Beck Company then resigned from Jones Co., effective mid-September 1951.]

Within six weeks after its formal opening, the defendant Scheideler, Beck & Werner, Inc., had in its employ seventy-one of the one hundred thirty-two persons formerly employed by plaintiff, including the defendants Scheideler, Werner, Beck, Hughes, Brooks, Hubbard and Hulshizer. Each of the defendants named above was a stockholder in the corporate defendant, and the defendants Scheideler, Werner, Hulshizer and Beck held the offices of president, vice president, secretary, and treasurer of the corporation respectively. * * *

Upon the question of accounts or customers, it appears that, at the time of its opening or shortly thereafter, defendant Scheideler, Beck & Werner, Inc., had as accounts Manhattan Soap Co., G.F. Heublein, International Salt, Wesson Oil, C.F. Mueller Company, The Borden Company, Marlin Fire Arms, McIlhenny Corp., Haskins Bros. and Continental Briar Pipe, all of which were customers of plaintiff prior to the formation of defendant Scheideler, Beck & Werner, Inc.

The foregoing evidence has led us to conclude that the conduct of the individual defendants-appellants as officers, directors or employees of the plaintiff corporation " * * * fell below the standard required by the law of one acting as an agent or employee of another." (*Lamdin* v. *Broadway Surface Adv. Corp.*, 272 N.Y. 133, 138.) Each of these defendants was " * * * prohibited from acting in any manner inconsistent with his agency or trust and [was] at all times bound to exercise the utmost good faith and loyalty in the performance of his duties." * * * The inferences reasonably to be drawn from the record justify the conclusion—reached by the jury and by a majority of the Appellate Division—that the individual defendants-appellants, while employees of plaintiff corporation, determined upon a course of conduct which, when subsequently carried out, resulted in benefit to themselves through destruction of plaintiff's business, in violation of the fiduciary duties * * * imposed on defendants by their close relationship with plaintiff corporation. * * *

Nor is it a defense to say that the defendants-appellants did not avail themselves of the benefit of the customers and personnel diverted from plaintiff until after defendants * * * had informed plaintiff of their intention to leave Duane Jones Company. Upon this record the jury might have found that the conspiracy originated in June or July while a fiduciary duty existed, and that the benefits realized when defendant Scheideler, Beck & Werner, Inc., commenced operation in September were merely the results of a predetermined course of action. In view of that circumstance, the individual defendants would not be relieved of liability for advantages secured by them, after termination of their employment, as a result of opportunities gained by reason of their employment relationship.

QUESTIONS AND NOTES

1.   Was it important that the defendants in this case were officers? What if they had been employees but not officers? What if they had been directors but not officers of Jones Co., rather than directors? Should it have been?

2.   Is *Jones Co.* consistent with *Meinhard v. Salmon?*

3.   Do we know whether the defendants had covenants not to compete with Jones Co.? Did the court need to know that?

4.   The classic remedy in a competing venture case appears to be the constructive trust. So if the breaching fiduciary goes into competition with his corporation and makes a profit, the corporation will recover that profit. On appropriate facts, the corporation may be able to obtain an injunction to stop the competition or—if the competition harmed the corporation in some way— damages may be available.

5.   Would the plaintiff have prevailed if the New York Court of Appeals followed the American Law Institute Principles of Corporate Governance? It provides:

§ 5.06   Competition With The Corporation

(a) *General Rule.* Directors and senior executives may not advance their pecuniary interests by engaging in competition with the corporation unless either:

(1) Any reasonably foreseeable harm to the corporation from such competition is outweighed by the benefit that the corporation may reasonably be expected to derive from allowing the competition to take place, or there is no reasonably foreseeable harm to the corporation from such competition;

(2) The competition is authorized in advance or ratified, following disclosure concerning the conflict of interest and the competition, by disinterested directors, or in the case of a senior executive who is not a director, is authorized in advance by a disinterested superior . . .; or

(3) The competition is authorized in advance or ratified, following such disclosure, by disinterested shareholders, and the shareholders' action is not equivalent to a waste of corporate assets

* * *

6.   Does a corporation's officer or director improperly compete if she also serves as a director for another corporation? Comment c to § 5.06 of ALI's Principles says no because the person is not pursuing his self-interest by serving on the other board.

7.   Suppose that a director of Bubba's Burritos, Inc. wants to open his own restaurant nearby that sells healthful burritos made with hemp and

recycled insect carcasses. Is there anything that he can do to reduce the risk of getting sued for competing with Bubba's?

b. "Usurping" a Corporate Opportunity

We encountered the notion of usurping a business opportunity briefly in connection with partnerships when reading *Meinhard v. Salmon*. In that case, the managing coadventurer took the real estate development opportunity for himself. The following case considers two questions: (1) what is a corporate opportunity? and (2) what does a director have to do when she is offered a corporate opportunity? In reading the case for the answers to these two legal questions, also consider the following:

1.   Was Nancy Harris a director? What if she had been a director of the corporation but not its president?

2.   How did Harris learn of the opportunity to buy the Gilpin property? The Smallidge parcel?

3.   Could the corporation afford to purchase the property? Would that matter?

NORTHEAST HARBOR GOLF CLUB, INC. V. HARRIS
Supreme Court of Maine, 1995
661 A.2d 1146

ROBERTS, JUSTICE. Northeast Harbor Golf Club, Inc., appeals from a judgment entered in the Superior Court (Hancock County, Atwood, J.) following a nonjury trial. The Club maintains that the trial court erred in finding that Nancy Harris did not breach her fiduciary duty as president of the Club by purchasing and developing property abutting the golf course. Because we today adopt principles different from those applied by the trial court in determining that Harris's activities did not constitute a breach of the corporate opportunity doctrine, we vacate the judgment.

Nancy Harris was the president of the Northeast Harbor Golf Club, a Maine corporation, from 1971 until she was asked to resign in 1990. The Club also had a board of directors that was responsible for making or approving significant policy decisions. The Club's only major asset was a golf course in Mount Desert. During Harris's tenure as president, the board occasionally discussed the possibility of developing some of the Club's real estate in order to raise money. Although Harris was generally in favor of tasteful development, the board always "shied away" from that type of activity.

In 1979, Robert Suminsby informed Harris that he was the listing broker for the Gilpin property, which comprised three noncontiguous parcels located among the fairways of the golf course. The property included an unused right-of-way on which the Club's parking lot and clubhouse were located. It was also encumbered by an easement in favor of the Club allowing foot traffic from the green of one hole to the next tee. Suminsby testified that he contacted Harris because she was the president of the Club and he believed that the Club would be interested in buying the property in order to prevent development.

Harris immediately agreed to purchase the Gilpin property in her own name for the asking price of $45,000. She did not disclose her plans to purchase the property to the Club's board prior to the purchase. She informed the board at its annual August meeting that she had purchased the property, that she intended to hold it in her own name, and that the Club would be "protected." The board took no action in response to the Harris purchase. She testified that at the time of the purchase she had no plans to develop the property and that no such plans took shape until 1988.

In 1984, while playing golf with the postmaster of Northeast Harbor, Harris learned that a parcel of land owned by the heirs of the Smallidge family might be available for purchase. The Smallidge parcel was surrounded on three sides by the golf course and on the fourth side by a house lot. It had no access to the road. With the ultimate goal of acquiring the property, Harris instructed her lawyer to locate the Smallidge heirs. At a board meeting in August 1985, Harris formally disclosed to the board that she had purchased the Smallidge property. The minutes of that meeting show that she told the board she had no present plans to develop the Smallidge parcel. Harris testified that at the time of the purchase of the Smallidge property she nonetheless thought it might be nice to have some houses there. Again, the board took no formal action as a result of Harris's purchase. Harris acquired the Smallidge property from ten heirs, paying a total of $60,000. In 1990, Harris paid $275,000 for the lot and building separating the Smallidge parcel from the road in order to gain access to the otherwise landlocked parcel.

The trial court expressly found that the Club would have been unable to purchase either the Gilpin or Smallidge properties for itself, relying on testimony that the Club continually experienced financial difficulties, operated annually at a deficit, and depended on contributions from the directors to pay its bills. On the other hand, there was evidence that the Club had occasionally engaged in successful fund-raising, including a two-year period shortly after the Gilpin purchase during which the Club raised $115,000. The Club had $90,000 in a capital investment fund at the time of the Smallidge purchase.

* * * In 1988, Harris, who was still president of the Club, and her children began the process of obtaining approval for a five-lot subdivision known as Bushwood on the lower Gilpin property. * * *

After Harris's plans to develop Bushwood became apparent, the board grew increasingly divided concerning the propriety of development near the golf course. * * *

In April 1991, after a substantial change in the board's membership, the board authorized the instant lawsuit against Harris for the breach of her fiduciary duty to act in the best interests of the corporation. The board simultaneously resolved that the proposed housing development was contrary to the best interests of the corporation.

The Club filed a complaint against Harris, her sons John and Shepard, and her daughter-in-law Melissa Harris. As amended, the complaint alleged that during her term as president Harris breached her fiduciary duty by purchasing the lots without providing notice and an opportunity for the Club to purchase the property and by subdividing the lots for future development. The Club sought an injunction to prevent development and also sought to impose a constructive trust on the property in question for the benefit of the Club.

The trial court found that Harris had not usurped a corporate opportunity because the acquisition of real estate was not in the Club's line of business. Moreover, it found that the corporation lacked the financial ability to purchase the real estate at issue. Finally, the court placed great emphasis on Harris's good faith. It noted her long and dedicated history of service to the Club, her personal oversight of the Club's growth, and her frequent financial contributions to the Club. The court found that her development activities were "generally * * * compatible with the corporation's business." This appeal followed.

Corporate officers and directors bear a duty of loyalty to the corporations they serve. As Justice Cardozo explained the fiduciary duty in *Meinhard v. Salmon*, 249 N.Y. 458, 164 N.E. 545, 546 (1928):

> A trustee is held to something stricter than the morals of the marketplace. Not honesty alone, but the punctilio of an honor the most sensitive, is then the standard of behavior. As to this there has developed a tradition that is unbending and inveterate. * * *

Despite the general acceptance of the proposition that corporate fiduciaries owe a duty of loyalty to their corporations, there has been much confusion about the specific extent of that duty when, as here, it is contended that a fiduciary takes for herself a corporate opportunity.

Various courts have embraced different versions of the corporate opportunity doctrine. The test applied by the trial court and embraced by Harris is generally known as the "line of business" test. The seminal case applying the line of business test is *Guth v. Loft, Inc.*, 5 A.2d 503 (Del. 1939). In *Guth*, the Delaware Supreme Court adopted an intensely factual test stated in general terms as follows:

> [I]f there is presented to a corporate officer or director a business opportunity which the corporation is financially able to undertake, is, from its nature, in the line of the corporation's

business and is of practical advantage to it, is one in which the corporation has an interest or a reasonable expectancy, and, by embracing the opportunity, the self-interest of the officer or director will be brought into conflict with that of his corporation, the law will not permit him to seize the opportunity for himself.

The "real issue" under this test is whether the opportunity "was so closely associated with the existing business activities . . . as to bring the transaction within that class of cases where the acquisition of the property would throw the corporate officer purchasing it into competition with his company." The Delaware court described that inquiry as "a factual question to be decided by reasonable inferences from objective facts."

The line of business test suffers from some significant weaknesses. First, the question whether a particular activity is within a corporation's line of business is conceptually difficult to answer. The facts of the instant case demonstrate that difficulty. The Club is in the business of running a golf course. It is not in the business of developing real estate. In the traditional sense, therefore, the trial court correctly observed that the opportunity in this case was not a corporate opportunity within the meaning of the *Guth* test. Nevertheless, the record would support a finding that the Club had made the policy judgment that development of surrounding real estate was detrimental to the best interests of the Club. The acquisition of land adjacent to the golf course for the purpose of preventing future development would have enhanced the ability of the Club to implement that policy. The record also shows that the Club had occasionally considered reversing that policy and expanding its operations to include the development of surrounding real estate. Harris's activities effectively foreclosed the Club from pursuing that option with respect to prime locations adjacent to the golf course.

Second, the *Guth* test includes as an element the financial ability of the corporation to take advantage of the opportunity. The court in this case relied on the Club's supposed financial incapacity as a basis for excusing Harris's conduct. Often, the injection of financial ability into the equation will unduly favor the inside director or executive who has command of the facts relating to the finances of the corporation. Reliance on financial ability will also act as a disincentive to corporate executives to solve corporate financing and other problems. In addition, the Club could have prevented development without spending $275,000 to acquire the property Harris needed to obtain access to the road. * * *

In an attempt to protect the duty of loyalty while at the same time providing long-needed clarity and guidance for corporate decisionmakers, the American Law Institute has offered the most recently developed version of the corporate opportunity doctrine. PRINCIPLES OF CORPORATE GOVERNANCE § 5.05 (May 13, 1992), provides as follows:

§ 5.05   Taking of Corporate Opportunities by Directors or Senior Executives

(a) *General Rule.* A director or senior executive may not take advantage of a corporate opportunity unless:

(1) The director or senior executive first offers the corporate opportunity to the corporation and makes disclosure concerning the conflict of interest [§ 1.14(a)] and the corporate opportunity [§ 1.14(b)];

(2) The corporate opportunity is rejected by the corporation; and

(3) Either:

(A) The rejection of the opportunity is fair to the corporation;

(B) The opportunity is rejected in advance, following such disclosure, by disinterested directors [§ 1.15], or, in the case of a senior executive who is not a director, by a disinterested superior, in a manner that satisfies the standards of the business judgment rule [§ 4.01(c)]; or

(C) The rejection is authorized in advance or ratified, following such disclosure, by disinterested shareholders [§ 1.16], and the rejection is not equivalent to a waste of corporate assets [§ 1.42].

(b) *Definition of a Corporate Opportunity.* For purposes of this Section, a corporate opportunity means:

(1) Any opportunity to engage in a business activity of which a director or senior executive becomes aware, either:

(A) In connection with the performance of functions as a director or senior executive, or under circumstances that should reasonably lead the director or senior executive to believe that the person offering the opportunity expects it to be offered to the corporation; or

(B) Through the use of corporate information or property, if the resulting opportunity is one that the director or senior executive should reasonably be expected to believe would be of interest to the corporation; or

(2) Any opportunity to engage in a business activity of which a senior executive becomes aware and knows is

closely related to a business in which the corporation is engaged or expects to engage.

(c) *Burden of Proof.* A party who challenges the taking of a corporate opportunity has the burden of proof, except that if such party establishes that the requirements of Subsection (a)(3)(B) or (C) are not met, the director or the senior executive has the burden of proving that the rejection and the taking of the opportunity were fair to the corporation.

(d) *Ratification of Defective Disclosure.* A good faith but defective disclosure of the facts concerning the corporate opportunity may be cured if at any time (but no later than a reasonable time after suit is filed challenging the taking of the corporate opportunity) the original rejection of the corporate opportunity is ratified, following the required disclosure, by the board, the shareholders, or the corporate decisionmaker who initially approved the rejection of the corporate opportunity, or such decisionmaker's successor.

(e) *Special Rule Concerning Delayed Offering of Corporate Opportunities.* Relief based solely on failure to first offer an opportunity to the corporation under Subsection (a)(1) is not available if: (1) such failure resulted from a good faith belief that the business activity did not constitute a corporate opportunity, and (2) not later than a reasonable time after suit is filed challenging the taking of the corporate opportunity, the corporate opportunity is to the extent possible offered to the corporation and rejected in a manner that satisfies the standards of Subsection (a).

The central feature of the ALI test is the strict requirement of full disclosure prior to taking advantage of any corporate opportunity. *Id.,* § 5.05(a)(1). "If the opportunity is not offered to the corporation, the director or senior executive will not have satisfied § 5.05(a)." *Id.,* cmt. to § 5.05(a). The corporation must then formally reject the opportunity. *Id.,* § 5.05(a)(2).

The ALI test defines "corporate opportunity" broadly. It includes opportunities "closely related to a business in which the corporation is engaged." *Id.,* § 5.05(b). It also encompasses any opportunities that accrue to the fiduciary as a result of her position within the corporation. This concept is most clearly illustrated by the testimony of Suminsby, the listing broker for the Gilpin property, which, if believed by the factfinder, would support a finding that the Gilpin property was offered to Harris specifically in her capacity as president of the Club. If the factfinder reached that conclusion, then at least the opportunity to acquire the Gilpin property would be a corporate opportunity. The state of the record concerning the Smallidge purchase precludes us from intimating any opinion whether that too would be a corporate opportunity.

Under the ALI standard, once the Club shows that the opportunity is a corporate opportunity, it must show either that Harris did not offer the opportunity to the Club or that the Club did not reject it properly. If the Club shows that the board did not reject the opportunity by a vote of the disinterested directors after full disclosure, then Harris may defend her actions on the basis that the taking of the opportunity was fair to the corporation. *Id.*, § 5.05(c). If Harris failed to offer the opportunity at all, however, then she may not defend on the basis that the failure to offer the opportunity was fair. *Id.*, cmt. to § 5.05(c).

* * * We follow the ALI test. The disclosure-oriented approach provides a clear procedure whereby a corporate officer may insulate herself through prompt and complete disclosure from the possibility of a legal challenge. The requirement of disclosure recognizes the paramount importance of the corporate fiduciary's duty of loyalty. At the same time it protects the fiduciary's ability pursuant to the proper procedure to pursue her own business ventures free from the possibility of a lawsuit.

* * * The question remains how our adoption of the rule affects the result in the instant case. The trial court made a number of factual findings based on an extensive record. The court made those findings, however, in the light of legal principles that are different from the principles that we today announce. Similarly, the parties did not have the opportunity to develop the record in this case with knowledge of the applicable legal standard. In these circumstances, fairness requires that we remand the case for further proceedings. Those further proceedings may include, at the trial court's discretion, the taking of further evidence.

The entry is: Judgment vacated.

Remanded for further proceedings consistent with the opinion herein.

QUESTIONS AND NOTES

1.   At the trial, the trial court found that the corporation "would have been unable to purchase either the Gilpin or Smallidge properties for itself." Is that relevant under ALI § 5.05? Should it be?

2.   Harris learned of the availability of the Smallidge property independent of her position with the corporation. Is that relevant under ALI § 5.05? Is it determinative?

3.   Robert Clark, then a professor at the Harvard Law School (and later Dean there), analogized usurpation of corporate opportunity to theft of corporate property: "At a general level therefore, the reasons for considering a manager's taking a corporate opportunity to be wrong are the same as the reasons for considering outright theft from the corporate treasury to be

wrong." Robert C. Clark, CORPORATE LAW 224 (1986). Is *Northeast Harbor* consistent with this analogy?

4.   On remand in *Northeast Harbor*, the court found that both land purchases were corporate opportunities but that the corporation's suit against Ms. Harris was barred by the statute of limitations. *See* Northeast Harbor Golf Club, Inc. v. Harris, 725 A.2d 1018 (Me. 1999).

In *Northeast Harbor*, the Maine Supreme Court discusses and criticizes the Delaware corporate opportunity test from *Guth v. Loft*. In the next case, the Delaware Supreme Court applies the Delaware corporate opportunity test from *Guth v. Loft*.

BROZ V. CELLULAR INFORMATION SYSTEMS, INC.
Supreme Court of Delaware, 1996
673 A.2d 148

[The defendant, Broz, was one of the directors of the plaintiff Cellular Information Systems, Inc. ("CIS"), a Delaware corporation in the business of providing cellular telephone service. Broz was also the sole stockholder and President of RFB Cellular, Inc. ("RFBC"), a competitor of CIS.

Mackinac Cellular Corp. ("Mackinac"), the owner of a Michigan-2 FCC cellular phone license for a portion of Michigan adjacent to an area served by RFBC, approached Broz about the possibility of RFBC's acquiring its license. Mackinac did not even contact CIS. CIS had recently emerged from a lengthy, contentious Chapter 11 bankruptcy case, had sold most of its license areas, and no longer had business operations in the Midwest.

Broz bought the license for RFBC without making formal disclosure to and obtaining the approval of the CIS board. Broz did mention his intentions to the CEO of CIS and to two other members of CIS's board—both of whom indicated that CIS was not interested in acquiring the Michigan-2 license.

An additional complicating (if not important) fact was that, during this time, PriCellular, Inc., ("PriCellular") was engaged in acquiring CIS. And, PriCellular was also interested in acquiring the Michigan-2 license.]

VEASEY, CHIEF JUSTICE. In this appeal, we consider the application of the doctrine of corporate opportunity. The Court of Chancery decided that the defendant, a corporate director, breached his fiduciary duty by not formally presenting to the corporation an opportunity which had come to the director individually and independent of the director's relationship with the corporation. Here the opportunity was not one in which the corporation in its current mode had an interest or which it had the financial ability to acquire, but, under the unique circumstances here, that mode was subject to change by virtue of the impending acquisition of the corporation by another entity.

We conclude that, although a corporate director may be shielded from liability by offering to the corporation an opportunity which has come to the director independently and individually, the failure of the director to present the opportunity does not necessarily result in the improper usurpation of a corporate opportunity. We further conclude that, if the corporation is a target or potential target of an acquisition by another company which has an interest and ability to entertain the opportunity, the director of the target company does not have a fiduciary duty to present the opportunity to the target company. Accordingly, the judgment of the Court of Chancery is REVERSED. * * *

The doctrine of corporate opportunity represents but one species of the broad fiduciary duties assumed by a corporate director or officer. A corporate fiduciary agrees to place the interests of the corporation before his or her own in appropriate circumstances. In light of the diverse and often competing obligations faced by directors and officers, however, the corporate opportunity doctrine arose as a means of defining the parameters of fiduciary duty in instances of potential conflict. The classic statement of the doctrine is derived from the venerable case of *Guth v. Loft, Inc.* [5 A.2d 503 (Del. 1939)]. In *Guth*, this Court held that:

> [I]f there is presented to a corporate officer or director a business opportunity which the corporation is financially able to undertake, is, from its nature, in the line of the corporation's business and is of practical advantage to it, is one in which the corporation has an interest or a reasonable expectancy, and, by embracing the opportunity, the self-interest of the officer or director will be brought into conflict with that of the corporation, the law will not permit him to seize the opportunity for himself.

The corporate opportunity doctrine, as delineated by *Guth* and its progeny, holds that a corporate officer or director may not take a business opportunity for his own if: (1) the corporation is financially able to exploit the opportunity; (2) the opportunity is within the corporation's line of business; (3) the corporation has an interest or expectancy in the opportunity; and (4) by taking the opportunity for his own, the corporate fiduciary will thereby be placed in a position inimical to his duties to the corporation. The Court in *Guth* also derived a corollary which states that a director or officer may take a corporate opportunity if: (1) the opportunity is presented to the director or officer in his individual and not his corporate capacity; (2) the opportunity is not essential to the corporation; (3) the corporation holds no interest or expectancy in the opportunity; and (4) the director or officer has not wrongfully employed the resources of the corporation in pursuing or exploiting the opportunity. *Guth*, 5 A.2d at 509.

Thus, the contours of this doctrine are well established. It is important to note, however, that the tests enunciated in *Guth* and subsequent cases provide guidelines to be considered by a reviewing court in balancing the equities of an individual case. No one factor is dispositive and all factors must be taken into account insofar as they are applicable. Cases involving a claim of usurpation of a corporate opportunity range over a multitude of factual settings. Hard and fast rules are not easily crafted to deal with such an array of complex situations. The determination of "[w]hether or not a director has appropriated for himself something that in fairness should belong to the corporation is 'a factual question to be decided by reasonable inference from objective facts.'" *Guth*, 5 A.2d at 513. In the instant case, we find that the facts do not support the conclusion that Broz misappropriated a corporate opportunity.

We note at the outset that Broz became aware of the Michigan-2 opportunity in his individual and not his corporate capacity. In fact, it is clear from the record that Mackinac did not consider CIS a viable candidate for the acquisition of Michigan-2. Accordingly, Mackinac did not offer the property to CIS. In this factual posture, many of the fundamental concerns undergirding the law of corporate opportunity are not present (e.g., misappropriation of the corporation's proprietary information). The burden imposed upon Broz to show adherence to his fiduciary duties to CIS is thus lessened to some extent. Nevertheless, this fact is not dispositive. The determination of whether a particular fiduciary has usurped a corporate opportunity necessitates a careful examination of the circumstances, giving due credence to the factors enunciated in *Guth* and subsequent cases.

We turn now to an analysis of the factors relied on by the trial court. First, we find that CIS was not financially capable of exploiting the Michigan-2 opportunity. Although the Court of Chancery concluded otherwise, we hold that this finding was not supported by the evidence. The record shows that CIS was in a precarious financial position at the time Mackinac presented the Michigan-2 opportunity to Broz. Having recently emerged from lengthy and contentious bankruptcy proceedings, CIS was not in a position to commit capital to the acquisition of new assets. Further, the loan agreement entered into by CIS and its creditors severely limited the discretion of CIS as to the acquisition of new assets and substantially restricted the ability of CIS to incur new debt.

The Court of Chancery based its contrary finding on the fact that PriCellular had purchased an option to acquire CIS' bank debt. At the time that Broz was required to decide whether to accept the Michigan-2 opportunity, PriCellular had not yet acquired CIS, and any plans to do so were wholly speculative. Thus, contrary to the Court of Chancery's finding, Broz was not obligated to consider the contingency of a PriCellular acquisition of CIS and the related contingency of PriCellular thereafter waiving restrictions on the CIS bank debt. Broz was required to consider the facts only as they existed at the time he determined to accept the Mackinac offer and embark on his efforts to bring the transaction to fruition.

Second, while it may be said with some certainty that the Michigan-2 opportunity was within CIS' line of business, it is not equally clear that CIS had a cognizable interest or expectancy in the license.* **[7]** Under the third factor laid down by this Court in *Guth*, for an opportunity to be deemed to belong to the fiduciary's corporation, the corporation must have an interest or expectancy in that opportunity. Despite the fact that the nature of the Michigan-2 opportunity was historically close to the core operations of CIS, changes were in process. At the time the opportunity was presented, CIS was actively engaged in the process of divesting its cellular license holdings. CIS' articulated business plan did not involve any new acquisitions.

Finally, the corporate opportunity doctrine is implicated only in cases where the fiduciary's seizure of an opportunity results in a conflict between the fiduciary's duties to the corporation and the self-interest of the director as actualized by the exploitation of the opportunity. In the instant case, Broz' interest in acquiring and profiting from Michigan-2 created no duties that were inimical to his obligations to CIS. Broz, at all times relevant to the instant appeal, was the sole party in interest in RFBC, a competitor of CIS. CIS was fully aware of Broz' potentially conflicting duties. Broz, however, comported himself in a manner that was wholly in accord with his obligations to CIS. Broz took care not to usurp any opportunity which CIS was willing and able to pursue.

In concluding that Broz had usurped a corporate opportunity, the Court of Chancery placed great emphasis on the fact that Broz had not formally presented the matter to the CIS board. In so holding, the trial court erroneously grafted a new requirement onto the law of corporate opportunity, viz., the requirement of formal presentation under circumstances where the corporation does not have an interest, expectancy or financial ability.

The teaching of *Guth* and its progeny is that the director or officer must analyze the situation *ex ante* to determine whether the opportunity

---

* **[7]** The language in the *Guth* opinion relating to "line of business" is less than clear:

Where a corporation is engaged in a certain business, and an opportunity is presented to it embracing an activity as to which it has fundamental knowledge, practical experience and ability to pursue, which, logically and naturally, is adaptable to its business having regard for its financial position, and is consonant with its reasonable needs and aspirations for expansion, it may properly be said that the opportunity is within the corporation's line of business. *Guth*, 5 A.2d at 514. This formulation of the definition of the term "line of business" suggests that the business strategy and financial well-being of the corporation are also relevant to a determination of whether the opportunity is within the corporation's line of business. Since we find that these considerations are decisive under the other factors enunciated by the Court in *Guth*, we do not reach the question of whether they are here relevant to a determination of the corporation's line of business.

is one rightfully belonging to the corporation. If the director or officer believes, based on one of the factors articulated above, that the corporation is not entitled to the opportunity, then he may take it for himself. Of course, presenting the opportunity to the board creates a kind of "safe harbor" for the director, which removes the specter of a *post hoc* judicial determination that the director or officer has improperly usurped a corporate opportunity. Thus, presentation avoids the possibility that an error in the fiduciary's assessment of the situation will create future liability for breach of fiduciary duty. It is not the law of Delaware that presentation to the board is a necessary prerequisite to a finding that a corporate opportunity has not been usurped. * * *

The corporate opportunity doctrine represents a judicially crafted effort to harmonize the competing demands placed on corporate fiduciaries in a modern business environment. The doctrine seeks to reduce the possibility of conflict between a director's duties to the corporation and interests unrelated to that role. In the instant case, Broz adhered to his obligations to CIS. We hold that the Court of Chancery erred as a matter of law in concluding that Broz had a duty formally to present the Michigan-2 opportunity to the CIS board. We also hold that the trial court erred in its application of the corporate opportunity doctrine under the unusual facts of this case, where CIS had no interest or financial ability to acquire the opportunity, but the impending acquisition of CIS by PriCellular would or could have caused a change in those circumstances.

Therefore, we hold that Broz did not breach his fiduciary duties to CIS. Accordingly, we REVERSE the judgment of the Court of Chancery holding that Broz diverted a corporate opportunity properly belonging to CIS and imposing a constructive trust.

QUESTIONS

1.   In *Meinhard v. Salmon*, it was important that Salmon learned of the opportunity because he was the managing coadventurer. Is it important that Broz's knowledge of the opportunity was not due to his position as a director of CIS? Is it determinative?

2.   What could Broz have done differently to avoid this litigation?

3.   Would the court have analyzed the case differently if it had applied the ALI approach from *Northeast Harbor*? Which is the better approach?

4.   Would the court have analyzed the *Broz* case differently if RFBC had shareholders other than Broz? Does the corporate opportunity doctrine present special challenges to a person who is the director of two companies in competing businesses? *See* Note, *Venture Capitalists' Corporate Opportunity Problem*, 2001 COLUM. BUS. L. REV. 473 (2001) ("[W]hen a venture capitalist serves on the boards of numerous companies that operate in similar fields of business, the application of these tests is impractical, and as I intend to

demonstrate, has the potential to harm capital formation and business development.").

5.   What is the relationship between improper competition with a corporation and usurpation of a corporate opportunity? The court in Broz noted that "the corporate opportunity doctrine is implicated only in cases where the fiduciary's seizure of an opportunity results in a conflict between the fiduciary's duties to the corporation and the self-interest of the director as actualized by the exploitation of the opportunity." If an officer or director usurps a corporate opportunity is she necessarily then also improperly competing with the corporation?

Reflecting the similarity between the two is the fact that the classic remedy is the imposition of a constructive trust. This means that the usurper will be required to hold the property he seized for the benefit of the corporation. If he still has that property, the constructive trust requires him to sell it to the corporation at his cost. If he has sold the property at a profit, the corporation would recover the profit.

We close the section on usurpation with a trial-court application of Delaware law:

IN RE EBAY, INC. SHAREHOLDERS LITIGATION
Delaware Chancery Court, 2004
2004 WL 25321

CHANDLER, J. Shareholders of eBay, Inc. filed these consolidated derivative actions against certain eBay directors and officers for usurping corporate opportunities. Plaintiffs allege that eBay's investment banking advisor, Goldman Sachs Group, engaged in "spinning," a practice that involves allocating shares of lucrative initial public offerings of stock to favored clients. In effect, the plaintiff shareholders allege that Goldman Sachs bribed certain eBay insiders, using the currency of highly profitable investment opportunities—opportunities that should have been offered to, or provided for the benefit of, eBay rather than the favored insiders. Plaintiffs accuse Goldman Sachs of aiding and abetting the corporate insiders breach of their fiduciary duty of loyalty to eBay.

The individual eBay defendants, as well as Goldman Sachs, have moved to dismiss these consolidated actions for failure to state a claim. * * * For reasons I briefly discuss below, I deny all of the defendants' motions to dismiss.

I.   BACKGROUND FACTS

The facts, as alleged in the complaint, are straightforward. In 1995, defendants Pierre M. Omidyar and Jeffrey Skoll founded nominal defendant eBay, a Delaware corporation, as a sole proprietorship. eBay is a pioneer in online trading platforms, providing a virtual auction community for buyers and sellers to list items for sale and to bid on items of interest. In 1998, eBay retained Goldman Sachs and other investment banks to underwrite an initial public offering of common stock. Goldman Sachs was the lead underwriter. The stock was priced at $18 per share. Goldman Sachs purchased about 1.2 million shares. Shares of eBay stock became immensely valuable during 1998 and 1999, rising to $175 per share in early April 1999. Around that time, eBay made a secondary offering, issuing 6.5 million shares of common stock at $170 per share for a total of $1.1 billion. Goldman Sachs again served as lead underwriter. Goldman Sachs was asked in 2001 to serve as eBay's financial advisor in connection with an acquisition by eBay of PayPal, Inc. For these services, eBay has paid Goldman Sachs over $8 million.

During this same time period, Goldman Sachs "rewarded" the individual defendants by allocating to them thousands of IPO shares, managed by Goldman Sachs, at the initial offering price. Because the IPO market during this particular period of time was extremely active, prices of initial stock offerings often doubled or tripled in a single day. Investors who were well connected, either to Goldman Sachs or to similarly situated investment banks serving as IPO underwriters, were able to flip these investments into instant profit by selling the equities in a few days or even in a few hours after they were initially purchased.

The essential allegation of the complaint is that Goldman Sachs provided these IPO share allocations to the individual defendants to show appreciation for eBay's business and to enhance Goldman Sachs' chances of obtaining future eBay business. In addition to co-founding eBay, defendant Omidyar has been eBay's CEO, CFO and President. He is eBay's largest stockholder, owning more than 23% of the company's equity. Goldman Sachs allocated Omidyar shares in at least forty IPOs at the initial offering price. Omidyar resold these securities in the public market for millions of dollars in profit. Defendant Whitman owns 3.3% of eBay stock and has been President, CEO and a director since early 1998. Whitman also has been a director of Goldman Sachs since 2001. Goldman Sachs allocated Whitman shares in over a 100 IPOs at the initial offering price. Whitman sold these equities in the open market and reaped millions of dollars in profit. Defendant Skoll, in addition to co-founding eBay, has served in various positions at the company, including Vice-President of Strategic Planning and Analysis and President. He served as an eBay director from December 1996 to March 1998. Skoll is eBay's second largest stockholder, owning about 13% of the company. Goldman Sachs has allocated Skoll shares in at least 75 IPOs at the initial offering price, which Skoll promptly resold on the open market, allowing him to realize millions of dollars in profit. Finally, defendant Robert C. Kagle has served as an eBay director since June 1997. Goldman Sachs allocated

Kagle shares in at least 25 IPOs at the initial offering price. Kagle promptly resold these equities, and recorded millions of dollars in profit.

II.   ANALYSIS

* * *

B.   Corporate Opportunity

Plaintiffs have stated a claim that defendants usurped a corporate opportunity of eBay. Defendants insist that Goldman Sachs' IPO allocations to eBay's insider directors were "collateral investments opportunities" that arose by virtue of the inside directors status as wealthy individuals. They argue that this is not a corporate opportunity within the corporation's line of business or an opportunity in which the corporation had an interest or expectancy. These arguments are unavailing.

First, no one disputes that eBay financially was able to exploit the opportunities in question. Second, eBay was in the business of investing in securities. The complaint alleges that eBay "consistently invested a portion of its cash on hand in marketable securities." According to eBay's 1999 10–K, for example, eBay had more than $550 million invested in equity and debt securities. eBay invested more than $181 million in "short-term investments" and $373 million in "long-term investments." Thus, investing was "a line of business" of eBay. Third, the facts alleged in the complaint suggest that investing was integral to eBay's cash management strategies and a significant part of its business. Finally, it is no answer to say, as do defendants, that IPOs are risky investments. It is undisputed that eBay was never given an opportunity to turn down the IPO allocations as too risky.

Defendants also argue that to view the IPO allocations in question as corporate opportunities will mean that every advantageous investment opportunity that comes to an officer or director will be considered a corporate opportunity. On the contrary, the allegations in the complaint in this case indicate that unique, below-market price investment opportunities were offered by Goldman Sachs to the insider defendants as financial inducements to maintain and secure corporate business. This was not an instance where a broker offered advice to a director about an investment in a marketable security. The conduct challenged here involved a large investment bank that regularly did business with a company steering highly lucrative IPO allocations to select insider directors and officers at that company, allegedly both to reward them for past business and to induce them to direct future business to that investment bank. This is a far cry from the defendants' characterization of the conduct in question as merely "a broker's investment recommendations" to a wealthy client.

Nor can one seriously argue that this conduct did not place the insider defendants in a position of conflict with their duties to the corporation. One can realistically characterize these IPO allocations as a form of commercial discount or rebate for past or future investment banking services. Viewed pragmatically, it is easy to understand how steering such commercial rebates to certain insider directors places those directors in an obvious conflict between their self-interest and the corporation's interest. It is noteworthy, too, that the Securities and Exchange Commission has taken the position that "spinning" practices violate the obligations of broker-dealers under the "Free-riding and Withholding Interpretation" rules. As the SEC has explained, "the purpose of the interpretation is to protect the integrity of the public offering system by ensuring that members make a bona fide public distribution of 'hot issue' securities and do not withhold such securities for their own benefit or use the securities to reward other persons who are in a position to direct future business to the member."

Finally, even if one assumes that IPO allocations like those in question here do not constitute a corporate opportunity, a cognizable claim is nevertheless stated on the common law ground that an agent is under a duty to account for profits obtained personally in connection with transactions related to his or her company. The complaint gives rise to a reasonable inference that the insider directors accepted a commission or gratuity that rightfully belonged to eBay but that was improperly diverted to them. Even if this conduct does not run afoul of the corporate opportunity doctrine, it may still constitute a breach of the fiduciary duty of loyalty. Thus, even if one does not consider Goldman Sachs' IPO allocations to these corporate insiders-allocations that generated millions of dollars in profit-to be a corporate opportunity, the defendant directors were nevertheless not free to accept this consideration from a company, Goldman Sachs, that was doing significant business with eBay and that arguably intended the consideration as an inducement to maintaining the business relationship in the future.

C.   Aiding and Abetting Claim

Plaintiffs' complaint adequately alleges the existence of a fiduciary relationship, that the individual defendants breached their fiduciary duty and that plaintiffs have been damaged because of the concerted actions of the individual defendants and Goldman Sachs. Goldman Sachs, however, disputes whether it "knowingly participated" in the eBay insiders' alleged breach of fiduciary duty. The allegation, however, is that Goldman Sachs had provided underwriting and investment advisory services to eBay for years and that it knew that each of the individual defendants owed a fiduciary duty to eBay not to profit personally at eBay's expense and to devote their undivided loyalty to the interests of eBay. Goldman Sachs also knew or had reason to know of eBay's investment of excess cash in marketable securities and debt. Goldman Sachs was aware (or charged with a duty to know) of earlier SEC interpretations that prohibited steering "hot issue" securities to persons in a position to direct future business to the broker-dealer. Taken together, these allegations allege a claim for aiding and abetting sufficient to withstand a motion to dismiss.

III. CONCLUSION

For all of the above reasons, I deny the defendants' motions to dismiss the complaint in this consolidated action.

c. Being on Both Sides of a Deal with the Corporation ("Self-Dealing" or "Interested Director Transactions")

Bubba's Burritos, Inc. prospers: more locations, more shareholders. The corporation is now considering leasing a building owned by Capel, who is a director and the majority shareholder. In such a transaction, Capel has divided loyalties: in her role as lessor, she has an incentive to have Bubba's overpay, because that will put more money in her own pocket; as a fiduciary of Bubba's, though, she should want Bubba's to pay the lowest possible price on the lease. Should a corporation be able to transact business with one of its directors? With the spouse of a director? With its majority shareholder? Should challenges to any such transactions be subject to the business judgment rule?

Common law allowed a business to void an interested director transaction if even one shareholder objected to it. This is a short-sighted view, though, because sometimes the interested director transaction may be a good deal for the corporation. In most states, there are statutes that permit the approval of self-dealing transactions.

HMG/COURTLAND PROPERTIES, INC. V. GRAY

Delaware Chancery Court, 1999
749 A.2d 94

[Gray and Fieber were two of the five directors of HMG/Courtland Properties, Inc., ("HMG"), a corporation that bought and sold commercial real estate. Gray was HMG's principal negotiator in these real estate transactions. On behalf of HMG, Gray negotiated a major sale of HMG real estate to NAF Associates ("NAF").

Fieber owned an interest in NAF, disclosed that interest to the other directors and abstained from voting on the proposed sale to NAF at the HMG directors meeting. Gray, through relatives and related business entities, also owned an interest in NAF. Gray did not disclose that interest to the other directors. Gray was one of the four directors of HMG who voted to approve the land sale to NAF. Fieber knew of Gray's interest but did not disclose Gray's interest to the other directors.]

STRINE, VICE CHANCELLOR. This case involves thirteen-year-old real estate sales transactions between HMG/Courtland Properties, Inc. as seller and two of HMG's directors, Lee Gray and Norman Fieber as buyers. While Fieber's self-interest in the transactions was properly disclosed, neither he nor Gray informed their fellow directors that Gray— who took the lead in negotiating the sales for HMG—had a buy-side interest. Gray's interest was concealed from HMG for a decade and was only discovered inadvertently by the company in 1996.

In this post-trial opinion, I find that Fieber and Gray breached their fiduciary duties of loyalty and care and defrauded the company. I award relief to HMG designed to remedy the harm caused by their misconduct.

This case directly implicates both the business judgment rule and § 144. Even though the business judgment rule and § 144 serve somewhat different purposes and cannot be interpreted identically, they are closely related.

In a case where § 144 is directly applicable, compliance with its terms should be a minimum requirement to retain the protection of the business judgment rule. The desirability of doctrinal and statutory coherence, where that can be accomplished without sacrificing public policy interests, also counsels that conclusion. In this case, both the business judgment rule as traditionally interpreted and § 144 point toward the entire fairness standard as the appropriate form of review.

Gray's interest in the * * * NAF Transactions implicates both the primary rationale for the entire fairness standard of review and the core concern of § 144—"self-dealing."

Gray's undisclosed, buy-side interest in the Transactions is a classic case of self-dealing. Proof of such undisclosed self-dealing, in itself, is sufficient to rebut the presumption of the business judgment rule and invoke entire fairness review.

Section 144 of the Delaware General Corporation Law dictates this conclusion. That statute is implicated whenever a corporation and "1 or more of its directors or officers * * * or partnership * * * or other organization in which 1 or more of its directors or officers * * * have a financial interest" engage in a transaction. 8 Del. C. § 144.

The interests of Gray and Fieber in the NAF Transactions trigger the statute. Section 144 provides that a self-dealing transaction will not be "void or voidable solely for this reason" if the transaction is ratified by a majority of the disinterested directors or by a shareholder vote. 8 Del. C. § 144(a)(1), (2). Such ratification is valid, however, only if the "material facts as [to the director's] relationship or interest and as to the contract or transaction are disclosed or are known to the [relevant ratifying authority]. . . ." Id. Neither Fieber nor Gray disclosed Gray's "interest" in the "[T]ransaction[s]" to the HMG Board. Id. In the absence of such disclosure, 8 Del. C. § 144(a)(1), the Transactions can only be rendered non-voidable if they were "fair as to [HMG] as of the time [they were] authorized."* **[24]** 8 Del. C. § 144(a)(3).

For all these reasons, Gray and Fieber must demonstrate the fairness of the NAF Transactions.

It is a well-settled principle of Delaware law that where directors stand on both sides of a transaction, they have "the burden of establishing its entire fairness, sufficient to pass the test of careful scrutiny by the courts." *Weinberger v. UOP, Inc.,* Del. Supr., 457 A.2d 701, 710 (1983) ("There is no 'safe harbor' for such divided loyalties in Delaware."). Directors will be found to have acted with entire fairness where they "demonstrate their utmost good faith and the most scrupulous inherent fairness of the bargain." Id.

* * *

The concept of entire fairness has two components: fair dealing and fair price. Fair dealing "embraces questions of when the transaction was timed, how it was initiated, structured, negotiated, disclosed to the directors, and how the approvals of the directors and the stockholders were obtained." Id. Fair price "relates to the economic and financial considerations of the proposed merger, including all relevant factors: assets, market value, earnings, future prospects, and any other elements that affect the intrinsic or inherent value of a company's stock." Id. In making a determination as to the entire fairness of a transaction, the Court does not focus on one component over the other, but examines all aspects of the issue as a whole.

i. Fair Dealing

The defendants have failed to convince me that the NAF Transactions were fairly negotiated or ratified. From the beginning of the negotiations, Gray, the primary negotiator for the seller in the Transactions, was interested in taking a position on the buyer's side. As such, Gray lacked the pure seller-side incentive that should have been applied on behalf of HMG—particularly in Transactions in which one director was already on the other side.

Given the intrinsically unique nature of real estate, the bargaining skills and incentives of HMG's negotiator were likely to be more important than if the negotiator was arranging for the sale of a financial

---

* **[24]** While non-compliance with §§ 144(a)(1), (2)'s disclosure requirement by definition triggers fairness review rather than business judgment rule review, the satisfaction of §§ 144(a)(1) or (a)(2) alone does not always have the opposite effect of invoking business judgment rule review that one might presume would flow from a literal application of the statute's terms. Rather, satisfaction of §§ 144(a)(1) or (a)(2) simply protects against invalidation of the transaction "solely" because it is an interested one. Id. As such, § 144 is best seen as establishing a floor for board conduct but not a ceiling.

asset. As the defendants' own expert conceded, in the context of a real estate sales transaction negotiation skills are "exceedingly important."

The process was thus anything but fair. Because neither Gray nor Fieber disclosed Gray's interest, the HMG Board unwittingly ratified Transactions in which a conflicted negotiator was relied upon by the Adviser to negotiate already conflicted Transactions.

ii.   Fair Price

The defendants attempt to meet their burden of demonstrating fair price by trying to convince me that the prices used in the Transactions were in a range of fairness, as proven by the 1984 Appraisals.

Once again, I believe the defendants misconceive their burden. On the record before me, I obviously cannot conclude that HMG received a shockingly low price in the Transactions or that the prices paid were not within the low end of the range of possible prices that might have been paid in negotiated arm's-length deals. In that narrow sense, the defendants have proven that the price was "fair." But that proof does not necessarily satisfy their burden under the entire fairness standard. As the American Law Institute corporate governance principles point out:

> A contract price might be fair in the sense that it corresponds to market price, and yet the corporation might have refused to make the contract if a given material fact had been disclosed * * *. Furthermore, fairness is often a range, rather than a point, so that a transaction involving a payment by the corporation may be fair even though it is consummated at the high end of the range. If an undisclosed material fact had been disclosed, however, the corporation might have declined to transact at that high price, or might have bargained the price down lower in the range. 1 Principles of Corporate Governance; Analysis and Recommendations Part V at 202 (1994).

The defendants have failed to persuade me that HMG would not have gotten a materially higher value for Wallingford and the Grossman's Portfolio had Gray and Fieber come clean about Gray's interest. That is, they have not convinced me that their misconduct did not taint the price to HMG's disadvantage. I base this conclusion on several factors.

First, the defendants' own expert on value, James Nolan, testified that his opinion that the prices paid in the Transactions were fair was premised on his assumption that Gray was not the leading negotiator from HMG's side. To the extent that Gray was a principal player in discussing terms with Fieber, Nolan said that his conclusion about the fairness of the price might well be different.* [28]

---

*   [28] Nolan is not a certified appraiser but has extensive experience in the real estate field so I decided to consider his testimony despite a credible challenge to his credentials mounted by HMG. Nolan did not perform a formal valuation of the affected properties as of 1986.

Second, the 1984 Appraisals understated the values of the Wallingford Property and the Portfolio as of early 1986. The Leased Fee Values in the 1984 Appraisals were generated through a discounted cash flow analysis utilizing 1983 actual rents and projected rents for 1984–1986. By 1986, it was clear that the Grossman's stores operating at Portfolio sites were performing better, and thereby generating higher lease payments (because a portion of the lease payments was tied to store sales) than estimated by the appraisers who conducted the 1984 Appraisals. If an update had been done in 1986, it would have produced values well in excess of the 1984 Appraisals. This conclusion is bolstered by appraisals done on six of the Portfolio properties in 1987 at the request of Chemical Bank, which selected the properties to be appraised. The 1987 appraisals indicated values 66% higher than the Leased Fee Values in the 1984 Appraisals. PX 396 (also indicating a 64.5% increase in the Fee Simple Values).

Third, a skilled and properly motivated negotiator could have done better than Leased Fee Value in price negotiations. As the defendants' expert Nolan testified, the skills of a negotiator are "exceedingly important" in a real estate transaction. Even without an updated appraisal, a properly motivated negotiator could have argued from the actual rents in 1984 and 1985 that the Leased Fee Value understated the value of the Portfolio. Furthermore, a properly motivated negotiator would have focused on the Fee Simple Value because of the likelihood that many of the Portfolio properties would come off lease from Grossman's. That eventuality—which came true—justified a higher price than the Leased Fee Value. I have no confidence that Gray negotiated with the Fiebers in any vigorous or skillful way. Since he wanted to participate on the buy-side, he had less than a satisfactory incentive to do so. Since the outcome of a real estate negotiation is often heavily influenced by the skills of the negotiators, this factor undercuts the claim that the price was fair to HMG. *See* 1 Principles of Corporate Governance: Analysis and Recommendations § 5.02 at 220 (1994) (in evaluating the fairness of a transaction, the court should consider the fact that the corporation was not represented by an unconflicted negotiator).

Finally, had Gray disclosed his interest, I believe that HMG would have terminated his involvement in the negotiations and have taken a much more traditional approach to selling the affected properties. To the extent that HMG continued to consider a sales transaction, I believe it would have commissioned new appraisals and would have sought purchasers other than Fieber.

While I believe Nolan sincerely attempted to give his honest opinion about the financial fairness of the Transactions, his rather unique "role playing" approach was heavily dependent on assumptions he made about the motivations and roles of the humans involved. Since those assumptions do not comport with my view of the evidence, I give little weight to his testimony.

Taken together, these factors lead me to conclude that the defendants have not demonstrated that they paid a fair price in the sense inherent in the entire fairness standard.

For the foregoing reasons, judgment shall be entered for HMG against defendants Gray and Fieber.* * * The parties shall report back to me in three weeks. If an agreed upon order is not presented, each party shall submit its position regarding the outstanding issues and an accompanying form of order.

QUESTIONS

1.   What did Fieber do wrong?

2.   Would the court have held Fieber and Gray liable if both Fieber and Gray had completely disclosed their interests in NAF and Fieber and Gray had abstained from voting?

a)   Is Delaware § 144(a)(1) exculpatory? Note the phrase "solely for this reason" in the prefatory paragraph of § 144(a).

b)   What is the relationship between § 144 and the business judgment rule?

c)   Under § 144, when is the fairness of the transaction to the corporation an issue?

3.   How would *HMG/Courtland* have been decided under MBCA §§ 8.60–8.63?

a)   Suppose we want disinterested directors to approve a self-dealing transaction. What would constitute a quorum under the Delaware statute? How about under the MBCA provisions? (BTW, can an interested director show up at the meeting under either legislation?)

b)   Are the MBCA provisions for approval by disinterested directors or disinterested shareholders exculpatory? In other words, does approval by disinterested shareholders or disinterested shareholders insulate the transaction from judicial scrutiny?

4.   We have omitted portions of the opinion discussing other claims against Fieber and Gray, claims against another defendant, and the measure of recovery. If you were representing HMG, what evidence would you present to establish the measure of recovery against Fieber and Gray for breach of duty of loyalty in connection with HMG's sale of real estate to NAF?

5.   Why didn't the Delaware court in *HMG* treat NAF's purchase of land from HMG as a usurpation of a corporate opportunity? What is the difference between "interested director transactions" and "corporate opportunities"? *Shapiro v. Greenfield*, 764 A.2d 270, 277 (Md. 2000), made the following comparison: a director transacting business with the

corporation as contrasted with a director taking business transactions away from the corporation. Is that helpful?

6. Looking back, how do the Delaware rules for interested director transactions in the *HMG/Courtland* case differ from the Delaware rules for corporate opportunities in *Broz*? *See generally* Eric G. Orlinsky, *Corporate Opportunity Doctrine and Interested Directors Transactions: A Framework for Analysis in An Attempt to Restore Predictability*, 24 DEL. J. CORP. L. 451 (1999).

7. We have seen that a corporation's top managers may also be directors. How does the board set such a manager's pay and benefits? Isn't the manager/director's negotiation of her compensation with the board an interested director transaction? Often a corporation's board will delegate compensation decisions to a "compensation committee" made up of directors other than those whose compensation is being established. As recent publicity about huge pay packages for some corporate managers have shown, such committees can be ineffective. Why?

Looking ahead, how do the Delaware rules for interested director transactions in the *HMG/Courtland* case differ from the Iowa (an MBCA state) rules in the next case? In reading the *Cookies Food Products* case, consider the following questions:

1. What were the interested director transactions?

2. Who approved the transactions?

3. In this litigation challenging the transactions, who proved what?

COOKIES FOOD PRODUCTS, INC. V. LAKES WAREHOUSE DISTRIBUTING, INC.

Supreme Court of Iowa, 1988
430 N.W.2d 447

NEUMAN, JUSTICE. This is a shareholders' derivative suit brought by the minority shareholders of a closely held Iowa corporation specializing in barbeque sauce, Cookies Food Products, Inc. (Cookies). The target of the lawsuit is the majority shareholder, Duane "Speed" Herrig and two of his family-owned corporations, Lakes Warehouse Distributing, Inc. (Lakes) and Speed's Automotive Co., Inc. (Speed's). Plaintiffs alleged that Herrig, by acquiring control of Cookies and executing self-dealing contracts, breached his fiduciary duty to the company and fraudulently misappropriated and converted corporate funds. Plaintiffs sought actual and punitive damages. Trial to the court resulted in a verdict for the defendants, the district court finding that Herrig's actions benefited, rather than harmed, Cookies. We affirm.

I. Background.

* * * L.D. Cook of Storm Lake, Iowa, founded Cookies in 1975 to produce and distribute his original barbeque sauce. Searching for a plant site in a community that would provide financial backing, Cook met with business leaders in seventeen Iowa communities, outlining his plans to build a growth-oriented company. He selected Wall Lake, Iowa, persuading thirty-five members of that community, including Herrig and the plaintiffs, to purchase Cookies stock. All of the investors hoped Cookies would improve the local job market and tax base. The record reveals that it has done just that.

Early sales of the product, however, were dismal. After the first year's operation, Cookies was in dire financial straits. At that time, Herrig was one of thirty-five shareholders and held only two hundred shares. He was also the owner of an auto parts business, Speed's Automotive, and Lakes Warehouse Distributing, Inc., a company that distributed auto parts from Speed's. Cookies' board of directors approached Herrig with the idea of distributing the company's products. It authorized Herrig to purchase Cookies' sauce for twenty percent under wholesale price, which he could then resell at full wholesale price. Under this arrangement, Herrig began to market and distribute the sauce to his auto parts customers and to grocery outlets from Lakes' trucks as they traversed the regular delivery routes for Speed's Automotive.

In May 1977, Cookies formalized this arrangement by executing an exclusive distribution agreement with Lakes. Pursuant to this agreement, Cookies was responsible only for preparing the product; Lakes, for its part, assumed all costs of warehousing, marketing, sales, delivery, promotion, and advertising. Cookies retained the right to fix the sales price of its products and agreed to pay Lakes thirty percent of its gross sales for these services.

Cookies' sales have soared under the exclusive distributorship contract with Lakes. Gross sales in 1976, the year prior to the agreement, totaled only $20,000, less than half of Cookies' expenses that year. By 1985, when this suit was commenced, annual sales reached $2,400,000.

As sales increased, Cookies' board of directors amended and extended the original distributorship agreement. In 1979, the board amended the original agreement to give Lakes an additional two percent of gross sales to cover freight costs for the ever-expanding market for Cookies' sauce. In 1980, the board extended the amended agreement through 1984 to allow Herrig to make long-term advertising commitments. Recognizing the role that Herrig's personal strengths played in the success of their joint endeavor, the board also amended the agreement that year to allow Cookies to cancel the agreement with Lakes if Herrig died or disposed of the corporation's stock.

In 1981, L.D. Cook, the majority shareholder up to this time, decided to sell his interest in Cookies. He first offered the directors an opportunity to buy his stock, but the board declined to purchase any of his 8100 shares. Herrig then offered Cook and all other shareholders $10 per share for their stock, which was twice the original price. Because of the overwhelming response to these offers, Herrig had purchased enough Cookies stock by January 1982 to become the majority shareholder. His investment of $140,000 represented fifty-three percent of the 28,700 outstanding shares.

Shortly after Herrig acquired majority control he replaced four of the five members of the Cookies' board with members he selected. Subsequent changes made in the corporation under Herrig's leadership formed the basis for this lawsuit.

First, under Herrig's leadership, Cookies' board has extended the term of the exclusive distributorship agreement with Lakes and expanded the scope of services for which it compensates Herrig and his companies. In April 1982, when a sales increase of twenty-five percent over the previous year required Cookies to seek additional short-term storage for the peak summer season, the board accepted Herrig's proposal to compensate Lakes at the "going rate" for use of its nearby storage facilities. The board decided to use Lakes' storage facilities because building and staffing its own facilities would have been more expensive.

Second, Herrig moved from his role as director and distributor to take on an additional role in product development. This created a dispute over a royalty Herrig began to receive. Herrig's role in product development began in 1982 when Cookies diversified its product line to include taco sauce. Herrig developed the recipe because he recognized that taco sauce, while requiring many of the same ingredients needed in barbeque sauce, is less expensive to produce. Further, since consumer demand for taco sauce is more consistent throughout the year than the demand for barbeque sauce, this new product line proved to be a profitable method for increasing year-round utilization of production facilities and staff. In August 1982, Cookies' board approved a royalty fee to be paid to Herrig for this taco sauce recipe. This royalty plan was similar to royalties the board paid to L.D. Cook for the barbeque sauce recipe. Although Herrig's rate is equivalent to a sales percentage slightly higher than what Cook receives, it yields greater profit to Cookies because this new product line is cheaper to produce.

Third, since 1982 Cookies' board has twice approved additional compensation for Herrig. In January 1983, the board authorized payment of a $1000 per month "consultant fee" in lieu of salary, because accelerated sales required Herrig to spend extra time managing the company. In August, 1983, the board authorized another increase in Herrig's compensation. Further, at the suggestion of a Cookies director who also served as an accountant for Cookies, Lakes, and Speed's, the Cookies board amended the exclusive distributorship agreement to allow Lakes an additional two percent of gross sales as a promotion allowance to expand the market for Cookies products outside of Iowa. As a direct result of this action, by 1986 Cookies regularly shipped products to several states throughout the country.

As we have previously noted, however, Cookies' growth and success has not pleased all its shareholders. The discontent is motivated by two factors that have effectively precluded shareholders from sharing in Cookies' financial success: the fact that Cookies is a closely held corporation, and the fact that it has not paid dividends. Because Cookies' stock is not publicly traded, shareholders have no ready access to buyers for their stock at current values that reflect the company's success. Without dividends, the shareholders have no ready method of realizing a return on their investment in the company. This is not to say that Cookies has improperly refused to pay dividends. The evidence reveals that Cookies would have violated the terms of its loan with the Small Business Administration had it declared dividends before repaying that debt. That SBA loan was not repaid until the month before the plaintiffs filed this action.

Through the exclusive distributorship agreements, taco sauce royalty, warehousing fees, and consultant fee, plaintiffs claimed that Herrig breached his fiduciary duties to the corporation and its shareholders because he allegedly negotiated for these arrangements without fully disclosing the benefit he would gain.

The court concluded that Herrig had breached no duties owed to Cookies or to its minority shareholders. * * *

On appeal from this ruling, the plaintiffs challenge: (1) the district court's allocation of the burden of proof with regard to the four claims of self-dealing; (2) the standard employed by the court to determine whether Herrig's self-dealing was fair and reasonable to Cookies; (3) the finding that any self-dealing by Herrig was done in good faith, and with honesty and fairness; (4) the finding that Herrig breached no duty to disclose crucial facts to Cookies' board before it completed deliberations on Herrig's self-dealing transactions; and (5) the district court's denial of restitution and other equitable remedies as compensation for Herrig's alleged breach of his duty of loyalty. After a brief review of the nature and source of Herrig's fiduciary duties, we will address the appellants' challenges in turn.

II. Fiduciary Duties.

Herrig, as an officer and director of Cookies, owes a fiduciary duty to the company and its shareholders. Herrig concedes that Iowa law imposed the same fiduciary responsibilities based on his status as majority stockholder.

* * * Appellants claim that Herrig violated his duty of loyalty to Cookies.

* * * The legislature enacted section 496A.34, quoted here in pertinent part, that establishes three sets of circumstances under which a director may engage in self-dealing without clearly violating the duty of loyalty:

> No contract or other transaction between a corporation and one or more of its directors or any other corporation, firm, association or entity in which one or more of its directors are directors or officers or are financially interested, shall be either void or voidable because of such relationship or interest * * * if any of the following occur:
>
>   1.   The fact of such relationship or interest is disclosed or known to the board of directors or committee which authorizes, approves, or ratifies the contract or transaction ... without counting the votes * * * of such interested director.
>
>   2.   The fact of such relationship or interest is disclosed or known to the shareholders entitled to vote [on the transaction] and they authorize * * * such contract or transaction by vote or written consent.
>
>   3.   The contract or transaction is fair and reasonable to the corporation.

Some commentators have supported the view that satisfaction of any one of the foregoing statutory alternatives, in and of itself, would prove that a director has fully met the duty of loyalty. We are obliged, however, to interpret statutes in conformity with the common law wherever statutory language does not directly negate it. Because the common law and section 496A.34 require directors to show "good faith, honesty, and fairness" in self-dealing, we are persuaded that satisfaction of any one of these three alternatives under the statute would merely preclude us from rendering the transaction void or voidable outright solely on the basis "of such [director's] relationship or interest." Iowa Code § 496A.34. To the contrary, we are convinced that the legislature did not intend by this statute to enable a court, in a shareholder's derivative suit, to rubber stamp any transaction to which a board of directors or the shareholders of a corporation have consented. Such an interpretation would invite those who stand to gain from such transactions to engage in improprieties to obtain consent. We thus require directors who engage in self-dealing to establish the additional element that they have acted in good faith, honesty, and fairness.

III. Burden of Proof.

Appellants contend that the district court improperly placed upon them the burden of proving that Herrig's self-dealing was not honest, in good faith, or fair to Cookies. The district court's ruling addressed Herrig's duties of care and loyalty in these circumstances, noting that in duty of care challenges the burden of proof is on plaintiffs because of the business judgment rule which affords directors the presumption that their decisions are informed, made in good faith, and honestly believed by them to be in the best interests of the company. *See Smith v. Van Gorkom*, 488 A.2d 858, 872 (Del.1985). The district court then noted the different burden imposed in challenges under Iowa's duty of loyalty statute, which, in its words "require[s] the director challenged in a self-dealing suit to carry the burden of establishing his good faith, honesty, and fairness."

After reviewing the record in light of the district court's ruling, we are persuaded that the court appropriately recognized the shifting burdens of proof in duty of loyalty cases.

IV. Standard of Law.

Next, appellants claim the district court applied an inappropriate standard of law to determine whether Herrig's conduct was fair and reasonable to Cookies. Appellants correctly assert that self-dealing transactions must have the earmarks of arms-length transactions before a court can find them to be fair or reasonable. The crux of appellants' claim is that the court should have focused on the fair market value of Herrig's services to Cookies rather than on the success Cookies achieved as a result of Herrig's actions.

We agree with appellants' contention that corporate profitability should not be the sole criteria [sic; should be "sole criterion"] by which to test the fairness and reasonableness of Herrig's fees. Applying such reasoning to the record before us, however, we cannot agree with appellants' assertion that Herrig's services were either unfairly priced or inconsistent with Cookies corporate interest.

There can be no serious dispute that the four agreements in issue—for exclusive distributorship, taco sauce royalty, warehousing, and consulting fees—have all benefited Cookies, as demonstrated by its financial success. Even if we assume Cookies could have procured similar services from other vendors at lower costs, we are not convinced that Herrig's fees were therefore unreasonable or exorbitant. Like the district court, we are not persuaded by appellants' expert testimony that Cookies' sales and profits would have been the same under agreements with other vendors.

V.   Denial of Equitable Relief.

* * * While both Iowa's statutes and case law impose a duty of disclosure on interested directors who engage in self-dealing, neither has delineated what information must be disclosed, or to whom. * * *

Examining Herrig's conduct under this duty of disclosure, we find no support for plaintiffs' assertion that Herrig owed the minority shareholders a duty to disclose any information before the board executed the exclusive distributorship, royalty, warehousing, or consultant fee agreements. These actions comprise management activity, and our statutes place the duty of managing the affairs of the corporation on the board of directors, not the shareholders. Because the shareholders had no role in making decisions concerning these agreements, we hold that Herrig owed these shareholders no duty to disclose facts concerning any aspect of these agreements before the board entered or extended them. We also note that plaintiffs did not complain at trial that the financial reports they regularly received concerning the affairs of the company were anything less than adequate.

With regard to the board of directors, the record before us aptly demonstrates that all members of Cookies' board were well aware of Herrig's dual ownership in Lakes and Speed's. We are unaware of any authority supporting plaintiffs' contention that Herrig was obligated to disclose to Cookies' board or shareholders the extent of his profits resulting from these distribution and warehousing agreements. * * *

We concur in the trial court's assessment of the evidence presented and affirm its dismissal of plaintiffs' claims.

AFFIRMED.

SCHULTZ, JUSTICE (dissenting). My quarrel with the majority opinion is not with its interpretation of the law, but with its application of the law to the facts. I would reverse the trial court's holding.

The majority opinion correctly stated the common law and statutory principles. When there is self-dealing by a majority stockholder which is challenged, the majority stockholder has the burden to establish that they have acted in good faith, honesty and fairness. This burden of fairness requires not just a showing of profitability, but also a showing of the fairness of the bargain to the interest of the corporation. I would hold that Herrig failed to sustain his burden. * * *

I believe that Herrig failed on his burden of proof by what he did not show. He did not produce evidence of the local going rate for distribution contracts or storage fees outside of a very limited amount of self-serving testimony. He simply did not show the fair market value of his services or expense for freight, advertising and storage cost. He did not show that his taco sauce royalty was fair. This was his burden. He cannot succeed on it by merely showing the success of the company. * * *

QUESTIONS AND NOTES

1.   Duane "Speed" Herrig was both a director and the majority shareholder. Would the court have decided this case differently if he had been only a director? Only a majority shareholder?

2.   Herrig has been elected to The American Royal Barbecue Hall of Fame which provides this biographical information: "Speed Herrig is known as the Sauceman, and is one of the founding members of the Iowa Barbecue Society. He owns Cookies Food Products and has been in the barbecue sauce business for over 35 years. He took a small one-man operation and turned it into one of the largest regional sauce manufacturers in the United States. Speed and his staff travel across the country each year in his famous 'Rib Wagon', bringing BBQ to crowds of sauce lovers." http://www.americanroyal. com/p/219. Here is a photo of Speed Herrig (left) with Mike Mills, who is four-time world champion barbecue pitmaster.

3.   Under the Iowa version of the MBCA, when is fairness of an interested director transaction an issue? Under the current version of the MBCA, when is fairness of an interested director transaction an issue? *See* MBCA § 8.61(b) and Official Comment 2 to § 8.61.

4.   Is the approach of the Iowa court in determining the fairness of Cookies' interested director transactions with Herrig's entities consistent with the approach of the Delaware court in determining the fairness of HMG's transaction with Gray's entity?

5.   If Cookies were a Delaware corporation, would the court have decided this case differently? How would it have come out under MBCA §§ 8.60–8.63?

6.   For more on Cookies' barbecue and taco sauces, see "Cookies Wild Web Page" at www.cookiesbbq.com.

3.   DUTY (OR OBLIGATION?) TO ACT IN GOOD FAITH

Everyone agrees that fiduciaries must act in good faith. This undeniable truth is codified at MBCA § 8.30(a)(1): "Each member of the board of directors, when discharging the duties of a director, shall act: (1) in good faith." And, courts have consistently described directors' "good faith" as a "key ingredient" of the business judgment rule.* *See also* MBCA § 8.31(a)(2)(i) (imposing liability for "action not in good faith").

Historically, claims against managers for lack of good faith were rare. It was not clear that such a claim added anything to an assertion that the defendant had breached the duty of care or duty of loyalty. In the past generation, however, the argument that a fiduciary did not act in good faith have become more common. Why? Remember that after *Smith v. Van Gorkom*, state legislatures enacted statutes to permit corporations to place exculpation provisions in the articles. These clauses eliminated directors' (and in some stated officers') liability for breaching the duty of care. *See, e.g.*, MBCA § 2.02(b)(4) and Delaware § 102(b)(7), which were discussed at page 224. Most of these statutes, however, like Delaware § 102(b)(7), do not permit a corporation to eliminate liability for "acts or omissions not in good faith." To avoid such clauses, plaintiffs now routinely assert that a fiduciary failed to act in good faith. In other words, acts not taken in good faith cannot be exculpated by an provision adopted under Delaware § 102(b)(7).

One obvious question is whether the requirement that a fiduciary act in good faith is a third "duty"—along with the duty of care and the duty of loyalty—owed to the corporation. Delaware courts did not forge a consistent answer until *Stone v. Ritter*, 911 A.2d 362 (2006). That case, as we saw in the Notes following the *Caremark* case above, involved claims that the board of directors had failed to monitor the activities of corporate

---

*   E.g., Chen v. Howard-Anderson, 2014 WL 1366551 (Del.Ch., April 08, 2014).

officers and employees. As noted there, the court in *Stone v. Ritter* held that a plaintiff making such a claim must show either that the directors failed completely to implement a reporting system or that they consciously failed to monitor the operation of such a system. Doing so would state a claim for breach of the duty of loyalty and of the obligation of good faith. The court also said that the requirement of good faith is not an independent fiduciary duty but, rather, is a component of the duty of loyalty.

Three months before deciding *Stone v. Ritter*, the Delaware Supreme Court issued its decision in the next case. It not only develops the law concerning good faith but also offers a window into the world of breathtaking CEO salaries. In 1995, Disney hired Hollywood super agent Michael Ovitz to serve as Disney's CEO. Fourteen months later, Disney fired him. It turns out that the Disney board had approved an employment contract under which the company paid Ovitz $130 million for his 14 months of service. Shareholders sued, alleging that the directors had breached the duty of care in various ways. In addition, they asserted that the directors had failed to act in good faith in approving such a lucrative buy-out provision. (There was no duty of loyalty claim because none of the directors had a conflict of interest.) The Delaware Supreme Court capped nine years of litigation with the following decision. The duty of care discussion will seem familiar. Our especial focus here is the court's treatment of good faith.

IN RE THE WALT DISNEY COMPANY DERIVATIVE LITIGATION
Supreme Court of Delaware, 2006
906 A.2d 27

JACOBS, JUSTICE. In August 1995, Michael Ovitz ("Ovitz") and The Walt Disney Company ("Disney" or the "Company") entered into an employment agreement under which Ovitz would serve as President of Disney for five years. In December 1996, only fourteen months after he commenced employment, Ovitz was terminated without cause, resulting in a severance payout to Ovitz valued at approximately $130 million.

In January 1997, several Disney shareholders brought derivative actions in the Court of Chancery, on behalf of Disney, against Ovitz and the directors of Disney who served at the time of the events complained of (the "Disney defendants"). The plaintiffs claimed that the $130 million severance payout was the product of fiduciary duty and contractual breaches by Ovitz, and breaches of fiduciary duty by the Disney defendants, and a waste of assets. * * * In August 2005, the Chancellor handed down a well-crafted 174 page Opinion and Order, determining that "the director defendants did not breach their fiduciary duties or commit waste." The Court entered judgment in favor of all defendants on all claims alleged in the amended complaint. * * *

We conclude, for the reasons that follow, that the Chancellor's factual findings and legal rulings were correct and not erroneous in any respect. Accordingly, the judgment entered by the Court of Chancery will be affirmed. * * *

The Court of Chancery held that the business judgment rule presumptions protected the decisions of the compensation committee and the remaining Disney directors, not only because they had acted with due care but also because they had not acted in bad faith. * * *

In its Opinion the Court of Chancery defined bad faith as follows:

> Upon long and careful consideration, I am of the opinion that the concept of *intentional dereliction of duty*, a *conscious disregard for one's responsibilities*, is an appropriate (although not the only) standard for determining whether fiduciaries have acted in good faith. Deliberate indifference and inaction *in the face of a duty to act* is, in my mind, conduct that is clearly disloyal to the corporation. It is the epitome of faithless conduct. * * *

[After rejecting the claims of bad faith for technical reasons, the court nonetheless discussed the requirements for a successful bad-faith claim.]

The precise question is whether the Chancellor's articulated standard for bad faith corporate fiduciary conduct—intentional dereliction of duty, a conscious disregard for one's responsibilities—is legally correct. In approaching that question, we note that the Chancellor characterized that definition as "*an* appropriate (*although not the only*) standard for determining whether fiduciaries have acted in good faith." That observation is accurate and helpful, because as a matter of simple logic, at least three different categories of fiduciary behavior are candidates for the "bad faith" pejorative label.

The first category involves so-called "subjective bad faith," that is, fiduciary conduct motivated by an actual intent to do harm. That such conduct constitutes classic, quintessential bad faith is a proposition so well accepted in the liturgy of fiduciary law that it borders on axiomatic. We need not dwell further on this category, because no such conduct is claimed to have occurred, or did occur, in this case.

The second category of conduct, which is at the opposite end of the spectrum, involves lack of due care—that is, fiduciary action taken solely by reason of gross negligence and without any malevolent intent. In this case, appellants assert claims of gross negligence to establish breaches not only of director due care but also of the directors' duty to act in good faith. Although the Chancellor found, and we agree, that the appellants failed to establish gross negligence, to afford guidance we address the issue of whether gross negligence (including a failure to inform one's self of available material facts), without more, can also constitute bad faith. The answer is clearly no. * * * [G]rossly negligent conduct, without more, does not and cannot constitute a breach of the fiduciary duty to act in good faith. . . . Both our legislative history and our common law jurisprudence distinguish sharply between the duties to exercise due care and to act in good faith, and highly significant consequences flow from that distinction.

The Delaware General Assembly has addressed the distinction between bad faith and a failure to exercise due care (*i.e.*, gross negligence). * * * Section 102(b)(7) of the DGCL * * *authorizes Delaware corporations, by a provision in the certificate of incorporation, to exculpate their directors from monetary damage liability for a breach of the duty of care. That exculpatory provision affords significant protection to directors of Delaware corporations. The statute carves out several exceptions, however, including most relevantly, "for acts or omissions not in good faith. . . ." Thus, a corporation can exculpate its directors from monetary liability for a breach of the duty of care, but not for conduct that is not in good faith. To adopt a definition of bad faith that would cause a violation of the duty of care automatically to become an act or omission "not in good faith," would eviscerate the protections accorded to directors by the General Assembly's adoption of Section 102(b)(7). * * *

Section 102(b)(7) * * * evidences the intent of the Delaware General Assembly to afford significant protections to directors * * * of Delaware corporations. To adopt a definition that conflates the duty of care with the duty to act in good faith by making a violation of the former an automatic violation of the latter, would nullify those legislative protections and defeat the General Assembly's intent. There is no basis in policy, precedent or common sense that would justify dismantling the distinction between gross negligence and bad faith.

That leaves the third category of fiduciary conduct, which falls in between the first two categories of (1) conduct motivated by subjective bad intent and (2) conduct resulting from gross negligence. This third category is what the Chancellor's definition of bad faith—intentional dereliction of duty, a conscious disregard for one's responsibilities—is intended to capture. The question is whether such misconduct is properly treated as a non-exculpable * * * violation of the fiduciary duty to act in good faith. In our view it must be, for at least two reasons.

First, the universe of fiduciary misconduct is not limited to either disloyalty in the classic sense (*i.e.*, preferring the adverse self-interest of the fiduciary or of a related person to the interest of the corporation) or gross negligence. Cases have arisen where corporate directors have no conflicting self-interest in a decision, yet engage in misconduct that is more culpable than simple inattention or failure to be informed of all facts material to the decision. To protect the interests of the corporation and its shareholders, fiduciary conduct of this kind, which does not involve disloyalty (as traditionally defined) but is qualitatively more culpable than gross negligence, should be proscribed. A vehicle is needed to address such violations doctrinally, and that doctrinal vehicle is the duty to act in good faith. The Chancellor implicitly so recognized in his Opinion, where he identified different examples of bad faith as follows:

The good faith required of a corporate fiduciary includes not simply the duties of care and loyalty, in the narrow sense that I have discussed them above, but all actions required by a true faithfulness and devotion to the interests of the corporation and its shareholders. A failure to act in good faith may be shown, for instance, where the fiduciary intentionally acts with a purpose other than that of advancing the best interests of the corporation, where the fiduciary acts with the intent to violate applicable positive law, or where the fiduciary intentionally fails to act in the face of a known duty to act, demonstrating a conscious disregard for his duties. There may be other examples of bad faith yet to be proven or alleged, but these three are the most salient.

Those articulated examples of bad faith are not new to our jurisprudence. Indeed, they echo pronouncements our courts have made throughout the decades.

Second, the legislature has also recognized this intermediate category of fiduciary misconduct, which ranks between conduct involving subjective bad faith and gross negligence. Section 102(b)(7)(ii) of the DGCL expressly denies money damage exculpation for "acts or omissions not in good faith or which involve intentional misconduct or a knowing violation of law." By its very terms that provision distinguishes between "intentional misconduct" and a "knowing violation of law" (both examples of subjective bad faith) on the one hand, and "acts . . . not in good faith," on the other. Because the statute exculpates directors only for conduct amounting to gross negligence, the statutory denial of exculpation for "acts . . . not in good faith" must encompass the intermediate category of misconduct captured by the Chancellor's definition of bad faith.

For these reasons, we uphold the Court of Chancery's definition as a legally appropriate, although not the exclusive, definition of fiduciary bad faith. We need go no further. To engage in an effort to craft (in the Court's words) "a definitive and categorical definition of the universe of acts that would constitute bad faith" would be unwise and is unnecessary to pose of the issues presented on this appeal.

Three months after Disney, the Delaware Supreme Court again addressed a director's duty to act in good faith in *Stone v. Ritter*, 911 A.2d 362 (Del.2006), holding "the plaintiffs' complaint seeks to equate a bad outcome with bad faith. The lacuna in the plaintiffs' argument is a failure to recognize that the directors' good faith exercise of oversight responsibility may not invariably prevent employees from violating criminal laws, or from causing the corporation to incur significant financial liability, or both, as occurred in this very case. In the absence of red flags, good faith in the context of oversight must be measured by the directors' actions "to assure a reasonable information and reporting system exists" and not by second-guessing after the occurrence of employee conduct that results in an unintended adverse outcome. Accordingly, we hold that the Court of Chancery properly applied *Caremark* and dismissed the plaintiffs' derivative complaint * * * "*

The *Ritter* opinion is more often cited for the following dictum: "although good faith may be described colloquially as part of a 'triad' of fiduciary duties that includes the duties of care and loyalty, the obligation to act in good faith does not establish an independent fiduciary duty that stands on the same footing as the duties of care and loyalty. Only the latter two duties, where violated, may directly result in liability, whereas a failure to act in good faith may do so, but indirectly. The second doctrinal consequence is that the fiduciary duty of loyalty is not limited to cases involving a financial or other cognizable fiduciary conflict of interest. It also encompasses cases where the fiduciary fails to act in good faith."†

QUESTIONS AND NOTES

1. Is the holding in *Disney* consistent with the holding in *Ritter*? Is the statement in *Ritter* that "good faith does not establish an independent fiduciary duty that stands on the same footing as the duties of care and loyalty" consistent with the *Disney* opinion?

2. What is the practical significance, if any, of conceptualizing the duty to in act in good faith as a part of the duty of loyalty? And, by the by‡, what is this duty of loyalty all about?

3. What do you think of this analysis?

Every time the issue of a director's good faith comes up in court, the court forces the complaining shareholder to prove that her directors acted affirmatively in bad faith as opposed to merely in the absence of good faith. The judiciary completely misses the point that acts lacking good faith are not always the same as acts affirmatively taken in bad faith. A director can act in the absence of good faith without going so far as to act affirmatively in bad faith. More troubling, the academics who write in the area of corporate law also completely miss the distinction between acts showing a lack of good faith—acts "not in good faith"—and acts in bad faith.

Elizabeth A. Nowicki, *Not in Good Faith*, 60 SMU L. REV. 441, 441 (2007).

---

*   911 A.2d at 373.

†   911 A.2d 370.

‡   Cf http://www.youtube.com/watch?v=argKVL–7GTs.

4.   D is a director of Pharmaceutical Company (PC). At monthly board meetings, senior officers make reports to the board that barely mention potential product liability issues. In light of recent highly-publicized product liability pharmaceutical cases against other companies, D develops a concern that the officers might not be reporting sufficiently on possible claims against PC. But at the board meetings, D does not raise her concern—the meetings are long anyway and she does not want to offend senior officers. Is D acting in the absence of good faith? Is D acting in bad faith? This excellent hypo is from Nowicki, *supra*, 60 SMU L. REV. at 466.

NOTE: POSTSCRIPT ON EXECUTIVE COMPENSATION

As the *Disney* case shows, chief executives of large companies in the U.S. get paid a lot. According to Forbes magazine, the CEOs of the Fortune 500 corporations made an average of $10.5 million per year in 2012. Of that, the average was $3.5 in salary, $3.8 million in other compensation (such as personal perquisite packages), and $3.2 million was realized in exercising stock options. The highest paid CEO that year was John Hammergren, of the health-care giant McKesson, whose total compensation was $131.2 million. Of that, $6.3 million was salary and $112 million came from his exercising stock options. Second highest was Ralph Lauren, whose compensation was $66.2 million.

Activists and the government have tried to control CEO pay in many ways. Many critics point to the gap between CEOs and those who work for them. In 1993, a CEO of a large company received on average 131 times as much as the average worker. In 2013, the CEOs of the 350 largest companies earned 273 times as much as the average worker.

In the early 1990s, the SEC began to require greater disclosure of executives' compensation. The hope was that disclosure would shame boards of directors into limiting the amounts. The government also limited the tax deductibility of executive salaries above $1 million. More recently, the government has attempted to limit the pay of the CEOs of companies that have received government bailouts.

Generally, such measures have not worked. For example, the disclosure requirement tended to increase compensation, not reduce it. Many CEOs demanded and received more pay when they found out how much other CEOs were making.

But are CEOs overpaid? CEOs argue that their pay is fair. For example, Harvey Golub, CEO of American Express Co., received total compensation of more than $250 million when he was CEO from 1993–2000. However, during his time as CEO, the value of the company's shares increased more than six times, and the company's value increased $55 *billion*, from $10 billion to $65 billion. "I made a lot of money. I became wealthy," he notes. "My shareholders became even wealthier. How much of the $55 billion should I get?" Joann S. Lublin & Scott Thurm, *Behind Soaring Executive Pay, Decades of Failed Restraints*, WALL ST. J., October 12, 2006, at A1.

Opponents respond that huge executive paydays are often the result not of worthy executive performance, but of failed oversight by directors. Suppose a CEO has demanded that his board of directors grant him a big pay raise. To avoid conflicts if officer-directors were to vote on their own pay, most boards delegate compensation decisions to a "compensation committee." The compensation committee often in turn then hires an outside consultant to advise it.

According to critics, compensation committees and consultants are poor watchdogs. Subtle conflicts of interests can exist. CEOs often influence who sits on the company's board. A compensation-committee member who opposes the CEO's pay demands may find herself not renominated to the board. A consultant who finds a CEO's pay demands excessive may not be rehired.

At minimum, the class of those who serve as large corporations' officers and directors is often seen as a cozy club whose members have little enthusiasm for opposing each other's demands. It should not be surprising that CEOs tend to believe that the CEO job is a difficult one that deserves big pay, whether it is their own job or that of a fellow CEO on whose board they sit. According to Warren Buffet, the famous investor, compensation committees are "tail-wagging puppy dogs meekly following recommendations by consultants." For a director to oppose such a recommendation "would be like belching at the dinner table."

A CEO's mammoth pay can cause special outrage when the CEO's company performs poorly. In the five years after Robert Nardelli joined Home Depot as CEO in 2000, Home Depot's stock price declined 12% while the stock price of its archrival Lowe's rose 175%. During the period, Nardelli received total compensation of $245 million, with the compensation committee giving him several big raises.

Of course, corporate executives are not the only people who might be overpaid. Think of how much Johnny Manziel makes for sitting on the bench of the Cleveland Browns or how much Adam Sandler gets paid for making movies like "You Don't Mess With the Zohan," or how much Epstein and Freer make for their bar review lectures. Many professional athletes make more than $10.5 million per year. Actors at the top in Hollywood often make more than $20 million per film. Oprah Winfrey routinely makes over $100 million per year, including $385 million in 2008. Yet no one seems interested in curbing compensation of entertainers and athletes. There seem to be no studies of how much more a star pitcher makes than the average fan at a baseball game.

C. ENFORCING THE DUTIES THROUGH SHAREHOLDER DERIVATIVE LITIGATION

1. BREACH OF DUTY CREATES A CLAIM FOR THE CORPORATION

We have said it before and say it again now: the fiduciary duties discussed in this chapter are owed to the *corporation* itself. So when a fiduciary breaches a duty, the corporation is harmed and the corporation holds a claim against the breaching fiduciary (or fiduciaries). To be sure, the shareholders suffer too—but only because they own part of a company that has been hurt by fiduciaries who fail to discharge their responsibilities appropriately. The direct harm is to the business, which may then sue the breacher(s).

The corporation may then decide to assert the claim and sue the wrongdoers. Whether to do so is a management decision, usually made by the board of directors. But wait. The suit may well be asserted against incumbent directors because they have allegedly breached duties owed to the corporation. Can we trust directors to determine whether the corporation should sue them (or their cronies)? The potential for having "the fox guard the henhouse" opens the door to the shareholder derivative suit.

2. WHAT IS A DERIVATIVE SUIT AND HOW DOES IT WORK?

a. Determining Whether a Claim Is Derivative

In a derivative suit, a shareholder sues to vindicate the *corporation's* claim. She stands in the shoes of the corporation in asserting the claim. The suit is "derivative" because the shareholder's right to bring it "derives" from the corporation's right. Some courts refer to these as "secondary" suits, because the shareholder's right to sue is secondary to the corporation's.

Allowing a shareholder to file such a suit reflects our concern—in at least two situations—that the board might not have the corporation file a suit it has a right to file. First, suppose Bubba's Burritos, Inc. has entered a contract with Tina's Tofu, which requires Tina's to provide one of the key ingredients for burritos in Bubba's Northern California stores. Tina's fails to deliver, and Bubba's has to cover by getting the ingredient from another supplier at a higher price. Although Bubba's has a contract claim against Tina's, the directors might decide *not* to file suit against Tina's. Why? Maybe there was such ambiguity in the contract that Bubba's might not win. Or maybe the cost of litigation might exceed any recovery. Or perhaps Bubba's has had an excellent overall relationship with Tina's, which both parties want to continue. The directors might decide that litigation would strain the relationship unduly, and that Tina's will "make things right" in the future.

Second, the directors might refuse to have the corporation bring suit for a more questionable motive. Suppose the directors of Bubba's—Capel, Propp, and Agee—want to have Bubba's take advantage of the national craze for eggplant by offering eggplant burritos. Capel tells her fellow directors about an offer from Edith's Eggplant Co., but does not tell them (1) that she (Capel) owns Edith's Eggplant Co. and (2) that the price charged by Edith's is higher than Bubba's could negotiate with another supplier. The Bubba's board votes unanimously to enter the deal with Edith's. The result, of course, is that Bubba's loses money because it has to pay too much for eggplant.

If Bubba's Burritos, Inc. has shareholders other than Agee, Capel and Propp, should we allow one or more of the other shareholders to vindicate the corporation's claim in either of these circumstances? In the first situation, allowing the shareholder to proceed would seem to violate the business judgment rule—after all, if the shareholder can assert the corporation's claim when the directors have opted not to, the shareholder would be permitted to second-guess a management decision. In the second situation, though, we are nervous about whether the directors will pursue the corporation's claim against the bad-guy director diligently.* Certainly Capel will not vote in favor of having Bubba's sue her for breaching her duty of loyalty to the corporation.† And we may harbor legitimate doubt that Propp and Agee would want to pursue litigation against their friend and fellow director. For these reasons, it makes sense to allow the shareholder to sue on behalf of the corporation here.

These examples illustrate the tension inherent in permitting shareholders to bring derivative suits. On the one hand, we do not want to permit untoward second-guessing of management. On the other, there may be cases in which we question the directors' ability to make an impartial decision about whether the corporation ought to sue. As a matter of policy, American law permits shareholders to bring derivative suits to vindicate corporate claims, but imposes significant procedural restrictions on doing so (which we discuss in subsection (b) below).

Derivative suits must be distinguished from *direct suits*, in which a shareholder seeks to vindicate her own *personal* claim growing out of her ownership of stock. Direct suits are simply "regular" litigation, to which the procedural restrictions applicable to derivative suits do not apply. Occasionally, a shareholder will claim that her suit is direct, and the

---

* By the way, why is this "the corporation's claim" at all? Remember: to whom do the directors owe the duties of care and loyalty?

† This sentence answered the question in the preceding footnote. But why would the deal described be an interested director transaction? Why would (1) the way in which it was approved and (2) its terms not satisfy the MBCA provision for approval of interested director deals?

corporation will take the position that the case is derivative. It does so to force the plaintiff shareholder to abide by the special procedural requirements for derivative suits. Some plaintiffs might find the restrictions so onerous that they will abandon the case rather than pursue a derivative action. The corporation took this tack in the following case. The main point of *Eisenberg* is to learn to distinguish between derivative and direct suits.

EISENBERG V. FLYING TIGER LINE, INC.
United States Court of Appeals, Second Circuit, 1971
451 F.2d 267

[Plaintiff, Eisenberg, owned stock in Flying Tiger Line, Inc. ("Flying Tiger"), which operated a freight and charter airline. That corporation formed a wholly-owned subsidiary called Flying Tiger Corporation ("FTC"). FTC, in turn, then formed a wholly-owned subsidiary, called FTL Air Freight Corporation ("FTL"). Then—and here it gets tough, so stick with it—Flying Tiger merged into FTL. That means Flying Tiger ceased to exist as a separate entity, and FTL survived. FTL took over running the airline. But the shareholders of Flying Tiger got stock not in FTL, but in FTC. Thus, Eisenberg and others (who used to own stock in an airline) now own stock in a holding company (FTC), a subsidiary of which (FTL) runs the airline.

Eisenberg sued, arguing that these machinations deprived him (and other minority shareholders of Flying Tiger) of any vote or influence over the affairs of the corporation that now runs the airline. Instead, he had been relegated to being a minority shareholder of a corporation that owned a corporation that ran an airline.

The defendants argued that Eisenberg's case was a derivative suit and thus that he was required to post a bond as "security-for-expenses" under § 627 of the New York Business Corporation Law. The trial court agreed, and ordered Eisenberg to post a bond of $35,000. When he refused to do so, the court dismissed the case. Here, the Court of Appeals reverses. It finds that Eisenberg's case was a direct suit. Therefore, Eisenberg did not have to satisfy the procedural requirements for a derivative suit.]

IRVING KAUFMAN, JUDGE. In this action, Eisenberg is seeking to overturn a reorganization and merger which Flying Tiger effected in 1969. He charges that a series of corporate maneuvers were intended to dilute his voting rights. * * *

* * * Eisenberg contends that the end result of this complex plan was to deprive minority stockholders [of Flying Tiger] of any vote or any influence over the affairs of the newly spawned company [FTL]. Flying Tiger insists the plan was devised to bring about diversification without

interference from the Civil Aeronautics Board, which closely regulates air carriers, and to better use available tax benefits. Even if any of these motives prove to be relevant, the alleged illegality is not relevant to the questions before this court. We are called on to decide, assuming Eisenberg's complaint is sufficient on its face, only whether he should have been required to post security for costs as a condition to prosecuting his action.

To resolve this question we look first to Cohen v. Beneficial Industrial Loan Corp., 337 U.S. 541 (1949), which instructs that a federal court with diversity jurisdiction must apply a state statute providing security for costs if the state court would require the security in similar circumstances. [The Court determined that New York law would apply, and that Eisenberg would have to post security in this case if he would be required to do so in a New York state court. The answer to that depends, of course, on whether Eisenberg's claim is direct or derivative.]

We are told that if the gravamen of the complaint is injury to the corporation, the suit is derivative, but "if the injury is one to the plaintiff as a stockholder and to him individually and not to the corporation," the suit is individual in nature. * * * This generalization is of little use in our case, which is one of those "borderline cases which are more or less troublesome to classify." * * * The essence of Eisenberg's claimed injury is that the reorganization has deprived him and fellow stockholders of their right to vote on the operating company affairs and that this right in no sense ever belonged to Flying Tiger itself. This right, he says, belonged to the stockholders per se. Flying Tiger notes, however, that the stockholders were harmed, if at all, only because their company was dissolved, and their vote can be restored only if that company is revived. It insists, therefore, that stockholders are affected only secondarily or derivatively because we must first breathe life back into their dissolved corporation before the stockholders can be helped.

Despite a leading New York case which would seem at first glance to support Flying Tiger's position, we find that its contention misses the mark by a wide margin in its failure to distinguish between derivative and non-derivative [cases]. In Gordon v. Elliman, 306 N.Y. 456 (1954), by a vote of 4 to 3, the Court of Appeals took an expansive view of the coverage of [the statute requiring plaintiff to post a bond in derivative suits]. The majority held that an action to compel the payment of a dividend was derivative in nature and security for costs could be required. The test formulated by the majority was "whether the object of the lawsuit is to recover upon a chose in action belonging directly to the stockholders, or whether it is to compel the performance of corporate acts which good faith requires the directors to take in order to perform a duty which they owe to the corporation, and through it, to its stockholders." 306 N.Y. at 459. Pursuant to this test it is argued that, if Flying Tiger's directors had a duty not to merge the corporation, that duty was owed to the corporation and only derivatively to its stockholders.

Both the 4–1 Appellate Division and the 4–3 Court of Appeals opinions [in *Gordon*] evoked the quick and unanimous condemnation of commentators. Moreover, this test, "which appears to sweep away the distinction between a [direct] and a derivative action," in effect classifying all stockholder [cases] as derivative, has been limited strictly to its facts by lower New York courts.* **[5]** * * * In [one such case, Lazar v. Knolls Cooperative Section No. 2, Inc., 130 N.Y.S.2d 407 (Sup. Ct. 1954)], a stockholder sought to force directors to call a stockholders' meeting. The court stated security for costs could not be required where a plaintiff

> "does not challenge acts of the management on behalf of the corporation. He challenges the right of the present management to exclude him and other stockholders from proper participation in the affairs of the corporation. He claims that the defendants are interfering with the plaintiff's rights and privileges as stockholders."

130 N.Y.S.2d at 410. In substance, this is a similar to what Eisenberg challenges here.

The legislature also was concerned with the sweeping breadth of *Gordon*. In the recodification of corporate statutes completed in 1963, it added three words to the definition of derivative suits contained in § 626. Suits are now derivative only if brought in the right of a corporation to procure a judgment "in its favor." This was to "forestall any such pronouncement in the future as that made by the Court of Appeals in *Gordon v. Elliman*." Hornstein, "Analysis of Business Corporation Law," 6 McKinney's Consolidated Laws of New York Ann. 483 (1963).

Other New York cases which have distinguished between derivative and [direct] actions are of some interest. In Horwitz v. Balaban, 112 F. Supp. 99 (S.D.N.Y.1949), a stockholder sought to restrain the exercise of conversion rights that the corporation had granted to its president. The court found the action [was direct] and refused to require security, setting forth the test as "where the corporation has no right of action by reason of the transaction complained of, the suit is * * * not derivative." Id. at 101. Similarly, actions to compel the dissolution of a corporation have been held [to be direct], since the corporation could not possibly benefit therefrom. Fontheim v. Walker, 141 N.Y.S.2d 62 (Sup. Ct. 1955). * * * And Lehrman v. Godchaux Sugars, Inc., [138 N.Y.S.2d 163 (Sup. Ct. 1955)] discloses that an action by a stockholder complaining that a proposed recapitalization would unfairly benefit holders of another class of stock was [direct]. These cases and *Lazar* are totally consistent with

---

* **[5]** In his dissenting opinion [in *Gordon*], Judge Fuld noted "in a very real sense, all suits against corporations * * * involve the actions of the directors or of officers responsible to the directors" so the majority's test would do away with representative actions altogether.

the postulates of the leading treatises. Professor Moore instructs that "where a shareholder sues on behalf of himself and all others similarly situated to * * * enjoin a proposed merger or consolidation * * * he is not enforcing a derivative right; he is, by an appropriate type of class suit enforcing a right common to all the shareholders which runs against the corporation."

Eisenberg's position is even stronger than it would be in the ordinary merger case. In routine merger circumstances the stockholders retain a voice in the operation of the company, albeit a corporation other than their original choice. Here, however, the reorganization deprived him and other minority stockholders of any voice in the affairs of their previously existing operating company.

It is thus clear to us that *Gordon* is factually distinguishable from the instant case. Moreover, a close analysis of other New York cases, the amendment to § 626 and the major treatises, lead us to conclude that *Gordon* has lost its viability as stating a broad principle of law.

Furthermore, we view as an objective of a requirement for security for costs the prevention of strike suits and collusive settlements. Where directors are sued for mismanagement, the risk of personal monetary liability is a strong motive for bringing the suit and inducing settlement. Here, no monetary damages are sought, and no individuals will be liable.

* * *

Reversed.

QUESTIONS

1. Why was Mr. Eisenberg's claim direct? Could it have been characterized in a way to make it derivative?

2. The court relied on the fact that the plaintiff was not seeking monetary recovery from any of the defendants. Why was that fact significant? Does this mean that all derivative suits seek to recover money?

3. In New York *today*, would a suit to force the directors to declare a dividend be derivative or direct?

4. According to the discussion in *Eisenberg*, how would you classify the following cases? Are they derivative or direct suits? Why?

   a) We will see below that shareholders have a right, in certain circumstances, to inspect the books and records of the corporation. Epstein sues the directors of Bubba's Burritos, Inc. because they improperly blocked his right to do so.

   b) Roberts sues the directors of Bubba's Burritos, Inc. for wasting corporate assets by paying themselves huge bonuses. Why is this a derivative suit?

c)   Shepherd sues the directors of Bubba's Burritos, Inc. for usurping corporate opportunities.

d)   Epstein sues the directors of Bubba's Burritos, Inc. for failing to exercise due care in purchasing supplies at a price much higher than could have been negotiated.

e)   Freer holds stock in a publicly-traded corporation. He attends a shareholders' meeting and asks difficult questions of the CEO. The CEO slugs him in the nose, causing enormous damage. Whom can Freer sue, and what kind of suit (direct or derivative) will it be?

b. Who Gets the Recovery and Pays the Expenses in a Derivative Suit?

Because a derivative suit vindicates the *corporation's* claim, the recovery in a successful case will go to the corporation. This may seem odd, however, because it is the shareholder who took the initiative and bore the burden of bringing suit. Most courts will allow the successful shareholder to recover her costs from the losing litigant and her attorneys' fees from the corporation. After all, by suing and winning, the shareholder has done the corporation a favor, and it should pick up the tab for the litigation.

In some circumstances, the derivative suit model does not make sense:

> Agee, Propp, and Capel are the only shareholders in a small corporation. Each owns one-third of the stock. Agee causes the company to buy supplies from another business, which he owns, for inflated prices. The company overpays $30,000. Agee breached the duty of loyalty. If Propp or Capel brings a derivative suit and wins, the company will recover $30,000. Because Agee owns one-third of the stock, though, the judgment in favor of the company essentially returns $10,000 to Agee.

To avoid this result, some courts will allow the innocent shareholders to sue Agee directly and to recover personally. Indeed, by statute in Texas, derivative claims in corporations having 35 or fewer shareholders may be treated as direct claims. TEX. BUS. ORGS. CODE, § 21.563. This means the innocent shareholders will not have to jump through the procedural hoops discussed below for bringing a derivative suit.

What happens if the shareholder loses the derivative suit? Generally, she bears her own costs and attorney's fees. (Usually, the shareholder's lawyer will have taken the case on a contingent fee, and thus will not recover here.) Under some statutes, the defendants may be able to recover *their* attorneys' fees from the shareholder if the court finds that she sued "without reasonable cause." In addition, the shareholder's loss is *res judicata* for other shareholders—they cannot sue to try to vindicate the corporation's claim a second time.

c.   Procedural Requirements for a Derivative Suit

The law of each state imposes a series of procedural hurdles on a shareholder bringing a derivative suit. We saw one of these in *Eisenberg* immediately above—that the shareholder be required to post a bond. Plaintiffs do not like this requirement because it means they must put up money to protect the defendants should the case turn out to be baseless. The bond provides a fund from which the defendants can recover expenses. Though some states still have such a requirement, most do not. The MBCA imposes no such bond requirement.

Plaintiffs in derivative suits are required to allege their claims with specificity, which means that the complaint must set forth details about the alleged wrongdoing by the defendants. In this regard, the shareholder's right to inspect corporate books and records may be enormously important, because it allows the shareholder to "get the goods" on the defendants. We address the inspection right in § D below.

(i) Contemporaneous Ownership

We focus on two main procedural requirements. The first is "contemporaneous ownership." MBCA § 7.41 is typical in this regard.

PROBLEMS

Study MBCA § 7.41 and answer the following:

1.   Roberts hears of some wrongdoing by directors of Bubba's Burritos, Inc. He wants to bring a derivative suit, but did not own stock in Bubba's when the claim arose. He buys one share of Bubba's stock. Why can he not bring a derivative suit? What would wrong with allowing him to purchase shares and purchase the right to sue at the same time? A few states do allow this, at least in some circumstances. *See* Cal. Corp. Code § 800(b).

2.   What might be examples of how stock could be transferred "by operation of law" so as to allow someone to bring suit even though she did not own stock when the claim arose? Why would such a transferee be a better candidate to serve as plaintiff than Roberts in Question 1?

3.   Must the plaintiff own stock of a particular value?

4.   What, if anything, does the requirement of MBCA § 7.41(2) add to that of contemporaneous ownership in § 7.41(1)?

(ii) Demand on the Board

Second—our major focus—is the historic requirement that the shareholder who wants to bring a derivative suit must make a demand on the board of directors that it authorize the corporation to sue. On the one hand, this requirement ensures that the management decision (of whether to have the corporation file suit) is placed squarely before the people who make management decisions. On the other hand, courts long ago decided that the shareholder should not be required to make such a demand if the demand would be "futile." It would be futile, for instance, if the suit would be brought against the incumbent directors themselves. In such cases, the demand on directors is "excused."

PROBLEM

Study MBCA § 7.42.

Does this statute recognize any exception to the demand requirement? If not, does it require the plaintiff shareholder to undertake a futile act?

The following opinion is the leading discussion of New York law on the subject of when a demand on directors will be excused. It is especially helpful because it also explains the Delaware and MBCA approaches to the topic.

MARX V. AKERS
New York Court of Appeals, 1996
88 N.Y.2d 189

SMITH, J. Plaintiff commenced this shareholder derivative action against International Business Machines Corporation (IBM) and IBM's board of directors without first demanding that the board initiate a lawsuit. The amended complaint (complaint) alleges that the board wasted corporate assets by awarding excessive compensation to IBM's executives and outside directors. The issues raised on this appeal are whether the Appellate Division abused its discretion by dismissing plaintiff's complaint for failure to make a demand and whether plaintiff's complaint fails to state a cause of action. We affirm the order of the Appellate Division because we conclude that plaintiff was not excused from making a demand with respect to the executive compensation claim and that plaintiff has failed to state a cause of action for corporate waste in connection with the allegations concerning payments to IBM's outside directors.

Facts and Procedural History

The complaint alleges that during a period of declining profitability at IBM the director defendants engaged in self-dealing by awarding excessive compensation to the 15 outside directors on the 18-member board. Although the complaint identifies only one of the three inside directors as an IBM executive (defendant Akers is identified as a former chief executive officer of IBM),* **[1]** plaintiff also appears to allege that the director defendants violated their fiduciary duties to IBM by voting for unreasonably high compensation for IBM executives.* **[2]**

Defendants moved to dismiss the complaint for (1) failure to state a cause of action, and (2) failure to serve a demand on IBM's board to initiate a lawsuit based on the complaint's allegations. The Supreme Court [the trial court in New York] dismissed, holding that plaintiff failed to establish the futility of a demand. [The] Supreme Court concluded that excusing a demand here would render Business Corporation Law § 626(c) "virtually meaningless in any shareholders' derivative action in which all members of a corporate board are named as defendants." Having decided the demand issue in favor of defendants, the court did not reach the issue of whether plaintiff's complaint stated a cause of action.

The Appellate Division affirmed the dismissal, concluding that the complaint did not contain any details from which the futility of a demand could be inferred. The Appellate Division found that plaintiff's objections to the level of compensation were not stated with sufficient particularity in light of statutory authority permitting directors to set their own compensation.

Background

A shareholder's derivative action is an action "brought in the right of a domestic or foreign corporation to procure a judgment in its favor, by a holder of shares or of voting trust certificates of the corporation or of a beneficial interest in such shares or certificates" (Business Corporation Law § 626 (a)). "Derivative claims against corporate directors belong to the corporation itself" (Auerbach v Bennett, 47 N.Y.2d 619, 631).

> The remedy sought is for wrong done to the corporation; the primary cause of action belongs to the corporation; recovery must enure to the benefit of the corporation. The stockholder brings the action, in behalf of others similarly situated, to vindicate the corporate rights and a judgment on the merits is a binding adjudication of these rights [citations omitted] (Isaac v Marcus, 258 N.Y. 257, 264).

Business Corporation Law § 626(c) provides that in any shareholders' derivative action, "the complaint shall set forth with particularity the efforts of the plaintiff to secure the initiation of such action by the board

---

*   **[1]** The other inside directors, although identified as Employee Directors, are never explicitly identified as executive officers in the complaint. However, the names of these directors appear on a chart disclosing "payments to certain executives."

*   **[2]** Executives at IBM are compensated through a fixed salary and performance incentives. Payouts on the performance incentives are based on IBM's earnings per share, return on equity and cash flow. Plaintiff's complaint criticizes only the performance incentive component of executive compensation as excessive because of certain accounting practices which plaintiff alleges artificially inflate earnings, return on equity and cash flow.

or the reasons for not making such effort." Enacted in 1961 * * * section 626(c) codified a rule of equity developed in early shareholder derivative actions requiring plaintiffs to demand that the corporation initiate an action, unless such demand was futile, before commencing an action on the corporation's behalf (Barr v. Wackman, 36 N.Y.2d 371, 377). The purposes of the demand requirement are to (1) relieve courts from deciding matters of internal corporate governance by providing corporate directors with opportunities to correct alleged abuses, (2) provide corporate boards with reasonable protection from harassment by litigation on matters clearly within the discretion of directors, and (3) discourage "strike suits" commenced by shareholders for personal gain rather than for the benefit of the corporation (*Barr*, 36 N.Y.2d, at 378). "[T]he demand is generally designed to weed out unnecessary or illegitimate shareholder derivative suits."

By their very nature, shareholder derivative actions infringe upon the managerial discretion of corporate boards. "As with other questions of corporate policy and management, the decision whether and to what extent to explore and prosecute such [derivative] claims lies within the judgment and control of the corporation's board of directors." (*Auerbach*, 47 N.Y.2d, at 631) Consequently, we have historically been reluctant to permit shareholder derivative suits, noting that the power of courts to direct the management of a corporation's affairs should be "exercised with restraint." (Gordon v Elliman, 306 N.Y. 456, 462)

In permitting a shareholder derivative action to proceed because a demand on the corporation's directors would be futile,

> the object is for the court to chart the course for the corporation which the directors should have selected, and which it is presumed that they would have chosen if they had not been actuated by fraud or bad faith. Due to their misconduct, the court substitutes its judgment ad hoc for that of the directors in the conduct of its business.

Achieving a balance between preserving the discretion of directors to manage a corporation without undue interference, through the demand requirement, and permitting shareholders to bring claims on behalf of the corporation when it is evident that directors will wrongfully refuse to bring such claims, through the demand futility exception, has been accomplished by various jurisdictions in different ways. One widely cited approach to demand futility which attempts to balance these competing concerns has been developed by Delaware courts and applies a two-pronged test to each case to determine whether a failure to serve a demand is justified. At the other end of the spectrum is a universal demand requirement which would abandon particularized determinations in favor of requiring a demand in every case before a shareholder derivative suit may be filed.

The Delaware Approach

Delaware's demand requirement, codified in Delaware Chancery Court Rule 23.1, provides, in relevant part,

> In a derivative action brought by 1 or more shareholders or members to enforce a right of a corporation . . . [the complaint shall allege] with particularity the efforts, if any, made by the plaintiff to obtain the action the plaintiff desires from the directors or comparable authority and the reasons for the plaintiff's failure to obtain the action or for not making the effort.

Interpreting Rule 23.1, the Delaware Supreme Court in *Aronson v Lewis* developed a two-prong test for determining the futility of a demand. Plaintiffs must allege particularized facts which create a reasonable doubt that,

> (1) the directors are disinterested and independent and (2) the challenged transaction was otherwise the product of a valid exercise of business judgment. Hence, the Court of Chancery must make two inquiries, one into the independence and disinterestedness of the directors and the other into the substantive nature of the challenged transaction and the board's approval thereof

The two branches of the *Aronson* test are disjunctive. Once director interest has been established, the business judgment rule becomes inapplicable and the demand excused without further inquiry. Similarly, a director whose independence is compromised by undue influence exerted by an interested party cannot properly exercise business judgment and the loss of independence also justifies the excusal of a demand without further inquiry. Whether a board has validly exercised its business judgment must be evaluated by determining whether the directors exercised procedural (informed decision) and substantive (terms of the transaction) due care.

The reasonable doubt threshold of Delaware's two-fold approach to demand futility has been criticized. The use of a standard of proof which is the heart of a jury's determination in a criminal case has raised questions concerning its applicability in the corporate context. The reasonable doubt standard has also been criticized as overly subjective, thereby permitting a wide variance in the application of Delaware law to similar facts * * *.

Universal Demand

A universal demand requirement would dispense with the necessity of making case-specific determinations and impose an easily applied bright line rule. The Business Law Section of the American Bar Association has proposed requiring a demand in all cases, without exception, and permits the commencement of a derivative proceeding within 90 days of the demand unless the demand is rejected earlier (Model Business Corporation Act § 7.42 [1] [1995 Supp]). However, plaintiffs may file suit before the expiration of 90 days, even if their demand has not been rejected, if the corporation would suffer irreparable injury as a result (Model Business Corporation Act § 7.42 [2]).

* * *

New York's Approach to Demand Futility

Although instructive, neither the universal demand requirement nor the Delaware approach to demand futility is adopted here. Since New York's demand requirement is codified in Business Corporation Law § 626(c), a universal demand may only be adopted by the Legislature. Delaware's approach, which resembles New York law in some respects, incorporates a "reasonable doubt" standard which, as we have already pointed out, has provoked criticism as confusing and overly subjective. An analysis of the *Barr* decision compels the conclusion that in New York, a demand would be futile if a complaint alleges with particularity that (1) a majority of the directors are interested in the transaction, or (2) the directors failed to inform themselves to a degree reasonably necessary about the transaction, or (3) the directors failed to exercise their business judgment in approving the transaction.

In *Barr v. Wackman*, we considered whether the plaintiff was excused from making a demand where the board of Talcott National Corporation (Talcott), consisting of 13 outside directors, a director affiliated with a related company and four interested inside directors, rejected a merger proposal involving Gulf & Western Industries (Gulf & Western) in favor of another proposal on allegedly less favorable terms for Talcott and its shareholders. The merger proposal, memorialized in a board-approved "agreement in principle," proposed exchanging one share of Talcott common stock for approximately $24 consisting of $17 in cash and 0.6 of a warrant to purchase Gulf & Western stock, worth approximately $7. This proposal was abandoned in favor of a cash tender offer for Talcott shares by Associates First Capital Corporation (a Gulf & Western subsidiary) at $20 per share—$4 less than proposed for the merger.

The plaintiff in *Barr* alleged that Talcott's board discarded the merger proposal after the four "controlling" inside directors received pecuniary and personal benefits from Gulf & Western in exchange for ceding control of Talcott on terms less favorable to Talcott's shareholders. As alleged in the complaint, these benefits included new and favorable employment contracts for nine Talcott officers, including five-year employment contracts for three of the controlling directors. In addition to his annual salary of $125,000 with Talcott, defendant Silverman (a controlling director) would allegedly receive $60,000 a year under a five-year employment contract with Associates First Capital, and an aggregate of $275,000 for the next five years in an arrangement with Associates First Capital to serve as a consultant. This additional compensation would be awarded to Silverman after control of Talcott passed to Associates First Capital and Gulf & Western. Plaintiff also alleged that Gulf & Western and Associates First Capital paid an excessive "finder's fee" of $340,000 to a company where Silverman's son was an executive vice-president. In addition to alleging that the controlling defendants obtained personal benefits, the complaint also alleged that Talcott's board agreed to sell a Talcott subsidiary at a net loss of $6,100,000 solely to accommodate Gulf & Western.

In *Barr*, we held that insofar as the complaint attacked the controlling directors' acts in causing the corporation to enter into a transaction for their own financial benefit, demand was excused because of the self-dealing, or self-interest of those directors in the challenged transaction. Specifically, we pointed to the allegation that the controlling directors "breached their fiduciary obligations to Talcott in return for personal benefits."

We also held in *Barr*, however, that as to the disinterested outside directors, demand could be excused even in the absence of their receiving any financial benefit from the transaction. That was because the complaint alleged that, by approving the terms of the less advantageous offer, those directors were guilty of a "breach of their duties of due care and diligence to the corporation." Their performance of the duty of care would have "put them on notice of the claimed self-dealing of the affiliated directors." The complaint charged that the outside directors failed "to do more than passively rubber-stamp the decisions of the active managers" resulting in corporate detriment. These allegations, the *Barr* Court concluded, also excused demand as to the charges against the disinterested directors.

Barr also makes clear that "[i]t is not sufficient . . . merely to name a majority of the directors as parties defendant with conclusory allegations of wrongdoing or control by wrongdoers" to justify failure to make a demand. Thus, *Barr* reflects the statutory requirement that the complaint "shall set forth with particularity the . . . reasons for not making such effort" (Business Corporation Law § 626 [c]).

Unfortunately, various courts have overlooked the explicit warning that conclusory allegations of wrongdoing against each member of the board are not sufficient to excuse demand and have misinterpreted *Barr* as excusing demand whenever a majority of the board members who approved the transaction are named as defendants [citations to five cases]. As stated most recently, "[t]he rule is clear in this State that no demand is necessary if 'the complaint alleges acts for which a majority of the directors may be liable and plaintiff reasonably concluded that the board would not be responsive to a demand.'" The problem with such an approach is that it permits plaintiffs to frame their complaint in such a way as to automatically excuse demand, thereby allowing the exception to swallow the rule.

We thus deem it necessary to offer the following elaboration of *Barr's* demand/futility standard. (1) Demand is excused because of futility when a complaint alleges with particularity that a majority of the board of directors is interested in the challenged transaction. Director interest may either be self-interest in the transaction at issue, or a loss of independence because a director with no direct interest in a transaction is "controlled" by a self-interested director. (2) Demand is excused because of futility when a complaint alleges with particularity that the board of directors did not fully inform themselves about the challenged transaction to the extent reasonably appropriate under the circumstances. The "long-standing rule" is that a director "does not exempt himself from liability by failing to do more than passively rubber-stamp the decisions of the active managers." (3) Demand is excused because of futility when a complaint alleges with particularity that the challenged transaction was so egregious on its face that it could not have been the product of sound business judgment of the directors.

The Current Appeal

Plaintiff argues that the demand requirement was excused both because the outside directors awarded themselves generous compensation packages and because of the acquiescence of the disinterested directors in the executive compensation schemes. The complaint states:

> Plaintiff has made no demand upon the directors of IBM to institute this lawsuit because such demand would be futile. As set forth above, each of the directors authorized, approved, participated and/or acquiesced in the acts and transactions complained of herein and are liable therefor. Further, each of the Non-Employee [outside] Directors has received and retained the benefit of his excessive compensation and each of the other directors has received and retained the benefit of the incentive compensation described above. The defendants cannot be expected to vote to prosecute an action against themselves. Demand upon the company to bring action [sic] to redress the wrongs herein is therefore unnecessary.

Defendants argue that neither the Supreme Court nor the Appellate Division abused its discretion in holding that plaintiff's complaint did not set forth the futility of a demand with particularity.

As in *Barr*, we look to the complaint here to determine whether the allegations are sufficient and establish with particularity that demand would have been futile. Here, the plaintiff alleges that the compensation awarded to IBM's outside directors and certain IBM executives was excessive.

Defendants' motion to dismiss for failure to make a demand as to the allegations concerning the compensation paid to IBM's executive officers was properly granted. A board is not interested "in voting compensation for one of its members as an executive or in some other nondirectorial capacity, such as a consultant to the corporation," although "so-called 'back-scratching' arrangements, pursuant to which all directors vote to approve each other's compensation as officers or employees, do not constitute disinterested directors' action" (1 ALI § 5.03, Comment g, at 250). Since only three directors are alleged to have received the benefit of the executive compensation scheme, plaintiff has failed to allege that a majority of the board was interested in setting executive compensation. Nor do the allegations that the board used faulty accounting procedures to calculate executive compensation levels move beyond "conclusory allegations of wrongdoing" (*Barr* at 379) which are insufficient to excuse demand. The complaint does not allege particular facts in contending that the board failed to deliberate or exercise its business judgment in setting those levels. Consequently, the failure to make a demand regarding the fixing of executive compensation was fatal to that portion of the complaint challenging that transaction.

However, a review of the complaint indicates that plaintiff also alleged that a majority of the board was self-interested in setting the compensation of outside directors because the outside directors comprised a majority of the board.

Directors are self-interested in a challenged transaction where they will receive a direct financial benefit from the transaction which is different from the benefit to shareholders generally * * * A director who votes for a raise in directors' compensation is always "interested" because that person will receive a personal financial benefit from the transaction not shared in by stockholders (see, 1 ALI § 5.03, Comment g, at 250 ["if the board votes directorial compensation for itself, the board is interested"]. Consequently, a demand was excused as to plaintiff's allegations that the compensation set for outside directors was excessive.

Corporate Waste

Our conclusion that demand should have been excused as to the part of the complaint challenging the fixing of directors' compensation does not end our inquiry. We must also determine whether plaintiff has stated a cause of action regarding director compensation, i.e., some wrong to the corporation. We conclude that plaintiff has not, and thus dismiss the complaint in its entirety.

Historically, directors did not receive any compensation for their work as directors. * * *

* * * Thus, a bare allegation that corporate directors voted themselves excessive compensation was sufficient to state a cause of action (* * *). Many jurisdictions, including New York, have since changed the common-law rule by statute providing that a corporation's board of directors has the authority to fix director compensation unless the corporation's charter or bylaws provides otherwise. Thus, the allegation that directors have voted themselves compensation is clearly no longer an allegation which gives rise to a cause of action, as the directors are statutorily entitled to set those levels. Nor does a conclusory allegation that the compensation directors have set for themselves is excessive give rise to a cause of action.

* * * Thus, a complaint challenging the excessiveness of director compensation must—to survive a dismissal motion—allege compensation rates excessive on their face or other facts which call into question whether the compensation was fair to the corporation when approved, the good faith of the directors setting those rates, or that the decision to set the compensation could not have been a product of valid business judgment.* **[6]**

Applying the foregoing principles to plaintiff's complaint, it is clear that it must be dismissed. The complaint alleges that the directors increased their compensation rates from a base of $20,000 plus $500 for each meeting attended to a retainer of $55,000 plus 100 shares of IBM stock over a five-year period. The complaint also alleges that "[t]his compensation bears little relation to the part-time services rendered by the Non-Employee Directors or to the profitability of IBM. The board's responsibilities have not increased, its performance, measured by the company's earnings and stock price, has been poor yet its compensation has increased far in excess of the cost of living."

These conclusory allegations do not state a cause of action. * * *

Accordingly, the order of the Appellate Division should be affirmed, with costs.

QUESTIONS AND NOTE

1. Would a demand on directors be required under (A) Delaware law; (B) the MBCA; and (C) New York law? In each, assume that the board consists of five directors.

---

*   **[6]** There is general agreement that the allocation of the burden of proof differs depending on whether the compensation was approved by disinterested directors or shareholders, or by interested directors. Plaintiffs must prove wrongdoing or waste as to compensation arrangements regarding disinterested directors or shareholders, but directors who approve their own compensation bear the burden of proving that the transaction was fair to the corporation. * * * However, at the pleading stage we are not concerned with burdens of proof.

    a)   The claim is that all five directors breached their duty of loyalty by engaging in competing ventures.

    b)   The claim is that two directors breached the duty.

    c)   The claim is that one director breached the duty, but that she is the dominant member of the board, and that the other four are under her control.

Since the decision in *Marx v. Akers*, Louisiana and Texas have adopted a universal-demand requirement.

    2.   If a shareholder-plaintiff makes the demand on the board, one of two things can happen. For one, the board can accept the recommendation and authorize the corporation to sue. At that point, the shareholder bows out. Because the corporation brings the case, it is not a derivative suit, and no shareholder involvement is required. The other possibility is that the board rejects the demand. At that point, the shareholder can (1) forget the whole thing or (2) file suit and assert that the board erred in its decision not to have the corporation sue.

The latter course will almost always be a loser. Why? Because the shareholder at that point is asserting that the directors violated the business judgment rule. And as we know, it is almost impossible to make such a showing. Plaintiff would have to show either (1) that the directors made their decision without any on-the-record-efforts to look like they were acting seriously or (2) that the decision was tainted by conflict of interest. *See* MBCA § 7.44(d).

Under Delaware law, it will be impossible to make the latter showing. According to the Delaware Supreme Court, the fact that the plaintiff made the demand constitutes an admission that the directors were disinterested. Spiegel v. Buntrock, 571 A.2d 767 (Del. 1990). In other words, making the demand admitted that demand was not futile.

d.   Motion to Dismiss a Derivative Suit

When a derivative suit is filed, the board of directors might have the corporation make a motion to have the case dismissed. In states in which the demand on the board can be excused (because making a demand would be futile), the corporation may assert that the suit is improper because the demand should have been made. At this point, the court must determine whether a majority of the board was tainted, as we saw in *Marx v. Akers*. If it was not, and thus the demand should have been made, the court will dismiss the derivative suit. The plaintiff should have made the demand, and because a majority of the board is not tainted, its decision not to sue is protected by the business judgment rule.

Or, regardless of whether a demand should have been made, the board might conclude that the suit is not in the company's best interest. For example, maybe the cost of litigation will exceed the projected recovery, or the claim will be difficult to win, or corporate resources would be better spent on expanding the business. What can the directors do? It was long considered appropriate for the board to authorize a motion to dismiss the derivative suit, *at least* when the case was against a third party. For example, suppose the claim is against a company that supplied defective goods to the corporation. The decision of whether to sue that company (or, instead, to work out the dispute in future deals with it) involves a business judgment. The board's decision should be final, unless it is irrational or galactically stupid.

But what about a case involving a claim of director wrongdoing? Here we are worried that the board will want the case dismissed to save its cronies from potential liability. Historically, then, everyone seemed to assume that the board could not authorize a motion to dismiss in such a case. That started to change in 1976, when one court permitted a disinterested committee of directors to bring a motion to dismiss a case for director misconduct because the case was not in the best interests of the corporation. Gall v. Exxon Corp., 418 F. Supp. 509 (S.D. N.Y. 1976). The court held hearings on whether the committee members in fact were independent of the defendants and concluded that dismissal could be appropriate. Today it is clear that though a shareholder has a right to bring suit (at least in demand-excused cases), she does not necessarily have the right to require the litigation proceed to adjudication. The corporation may be able to get the case dismissed.

A corporation's motion to dismiss must be based upon findings by independent and disinterested directors—that is, people who are not implicated in the claim asserted and are not closely related to someone who will is implicated. Such persons are usually appointed to a committee (usually called a "special litigation committee" (SLC)) to investigate and determine whether the derivative suit is in the corporation's best interest.

Courts disagree, however, on what the court is to assess in ruling on the motion to dismiss. In most states, the court will assess only procedural matters: whether the SLC consisted of truly independent persons and whether they undertook an adequate investigation in good faith. If they were independent and if they did appropriate homework, the court will grant the motion to dismiss. Delaware courts, however, go beyond this. In *Zapata Corporation v. Maldonado*, 430 A.2d 779, 788–789 (Del. 1981), the Delaware Supreme Court agreed that trial courts must review the procedural matters of whether the members of the SLC were independent and whether the SLC made an appropriate investigation. In addition, the court undertakes an independent substantive review of the SLC's recommendation. The court is to apply its "own independent business judgment" to determine whether the case is in the corporation's best interest. This substantive component is surprising because it requires the court to make the kind of business assessments that courts are not trained to undertake.

PROBLEMS

Recall that under the MBCA, the demand on directors is never excused. So there is no bifurcation—as there is in non-MBCA states—between "demand required" and "demand excused" cases. Apply MBCA § 7.44 to these Problems.

1.   Does the standard for dismissal under § 7.44(a) adopt or reject the Delaware approach in *Zapata* (discussed in the previous paragraph)?

2.   Who makes the recommendation that the suit be dismissed?

3.   What is a "qualified" director? (MBCA § 1.43 is relevant here.)

4.   How and by whom must members of a SLC be appointed?

5.   Does it matter whether a majority of the board was tainted at the time the determination was made (the determination that the suit was not in the company's best interest)?

D. SHAREHOLDERS' RIGHT TO INSPECT CORPORATE DOCUMENTS

If a derivative suit survives the gauntlet of procedural pre-requisites, the plaintiff will be able to use discovery tools to uncover evidence of wrongdoing. Before that, however, how can a shareholder find out about whether managers have engaged in actionable shenanigans? In every state, shareholders have a statutory (and possibly a common law) right to inspect books and records of the corporation. *See* Delaware § 220(b) and MBCA § 16.02. There are many legitimate reasons for a shareholder to want access to these materials. In small corporations (in which there is no public market for the stock), a common reason for inspection is to determine the value of a shareholder's stock. In any corporation, one reason for inspection is to support derivative litigation against managers who have breached their fiduciary duties. The following case is a good example.

The case involves back-dating (that is, putting an earlier date) on options to buy a company's stock.

MELZER V. CNET NETWORKS, INC.

Chancery Court of Delaware, 2007
934 A.2d 912

CHANDLER, CHANCELLOR. This should have been a very easy case. Plaintiffs, who are shareholders of CNET, initiated this action under 8 *Del. C.* § 220 to seek books and records relating to stock options backdating—a practice in which the company has already admitted it engaged—after being ordered to do so by a federal judge in California. This seeming simplicity notwithstanding, CNET opposed the demand for inspection, the parties battled over discovery via a contentious motion to compel, and only on the brink of trial did CNET agree to share certain documents with plaintiffs. This agreement was not, however, all encompassing, and now the parties dispute the scope of books and records to which plaintiffs are entitled. Summarized as succinctly as possible, the issue is whether plaintiffs are entitled to documents relating to options granted before plaintiffs owned stock in CNET. Because plaintiffs' purpose in this action is to obtain the particularized facts they need to adequately allege demand futility (rather than to investigate potential claims that plaintiffs have no standing to assert), plaintiffs may have access to certain documents pertaining to options granted before they owned shares.

I.   FACTUAL AND PROCEDURAL BACKGROUND

This case, like so many others concerning backdated stock options, found its genesis in a March 18, 2006 article in the *Wall Street Journal* that suggested many large corporations were engaging in an options-granting practice that contravened corporate charters far and wide. * * *

CNET's options issues first came to light in May 2006, when the Center for Financial Research and Accountability ("CFRA") published an analysis of option-granting practices of one hundred publicly traded companies. The CFRA report specifically identified CNET as a company whose pattern of granting options indicated backdating. On June 27, 2006, CNET disclosed that its option granting practices were under investigation by the U.S. Attorney for the Northern District of California and by the Securities and Exchange Commission. The next month, CNET announced that an internal investigation conducted by a special committee confirmed the CFRA report and announced that the company would need to restate its financial statements from 2003–05. In mid-October 2006, CNET released further, more specific findings from the special committee, which concluded backdating had been a problem for the company from the time of its IPO in 1996.

On June 19, 2006, plaintiffs filed their initial complaint in the District Court for the Northern District of California alleging federal securities and state law claims against CNET and its directors relating to backdated stock options. After CNET's disclosures in the fall, plaintiffs amended their derivative complaint, and the defendants moved to dismiss for failure to make a demand on the CNET board. Applying the *Aronson** [4] test for demand futility, the district court granted the motion to dismiss.

Plaintiffs had alleged several theories to support their contention that demand on the CNET board would have been futile. First, to the extent a director materially benefited from a backdated option, he or she

---

*   [4] *Aronson v. Lewis,* 473 A.2d 805 (Del.1984). [Note from your casebook authors: The *Aronson* test was discussed by the court in *Marx v. Akers,* which we read in § C above.]

would not be disinterested under the first prong of the *Aronson* test. Thus, to the extent that plaintiffs could plead with particularity facts demonstrating that a majority of the directors received backdated options, demand would be excused. Second, to the extent a director knowingly backdated a stock option in violation of the company's charter, that director's action is *ultra vires* and is not the product of valid business judgment. If a majority of the current board engaged in backdating, demand would be excused.

Thus, key to establishing demand futility was particularized facts demonstrating that backdating occurred and either that (1) a majority of the current board received backdated options or (2) a majority of the current board engaged in backdating itself. The district court analyzed individually the eight option grants that plaintiffs alleged were backdated and concluded that plaintiffs successfully pleaded particularized facts with respect to only the grants on June 3, 1998, April 17, 2000, and October 8, 2001. Consequently, plaintiffs had demonstrated that only *one* member of the then-current board received backdated options. Judge Alsup also found unpersuasive plaintiffs' attempts to show demand futility under the second prong of *Aronson,* concluding that plaintiffs failed to allege the particularized facts necessary to demonstrate that board members actually engaged in the process of backdating.

After dismissing plaintiffs' amended complaint, however, Judge Alsup granted further leave to amend, and issued a stay pending a books and records demand in Delaware. The stay specifically requested that CNET cooperate and expedite the inspection because "CNET itself raised the availability of such an inspection in its recent memoranda." Judge Alsup listed four categories of books and records that would be helpful in the California action.

* * *

[O]n May 14, 2007, plaintiffs sent their demand to inspect books and records to CNET via certified mail. In this demand letter, plaintiffs made six requests:

1.   All books and records created by, distributed to, or reviewed by CNET's Board of Directors (the "Board"), or any member or committee thereof, showing the extent to which the CNET Compensation Committee delegated (or did not delegate) to management, either stock options under CNET's 1997 Stock option Plan ("1997 Plan") and, if such delegation occurred, the extent to which the Compensation Committee was made aware of the exercise prices and dates selected.

2.   All books and records establishing the specific chronology and events leading to the stock option grants alleged in the Amended   Consolidated   Verified   Shareholder   Derivative

Complaint and exercise prices and grant dates associated therewith.

3.   All books and records needed to determine whether John C. Colligan and/or Eric Robison received stock options that were backdated, misdated, mispriced or incorrectly dated.

4.   All books and records necessary to show the extent to which any minutes or unanimous written consents for the Compensation Committee (while Colligan and Robison were members) were backdated, at least as to those minutes involving or relating to stock option grants.

5.   The written report and findings of the Special Committee of the CNET Board on the Company's option granting practices and procedures.

6.   All documents that CNET provided to the Securities and Exchange Commission ("SEC") in connection with the SEC's investigation into the stock option granting practices and procedures at CNET.

In this demand letter, the plaintiffs identified their purpose as "investigating possible violations of law ... in connection with the Company's granting practices" and "determining whether the Company's officers and directors are independent and/or disinterested and whether they have acted in good faith."

CNET, unmoved by Judge Alsup's request for cooperation, did not comply, and plaintiffs initiated the present action in this Court on June 14, 2007. * * * Specifically, the parties disagree about whether plaintiffs may properly inspect books and records predating plaintiffs' ownership of stock. It is that question this opinion now resolves.

II. LEGAL ANALYSIS

A.   Investigation of admitted stock option backdating constitutes a proper purpose under Section 220.

Section 220 provides shareholders of Delaware corporations with a qualified right to inspect corporate books and records. In relevant part, the statute reads:

> Any stockholder, in person or by attorney or other agent, shall, upon written demand under oath stating the purpose thereof, have the right during the usual hours for business to inspect for any proper purpose, and to make copies and extracts from: (1) The corporation's stock ledger, a list of its stockholders, and its other books and records. * * *

The statute is an expansion of the common law right of shareholders to protect themselves by keeping abreast of how their agents were conducting corporate affairs, but it does not permit unfettered access. Before shareholders may inspect books and records, they must (1) comply with the technical requirements of section 220 and (2) demonstrate a proper purpose for seeking inspection. There is no shortage of proper purposes under Delaware law, but perhaps the most common "proper purpose" is the desire to investigate potential corporate mismanagement, wrongdoing, or waste. Merely stating that one has a proper purpose, however, is necessarily insufficient. For example, a shareholder seeking a books and records inspection under section 220 in order to investigate mismanagement or wrongdoing "must present 'some evidence' to suggest a 'credible basis' from which a court can infer that mismanagement, waste or wrongdoing may have occurred."* **[19]**

Here, as noted above, the plaintiffs have identified two purposes, but both really relate to plaintiffs' desire to bring * * * a [derivative] suit alleging a breach of fiduciary duty in connection with backdated options granted by CNET. Defendant does not dispute this characterization. In fact, defendant relies on this characterization to support its chief argument: plaintiffs are not entitled to books and records from the time period before plaintiffs owned stock in CNET, because plaintiffs lack standing under 8 *Del. C.* § 327 to bring a derivative suit for any claims that accrued before they owned such stock. Thus, all parties agree that plaintiffs have a proper purpose. At issue, however, is the scope of the investigation that plaintiffs' proper purpose will permit.

B.   A stockholder must be given sufficient access to books and records to effectively address the problem of backdating through derivative litigation.

Section 220 does not sanction a "broad fishing expedition," but "where a § 220 claim is based on alleged corporate wrongdoing, . . . the stockholder should be given enough information to effectively address the problem. . . ." Generally, this Court has "wide latitude in determining the proper scope of inspection," and this Court must "tailor the inspection to the stockholder's stated purpose."

---

* **[19]** *Seinfeld v. Verizon Commc'ns, Inc.,* 909 A.2d 117, 118 (Del.2006). Delaware courts have been harshly criticized for this requirement. *See, e.g.,* J. Robert Brown's *Inspection Rights under Delaware Law,* http://www.thereacetothebottom.org (Nov. 20, 2007, 6:16 a.m.) (arguing that the *Seinfeld* decision "illustrates that courts deliberately discourage the use of inspection rights by shareholders, using not the language in the statute but excessive pleading standards"). Such sensationalized criticism may make for an entertaining blog, but it is both unfair and incorrect. First, there is nothing "excessive" about requiring a petitioner to plead the elements of the statute under which he or she petitions the court. Section 220 makes inspection available only for shareholders with a "proper purpose." If a shareholder could satisfy this burden by conclusorily repeating words previously used to describe a proper purpose, the requirement would be rendered meaningless, and well settled canons of statutory construction prevent such absurd results. Second, as Justice Holland explained in *Seinfeld,* permitting a single shareholder to hound a corporation with exclusively personal requests for books and records is a waste of corporate resources that engenders no benefit for the shareholders in general. The proper purpose requirement protects against such wealth-reducing outcomes. Finally, the "credible basis" standard is "the lowest possible burden of proof" in Delaware jurisprudence, and this can hardly be characterized as an excessive pleading standard. *Seinfeld,* 909 A.2d 117 at 123.

Defendant argues that plaintiffs should be barred from inspecting any books and records that predate plaintiffs' ownership of CNET stock. Because plaintiffs are only seeking to bring a derivative claim, defendant argues, and because plaintiffs can only bring claims for wrongs that occurred after plaintiffs purchased stock, there is no reason for plaintiffs to inspect documents before the purchase date. In so arguing, defendant relies heavily on *Polygon Global Opportunities Master Fund v. West Corp.* and *West Coast Management & Capital, LLC v. Carrier Access Corp.* * * * [D]efendant also cites language from the Supreme Court's opinion in *Saito* that indicates "if the stockholder's only purpose [in pursuing a section 220 books and records inspection] was to institute derivative litigation," one might reasonably question "whether the stockholder's purpose was reasonably related to his or her interest as a stockholder."

However, *Polygon* and *West Coast* are distinguishable, and *Saito*, while instructive, mandates a different result than what defendant proposes.

* * *

Judge Alsup told plaintiffs to go to Delaware to find the particularized facts they needed to properly plead demand futility. There are several ways plaintiffs can attempt to accomplish this, one of which is the second prong of *Aronson v. Lewis.* To plead demand futility under the second prong of *Aronson,* a shareholder must allege particularized facts that create a reasonable doubt that the "challenged transaction was * * * the product of a valid exercise of business judgment." This invites an inquiry "into the substantive nature of the challenged transaction and the board's approval thereof." One potential way to show that the board was not exercising valid business judgment is to show that there was a "sustained or systematic failure of the board to exercise oversight"—a violation of the board's duty of loyalty by way of bad faith. To show a "sustained or systematic failure of the board to exercise oversight," the plaintiffs might reasonably need to consult documents that predate their ownership of CNET stock.

In *Polygon*, the shareholder's articulated purpose was solely to investigate potential claims—claims that the shareholder would be barred from bringing. Here, plaintiffs are seeking particularized facts to replead demand futility; they are not fishing for new claims. In *West Coast*, the federal judge overseeing the derivative action explicitly barred the shareholder from repleading demand futility. Here, Judge Alsup explicitly asked plaintiffs to do just that. Indeed, *Saito* is ultimately controlling. There, Justice Berger defined the appropriate scope of a books and records investigation as "enough information to *effectively address the problem.* . . ." Here, plaintiffs cannot effectively address the alleged problem through a derivative suit unless they can properly plead demand futility. Because *Stone v. Ritter* held that a violation of the duty of loyalty/good faith described in *Caremark* can, in theory, excuse demand, and because plaintiffs might need older documents to establish a "sustained or systematic failure" of oversight, I must conclude that plaintiffs' request for the documents here is reasonably related to their proper purpose as shareholders of CNET.

III. CONCLUSION

Plaintiffs should have access to books and records that predate their purchase of stock in order to allow them to explore a potential lapse in the good faith of the CNET board that would excuse demand in the California derivative suit. The outer bounds of this disclosure are defined by plaintiffs' demand letter itself; not by plaintiffs' interrogatories. It is about time defendant takes Judge Alsup's advice, provides the requested documents, and gets "going, going/back, back/to Cali, Cali."

QUESTIONS AND NOTES

1.   In light of the contemporaneous ownership requirement (that the shareholder must have owned stock when the claim arose), how can the plaintiffs in this case gain access to documents that pre-date their ownership?

2.   Does the court order access to the records under Delaware § 220 or as part of discovery in the derivative suit?

3.   Does the court require the shareholder to make a substantive showing of wrongdoing to gain access to the corporate records? If not, how does the court protect the corporation from "fishing expeditions" by shareholders who have nothing more than a hunch that managers breached a fiduciary duty?

4.   Study Delaware § 220 and MBCA § 16.02.

   a).   Can a shareholder gain access to any documents under Delaware law or the MBCA without stating a "proper purpose" for inspection?

   b)   If so, are they the types of documents that would make the board of directors nervous?

   c)   By the way, should *directors* have broader access to corporate books and records than shareholders? Take a look at Delaware § 220(d) and MBCA § 16.05(a).

E. WHO REALLY PAYS?

Remember the McDonald's directors—who they are, how much they are being paid for serving as directors of McDonald's, how much other money they probably have. These folks—like their counterparts at smaller corporations such as Bubba's Burritos, Inc.—do not want to have to "pay" for the honor of serving as a director of a corporation. They want to be protected from liability: from civil damages, from criminal penalties, from litigation costs.

We have previously considered one form of such protection—statutes allowing corporations to limit or eliminate director liability to the corporation of its shareholders for breach of duty of care. Please re-read (read?) the provisions concerning such exculpation clauses at MBCA § 2.02(b)(7) and Delaware § 1.02(b)(7). Recall the two obvious limitations on the protection from such statutes. First, the statutes only affect claims against directors by the corporation or its shareholders, and not by third parties. Second, the statutes do not affect all claims asserted by such plaintiffs. They usually exculpate only for violations of the duty of care (not violations of the duty of loyalty or acts not undertaken in good faith).

We need to consider two other forms of director protection: indemnification and insurance.

1. INDEMNIFICATION

Directors do not have a common law right to indemnification from the corporation for any judgment or settlement that they have to pay or for the litigation costs they incur in connection with their corporate duties. Under general agency principles, an agent has a right to be indemnified by its principal. But, under the same agency principles, a director is not an agent of the corporation. *See* Restatement (Second) of Agency § 14D.

Accordingly, the legal bases for a corporation's indemnification of a director are found in indemnification statutes, the articles of incorporation, the bylaws, and contracts between a corporation and its directors. Indemnification in this context means reimbursement for the various expenses the director incurred as a result of the suit against her. These include litigation costs, attorney's fees, maybe a fine incurred or a judgment imposed or payment made to settle the underlying case against her. The litigation against the director usually will be for alleged breach of fiduciary duty. She is thus sued by or on behalf of the corporation.

Relevant statutes typically differentiate between situations in which a corporate is *permitted* to indemnify its directors (*See* MBCA §§ 8.51 and 8.55) and situations in which a corporation is *required* to indemnify its directors (*See* MBCA § 8.52). Please apply the MBCA indemnification provisions to the following questions.

PROBLEMS

1. Capel, a director of Bubba's Burritos, Inc., is sued for breach of the duty of care. The articles do not contain an exculpation provision.

a)   After trial, the court finds that Capel is not liable. Does Capel have a right to be reimbursed by the corporation for her litigation costs and attorneys' fees? *See* MBCA § 8.52.

b)   Would your answer be different if Capel prevailed because of a "legal technicality" such as the statute of limitations?

c)   After trial, the courts finds that Capel breached the duty of care and assesses damages against Capel. Capel seeks reimbursement of her expenses, attorney's fees, and the judgment she paid. What result?

d)   Capel settles the case with the plaintiff, and writes a check for the settlement amount. Capel seeks reimbursement from the corporation of her expenses, attorney's fees, and the amount she paid to settle the case. What result?

e)   Would your answer to any of these questions be different if Capel were an officer and not a director? (*See* MBCA § 8.56(a).)

2.   Agee, a director of Bubba's Burritos, Inc., is sued by the Securities and Exchange Commission for violation of the federal securities laws. The court assesses damages and fines against Agee.

a)   Does Agee have a right to be indemnified by the corporation for his attorneys' fees? *See* MBCA §§ 8.51 and 8.52.

b)   Would your answers be different if the Articles of Bubba's Burritos contain the following provision regarding indemnification:

ARTICLE VI

INDEMNIFICATION

Section 6.1   <u>Indemnification</u>. The Corporation shall, to the full extent permitted by applicable law, indemnify any person (and the heirs, executors and administrators of such person) who, by reason of the fact that he is or was a Director, officer, employee or agent of the Corporation or of a constituent corporation absorbed by the Corporation in a consolidation or merger or is or was serving at the request of the Corporation or such constituent corporation as a director, officer, employee or agent of any other corporation, partnership, joint venture, trust or other enterprise, was or is a party or is threatened to be a party to:

(a) any threatened, pending or completed action, suit or proceeding, whether civil, criminal, administrative or investigative (other than an action by or in the right of the Corporation), against expenses (including attorneys' fees), judgments, fines and amounts paid in settlement actually and reasonably incurred by such person in connection with any such action, suit or proceeding, or,

(b) any threatened, pending or completed action or suit by or in the right of the Corporation to procure a judgment in its favor, against expenses (including attorneys' fees) actually and reasonably incurred by him in connection with the defense or settlement of such action or suit.

Expenses incurred by a Director, officer, employee or agent of the Corporation in defending an action, suit or proceeding described in subsections (a) and (b) above may be paid by the Corporation in advance of the final disposition of such action, suit or proceeding upon receipt by the Corporation of an undertaking by or on behalf of the Director, officer, employee or agent to repay such amount if and to the extent that it shall ultimately be determined that he is not entitled to be indemnified by the Corporation as authorized in this Section 6.1.

Any indemnification or advancement of expenses by the Corporation pursuant hereto shall be made only in the manner and to the extent authorized by applicable law, and any such indemnification or advancement of expenses shall not be deemed exclusive of any other rights to which those seeking indemnification may otherwise be entitled.

Section 6.2   Indemnification Insurance. The Corporation shall have power to purchase and maintain insurance on behalf of any person who is or was a Director, officer, employee or agent of the Corporation, or is or was serving at the request of the Corporation as a Director, officer, employee or agent of another corporation, partnership, joint venture, trust or other enterprise against liability asserted against him and incurred by him in any such capacity, or arising out of his status as such, whether or not the Corporation would have the power to indemnify him against such liability under applicable law.

2. INSURANCE

MBCA § 8.57 authorizes a corporation to buy liability insurance for its directors and officers. Most states have similar provisions, authorizing corporations to purchase and maintain such "D&O" insurance. Generally, there is no corporate law question as to whether a corporation has the legal authority to buy D&O insurance. The common questions are (i) the business questions such as whether to buy D&O insurance and, if so, what kind; and (ii) the contract law questions such as what is covered by the policy and who makes what decisions with respect to litigating and settling claims.

The following part of an article by two Chicago lawyers specializing in D & O insurance discusses some of these questions.

Companies may buy D&O insurance for a variety of reasons. Indemnification may be insufficient protection if a company has assets that may not be adequate to allow the corporation to easily satisfy its indemnification obligations. Insurance coverage may also be available in some situations where a director or officer does not meet a standard of "good faith" required for indemnification by the corporation (such as where conduct was opposed to the best interests of the corporation but not intentionally dishonest and thus excluded by the D&O policy). There may also be restrictions on the corporation's ability to indemnify directors and officers in some jurisdictions for derivative judgments and settlements.

In some circumstances (for example, a healthy corporation with strong indemnification provisions and a low risk of claims), corporations may opt not to purchase D&O insurance or to only buy direct coverage for directors and officers where the corporation cannot or does not indemnify its directors and officers.

This direct coverage for directors and officers is often referred to as "Side A" or "last resort" coverage. It is usually much cheaper than traditional D & O insurance because it only comes into play when the corporation cannot (because of insolvency or the failure to meet a standard of care, for example), or does not, indemnify the directors and officers. This is a relatively infrequent occurrence, usually arising where there has been a dispute regarding corporate control.

Given the severity and expense of potential claims, however, many companies, especially public corporations, purchase traditional D&O insurance to cover not only unindemnified claims made against the directors and officers but also to reimburse the company for its costs in providing indemnification. Under this corporate reimbursement, or "Side B" coverage, the insurer agrees to "pay on behalf of" or "reimburse" the corporation for amounts the corporation has paid or is required to pay in indemnifying its directors and officers.

D&O insurance typically covers "loss" arising from claims made against directors and officers (or in some instances against the company or employees) for negligent, rather than intentionally dishonest, conduct causing economic injury. A typical definition of "wrongful act" is "any breach of duty, neglect, error, misstatement, misleading statement, omission or act by the directors or officers in their respective capacities as such, or any matter claimed against them solely by reason of their status as directors or officers of the company." (American International Companies Directors, Officer and Corporate Liability Insurance Policy, Form 62334 (5/95), Section 2(m).)

Most D&O policies generally provide "claims made" coverage. Coverage is triggered and provided by the policy in effect when the claim is made, not when the allegedly wrongful conduct took place.

Because the trigger of coverage under a D&O policy generally is when a claim is made, the definition of "claim" is important. Insureds negotiating coverage should seek a broad definition of "claim" that encompasses written demands for relief, lawsuits, civil, criminal, administrative and regulatory proceedings and investigations.

Most D&O policies allow the insured to select counsel to defend the claim, with the carrier's consent, but the payment of defense costs is charged against the limits of the policy. The defense costs are incurred by the insureds and typically indemnified by the corporation, which then seeks reimbursement from the carrier for the amounts paid.

The policy provisions and issues discussed above are a sampling of the items that can be negotiated. One thing is certain: Negotiating terms at the inception of the policy is infinitely better than discovering policy pitfalls after a claim arises.

Carolyn Rosenberg & Duane Sigleko, *The Armor Plated Board—Yes D&O Coverage Needs to be Negotiated,* Business Law Today Oct. 1999, p. 20.

PROBLEMS

1. Roberts serves as an outside director of Bubba's Burritos, Inc. Does he care whether Bubba's Burritos maintains D&O insurance after he leaves the board?

2. Professor James D. Cox of the Duke University Law School studied D&O insurance and concluded:

We should understand that both the employee and the corporation face a good deal of uncertainty as to whether the liability arising from the employee's misbehavior and the entity's vicarious responsibility will ultimately be borne by their insurer. First, there are some inconveniences and burdens of such litigation, such as its distractions or any accompanying loss of reputation, for which insurance provides no protection. Of greater concern is whether the misconduct falls within one of the numerous exclusions. Because willful misconduct is beyond the scope of the policy, exclusions have their greatest impact on the willful violator. With insurance unavailable, the only basis for arguing that insurance undercuts the deterrence effects of private liability is if the plaintiff's lawyer drafts the complaint so as to allege misconduct that is not excluded from the policy's coverage. Here, the evidence * * * regarding coverage disputes between carriers and their insureds serves as a sobering reminder to those considering whether to misbehave; they then proceed on less than certain ground. Further uncertainty arises because of the uncertainty that insurance will be available when the claim is asserted. As most D&O insurance is on a claims-made basis and the insurer can be expected to dispute coverage if the application for insurance does not fully disclose the events and the facts that underlie the asserted claim. Moreover, the insurance cycle may rear its historic ugly head so that deductions are raised and coverage amounts lowered from the levels available when the misconduct occurred that gave rise to the claim.

James D. Cox, *Private Litigation and the Deterrence of Corporate Misconduct*, 60 Law & Contemp. Probs. 1, 36–37 (1997).

3.   Capel, a director of Bubba's Burritos, Inc., is sued in a shareholder derivative suit and held liable to the corporation for $400,000 for breach of the duty of care. Will Bubba's Burritos D&O liability insurance cover the judgment amount, or Capel' litigation costs, or Capel's attorney's fees?

4.   What is the rationale for permitting the corporation to pay for D&O insurance, but not for reimbursing expenses incurred because of certain director action? What is the rationale for permitting the corporation or its shareholders to sue directors for damages and then, through D&O insurance and indemnification statutes, to permit the directors to pay these damages by using money provided directly or indirectly by the corporation and its shareholders? *See generally* Ehud Kamar, *Shareholder Litigation Under Indeterminate Corporate Law*, 66 U. CHI. L. REV. 887 (1999).

CHAPTER 7

CLOSE CORPORATIONS

■ ■ ■

A. WHAT IS A CLOSE CORPORATION?

In the discussion of *Hobby Lobby* on pages 10–11, and more recently in Chapter 5, we encountered the concept of the "close" or "closely held" corporation. It is a real corporation, formed like an ordinary corporation, but it generally has three characteristics: it has few shareholders, its stock is not publicly traded, and the shareholders often participate in managing the corporation (because they are either board members or managers who run the business). We contrasted this with the "public" corporation, which has thousands of shareholders who do not manage the corporation (either as board members or operating managers), and the stock is bought and sold daily on public stock markets. Although many corporations fall between these two extremes, the difference between close and public corporations is important.

As long as it has the necessary characteristics, a close corporation need not be small. The largest close corporation in the United States is Cargill, the agribusiness giant, with over $100 billion in revenues and 126,000 employees. This is not typical, though, and most close corporations are small, local companies.

In Chapter 5, we saw that, for close corporations, there are two other unique possibilities. First, in some (exceptional) circumstances, shareholders of a close corporation may be held personally liable for business debts. Liability is imposed through the judicially-created doctrine of "piercing the corporate veil" (remember the *DeWitt* case on page 149). Second, under modern statutes, the proprietors of a close corporation can avoid the traditional corporate management structure by entering a shareholder management agreement, which we studied on pages 191–198. For instance, they might eliminate the board and run the company directly or appoint someone as manager. Neither of these things—piercing the corporate veil or direct shareholder management—can happen in public corporations.

In this Chapter, we focus in more detail on the close corporation. We start by contrasting the expectations of people who invest in a close corporation with those who invest in a public entity. Although some close corporations are founded and financed by a single person, many are established by a group of family members or friends. Their expectations are like those of people who enter a partnership. They want to own the business, share profits and losses, share in management decisions, and be employed by the business. They do not see their investment in the business as "liquid." That means they do not expect to make money by selling their stock, at least in the near term. Instead, they often expect financial return through their employment.

People who invest in public corporations have completely different expectations. They have no effective voice in management of the business (they do not own enough stock to affect company policy). They do not expect to have a job with the company. They view their investment as liquid—that is, they hope to sell their stock for more money than they paid to buy it (they also may expect to receive dividends).

So, in general, the owners of a close corporation have the same expectations as the partners in a partnership. But they did not form a partnership. They formed a corporation. In this Chapter, we discuss three areas of tension between these expectations and the corporate business structure.

First, remember that partners cannot transfer their entire interest in the business to a third party. They can transfer only their financial interest, and not rights to management. And remember that new partners can be admitted only upon the unanimous vote of the partners (unless the partnership agreement says otherwise). As a result, the original proprietors cannot be forced to accept a new partner.

In the corporation, however, a transfer of stock normally transfers *all* rights, including any management rights. So one shareholder can unilaterally disrupt the closely-held character of the business by giving or selling her stock to a third party. Part B of this Chapter addresses how the corporation can change the normal rule and keep outsiders out.

This Chapter also discusses the opposite side of the close corporation's being able to keep outsiders out: a close corporation's illiquidity problem. Suppose a shareholder retires from the business. She might like to have her interest bought out (as a partnership buys out the interest of a departing partner). But there is no public market for the stock. The same problem arises when a shareholder dies (we saw that in the partnership in *Creel v. Lilly* at page 105). We will see that good planning will provide for a "buy-sell" agreement to require the business or other shareholders to buy the stock.

Second, in Part C of this Chapter, we address the relationship among the shareholders. If the corporation functions as a partnership, should the shareholders owe each other the fiduciary duties that generally apply among partners? In other words, do shareholders in a close corporation have to treat each other in accordance with the strict rules of *Meinhard v. Salmon*, which we saw on page 77? Specifically, does a majority shareholder in a close corporation breach a fiduciary duty by harming a minority shareholder? Or similarly, does a minority shareholder have a statutory right to be free of "oppression" by majority shareholders?

Third, in Part D of this Chapter, we discuss the law concerning the way in which most shareholders in close corporations expect to make money: by employment.

Before tackling these issues, we need to learn about a "statutory close corporation." Historically, the law of close corporations consisted of common law adjustments to the operation of ordinary corporations. However, in recent years, about 20 states have adopted legislation in the area. They have not done so with separate codes, but with "supplements" to the general corporate law. The MBCA has such a supplement. A statutory close corporation is one formed under such provisions. Like common-law close corporations, the stock is not publicly traded and there are few shareholders—though here, unlike the common law version, there is usually a statutory maximum number of shareholders (often 50).

The difference between common law and statutory close corporations is generally not important. Even in states with such statutes, you can form a close corporation without being a statutory close corporation: proprietors remain free to form their corporation under the general corporate code and operate under that state's common-law gloss for close corporations. Theirs is a close corporation as long as it has the characteristics of a close corporation. For some years, statutory close corporations had the advantage of allowing flexible management structure. However, as we saw in Chapter 5, statutes now allow this flexibility in all close corporations.

B. HOW DO THE OWNERS OF A CLOSE CORPORATION KEEP OUTSIDERS OUT?

1. KEEPING IT IN THE FAMILY

As noted, the proprietors of a close corporation choose to own and operate the business with each other. Because stock is normally freely transferable, they may take steps to ensure that outsiders do not become shareholders. Because the company can issue new stock, they also may take steps to ensure that their relative ownership interests are not altered.

a. Preemptive Rights

Assume that Agee, Propp and Capel are the only shareholders of Bubba's Burritos and that each owns one-third of the outstanding shares. If the corporation subsequently issues 150 new shares to each of the existing three shareholders, then the percentage of ownership remains unchanged. If, however, Bubba's Burritos subsequently issues 300 shares to a new shareholder or to Agee and Propp, then Capel's ownership interest will be decreased, or "diluted." What are the potential harms to Capel from dilution? Are there situations in which dilution would not harm him?

Existing shareholders can be protected from such dilution if they have "preemptive rights." A shareholder with preemptive rights has the right to purchase that number of shares of any new issuance of shares that will enable the shareholder to maintain her percentage of ownership. For example, if Capel owns one-third of the outstanding stock, preemptive rights means that Capel has the right to buy one-third of the new issuance.

Whether a shareholder has preemptive rights depends upon (1) what the state corporation code says about preemptive rights, (2) what the articles of incorporation say about preemptive rights, and (3) what the purpose of the issuance is. Please read MBCA § 6.30 and answer the following questions.

QUESTIONS

1.   Under MBCA § 6.30, if the articles say nothing about preemptive rights, do they exist? Why is the MBCA an "opt in" statute? The corporate codes of some states are "opt out" provisions. Under these, preemptive rights exist unless the articles provide that they do not.

2.   What is the practical significance of preemptive rights? Does a shareholder with preemptive rights get the new stock for free? Does she get it at a reduced price?

3.   Is a shareholder with preemptive rights *required* to exercise the rights?

4.   Bubba's Burritos, Inc. has issued 10,000 shares. Shepherd owns 2,000 of these. Assume Bubba's is planning to issue an additional 5,000 shares, the consideration for which is to be cash. If Shepherd has preemptive rights, how many shares can he purchase of the new issuance?

5.   Same facts as in Question 4, except the new issuance of 5,000 shares is to Roberts in exchange for Roberts's sale to the corporation of his racing yacht. Why does Shepherd *not* have preemptive rights as to this issuance under MBCA § 6.30? Does the lack of preemptive rights in this scenario make sense?

6.   Capel owns 1000 shares of Bubba's Burritos stock. Agee and Propp each own 200 shares. If Capel agrees to sell all of her 1000 shares to Agee, can Propp assert preemptive rights?

b. Stock Transfer Restrictions

Read MBCA § 6.27.

PROBLEMS

1.   Agee, Propp, and Capel each owns one-third of the shares of Bubba's Burritos, Inc., which is a close corporation. Agee needs cash to pay college tuition for her children. She finds a buyer for her stock and sells to him. Why might Propp and Capel be upset about this?

2.   To avoid such transfers to third parties, how might each shareholder's right to transfer her stock be limited?

3.   Suppose the Bubba's articles impose a stock transfer restriction requiring that, before any shareholder transfers her stock, she offer it first to the corporation (this is called a "right of first refusal"). Suppose Agee finds a third party who is willing to pay her $30,000 for her stock. Pursuant to the stock transfer restriction, Bubba's offers Agee $5,000 for the stock. Is the restriction valid?

4.   Suppose Agee simply sells her stock to a third party without first offering it to the corporation. Can the corporation have the sale rescinded?

2.   THE ILLIQUIDITY PROBLEM: BUY-SELL AGREEMENTS

To whom can a shareholder sell her shares? This is not a hard question for a shareholder of a large, public corporation like McDonald's. There is a public market for such shares. You can sell your shares instantly by going online or calling your stockbroker.

What about the shareholder of a small, closely held corporation? If Propp, one of three shareholders of Bubba's Burritos, Inc., wants to sell his shares, who are the likely buyers? If Propp is unable to find any other buyer, is the corporation legally obligated to repurchase Propp's shares?

Recall partnership law and the RUPA concept of "dissociation." In many situations, a partner who desired to leave the partnership was entitled to have the partnership buy her out. There is no MBCA counterpart to dissociation in partnership law. Neither corporate codes nor case law creates a "redemption" right—a general right for a shareholder to be able to "redeem" or sell her stock back to the corporation. So a shareholder in a close corporation may have great difficulty in selling her shares.[*]

This difficulty and acrimony (and litigation) can be avoided, though, if the shareholders plan ahead. One of the most important planning tools is the "buy-sell agreement." As the label suggests, this is simply a

---

[*]   "Savorers of political fare recall with glee the tale of two brothers: one who went off to sea, the other who became Vice-President of the United States and neither was ever heard of again. If there had been a third sibling of this dubious duo who had suffered the same fate, it could only be because he was a minority shareholder in a closely held Alabama corporation. Simply put, no buyer in his right mind would pay cash for paper stock carrying no rights, including the right to income therefrom." Andrew P. Campbell, *Litigating Minority Shareholder Rights and the New Tort of Oppression*, 53 ALA. LAWYER 108 (1992).

contract that requires the corporation or the majority shareholders of the corporation to purchase shares in specified situations at a specified price. The price may be a formula or multiple of some financial metric like sales or profits.

A well-drafted buy-sell agreement will specify the situations that trigger the buy-sell, how the purchase price is determined, and—sometimes—where the funds will come from. The fundamental premise of the agreement is that the stock will not be transferred to a third party.

Of course, the parties to the buy-sell agreement are free to ignore the agreement and allow transfer to a third party. Or, they may agree to find an outside buyer for the entire business. But these waivers require agreement of all of the parties to the buy-sell agreement.

The buy-sell is valuable in a circumstance where a minority shareholder wants to exit the business and would otherwise be forced—because of the controlling shareholder's power—to sell his shares to the majority owner at a price set solely by that owner's whim. The buy-sell provision gives the minority owner rights both to sell and to be paid a fairer price—at least a price that was agreed upon in the agreement.

Several circumstances that may lead to the need for a shareholder to sell her shares:

- a shareholder may die or become disabled, and her heirs or guardian want to sell the stock;
- a minority (or even equal) shareholder may tire of the business, want to retire, or have a falling out with her co-owners;
- a shareholder may feel that the business is in decline (think printing color photos from film at the beginning of digital photography) and wish to get out while the getting is good; or,
- a shareholder may simply have some special need for cash (maybe her kids decide to go to law school).

Thus, the buy-sell agreement will typically specify what happens in the event of death or disability of a shareholder and may give any shareholder the right to initiate the buy-sell process.

At that point, the key issue becomes the price at which the shares will be bought and sold. There are several ways in which the entity can be valued. The buy-sell agreement might specify a formula for determining the price of the business. For example, it might value the business at "seven times the average profit of the last three calendar years" or "five times the book value of the company's assets, less its liabilities." There are an infinite number of formulas, but a reasonable one attempts to value the business fairly.

Another approach is a simple children's rule of "you cut the cake and I'll pick my slice." In this method, the "moving party" triggers the buy-sell and states a per share price (or values the entire company). The other party can then choose to be a buyer or a seller at that price.

Another possibility is an auction, where one party triggers the buy-sell. Here, both parties submit their bid, and the winner buys the loser's shares. Sometimes the winner buys the loser out at the winner's bid, sometimes at the loser's bid, and sometimes at an average of the two. Though these examples consider the case of two parties, the principles can be extended to three or even more parties.

If the company buys the shares, it will retire them. This increases the remaining shareholder's ownership stake as if she had repurchased the shares herself.

Where does the money come from? In the case of a buyout when a shareholder dies, the cash could come from a life insurance policy owned by the company. Or the company may take out a loan to buy the stock, or some buy-sell agreements specify that the company will buy the shares over X years at a Y% interest rate. Sometimes, the buyer simply has to come up with the cash.

Just as many couples in the throes of passion bristle at the thought of a prenuptial agreement, people forming a business sometimes fail to create a buy-sell agreement because they are swept away by their excitement. This is usually a mistake. The details of buying out an owner should be resolved at the outset of the relationship. You are likelier to craft a fair agreement at the beginning of the journey, when you are unsure which side of the deal you will be on when you decide to dissolve the relationship, than at the end, when everyone is grasping for everything they can get.

One final note. Under most corporation codes, to the extent that a buy-sell agreement restricts the right of a shareholder to sell her shares to third parties, the restriction is effective only if either (i) the buyer knows of the restriction or (ii) the restriction is "noted conspicuously" on the stock certificate or contained in the information required for shares without certificates. *See* MBCA § 6.27(b).

C. FIDUCIARY DUTIES AMONG SHAREHOLDERS OF A CLOSE CORPORATION

Traditionally, shareholders, whether they control the corporation or not, owed no fiduciary duties to the corporation or to other shareholders. That is, shareholders could exercise their power in whatever way they wanted, even if it harmed other shareholders. For example, suppose the CEO of Burger King, Inc. buys a share of McDonald's, Inc. The Burger-King CEO is permitted to vote to elect McDonald's directors who she knows are incompetent. This is so even if the Burger-King CEO is trying to harm McDonalds.

The shareholders of a close corporation might change the rule by entering a shareholder management agreement under MBCA § 7.32 or a similar statute (we saw § 7.32 at pages 192–193). But suppose that a corporation has no 7.32 agreement.

In some states, the rule that shareholders have no fiduciary duties has been modified for close corporations. Recall that a close corporation resembles a partnership, except that it offers its owners limited liability. Like the typical partnership, a close corporation has few owners, they can't freely transfer their ownership, and the owners are often involved in management. As we saw in *Meinhard*, the owners of a partnership owe strong fiduciary duties to each other and to the partnership.

As the next case, *Donahue v. Rodd Electrotype,* shows, it was not much of a leap for a Massachusetts court to rule that, because of close corporations' similarities to partnerships, shareholders in close corporations should have the same fiduciary duties as partners. Some states have followed *Donahue*. Some others have not. We now examine *Donahue* and another case, both of which address attempts by minority shareholders to sell shares back to corporations.

Suppose a shareholder of a close corporation would like to sell her shares back to her corporation, but the shareholders have failed to create a buy-sell agreement. A close corporation has no general obligation to repurchase its shareholders shares. This is no problem if the shareholder owns a majority of the corporation's shares; because she controls the corporation, she can cause the corporation to buy back her shares. But if the majority shareholder does this, can the minority shareholder insist that the corporation buy his shares too?

In reading the case, please consider the following:

1. Who decided that the corporation would buy Harry Rodd's stock?

2. Who decided the price that the corporation would pay for Harry Rodd's stock? Was there any evidence that the price paid for the stock was excessive?

3. Make sure that you understand the difference between a redemption right, under which a shareholder is entitled to *sell* her shares to the corporation, and preemptive right (which we've already discussed), under which the shareholder is entitled to *buy* additional shares.

DONAHUE V. RODD ELECTROTYPE COMPANY
OF NEW ENGLAND, INC.

Supreme Judicial Court of Massachusetts, 1975
328 N.E.2d 505

TAURO, CHIEF JUSTICE. The plaintiff, Euphemia Donahue, a minority stockholder in the Rodd Electrotype Company of New England, Inc. (Rodd Electrotype), a Massachusetts corporation, brings this suit against the directors of Rodd Electrotype, Charles H. Rodd, Frederick I. Rodd and Mr. Harold E. Magnuson, against Harry C. Rodd, a former director, officer, and controlling stockholder of Rodd Electrotype and against Rodd Electrotype (hereinafter called defendants). The plaintiff seeks to rescind Rodd Electrotype's purchase of Harry Rodd's shares in Rodd Electrotype and to compel Harry Rodd "to repay to the corporation the purchase price of said shares, $36,000, together with interest from the date of purchase." The plaintiff alleges that the defendants caused the corporation to purchase the shares in violation of their fiduciary duty to her, a minority stockholder of Rodd Electrotype.* **[4]**

The trial judge, after hearing oral testimony, dismissed the plaintiff's bill on the merits. He found that the purchase was without prejudice to the plaintiff and implicitly found that the transaction had been carried out in good faith and with inherent fairness. The Appeals Court affirmed with costs.

[Plaintiff owned 45 shares of Rodd Electrotype. Harry Rodd and his children owned the remaining 189 outstanding shares. More specifically, Harry Rodd owned 81 shares and each of his three children owned 36 shares].

* * * We come now to the events of 1970 which form the grounds for the plaintiff's complaint. In May of 1970, Harry Rodd was seventy-seven years old. The record indicates that for some time he had not enjoyed the best of health and that he had undergone a number of operations. His sons wished him to retire. Mr. Rodd was not averse to this suggestion. However, he insisted that some financial arrangements be made with respect to his remaining eighty-one shares of stock. A number of conferences ensued. Harry Rodd and Charles Rodd (representing the company) negotiated terms of purchase for forty-five shares which, Charles Rodd testified, would reflect the book value and liquidating value of the shares.

---

* **[4]** In form, the plaintiff's bill of complaint presents, at least in part, a derivative action, brought on behalf of the corporation, and, in the words of the bill, 'on behalf of . . . (the) stockholders' of Rodd Electrotype. Yet, the plaintiff's bill, in substance, was one seeking redress because of alleged breaches of the fiduciary duty owed to her, a minority stockholder, by the controlling stockholders.

We treat that bill of complaint (as have the parties) as presenting a proper cause of suit in the personal right of the plaintiff.

A special board meeting convened on July 13, 1970. As the first order of business, Harry Rodd resigned his directorship of Rodd Electrotype. The remaining incumbent directors, Charles Rodd and Mr. Harold E. Magnuson (clerk of the company [what most states call the corporate "secretary"] and a defendant and defense attorney in the instant suit), elected Frederick Rodd to replace his father. The three directors then authorized Rodd Electrotype's president (Charles Rodd) to execute an agreement between Harry Rodd and the company in which the company would purchase forty-five shares for $800 a share ($36,000). * * *

A few weeks after the meeting, the Donahues, acting through their attorney, offered their shares to the corporation on the same terms given to Harry Rodd. Mr. Harold E. Magnuson replied by letter that the corporation would not purchase the shares and was not in a financial position to do so. This suit followed.

In her argument before this court, the plaintiff has characterized the corporate purchase of Harry Rodd's shares as an unlawful distribution of corporate assets to controlling stockholders. She urges that the distribution constitutes a breach of the fiduciary duty owed by the Rodds, as controlling stockholders, to her, a minority stockholder in the enterprise, because the Rodds failed to accord her an equal opportunity to sell her shares to the corporation. The defendants reply that the stock purchase was within the powers of the corporation and met the requirements of good faith and inherent fairness imposed on a fiduciary in his dealings with the corporation. They assert that there is no right to equal opportunity in corporate stock purchases for the corporate treasury. For the reasons hereinafter noted, we agree with the plaintiff and reverse the decree of the Superior Court. However, we limit the applicability of our holding to "close corporations," as hereinafter defined. Whether the holding should apply to other corporations is left for decision in another case, on a proper record.

In previous opinions, we have alluded to the distinctive nature of the close corporation, but have never defined precisely what is meant by a close corporation. There is no single, generally accepted definition. Some commentators emphasize an "integration of ownership and management" in which the stockholders occupy most management positions. Others focus on the number of stockholders and the nature of the market for the stock. In this view, close corporations have a few stockholders; there is little market for corporate stock. The Supreme Court of Illinois adopted this latter view in *Galler v. Galler*, 32 Ill.2d 16, 203 N.E.2d 577 (1964): "For our purposes, a close corporation is one in which the stock is held in a few hands, or in a few families, and wherein it is not at all, or only rarely, dealt in by buying or selling." *See, generally*, F. H. O'Neal, CLOSE

CORPORATIONS: LAW AND PRACTICE, § 1.02 (1971).* **[11]** We accept aspects of both definitions. We deem a close corporation to be typified by: (1) a small number of stockholders; (2) no ready market for the corporate stock; and (3) substantial majority stockholder participation in the management, direction and operations of the corporation.

As thus defined, the close corporation bears striking resemblance to a partnership. Commentators and courts have noted that the close corporation is often a little more than an "incorporated" or "chartered" partnership. The stockholders "clothe" their partnership "with the benefits peculiar to a corporation, of limited liability, perpetuity and the like. In essence, though, the enterprise remains one in which ownership is limited to the original parties or transferees of their stock to whom the other stockholders have agreed, in which ownership and management are in the same hands, and in which the owners are quite dependent on one another for the success of the enterprise. Many close corporations are 'really partnerships, between two or three people who contribute their capital, skills, experience and labor.'" Just as in a partnership, the relationship among the stockholders must be one of trust, confidence and absolute loyalty if the enterprise is to succeed. Close corporations with substantial assets and with more numerous stockholders are no different from smaller close corporations in this regard. All participants rely on the fidelity and abilities of those stockholders who hold office. Disloyalty and self-seeking conduct on the part of any stockholder will engender bickering, corporate stalemates, and, perhaps, efforts to achieve dissolution.

In *Helms v. Duckworth*, 249 F.2d 482 (1957), the United States Court of Appeals for the District of Columbia Circuit had before it a stockholders' agreement providing for the purchase of the shares of a deceased stockholder by the surviving stockholder in a small "two-man" close corporation. The court held the surviving stockholder to a duty "to deal fairly, honestly, and openly with . . . [his] fellow stockholders." Judge Burger, now Chief Justice Burger, writing for the court, emphasized the resemblance of the two-man close corporation to a partnership: "In an intimate business venture such as this, stockholders of a close corporation occupy a position similar to that of joint adventurers and partners. While courts have sometimes declared stockholders 'do not bear toward each other that same relation of trust and confidence which prevails in partnerships,' this view ignores the practical realities of the organization and functioning of a small 'two-man' corporation organized to carry on a small business enterprise in which the stockholders, directors, and managers are the same persons" (footnotes omitted).

---

* **[11]** O'Neal restricts his definition of the close corporation to those corporations whose shares are not generally traded in securities markets. F.H. O'Neal, CLOSE CORPORATIONS: LAW AND PRACTICE, § 1.02 (1971).

Although the corporate form provides the above-mentioned advantages for the stockholders (limited liability, perpetuity, and so forth), it also supplies an opportunity for the majority stockholders to oppress or disadvantage minority stockholders. The minority is vulnerable to a variety of oppressive devices, termed "freeze-outs," which the majority may employ. An authoritative study of such "freeze-outs" enumerates some of the possibilities: "The squeezers (those who employ the freeze-out techniques) may refuse to declare dividends; they may drain off the corporation's earnings in the form of exorbitant salaries and bonuses to the majority shareholder-officers and perhaps to their relatives, or in the form of high rent by the corporation for property leased from majority shareholders . . .; they may deprive minority share-holders of corporate offices and of employment by the company; they may cause the corporation to sell its assets at an inadequate price to the majority shareholders. . . ." F. H. O'Neal and J. Derwin, EXPULSION OR OPPRESSION OF BUSINESS ASSOCIATES 42 (1961). In particular, the power of the board of directors, controlled by the majority, to declare or withhold dividends and to deny the minority employment is easily converted to a device to disadvantage minority stockholders.

The minority can, of course, initiate suit against the majority and their directors. Self-serving conduct by directors is proscribed by the director's fiduciary obligation to the corporation. However, in practice, the plaintiff will find difficulty in challenging dividend or employment policies. Such policies are considered to be within the judgment of the directors. This court has said: "The courts prefer not to interfere . . . with the sound financial management of the corporation by its directors, but declare as a general rule that the declaration of dividends rests within the sound discretion of the directors, refusing to interfere with their determination unless a plain abuse of discretion is made to appear." Judicial reluctance to interfere combines with the difficulty of proof when the standard is "plain abuse of discretion" or bad faith to limit the possibilities for relief. * * *

Thus, when these types of "freeze-outs" are attempted by the majority stockholders, the minority stockholders, cut off from all corporation-related revenues, must either suffer their losses or seek a buyer for their shares. Many minority stockholders will be unwilling or unable to wait for an alteration in majority policy. * * *

At this point, the true plight of the minority stockholder in a close corporation becomes manifest. He cannot easily reclaim his capital. In a large public corporation, the oppressed or dissident minority stockholder could sell his stock in order to extricate some of his invested capital. By definition, this market is not available for shares in the close corporation. In a partnership, a partner who feels abused by his fellow partners may cause dissolution by his "express will . . . at any time" and recover his share of partnership assets and accumulated profits. If dissolution results in a breach of the partnership articles, the culpable partner will be liable in damages. By contrast, the stockholder in the close corporation or "incorporated partnership" may achieve dissolution and recovery of his share of the enterprise assets only by compliance with the rigorous terms of the applicable chapter of the General Laws. "The dissolution of a corporation which is a creature of the Legislature is primarily a legislative function, and the only authority courts have to deal with this subject is the power conferred upon them by the Legislature." To secure dissolution of the ordinary close corporation the stockholder, in the absence of corporate deadlock, must own at least fifty per cent of the shares or have the advantage of a favorable provision in the articles of organization. The minority stockholder, by definition lacking fifty per cent of the corporate shares, can never "authorize" the corporation to file a petition for dissolution. He will seldom have at his disposal the requisite favorable provision in the articles of organization.

Thus, in a close corporation, the minority stockholders may be trapped in a disadvantageous situation. No outsider would knowingly assume the position of the disadvantaged minority. The outsider would have the same difficulties. To cut losses, the minority stockholder may be compelled to deal with the majority. This is the capstone of the majority plan. Majority "freeze-out" schemes which withhold dividends are designed to compel the minority to relinquish stock at inadequate prices. When the minority stockholder agrees to sell out at less than fair value, the majority has won.

Because of the fundamental resemblance of the close corporation to the partnership, the trust and confidence which are essential to this scale and manner of enterprise, and the inherent danger to minority interests in the close corporation, we hold that stockholders* [17] in the close corporation owe one another substantially the same fiduciary duty in the operation of the enterprise that partners owe to one another. In our previous decisions, we have defined the standard of duty owed by partners to one another as the "utmost good faith and loyalty." Stockholders in close corporations must discharge their management and stockholder responsibilities in conformity with this strict good faith standard. They may not act out of avarice, expediency or self-interest in derogation of their duty of loyalty to the other stockholders and to the corporation.

We contrast this strict good faith standard with the somewhat less stringent standard of fiduciary duty to which directors and stockholders of all corporations must adhere in the discharge of their corporate

---

* [17] We do not limit our holding to majority stockholders. In the close corporation, the minority may do equal damage through unscrupulous and improper "sharp dealings" with an unsuspecting majority.

responsibilities. Corporate directors are held to a good faith and inherent fairness standard of conduct and are not "permitted to serve two masters whose interests are antagonistic." "Their paramount duty is to the corporation, and their personal pecuniary interests are subordinate to that duty."

The more rigorous duty of partners and participants in a joint adventure,* **[21]** here extended to stockholders in a close corporation, was described by then Chief Judge Cardozo of the New York Court of Appeals in *Meinhard v. Salmon*, 249 N.Y. 458, 164 N.E. 545 (1928): "Joint adventurers, like copartners, owe to one another, while the enterprise continues, the duty of the finest loyalty. Many forms of conduct permissible in a workaday world for those acting at arm's length, are forbidden to those bound by fiduciary ties. . . . Not honesty alone, but the punctilio of an honor the most sensitive, is then the standard of behavior."* **[22]** * * *

Under settled Massachusetts law, a domestic corporation, unless forbidden by statute, has the power to purchase its own shares. An agreement to reacquire stock "(is) enforceable, subject, at least, to the limitations that the purchase must be made in good faith and without prejudice to creditors and stockholders." When the corporation reacquiring its own stock is a close corporation, the purchase is subject to the additional requirement, in the light of our holding in this opinion, that the stockholders, who, as directors or controlling stockholders, caused the corporation to enter into the stock purchase agreement, must have acted with the utmost good faith and loyalty to the other stockholders.

To meet this test, if the stockholder whose shares were purchased was a member of the controlling group, the controlling stockholders must cause the corporation to offer each stockholder an equal opportunity to sell a ratable number of his shares to the corporation at an identical price. Purchase by the corporation confers substantial benefits on the members of the controlling group whose shares were purchased. These benefits are not available to the minority stockholders if the corporation does not also offer them an opportunity to sell their shares. The controlling group may not, consistent with its strict duty to the minority, utilize its control of the corporation to obtain special advantages and disproportionate benefit from its share ownership.

The benefits conferred by the purchase are twofold: (1) provision of a market for shares; (2) access to corporate assets for personal use. By

---

*   **[21]** We have indicated previously that the duty owed by partners *inter sese* and that owed by coadventurers *inter sese* are substantially identical.

*   **[22]** These pages of the *Meinhard* case are cited with approval as authority for the standard of duty applicable to joint adventurers and partners and as authority for "the special liabilities of joint venturers."

definition, there is no ready market for shares of a close corporation. The purchase creates a market for shares which previously had been unmarketable. It transforms a previously illiquid investment into a liquid one. If the close corporation purchases shares only from a member of the controlling group, the controlling stockholder can convert his shares into cash at a time when none of the other stockholders can. Consistent with its strict fiduciary duty, the controlling group may not utilize its control of the corporation to establish an exclusive market in previously unmarketable shares from which the minority stockholders are excluded.

The purchase also distributes corporate assets to the stockholder whose shares were purchased. Unless an equal opportunity is given to all stockholders, the purchase of shares from a member of the controlling group operates as a preferential distribution of assets. In exchange for his shares, he receives a percentage of the contributed capital and accumulated profits of the enterprise. The funds he so receives are available for his personal use. The other stockholders benefit from no such access to corporate property and cannot withdraw their shares of the corporate profits and capital in this manner unless the controlling group acquiesces. Although the purchase price for the controlling stockholder's shares may seem fair to the corporation and other stockholders under the tests established in the prior case law, the controlling stockholder whose stock has been purchased has still received a relative advantage over his fellow stockholders, inconsistent with his strict fiduciary duty—an opportunity to turn corporate funds to personal use.

The rule of equal opportunity in stock purchases by close corporations provides equal access to these benefits for all stockholders. We hold that, in any case in which the controlling stockholders have exercised their power over the corporation to deny the minority such equal opportunity, the minority shall be entitled to appropriate relief. * * *

We turn now to the application of the learning set forth above to the facts of the instant case. The strict standard of duty is plainly applicable to the stockholders in Rodd Electrotype. Rodd Electrotype is a close corporation. Members of the Rodd and Donahue families are the sole owners of the corporation's stock. * * * We reject the defendants' contention that the Rodd family cannot be treated as a unit for this purpose. From the evidence, it is clear that the Rodd family was a close-knit one with strong community of interest. Harry Rodd had hired his sons to work in the family business, Rodd Electrotype. As he aged, he transferred portions of his stock holdings to his children. Charles Rodd and Frederick Rodd were given positions of responsibility in the business as he withdrew from active management. In these circumstances, it is realistic to assume that appreciation, gratitude, and filial devotion would prevent the younger Rodds from opposing a plan which would provide funds for their father's retirement.

Moreover, a strong motive of interest requires that the Rodds be considered a controlling group. When Charles Rodd and Frederick Rodd were called on to represent the corporation in its dealings with their father, they must have known that further advancement within the corporation and benefits would follow their father's retirement and the purchase of his stock. * * *

On its face, then, the purchase of Harry Rodd's shares by the corporation is a breach of the duty which the controlling stockholders, the Rodds, owed to the minority stockholders, the plaintiff and her son. The purchase distributed a portion of the corporate assets to Harry Rodd, a member of the controlling group, in exchange for his shares. The plaintiff and her son were not offered an equal opportunity to sell their shares to the corporation. In fact, their efforts to obtain an equal opportunity were rebuffed by the corporate representative. As the trial judge found, they did not, in any manner, ratify the transaction with Harry Rodd.

Because of the foregoing, we hold that the plaintiff is entitled to relief. Two forms of suitable relief are set out hereinafter. The judge below is to enter an appropriate judgment. The judgment may require Harry Rodd to remit $36,000 with interest at the legal rate from July 15, 1970, to Rodd Electrotype in exchange for forty-five shares of Rodd Electrotype treasury stock. This, in substance, is the specific relief requested in the plaintiff's bill of complaint. In the alternative, the judgment may require Rodd Electrotype to purchase all of the plaintiff's shares for $36,000 without interest. In the circumstances of this case, we view this as the equal opportunity which the plaintiff should have received. Harry Rodd's retention of thirty-six shares, which were to be sold and given to his children within a year of the Rodd Electrotype purchase, cannot disguise the fact that the corporation acquired one hundred per cent of that portion of his holdings (forty-five shares) which he did not intend his children to own. The plaintiff is entitled to have one hundred per cent of her forty-five shares similarly purchased.

The final decree, in so far as it dismissed the bill as to Harry C. Rodd, Frederick I. Rodd, Charles J. Rodd, Mr. Harold E. Magnuson and Rodd Electrotype Company of New England, Inc., and awarded costs, is reversed. The case is remanded to the Superior Court for entry of judgment in conformity with this opinion. * * *

WILKINS, JUSTICE (concurring).

I agree with much of what the Chief Justice says in support of granting relief to the plaintiff. However, I do not join in any implication that the rule concerning a close corporation's purchase of a controlling stockholder's shares applies to all operations of the corporation as they affect minority stockholders. That broader issue, which is apt to arise in connection with salaries and dividend policy, is not involved in this case. The analogy to partnerships may not be a complete one.

QUESTIONS

1.   Professor Douglas K, Moll, a co-author of one of Freer's other books (bless his heart), describes *Donahue* as a "landmark case" and explains that "*Donahue* played a significant role in spawning a new era of judicial activity that focused on providing protection to minority shareholders in closely held corporations from abusive majority conduct. *Donahue*'s influence in this 'movement' has been far-reaching, as a number of courts outside of Massachusetts have also imposed a fiduciary duty between shareholders in closely held corporations. Indeed, due in no small part to decisions like *Donahue*, most jurisdictions have gradually come to recognize that closely held corporations and their publicly held counterparts, as well as the expectations of the shareholders in those ventures, are sufficiently distinct to warrant a different legal treatment." Douglas K, Moll, *Of Donahue and Fiduciary Duty: Much Ado About . . .?*, 33 W.New Eng. L. Rev. 471 (2011).

2.   *Donahue*'s equal access rule requires a close corporation not to discriminate in repurchasing shares. To do so breaches a fiduciary obligation owed to the minority shareholders. Where the rule is accepted, as in Massachusetts, it is limited to the close corporation. Why would a court limit the equal access rule to close corporations? In the states that reject the equal access rule even for close corporations, is there any way that minority shareholders can protect themselves? We have already discussed buy-sell agreements. Also take another look at the redemption rights in the Silicon Gaming document at pages 134–136.

3.   Recall that the court treated this case as a direct, rather than as a derivative, action. Why? Do you agree with attorneys and judges who read *Donahue* as "converting all intracorporate disputes that would normally be characterized as derivative actions into direct actions whenever the case involves a closely held corporation"? *Cf.* AMERICAN LAW INSTITUTE PRINCIPLES OF CORPORATE GOVERNANCE § 7.01, comment (e); Brown v. Brown, 731 A.2d 1212, 1214–18 (N.J. Sup. Ct. App. Div. 1999) (which misspells and discusses the ALI "Principals").

4.   Comparisons

a)   The court compares the stockholders of close corporations with partners of partnerships. What are the similarities? The differences? Does *Donahue* blur the line between close corporations and partnerships?

b)   The court also compares the fiduciary duties of directors of corporations with the fiduciary duties of shareholders of close corporations. What are the differences? To whom does the director of a corporation owe a fiduciary duty? To whom does the shareholder of a close corporation owe a fiduciary duty? For whom is a "punctilio of any honor the most sensitive" the standard of behavior? Recall the statement from the *Zidell* case in Chapter 7, Part B, § 3: "Those in control of corporate affairs have fiduciary duties of good faith and fair dealing to minority shareholders." Is that statement from *Zidell* consistent with the statements in *Donahue*?

       c)   Here is one final comparison of different ways in which a corporation can get money to its shareholders. Compare a corporation's decision to redeem stock with a corporation's decision to declare dividends. How did the $36,000 stock redemption affect Rodd Electrotype's balance sheet? How would $36,000 in dividends affect Rodd Electrotype's balance sheet? *Cf.* MBCA § 14.06 ("A distribution may be in the form of a declaration or payment of a dividend; a purchase, redemption or other acquisition of shares; a distribution of indebtedness; or otherwise.")

5.   Would the court have decided this case differently if there had been a bylaw provision that the corporation may purchase shares from one shareholder without offering the other shareholders an equal opportunity to sell their shares to the corporation?

6.   Would the court have decided this case differently if none of the shareholders were a relative? One article emphasizes that the control group in *Donahue* was a family group: "One may worry that the payment to Dad is disguised self-dealing, the more Dad gets for his shares the less the children in the business will have to contribute to buy him an apartment in Miami." Edward B. Rock & Michael L. Wachter, *Waiting for the Omelet to Set: Match-Specific Assets and Minority Oppression in Close Corporations*, 24 J. CORP. L. 913 (1999).

7.   What is "book value"? "Liquidating value"? Are the two the same?

      As we will see in the cases that follow, *Donahue* has been widely cited and followed in states in addition to Massachusetts. However, not all states do. Some states, including important states such as Delaware, refuse to recognize special common-law fiduciary duties that protect minority shareholders of closely held corporations. Nixon v. Blackwell, 626 A.2d 1366 (1993). For example, in Ritchie v. Rupe, 29014 WL 2788335 (2014), the Texas Supreme Court reversed a trial court judgment ordering Rupe Investment Corporation (RIC), a closely held corporation, to purchase the shares of Ann Rupe (AR), a minority shareholder, for $7.3 million. AR asked the court to recognize a common law cause of action for "minority shareholder oppression," alleging that RIC's other shareholders (who were also RIC's directors) refused to either buy her shares for fair value or even meet with prospective buyers of her RIC shares.

In refusing to create a common law cause of action for minority shareholder oppression, the Texas Supreme Court acknowledged that there will be a gap in the legal protection available to minority shareholders since directors may be able to take actions that are defensible as being in the best interest of the corporation but still harm a minority shareholder. The court concluded, however, that the benefits of protecting minority shareholders were outweighed by public policy concerns: "The Legislature has crafted a statutory scheme governing domestic corporations. The statutes are detailed and extensive, reflecting legislative policy judgments about when the government should step in to impose rights and obligations . . . and when the parties should be free to dictate their own rights vis-à-vis each other and the business. This Court has the prerogative to superimpose a common-law cause of action upon this statutory framework . . . but we exercise that power sparingly. . . ."

In states whose courts reject both *Donahue* and the shareholder-oppression theory, minority shareholders in close corporations are not defenseless. They can protect themselves by insisting on protections *before* they invest in the close corporation. For example, they can demand a unanimous shareholder agreement, such as under MBCA § 7.32, that will guarantee them employment. Or they can require a buy-sell agreement that will allow them to sell their shares for a fair price.

However, the number of minority shareholders who do not protect themselves is substantial. Common examples are people who become shareholders in small family corporations with no foresight that the rest of the family would later mistreat them. In such corporations in such states, the life of a minority shareholder may not be happy.

In some states, legislation offers some protection for minority shareholders in the close corporation by permitting them, if they have been "oppressed," to sue for involuntary dissolution of the corporation. Section 14.30 of MBCA is an example. The presence of such a statute raises an important question: for violation of such a statute, is dissolution the sole remedy? In other words, if the legislature prescribes only one remedy (dissolution), are courts free to infer another remedy (a right to sue for damages without dissolving the corporation)? Two cases in the following section will reflect inconsistent answers to the question. In *Hollis v. Hill*, page 331, the court will infer a right of action absent dissolution. The dissenting judge will take the court to task for doing so. And in *Giannotti v. Hamway*, page 346, the court refuses to recognize a right to sue because the legislature prescribed dissolution as the appropriate remedy. Thus, as Professor Moll concludes: "oppression has evolved from a statutory ground for involuntary dissolution to a statutory ground for a wide variety of relief."* But courts have been inconsistent on exactly what relief that should be.

———————

Let's look at another application of *Donahue*'s fiduciary duty. Even if a close corporation has a buy-sell agreement, the corporation's controlling shareholders could still harm the minority shareholders by not informing them about important information; without the information, the minority shareholders might sell back their shares for a low price.

In *Berreman*, our next case, West redeemed its shares from shareholder Berreman at $2,088.90 a share. However, West did not tell Berreman that it was planning to sell the company. Berreman sued the corporation and three of its directors (who were also shareholders), alleging, inter alia, breach of fiduciary duty. The following is a portion of the Minnesota Court of Appeals' decision where the court both applied *Donahue* and interpreted it to require the company to reveal to its minority shareholders material information.

BERREMAN V. WEST PUBLISHING COMPANY

Minnesota Court of Appeals, 2000
615 N.W.2d 362

LANSING, JUDGE. Thomas Berreman appeals from summary judgment dismissing his action against West Publishing Company and three West directors (collectively "West"). Berreman's claims were based on his assertion that West had a duty to disclose to him, before Berreman retired from West and sold his stock back to the company in June 1995, that three of West's directors had begun to consider the sale of West and had engaged an investment-banking firm to explore West's options. On cross-motions for summary judgment, the district court granted summary judgment to West on all of Berreman's claims. We affirm.

FACTS

The facts are undisputed. In April 1995, Thomas Berreman, a 25-year employee of West Publishing Company, told West's Chief Executive Officer, Dwight Opperman, that he intended to retire effective June 1, 1995. Berreman had worked for West's law school division since 1970. West promoted him to assistant manager of the division in 1977 and to division head in 1992.

Beginning in 1974, Berreman bought West stock through a stock-option program for high-level managers and sales representatives that granted options at Dwight Opperman's discretion. Berreman bought his stock subject to a written agreement for purchase, sale, and resale, which

———————

* Douglas K. Moll, *Shareholder Oppression and "Fair Value": Of Discounts, Dates, and Dastardly Deeds in the Close Corporation,* 54 Duke L.J. 293 (2002).

provided that if he decided to sell his stock or in the event of his death, incompetency, or termination of employment, West could exercise an option to repurchase the stock at book value. * * *

Berreman's last day at West was May 31, 1995. On June 1, 1995, with Berreman's authorization, West redeemed Berreman's stock at the current book value of $2,088.90 per share and paid off a bank loan secured by the stock. On June 15, 1995, Chief Financial Officer Grant Nelson gave Berreman a check for approximately $2.8 million.

As of May 31, 1995, West had about 200 employee shareholders, 25 non-employee shareholders, and 328,908 shares outstanding. Dwight Opperman, Nelson, and board president Vance Opperman, in addition to being directors, were each shareholders. Together they held 23 percent of West's outstanding shares. Until its sale to Thomson Corporation in 1996, West was a privately held corporation. And until West announced the possibility of a sale in August 1995, West directors had publicly expressed their commitment to remaining privately held.

During 1994 and 1995, West was facing an increasingly competitive legal publications market. Two of West's competitors, Mead Data, owner of Lexis-Nexis, and Prentice Hall Law & Business, merged into international publishing companies in 1994. That same year West received unsolicited materials on possible mergers from investment-banking firms Goldman-Sachs and A.G. Edwards, which included information about Thomson Corporation. In response to the increasingly competitive conditions, West's board increased its acquisition fund from $70 million to $300 million in October 1994.

During the second week of May 1995, while on vacation, Nelson reflected on the future of West in light of the changing legal-publications market. Nelson was concerned about West's future given increasing competition, changing technology, and pending antitrust investigations. Nelson concluded that rather than making an acquisition, West should consider being acquired or entering into a joint venture.

On May 15, 1995, Nelson met with Dwight Opperman, who listened to Nelson's concerns and told him, "I think you may be right." Nelson and Dwight Opperman met with Vance Opperman the next day, and the three decided to engage A.G. Edwards to explore West's options. Nelson called Ray Kalinowski at A.G. Edwards the same day and told him that West wanted advice on the company's future financial options, including a possible sale of the company. On May 17, 1995, A.G. Edwards representatives met with the West directors. The directors authorized A.G. Edwards to retain another investment-banking firm if necessary.

The West board met on May 23, 1995. During that meeting, the board again addressed its potential acquisitions and authorized A.G. Edwards to explore financing options beyond West's local bank. The board did not discuss the possibility of selling the company. This meeting was the last board meeting before Berreman's June 1 retirement.

On August 28, 1995, A.G. Edwards made a presentation to the West board outlining four options: recapitalization, public offering, status quo, and sale. The board engaged A.G. Edwards and Goldman-Sachs to advise and assist West in evaluating its options and authorized West management to take necessary steps, including contacting potential buyers and developing acquisition proposals.

On August 29, 1995, West announced to its employees and to the public that it had engaged investment bankers and was considering alternative financial options including public offering, entering into a joint venture, joining a strategic partner, recapitalization, sale, or any other available option. In September 1995, West sent invitations for bids to 45 potential purchasers. The bids were due by February 1996, and West eventually received four bids, including one from Thomson Corporation. West accepted Thomson Corporation's bid, and the companies entered into a merger agreement on February 25, 1996. After a shareholder vote and review by the Department of Justice, West concluded the sale to Thomson in June 1996. Thomson paid $10,445 per share to acquire West, about five times the amount Berreman received when he sold his stock back to the company in June 1995. Berreman's action against West followed. * * *

Common Law Fiduciary Duty

At common law, the shareholders in a close corporation owe one another a fiduciary duty. Courts impose the fiduciary duty because they find that close corporations are really more like "partnership[s] in corporate guise." *Donahue v. Rodd Electrotype Co.*, 367 Mass. 578, 328 N.E.2d 505, 512 (1975) ("Commentators and courts have noted that the close corporation is often little more than an 'incorporated' or 'chartered' partnership.").

Attributes of Close Corporation

Courts generally identify common law close corporations by three characteristics: (1) a small number of shareholders; (2) no ready market for corporate stock; and (3) active shareholder participation in the business. In addition, dividends are rarely distributed in a close corporation. Rather, "shareholders derive their income mainly from salaries and perquisites." Id.

In May 1995, West exhibited characteristics of a close corporation. First, West was not publicly traded; thus, there was no ready public market for its stock. This court has recognized the lack of a public market as the dominant characteristic of a common law close corporation. Additionally, West offered its stock only to high-level managers and sales people at Dwight Opperman's discretion. The lack of a public market for

West stock, combined with the managerial role West's shareholders occupied, supports the characterization of West as a common-law close corporation.

Second, the rationale for distinguishing close corporations from other corporations supports the characterization of West as a close corporation. Courts have recognized that because majority shareholders of a close corporation can deny minority shareholders income from their investment, minority shareholders are in a vulnerable position. That West's corporate structure would have allowed this type of "freeze out" supports its characterization as a close corporation.

On the other hand, West's 200 shareholders far exceed the number of shareholders in any corporation that Minnesota courts have recognized as a close corporation. To categorize West as a close corporation under Minnesota common law would substantially extend the definition's numerical boundaries. Berreman argues that because 94% of the stock was held by employees and subject to repurchase agreements, West's decision-making was concentrated in only a few individuals, and West's numerical structure should be analyzed from that viewpoint. These arguments have persuasive force and a fact-finder could draw inferences that would credit Berreman's arguments. Because we are reviewing a summary judgment against Berreman's claims, he is entitled to review in a light most favorable to the evidence supporting his claims, and thus we assume for purposes of our analysis that West may be categorized as a close corporation. * * *

Scope of Common Law Fiduciary Duty

We turn next to the scope of the common law fiduciary duty. While it is well established that shareholders in a close corporation owe a fiduciary duty to one another, the scope of the duty has never been well defined. In *Donahue v. Rodd Electrotype Co.*—often cited as a leading case on fiduciary duty in the close corporation context—the Massachusetts Supreme Court held that "stockholders in a close corporation owe[d] one another substantially the same fiduciary duty in the operation of the enterprise that partners owe one another." 328 N.E.2d at 515 (footnote omitted). The court described the duty as one of "utmost good faith and loyalty" and went on to hold that a corporation that buys shares from one shareholder must offer to buy shares from all other shareholders at the same rate. This has since been called the equal-opportunity rule. *Donahue* is probably the broadest statement of the fiduciary duty in the close corporation context. Even the Massachusetts Supreme Court later qualified its holding by recognizing that there may be legitimate business reasons for treating shareholders differently. *Wilkes v. Springside Nursing Home, Inc.*, 370 Mass. 842, 353 N.E.2d 657, 663 (1976) (establishing that when corporation demonstrates legitimate business interest, plaintiff, to succeed on fiduciary claim, must show less harmful alternative to achieve that interest). * * *

The Minnesota cases have not addressed whether the fiduciary duty in [the] close corporation context includes a duty to disclose. The [state] supreme court has, however, ruled that "[o]ne who stands in a confidential or fiduciary relation to the other party to a transaction must disclose material facts." And this court has applied the duty to disclose material facts in the analogous partnership context.

Relying on the principles expressed in the Minnesota cases addressing disclosure, we conclude that the fiduciary duties of shareholders in a close corporation include the duty to disclose material information about the corporation. Our holding is consistent with federal cases recognizing the duty to disclose material facts as within the fiduciary duties of shareholders in a close corporation. Jordan v. Duff & Phelps, Inc., 815 F.2d 429, 435 (7th Cir.1987) (stating that "[c]lose corporations buying their own stock, like knowledgeable insiders of closely held firms buying from outsiders, have a fiduciary duty to disclose material facts").

Materiality of Undisclosed Facts

The recognition that shareholders in a close corporation have a duty to disclose material facts leads us to the second part of the question: What facts are material and thus fall within the scope of that duty? In the context of the federal securities laws, the U.S. Supreme Court has held that an omitted fact is material "if there is a substantial likelihood that a reasonable shareholder would consider it important in deciding how to vote." *Basic Inc. v. Levinson*, 485 U.S. 224, 231, 108 S.Ct. 978, 983 (1988) (citation omitted). * * *

In *Basic v. Levinson*, the Supreme Court adopted the probability-magnitude approach for determining whether preliminary merger discussions are material. Under that test, materiality "will depend at any time upon a balancing of both the indicated probability that the event will occur and the anticipated magnitude of the event in light of the totality of the company activity." Probability should be assessed by evaluating the "indicia of interest in the transaction at the highest corporate levels." Magnitude should be assessed by considering "such facts as the size of the two corporate entities and of the potential premiums over market value." * * *

Application of Probability-Magnitude Test to Undisclosed Facts

Applying the probability-magnitude test to this case, we hold that the facts known to West at the time Berreman resigned were immaterial as a matter of law. By the end of May 1995, Nelson, Dwight Opperman, and Vance Opperman had decided to explore options for the future of West including a possible sale, and they had hired an investment-banking firm to investigate West's options. West, however, had made no decision to solicit bids for the sale of West, much less initiated discussions with any potential buyers. The federal courts have been reluctant to find materiality in the absence of evidence that the corporation engaged in discussions with potential buyers. Even in the close-corporation context, the Seventh Circuit has gone no further than to say that a corporation's decision to seek a buyer may be material. We agree that tentative, speculative discussions about merger are not material.

Berreman urges that the early discussions among the West directors about the possibility of merger should be found material because the magnitude of any potential merger was substantial. West had always been a privately held corporation, and until August 1995, its directors were vocally committed to being privately held. That any merger would have been such a sharp departure from West's long history of being privately held supports the magnitude of the merger discussions. But the magnitude of the discussions does not overcome the low probability that the merger would ever occur. The initial discussions were among West's top directors, which supports probability. But even these three directors had decided only to explore West's financial options. Thus, the discussions were not material. * * *

As a matter of law, West did not breach a fiduciary duty * * * to Berreman. * * * Accordingly, we affirm summary judgment for West.

QUESTIONS

1.   Why did the court discuss the fiduciary duty of shareholders instead of the fiduciary duty of directors?

2.   Was West Publishing Company a close corporation?

3.   What could West's CEO have told Berreman in June of 1995? Why didn't West's CEO tell Berreman that "three of West's directors had begun to consider the sale of West and had engaged an investment banking firm to explore West's options"?

D. RECEIVING SALARIES FROM THE CORPORATION

How does a shareholder of a closely held corporation hope to make money? Shareholders in a close corporation (like partners in a partnership) do not expect to make money primarily by selling their interest to a third party; by definition, there is no ready market in the close corporation's shares. As shown by *Berreman* and *Donahue,* the best that they can hope to do is sell their shares under a buy-sell agreement back to the corporation or to the other few shareholders.

They also do not expect to make money by receiving dividends. Most close corporations do not pay significant dividends. This is because, unlike salaries, dividends are not tax-deductible by the company. A corporation's profits are taxed in two ways. First, the corporation pays a corporate tax of a percentage of its profits. Second, when whatever remains is distributed to the shareholders, it is taxed at the individual level. If a corporation pays a $100,000 dividend to a shareholder, the dividend is not tax-deductible by the firm. In contrast, if the $100,000 is distributed as a reasonable salary, then the full amount is deductible from the corporation's reported net income, reducing the corporation's taxes. In effect, paying salaries rather than distributing dividends eliminates the so-called "double taxation" of corporations; because salaries are tax-deductible for the corporation, they are taxed only at the individual level. We discuss dividends further in Chapter 8, at page 431.

Instead, shareholders in a close corporation often expect to benefit from the business by being employed by the business. Shareholders who work for the corporation expect to earn salaries and bonuses. This raises three questions: (1) Who decides which shareholders get salaries? (2) Who decides how much the salaries will be? And (3) what are the legal limitations, if any, on such salary decisions?

None of the three questions is expressly answered by the MBCA. Section 6.40 deals with "distributions" to shareholders. But a salary for services to the corporation is not a "distribution" as defined in § 1.40(6) ("transfer of money or other property * * * in respect of any of its shares").

More relevant to the question of who decides what salaries a corporation pays to its shareholders is § 8.01, which generally authorizes the board of directors to manage "the business and affairs of the corporation." Please read §§ 8.01 and 7.32.

1. WHO DECIDES WHO GETS WHAT SALARY?

"A guaranty of employment may have been one of the basic reasons why a minority owner has invested capital in the firm. The minority shareholder typically depends on his salary as the principal return on his investment since the earnings of a close corporation * * * are distributed in major part in salaries, bonus and retirement benefits." Wilkes v. Springside Nursing Home, Inc., 353 N.E.2d 657 (Mass. 1976).

In that case, Wilkes was one of four shareholders of a corporation that owned and operated a nursing home. Initially, all of the shareholders worked at the nursing home and were paid salaries for their work. After a falling out with his fellow shareholders, they forced Wilkes out of his nursing home job and salary.

Wilkes sued the other shareholders, alleging a breach of the fiduciary duty owed to him by the majority shareholders. The Massachusetts court held for Wilkes because the majority had not shown a "legitimate business purpose" in firing Wilkes.

The next case, *Hollis v. Hill*, also involves a shareholder (Hollis) who lost his job and salary with the corporation and who relies on *Wilkes* in suing the shareholder (Hill) who, he argued, oppressed him. In reading the Fifth Circuit's decision, note that the court applies the same fiduciary duty running from a majority shareholder to a minority shareholder from the *Donahue* case, a few pages back. Also, please consider these questions:

1.   When he became a shareholder in FFUSA, did the plaintiff Hollis expect that he would have a job with the corporation and receive a salary from FFUSA?

2.   Do we know whether Hollis had a contract either with FFUSA or with Hill that provided for such a job and salary?

3.   Do we know whether FFUSA needed Hollis to work at the Florida office? Do we know whether FFUSA needed a Florida office? Do we know whether FFUSA needed Hollis to work with Hill at the Texas office? Do we know whether FFUSA needed Hollis to work?

4.   What did Hill do wrong?

HOLLIS V. HILL

United States Court of Appeals, Fifth Circuit, 2000
232 F.3d 460

POLITZ, CIRCUIT JUDGE. James P. Hollis seeks a court-ordered buy-out of his 50% interest in a Nevada corporation. The district court found that Dan Hill, holder of the other 50% interest, breached the fiduciary duty he owed to Hollis and ordered a buy-out of Hollis' shares based on the corporation's value more than one year prior to the date of judgment. Hill timely appeals. For the reasons assigned, we affirm in part and vacate and remand in part.

BACKGROUND

In early 1995, Hill and Hollis jointly founded First Financial USA, Inc. (FFUSA), a Nevada corporation which marketed first lien mortgage notes and other non-security financial products. All of the whole mortgage notes placed by FFUSA were obtained from and serviced by South Central Mortgage.* **[1]** Hill and Hollis also owned equal shares of First Financial United Investments, Ltd., L.L.P. (FFUI), a Texas limited liability partnership organized in June 1996 to sell securities products as

---

* **[1]** Hill explained that FFUSA relied heavily on South Central Mortgage for two reasons: Hill's experience with South Central and his relationship with its president, Todd Etter, persuaded him that the company could be relied upon to service the notes properly. This was particularly important in the event that a note was defaulted. In addition, South Central was among the few firms outsourcing the marketing of its notes. Most other mortgage companies preferred to keep the entire operation in-house by maintaining their own sales forces. As FFUSA was strictly a marketing company, few other firms would complement its business as well as South Central.

a broker/dealer. This action focuses on the parties' rights and obligations respecting FFUSA.

Hill was a 50% owner of FFUSA, was a director and served as its president, and operated its Houston office. He testified his duties were "to set up the company, set up all the administration, hire the personnel, set up the tracking systems, support reps, recruit reps, and generally help in the strategizing of the company's direction." Hollis owned the other 50% interest in FFUSA, was a director and served as its vice president. Hollis operated its Melbourne, Florida office, with duties including recruiting, training and supporting representatives in their marketing efforts, seeking out new revenue sources, and participating in management. Their wives completed the board of directors and were employed by the firm.

From its inception through 1997, FFUSA did very well financially and paid substantial salaries to Hill and Hollis. In early December 1997, however, Hill began to complain that Hollis was not carrying an equal share of the firm's workload and made known his belief that Hollis was getting more money than he deserved. He stopped paying Hollis' salary. Hollis proposed several ways to resolve the dispute, including mediation, relocating to Houston, placing a disinterested person on the board to break the deadlock, or exchanging his interest in FFUI for Hill's interest in FFUSA. Hill rejected all of the proposals. In March 1998, Hill proposed to buy Hollis' interest in FFUSA in exchange for a ten-year, $1.5 million consultant agreement.* **[2]** When Hollis rejected the proposal, Hill threatened to close FFUI and establish his own broker/dealer business.

Meanwhile, Hill took FFUSA's annuity business and, without Hollis' knowledge, placed it into a sole proprietorship called "Dan Hill d.b.a. First Financial U.S.A." Hill explained that this move was in response to a cease and desist letter FFUSA received from the State of Texas prohibiting it, as a corporation not licensed in Texas, from marketing insurance products. Hill, a resident of Texas, created the sole proprietorship so that FFUSA could continue the marketing of insurance products and executed a contemporaneous assignment transferring all accounts of the sole proprietorship back to FFUSA. Hill charged the corporation a fee for providing this "service." He later split this fee with Hollis.

Hill also stopped sending FFUSA financial reports to Hollis. On May 11, 1998, Hollis visited the Houston office of FFUSA and FFUI and requested copies of financial reports and other documents. Hill refused, claiming that he and the key Houston office employees had appointments that day and that they did not have time to go over the books with Hollis. Hollis later, through his attorney, asserted his right as a shareholder of

---

    *   **[2]** A valuation report by Dixon & Company dated December 17, 1997, estimated the company's value to be between $1.3 million and $3.5 million.

FFUSA and limited partner of FFUI to inspect the books and records of the two firms. On the eve of the inspection, Hill and Hollis agreed to negotiate. Hollis testified that the result was an agreement under which Hill would acquire Hollis' interest in FFUI and would draw a salary of $200,000 from FFUSA, and Hollis would draw an annual salary of $120,000 therefrom for encouraging FFUSA's representatives to produce business and for supplying them with the necessary paperwork. Under the agreement, both men retained a 50% interest in FFUSA.

By August 1998, the tension between Hollis and Hill resurfaced. Hill stopped sending company reports to Hollis and unilaterally undertook a number of measures he claims were intended to lower the firm's costs, including reducing officer salaries by 50%. On October 16, 1998, he informed Hollis that he had decided to reduce his own annual salary to $80,000 and would reduce Hollis' salary to zero dollars. In a November 1998 letter, Hill told Hollis that: "[his] position as an inactive officer commands no salary;" phone service in the Florida office would be canceled; and the lease for the Florida office would be terminated. Hollis was informed that he was no longer authorized to use the company cellular phone and that FFUSA would no longer pay the expense of his leased vehicle. Hill terminated the employment of Hollis' wife. * * *

Hollis filed the instant action on December 8, 1998, alleging shareholder oppression. A few weeks later Hill terminated Hollis as vice-president and eliminated all of his company benefits. Hollis continued as corporate secretary, board member, and 50% shareholder. The financial condition of FFUSA worsened and, according to Hill's expert, the firm had decreased in value to $100,000 by May 11, 1999. On April 30, 1999, Hill, acting through his attorney, made an unsuccessful "capital call" on Hollis. [A capital call requires principals to contribute more capital to the business.]

The district court, applying Nevada law, concluded that Hill's conduct was oppressive and ordered him to buy Hollis' shares in FFUSA. The court cited the capital call and the firing of Hollis as the "easiest objective data" supporting the claim of oppression, and added that the "more egregious" act of moving the annuity business to the Hill-sole-proprietorship should not have occurred without the approval of the board of directors. The court also suggested that Hill's interference with the flow of information to Hollis and his threat to start a business that competed with FFUI were oppressive acts.* [3] The court ordered Hill to

---

* [3] In ruling from the bench, the district court opined that the absence of a non-compete agreement was of no consequence and that Hill's actions were subject to the corporate opportunity doctrine. Any finding of the breach of duty of loyalty based on usurpation of a corporate opportunity necessarily related to opportunities available to FFUI. Hollis has made no claims as an FFUI shareholder and has not claimed that Hill usurped a corporate opportunity. The trial court appropriately did not specifically find a violation of the corporate opportunity doctrine. We assume that the district court intended this discussion to support its finding of oppression.

purchase Hollis' shares for $667,950, which represented the value of the corporation on February 28, 1998, the date the court found that the oppression began. Adding attorney's and expert's fees, the total award to Hollis was $792,915. This appeal followed.

ANALYSIS

We apply Texas law in this diversity action. Texas, like most other states, follows the "internal affairs doctrine." That is, the internal affairs of the foreign corporation, "including but not limited to the rights, powers, and duties of its board of directors and shareholders and matters relating to its shares," are governed by the laws of the jurisdiction of incorporation. Nevada corporate law therefore determines the existence and scope of duties between Hollis and Hill. "In order to determine state law, federal courts look to final decisions of the highest court of the state. When there is no ruling by the state's highest court, it is the duty of the federal court to determine as best it can, what the highest court of the state would decide."

Generally, in determining what a state's highest court would hold with respect to a particular issue, "we may consider relevant state precedent, analogous decisions, considered dicta, scholarly works and any other reliable data." In the present situation, however, the most reliable source of assistance, namely dispositive decisions from the Nevada courts, are non-existent. In addition, the corporate law of Nevada gives limited guidance, and determining where the Nevada Supreme Court would look for such guidance on the issues presented herein presents a challenge.
* * *

Nearly every state statutorily permits holders of a certain percentage of corporate shares to petition the courts for dissolution under particular enumerated circumstances. Thirty-six states list the oppression of minority shareholders by controlling shareholders as grounds for dissolution. Nevada does not. Hollis, however, has not sought dissolution of FFUSA under Nev.Rev.Stat. § 78.650. Instead, he contended, and the district court found, that Hill's actions amount to a breach of fiduciary duty owed him and that equitable relief is therefore available. Before us, then, is the question whether a duty of loyalty was breached by Hill and, if so, whether the district court erred in granting a retroactive buy-out remedy.

A.   *Existence of a Fiduciary Duty*

We find that a fiduciary duty existed between Hollis and Hill. The facts reveal that they agreed to begin a business together, incorporating it under the name FFUSA. They retained equal ownership in the corporation, and became officers and directors, agreeing to the work obligations and salary of the other. With only two shareholders and management responsibilities divided between them, a fiduciary relationship was created not unlike that in a partnership.

We find this case analogous to *Clark v. Lubritz*, [944 P.2d 861 (Nev. 1997)]. [In *Clark*, the Nevada Supreme court upheld a claim for oppression by one of five members of a medical practice. The other four secretly reduced the plaintiff's share of proceeds. The medical practice had been operated as a partnership. Though it was then incorporated, the doctors never operated it as a corporation. The court thus found that the duty of good faith and fair dealing among partners should apply.] * * * [W]e see no reason why the Nevada Supreme Court would not treat the agreement between Hollis and Hill in the same manner as the agreement in *Clark*.* **[16]**

We find our decision buttressed by the legal authority dealing with close corporations.* **[17]** We concede that many of Hill's alleged "oppressive" acts, including the diminution and eventual termination of salary, the failure to deliver financial information, the closing of one of the company's offices, termination of employment, and the cessation of benefits, are classic examples of acts typically shielded from judicial scrutiny under the business judgment rule. Generally, employees who are adversely affected by such officer and director decisions may not claim oppression by those in control of the corporation, even if they are also shareholders of the corporation.* **[18]** Certain actions by a director, however, receive much different treatment when the corporation only has a few shareholders, including that director.

In the context of a closely held corporation, many classic business judgment decisions can also have a substantial and adverse effect on the "minority's" interest as shareholder. Close corporations present unique opportunities for abuse because the expectations of shareholders in

---

* **[16]** We note that both parties argue over the relevance of Hollis' status as an "equal" rather than "minority" shareholder. We find this distinction immaterial to the present dispute. While we acknowledge that in *Clark* the plaintiff truly was a "minority" shareholder, in the sense that he owned only one-fifth of the stock, we find this difference insignificant in light of Hill's virtually unfettered control of FFUSA. Further, the court in *Clark* never spoke of "minority" shareholder status, partially because it treated the organization as a de facto partnership, but also because the partners who decreased his salary clearly controlled the organization, much like Hill controlled FFUSA in the case at bar. Furthermore, other jurisdictions have agreed that the question of minority versus majority should not focus on mechanical mathematical calculations, but instead, "The question is whether they have the power to work their will on others—and whether they have done so improperly."

* **[17]** FFUSA was not incorporated as a close corporation, but, * * * this does not affect our analysis in the instant action. Relevant references herein to "close corporation" also mean "closely held" corporation.

* **[18]** As one court has observed, "a 'fiduciary' duty to every baggage handler at United Airlines just because the employee owns a share of stock would put employee-owned firms at such a competitive disadvantage that they would soon collapse." *Nagy v. Riblet Products Corp.*, 79 F.3d 572, 577 (7th Cir.1996).

closely held corporations* [19] are usually different from those of share-holders in public corporations. As a leading commentator has noted:

> Unlike the typical shareholder in a publicly-held corporation, who may be simply an investor or a speculator and does not desire to assume the responsibilities of management, the shareholder in a close corporation considers himself or herself as a co-owner of the business and wants the privileges and powers that go with ownership. Employment by the corporation is often the shareholder's principal or sole source of income. Providing employment may have been the principal reason why the shareholder participated in organizing the corporation. Even if shareholders in a close corporation anticipate an ultimate profit from the sale of shares, they usually expect (or perhaps should expect) to receive an immediate return in the form of salaries as officers or employees of the corporation, rather than in the form of dividends on their stock. Earnings of a close corporation are distributed in major part in salaries, bonuses and retirement benefits. . . .* [20]

In this setting, it is not difficult for a controlling stockholder to frustrate such expectations and deny a return on investment through means that would otherwise be legitimate.* [21]

For this reason, a number of jurisdictions, including Massachusetts in the landmark case *Donahue v. Rodd Electrotype Co.*, have held that the duty existing between controlling and minority shareholders in close corporations is the same as the duty existing between partners.* [23] In *Donahue*, the court required a majority shareholder, whose shares were purchased by the corporation, to make available to the minority an equal opportunity to sell a ratable number of shares to the corporation at an identical price. While *Donahue's* equal opportunity principle has been rejected by some courts, its recognition of special rules of fiduciary duty applicable to close corporations has gained widespread acceptance. * * *

---

    *   **[19]** Closely held corporations are characterized by a small number of stockholders, the absence of a ready market for the corporate stock, and substantial majority stockholder participation in the management, direction, and operation of the company. *Donahue v. Rodd Electrotype Co.*, 367 Mass. 578, 328 N.E.2d 505 (1975).

    *   **[20]** F. Hodge O'Neal & Robert B. Thompson, 1 O'Neal's Close Corporations § 1:08, at 31–32 (3d ed. 1998).

    *   **[21]** It is not critical that Hill and Hollis each owned 50% of FFUSA and therefore neither was a majority shareholder. A fiduciary duty exists between shareholders by virtue of the fact that one of the shareholders has control over the corporation's assets. Indeed, a duty has been found to run from the minority to the majority where the minority shareholder had veto power over corporate action. Hill acknowledges that he had control over FFUSA.

    *   **[23]** The Massachusetts court borrowed this oft-quoted statement from then-Chief Judge Cardozo: "Joint adventurers, like copartners, owe to one another, while the enterprise continues, the duty of the finest loyalty. Many forms of conduct permissible in a workaday world for those acting at arm's length, are forbidden to those bound by fiduciary ties . . . Not honesty alone, but the punctilio of an honor the most sensitive, is then the standard of behavior." Id. at 516 (quoting *Meinhard v. Salmon*, 164 N.E. 545 (N.Y. 1928)).

We * * * decline Hill's invitation to apply the law of Delaware. While mindful of the cases cited by Hill where courts applying Nevada law have looked to Delaware on unrelated issues of corporate law, we conclude that cases such as *Clark* remain a better indication of the Nevada court's position with respect to issues involving close and closely held corporations. The opinions of the Delaware courts are often influential in matters of corporate law, but no more so in Nevada than any of the other states that have followed *Donahue.** [28]

Nor do we accept Hill's suggestion that our analysis should reflect Nevada's desire to provide management-friendly corporate law. If indeed that is Nevada's desire, it would not necessarily be furthered in the context of the close or closely held corporation where disputes typically pit manager/share-holder against manager/shareholder.

B.   Breach of Fiduciary Duty

Convinced of the existence of a fiduciary duty between shareholders in a close corporation, we turn to the scope of that duty and examine whether Hill breached his duty in the case at bar. As previously noted, the scope of this fiduciary duty has varied among the jurisdictions which have adopted *Donahue*. One context in which the scope has been frequently litigated has been with regard to salary and employment decisions. Again, Nevada has not addressed this issue and we must look to the law of other jurisdictions for guidance.

[The court relied upon another Massachusetts case, *Wilkes v. Springside Nursing Home*, which we discussed on page 330. In *Wilkes*, three shareholders in a close corporation ganged up on the fourth. They fired him from employment, refused to purchase his stock, and refused to pay dividends. Thus, they deprived the plaintiff of all perquisites of ownership and of the reasonable expectations of a shareholder in a close corporation. The Massachusetts court upheld a claim for oppression, but permitted the defendants to show that their actions were supported by legitimate business purposes. If they showed that, the plaintiff would still prevail if he showed that the legitimate purpose could be satisfied in a way that was less disruptive to his shareholder expectations.] * * *

That a controlling shareholder cannot, consistent with his fiduciary duty, effectively deprive a minority shareholder of his interest as a shareholder by terminating the latter's employment or salary has been widely accepted. The states considering the issue directly essentially have adopted the approach of *Wilkes*. In addition, shareholder oppression

---

*   [28] While it is true that some of the Delaware opinions, most notably *Nixon v. Blackwell*, 626 A.2d 1366 (Del.1993), contain very forceful dicta indicating that Delaware is likely not to apply heightened fiduciary duties to participants in close corporations, the Delaware Supreme Court has yet to consider the precise issue in this case, namely whether a controlling shareholder is liable for actions taken with the purpose and effect of freezing out another shareholder.

under the dissolution statutes, which is often defined in the same terms as the fiduciary duty between shareholders, frequently has been found under circumstances similar to those described in *Wilkes*. The opinions make clear, however, that shareholders do not enjoy fiduciary-rooted entitlements to their jobs. Such a result would clearly interfere with the doctrine of employment-at-will. Rather, the courts have limited relief to instances in which the shareholder has been harmed as a shareholder. The fiduciary duty in the close corporation context, as in the context of public corporations, appropriately is viewed as a protection of the shareholder's investment. The precise nature of an investment in a close corporation often is not clear, particularly when the shareholder is also an employee. It is therefore important to distinguish investors who obtain their return on investment through benefits provided to them as employees from employees who happen also to be investors. To that end, courts may consider the following non-exclusive factors: whether the corporation typically distributes its profits in the form of salaries; whether the shareholder/employee owns a significant percentage of the firm's shares; whether the shareholder/employee is a founder of the business; whether the shares were received as compensation for services; whether the shareholder/employee expects the value of the shares to increase; whether the share-holder/employee has made a significant capital contribution; whether the shareholder/employee has otherwise demonstrated a reasonable expectation that the returns from the investment will be obtained through continued employment; and whether stock ownership is a requirement of employment. The minority's shareholder interest is not injured, however, if the corporation redeems shares at a fair price or a price determined by prior contract or the shareholder is otherwise able to obtain a fair price.

Overlaying these factors to the relevant facts at bar, we conclude that Hollis demonstrated an injury as a shareholder. * * *

C. Remedy

The district court found Hill liable for breach of his fiduciary duty and ordered a buy-out of Hollis' shares. The court determined that Hill began his oppressive conduct on February 28, 1998, and thus ordered the buy-out as of that date, calculating the value of the shares at $667,950. While we essentially agree with the district court's remedial approach, we conclude that its decision to backdate the buy-out to February 28 is clear error. * * *

Although Hollis' relationship with Hill began to decline significantly in February 1998, many of the actions upon which we base our finding of oppression occurred after this date. Hollis continued to receive his agreed upon salary until September of 1998, when it was reduced by 50%. His salary was not reduced to zero until October of 1998. Hill's unilateral decision to close the Florida office, discontinue the car lease payments, and terminate phone service was not communicated to Hollis until November of 1998. Hollis' original complaint was filed in the district court in December of 1998. As an equal shareholder, [Hollis] commanded as much authority to assert control over the corporation as did [Hill]. His failure to act on this authority until December of 1998 was his choice. The presumptive valuation date for other states allowing buy-out remedies is the date of filing unless exceptional circumstances exist which require an earlier or later date to be chosen. No such circumstances exist in this case. Therefore, we conclude that the date of valuation for the court ordered buy-out should be the date suit was filed herein. Use of this date will take into consideration all of Hill and Hollis' actions, inactions, and prudent and imprudent business decisions which affected the value of the business during the intervening period.

We therefore vacate the calculation of the value of Hollis' shares by the district court and remand for further proceedings to determine the proper valuation of Hollis' shares consistent herewith. We likewise vacate the award of attorneys' fees and the fees of expert witnesses, and remand for reconsideration of those settings in light of relevant Nevada law. In all other respects, the decision appealed is affirmed.

E. GRADY JOLLY, CIRCUIT JUDGE, dissenting. Because I find that the cause of action and remedy here would not be adopted by Nevada courts, I respectfully dissent.

The question that needs to be answered in this case, whether framed as a breach of fiduciary duty or a statutory right, is whether Nevada recognizes a cause of action for oppression of minority shareholders. I find no basis to conclude that it does. The Nevada dissolution statute, Nev.Rev.Stat. § 78.650, sets out a statutory basis for the remedy effectively imposed here, and the statute does not allow dissolution for the oppression of minority stockholders. The Nevada case cited to justify the extension of fiduciary duty to cover shareholder oppression, *Clark v. Lubritz*, treated the business as a partnership because the parties treated the corporation as a partnership. To follow *Clark* here, where there is nothing in the past history or present arrangement indicating that the parties have treated the business as anything other than a corporation, effectively finds that Nevada will ignore corporate structure, when, on a case-by-case basis, equity justifies it.

Furthermore, all indications are that Nevada attempts to pattern its corporate law after the management-friendly approach of Delaware, a state that clearly prohibits a cause of action for oppression of minority shareholders. *See Nixon v. Blackwell*, 626 A.2d 1366, 1380–81 (Del.1993) (finding that majority shareholders owe no special fiduciary duties to minority shareholders). Even if Nevada is not as friendly to corporate structures and management as Delaware, there is no basis to find that Nevada would adopt the law of Massachusetts, which seems to be at the other end of the spectrum respecting corporate formalities. In sum, I am convinced that, given the general acknowledgment that Nevada is corporate friendly, as shown through its statutory dissolution provision and its tendency to follow Delaware law, the cause of action and remedy here would not be recognized. I therefore respectfully dissent.

QUESTIONS AND NOTE

1.   At the time of the litigation, FFUSA's only office was in Houston. FFUSA was incorporated in Nevada. Why was FFUSA incorporated in Nevada? Why does Judge Politz, who is from Louisiana, rely on Massachusetts law? Why does Judge Jolly, who is from Mississippi, rely on Delaware law?

2.   The plaintiff Hollis was a 50% shareholder. The defendant Hill was a 50% shareholder. Hill, Hollis, and their wives were the four directors of FFUSA. Why was Hill able to make decisions for FFUSA?

3.   Did Hollis have a legal right to receive the same salary from FFUSA as Hill? Would Hollis be able to compel Hill to buy his stock if Hollis's salary was $200,000 and Hill's salary was only $120,000? What if Hollis's salary was $100,000 and Hill's salary was $20,000?

4.   Is this decision consistent with the business judgment rule? With the "legitimate business purpose" rule of *Wilkes*?

5.   Two professors are critical of the decision in the *Wilkes* nursing home case:

> Could the other shareholders in Wilkes have been behaving opportunistically? Could they have terminated Wilkes' relationship with the firm in order to expropriate his investment, considering that he had already committed whatever special skills and knowledge he possessed? Absolutely. Opportunistic behavior is clearly possible in such circumstances. Yet that alone is not sufficient to justify the court's response, which was namely a case-by-case analysis of terminations to determine if the firm acted with a "legitimate business purpose" and with no "less harmful alternatives." That is the same as stating that because opportunistic behavior is possible in the employment relationship, a court should scrutinize each termination to see if it was for just cause.

> The *Wilkes* case is a good example of the difficulties courts have with the employment issues that frequently overlay close corporation cases. For example, was the court correct in saying that there was no legitimate business purpose in terminating Wilkes' employment? On the one hand, we are told that there was no misconduct and that Wilkes "had always accomplished his assigned share of the duties competently." The court, however, made no attempt to determine whether Wilkes' services were still needed. Apparently he was not replaced, suggesting overstaffing. By not

appreciating the norms of the employment relation, the court stumbled badly, inferring a right to continued employment, subject only to proof of misconduct. Such a right is so far at variance with employment practice anywhere that its insertion in the case undermines the logical application of the legitimate business purpose standard.

Edward B. Rock & Michael L. Wachter, *Waiting for the Omelet To Set: Match-Specific Assets and Minority Oppression in Close Corporations,* 24 J.CORP.L. 913, 933–34 (1999).

6.   In a recent Massachusetts case, a minority shareholder contended that the majority shareholder had frozen him out by firing him from his job with the corporation. The court noted, citing *Donahue*:

> In a close corporation, shareholders owe each other a fiduciary duty of utmost good faith and loyalty. That duty is held to be analogous to the duties partners in a general partnership owe to one another. * * * Here, plaintiff [asserted that] there have been payments to shareholders in violation of the directors' and controlling shareholders' fiduciary duties. The possibility of such wrongdoing is well recognized when a shareholder in a close corporation claims to have been frozen out (a typical element of freeze out may be the payment of exorbitant salaries in lieu of dividends).

Bernstein v. Pritsker, 30 Mass.L.Rptr. 636 (Mass.Super. 2013).

7.   If Hollis and Hill had formed a partnership, what could Hollis have done as soon as Hill started treating him badly? Would he have been able to get the remedy he sought without having to file suit?

2.   WHAT ARE THE LEGAL LIMITS ON SALARIES?

The MBCA and other state corporate codes do not set limits on the salaries that a corporation pays its officers or directors. Federal income tax law, however, does limit the amount of salary payment that a corporation can deduct from its taxable income as an ordinary and necessary business expense.

Recall that a corporation is a separate taxpayer. It must pay taxes on its income after deducting its ordinary and necessary business expenses.* Salaries can be a reasonable and necessary business expense. In contrast, dividends and other distributions to shareholders cannot be claimed as an ordinary and necessary business expense deduction.

Accordingly, there can be a strong tax incentive for corporations to set salaries to shareholders as high as possible. So the Internal Revenue Service has a strong incentive to review the reasonableness of salaries

---

*   An exception to this rule is the S Corporation, mentioned briefly in Chapter 1, which enjoys flow-through taxation, like a partnership.

that corporations pay to shareholders. With regard to the next case, consider the following:

1.   Whose money is being used to pay Heitz's salary?

2.   Who approved Heitz's salary?

3.   Are any of the shareholders receiving a salary from the corporation?

4.   Are the shareholders receiving dividends from the corporation?

EXACTO SPRING CORP. V. COMMISSIONER OF INTERNAL REVENUE

United States Court of Appeals, Seventh Circuit, 1999
196 F.3d 833

POSNER, CHIEF JUDGE. This appeal from a judgment by the Tax Court requires us to interpret and apply 26 U.S.C. § 162(a)(1), which allows a business to deduct from its income its "ordinary and necessary" business expenses, including a "reasonable allowance for salaries or other compensation for personal services actually rendered." In 1993 and 1994, Exacto Spring Corporation, a closely held corporation engaged in the manufacture of precision springs, paid its cofounder, chief executive, and principal owner, William Heitz, $1.3 and $1.0 million, respectively, in salary. The Internal Revenue Service thought this amount excessive, that Heitz should not have been paid more than $381,000 in 1993 or $400,000 in 1994, with the difference added to the corporation's income, and it assessed a deficiency accordingly, which Exacto challenged in the Tax Court. That court found that the maximum reasonable compensation for Heitz would have been $900,000 in the earlier year and $700,000 in the later one—figures roughly midway between his actual compensation and the IRS's determination—and Heitz has appealed.

In reaching its conclusion, the Tax Court applied a test that requires the consideration of seven factors, none entitled to any specified weight relative to another. The factors are, in the court's words, "(1) the type and extent of the services rendered; (2) the scarcity of qualified employees; (3) the qualifications and prior earning capacity of the employee; (4) the contributions of the employee to the business venture; (5) the net earnings of the employer; (6) the prevailing compensation paid to employees with comparable jobs; and (7) the peculiar characteristics of the employer's business." 75 T.C.M. at 2525. It is apparent that this test, though it or variants of it (one of which has the astonishing total of 21 factors) are encountered in many cases, leaves much to be desired—being, like many other multi-factor tests, "redundant, incomplete, and unclear."

To begin with, it is nondirective. No indication is given of how the factors are to be weighed in the event they don't all line up on one side. And many of the factors, such as the type and extent of services rendered, the scarcity of qualified employees, and the peculiar characteristics of the employer's business, are vague.

Second, the factors do not bear a clear relation either to each other or to the primary purpose of section 162(a)(1), which is to prevent dividends (or in some cases gifts), which are not deductible from corporate income, from being disguised as salary, which is. Suppose that an employee who let us say was, like Heitz, a founder and the chief executive officer and principal owner of the taxpayer rendered no services at all but received a huge salary. It would be absurd to allow the whole or for that matter any part of his salary to be deducted as an ordinary and necessary business expense even if he were well qualified to be CEO of the company, the company had substantial net earnings, CEOs of similar companies were paid a lot, and it was a business in which high salaries are common. The multifactor test would not prevent the Tax Court from allowing a deduction in such a case even though the corporation obviously was seeking to reduce its taxable income by disguising earnings as salary. The court would not allow the deduction, but not because of anything in the multi-factor test; rather because it would be apparent that the payment to the employee was not in fact for his services to the company.

Third, the seven-factor test invites the Tax Court to set itself up as a superpersonnel department for closely held corporations, a role unsuitable for courts. The judges of the Tax Court are not equipped by training or experience to determine the salaries of corporate officers; no judges are.

Fourth, since the test cannot itself determine the outcome of a dispute because of its nondirective character, it invites the making of arbitrary decisions based on uncanalized discretion or unprincipled rules of thumb. The Tax Court in this case essentially added the IRS's determination of the maximum that Mr. Heitz should have been paid in 1993 and 1994 to what he was in fact paid, and divided the sum by two. It cut the baby in half. One would have to be awfully naive to believe that the seven-factor test generated this pleasing symmetry.

Fifth, because the reaction of the Tax Court to a challenge to the deduction of executive compensation is unpredictable, corporations run unavoidable legal risks in determining a level of compensation that may be indispensable to the success of their business. * * *

Finally, under factor (7) ("peculiar characteristics"), the court first and rightly brushed aside the IRS's argument that the low level of dividends paid by Exacto (zero in the two years at issue, but never very high) was evidence that the corporation was paying Heitz dividends in the form of salary. The court pointed out that shareholders may not want dividends. They may prefer the corporation to retain its earnings, causing the value of the corporation to rise and thus enabling the shareholders to obtain corporate earnings in the form of capital gains taxed at a lower rate than ordinary income. The court also noted that while Heitz, as the owner of 55 percent of Exacto's common stock, obviously was in a position to influence his salary, the corporation's two other major shareholders, each with 20 percent of the stock, had approved it. They had not themselves been paid a salary or other compensation, and are not relatives of Heitz; they had no financial or other incentive to allow Heitz to siphon off dividends in the form of salary. * * *

* * * The Internal Revenue Code limits the amount of salary that a corporation can deduct from its income primarily in order to prevent the corporation from eluding the corporate income tax by paying dividends but calling them salary because salary is deductible and dividends are not. (Perhaps they should be, to avoid double taxation of corporate earnings, but that is not the law.) In the case of a publicly-held company, where the salaries of the highest executives are fixed by a board of directors that those executives do not control, the danger of siphoning corporate earnings to executives in the form of salary is not acute. The danger is much greater in the case of a closely held corporation, in which ownership and management tend to coincide; unfortunately, as the opinion of the Tax Court in this case illustrates, judges are not competent to decide what business executives are worth.

There is, fortunately, an indirect market test, as recognized by the Internal Revenue Service's expert witness. A corporation can be conceptualized as a contract in which the owner of assets hires a person to manage them. The owner pays the manager a salary and in exchange the manager works to increase the value of the assets that have been entrusted to his management; that increase can be expressed as a rate of return to the owner's investment. The higher the rate of return (adjusted for risk) that a manager can generate, the greater the salary he can command. If the rate of return is extremely high, it will be difficult to prove that the manager is being overpaid, for it will be implausible that if he quit if his salary was cut, and he was replaced by a lower-paid manager, the owner would be better off; it would be killing the goose that lays the golden egg. The Service's expert believed that investors in a firm like Exacto would expect a 13 percent return on their investment. Presumably they would be delighted with more. They would be overjoyed to receive a return more than 50 percent greater than they expected—and 20 percent, the return that the Tax Court found that investors in Exacto had obtained, is more than 50 percent greater than the benchmark return of 13 percent.

When, notwithstanding the CEO's "exorbitant" salary (as it might appear to a judge or other modestly paid official), the investors in his company are obtaining a far higher return than they had any reason to expect, his salary is presumptively reasonable. We say "presumptively" because we can imagine cases in which the return, though very high, is not due to the CEO's exertions. Suppose Exacto had been an unprofitable company that suddenly learned that its factory was sitting on an oil field, and when oil revenues started to pour in its owner raised his salary from $50,000 a year to $1.3 million. The presumption of reasonableness would be rebutted. There is no suggestion of anything of that sort here and likewise no suggestion that Mr. Heitz was merely the titular chief executive and the company was actually run by someone else, which would be another basis for rebuttal.

The government could still have prevailed by showing that while Heitz's salary may have been no greater than would be reasonable in the circumstances, the company did not in fact intend to pay him that amount as salary, that his salary really did include a concealed dividend though it need not have. This is material (and the "independent investor" test, like the multifactor test that it replaces, thus incomplete, though invaluable) because any business expense to be deductible must be, as we noted earlier, a bona fide expense as well as reasonable in amount. The fact that Heitz's salary was approved by the other owners of the corporation, who had no incentive to disguise a dividend as salary, goes far to rebut any inference of bad faith here, which in any event the Tax Court did not draw and the government does not ask us to draw.

The judgment is reversed with directions to enter judgment for the taxpayer.

QUESTIONS

1.   What is the "danger that is much greater in the case of a closely held corporation in which ownership and management tend to coincide"?

2.   If the other shareholders of Exacto Spring Corporation are not receiving salaries or dividends from the corporation, how are they making money from their ownership of the business? Exacto Spring Corporation is not publicly-traded. If a shareholder offered to sell her stock to you, would you be interested? Is that true of the stock of most close corporations we've read about?

3.   How did the Internal Revenue Service's expert witness determine that 13% is a reasonable return for Exacto's investors? How did the Court determine that Exacto's stockholders had received a 20% return on their investment? How important are such determinations in applying the holding in this case?

One can understand why shareholders of a closely held corporation who do not have jobs with the corporation might object if high salaries are paid to other shareholders. We also understand that these shareholders would prefer that the same sum be distributed in the form of a dividend to all shareholders (even though the tax obligations of the corporation might thereby be higher). The next case involves such an objection. In reading the case, consider the following:

1. Who set the salaries that the corporation paid the defendants?

2. Were the defendants both officers and directors?

3. What did the plaintiffs ask the court to do?

4. Who made money as a result of the court's ruling in this case?

GIANNOTTI V. HAMWAY

Supreme Court of Virginia, 1990
387 S.E.2d 725

COMPTON, JUSTICE. In this intracorporate dispute arising in a close corporation, we examine the correctness of the trial court's decision to order liquidation of the corporate assets and business.

Because this suit was filed in 1980, former Code § 13.1–94 (Repl.Vol.1978) (now Code § 13.1–747) applies. As pertinent to the controversy, the statute provided:

> Any court of record, with general equity jurisdiction . . ., shall have full power to liquidate the assets and business of [a] corporation . . .:

> (a) In an action by a stockholder when it is established: * * *

> (2) That the acts of the directors or those in control of the corporation are illegal, oppressive or fraudulent; or * * *

> (4) That the corporate assets are being misapplied or wasted.

In September 1980, appellees Alexander Hamway, Leroy Steiner, and Louis Adelman filed a bill of complaint against Libbie Rehabilitation Center, Inc. (Libbie), Frank R. Giannotti, Alex Grossman, Henry C. Miller, Ernest H. Dervishian, and Lewis T. Cowardin (defendants). The plaintiffs asserted that Libbie was a duly organized Virginia corporation and that the defendants were directors of Libbie holding the following offices: Giannotti—Chairman of the Board and Chief Executive Officer; Grossman—President; Miller—Vice President; Dervishian—Secretary and Corporate Attorney; and, Cowardin—Treasurer. The corporation was engaged in the development and operation of nursing homes.

The plaintiffs also asserted that the defendants, either individually or through corporations they controlled, owned or controlled a majority of the 209,054 shares of the then outstanding Libbie common stock. The plaintiffs also alleged that they were minority stockholders owning a total of approximately 74,500 shares of Libbie common stock. * * *

The plaintiffs specifically charged defendants with authorizing and making payments from corporate funds to themselves for directors' fees and officers' salaries "grossly in excess of the value of the services they have rendered to Libbie." * * *

Plaintiffs also charged that defendants, acting in bad faith, had "refused to declare dividends on Libbie common stock which, with due regard to the condition of the property and affairs of Libbie, should have been declared." * * *

Asserting that they were "unable to prevent the continuing oppression, * * * mismanagement, waste and self-dealing practiced by the defendants," plaintiffs asked the court, pursuant to Code §§ 13.1–94 and –95, to appoint a receiver pending the suit, to require defendants, "jointly and severally to restore to Libbie such funds as have been misspent or lost by Libbie as a result of their oppressive acts, and mismanagement, breach of fiduciary duty and improper self-dealing," and to "order the liquidation of the assets and business of Libbie."

The defendants filed a demurrer and answer to the bill, generally contending that the plaintiffs had not alleged any facts which would support their prayer for relief and specifically denying the allegations of wrongful conduct. [The court overruled the demurrer and the litigation continued.]

The trial eventually was held and the chancellor heard evidence *ore tenus* [that's what Virginia courts say when they want to tell us that the witnesses testified orally (rather than having their depositions read by the judge)] for 20 days from November 1985 to February 1986. The parties submitted proposed findings of fact and conclusions of law to the trial court in April 1986. The plaintiffs filed 265 proposals; the defendants filed 153. In November 1987, the chancellor announced his decision by letter opinion, finding in favor of the plaintiffs and ordering dissolution of the corporation. The trial court refused plaintiffs' request to order the defendants to restore certain assets to the corporation. These rulings were incorporated in a February 1988 final decree in which the court appointed a receiver to liquidate the corporate assets. * * *

The evidence relating to excessive compensation focused on officers' salaries, directors' fees, bonuses, expense allowances, and other payments, all authorized by the recipients. * * *

The plaintiffs' evidence of inadequate dividends showed that from June 1975 through September 30, 1985, defendants' compensation totalled $2,799,006 while during the same period the plaintiffs received $50,000 of $132,000 in common stock dividends. The plaintiffs showed that after-tax profits during the period amounted to $1,042,350, which, according to plaintiffs, meant that for every dollar of profit earned, defendants received $2.67 in compensation. This comparison, the plaintiffs urged, did not take into account an additional $1.4 million attributable to unnecessary loan and interest costs incurred in order to enable those payments to be made to defendants. The plaintiffs claimed that when profits are compared to the total cost of compensation, the ratio of compensation to profits is 4 to 1. * * *

The trial court found "that plaintiffs have borne their burden as to the substance of their claims," relying principally on the testimony of the administrators of each of the three Libbie facilities "as most telling regarding the lack of sufficient work and supervision to justify officer salaries, fees and other benefits." * * *

Finally, the chancellor made the specific finding "that defendants by their actions have been oppressive to the minority plaintiff shareholders in breach of their fiduciary duties in their capacity as majority controllers of the corporation by effectively freezing out plaintiffs from a reasonable opportunity to receive a reasonable return on their investment given the financial condition of the corporation during the period." * * *

As used in § 13.1–94, "oppressive" means conduct by corporate managers toward stockholders which departs from the standards of fair dealing and violates the principles of fair play on which persons who entrust their funds to a corporation are entitled to rely. The term does not mean that a corporate disaster may be imminent and does not necessarily mean fraudulent conduct. Indeed, "oppressive" is not synonymous with the statutory terms "illegal" or "fraudulent." The term can contemplate a continuous course of conduct and includes a lack of probity in corporate affairs to the prejudice of some of its shareholders.

A corporate officer has the same duties of fidelity in dealing with the corporation that arise in dealings between a trustee and a beneficiary of the trust. Thus, "a director of a private corporation cannot directly or indirectly, in any transaction in which he is under a duty to guard the interests of the corporation, acquire any personal advantage, or make any profit for himself, and if he does so, he may be compelled to account therefor to the corporation." * * *

Courts are hesitant to question the reasonableness of a corporate officer's compensation when it is set by a disinterested board. However, as in this case, where the directors of a close corporation elect themselves as officers and set their own salaries, and they are all accused of combining to fix excessive salaries for each other, it is impossible to have a "disinterested board."

Further, when a plaintiff "demonstrates that a director had an interest in the transaction at issue, the burden shifts to the director to prove that the transaction was fair and reasonable to the corporation." In defendants' words, they "have not contested in this appeal that the ultimate burden of proof lies with them on the issue of the reasonableness of compensation."

Against the background of these settled principles, our study of this record convinces us that the chancellor's findings of fact are neither plainly wrong nor without evidence to support them. Indeed, there is abundant, credible evidence to support the trial court's conclusions that defendants engaged in oppressive conduct and that they misapplied and wasted corporate assets. * * *

The defendants came to the Libbie enterprise with few qualifications to operate a nursing home. Giannotti had been a carpet and tile retailer, Grossman a pharmacist, Miller a retired real estate developer, Dervishian a lawyer, and Cowardin a retail jeweler. While Giannotti and Dervishian had operated a small nursing home in the city of Richmond for a while before becoming associated with Libbie, none of the defendants, either by education or training, had any expertise in the operation of nursing homes.

The nature, extent, and scope of defendants' work in attending to corporate affairs were very limited. Giannotti was the main actor in directing the affairs of Libbie, although he principally was involved in approving administrators' decisions regarding the day-to-day operation of the facilities. While Grossman received compensation from all three facilities, his activities were limited almost exclusively to Libbie Convalescent. Miller had few work responsibilities. Dervishian's role was limited. He was a friend and advisor of Giannotti, but his corporate responsibilities were duplicated by his assignments as general counsel. Cowardin, Libbie's finance officer, demonstrated no knowledge of the Medicare and Medicaid programs, the principal sources of Libbie's income. While he claimed to have spent 20–25 hours per week on his corporate duties, about 50 percent of a normal 40-hour work week, Cowardin reported on tax returns for his jewelry business that he spent 90 percent of his working time in that business for its fiscal years ending in 1978 and 1979; 80 percent of his time during fiscal 1980, 1981, and 1983; 75 percent of his time during fiscal 1984; and 40 percent of his time in 1985. From the standpoint of hours worked for Libbie, defendants were part-time employees with significant outside business interests.

The difficulties of the business can justify officers' and directors' compensation. But, the complexities of nursing home operation were handled by the administrators of Libbie's facilities. The respective parties offered expert testimony on the reasonableness of the compensation, which included comparisons with amounts paid to officers in similar businesses. The credibility of defendants' main expert was challenged, and the trial court accepted the opinion of one of plaintiffs' experts that "the work that was performed was not of sufficient scope and complexity to justify the salary, bonuses, fringe benefits and other compensation which was paid to these individuals." According to another plaintiffs' expert, five men were performing management functions that could have been performed by one individual.

Defendants rely heavily on Libbie's purported success in attempting to convince us that they sustained their burden of proving that the compensation was reasonable. The defendants offered evidence comparing their salary and efforts with two other nursing homes in Central Virginia. The comparison showed, however, that Libbie has not been operated profitably by the standards of the other homes upon which defendants relied. During the period of 1980 to 1985, the average, before-tax profit per bed was $2,009 in one case and $2,975 in another. During the same period, Libbie's profits were $1,107 per bed. The trial court was justified in finding, under the evidence as a whole, that Libbie would have been more profitable except for the excessive compensation extracted from the corporation by defendants. * * *

Having concluded that the chancellor did not err in finding defendants guilty of oppressive conduct, which involved misapplication and waste of corporate funds, including failure to pay adequate dividends, we turn to the correctness of the relief awarded below. Defendants argue that the "corporate death penalty" should not be imposed on a viable, solvent corporation.

As the trial court recognized, courts generally should be reluctant to order liquidation of a functioning corporation at the instance of minority stockholders. However, the General Assembly has cloaked courts of equity with, in the words of the statute, "full power" to liquidate in a proper case where oppressive conduct has been established. The remedy specified by the legislature, while discretionary, is "exclusive," and does not permit the trial court to fashion other, apparently equitable remedies. Because the trial court's finding of oppression in this case is not plainly wrong or without evidence to support it, we cannot say, under these circumstances, that the court abused its discretion in decreeing dissolution. * * *

This brings us to the assignments of cross-error. Plaintiffs contend that the trial court erred in refusing to require defendants to restore corporate funds which the court found the defendants had misapplied or wasted. * * *

We hold that the trial court did not err in refusing to require restoration of funds at this stage of the proceeding. Former Code § 13.1–95 (1978 Repl.Vol.) (now, in substance, § 13.1–748) prescribes the procedure to be employed after dissolution has been decreed under the judicial dissolution statute and allows the liquidating receiver to maintain suits in his name as receiver of the corporation. Indeed, the final decree in this case empowers the receiver "to institute and prosecute all suits as may be necessary . . . to collect the . . . obligations due to Libbie." And, defendants represent on brief that this receiver, relying on the trial court's findings of excessive compensation and improper related party transactions, instituted an action against them in May 1988 seeking to recover certain sums. * * *

Accordingly, we hold that the assignments of cross-error have no merit. For these reasons, the final decree of the trial court will be affirmed and the cause will be remanded for the court to supervise the liquidation as provided in its decree.

* * *

GORDON, JUSTICE (RETIRED), dissenting. To liquidate the corporation is to kill the goose that laid the golden egg. The history, as shown by the record, since the individual defendants assumed control proves the point:

Financial Data	1975	1985	Percentage Increase
Total Assets	$1,720,076	$6,392,997	272%
Current Ratio	1.31	2.64	
Total Operating Revenues	1,514,686	6,807,902	349%
Retained Earnings	181,984	922,473	406%
Common Stockholders Equity	602,363	1,274,851	112%
Book Value of Common Stock	2.41	5.85	143%
Net Income Before Taxes	150,000	330,000	220%
Net Income After Taxes	89,473	191,407	114%

During the period, the corporation opened additional facilities, requiring the expenditure of substantial sums. Bed capacity increased from 195 to 443.

Neither the corporation nor the plaintiff-stockholders have suffered from oppressive actions by the defendants. The record discloses that the plaintiff-stockholders have suffered only the usual and legal burdens borne by minority stockholders.

The complainants rely on the individual defendants' failure to declare dividends as a ground for liquidation. In *Penn v. Pemberton & Penn*, 53 S.E.2d 823 ([Va.] 1949) (affirming the trial court's refusal to order liquidation under a statute then in force), the Court said:

> The general rule is that in the absence of a special contract or statute the board of directors, in its discretion, determines whether to declare dividends on the stock, or to apply the earnings and surplus to operating capital, or to some other corporate purpose. If the directors act in good faith, a court of equity usually will not interfere with the exercise of their discretion. However, if the action of the board in refusing to declare a dividend when there are sufficient earnings or surplus not necessarily needed in the business, is so arbitrary, or so

unreasonable, as to amount to a breach of trust, such action is subject to judicial review. * * *

The complainants' remedy here (if any) is the enforced declaration of a dividend, not liquidation. But in view of the expanded corporate business and finances, the record does not support even that remedy.

I would reverse the decree and dismiss the bill of complaint.

QUESTIONS

1. Why did the defendants have the burden of proof? How could the defendants have satisfied that burden of proof?

2. Why didn't the plaintiffs sue for money damages instead of dissolution?

3. Why didn't the plaintiffs simply sell their stock?

CHAPTER 8

CORPORATE FINANCE, SECURITIES REGULATION, AND DIVIDENDS

■ ■ ■

We now address three related issues about how money flows from investors to the corporation, and then back to investors. We first explore corporate finance, the process by which the corporation obtains the money that it needs to operate. We'll see that the company can raise money by retaining its earnings, by issuing debt (that is, borrowing money), or by selling stock. Second, we'll examine securities regulation, the law that governs the sale of stock or issuance of debt. Third, we examine what happens when the corporation seeks to do the opposite of raise money; that is, when the company seeks to give money back to shareholders, via dividends.

A. CORPORATE FINANCE

We have seen that the objective of a business is typically making money. Money goes into a business, works within that business (e.g., buying needed equipment and inventory, paying employees and other operating costs), and then comes out of the business. If the business is successful, more comes out than went in.

Of course, such financial capital isn't the only thing that's working in the business. Also hard at work are human and intellectual capital. But they are regulated by different sets of legal rules—labor law and IP law—that you will learn in other courses. In this book, "capital" refers to financial capital.

Financial capital can generally be of two types: debt and equity. Businesses issue "securities" as the evidence of their obligations and responsibilities to the individuals and firms that have provided that capital. In the world of corporate finance, a security is any piece of paper (and now, more often, an electronic record) of a company's promise to do something tomorrow in exchange for your money today. Stocks and preferred stocks are "equity securities." Bonds, notes and debentures are "debt securities," as are commercial paper, mortgage-backed securities and many other forms of debt. For our purposes, you don't need to know how these various securities differ from one another, other than to understand the difference between debt and equity, about which we'll say more below.

Lenders and investors have invented many complicated securities. Whenever there is a problem or misunderstanding, the lawyers modify the securities' legal documents to attempt to prevent that problem from occurring again.

All those legal documents have as their foundation the basic economic or business deal that underpins the transaction, and it is worth understanding the basic economics that drive the parties on both sides.

We now describe two things. First, we describe the basic economic forces that apply when companies issue securities. Second, we describe the law that governs the sale of securities. We discuss both because you need to understand the economics to understand the law.

1.   INITIAL INVESTMENT BY THE FOUNDERS

The first investment in the business almost always will be from the business' founder(s). One reason is that, by investing in her own business, the entrepreneur can demonstrate her commitment to the business. Investors and lenders recognize that the entrepreneur will be more committed to the venture if she has invested her personal assets in it.

There is another, more practical, reason this start-up phase will usually be financed with the entrepreneur's own funds. To raise money from others, you typically need more than an idea. Before others will be willing to invest, the entrepreneur will have to invest some money in the idea, perhaps to build a prototype or to do a market study.

These funds need not be the owner's own money in the purest sense. The entrepreneur can obtain these funds by mortgaging personal assets like a house or car, borrowing from friends or relatives, or even by using a personal bank loan or credit card advances. Once the founder has pulled together these personal funds, either from savings or by borrowing personally, she can inject these funds into the business as either debt or equity—that is, by either loaning her company money or buying her company's stock. Generally, a risky startup is better off without the added risk imposed by having to make fixed interest payments and principal repayments on debt. If the founder subsequently seeks to secure outside financing—other people's money—the outside investors will typically not like to see the founder's funds as debt on the balance sheet. That would mean that the founder would get her debt repaid before the outsider investors get their funds. Outside investors want to see the founder standing in line *behind* them, not in front of them.

2.   RETAINING EARNINGS INSTEAD OF PAYING DIVIDENDS OR BUYING BACK STOCK

An additional—and simple way—for the corporation to obtain more capital is to earn it and then plow it back into the business. Assume that

Bubba's Burritos, Inc. had a profitable 2015. After taking account of its revenues and expenses, the business earned a profit of $100,000.

Bubba's board of directors could decide to retain that $100,000 to use in expanding its business by advertising more or opening a new store. If it did that, it wouldn't have to raise as much money through additional borrowing or selling more stock.

However, the board could decide that instead, it wished to return those funds to its shareholders. If it chose this latter course, it would have two choices: (1) pay dividends; or (2) buy back its stock. We will explore the details of dividends and share buy-backs at the end of this chapter, where we will also discuss how the corporation decides between such distributions of its earnings to shareholders and retaining the earnings instead.

3. OTHER PEOPLE'S MONEY—AN OVERVIEW OF DEBT AND EQUITY

You will recall from our discussion in Chapter 1 that the balance sheet has two main sections. First is assets. Second is the company's capital: its liabilities and its equity. This "liabilities and equity" section reflects the two ways in which the business can obtain money from outsiders: debt and equity financing. Debt is borrowing (a liability). Equity represents an ownership stake in the business, and is accomplished by selling shares.

a. The Balance Sheet Revisited

A company's balance sheet describes its "capital structure": the nature and amount of its debt and equity. Consider the balance sheet below:

Bubba's Burritos, Inc.
Balance Sheet as of December 31, 2014

ASSETS	
Cash	281,733
Accounts Receivable	40,341
Inventory	104,180
Prepaid expenses	47,508
Security deposits	72,151
Net fixed assets	2,209,053
Total assets	2,754,966

LIABILITIES AND SHAREHOLDERS' EQUITY

Accounts payable	259,726
Meals tax payable	15,193
Bank debt (long term)	491,247
Total liabilities	766,166
Shareholders' equity	1,998,800
Total liabilities + equity	2,754,966

The assets section of the balance sheet shows how the company has used its capital. It shows the different asset categories in which capital is invested and working: inventory, equipment, accounts receivable and even cash, which the business needs to pay its bills.

The liabilities and equity section shows where the money is coming from—the source of that capital. Debt comes from lenders. Equity comes from investors who purchase stock.

Recall from Chapter 1 that the total capital of the business (that is, its total assets) must equal the business' debt (or liabilities) plus its equity. That is, the company's assets are what the business uses to make money. The list of liabilities and equity shows how the company has paid for the assets it's using. Note that "paid for" includes the concept of retaining earnings, earnings which could otherwise have been used to pay dividends. Thus, shareholders' equity includes both the capital originally invested in the business ("paid-in capital") as well as retained earnings that are "left inside" the business and can continue to be used to fund its operations and growth.

PROBLEMS

1. Using the sample balance sheet presented above, describe Bubba's Burritos' most significant asset? Its biggest liability? What do you think would happen if the bank "called" the loan (i.e., asked for it to be repaid immediately)? Can you tell from the balance sheet how well Bubba's is performing as a business?

2. Again, using the sample balance sheet, what is the ratio of debt to total equity? Can you think of some other statistics that you could compute— if you had available more information about the company's financials and its bank loan—that could help you judge how risky its debt structure is? If you were a bank, what statistics would you look at to decide how much money to loan a business?

b. Comparison of Debt and Equity

All financing for a business is either (1) debt or (2) equity. Debt is a loan that the business is legally obligated to repay, generally with interest. In contrast, equity funding is an investment that the business receives for selling part ownership in the business. Unlike with a loan, the business is not legally obligated to repay this investment.

Debt and equity financing differ in several ways. First, each presents different risk to the provider of funds. When a business borrows money, the creditor is entitled to receive both repayment of the amount borrowed—the principal—and interest on that principal, according to a set schedule.

In contrast, if someone provides equity funds, the business is not legally obligated to pay her anything, although the business may choose to distribute some cash as dividends. The main benefit these equity holders receive is an ownership interest in the firm. Compared to being a creditor, being an owner has a much wider variety of potential outcomes, both good and bad. The risk is higher, but so is the potential return. A creditor can expect at most repayment of the debt with interest. In contrast, the owner can get fabulously rich if the business does incredibly well. However, the owner can also lose everything. The creditors of a failing business must be paid in full before anything is distributed to the business's owners. If nothing is left after paying creditors, the owners get nothing.

The second difference between debt and equity is the degree of risk that they represent to the business. Debt is riskier to the business. Suppose that the business borrows money, and then times get tough. If the business fails to repay either the debt or the required interest, the lender can sue and even force the business into bankruptcy.

This is not true with equity. The equity owner has no right to repayment. So an equity investment will permit a business to weather hard times easier than will a loan of equal size. Indeed, if the business keeps on borrowing—getting more "leveraged"—then its interest obligation may grow so large that even a modest downturn in sales will endanger the company's survival. In contrast, selling additional equity will not make the company riskier.

Finally, debt and equity differ in their cost to the business. Debt has a fixed cost: the cost of those funds is the interest rate the business pays to borrow the money. In contrast, at the time the equity is sold to investors, the cost to the business of that equity is uncertain. If the owners of the company sell equity to investors, then those investors share in the success of the company. If the company does extremely well and the equity becomes worth a great deal, then the cost to the initial owners is large—compared to the money they could have made if they had held on to that equity, instead of "diluting" their ownership by selling it to others. The new investors get some of the large value of the company, instead of the original entrepreneur's getting all of it. In contrast, if the company does poorly or fails, the ownership that the first owners have sacrificed is worth little.

Another cost of equity is the control that the initial owners give up. Equity investors often have a vote in how to run the business. In contrast, creditors are not entitled to any control over the company, unless they bargain for it specifically and specify these controls in the contractual "covenants" that establish the loan.

We've discussed the two main sources of capital for a business: debt and equity. There are entire courses in business school devoted to thinking about exactly how much debt and how much equity should be in a corporation's capital structure. Indeed, this is one of the two or three most significant issues in the entire field of finance.

Let's talk a little about how corporations make such decisions. There are two forces that cause a corporation to use debt as much as possible, rather than equity. First, recall that lenders incur less risk than equity investors. Accordingly, a corporation's lenders tend to receive a lower return than equity investors. Lower risk means lower return. This is the same as saying that the company pays a lower price for debt than for equity. This alone causes companies to prefer debt to equity.

Second, debt enjoys a tax advantage. A corporation can deduct the interest payments from its reported income and thus lower its taxes. In contrast, the corporation cannot deduct dividend payments on equity. In effect, the federal government subsidizes debt, but not equity.

So why wouldn't a corporation finance itself only with debt? There are two forces that put the brakes on the inclination to rely exclusively on debt. First, lenders understand this phenomenon, and work hard to lend only what they are sure will be paid back. This is the primary work of bankers—figuring out how much is safe to lend to which borrowers.

Second, the corporation itself will fear not being able to pay its debts. Every corporation's cash flow varies somewhat from month to month. A corporation's managers understand these ups-and-downs, and if the corporation borrows too much, then, in a year when cash flow is low, the corporation might not be able to make the required interest and principal payments. Bankruptcy might result. In contrast, this risk is reduced if the company's capital structure instead uses more equity. Replacing debt with equity lowers the fixed annual costs associated with the company's outstanding debt.

Companies have different levels of exposure to risk. For example, small technology companies might be more exposed to downturns in the economy than electric utilities and grocery stores. Skilled business managers carefully weigh the risk of increased debt against the larger returns to the equity holders that debt leverage provides. The end result might be that the small technology company would use a lower proportion of debt, and the electric utility a higher proportion.

4. DEBT FINANCING

We have seen that a business has two ways of raising money from outsiders. The first is borrowing it—or, equivalently, "issuing debt." We'll look at equity in the next part of the text. Any business form, not just a corporation, may eventually need to borrow money from banks or individuals outside the business. Such debt financing can be examined from several perspectives.

a. Lawyers' View of Debt

Often, lawyers are central participants in a corporation's efforts to grow by borrowing money. Lawyers, of course, draft the loan documents. In addition, the best lawyers understand both the economics of the possible financing choices and their clients' business objectives.

These deals can be structured in many ways. The loan documents will spell out not only the basic loan payment and repayment terms, but also the parties' other rights and responsibilities.

It may sound counterintuitive, but banks and other lenders like to make loans to borrowers who really don't need the money. Ideal borrowers have the assets and earnings history to be able to assure lenders that they won't default. At the very least, lenders prefer borrowers who have unencumbered assets that can be used as collateral for the loan. In the event of default, the lender can then seize and sell this collateral to collect its debt. So the potential borrower must consider what is available to offer as collateral for the loan. Real estate is a classic example of an asset where the lender may be willing to lend a relatively high proportion of the value of the property because they feel confident of being able to sell the asset quickly for a good price. Specialized manufacturing equipment may be viewed quite differently. Lenders are skilled in evaluating the loan collateral and deciding how much they are comfortable "loaning against it."

Of course, in this negotiation, the business owner is trying to get the loan on the most favorable terms, and the bank (or other lender) is trying to loan the money at an attractive (i.e., high) interest rate and minimize their risk. The negotiable issues include:

- What covenants will the lender require? Lenders reduce their risks by requiring financial and operational commitments from the borrower until the loan has been repaid. Such covenants limit the business's ability to do things that might make it more difficult for the corporation to meet its obligations. Typical loan covenants include limits on large expenditures. They also include restrictions on both distributions to owners and issuance of new debt that would need to be repaid before existing debt. Other covenants may set financial metrics that must be met, like cash flow, debt to equity ratio, profitability, etc. If the business fails to live up to these performance measures, the lender gets certain additional rights, including the right to require the borrower to pay back the loan immediately.

- What is the security for the loan? Here, "security" means collateral, i.e., a back-up plan if the business fails to make its payment and the bank has to step in and claim some other asset instead. Typical collateral can include real estate, furniture and fixtures, inventory, and accounts receivable. Of course, collateral is less valuable if someone else has a prior claim on it.

- What are the loan details? How is the business going to service the debt, i.e., pay the monthly interest and then repay the loan? What is the term of the loan? Will principal be paid along the way? In equal installments? Or, will 100% of it be paid at the completion of the loan (a so-called "bullet" payment)? Can the business generate sufficient cash to make the loan payments?

- What happens if the business defaults? Lenders may require that owners personally guarantee repayment. The loan documents will generally define default much more broadly than a single late or missed payment. For example, the documents might provide that the loan defaults, and so must immediately be repaid, if the business's cash declines below a certain level.

QUESTIONS

1. Bubbba's Burritos, Inc. borrows $500,000 from Acme Bank. How does this transaction affect Bubba's Burritos balance sheet?

2. Would your answer to 1 change if a second mortgage on Bubba's Burritos building was collateral for the loan?

3. If we say that Bubba's Burritos financial capital is $500,000, does that mean that Bubba's Burritos now has cash or other liquid assets of $500,000?

4. One of the financial covenants in the Bubba's Burritos, Inc./Acme loan requires that Bubba's Burritos, Inc. monthly gross revenues are at least $100,000. While Bubba's Burritos is current on its loan payment obligations, its revenues for each of the last two months is less than $90,000. What can Acme Bank do? What do you think Acme Bank will do?

b. Business Owners' View of Debt

Business owners are concerned about return on equity (ROE). This statistic measures the rate of return that the business earns on the money invested. For example, if a business in which $1,000,000 has been invested generates $100,000 of annual cash flow, then the business would be earning a 10% return on capital. It will be no surprise to you that the owners and managers of businesses are generally trying to maximize the return on capital. If you invested $1,000, would you rather get back $100 or $200?

(i) Debt and Return on Equity Capital

Suppose you owned the company we described above, which makes a 10% return on equity, or ROE (the annual cash flow of $100,000 divided by your equity investment of $1,000,000). Now, let's suppose you could borrow half of the total capital required at a 5% interest rate, so you only had to invest $500,000 of your own money to create a business with $1,000,000 of total capital. Well, the cash flow of the business will drop slightly, because now it has a new expense: interest of 5% on borrowings of $500,000 is $25,000, so the cash flow drops to $75,000. But the ROE shoots up because the equity capital invested dropped in half; you invested only $500,000 of your own money, rather than $1,000,000. $75,000 divided by $500,000 in equity is 15%. Your ROE has increased by 50%, from 10 to 15%.

What if, instead, you borrowed 90% of the $1,000,000 of required capital—$900,000? Now your cash flow drops by the $45,000 in interest expenses ($900,000 × 5%), so cash flow is only $55,000. But, since equity is only $100,000, the ROE is now 55%.

Let's consider an even further extreme. Imagine how impressive your ROE would be if you borrowed $999,999 and put in just $1 of equity!

(ii) Debt and Risk to the Business

Does this mean that it's always best to borrow as much as possible? No. That's because we have discussed only the increased return on equity. We have ignored the risk of debt.

To understand how and why debt increases the risk of a business, just imagine a business, Epstein Co., with no debt, where investors had invested $1,000,000 in equity. The business has $600,000 of fixed yearly costs, and $1,000,000 of sales revenues, where the cost of goods sold (COGS) is 30% of revenues or $300,000. With $1,000,000 in revenues, the company can pay its $600,000 of fixed costs, $300,000 of COGS, and make $100,000 of net profit, for a ROE of 10%.

Now, suppose we have Freer Company, identical to Epstein Co. except for one thing. Instead of having no debt, this company had begun its operations with investors putting in only $100,000 of equity and taking out a loan of $900,000 at 5% interest. Its fixed costs go up (by the $45,000 of interest expense) and it now has $645,000 of fixed costs. As long as the economy stays healthy and revenues continue at $1,000,000 per year, then the investors are doing great. Profit is $55,000—$1,000,000 revenues minus $645,000 fixed costs and $300,000 of COGS. Because the investors have invested only $100,000 of their own money, the ROE is much higher: $55,000 divided by $100,000, or 55%. The investors in this highly-leveraged company are delighted when the economy is thriving.

However, look what happens when the economy stops booming. Suppose the economy then goes into a recession and sales revenues drop to $900,000. Unleveraged Epstein Co. would still be OK. Its fixed costs will remain $600,000 and its COGS will fall to $270,000, so that it will still have positive net revenue of $30,000. The investors' return on equity will have fallen to 3%. But the company can still pay its bills.

In contrast, Freer Company is in peril. Its costs will exceed its revenues. Costs will be $915,000 (fixed costs and interest of $645,000 plus COGS of $270,000), compared to $900,000 revenue. Unless it has saved money from earlier years, the company will be unable to pay its bills. The company will be insolvent, and the investors will not only have a return on their equity of zero, they are in danger of losing their $100,000 investment completely.

This is how leveraged companies get into financial trouble, explaining a lot of what happens in financial crises. Without the added fixed costs of debt, the company would have more flexibility to cushion these fluctuations in the cash flow. (Please note that these simple examples consider just the fixed interest cost, and ignore the additional cash expenditure associated with paying back the principal amount of the loan.)

So now you see the downside of leverage. The examples above show the intimate relationship between risk and return. We can raise our return (when things go well) by bearing more risk. But, that risk means a higher probability of things going wrong, and a worse outcome when they do. To put it another way, as Warren Buffet has: "When the tide goes out, you see who's been swimming naked." So we need to understand why companies use so much debt in their capital structures, and how it can come back to bite them.

PROBLEMS

1.   You are an attorney negotiating with a bank on behalf of Bubba's Burritos. The company is seeking a $1.2 million loan to be paid back over 10 years, in equal monthly installments i.e., $10,000 per month. The money will be used—along with available cash—to open two new restaurants. Interest will be computed at 5% on the average balance outstanding each month, and due with the principal payment on the last day of each month. How would respond to some of the bank's requested terms, below:

    a)   Each year, the company must provide the bank with audited financial statements, for its prior year, by the 15th of March.

    b)   For each year, the company must show profits equal to the average of its last 3 years profit figure, or else the loan shall be in default and immediately due.

    c)   The company must pledge a first security interest in all plant and equipment, inventory and accounts receivable against the outstanding balance of the loan.

    d)   The CEO, a non-shareholder, must personally guarantee the loan.

    e)   The 4 shareholders, each of whom owns 25% of the company, must each personally guarantee the loan on a joint and several basis.

2.   Using the sample balance sheet for Bubba's Burritos, above, imagine it has $450,000 in pretax profit and $300,000 in after tax profit. What is the company's Return on total Capital (ROC)? Return on Equity (ROE)?

3.   Same company, same financial performance, except it doesn't borrow $1.2 million, as above. Instead, the company borrows $1 million and pays it out in a dividend to the shareholders. The company pays $60,000 per year in interest, and the loan must be fully repaid, in a single payment, at the end of 10 years. Now, what is the company's ROC? Its ROE?

4.   Is a company with a return on equity of 50% more profitable than a company with return on equity of 25%?

c.   An Overview of Publicly-Traded Debt

In addition to negotiating a specific loan from a specific lender, a corporation might borrow $1000 from many people at the same time on the same terms. The government can also borrow like this. Whether public or private, debt instruments of less than one year in maturity are typically referred to as "notes" and longer than one year as "bonds," and we'll just use "bonds" for simplicity's sake. Regardless of the debt's maturity, once the money has been borrowed in this way—or, equivalently, once the bonds have been sold—the bonds can be resold on secondary markets: just like owners of stock, owners of bonds can resell them to others, and there will be market prices quoted for the bonds.

The debt market is much bigger than the stock market. At the end of 2013, U.S. stocks had a total value of about $20 trillion. In contrast, $40 trillion of bond instruments were outstanding. This included $11.9 trillion of U.S. Treasury debt, $9.6 trillion for corporate debt, and other large sums for selected U.S. agencies and municipalities.

A few words about government debt. Government debt serves as the benchmark for pricing other forms of debt (that is, determining the interest rate it will bear). The federal government spends more than it takes in, and it makes up this difference by issuing debt. Because U.S. government debt is perceived as riskless, it enjoys the lowest interest rate of any debt. All other debt is perceived to have some risk, and therefore it has to pay a higher interest rate. The higher the risk, the higher the interest rate.

Now, you need to remember that—in the world of bonds—a higher interest rate is the equivalent of a lower price. Perform this simple mental experiment: Imagine you lend a business $1,000 for 20 years at 5% interest. You believe that the 5% accurately compensates you for the risk you are taking. The next day, someone initiates a big lawsuit against the company, a lawsuit that could wipe out the business if it succeeds. Well, you want to sell the bond and avoid the risk. The bond is paying $50 in interest—the 5% on the $1,000 face value. The prospective buyer no longer believes 5% is enough return to compensate him for the risk he is taking. He wants 10%. Intuitively, he is willing to pay you only $500 for the bond so he can get his 10% interest—the $50 in interest on the new lower price of $500 he is paying.* When risk increases, interest rates must increase, and the price of a given bond will fall to adjust so that its nominal dollar interest paid equates to a new, effective interest rate, when divided by the new, market price of the bond. This new interest rate (10% in our example) is the "effective yield." This contrasts with the stated interest rate or "coupon" (in our example, 5%).

Bonds can vary in their maturities—that is, when the borrower needs to repay the loans. For example, maturities can be 5 years or 10 years.

As we've discussed, bonds can also vary in their risk. The risk is measured by the bond's rating or "grade." The grades are given to each bond by rating agencies, which include Standard & Poor's, Moody's, and Fitches. The grade is an attempt to evaluate the issuer's risk: its ability to cover its financial commitments. Companies that have plenty of cash to spare can suffer a deterioration in their business operations and still make their debt payments, and cover other financial commitments.

---

* This is an oversimplification because it ignores the fact that the new buyer will get the $1000 face value back when he redeems the bond in 20 years—assuming the business is not bankrupt.

Companies that have almost all of their anticipated cash flow pledged to cover their debt payments are on a knife edge; if they have a hiccup in their business they may default on some of their payments.

Standard & Poor's (S&P) is the best-known rating agency. For S&P, AAA is the highest, and the grades go all the way as low as D, for a bond that has already defaulted—that is, the issuer has failed to make a scheduled payment. Here are the definitions of some of the S&P ratings*:

- AAA—Extremely strong capacity to meet financial commitments.
- A—Strong capacity to meet financial commitments, but somewhat susceptible to adverse economic conditions and changes in circumstances.'
- BBB—Adequate capacity to meet financial commitments, but more subject to adverse economic conditions.
- BBB—Considered lowest investment grade by market participants
- CCC—Currently vulnerable and dependent on favorable business, financial and economic conditions to meet financial commitments.
- D'—Payment default on financial commitments.

S&P also appends a "+" or "-" sign to ratings to create even finer gradations.

BBB is considered the lowest "investment grade" bond, meaning that the issuer is considered highly likely to meet its principal and interest obligations, and the bond is therefore a "reasonable" one to hold in a conservative investment portfolio. Bonds below that grade are more speculative. They are often referred to as "junk" bonds, or, more politely, as "high yield" bonds. Banks are prohibited from holding bonds of a lower grade than BBB.

The next table below shows the effective yields on several types of bonds on July 30, 2014. Note that the table has three patterns.

Bond Rating	5-Year Yield	10-Year Yield
US Treasury	1.76	2.55
AAA	1.95	2.9
A	2.21	3.4
BBB	5.82	6.24

First, bonds issued by the US government, or "treasuries," have the lowest yields. That is because they are considered the lowest-risk bonds available. Just about everyone expects the US government to make good

---

* https://www.globalcreditportal.com/ratingsdirect/renderArticle.do?articleId=1331219& SctArtId=257653&from=CM&nsl_code=LIME&sourceObjectId=5435305&sourceRevId=7&fee_ ind=N&exp_date=20240818-02:07:33.

on its obligations. So those bonds have the lowest yield. All other bonds are considered to have more risk, and all other bonds are priced in reference to US treasuries. If the effective interest rate rises or falls on US treasury bonds, then the stated interest rates paid on all other subsequently issued bonds change as well. Moreover, the effective interest rate paid on already-issued bonds will change when those bonds are sold in the secondary market, because their price will change to reflect the new interest rate environment, as discussed above. And, even if an investor does not sell her bonds, those bonds are worth less if interest rates have risen, and worth more if rates have fallen. Let's emphasize that important relationship: if market interest rates fall, then bond prices rise; if market interest rates rise, then bond prices fall.

The second pattern to note is that interest rates rise as bond rating drops—i.e., as the bond gets more risky. This is exactly what you would expect.

Third, note that the interest rate on 10-year bonds is higher than that on 5-year bonds. This is the normal pattern: the longer the time until a bond matures, the higher the interest rate because there is higher risk for the longer-term bond. For example, the longer the term of the bond, the greater the chance that the borrower will go bankrupt during the term, and be unable to repay what it has borrowed. Likewise, the longer a bond's term, the more that the bond's market price will fluctuate in response to changes in market interest rates—again creating more risk for the bondholder.

In the rare situation where long-term bonds have lower interest rates than short-term bonds, investors must expect that interest rates in the future will fall. So investors will lock in the current high yields now by buying long-term bonds. This will cause the price of long-term bonds to rise, which necessarily reduces their yield.

The next article describes how people think about rating the debt of a business, and why it matters.

MOODY'S DOWNGRADES VERMONT LAW SCHOOL REVENUE BONDS

Moody's Investors Service, an investment assessment services company, downgraded Vermont Law School's $10.3 million in 2011 revenue bonds this week. Moody's lowered its rating for the school's bonds from Baa2 to Ba1 this week. [Note: on the S&P scale, this corresponds to a drop from BBB to BB+]

The downgrade drops Vermont Law School by two rating categories. * * * Moody's gave the school a negative outlook because a covenant written into the debt service contract requires that the school maintain a rating of Baa2 or higher. [The bond holders] could demand an accelerated repayment of the debt, according to Emily Schwarz and Edith Behr, the Moody's analysts who authored the report. The downgrade is based on "substantial declines" in law school enrollments because of reduced national demand for juris doctorate programs and an expectation that revenues from student tuition will be lower at Vermont Law School. This loss of revenue, Moody's says, will put pressure on the school's cash flow and debt service coverage.

In a statement, Peter Glenshaw, a spokesman for the Vermont Law School, tied the downgrade to national trends in the legal field. There has been a decline in the number of students taking the LSAT entrance exam and declining enrollments in law schools across the country, he said. Glenshaw says Vermont Law School has taken steps to stabilize its finances: "We expect to finish this year with a surplus, and our fiscal health remains stable," Glenshaw wrote. "As Moody's noted, we have carefully managed this situation. We have increased enrollment in our distance learning program and have announced numerous partnerships with other colleges and universities. In addition, this year we have announced $2 million in new gifts to the law school and $700,000 in grants. We will continue to carefully steward our fiscal resources as we consider the future of Vermont Law School."

* * * Moody's says Vermont Law School's declining enrollment and small size are a particular challenge because the school is a standalone institution.

Vermont Law School relies heavily on tuition as a source of revenue and has faced a decline in applicants * * *. Enrollments at the Vermont Law School declined 3.5 percent in 2013 for all programs and a 45 percent drop in the number of new applicants in the J.D. program from the fall of 2009 to the fall of 2013, according to Moody's: "Net tuition per student has stagnated or declined for four years, and is projected to decline further in FY 2014 and FY 2015," according to the rating agency report.

Moody's took into account two important factors that add to the institution's risk: the Vermont Law School's small size ($28.2 million revenue in fiscal year 2013) and unlike most law schools around the country, the Vermont Law School is a standalone institution with no backing from a larger university or college. * * * [Moody's said] "Fiscal diligence will be critical in the future as revenues continue to decline," Moody's analysts reported. The law school can improve its bond rating by "stabilizing" enrollments and net tuition revenue growth.

Anne Galloway, VTDigger.Org, April 17, 2014.*

In a similar vein, the following article discusses what happens when a business misses a bond payment.

---

* http://vtdigger.org/2014/04/17/moodys-downgrades-vermont-law-school-revenue-bonds/.

THOMAS JEFFERSON SCHOOL OF LAW GETS REPRIEVE AFTER MISSED BOND PAYMENT

Thomas Jefferson School of Law is scrambling to restructure its debt after blowing a bond payment deadline.

The downtown San Diego private law school has disclosed in a financial filing that it failed to meet its entire debt obligations in June. But an agreement the school struck with creditors staves off doomsday at least until Oct. 17, while requiring it to come up with another $2 million.

School officials say they're counting on reaching a restructuring deal with bondholders, who've agreed not to pursue legal remedies for the time being.

"As part of the negotiations, various potential structures and restructuring alternatives have been discussed," the school said in a statement Tuesday evening following a report by the Above the Law blog about its borrowing woes.

"The parties have a mutual interest in restructuring the law school's debt in a way that will allow the school to remain in operation and prosper," the statement said.

Stand-alone law schools, like Thomas Jefferson, have had a rougher time recovering from the last financial downturn and dealing with a broader decline among college graduates in demand for law degrees, according to financial analysts. Unattached to broader universities, independent schools lack the financial backstop of a bigger institution when cash runs out.

Between 2007 and 2013, applications to Thomas Jefferson fell 45% as its acceptance rate jumped to 81% from 45%, according to its figures. The school last year slashed teaching and administrative positions after missing its enrollment targets. It also hired a new dean, Thomas Guernsey.

While trying to escape a budget hole, the school has been literally digging. In 2011, it cut the ribbon on a 305,000 square-foot "luxurious" new building, whose $90 million construction became mired in litigation.

The school last year enrolled about 1,000 students and employed 42 full-time faculty members—with an operating budget of around $40 million, according to financial and enrollment records.

In October, Thomas Jefferson's credit rating was downgraded two notches to B+—junk-bond status—with a negative outlook.

A December 2013 credit-rating analysis by Standard & Poor's Ratings Services sized up the school's predicament:

"We believe the law school's large amount of debt and very high debt service, which resulted from the construction of a new facility that the school put into service during 2011, are credit weaknesses. In our opinion, there is also enrollment risk given the declining number of law students nationally and recent weakness in headcount that will likely compress operating margins, particularly since the school has no track record of fundraising."

Wall St. Journal Law Blog, Sept 17.[*]

PROBLEMS

1.   Does a company that issues bonds care about whether its bonds are rated AAA or some lower rating? If so, why?

2.   What happens if a business can't make its debt payments and defaults on its loan or bonds? What determines how happy or unhappy the lender will be in the event of a default?

3.   Why do you suppose Thomas Jefferson School of Law was able to successfully negotiate with its bondholders? What do you think the "doomsday" in the article would look like?

4.   If Acme Corp issues 5% bonds payable in 10 years and Acme's business performance declines during that 10-year period, how does that affect Roberts who had purchased $100,000 of Acme bonds?

5.   Why would longer duration bonds pay a higher interest rate than shorter duration ones? Why might they pay a lower interest rate? Why might some buyers choose to buy 10-year rather than 5-year bonds?

6.   If you hold a $1,000 bond paying 4%, and interest rates fall, is your bond worth more or less? Why?

5.   EQUITY FINANCING

Now that we have explored debt, let's look at the other way that a business can raise money from outsiders. It can sell equity in itself, also known as selling its shares or selling its stock. By selling stock, the company does not borrow money. Instead, the company makes new people part-owners in the company. The company can sell stock broadly to the public, and so become a "public company." We'll talk about that a bit later. We examine now how a company might sell stock instead just to a single person, or to a single company. A company that needs outside funding might first sell stock to an "angel investor." These are rich people who enjoy investing in young companies. Their investments are typically $1 million or $2 million. If the company still needs more money than this, it might sell stock to a "venture capital company" or "VC." An investment from a VC might typically be $10 million.

---

[*]   2014 http://blogs.wsj.com/law/2014/09/17/thomas-jefferson-school-of-law-gets-reprieve-after-missed-bond-payment/.

a. Issuing Stock to a Venture Capital Fund

Venture capital is a specialized type of equity financing used by rapidly-growing, high-potential start-ups. There is no separate law regarding venture capital. There is, however, a lore regarding venture capitalists. As Bob Zider, an entrepreneur and observer of venture capitalists in Silicon Valley, noted in the *Harvard Business Review*: "[T]he entrepreneur is the modern day cowboy, roaming new industrial frontiers much the same way the earlier Americans explored the West. At his [or her] side stands the venture capitalist, a trail-wise sidekick ready to help the hero through all the tight spots—in exchange of course for a piece of the action." Bob Zider, *How Venture Capital Works*, HARVARD BUSINESS REVIEW 131 (Nov.–Dec. 1998).

Professor Dent of the Case Western Reserve Law School provides a less picturesque but clearer picture of venture capital:

> Venture capital is a substantial equity investment in a non-public enterprise that does not involve active control of the firm. It is often associated with the financing of high technology start-up companies, where it has achieved its most spectacular successes. But, many companies financed with venture capital are neither high technology nor start-up companies. Indeed, companies past the start-up stage often raise additional venture capital when they are unable to finance through more conventional sources. These later round financings are often called "second tier," or "mezzanine" financings. Furthermore, once-successful companies that have fallen on hard times may also obtain financing from venture capitalists; these investors are often called "angels."

> Entrepreneurs usually seek venture capital when they need capital but are unable to raise it elsewhere. Retained earnings are a manager's favorite source of funding. However, this source of funding is unavailable for start-up companies since they have not yet produced earnings to retain; and even after the start-up, a growing company usually requires more capital than its cash flow provides. Debt is often the managers' second choice for capital. Debt financing is generally preferred over equity because equity investors demand a higher return on their investment than lenders. Moreover, sales of stock dilute managers' equity interest and voting power. However, loans are unavailable to most start-up and growth companies because of the high risk of loss. In theory, lenders can offset increased risk by charging a high interest rate. In practice, however, usury laws, as well as regulations that require institutional lenders (such as banks and insurance companies) to be conservative, preclude such high interest loans. Moreover, few start-up companies generate

sufficient cash flow to service high interest charges. For these companies such a loan would rapidly lead to insolvency. Even more-established firms may need more capital than they can borrow.

Most companies that seek venture capital are unstable and risky. In fact, one-third of venture capital-financed companies wind up in bankruptcy. Another one-third end up in "limbo" or as "living dead"—limping along, able to pay expenses (including managers' salaries), but unable to go public or pay significant dividends. Only one-third of the companies that use venture capital financing succeed.* Venture capitalists demand high returns because the successful one-third of their investments must cover the losses generated by the other two-thirds, as well as the high transactions costs that venture capitalists pay in seeking, monitoring, and evaluating their investments.

Venture capitalists also demand high returns because they cannot reduce risks by diversifying. Although modern portfolio theory advises investors not to put all their eggs in one basket, venture capitalists are forced to ignore this advice. High transaction costs of choosing, monitoring, and evaluating private equity investments limit the venture capitalist to a few major purchases rather than many small investments.

Illiquidity also requires venture capitalists to demand a higher return on their investment. The inability of venture capitalists to sell their stock at a fair price whenever they choose is a burden for which they must be compensated. Thus, venture capitalists demand higher returns than the yield typically paid on debt or even on other types of equity investments.

Venture capitalists usually obtain a significant voice in the control of the firm. Venture capitalists also demand protective covenants.

Although contracts are quite standardized in many areas, the varied business contexts of venture capital discourage uniformity. For example, an investor who has the power to choose a majority of the board of directors has needs far different from an investor who lacks even a veto power over the board's decisions. The variety of terms in venture capital contracts also mirrors the diverse preferences of the parties involved. Venture capitalists range from pension funds and other huge financial institutions to individual investors of modest means. In addition,

---

* New research indicates that about three-quarters of venture-backed firms in the U.S. don't return investors' capital, according to Shikhar Ghosh, a senior lecturer at Harvard Business School   http://online.wsj.com/news/articles/SB1000087239639044372020457800498804 76429190.

managers have varied preferences, such as differing levels of risk aversion. Another factor is the parties' level of sophistication. Unusual terms may reflect either mutual ignorance or overreaching by a more sophisticated party.

George W. Dent, Jr., *Venture Capital and the Future of Corporate Finance*, 70 WASH. U.L.Q. 1029, 1031 et seq. (1992).

A venture capitalist is a shareholder, but often a shareholder with special rights. The special rights might include "downside protection," such as a liquidation preference that requires the venture capitalist to be paid first if the company's assets are sold off. They might include "upside opportunities" such as the right to acquire additional stock at a predetermined price. They might include rights to influence how the company is run, such as special voting and veto rights. Finally, the venture capitalist's rights might "exit opportunities," such as a "redemption" right to sell the shares back to the corporation.*

Note that venture capitalists are able to carve out such rights for themselves via preferred shares. As their name implies, and Chapter 4, page 133 explains, preferred shares enjoy various preferences. These preferences are relative to the common stock, which is held by the founders and early employees.†

b. Issuing Stock to the Public

We have considered corporations' issuing shares to a limited number of people such as its existing shareholders, an angel, or a venture capital fund. A corporation can also offer its shares to the public. Such an issuance of stock is, reasonably enough, called a "public offering." The first time a corporation issues its stock to the public is called its "initial public offering" or "IPO." A company that conducts an IPO is said to "go public."‡ This section focuses on why and how a business structured as a corporation goes public.

Why go public? The reason to go public is to raise money. After receiving investments from VCs, successful, growing companies often require more money. The public markets are viewed as the largest and

---

*   We have already seen an example of such provisions in the discussion of Silicon Gaming's preferred stock in Chapter 4 § (B)(4).

†   Other early employees may have stock options, which are options to purchase common stock at a set price, and which are popular because they receive favorable tax treatment i.e., they are not treated as income to the recipient when issued, because of the theory that they have no value as long as they were issued at the then fair market value. The recipient is then taxed on the increase in value when that increase is recognized by the employee at the time of exercise of the option and a sale of the security In exchange of this benefit, the income is taxed as ordinary income, rather than as a capital gain.

‡   And the term "going public" is used in other contexts. http://www.youtube.com/watch?v=_iEkj8JU5MQ.

least expensive source of capital. Typically, firms that desire to go public have a record of sales and earnings that allows prospective investors—purchasers of the shares—to have some confidence in the long run profitability of the company, and thus, the value of their shares. Often, it takes several years—and successive rounds of private financing, perhaps venture capital—to reach this point. The private financing is more expensive for the firm's owners than public financing; that is, to obtain private financing, the owners have to give up a relatively larger fraction of their ownership or equity.

Thus, when the firm has reached a stage in its evolution where it believes it has proven its business model, a public offering can be an attractive means of funding business growth. The question then arises: how much money to raise?

How much money to raise? In part, this is a function of the amount of capital the firm will need to finance its growth. A very rapidly-growing firm in a capital-intensive business will need more capital than a more slowly-growing company. Because the fixed costs of going public, such as legal and accounting fees, can be significant (costs often reach more than 10% of the amount raised), it can be in the firm's interest to seek as much money as possible.

In deciding how much money to raise, the company will balance fear against greed. First, the greed. Suppose that the company is a big success after its initial public offering. If the company accomplishes what it hopes to, it will grow, become more profitable, and its value will increase. If this hugely successful corporation later needs more money to grow, it will be able to get that financing by giving up less ownership to the new investors. Greed then argues for raising as little money as possible to get to the next milestone.

Now, the fear. What if, after the first public offering, the company is not as successful as anticipated? If the company falters after the IPO, it will wish it had raised as much money as it could have in the first public offering. The extra cash is money in the bank that buys time to try new things to get the business back on track.

How does this balancing of greed and fear generally resolve itself? Companies tend to use a public offering to raise enough money to meet anticipated needs for at least two years.

How many shares, at what price? To raise its chosen amount, the company will need to think carefully about how many shares it will attempt to sell, and at what price.

The company will first calculate what it is currently worth. For a corporation whose shares are traded publicly, it's easy to see what the consensus is about the firm's value. The company's market value—the market capitalization or "market cap"—is simply the price per share at which the shares trade times the number of shares outstanding. The price per share is printed in some newspapers each day and is available online.

The price per share is a reflection of the give and take that takes place every day in the stock market on these relative values. The number of shares sold has to equal the number bought. If the price is such that many people think the stock is a good deal, then the price has to rise to coax out the shares required to clear the market. If the number of willing sellers is high for the opposite reason, then the price falls to coax out the buyers.

In contrast, before a corporation's stock is freely tradable (i.e., before an initial public offering while it is still a private company), the valuation is harder to calculate. The firm will need to estimate its future earnings as best it can. This is a science and an art. Note that the firm's value depends on its *future* earnings, not its earnings in the past. Even companies that have never had any earnings can be worth lots of money if people expect them to have large earnings in the future. Examples would be a company that is developing a drug that promises to cure cancer, or an internet start-up with a great idea that is not yet developed. However, in estimating future earnings, past earnings are not irrelevant. They often are the best evidence of what earnings will be in the future.

Based on this estimate of future earnings, the firm will then calculate its *current* value. One way for a company to do this is to look at "comparable companies"—businesses like theirs—that are publicly traded, and determine the market value of these enterprises. If several fast food chains sell for about 20 times their expected future earnings, then, the logic goes, Bubba's Burritos, Inc., should be worth about 20 times *its* expected future earnings. If Bubba's expects to earn $10 million per year into the future, then it should be valued at $200 million.* Think of this as the value of the firm's equity pre-IPO. To determine the value per share, we need to divide this total value by the number of shares. Suppose the number of shares is 20 million. Then the value per share is $10.

Now, let's suppose the company expects to raise $30 million from the public offering. If the company was worth $200 million before the IPO, then it must be worth $230 million once an additional $30 million drops onto its balance sheet. This is the post-IPO value (more generally called the "post money" valuation).

Next, we need to decide how many shares to sell to raise the $30 million, and at what price. For the current owners, it is obviously best to sell the fewest shares possible at the highest price possible; the current owners want the company to get the $30 million in exchange for as small

---

    *   Another, more sophisticated way to calculate the firm's value is to calculate the present discounted value of the firm's expected future earnings. You can learn how to do this in a course in Corporate Finance, either at the law school or business school.

a proportion of the company as possible. The current owners would be delighted if they could obtain the whole $30 million by selling one share. But investors won't be willing to pay that much per share. Investors will be willing to pay no more than the value of the shares. What is the value per share if they sell one share for $30 million? The value of the share is the value of the company ($230 million, as we determined above) divided by the number of shares (20,000,001). So the value that the buyer of the one share would receive for her $30 million would be only $11.50 ($230,000,000 / 20,000,001). So the buyer would never pay $30 million for the one share. If the company's offering price was $30 million per share, then the offering would fail.

What is the highest price per share that that the company can charge for the shares and still (1) raise the $30 million and (2) shareholders will be willing to buy them? It turns out that it's $10/share, the pre-IPO value per share. At that price, investors are receiving for their $10 payment exactly $10 of value. To see this, let's do the same calculation as before. Raising $30 million at $10 per share would require issuing 3 million more shares. After this IPO, the value of each share, including the new ones, would be $230 million / 23 million shares = $10. So $10 is the highest price that could be charged per share and still raise the $30 million.

Why not, to raise the $30 million, sell even more shares, at a lower price? Because this would harm the pre-existing shareholders. The company would receive the same $3 million as it would receive from selling at $10/share, but pre-existing shareholders would own less of the company; the new shareholders would own more shares than if the shares were sold at $10. For example, suppose the company raised $30 million by selling shares at $5/share. They would have to sell 6 million shares. After the IPO, the value per share would be $230 million / 26 million = $8.85. The new shareholders would get a bargain: they pay $5 for a share worth $8.85. However, the pre-existing shareholders are harmed. Before the IPO, each of their shares was worth $10. Now they are worth $8.85. They have been harmed because of dilution; in the $30 million IPO, the company gave up more of the company than was necessary.

Let's look at this from another angle. Suppose that company decides not to raise a certain amount of money, but instead to sell a certain number of shares. The company will try to ensure that it doesn't price them too high or too low. If it prices them at more than they are worth, people won't buy them, and the offering will fail. In contrast, if it sets the price too low, then it won't raise as much money as it could have. The shares' buyers will be delighted to have received a bargain. But the company will have thrown away money.

What are stock splits? Many companies like for their stock to trade at around $25 or $30 per share (although we've left it at $10 in the previous example to make the math simpler). Any higher than the $25 to $30 range, and investors with few funds may be unable to purchase even one share. Any lower, and the price is so cheap that the public's perception of the company itself is cheapened. There are techniques that the company can use to adjust the price into the sweet spot. If the market-clearing price is too high—say $50—the company can perform a "stock split": it exchanges each existing share for two shares. This will cut the market price of each share in half, to $25. If the price is too low, the company uses a "reverse stock split." For example, the company will swap two old shares for one new share. Stock splits and reverse stock splits do not affect the underlying value of each shareholder's investment in the company. After the stock split or reverse stock split, each shareholder owns exactly the same proportion of the company that they owned before.

Such techniques are sometimes used in public offerings. Suppose that, before an IPO, the optimal price per share for the offering is outside the $25–$30 range? Before the IPO, the company can conduct a stock spilt (or a reverse stock split) to readjust the number of shares held by existing shareholders so that the optimal offering price moves into the sweet spot.

How does a corporation make a public offering? In part, a public offering is about a "registration process"—involving documents such as a registration statement and prospectus prepared by lawyers and accountants and filed with and approved by the Securities and Exchange Commission (SEC). We will consider this "law" component of a public offering later, on page 385. There is also a business component of a public offering that is important for lawyers to understand.

When a company starts down the road to an IPO, one of the first tasks is selecting an underwriter. The underwriter is typically an investment bank—for example, Morgan Stanley or Goldman Sachs. The process of selecting an underwriter is generally driven by the company's sense of who can obtain the best price for its stock, particularly if market conditions sour. This in turn depends on which investment bank has the relationships and reputation to get a deal done.

One factor that corporations use to select an underwriter is the underwriter's past experience in the industry. For example, does the underwriter have a reputation for bringing good companies public in the corporation's particular industry. This, in turn, is often a function of the firm's research analysts. So, if an underwriter is known to have a very strong research analyst in the optical communications industry, then an optical communications company that wants to go public might choose that underwriter. That way, that underwriter's analyst will follow the stock, thus marketing it to investment professionals.*

---

* While it is tempting to think of the underwriter's analysts as neutral, objective reporters on a company's prospects, it is widely believed that they sometimes act as part of the underwriter's marketing force, attracting clients and then supporting their shares with favorable reports.

The underwriter manages the process of drawing up the offering memorandum that is filed with the SEC. More important, the underwriter is responsible for advice on structuring the offering, pricing the securities, and maintaining a market for the securities after the offering. The underwriter and the company executives go on a "road show" where they speak with the likely buyers of the shares—people who run mutual funds or otherwise manage large pools of money. Buyers provide an "indication of interest" in buying the stock at the various prices within the range that the firm is considering offering its shares. All of this sales effort comes to a head when the SEC approves the registration materials (sometimes after several rounds of comments and responses) and the offering is said to be "effective."

The shares of stock hit the market the next morning at a price set the night before. That is, the price at which the stock will be publicly offered is set only just before the offering actually begins. It is not set earlier at the time the corporation decided to make the public offering. It is also not set at the time that the corporation selected its underwriter. It is not set before the corporation has spent hundreds of thousands of dollars (if not millions) on attorneys and accountants. Why is this? It will take at least three or four months from the time a company makes the decision to go public to the time that the SEC makes the decision that the registration is effective. The company must wait to set the price because the market— and the best price for the offering—may change dramatically during that time.

Until relatively recently, virtually all companies that went public had earnings, and most fit within some well-established peer group. So, if a new pharmaceutical company was conducting an IPO, it was a straightforward matter to look at comparable companies, see the kind of P/E (price-to-earnings ratio) at which they traded, and price the new company's offering at a similar level.

Recently, however, companies have been going public far earlier in their life cycles, before they even have earnings. This makes the problem of valuing the company's stock more difficult. Faced with this uncertainty, and to make sure that the shares sell, the company and its underwriters may set the price relatively low. Thus, it is not uncommon for the stock price to rise quickly after the IPO when they are resold on the secondary market.

Can you see why a soaring stock price directly after an IPO should cause the company's managers to weep, not cheer?

Facebook and Twitter were two IPOs in which the IPO pricing received a lot of scrutiny. In both these cases, the firms were sufficiently new—and generating little or no earnings—that it was difficult to value the shares by traditional financial metrics.

For example, Facebook's May 16, 2012 prospectus, filed just as it was going public, offered up the latest financial data, showing that the company had earnings (on a fully-diluted basis) of $0.43 per share for the full year ended Dec. 31, 2011, and $0.09 per share for the first three months of 2012. At an IPO offering price of $38.00 per share, the stock was thus valued at 88 times the prior 12 months earnings. This valued the entire company at $104 billion.

On the day of the IPO, there was weaker than expected demand— and more selling—of Facebook shares than anticipated. There were also technical problems with the NASDAQ trading system, and by the day's end, the stock stood only $0.23 above the offering price. By the end of the first week, the stock was at $29.60, down 22% from the offering price.

Some blamed Facebook and its underwriters for over-pricing the stock. Others blamed them for deciding to increase the number of shares being sold only days before the offering. It also emerged that the lead underwriter's internal research analysts had cut their earnings forecasts for Facebook, but had selectively transmitted that information to their best clients leaving retail investors in the dark. (Are you seeing a pattern here?) Naturally, there were lawsuits—against NASDAQ, the underwriters, Facebook itself.

Twitter's IPO followed a different path. On November 7, 2013, the company went public, selling 70 million shares at $26. The stock quickly traded up to about $50.00 and closed at near $45. A good ending or bad? Well, if the stock was really worth $45 per share, then Twitter left 70 million times $19, or over $1.3 billion on the table by not fully pricing the stock at its $45. For all of 2012, Twitter had a loss of $0.18 per share, and for the first 9 months of 2013, a loss of $0.28 per share. Clearly, the company was not being valued on a multiple of its (negative) earnings. Valuations were based on forecasts—in many cases by investment bank analysts—of the future revenues and profits, driven by as-yet unexplored advertising models for the company. With so many untested variables driving the math, it is not surprising that different people ended up with different conclusions about the future, and thus the current, value of the company.

Underpricing may also occur for a more sinister reason. Occasionally, unscrupulous underwriters may have an incentive to underprice the shares for their own selfish purposes. They might hope to funnel the bargain shares to their other clients to create loyalty and future business for themselves.

For example, the complaint in the eBay case discussed in Chapter 6 at page 247 alleged that Goldman Sachs allocated shares from many IPOs to eBay's officers "to show appreciation for eBay's business and to enhance Goldman Sachs' chances of obtaining future eBay business." One of the defendants, Meg Whitman, eBay's CEO and a director, (and in mid-

2014 CEO of Hewlett Packard), was alleged to have received "shares in over 100 IPOs at the initial offering price. Whitman sold these equities in the open market and reaped millions of dollars in profit."

Where does the money come from? Underwriting activities are conducted on either a "firm commitment" or a "best efforts" basis. In a firm commitment underwriting, the money comes from the underwriter. The underwriter actually buys all of the shares in the public offering from the issuing company at the public offering price, less a negotiated discount. The underwriter then resells the shares to other investment bankers and the public.

In contrast, in a "best efforts underwriting," the money comes from the public, not the underwriter. Rather than buying the stock itself and then reselling it, the underwriter instead uses its best efforts to help the issuer to find buyers for the stock. The corporation, not the underwriter, bears the risk that shares cannot be sold at the offering price. Most underwritings are on a "firm commitment" basis. However, it is not very likely that the underwriter will be unable to sell the stock. This is because the underwriter has spent weeks or months on the road show selling the stock, its clients have indicated their interest in buying shares, and the underwriter has set a price it believes will clear the market. Moreover, the risk is low because the underwriter doesn't formally sign the underwriting agreement making this firm commitment until after these steps have been completed.

Where does the money go? Now, for the interesting question—what happens to the money that is raised in the IPO? Let's take an example where 10 million shares are sold to the public at $10 per share—this would result in $100 million. Once we subtract the 7.5% that the investment bank gets for its underwriting fee plus fees for other professionals such as lawyers and accountants, there is a transfer of the remaining $90 million or so from the public to someone. Who gets the money?

The answer depends on who is selling the shares. If the company *itself* is selling shares, then the company gets the money (those are called "primary" or newly issued shares). If the *existing owners* of the company are selling shares that they own (referred to as "secondary shares"), then these people get the money, and the company does not. The prospectus* will always have a table that describes in great detail the source of the shares.

You might ask whether the potential buyer of the stock—the public— cares about any of this. If a share of stock represents a proportional claim

---

* The prospectus is a document an issuer provides to potential purchasers, describing the security being sold, the issuing company, and the risk characteristic of the security. As we will see below, the prospectus is an important part of a registration statement under federal securities laws.

of the company's value, does it matter whether you bought it from an original owner or the company itself?

There are two components to answering this question. First, in the above example, suppose all 10 million shares were shares that other shareholders already owned. Then after the offering, the company would have the same amount of money in the bank as it did before the offering; all of the money goes to shareholders who owned the shares, not the company. If instead the offering sold only newly issued shares, then the company would have $90 million more in the bank the day after the offering than the day before. So, part of the answer is that the company will benefit more if the money goes into the company, where it can be invested to generate earnings, rather than if it goes to the former shareholders to make them rich. So you should be willing to pay more for your share of stock if the money is going onto the company. (Review the math above of how we determined the value of Bubba's in its IPO, and you'll see how the money it was planning to raise in its hypothetical IPO was added to the company's value.)

A second part of the answer depends on which shareholders are selling. If, for example, a company was backed by a venture capital (VC) firm, and that firm is selling some or all of its shares, then that needn't worry the new shareholders. The VC firm has investors of its own and they expect to get their money back. On the other hand, suppose the company's CEO is selling a large percentage of her shares. Presumably, this person knows a lot more about the company than you do. Do you want to be buying if she is selling?

Of course, there are sound reasons why an executive might sell some stock—to diversify her own financial situation, for instance. But many investors look unfavorably on a company's prospects when an executive sells a significant fraction of her shares.

Although a corporation going public gets money only at the time of the public offering, the offering will require the company to continue to spend money. It will continue spending money on attorneys and accountants to comply with various SEC reporting requirements that will now extend indefinitely.

There are other, less direct costs. Once a company goes public, the world changes. The company and its performance are much more in the public eye because the company must now comply with its public disclosure obligations. Investors attempt to gauge the value of the stock as a function of forecast earnings. Analysts develop earnings models and tweak them quarterly as the company publicly discloses its actual performance. Missing the analysts' estimates can quickly cause investors to sour on a company. If these professional investors abandon the stock, the market for its shares can dry up, allowing relatively small sales or purchases to produce large swings in the stock's price. Employees—

especially those with stock options—begin to pay a great deal of attention to the price of the stock, and its gyrations can have a significant effect on employee morale, and on the job prospects of the company's managers.

QUESTIONS AND NOTE

1. At what point in the public offering process,

    • does the issuing corporation make money?

    • does the underwriter make money?

    • do the attorneys and accountants make money?

2. In a firm commitment underwriting, does the underwriter have a financial incentive to set the offering price as low as is acceptable to the issuing company? A financial incentive to set the issuing price as high as is acceptable to prospective buyers?

3. Bubba's Burritos, Inc. makes a firm commitment public offering at $20 a share. Who pays the $20 a share? Who gets the $20 a share?

4. The next day, Bubba's Burritos stock is selling at $22 a share. Who benefits from this increase?

5. If Bubba's Burritos makes a public offering of 200,000 shares at $20 a share, will that affect the company's balance sheet? Would a second day increase in the market price of Bubba's shares affect Bubba's Burrito's balance sheet?

B. SECURITIES REGULATION

1. A FIRST LOOK AT REGISTRATION AND EXEMPTIONS

Now that you understand what an underwriter is and part of what your client might have learned from B-School, let's look at the laws implicated by a corporation's issuance of its shares to the public. The most important such laws are federal statutes.

Federal securities statutes are a product of the stock market crash of the 1920s and the New Deal of the 1930s. The two most significant federal statutes are the Securities Act of 1933 (the " '33 Act") and the Securities Exchange Act of 1934 (you guessed it, the " '34 Act").

In general, the '33 Act governs the issuance of securities by the corporation itself. In contrast, the '34 Act provides information to the markets for new securities and resales by requiring many corporations continually to provide detailed public reports about their operations. The securities that the acts cover include not only stock, but also securities such as bonds by which investors lend the company money.

The federal securities laws protect investors in two ways. First are disclosure requirements: companies that issue securities must provide specific detailed information to investors about themselves and the securities. Second, the laws permit investors to sue issuers who have sold securities by using false or misleading information. We now provide a very general introduction to the '33 Act's disclosure requirements. We'll look at state and federal antifraud laws a little further on.

The '33 Act contemplates that a corporation issuing securities will first file a detailed and extensive "registration statement" with the SEC and will provide a copy of the main part of that registration statement (the "prospectus") to all people to whom the securities are offered. Only after the SEC staff reviews the registration statement carefully for adequacy of information will it permit the statement to be effective and prospectuses distributed to the public.

In essence, federal regulation of the issuance of securities to the public is based on disclosure. As long as full disclosure is made through the registration process, the government will not prevent a security from being sold to the public because of its lack of investment merit.

The '33 Act also provides for a number of exemptions from the "dangerously complicated"* registration process. And, "dangerously complicated law" also determines what types of stock issuances are exempt from registration. Put generally, federal and state securities laws tend to treat a corporation's offering of a limited amount of its stock to a limited number of investors differently than they do a corporation's offering of a substantial amount of its stock to the public.

In particular, the securities regulations attempt to carve out space for "accredited" investors. Basically, the main objective of the law is to restrict the investment in unregistered (i.e., non-public) securities to people who are wealthy enough to be able to bear the loss of their money in a risky investment.

In addition to federal registration requirements, there are also registration requirements, and exemptions, in many states. State requirements are often called "Blue Sky Laws," because the laws protect against shady promoters who would sell stock by promising the buyer the whole blue sky.

QUESTIONS AND NOTES

1.   What is the reason for the SEC's requiring and reviewing registration statements? Who is protected? From what?

2.   One professor has speculated about the problems the Wright brothers would have encountered if they had needed to raise money to pursue

---

*   "Dangerously complicated" are Roberts' words. These are the words that a B-School prof uses—words that your clients will have heard and will identify with public offerings.

their dreams of manned flight under today's federal securities laws. He imagines that the brothers' lawyer, Horace, would give the following advice:

"Boys," he started, "I have to tell you that these new securities laws are not helpful. They're supposed to protect the public against fraudulent schemes, but it looks to me like they mostly hurt young inventors like you."

"We're not doing anything fraudulent," responded Wilbur, "so we should have no worries about that."

"You'd think so," Horace replied, "but these registration provisions are so time-consuming and costly that they make it near-impossible for young entrepreneurs like you to raise money. Here's what I've found. First, for federal law purposes, you have to file a registration statement unless you can qualify for an exemption. Preparing a registration statement will probably take a couple of months, then the SEC will have to review it. And meanwhile, you can't sell a single share of stock. You're stuck in a long timetable and running up expenses with no way to pay for them. Once you've got the SEC go-ahead, the questions become how much can you raise, and how quickly? Who knows? You're a new and untested company. What's more, registration entails potential liabilities that might not be imposed in unregistered offerings. In a nutshell, registration involves huge problems in terms of time, costs, and potential liabilities, all the while not knowing whether an offering will even be successful."

"Anything that takes several months won't work," Orville noted. "We've got to have money in hand within a month to prepare for our North Carolina experiments."

"That's why I've abandoned the registration idea. We need to fit the offering into a registration exemption."[*]

3.   Yet another law professor suggests that the registration exemptions are inconsistent with the reasons for the registration requirements:

Although the exemptions for small businesses reduce the expense for businesses seeking to raise capital, the exemptions are not without costs. Paradoxically those companies where investors require the greatest protection—small, unknown business—are also those companies with the greatest ability to skirt securities regulatory protections.[†]

---

[*]   Stuart R. Cohn, *The Impact of Securities Laws on Developing Companies: Would the Wright Brothers Have Gotten Off the Ground?* 3 J. SMALL & EMERGING BUS. L. 315, 326–28 (1999).

[†]   Stephen J. Choi, *Gatekeepers and the Internet: Rethinking the Regulation of Small Business Capital Formation,* 2 J. SMALL & EMERGING BUS. L. 27, 33 (1998).

2. AN EARLY (TOO EARLY?) LOOK AT CROWDFUNDING

With the rise of the internet, and particularly the social networking dimensions that were popularized more recently, "crowdfunding" became a new source of funds for start-ups. The most popular of these sites was kickstarter (www.kickstarter.com), where new ventures could describe their hoped-for product or service and seek funding to finance its development. Typically, subscribers would be offered one of the products when development was complete.

While this funding had its uses, it was really more "preselling" a product than it was raising equity funding. The start-up made no promise about what it would deliver and the person who wrote the check was not an investor in the business, as she had no upside or right to profit from its success.

In the JOBS (Jumpstart our Business Startups) Act of 2012, Congress and the President sought to make it easier for small private companies and start-ups to raise equity financing. By tying this idea to the notion of creating more jobs, they created the political tailwind to get the bill passed and signed in what was otherwise a contentious legislative climate.

The key hurdles that the JOBS Act sought to overcome were principally related to the existing securities laws, which place significant restrictions on the ability of a company to raise money. These restrictions take the form of 1) disclosure requirements, which often require registration of securities with the SEC; and, 2) standards (around wealth and income) that investors must typically meet in order to be eligible to invest in the newer companies that can't meet the strict disclosure requirements of registration. (See earlier pp. 381–382) Moreover, existing regulations required significant legal and accounting expenditures on the part of companies to attempt to meet these requirements.

Among the Act's many provisions, the key ones related to start-up funding were the creation of exemptions for "emerging businesses" (less than $1 billion in revenues) that are raising less than $1 million (in any 12 month period). Limitations were also placed on the amount that any individual could invest: individual investors are limited to the greater of $2,000 or 5% of annual net income or net worth (if annual income or net worth is less than $100,000); or, 10% of annual net income or net worth (not to exceed $100,000) for investors with annual incomes or net worth over $100,000.

The Act also requires offerings to be made via approved intermediaries or "portals" that allow companies to provide information and also allow prospective investors to share their own information, due diligence and opinions with each other.

It seems likely that the Act will permit a hitherto unfunded group of companies to raise money from a group of individuals who would otherwise have been unable to invest in these high-risk and (potentially) high-return start-ups. Whether these investments turn out to be profitable ones is another matter. While the public imagination is captured by the huge returns made on Facebook and Twitter, the fact remains that—on average—the overwhelming majority of venture capital investments lose money. Over the past decade, for venture capitalists who do this all day every day for a living, and who invest tremendous amounts of time and energy in researching and working with companies, venture capital returns have been close to zero. Thus, it is not obvious that amateur investors, devoting less time and energy to the investment process, will be able to improve on this performance.

The JOBS Act's crowdfunding exemption is not self-executing but, instead, requires regulatory implementation by the SEC. Proposed regulations are still under review.

3. WHAT ARE THE LEGAL DUTIES RELATING TO BUYING, SELLING, AND RESELLING STOCKS AND BONDS?

a. Available Information

If you are considering buying or selling McDonald's stock, it is relatively easy to learn what McDonald's stock is worth—or at least the market price for McDonald's shares. Go to the "Business" section of any newspaper (even THE NEW YORK POST). Or go on-line to any of a variety of sources providing stock quotes (e.g., www.schwab.com). One important internet source for a wide variety of information about publicly-traded corporations is EDGAR, which provides online access to the reports that public corporations file with the SEC (Securities & Exchange Commission). Such publicly traded corporations are "registered," as we discussed at pp. 381–382.

We are used to hearing about the major stock exchanges, such as the New York Stock Exchange and NASDAQ. These exchanges set prices for publicly-traded stocks each trading day. For some smaller corporations, similar information may be available online through the OTC Link—still called by some the Pink Sheets because the information was originally printed on pink sheets. The SEC provides this explanation and "warning":

> TC Link LLC (OTC Link) is owned by OTC Markets Group Inc., formerly known as Pink OTC Markets Inc. OTC Link is an electronic inter-dealer quotation system that displays quotes from broker-dealers for many over-the-counter (OTC) securities. "Market makers" and other broker-dealers who buy and sell OTC securities can use OTC Link to publish their bid and ask

quotation prices. OTC Link is registered with the SEC as a broker-dealer and as an alternative trading system, and is a member of FINRA. OTC Link does not require companies whose securities are quoted on its systems to meet any listing requirements. With the exception of some foreign issuers, the companies quoted on OTC Link tend to be closely held, extremely small and/or thinly traded. Most of these issuers do not meet the minimum listing requirements for trading on a national securities exchange, such as the New York Stock Exchange or the Nasdaq Stock Market. Many of these companies do not file periodic reports or audited financial statements with the SEC, making it very difficult for investors to find current, reliable information about those companies. For all of these reasons, companies quoted on OTC Link can be among the most risky investments. That's why you should take extra care to thoroughly research any company quoted exclusively on OTC Link."[*]

Not all close corporations are traded on the pink sheets. Indeed, most are not. For smaller close corporations such as Bubba's Burritos, whose securities are not traded on formal exchanges or in the pink sheets, how does one get information about appropriate pricing? Recall the earlier consideration of the information provided by financial statements and the earlier consideration of the statutory rights of an existing shareholder to look at the books and records.

Can you rely on what you find in the books and records of a corporation? Consider the following answer by an "experienced chancery practitioner" and a "qualified forensic accountant":

There exist no definitive guidelines regarding the form and content of "books and records of account" that are required to be maintained by a corporation under the statute (the New Jersey counterpart to MBCA § 2.20). The Internal Revenue Code offers some guidance, but only of a general nature.

Although a company may maintain what appears to be accurate books and records, those records may be a product of manipulation and fraud. An experienced chancery practitioner, assisted by a qualified forensic accountant, is essential in effectively representing the interests of a minority shareholder who wishes to exercise his or her statutory inspection rights and protect his or her overall financial interests in the corporation.

Michael J. Faul, Jr. and Robert Dipasquale, *A Minority Shareholder's Inspection Rights Under N.J.S.A. 14A:5–28*, NEW JERSEY LAWYER, 2004-Aug NJLAW 8.

---

[*]   http://www.sec.gov/answers/pink.htm.

b. Reliability of Information in Sales and Resales: Common Law Fraud and Rule 10b–5

Investors are protected not only by federal and state registration requirements, but also by antifraud provisions of both federal and state law. Unlike the registration requirements, the antifraud provisions include no exemptions; they apply to a sale or purchase of stock regardless of whether the transaction is exempt from registration.

As to state law, a person who buys stock from a corporation as a result of that corporation's false or misleading statement can invoke the contract law of misrepresentation to avoid her contract to buy the stock, or she can invoke the tort law of fraud or deceit to recover damages from the corporation. The contract law of misrepresentation was (supposed to be) covered in your contracts course; the law of fraud or deceit was (supposed to be) covered in your torts course.

In addition to state law, federal law provides strong antifraud protections. Rule 10b–5, the securities antifraud rule promulgated by the SEC under section 10 of the '34 Act, has been described as "a bedrock of protection for those who purchase and sell securities. Every securities transaction lives under its protective shade and menacing shadow." Alan R. Palmiter, CORPORATIONS—EXAMPLES AND EXPLANATIONS 413 (6th ed. 2009).

Rule 10b–5 was promulgated in 1948 and provides:

It shall be unlawful for any person, directly or indirectly, by the use of any means or instrumentality of interstate commerce, or the mails or of any facility of any national securities exchange,

(a) To employ any device, scheme, or artifice to defraud,

(b) To make any untrue statement of a material fact or to omit to state a material fact necessary in order to make the statements made, in the light of the circumstances under which they were made, not misleading, or

(c) To engage in any act, practice, or course of business which operates or would operate as a fraud or deceit upon any person

in connection with the purchase or sale of any security.

Most of the content of Rule 10b–5 is the result of decades of case law.* Most of those cases involve fraud, misrepresentations, or omissions in connection with *re*sales of stock or in connection with corporate combinations such as mergers—and not fraud, misrepresentation or

---

*   The Supreme Court has described 10b–5 law as "a judicial oak which has grown from little more than a legislative acorn." *Blue Chip Stamps v. Manor Drug Stores,* 421 U.S. 723, 737 (1975).

omissions by corporations in connection with their initial issuance of stock. Apply Rule 10b–5 and common sense to the following easy (we hope) issuance problems.

PROBLEMS

1.   Agee, Capel and Propp are the only three shareholders of Bubba's Burritos, Inc. Each owns 1,000 shares. Roberts is considering buying 1,000 shares from Bubba's for $100,000. Agee, the CEO of Bubba's, tells Roberts that Bubba's has never received a Health Department rating lower than "VG" (Very Good). In reliance on that representation, Roberts buys the 1,000 shares from Bubba's. Roberts later learns that Bubba's had received seven Health Department ratings of UB—Unbelievably Bad. Advise Roberts as to possible recourse.

2.   Same facts as Problem 1 except that Bubba's had not received a Health Department rating lower than VG. However, the day before Agee told Roberts that Bubba's had never received a Health Department rating lower that VG, the Health Department had inspected Bubba's and the inspector had met with Agee and told Agee that there were major problems and that it was almost certain that the company would receive the lowest possible rating. While Agee tells Roberts about Bubba's history of good Health Department ratings, he does not mention this conversation with the inspector. After Roberts buys the stock from Bubba's, the Health Department announces Bubba's UB (Unbelievably Bad) rating and Roberts learns of the inspector's conversation with Agee. Advise Roberts as to possible recourse.

3.   Same facts as Problem 2 except that Agee does not say anything about Health Department ratings. He does not say that past ratings have been good and he does not disclose that a bad rating is coming. Roberts buys the stock from Bubba's. Later he learns of the bad Health Department rating. Advise Roberts as to possible recourse.

4.   Now, man bites dog. Bubba's is considering acquiring a building from Epstein in exchange for 1,000 shares of Bubba's stock. Epstein tells Agee, Bubba's CEO, that the building has never had any termite problems. In reliance on Epstein's representation, Bubba's issues 1,000 shares of its stock to Epstein and takes title to the building. Bubba's later learns that Epstein's representation was a lie—that Epstein was aware of the building's past and present termite problems. Advise Bubba's as to possible recourse. Note from this Problem that Rule 10b–5 does not require that the issuer be the bad guy. Also, Rule 10b–5 condemns misrepresentations not only by sellers of securities, but also by buyers.

5.   Does Rule 10b–5 apply if the Bubba's CEO lies to sell his own Bubba's stock, rather than the stock of the company?

6.   In the hypos so far, the defendant shareholder was an officer of the corporation. Is Rule 10b–5 limited to situations where the buying or selling shareholder is involved in the management of the corporation?

7.   Suppose that a mining company knows that there are valuable mineral deposits under a farmer's land. Does the mineral company violate rule 10b–5 if it buys the land from the farmer at a low price without disclosing the existence of the mineral deposits?

c.   Materiality and Reliance

Two of the requirements for a 10b–5 claim are materiality and reliance. The materiality requirement means that not all false statements produce liability. There is liability only for "material" statements, not ones that are minor or unimportant. The trick is determining which statements are material and which ones are not.

The second requirement, the reliance requirement, requires that the securities plaintiff have been aware of the defendant's false statement and have relied on it in deciding to purchases or sell securities.

The next case discusses how to identify material statements. It also introduces a presumption that can substitute for reliance, so that a plaintiff can win a 10b–5 lawsuit even if she was not aware of the defendant's false statements.

In reading the case, please consider the following:

1.   Were Basic's statements in footnote 4 untrue?

2.   Who are the plaintiffs? Did the plaintiffs read the October 21, 1977 edition of the *Cleveland Plain Dealer*? What is the "fraud on the market theory"?

3.   Did Max Muller, the President of Basic, act with "scienter"? Could he spell "scienter"? Can you pronounce "scienter"? Is Scienter the name of a trendy perfume?

BASIC INC. V. LEVINSON
United States Supreme Court, 1988
485 U.S. 224

BLACKMUN, J. Prior to December 20, 1978, Basic Incorporated was a publicly traded company primarily engaged in the business of manufacturing chemical refractories for the steel industry. As early as 1965 or 1966, Combustion Engineering, Inc., a company producing mostly alumina-based refractories, expressed some interest in acquiring Basic. * * *

Beginning in September 1976, Combustion representatives had meetings and telephone conversations with Basic officers and directors, including petitioners here, concerning the possibility of a merger. During 1977 and 1978, Basic made three public statements denying that it was engaged in merger negotiations.* **[4]** On December 18, 1978, Basic asked the New York Stock Exchange to suspend trading in its shares and issued a release stating that it had been "approached" by another company concerning a merger. On December 19, Basic's board endorsed Combustion's offer of $46 per share for its common stock, and on the following day publicly announced its approval of Combustion's tender offer for all outstanding shares.

Respondents are former Basic shareholders who sold their stock after Basic's first public statement of October 21, 1977, and before the suspension of trading in December 1978. Respondents brought a class action against Basic and its directors, asserting that the defendants issued three false or misleading public statements and thereby were in violation of § 10(b) of the 1934 Act and of Rule 10b–5. Respondents alleged that they were injured by selling Basic shares at artificially depressed prices in a market affected by petitioners' misleading statements and in reliance thereon.

The District Court adopted a presumption of reliance by members of the plaintiff class upon petitioners' public statements that enabled the court to conclude that common questions of fact or law predominated over particular questions pertaining to individual plaintiffs.† The District Court therefore certified respondents' class. On the merits, however, the District Court granted summary judgment for the defendants. It held that, as a matter of law, any misstatements were immaterial: there were no negotiations ongoing at the time of the first statement, and although negotiations were taking place when the second and third statements were issued, those negotiations were not "destined, with reasonable certainty, to become a merger agreement in principle."

---

* **[4]** On October 21, 1977, after heavy trading and a new high in Basic stock, the following news item appeared in the *Cleveland Plain Dealer*:

"[Basic] President Max Muller said the company knew no reason for the stock's activity and that no negotiations were under way with any company for a merger. He said Flintkote recently denied Wall Street rumors that it would make a tender offer of $25 a share for control of the Cleveland-based maker of refractories for the steel industry."

On September 25, 1978, in reply to an inquiry from the New York Stock Exchange, Basic issued a release concerning increased activity in its stock and stated that: "management is unaware of any present or pending company development that would result in the abnormally heavy trading activity and price fluctuation in company shares that have experienced in the past few days."

On November 6, 1978, Basic issued to its shareholders a "Nine Months Report 1978." This Report stated:

With regard to the open stock market activity in the Company's shares, we remain unaware of any present or pending developments which would account for the high volume of trading and price fluctuations in recent months.

† [Note from your authors: To certify a class action under Federal Rule 23 (b)(3), as plaintiffs sought here, one must show that common questions predominate over individual questions.]

The United States Court of Appeals for the Sixth Circuit affirmed the class certification, but reversed the District Court's summary judgment, and remanded the case. The court reasoned that while petitioners were under no general duty to disclose their discussions with Combustion, any statement the company voluntarily released could not be "so incomplete as to mislead." In the Court of Appeals' view, Basic's statements that no negotiations where taking place, and that it knew of no corporate developments to account for the heavy trading activity, were misleading. With respect to materiality, the court rejected the argument that preliminary merger discussions are immaterial as a matter of law, and held that "once a statement is made denying the existence of any discussions, even discussions that might not have been material in absence of the denial are material because they make the statement made untrue."

The Court of Appeals joined a number of other Circuits in accepting the "fraud-on-the-market theory" to create a rebuttable presumption that respondents relied on petitioners' material misrepresentations, noting that without the presumption it would be impractical to certify a class under Federal Rule of Civil Procedure 23(b)(3).

We granted certiorari to resolve the split among the Courts of Appeals as to the standard of materiality applicable to preliminary merger discussions, and to determine whether the courts below properly applied a presumption of reliance in certifying the class, rather than requiring each class member to show direct reliance on Basic's statements.

II

The 1934 Act was designed to protect investors against manipulation of stock prices. Underlying the adoption of extensive disclosure requirements was a legislative philosophy: "There cannot be honest markets without honest publicity. Manipulation and dishonest practices of the market place thrive upon mystery and secrecy." * * *

Pursuant to its authority under § 10(b) of the 1934 Act, the Securities and Exchange Commission promulgated Rule 10b–5.* [6] Judicial interpretation and application, legislative acquiescence, and the passage of time have removed any doubt that a private cause of action exists for a violation of § 10(b) and Rule 10b–5, and constitutes an essential tool for enforcement of the 1934 Act's requirements.

---

* [6] In relevant part, Rule 10b–5 provides:

"It shall be unlawful for any person, directly or indirectly, by the use of any means or instrumentality of interstate commerce, or of the mails or of any facility of any national securities exchange,

(b) To make any untrue statement of a material fact or to omit to state a material fact necessary in order to make the statements made, in the light of the circumstances under which they were made, not misleading . . . "in connection with the purchase or sale of any security."

The Court previously has addressed various positive and common-law requirements for a violation of § 10(b) or of Rule 10b–5. *See, e.g., Blue Chip Stamps v. Manor Drug Stores,* ("in connection with the purchase or sale" requirement of the Rule); *Dirks v. SEC,* (duty to disclose); *Ernst & Ernst v. Hochfelder,* (scienter); *see TSC Industries, Inc. v. Northway, Inc.,* concluding in the proxy-solicitation context that "[a]n omitted fact is material if there is a substantial likelihood that a reasonable shareholder would consider it important in deciding how to vote." The Court was careful not to set too low a standard of materiality; it was concerned that a minimal standard might bring an overabundance of information within its reach, and lead management "simply to bury the shareholders in an avalanche of trivial information—a result that is hardly conducive to informed decisionmaking." It further explained that to fulfill the materiality requirement "there must be a substantial likelihood that the disclosure of the omitted fact would have been viewed by the reasonable investor as having significantly altered the 'total mix' of information made available." * * *

III

The application of this materiality standard to preliminary merger discussions is not self-evident. Where the impact of the corporate development on the target's fortune is certain and clear, the *TSC Industries* materiality definition admits straightforward application. Where, on the other hand, the event is contingent or speculative in nature, it is difficult to ascertain whether the "reasonable investor" would have considered the omitted information significant at the time. Merger negotiations, because of the ever-present possibility that the contemplated transaction will not be effectuated, fall into the latter category. * * *

This case does not concern the timing of a disclosure; it concerns only its accuracy and completeness. We face here the narrow question whether information concerning the existence and status of preliminary merger discussions is significant to the reasonable investor's trading decision. Arguments based on the premise that some disclosure would be "premature" in a sense are more properly considered under the rubric of an issuer's duty to disclose. The "secrecy" rationale is simply inapposite to the definition of materiality. * * *

Even before this Court's decision in *TSC Industries,* the Second Circuit had explained the role of the materiality requirement of Rule 10b–5, with respect to contingent or speculative information or events, in a manner that gave that term meaning that is independent of the other provisions of the Rule. Under such circumstances, materiality "will depend at any given time upon a balancing of both the indicated probability that the event will occur and the anticipated magnitude of the event in light of the totality of the company activity." *SEC v. Texas Gulf*

Sulphur Co., 401 F.2d [833, 849 (2d Cir. 1968)]. Interestingly, neither the Third Circuit decision adopting the agreement-in-principle test nor petitioners here take issue with this general standard. Rather, they suggest that with respect to preliminary merger discussions, there are good reasons to draw a line at agreement on price and structure.

In a subsequent decision, the late Judge Friendly, writing for a Second Circuit panel, applied the *Texas Gulf Sulphur* probability/magnitude approach in the specific context of preliminary merger negotiations. After acknowledging that materiality is something to be determined on the basis of the particular facts of each case, he stated: "Since a merger in which it is bought out is the most important event that can occur in a small corporation's life, to wit, its death, we think that inside information, as regards a merger of this sort, can become material at an earlier stage than would be the case as regards lesser transactions—and this even though the mortality rate of mergers in such formative stages is doubtless high."

We agree with that analysis.

Whether merger discussions in any particular case are material therefore depends on the facts. Generally, in order to assess the probability that the event will occur, a factfinder will need to look to indicia of interest in the transaction at the highest corporate levels. Without attempting to catalog all such possible factors, we note by way of example that board resolutions, instructions to investment bankers, and actual negotiations between principals or their intermediaries may serve as indicia of interest. To assess the magnitude of the transaction to the issuer of the securities allegedly manipulated, a factfinder will need to consider such facts as the size of the two corporate entities and of the potential premiums over market value. No particular event or factor short of closing the transaction need be either necessary or sufficient by itself to render merger discussions material.* **[17]**

As we clarify today, materiality depends on the significance the reasonable investor would place on the withheld or misrepresented information. Because the standard of materiality we have adopted differs from that used by both courts below, we remand the case for

---

*   **[17]** To be actionable, of course, a statement must also be misleading. Silence, absent a duty to disclose, is not misleading under Rule 10b–5. "No comment" statements are generally the functional equivalent of silence. It has been suggested that given current market practices, a "no comment" statement is tantamount to an admission that merger discussions are underway. That may well hold true to the extent that issuers adopt a policy of truthfully denying merger rumors when no discussions are underway, and of issuing "no comment" statements when they are in the midst of negotiations. There are, of course, other statement policies firms could adopt; we need not now advise issuers as to what kind of practice to follow, within the range permitted by law. Perhaps more importantly, we think that creating an exception to a regulatory scheme founded on a prodisclosure legislative philosophy, because complying with the regulation might be "bad for business," is a role for Congress, not this Court.

reconsideration of the question whether a grant of summary judgment is appropriate on this record.

IV

A

We turn to the question of reliance and the fraud-on-the-market theory. Succinctly put:

> The fraud on the market theory is based on the hypothesis that, in an open and developed securities market, the price of a company's stock is determined by the available material information regarding the company and its business. . . . Misleading statements will therefore defraud purchasers of stock even if the purchasers do not directly rely on the misstatements. . . . The causal connection between the defendants' fraud and the plaintiffs' purchase of stock in such a case is no less significant than in a case of direct reliance on misrepresentations.

Our task, of course, is not to assess the general validity of the theory, but to consider whether it was proper for the courts below to apply a rebuttable presumption of reliance, supported in part by the fraud-on-the-market theory.

This case required resolution of several common questions of law and fact concerning the falsity or misleading nature of the three public statements made by Basic, the presence or absence of scienter, and the materiality of the misrepresentations, if any. In their amended complaint, the named plaintiffs alleged that in reliance on Basic's statements they sold their shares of Basic stock in the depressed market created by petitioners. Requiring proof of individualized reliance from each member of the proposed plaintiff class effectively would have prevented respondents from proceeding with a class action, since individual issues then would have overwhelmed the common ones. The District Court found that the presumption of reliance created by the fraud-on-the-market theory provided "a practical resolution to the problem of balancing the substantive requirement of proof of reliance in securities cases against the procedural requisites of [Federal Rules of Civil Procedure, Rule] 23." The District Court thus concluded that with reference to each public statement and its impact upon the open market for Basic shares, common questions predominated over individual questions, as required by Federal Rules of Civil Procedure 23(a)(2) and (b)(3).

Petitioners and their amici complain that the fraud-on-the-market theory effectively eliminates the requirement that a plaintiff asserting a claim under Rule 10b–5 prove reliance. * * *

We agree that reliance is an element of a Rule 10b–5 cause of action. Reliance provides the requisite causal connection between a defendant's misrepresentation and a plaintiff's injury. There is, however, more than one way to demonstrate the causal connection. * * *

The modern securities markets, literally involving millions of shares changing hands daily, differ from the face-to-face transactions contemplated by early fraud cases, and our understanding of Rule 10b–5's reliance requirement must encompass these differences.

* * * The courts below accepted a presumption, created by the fraud-on-the-market theory and subject to rebuttal by petitioners, that persons who had traded Basic shares had done so in reliance on the integrity of the price set by the market, but because of petitioners' material misrepresentations that price had been fraudulently depressed. Requiring a plaintiff to show a speculative state of facts, i.e., how he would have acted if omitted material information had been disclosed, or if the misrepresentation had not been made, would place an unnecessarily unrealistic evidentiary burden on the Rule 10b–5 plaintiff who has traded on an impersonal market. * * *

The presumption is also supported by common sense and probability. Recent empirical studies have tended to confirm Congress' premise that the market price of shares traded on well-developed markets reflects all publicly available information, and, hence, any material misrepresentations. Because most publicly available information is reflected in market price, an investor's reliance on any public material misrepresentations, therefore, may be presumed for purposes of a Rule 10b–5 action.

The Court of Appeals found that petitioners "made public, material misrepresentations and [respondents] sold Basic stock in an impersonal, efficient market. Thus the class, as defined by the district court, has established the threshold facts for proving their loss." The court acknowledged that petitioners may rebut proof of the elements giving rise to the presumption, or show that the misrepresentation in fact did not lead to a distortion of price or that an individual plaintiff traded or would have traded despite his knowing the statement was false.

Any showing that severs the link between the alleged misrepresentation and either the price received (or paid) by the plaintiff, or his decision to trade at a fair market price, will be sufficient to rebut the presumption of reliance. For example, if petitioners could show that the "market makers" were privy to the truth about the merger discussions here with Combustion, and thus that the market price would not have been affected by their misrepresentations, the causal connection could be broken: the basis for finding that the fraud had been transmitted through market price would be gone. Similarly, if, despite petitioners' allegedly fraudulent attempt to manipulate market price, news of the merger discussions credibly entered the market and dissipated the effects of the misstatements, those who traded Basic shares after the corrective statements would have no direct or indirect connection with the fraud. Petitioners also could rebut the presumption of reliance as to plaintiffs who would have divested themselves of their Basic shares without relying on the integrity of the market. For example, a plaintiff who believed that Basic's statements were false and that Basic was indeed engaged in merger discussions, and who consequently believed that Basic stock was artificially underpriced, but sold his shares nevertheless because of other unrelated concerns, e.g., potential antitrust problems, or political pressures to divest from shares of certain businesses, could not be said to have relied on the integrity of a price he knew had been manipulated.

In summary:

* * *

Materiality in the merger context depends on the probability that the transaction will be consummated, and its significance to the issuer of the securities. Materiality depends on the facts and thus is to be determined on a case-by-case basis.

It is not inappropriate to apply a presumption of reliance supported by the fraud-on-the-market theory.

That presumption, however, is rebuttable.

The judgment of the Court of Appeals is vacated, and the case is remanded to that court for further proceedings consistent with this opinion.

QUESTIONS AND NOTE

1.   What do the plaintiffs have to prove on remand?

2.   "Petitioners and their amici complain that the fraud on the market theory effectively eliminates the requirement that a plaintiff asserting a claim under Rule 10b–5 prove reliance." Do you agree with this assertion? Did the Court?

3.   Your client T (for "target"), a publicly traded corporation, is involved in preliminary, secret merger discussions with A ("acquirer"), which is also a publicly traded company. A has repeatedly told T that if news of their merger discussion is disclosed prematurely, A will "walk away from the deal." T's CEO gets a telephone message from the business reporter of the local newspaper that he has heard rumors that T and A are negotiating a merger. The reporter wants to talk with the CEO about T and A. On the basis of *Basic*, how would you advise T's CEO?

4.   Basic's fraud-on-the-market theory has been controversial. For example, Professors Arlen and Carney use economic analysis to criticize the theory. They indicate that most fraud on the market cases simply transfer

wealth from one set of stockholders to another, while incurring large transactions costs. Jennifer Arlen and William Carney, *Vicarious Liability for Fraud on the Securities Markets*, 1992 U. ILL. L. REV. 691.

However, the Supreme Court recently affirmed the theory. In *Halliburton Co. v. Erica P. John Fund, Inc.*, 134 S. Ct. 2398 (2014), the defendants in a securities class action urged that *Basic*'s acceptance of the theory should be overruled. Among other arguments, they suggested that the economic assumption that underlay the theory—that markets were efficient—was incorrect. In a unanimous decision, the Court preserved *Basic* and affirmed the fraud-on-the-market theory.

Although the *Haliburton* opinion helped plaintiffs by preserving the fraud on the market theory, it also helped securities defendants in an important way. Recall that the fraud-on-the-market theory creates a presumption that the plaintiff relied on the defendant's misleading statements. But the presumption is rebuttable. Until *Halliburton*, the defendant could not attempt to rebut the presumption at the stage of the litigation when the judge was deciding whether to certify a class action. Instead, the defendant had to wait until the later stages of litigation that address the merits. But, by then, the case has often settled, with the defendants paying large amounts. In *Halliburton*, the court held that defendants could present evidence to rebut the presumption before class-certification. This may lead fewer cases to gain class-certification and may lead to smaller settlement amounts.

d. The Bespeaks Caution Defense

We have explored the general definition of materiality. In addition, there is a special way that a defendant in a securities suit can show that a false statement was not material. This is the court-created "bespeaks caution" doctrine. The doctrine has also been adopted in a federal statute: the Private Securities Litigation Reform Act of 1995.

EP MEDSYSTEMS, INC. V. ECHOCATH, INC.
United States Court of Appeals, Third Circuit, 2000
235 F.3d 865

SLOVITER, CIRCUIT JUDGE. EP MedSystems, Inc. appeals the dismissal with prejudice of its securities action against EchoCath, Inc. According to the complaint, the Chief Executive Officer of EchoCath enticed MedSystems into investing $1.4 million in EchoCath by assuring MedSystems that lengthy negotiations had already taken place with four prominent companies to market certain new EchoCath products and that contracts with these companies were "imminent." Relying on cautionary language contained in several public documents filed by EchoCath with the Securities Exchange Commission, the District Court held that these representations, as well as other related representations, were immaterial as a matter of law under the "bespeaks caution" doctrine and the general test for materiality. It also held that MedSystems failed to adequately plead scienter, reasonable reliance, and loss causation and could not do so. It accordingly dismissed the complaint without leave to amend.

Our review of a decision granting a motion to dismiss is plenary.

BACKGROUND

The following facts are drawn largely from the amended complaint and the documents attached to the pleadings by the parties, including several EchoCath public filings with the Securities Exchange Commission (SEC).

EchoCath is a small New Jersey research and development company engaged in developing, manufacturing, and marketing medical devices to enhance and expand the use of ultrasound technology for medical applications and procedures. Among the products that EchoCath has developed with the company's proprietary ultrasound technology are ColorMark, which highlights metallic objects such as needles and other interventional instruments in color to permit them to be seen on existing ultrasound imaging screens, and EchoMark, which electronically marks and displays the position of non-metallic objects such as catheters within the body. The parties refer to these two products as the "women's health products." EchoCath describes its women's health products as enabling physicians to perform procedures such as needle biopsies, catheterizations, and intravascular imaging more safely and efficiently.

EchoCath consummated its initial public offering on January 17, 1996 and issued a lengthy Prospectus that included details of the company's technologies, future plans, capitalization, collaborative agreements, and selected financial data. The Prospectus also included the caution that "[a]n investment in the securities offered . . . is speculative in nature and involves a high degree of risk," and set forth several pages of risk factors. In particular, EchoCath cautioned investors that the company "intend[ed] to pursue licensing, joint development and other collaborative arrangements with other strategic partners . . . [but] [t]here can be no assurance . . . that the Company will be able to successfully reach agreements with any strategic partners, or that other strategic partners will ever devote sufficient resources to the Company's technologies."

More than six months after the public offering, MedSystems began consideration of a sizable investment in EchoCath. * * *

Frank DeBernardis, the Chief Executive Officer (CEO) of EchoCath, made a lengthy presentation during the August meeting to David Jenkins, MedSystems President and CEO, James Caruso, its Chief Financial Officer (CFO), and Anthony Varrichio, a Director. DeBernardis represented that EchoCath had engaged in lengthy negotiations to license its products and was on the verge of signing contracts with a number of prominent medical companies, which he identified as including UroHealth, Johnson & Johnson, Medtronic, and C.R. Bard, Inc., to develop and market EchoCath's women's health products.

* * * Throughout the negotiations and until the closing in February 1997, EchoCath's CEO continued to represent to MedSystems officials that EchoCath was actively moving forward with the line of women's health products described in the August meeting, and that the contracts with UroHealth, Johnson & Johnson, Medtronic and C.R. Bard to develop these products were "imminent." * * *

* * * On February 27, 1997, MedSystems entered into a subscription agreement with EchoCath to purchase 280,000 shares of preferred EchoCath stock for $1,400,000. In the agreement, MedSystems specified that it "ha[d] not relied upon any representation or other information (oral or written) other than as contained in documents or answers to questions so furnished to [MedSystems] by [EchoCath]," that it had "relied on the advice of, or has consulted with, only its own Advisors," and acknowledged that "an investment in the Shares involves a number of very significant risks and [MedSystems was] able to bear the loss of its entire investment." Nonetheless, MedSystems alleges in the complaint that it relied on the representations from EchoCath's CEO of imminent contracts. * * *

In the fifteen months after MedSystems made its investment, EchoCath failed to enter into a single contract or to receive any income in connection with the marketing and development of the women's health products. * * *

MedSystems filed suit in the United States District Court for the District of New Jersey, alleging that EchoCath intentionally or recklessly made misrepresentations to MedSystems in connection with the sale of securities in an effort to induce MedSystems to purchase its securities, in violation of Section 10 of the Securities Exchange Act of 1934, 15 U.S.C. S 78j, and Rule 10b–5. MedSystems also alleged a supplemental state law fraud claim. * * *

EchoCath moved to dismiss the complaint. It attached to its motion: (1) the January 17, 1996 Prospectus; (2) the February 27, 1997 Subscription Agreement between EchoCath and MedSystems for the purchase of the stock; (3) its annual 10-KSB report filed with the SEC on December 12, 1996 for the 1996 fiscal year ending August 31, 1996 ("Annual Report"), which reported, inter alia, that as of August 31, 1996, EchoCath's operations had not generated significant revenues and which contained substantial cautionary language;* [1] (4) EchoCath's quarterly

---

*   [1] Among the cautions contained in the Annual Report were statements that "[n]o assurance can be given that the Company will successfully commercialize any of its products or achieve profitable operations," that the report contained "forward-looking statements" within the

update filed with the SEC on January 21, 1997 for the three months ending on November 30, 1996 ("Quarterly Report"), which reported that EchoCath anticipated additional cash resources that would be provided by the completion of unspecified licensing agreements and strategic alliances, but that there "can be no assurances that the Company will be able to complete the aforementioned license agreements and strategic alliances on acceptable terms." EchoCath took the position that these documents established that any alleged misrepresentations were immaterial under the "bespeaks caution" doctrine because they contained sufficient cautionary language.

* * * There is no indication that MedSystems ever received a copy of these documents, but they were readily available to the public. * * *

The District Court then dismissed the complaint with prejudice. In an exhaustive and lengthy opinion, the court concluded that the representations were immaterial as a matter of law under the "bespeaks caution" doctrine because of the cautionary language accompanying these alleged misrepresentations. The court also stated that MedSystems had failed to plead scienter with sufficient particularity as required by 15 U.S.C. § 78u–4(b)(2). Next, the court found that MedSystems could not have reasonably relied on EchoCath's optimistic financial projections. Finally, the court concluded that MedSystems failed to plead loss causation. Having dismissed the federal securities claim, the District Court declined to retain jurisdiction over the remaining state law fraud claim. * * *

DISCUSSION

* * * Rule 10b–5 makes it unlawful for a person to "make any untrue statement of a material fact or to omit to state a material fact necessary in order to make the statements made, in the light of the circumstances under which they were made, not misleading . . . in connection with the purchase or sale of any security." * * *

Under the legal principles governing actions alleging securities fraud, MedSystems must prove that EchoCath (1) made misstatements or omissions of material fact; (2) with scienter; (3) in connection with the purchase or sale of securities; (4) upon which MedSystems relied; and (5) that MedSystems' reliance was the proximate cause of its injury. The District Court relied on these principles, and the precedents applying them, in dismissing MedSystems' complaint as a matter of law.

At the outset, it is important to recognize that there are important distinctions between this case and the usual securities actions for which

---

meaning of the Private Securities Litigation Reform Act of 1995, and that many known and unknown risks may cause the actual results to be materially different from the company's future predictions.

these principles were developed. Although EchoCath, like the companies sued in those cases, sought to sell its securities in the market by an offering accompanied by the January 1996 Prospectus, MedSystems does not base its claim on public misrepresentations or omissions that affected the price of the stock it purchased. Instead, it contends that it was induced to make the substantial $1.4 million investment as a result of personal representations directly made to its executives by EchoCath's executives and that those representations were false and misleading.

In one sense, this action is more akin to a contract action than a securities action, and that may be the claim encompassed in its state law fraud count that the District Court did not consider. The distinction between the fact pattern alleged here and that in the typical securities cases explains why it is difficult to apply the precedent from those cases to many of the issues. It is like the proverbial difficulty of fitting a square peg in a round hole. While the question whether EchoCath's alleged misrepresentations are immaterial as a matter of law can be readily considered under the precedent, it is far more difficult to do so with the subsequent issues, such as whether MedSystems pled scienter with sufficient particularity, failed to plead reasonable reliance, and failed to plead loss causation. We consider each of these issues hereafter, keeping in mind throughout not only this distinction but also that the District Court dismissed the complaint without leave to amend.

A.   General Principles of Materiality

That materiality is a prerequisite to a viable securities action based on a misrepresentation is too well established to require citation. Nor can there be any disagreement as to the general definition of materiality under the securities laws. As the Supreme Court has defined it, a misrepresentation or omitted fact "is material if there is a substantial likelihood that a reasonable shareholder would consider it important in deciding how to [act]." *TSC Industries, Inc. v. Northway, Inc.*, [426 U.S. 438 (1976)]. Although the *TSC Industries* case involved a proxy solicitation dispute, the *TSC Industries* standard of materiality was expressly applied by the Court to Rule 10b–5 in *Basic Inc. v. Levinson*, [485 U.S. 224 (1988)]. According to the Court, for a misrepresentation or omission to be material "there must be a substantial likelihood that the disclosure of the omitted fact [or misrepresentation] would have been viewed by the reasonable investor as having significantly altered the 'total mix' of information made available." * * *

The materiality requirement has been further refined in recent years. In 1995, Congress enacted the Private Securities Litigation Reform Act (the "Reform Act") because of significant evidence of abuse in private securities litigation, particularly the filing of frivolous suits alleging securities violations designed solely to coerce companies to settle quickly and avoid the expense of litigation. The Reform Act contains, inter alia, a statutory safe harbor for forward-looking written or oral statements.* **[2]** Under that provision, an issuer is not liable for a forward-looking statement if it is "identified as a forward-looking statement, and is accompanied by meaningful cautionary statements identifying important factors that could cause actual results to differ materially from those in the forward-looking statement." The safe harbor is also available for oral forward-looking statements under certain conditions.

In this case, the District Court did not rely on, nor did EchoCath cite, the safe harbor provision as a basis for finding the representations at issue immaterial as a matter of law. This may be because the oral misrepresentations on which MedSystems brought suit were not identified as forward-looking as required by the safe harbor provision. Instead, the District Court found that the misrepresentations were immaterial under the "bespeaks caution" doctrine as adopted by this court in *In re Donald J. Trump Casino Sec. Litig.*, 7 F.3d 357 (3d Cir.1993).

Under the "bespeaks caution" doctrine, "cautionary language, if sufficient, renders the alleged omissions or misrepresentations immaterial as a matter of law." In *In re Trump Casino Sec. Litig.*, we held that a suit brought by a class of investors who purchased bonds to provide funding for the acquisition and completion of the Taj Mahal, a lavish casino/hotel on the boardwalk of Atlantic City, could not be maintained because the alleged misrepresentations and omissions in the prospectus were accompanied by warning signals in the text of the prospectus that conveyed to potential investors the extreme risks inherent in the venture and the variety of obstacles the venture would face. We stated that "bespeaks caution" represents new nomenclature, but it "is essentially shorthand for the well-established principle that a statement or omission must be considered in context, so that accompanying statements may render it immaterial as a matter of law." * * *

---

*   **[2]** The Act defines "forward-looking statement" to include:

(A) a statement containing a projection of revenues, income (including income loss), earnings (including earnings loss) per share, capital expenditures, dividends, capital structure, or other financial items;

(B) a statement of the plans and objectives of management for future operations, including plans or objectives relating to the products or services of the issuer;

(C) a statement of future economic performance, including any such statement contained in a discussion and analysis of financial condition by the management or in the results of operations included pursuant to the rules and regulations of the Commission;

(D) any statement of the assumptions underlying or relating to any statement described in subparagraph (A), (B), or (C);

(E) any report issued by an outside reviewer retained by an issuer, to the extent that the report assesses a forward-looking statement made by the issuer; or

(F) a statement containing a projection or estimate of such other items as may be specified by rule or regulation of the Commission.

By its terms, the "bespeaks caution" doctrine, like the safe harbor provision in the Reform Act, is directed only to forward-looking statements. * * *

We have also recognized that for the "bespeaks caution" doctrine to apply, the cautionary language must be directly related to the alleged misrepresentations or omissions. * * *

We turn to consideration of the misrepresentations alleged by MedSystems in light of these general principles to determine if dismissal at the pleading stage should be upheld.

B. *Alleged Misrepresentations*

The principal allegation of MedSystems is that EchoCath repeatedly misrepresented the existence of imminent contracts for its women's health products. The complaint alleges that EchoCath's CEO represented that it "had engaged in lengthy negotiations with and was on the verge of signing contracts with a number of companies including UroHealth, Johnson & Johnson, Medtronic and C.R. Bard, Inc. to develop and market [EchoCath's] women's health products." MedSystems also alleges that "[t]hroughout the negotiations and until the closing in February, 1997," EchoCath "continued to represent . . . that EchoCath was actively moving forward with the line of women's health products. . . ." * * *

As we noted earlier, the "bespeaks caution" doctrine applies only to forward-looking statements. On review, we cannot say as a matter of law that the representation was not a present statement of fact. EchoCath's CEO had told MedSystems that lengthy negotiations with the four companies had already taken place and that the contracts were "imminent." An event is "imminent" if it is "ready to take place." WEBSTER'S THIRD NEW INTERNATIONAL DICTIONARY 1130 (1976). A statement by the CEO of EchoCath that contracts with four companies were "ready to take place" may reasonably be construed as a representation about the current state of negotiations between EchoCath and the four companies it had identified. As such, the representation could be reasonably construed by a trier of fact to be a statement of fact rather than a prediction of future events. * * *

There is also a question whether the cautionary language cited by the District Court was sufficiently proximate to the imminent contracts representations to meet the relatedness test established by our precedent. The representations were not accompanied by any cautionary language. * * *

C. *Scienter*

EchoCath argues on appeal that the District Court correctly held that dismissal of the complaint was also warranted on the ground that MedSystems failed to meet the heightened pleading required for the scienter element in securities fraud cases. Rule 9(b) of the Federal Rules of Civil Procedure, which applies to all complaints filed in federal court, provides that "[i]n all averments of fraud or mistake, the circumstances constituting fraud or mistake shall be stated with particularity." Fed.R.Civ.P. 9(b). The 1995 Reform Act requires, inter alia, that a "complaint shall, with respect to each act or omission alleged to violate [the Securities Exchange Act], state with particularity facts giving rise to a strong inference that the defendant acted with the required state of mind." 15 U.S.C.A. § 78u–4(b)(2) (West Supp.2000). * * *

MedSystems' complaint alleges that "[c]ontrary to EchoCath's repeated representations to EP MedSystems, EchoCath was not on the verge of signing contracts with UroHealth, Johnson & Johnson, Medtronic, C.R. Bard, Inc. or any other company to market and develop a line of women's health products in September, 1996 or at any other time up to the closing of February 27, 1997." Moreover, "EchoCath knew at all times relevant hereto that it had no reasonable prospects of entering into the contracts it had identified to EP MedSystems." The complaint then notes that "EchoCath has failed to entered [sic] into a single contract and has yet to receive any income from the sale of women's health products" since September 1996.

* * * The District Court, on the other hand, viewed the complaint as merely alleging fraud by hindsight. It is, of course, true that we generally require more than a showing that a predicted event did not occur in order to sustain a claim of fraud. * * *

As we noted earlier, this case presents a factual situation unlike that in our prior precedent and, indeed, unlike those that were the basis for the 1995 Reform Act. The legislative history of the Reform Act makes clear that it was primarily directed at the abuse and misuse of securities class action lawsuits where defendant companies "choose to settle rather than face the enormous expense of discovery and trial." As the Senate Report states: The fact that many of these lawsuits are filed as class actions has had an in terrorem effect on Corporate America. A whole stable of "professional plaintiffs," who own shares—or sometimes fractions of shares—in many companies, stand ready to lend their names to class action complaints.

* * *

The "victims" on whose behalf these lawsuits are allegedly brought often receive only pennies on the dollar in damages. Even worse, long-term investors ultimately end up paying the costs associated with the lawsuits. As the Council for Institutional Investors advised: "We are * * * hurt if a system allows someone to force us to spend huge sums of money in legal costs by merely paying ten dollars and filing a meritless cookie cutter complaint against a company or its accountants when that plaintiff is disappointed in his or her investment."

MedSystems stands in contrast to the professional plaintiffs who were the focus of the statute. MedSystems invested the substantial sum of $1.4 million in EchoCath. It did so on the basis of personal representations by EchoCath executives to MedSystems officers concerning negotiations that had occurred and the imminent results expected of those negotiations. MedSystems' complaint is not a "cookie cutter complaint" or a class action brought by shareholders with an insignificant interest in the company; it is an individual action, based on a transaction arising from direct negotiations between the parties to the action.

It is difficult to see how MedSystems could have pled fraud or scienter with more specificity without having been given the opportunity to conduct any discovery. Here, the necessary information as to the status of EchoCath's negotiations with the four companies lies in the defendant's hands. We acknowledge the Reform Act's heightened pleading requirement for the defendant's state of mind, but we believe that MedSystems' allegations are sufficient under the particular facts of this case, which is not the typical class action that Congress intended to target. * * *

D.   Reliance

It is undisputed that a plaintiff seeking relief under Rule 10b–5 must show reasonable reliance on a false statement or omission of material fact. MedSystems' complaint alleges that its executives believed the "representations concerning EchoCath's line of women's health products were true and would not have made its substantial investment in EchoCath if it had known these representations were false." The District Court treated the imminent contracts representation as involving future predictions by EchoCath that contained no guarantee that the contracts would be consummated. The court repeated its position that the representation was contradicted by disclaimers and cautionary language in the 1996 Prospectus, the Annual Report, and the Quarterly Report filed with the SEC. Thus, the court found that any reliance by MedSystems on the representation was unreasonable as a matter of law.

Our consideration of the District Court's analysis leads us to a conclusion similar to that we reached in our discussion on materiality where we concluded that none of the documents containing cautionary language sufficiently neutralized the materiality of the imminent contracts representation. It follows that reliance on the repeated oral representations by EchoCath's CEO was not unreasonable as a matter of law because of those documents. * * *

E. *Loss Causation*

Finally, we turn to EchoCath's contention that dismissal was appropriate because the complaint fails to plead loss causation. The Reform Act provides that in a securities law action, "the plaintiff shall have the burden of proving that the act or omission of the defendant . . . caused the loss for which the plaintiff seeks to recover damages." 15 U.S.C.A. § 78u–4(b)(4) (West Supp.2000). Although this provision does not deal with pleading, the District Court concluded that MedSystems failed to plead loss causation. The court stated that the plaintiff must show that the misrepresentations "caused the decline in value rather than merely inducing the transaction." * * *

In considering loss causation, it is important to recognize once again how this case differs from the usual securities action. In the usual securities action, plaintiffs complain because some announcement emanating from the company, whether regarding a tender offer, earnings, projected earnings, or the company's financial condition, fraudulently represented the actual state of affairs. Plaintiffs claim that, as a result, they purchased the securities at a price that was artificially inflated, only to suffer a loss when the true situation was made known.

This case differs. In this case, MedSystems claims that as a result of fraudulent misrepresentations made in personal communications by EchoCath executives, it was induced to make an investment of $1.4 million which turned out to be worthless. * * *

The causation issue becomes most critical at the proof stage. Whether the plaintiff has proven causation is usually reserved for the trier of fact. MedSystems' complaint was dismissed at the pleading stage. Although, as noted above, the allegation that it "sustained substantial financial losses as a direct result of the aforementioned misrepresentations and omissions on the part of EchoCath" could have more specifically connected the misrepresentation to the alleged loss, i.e., investment in a company with little prospects, when we draw all reasonable inferences in plaintiff's favor, we conclude that MedSystems has adequately alleged loss causation.

* * *

CONCLUSION

* * * Specifically, we have concluded that MedSystems' central allegation, that EchoCath's CEO gave MedSystems executives assurances that, after lengthy negotiations, contracts with four identified companies were "imminent" and provided sales projections that were an integral part of these assurances, should not have been dismissed. This was a statement of fact in the context in which presented by MedSystems' complaint that could be found to meet the requirement of materiality. The allegation that EchoCath knew or had reason to know that this was not

the case adequately met the requirement of pleading scienter. A trier of fact could find that reliance was reasonable and that there was the requisite causal connection between the assurances and MedSystems' loss, i.e., its investment.

* * * It follows that we will reverse the dismissal of the complaint, and also direct reinstatement of the state fraud count. * * *

QUESTIONS

1.   Are there any differences between the "forward-looking statement" safe harbor in the Private Securities Litigation Reform Act and the judicially created "bespeaks caution" principle?

2.   Would the Third Circuit have decided the case differently if, after each of his statements about EchoCath's being "on the verge of signing contracts with a number of prominent medical companies," DeBernardis had added the statement "Of course, that is just my opinion. I could be wrong."?

3.   Recall that the Third Circuit merely reversed and remanded the case for trial. If you were representing EchoCath, what would you recommend that your client offer in settlement?

4.   The Private Securities Litigation Reform Act imposes "loss causation" as a requirement in addition to regular but-for causation. But-for causation simply requires that the plaintiff would not have entered the transaction if it were not for the defendant's fraudulent behavior. In essence, the plaintiff must be able to say "I bought this stock *because* defendant lied to me." In contrast, loss causation requires the plaintiff to show that the lie caused the plaintiff not only to buy the stock, but also to suffer a loss.

For example, suppose D tells P that the corporation will do very well because it has just perfected a new method for marketing widgets. It is a lie. The corporation does not have a new method for anything. P buys stock in the corporation because of this misrepresentation. Now suppose the stock plummets in value for reasons wholly unrelated to D's lie. For example, suppose the market for widgets simply dries up because of macroeconomic forces.

In this case, P can show but-for causation, because she would not have bought the stock but for D's misrepresentation. But she cannot show loss causation; the stock lost value for reasons unrelated to D's misrepresentation. Thus, under the Private Securities Litigation Reform Act, P cannot recover. As *EP Medsystems* makes clear, the plaintiff has the burden of proving loss causation.

5.   Now, having read *EP Medsystems*, reconsider Questions 1 through 3 on page 388.

Recall that Rule 10b–5 ends with the phrase "in connection with the purchase or sale of any security" and that the plaintiffs in *EchoCath* had bought EchoCath stock, and the plaintiffs in *Basic* had sold their Basic stock. What protects the shareholder who decides *not to sell* because of a false or misleading statement? Not Rule 10b–5.

In *Birnbaum v. Newport Steel Corp.*, 193 F.2d 461 (2d Cir. 1952), the court held that only those who bought or sold in reliance on a false or misleading statement may bring a private claim for damages. The Supreme Court adopted this interpretation of "in connection with the purchase or sale of any security" in *Blue Chip Stamps v. Manor Drug Stores*, 421 U.S. 723 (1975). (Still, many refer to this as the "*Birnbaum* rule.") Thus folks who sit on the sidelines and do not buy or sell in the face of a false or misleading statement may not bring a private case for damages under Rule 10b–5.

Perhaps the courts are restrictive in this area because Rule 10b–5 does not expressly provide for a private right of action. Rule 10b–5 simply provides that various misstatements or omissions are "unlawful." Clearly, the SEC can enforce the rule through civil actions or administrative enforcement proceedings. The SEC can also refer suspected violations to the Department of Justice for criminal prosecution. Nonetheless lower courts inferred from the existence of the rule that a private right of action should be recognized, allowing suits for damages by those defrauded. *See Kardon v. National Gypsum Co.*, 73 F.Supp. 798 (E.D. Pa. 1947). The Supreme Court finally embraced this position expressly in *Herman & MacLean v. Huddleston*, 459 U.S. 375 (1983). According to the Court, the fact that lower courts had long recognized the private right to sue, coupled with the fact that neither Congress nor the SEC had attempted to change that understanding, indicated that such an action was consistent with Congress's intent.

e. Insider Trading

In our cases so far, we have seen Rule 10b–5 applied when there was an alleged misrepresentation upon which someone relied in buying or selling securities. There, Rule 10b–5 complements common law fraud in providing a remedy for an aggrieved buyer or seller.

Rule 10b–5 has also had a large impact in punishing insider trading. In the last decades, the news regularly presents images of high-paid corporate officials and bankers in expensive suits being handcuffed, arrested for insider trading under rule 10b–5, and doing the perp walk.

With insider trading, there is no misrepresentation. Instead, someone privy to confidential business information (an "insider") uses it (or perhaps passes it along to another) to trade in securities of that business (or perhaps another business). Despite the lack of a

misrepresentation, courts have held that insider trading violates Rule
10b–5. *Chiarella v. United States*, 445 U.S. 222 (1980).

Rule 10b–5 does not prohibit all transactions in which a buyer or
seller of securities has more information than the other party to the
transaction. The Securities and Exchange Commission had suggested
such a broad rule. *SEC v. Texas Gulf Sulphur Co.*, 401 F.2d 833 (2d Cir.
1968). But the Supreme Court rejected it, holding that "not every instance
of financial unfairness constitutes fraudulent activity under § 10(b).
[There is not] a general duty between all participants in market
transactions to forgo actions based on material, nonpublic information."
Chiarella, 445 U.S. at 233.

Instead, in a series of cases, the Supreme Court indicated which uses
of nonpublic information violate the law, and which do not. Courts first
held that it is illegal for a corporate insider, such as a director, officer, or
employee, to use material, nonpublic information to trade in the
corporation's own stock. *Chiarella*, 445 U.S. at 228–29. This is called
"classic" or "traditional" insider trading. For example, let's suppose that
the CEO of Bubba's Burritos secretly learned that the results of testing
showed that the consumption of the company's burritos eliminated acne
in teenagers. The CEO expects that, when the information becomes
public, his company's stock will soar in value as teens switch to the
Bubba's Burritos Diet. It would violate Rule 10b–5 for the CEO to call his
stockbroker and purchase his company's stock.

Similarly, suppose instead that a Bubba's employee overheard the
company's top officials conduct a crisis meeting, in which they discussed
secret test results that would show that methane emissions after
consumption of the burritos would cause innocent bystanders to suffer
brain damage. It would be illegal for the employee to sell his stock, in
anticipation of the price decline that would occur when negative
information became public.

But what about the following other common situations?

QUESTIONS

1.   A law student is standing in an elevator minding her own business,
and she overhears Bubba's CEO discussing the company's acne test results.
Does it violate Rule 10b–5 if the student buys stock in Bubba's?

2.   Bubba's has hired a law firm. While representing Bubba's, one of
the firm's lawyers hears about the acne results. Does it violate Rule 10b–5 if
the lawyer then buys Bubba's stock?

3.   Bubba's CEO decides that Bubba's will purchase another company,
Walter's Wraps. Does it violate Rule 10b–5 if the CEO purchases stock not in
Bubba's, but in Walter's, anticipating that Walter's stock price will jump
when the acquisition is announced?

4.   Bubba's CEO tells one of the players on his ultimate frisbee team about the acne test results. The teammate pays the CEO $5000 for the information. Has the teammate done anything wrong when he buys Bubba's stock?

5.   Bubba's hires a printing company to print the legal documents for its purchase of Walter's. A receptionist at the printing company rummages through the garbage, finds drafts of the documents, figures out that Walter's is the acquisition target, and purchases stock in Walter's. Has the receptionist engaged in illegal insider trading?

The following two cases deal specifically with questions 4 and 5. However, they also indicate how to answer 1–3. See if you can use the cases to answer all of the questions.

DIRKS V. SECURITIES & EXCHANGE COMMISSION

United States Supreme Court, 1983
463 U.S. 646

POWELL, J. Petitioner Raymond Dirks received material nonpublic information from "insiders" of a corporation with which he had no connection. He disclosed this information to investors who relied on it in trading in the shares of the corporation. The question is whether Dirks violated the antifraud provisions of the federal securities laws by this disclosure.

I

In 1973, Dirks was an officer of a New York broker-dealer firm who specialized in providing investment analysis of insurance company securities to institutional investors. On March 6, Dirks received information from Ronald Secrist, a former officer of Equity Funding of America. Secrist alleged that the assets of Equity Funding, a diversified corporation primarily engaged in selling life insurance and mutual funds, were vastly overstated as the result of fraudulent corporate practices. Secrist also stated that various regulatory agencies had failed to act on similar charges made by Equity Funding employees. He urged Dirks to verify the fraud and disclose it publicly.

Dirks decided to investigate the allegations. He visited Equity Funding's headquarters in Los Angeles and interviewed several officers and employees of the corporation. The senior management denied any wrongdoing, but certain corporation employees corroborated the charges of fraud. Neither Dirks nor his firm owned or traded any Equity Funding stock, but throughout his investigation he openly discussed the information he had obtained with a number of clients and investors. Some of these persons sold their holdings of Equity Funding securities, including five investment advisers who liquidated holdings of more than $16 million.

While Dirks was in Los Angeles, he was in touch regularly with William Blundell, the Wall Street Journal's Los Angeles bureau chief. Dirks urged Blundell to write a story on the fraud allegations. Blundell did not believe, however, that such a massive fraud could go undetected and declined to write the story. He feared that publishing such damaging hearsay might be libelous.

During the two-week period in which Dirks pursued his investigation and spread word of Secrist's charges, the price of Equity Funding stock fell from $26 per share to less than $15 per share. This led the New York Stock Exchange to halt trading on March 27. Shortly thereafter California insurance authorities impounded Equity Funding's records and uncovered evidence of the fraud. Only then did the Securities and Exchange Commission (SEC) file a complaint against Equity Funding and only then, on April 2, did the Wall Street Journal publish a front-page story based largely on information assembled by Dirks. Equity Funding immediately went into receivership.

The SEC began an investigation into Dirks' role in the exposure of the fraud. After a hearing by an Administrative Law Judge, the SEC found that Dirks had aided and abetted violations of [other federal securities provisions and] SEC Rule 10b–5 by repeating the allegations of fraud to members of the investment community who later sold their Equity Funding stock. The SEC concluded: "Where 'tippees'—regardless of their motivation or occupation—come into possession of material 'corporate information that they know is confidential and know or should know came from a corporate insider,' they must either publicly disclose that information or refrain from trading." 21 S.E.C. Docket 1401, 1407 (1981) (quoting Chiarella v. United States, 445 U.S. 222, 230, n. 12 (1980)). Recognizing, however, that Dirks "played an important role in bringing [Equity Funding's] massive fraud to light," * * * the SEC only censured him.

Dirks sought review in the Court of Appeals for the District of Columbia Circuit. The court entered judgment against Dirks * * *.

In view of the importance to the SEC and to the securities industry of the question presented by this case, we granted a writ of certiorari. * * * We now reverse.

II

In the seminal case of *In re Cady, Roberts & Co.*, 40 S.E.C. 907 (1961), the SEC recognized that the common law in some jurisdictions imposes on "corporate 'insiders,' particularly officers, directors, or controlling stockholders" an "affirmative duty of disclosure . . . when dealing in securities." The SEC found that not only did breach of this common-law duty also establish the elements of a Rule 10b–5 violation, but that individuals other than corporate insiders could be obligated either to disclose material nonpublic information before trading or to abstain from trading altogether. In *Chiarella*, we accepted the two elements set out in *Cady, Roberts* for establishing a Rule 10b–5 violation: "(i) the existence of a relationship affording access to inside information intended to be available only for a corporate purpose, and (ii) the unfairness of allowing a corporate insider to take advantage of that information by trading without disclosure." In examining whether Chiarella had an obligation to disclose or abstain, the Court found that there is no general duty to disclose before trading on material nonpublic information, and held that "a duty to disclose under § 10(b) does not arise from the mere possession of nonpublic market information." Such a duty arises rather from the existence of a fiduciary relationship.

Not "all breaches of fiduciary duty in connection with a securities transaction," however, come within the ambit of Rule 10b–5. Santa Fe Industries, Inc. v. Green, 430 U.S. 462, 472 (1977). There must also be "manipulation or deception." In an inside-trading case this fraud derives from the "inherent unfairness involved where one takes advantage" of "information intended to be available only for a corporate purpose and not for the personal benefit of anyone." In re Merrill Lynch, Pierce, Fenner & Smith, Inc., 43 S.E.C. 933, 936 (1968). Thus, an insider will be liable under Rule 10b–5 for inside trading only where he fails to disclose material nonpublic information before trading on it and thus makes "secret profits."

III

We were explicit in *Chiarella* in saying that there can be no duty to disclose where the person who has traded on inside information "was not [the corporation's] agent, . . . was not a fiduciary, [or] was not a person in whom the sellers [of the securities] had placed their trust and confidence." Not to require such a fiduciary relationship, we recognized, would "[depart] radically from the established doctrine that duty arises from a specific relationship between two parties" and would amount to "recognizing a general duty between all participants in market transactions to forgo actions based on material, nonpublic information." This requirement of a specific relationship between the shareholders and the individual trading on inside information has created analytical difficulties for the SEC and courts in policing tippees who trade on inside information. Unlike insiders who have independent fiduciary duties to both the corporation and its shareholders, the typical tippee has no such relationships.* [14] In view of this absence, it has been unclear how a

---

*   [14] Under certain circumstances, such as where corporate information is revealed legitimately to an underwriter, accountant, lawyer, or consultant working for the corporation, these outsiders may become fiduciaries of the shareholders. The basis for recognizing this fiduciary duty is not simply that such persons acquired nonpublic corporate information, but

tippee acquires the *Cady, Roberts* duty to refrain from trading on inside information.

A

The SEC's position, as stated in its opinion in this case, is that a tippee "inherits" the *Cady, Roberts* obligation to shareholders whenever he receives inside information from an insider:

> In tipping potential traders, Dirks breached a duty which he had assumed as a result of knowingly receiving confidential information from [Equity Funding] insiders. Tippees such as Dirks who receive non-public, material information from insiders become "subject to the same duty as [the] insiders." Such a tippee breaches the fiduciary duty which he assumes from the insider when the tippee knowingly transmits the information to someone who will probably trade on the basis thereof. . . . Presumably, Dirks' informants were entitled to disclose the [Equity Funding] fraud in order to bring it to light and its perpetrators to justice. However, Dirks—standing in their shoes—committed a breach of the fiduciary duty which he had assumed in dealing with them, when he passed the information on to traders.

This view differs little from the view that we rejected as inconsistent with congressional intent in *Chiarella*. In that case, the Court of Appeals agreed with the SEC and affirmed Chiarella's conviction, holding that "[anyone]—corporate insider or not—who regularly receives material nonpublic information may not use that information to trade in securities without incurring an affirmative duty to disclose." United States v. Chiarella, 588 F.2d 1358, 1365 (CA2 1978). Here, the SEC maintains that anyone who knowingly receives nonpublic material information from an insider has a fiduciary duty to disclose before trading.* [15]

---

rather that they have entered into a special confidential relationship in the conduct of the business of the enterprise and are given access to information solely for corporate purposes. * * * When such a person breaches his fiduciary relationship, he may be treated more properly as a tipper than a tippee. *See* Shapiro v. Merrill Lynch, Pierce, Fenner & Smith, Inc., 495 F.2d 228, 237 (CA2 1974) (investment banker had access to material information when working on a proposed public offering for the corporation). For such a duty to be imposed, however, the corporation must expect the outsider to keep the disclosed nonpublic information confidential, and the relationship at least must imply such a duty.

    * **[15]** Apparently, the SEC believes this case differs from *Chiarella* in that Dirks' receipt of inside information from Secrist, an insider, carried Secrist's duties with it, while Chiarella received the information without the direct involvement of an insider and thus inherited no duty to disclose or abstain. The SEC fails to explain, however, why the receipt of non-public information from an insider automatically carries with it the fiduciary duty of the insider. As we emphasized in *Chiarella*, mere possession of nonpublic information does not give rise to a duty to disclose or abstain; only a specific relationship does that. And we do not believe that the mere receipt of information from an insider creates such a special relationship between the tippee and the corporation's shareholders.

In effect, the SEC's theory of tippee liability in both cases appears rooted in the idea that the antifraud provisions require equal information among all traders.* **[16]** This conflicts with the principle set forth in *Chiarella* that only some persons, under some circumstances, will be barred from trading while in possession of material nonpublic information. Judge Wright [in the Court of Appeals' consideration of this case] correctly read our opinion in *Chiarella* as repudiating any notion that all traders must enjoy equal information before trading: "[The] 'information' theory is rejected. Because the disclose-or-refrain duty is extraordinary, it attaches only when a party has legal obligations other than a mere duty to comply with the general antifraud proscriptions in the federal securities laws." We reaffirm today that "[a] duty [to disclose] arises from the relationship between parties . . . and not merely from one's ability to acquire information because of his position in the market."

Imposing a duty to disclose or abstain solely because a person knowingly receives material nonpublic information from an insider and trades on it could have an inhibiting influence on the role of market analysts, which the SEC itself recognizes is necessary to the preservation of a healthy market. It is commonplace for analysts to "ferret out and analyze information," and this often is done by meeting with and questioning corporate officers and others who are insiders. And information that the analysts obtain normally may be the basis for judgments as to the market worth of a corporation's securities. The analyst's judgment in this respect is made available in market letters or otherwise to clients of the firm. It is the nature of this type of information, and indeed of the markets themselves, that such information cannot be made simultaneously available to all of the corporation's stockholders or the public generally.

B

The conclusion that recipients of inside information do not invariably acquire a duty to disclose or abstain does not mean that such tippees always are free to trade on the information. The need for a ban on some tippee trading is clear. Not only are insiders forbidden by their fiduciary relationship from personally using undisclosed corporate information to their advantage, but they also may not give such information to an outsider for the same improper purpose of exploiting the information for their personal gain. * * * Thus, the tippee's duty to disclose or abstain is

---

Apparently recognizing the weakness of its argument in light of *Chiarella*, the SEC attempts to distinguish that case factually as involving not "inside" information, but rather "market" information, i.e., "information originating outside the company and usually about the supply and demand for the company's securities." This Court drew no such distinction in *Chiarella* and, as THE CHIEF JUSTICE noted, "[it] is clear that § 10(b) and Rule 10b–5 by their terms and by their history make no such distinction."

* **[16]** In *Chiarella*, we noted that formulation of an absolute equal information rule "should not be undertaken absent some explicit evidence of congressional intent." * * *

derivative from that of the insider's duty. As we noted in Chiarella, "[the] tippee's obligation has been viewed as arising from his role as a participant after the fact in the insider's breach of a fiduciary duty."

Thus, some tippees must assume an insider's duty to the shareholders not because they receive inside information, but rather because it has been made available to them improperly. And for Rule 10b–5 purposes, the insider's disclosure is improper only where it would violate his Cady, Roberts duty. Thus, a tippee assumes a fiduciary duty to the shareholders of a corporation not to trade on material nonpublic information only when the insider has breached his fiduciary duty to the shareholders by disclosing the information to the tippee and the tippee knows or should know that there has been a breach. As Commissioner Smith perceptively observed in In re Investors Management Co., 44 S.E.C. 633 (1971): "[Tippee] responsibility must be related back to insider responsibility by a necessary finding that the tippee knew the information was given to him in breach of a duty by a person having a special relationship to the issuer not to disclose the information. . . ." Tipping thus properly is viewed only as a means of indirectly violating the *Cady, Roberts* disclose-or-abstain rule.

C

In determining whether a tippee is under an obligation to disclose or abstain, it thus is necessary to determine whether the insider's "tip" constituted a breach of the insider's fiduciary duty. All disclosures of confidential corporate information are not inconsistent with the duty insiders owe to shareholders. In contrast to the extraordinary facts of this case, the more typical situation in which there will be a question whether disclosure violates the insider's *Cady, Roberts* duty is when insiders disclose information to analysts. * * * In some situations, the insider will act consistently with his fiduciary duty to shareholders, and yet release of the information may affect the market. For example, it may not be clear—either to the corporate insider or to the recipient analyst—whether the information will be viewed as material nonpublic information. Corporate officials may mistakenly think the information already has been disclosed or that it is not material enough to affect the market. Whether disclosure is a breach of duty therefore depends in large part on the purpose of the disclosure. This standard was identified by the SEC itself in *Cady, Roberts*: a purpose of the securities laws was to eliminate "use of inside information for personal advantage." Thus, the test is whether the insider personally will benefit, directly or indirectly, from his disclosure. Absent some personal gain, there has been no breach of duty to stockholders. And absent a breach by the insider, there is no derivative breach. As Commissioner Smith stated in *Investors Management Co.*: "It is important in this type of case to focus on policing insiders and what they do . . . rather than on policing information *per se* and its possession. . . ."

The SEC argues that, if inside-trading liability does not exist when the information is transmitted for a proper purpose but is used for trading, it would be a rare situation when the parties could not fabricate some ostensibly legitimate business justification for transmitting the information. We think the SEC is unduly concerned. In determining whether the insider's purpose in making a particular disclosure is fraudulent, the SEC and the courts are not required to read the parties' minds. Scienter in some cases is relevant in determining whether the tipper has violated his *Cady, Roberts* duty. But to determine whether the disclosure itself "[deceives], [manipulates], or [defrauds]" shareholders, *Aaron v. SEC*, 446 U.S. 680, 686 (1980), the initial inquiry is whether there has been a breach of duty by the insider. This requires courts to focus on objective criteria, i. e., whether the insider receives a direct or indirect personal benefit from the disclosure, such as a pecuniary gain or a reputational benefit that will translate into future earnings. * * * There are objective facts and circumstances that often justify such an inference. For example, there may be a relationship between the insider and the recipient that suggests a *quid pro quo* from the latter, or an intention to benefit the particular recipient. The elements of fiduciary duty and exploitation of nonpublic information also exist when an insider makes a gift of confidential information to a trading relative or friend. The tip and trade resemble trading by the insider himself followed by a gift of the profits to the recipient.

Determining whether an insider personally benefits from a particular disclosure, a question of fact, will not always be easy for courts. But it is essential, we think, to have a guiding principle for those whose daily activities must be limited and instructed by the SEC's inside-trading rules, and we believe that there must be a breach of the insider's fiduciary duty before the tippee inherits the duty to disclose or abstain. In contrast, the rule adopted by the SEC in this case would have no limiting principle.

IV

Under the inside-trading and tipping rules set forth above, we find that there was no actionable violation by Dirks. It is undisputed that Dirks himself was a stranger to Equity Funding, with no pre-existing fiduciary duty to its shareholders. He took no action, directly or indirectly, that induced the shareholders or officers of Equity Funding to repose trust or confidence in him. There was no expectation by Dirks' sources that he would keep their information in confidence. Nor did Dirks misappropriate or illegally obtain the information about Equity Funding. Unless the insiders breached their *Cady, Roberts* duty to shareholders in disclosing the nonpublic information to Dirks, he breached no duty when he passed it on to investors as well as to the *Wall Street Journal*.

It is clear that neither Secrist nor the other Equity Funding employees violated their *Cady, Roberts* duty to the corporation's shareholders by providing information to Dirks. The tippers received no monetary or personal benefit for revealing Equity Funding's secrets, nor was their purpose to make a gift of valuable information to Dirks. As the facts of this case clearly indicate, the tippers were motivated by a desire to expose the fraud. In the absence of a breach of duty to shareholders by the insiders, there was no derivative breach by Dirks. Dirks therefore could not have been "a participant after the fact in [an] insider's breach of a fiduciary duty." *Chiarella*, 445 U.S. at 230, n. 12.

V

We conclude that Dirks, in the circumstances of this case, had no duty to abstain from use of the inside information that he obtained. The judgment of the Court of Appeals therefore is Reversed.

* * *

BLACKMUN, J., with whom BRENNAN and MARSHALL, J.J. join, dissenting.

The Court today takes still another step to limit the protections provided investors by § 10(b) of the Securities Exchange Act of 1934. *See* Chiarella v. United States, 445 U.S. 222, 246 (1980) (dissenting opinion). The device employed in this case engrafts a special motivational requirement on the fiduciary duty doctrine. This innovation excuses a knowing and intentional violation of an insider's duty to shareholders if the insider does not act from a motive of personal gain. Even on the extraordinary facts of this case, such an innovation is not justified. * * *

QUESTIONS AND NOTES

1.   What did Dirks do wrong? Did he deserve punishment, or a reward?

2.   According to the Court in *Dirks*, what must be shown to impose liability on someone as a tipper?

3.   What must be shown to impose liability on someone as a tippee?

4.   If a tipper tips a tippee, but the tippee does not act on the tip, has anyone violated Rule 10b–5?

5.   Why can there be no tippee liability under Rule 10b–5 if there is no tipper?

6.   Note that when the case was filed, Secrist was a *former* officer of Equity Funding. This fact could not help him under Rule 10b–5, however, because he allegedly obtained the information while serving as an officer.

7.   Footnote 14 discusses the possibility of "temporary insiders," also described by those familiar with *Dirks* as "footnote 14 insiders." For the purposes of insider trading, the law treats people in a law firm, accounting firm, or other professional group that is working for a corporation the same as if they were full-time employees of the corporation. For example, if a

lawyer whom the corporation has temporarily hired trades on the corporation's inside information, the lawyer violates Rule 10b–5 just as if he were the corporation's full-time employee. This answers Question 2 before *Dirks*.

8. Does *Dirks* permit us to answer Question 4 before the case? Yes. The CEO would be liable because he disclosed confidential information to his teammate, he received a benefit for his disclosure because the teammate paid him for the information, and the teammate traded on the information.

9. Since 1966, Dean Henry Manne has argued that insider trading would be an efficient way to compensate insiders without harming investors. Indeed, Manne and others have argued that permitting corporate officers to make money by using confidential inside information could increase the value of the corporation for which the insider works: the opportunity to reap trading profits because good things had happened for the corporation that the public did not yet know about would motivate these insiders to make such good things happen. *See generally* Henry G. Manne, INSIDER TRADING AND THE STOCK MARKET 138–41 (1996); Symposium, *The Legacy of Henry G. Manne—Pioneer in Law & Economics and Innovator in Legal Education*, 50 CASE W. RES. L. REV. 1 (1999). Are there ways other than insider trading that an officer can be compensated if she improves her corporation's performance?

Manne also pointed out that shareholders who just randomly happen to sell their shares during the period when insiders are purchasing shares based on inside information actually *benefit* from the insider trading. Can you see why?

10. Barry Switzer, the former coach of the Dallas Cowboys and Oklahoma sooners, was once sunbathing in the stands at his son's track meet. He happened to overhear the CEO of a company and the CEO's wife talking below him about how several other companies had begun bidding for the CEO's company. Switzer quickly bought shares in the CEO's company. Applying the *Dirks* test, was Switzer guilty of insider trading? The court said no, because the CEO had not received any benefit when Switzer heard him. "Rule 10b–5 does not bar trading on the basis of information inadvertently revealed by an insider." Nor was the CEO liable. *SEC v. Switzer*, 590 F.Supp. 756 (W.D. Okla. 1984). So we now have the answer to Question 1 before *Dirks*.

11. Although inadvertent disclosure will not lead to liability for insider trading, it can lead to great trouble. The American Lawyer published an article about lawyer tipping from which the following is an excerpt. It reminds us of the posters from World War II: "Loose lips sink ships."

> In January, Julie Freese was one of the young associates at San Francisco's Brobeck, Phleger & Harrison we wrote about in "Still Golden." Freese, we noted, was running her own deals, characteristic of the responsibility given to Brobeck associates during the dot-com boom.

Like the stock market itself, Freese has since fallen to earth. The second-year M & A associate resigned from the firm's Palo Alto office in March in the wake of an insider trading investigation of Joel Mesplou, a Palo Alto stock trader.

Mesplou made more than $400,000 after he learned privileged information from Freese about Sun Microsystems, Inc.'s acquisition of Cobalt Networks.

Freese—who is simply referred to as an associate at Brobeck in the court papers—has not been charged with anything. Her lawyer, Nanci Clarence, says Mesplou was already familiar with the possibility of the pending transaction when Freese unintentionally mentioned something about it. "She made an inadvertent statement while talking about the nature of her work," says Clarence.

Clarence explains that her client had met Mesplou at a "very crowded party" last September. A couple of weeks later—after working grueling hours on the deal—Freese ran into Mesplou a second time and indirectly mentioned what was keeping her so busy, Clarence says.

James Burns, Jr., Brobeck's managing partner, says that the firm learned of the investigation and Freese's connection to it in mid-January, when Freese told the lead partner on the Sun-Cobalt transaction that she had been questioned by authorities. Soon afterward, when Freese was questioned further, she was placed on administrative leave according to firm policy. In March she voluntarily resigned.

Amy Fantini, *Youthful Indiscretions,* THE AMERICAN LAWYER (May 2001).

12. The fact that you might not be liable under Rule 10b–5 does not mean that you are home free. There are many other securities laws that might impose liability, as well as other federal statutes such as those involving mail fraud. You can study all of the legal traps in a course on securities regulation or white collar crime.

But let's discuss one example. Section 14(e) of the '34 Act (added in the Williams Act) is aimed at fraud in connection with tender offers—where someone, in order to gain control of a company, attempts to purchase a large number of a company's shares from the existing shareholders. Under this statute, the SEC promulgated Rule 14e–3(a), which makes it unlawful to trade on material nonpublic information concerning a tender offer. Under that Rule, the information might come from the acquiring company or the target or insiders or others working for either the acquiring or target company—just so the defendant knows or should know that the information is nonpublic. Thus, a person who overheard information about a tender offer might violate Rule 14e–3(a) even though he did not violate Rule 10b–5.

13. One important question is whether "secondary" violators can be held liable under the disclosure requirements of Rule 10b–5. For example,

suppose a corporation violated Rule 10b–5 in issuing its stock. Obviously, defrauded investors can sue the corporation. Often, however, the business has no assets. So plaintiffs routinely joined "secondary" or "collateral" participants—such as the corporation's accountants, bankers, directors, and officers—for aiding and abetting the corporation's violation of Rule 10b–5.

The Supreme Court rejected the effort in *Central Bank of Denver, N.A. v. First Interstate Bank of Denver, N.A.*, 511 U.S. 164 (1994), by holding that there can be no liability—at least in a civil case—for aiding and abetting a violation of Rule 10b–5.

We note two reactions to the holding in *Central Bank of Denver*. First, Congress, in the Private Securities Litigation Reform Act of 1995, expressly embraced liability for "aiding and abetting" violations of the securities laws (including, obviously, Rule 10b–5). The provision does so, however, only for cases brought by the Securities and Exchange Commission; so aiding and abetting is not a viable theory in private actions.

Second, enterprising plaintiffs' lawyers attempted to find ways around the holding in *Central Bank of Denver. See, e.g., In re Enron Corporation Securities, Derivative & ERISA Litig.*, 235 F.Supp.2d 549 (S.D. Tex. 2002) (concerning potential liability of such secondary actors as law and accounting firms and banks in the collapse of Enron). One such effort was something called "scheme liability," essentially arguing that secondary players are part of the same scheme as the primary violator of Rule 10b–5.

The Supreme Court rejected the effort and reaffirmed its holding from *Central Bank of Denver* in *Stoneridge Investment Partners, LLC v. Scientific-Atlanta, Inc.*, 552 U.S. 148 (2008). In that case, the operator of a cable television system agreed to pay two companies (Motorola and Scientific-Atlanta) additional funds for cable boxes; those companies then returned a portion of the money to the cable operator, as part of an effort to make its books look better, in violation of Rule 10b–5. The Court held that Motorola and Scientific-Atlanta could not be held liable because they had neither made statements to investors nor participated in the cable operator's statements to investors. Accordingly, investors in the cable operator could not have relied upon anything Motorola or Scientific-Atlanta said. Without reliance, there could be no Rule 10b–5 violation.

What about the situation in Question 5 before *Dirks*, where a person trades on confidential information about a corporation, where he has stolen the information from some other business where he works? The Supreme Court finally addressed the "misappropriation theory" definitively in the following case, which involves the sad story of a badly-behaved lawyer in Minnesota.

UNITED STATES V. O'HAGAN

United States Supreme Court, 1997
521 U.S. 642

GINSBURG, J. [O'Hagan was a partner in the Minneapolis law firm of Dorsey & Whitney. In July 1988, an English company (Grand Metropolitan PLC, or "Grand Met") retained the firm concerning a potential tender offer to acquire Pillsbury Company, which was headquartered in Minneapolis. The tender offer was announced publicly on October 4, 1988. Although O'Hagan was not working on the Grand Met-Pillsbury transaction, he learned of it. In August and September 1988, he bought Pillsbury stock and options to acquire Pillsbury stock. After the tender offer was announced and the price of Pillsbury stock rose, O'Hagan sold the stock for a profit of $4,300,000.

He was charged in a 57-count federal indictment, which included 17 counts of securities fraud in violation of Rule 10b-5. According to the indictment, by the way, O'Hagan used the profits from the alleged insider trading to replenish client trust funds from which he had converted money. O'Hagan was convicted on this point in state court and was, not surprisingly, disbarred. A jury convicted O'Hagan of all 57 federal counts, and O'Hagan appealed to the United States Court of Appeals for the Eighth Circuit.

That court reversed the convictions on all counts. The Supreme Court agreed to hear the case. In the portion of the opinion set forth below, the Supreme Court addresses whether O'Hagan should be convicted under Rule 10b-5. The Court concludes that he should, and adopts a version of the "misappropriation theory" of Rule 10b-5.]

* * *

II

We address first the Court of Appeals' reversal of O'Hagan's convictions under § 10(b) and Rule 10b-5. Following the Fourth Circuit's lead, the Eighth Circuit rejected the misappropriation theory as a basis for § 10(b) liability. We hold, in accord with several other Courts of Appeals, that criminal liability under § 10(b) may be predicated on the misappropriation theory.* **[4]**

A

* * *

---

*   **[4]** Twice before we have been presented with the question whether criminal liability for violation of § 10(b) may be based on a misappropriation theory. In *Chiarella v. United States*, 445 U.S. 222, 235–237 (1980), the jury had received no misappropriation theory instructions, so we declined to address the question. In Carpenter v. United States, 484 U.S. 19, 24 (1987), the Court divided evenly on whether, under the circumstances of that case, convictions resting on the misappropriation theory should be affirmed. * * *

Under the "traditional" or "classical theory" of insider trading liability, § 10(b) and Rule 10b–5 are violated when a corporate insider trades in the securities of his corporation on the basis of material, nonpublic information. Trading on such information qualifies as a "deceptive device" under § 10(b), we have affirmed, because "a relationship of trust and confidence [exists] between the shareholders of a corporation and those insiders who have obtained confidential information by reason of their position with that corporation." Chiarella v. United States, 445 U.S. 222, 228 (1980). That relationship, we recognized, "gives rise to a duty to disclose [or to abstain from trading] because of the 'necessity of preventing a corporate insider from . . . taking unfair advantage of . . . uninformed . . . stockholders.' " The classical theory applies not only to officers, directors, and other permanent insiders of a corporation, but also to attorneys, accountants, consultants, and others who temporarily become fiduciaries of a corporation. *See* Dirks v. SEC, 463 U.S. 646, 655, n. 14 (1983).

The "misappropriation theory" holds that a person commits fraud "in connection with" a securities transaction, and thereby violates § 10(b) and Rule 10b–5, when he misappropriates confidential information for securities trading purposes, in breach of a duty owed to the source of the information. * * * Under this theory, a fiduciary's undisclosed, self-serving use of a principal's information to purchase or sell securities, in breach of a duty of loyalty and confidentiality, defrauds the principal of the exclusive use of that information. In lieu of premising liability on a fiduciary relationship between company insider and purchaser or seller of the company's stock, the misappropriation theory premises liability on a fiduciary-turned-trader's deception of those who entrusted him with access to confidential information.

The two theories are complementary, each addressing efforts to capitalize on nonpublic information through the purchase or sale of securities. The classical theory targets a corporate insider's breach of duty to shareholders with whom the insider transacts; the misappropriation theory outlaws trading on the basis of nonpublic information by a corporate "outsider" in breach of a duty owed not to a trading party, but to the source of the information. The misappropriation theory is thus designed to "protect the integrity of the securities markets against abuses by 'outsiders' to a corporation who have access to confidential information that will affect the corporation's security price when revealed, but who owe no fiduciary or other duty to that corporation's shareholders."

In this case, the indictment alleged that O'Hagan, in breach of a duty of trust and confidence he owed to his law firm, Dorsey & Whitney, and to its client, Grand Met, traded on the basis of nonpublic information regarding Grand Met's planned tender offer for Pillsbury common stock.

This conduct, the Government charged, constituted a fraudulent device in connection with the purchase and sale of securities.* **[5]**

B

We agree with the Government that misappropriation, as just defined, satisfies § 10(b)'s requirement that chargeable conduct involve a "deceptive device or contrivance" used "in connection with" the purchase or sale of securities. We observe, first, that misappropriators, as the Government describes them, deal in deception. A fiduciary who "[pretends] loyalty to the principal while secretly converting the principal's information for personal gain," * * * "dupes" or defrauds the principal. * * *

We addressed fraud of the same species in *Carpenter v. United States*, 484 U.S. 19 (1987), which involved the mail fraud statute's proscription of "any scheme or artifice to defraud," 18 U.S.C. § 1341. Affirming convictions under that statute, we said in *Carpenter* that an employee's undertaking not to reveal his employer's confidential information "became a sham" when the employee provided the information to his co-conspirators in a scheme to obtain trading profits. A company's confidential information, we recognized in *Carpenter*, qualifies as property to which the company has a right of exclusive use. The undisclosed misappropriation of such information, in violation of a fiduciary duty, the Court said in *Carpenter*, constitutes fraud akin to embezzlement—"the fraudulent appropriation to one's own use of the money or goods entrusted to one's care by another." *Carpenter's* discussion of the fraudulent misuse of confidential information, the Government notes, "is a particularly apt source of guidance here, because [the mail fraud statute] (like Section 10(b)) has long been held to require deception, not merely the breach of a fiduciary duty." * * *

Deception through nondisclosure is central to the theory of liability for which the Government seeks recognition. As counsel for the Government stated in explanation of the theory at oral argument: "To satisfy the common law rule that a trustee may not use the property that [has] been entrusted [to] him, there would have to be consent. To satisfy the requirement of the Securities Act that there be no deception, there would only have to be disclosure."* **[6]**

---

*   **[5]** The Government could not have prosecuted O'Hagan under the classical theory, for O'Hagan was not an "insider" of Pillsbury, the corporation in whose stock he traded. Although an "outsider" with respect to Pillsbury, O'Hagan had an intimate association with, and was found to have traded on confidential information from, Dorsey & Whitney, counsel to tender offeror Grand Met. Under the misappropriation theory, O'Hagan's securities trading does not escape Exchange Act sanction, as it would under the dissent's reasoning, simply because he was associated with, and gained nonpublic information from, the bidder, rather than the target.

*   **[6]** Under the misappropriation theory urged in this case, the disclosure obligation runs to the source of the information, here, Dorsey & Whitney and Grand Met. Chief Justice Burger, dissenting in *Chiarella*, advanced a broader reading of § 10(b) and Rule 10b–5; the disclosure obligation, as he envisioned it, ran to those with whom the misappropriator trades. 445 U.S. at

The misappropriation theory advanced by the Government is consistent with *Santa Fe Industries, Inc. v. Green*, 430 U.S. 462 (1977), a decision underscoring that § 10(b) is not an all-purpose breach of fiduciary duty ban; rather, it trains on conduct involving manipulation or deception. In contrast to the Government's allegations in this case, in *Santa Fe Industries*, all pertinent facts were disclosed by the persons charged with violating § 10(b) and Rule 10b–5, therefore, there was no deception through nondisclosure to which liability under those provisions could attach. Similarly, full disclosure forecloses liability under the misappropriation theory: Because the deception essential to the misappropriation theory involves feigning fidelity to the source of information, if the fiduciary discloses to the source that he plans to trade on the nonpublic information, there is no "deceptive device" and thus no § 10(b) violation—although the fiduciary-turned-trader may remain liable under state law for breach of a duty of loyalty.* **[7]**

We turn next to the § 10(b) requirement that the misappropriator's deceptive use of information be "in connection with the purchase or sale of [a] security." This element is satisfied because the fiduciary's fraud is consummated, not when the fiduciary gains the confidential information, but when, without disclosure to his principal, he uses the information to purchase or sell securities. The securities transaction and the breach of duty thus coincide. This is so even though the person or entity defrauded is not the other party to the trade, but is, instead, the source of the nonpublic information. * * * A misappropriator who trades on the basis of material, nonpublic information, in short, gains his advantageous market position through deception; he deceives the source of the information and simultaneously harms members of the investing public.

The misappropriation theory targets information of a sort that misappropriators ordinarily capitalize upon to gain no-risk profits through the purchase or sale of securities. Should a misappropriator put such information to other use, the statute's prohibition would not be implicated. The theory does not catch all conceivable forms of fraud involving confidential information; rather, it catches fraudulent means of capitalizing on such information through securities transactions.

      * * *

The misappropriation theory comports with § 10(b)'s language, which requires deception "in connection with the purchase or sale of any

---

240 ("a person who has misappropriated nonpublic information has an absolute duty to disclose that information or to refrain from trading"). * * * The Government does not propose that we adopt a misappropriation theory of that breadth.

   * **[7]** Where, however, a person trading on the basis of material, nonpublic information owes a duty of loyalty and confidentiality to two entities or persons—for example, a law firm and its client—but makes disclosure to only one, the trader may still be liable under the misappropriation theory.

security," not deception of an identifiable purchaser or seller. The theory is also well-tuned to an animating purpose of the Exchange Act: to insure honest securities markets and thereby promote investor confidence. * * * Although informational disparity is inevitable in the securities markets, investors likely would hesitate to venture their capital in a market where trading based on misappropriated nonpublic information is unchecked by law. An investor's informational disadvantage vis-a-vis a misappropriator with material, nonpublic information stems from contrivance, not luck; it is a disadvantage that cannot be overcome with research or skill. * * *

In sum, considering the inhibiting impact on market participation of trading on misappropriated information, and the congressional purposes underlying § 10(b), it makes scant sense to hold a lawyer like O'Hagan a § 10(b) violator if he works for a law firm representing the target of a tender offer, but not if he works for a law firm representing the bidder. The text of the statute requires no such result. The misappropriation at issue here was properly made the subject of a § 10(b) charge because it meets the statutory requirement that there be "deceptive" conduct "in connection with" securities transactions.

C

The Court of Appeals rejected the misappropriation theory primarily on two grounds. First, as the Eighth Circuit comprehended the theory, it requires neither misrepresentation nor nondisclosure. As just explained, however, deceptive nondisclosure is essential to the § 10(b) liability at issue. Concretely, in this case, "it [was O'Hagan's] failure to disclose his personal trading to Grand Met and Dorsey, in breach of his duty to do so, that made his conduct 'deceptive' within the meaning of [§]10(b)."

Second and "more obvious," the Court of Appeals said, the misappropriation theory is not moored to § 10(b)'s requirement that "the fraud be 'in connection with the purchase or sale of any security.'" According to the Eighth Circuit, [*Chiarella* and other] of our decisions reveal that § 10(b) liability cannot be predicated on a duty owed to the source of nonpublic information * * *.

* * *

The Court did not hold in *Chiarella* that the only relationship prompting liability for trading on undisclosed information is the relationship between a corporation's insiders and shareholders. That is evident from our response to the Government's argument before this Court that the printer's misappropriation of information from his employer for purposes of securities trading—in violation of a duty of confidentiality owed to the acquiring companies—constituted fraud in connection with the purchase or sale of a security, and thereby satisfied the terms of § 10(b). The Court declined to reach that potential basis for the printer's liability, because the theory had not been submitted to the jury. But four Justices found merit in it. * * *

Chiarella thus expressly left open the misappropriation theory before us today. * * *

Dirks, too, left room for application of the misappropriation theory in cases like the one we confront. * * *

QUESTIONS AND NOTES

1. Can you see how, under *O'Hagan,* Question 5 from before *Dirks* would come out—the one about the printing company? The receptionist would be liable, wouldn't he, because he stole his company's information just like Mr. O'Hagan?

2. The case also shows how to answer Question 3 before *Dirks*. Mr. O'Hagan was liable even though he purchased stock in the *target* company about which he had inside information, rather than in the *acquiring* company for which his law firm was working.

3. Could O'Hagan have been charged as a temporary insider, as defined in footnote 14 of *Dirks?*

4. What if, before purchasing the Pillsbury stock, O'Hagan had told his law firm about his intentions to do that?

5. Could Grand Met have sued Whitney & Dorsey for misappropriation by O'Hagan? Could Grand Met have sued the other partners of the law firm? Interestingly, that firm did not become a limited liability partnership until 1996. Recall from Chapter 3 that in a limited liability partnership, individual partners are not on the hook for business debts. Do you think the *O'Hagan* case might have been a reason for adopting LLP status?

6. It appears that Osama Bin Laden and his terrorist network, knowing in advance of the September 11, 2001 attacks on the World Trade Center, may have sold short stocks of various U.S. airlines and purchased put options on them. Short sales and put options are both financial bets that the stocks will decline in price. Because the prices of the airline stocks declined sharply after 9/11, the short sales and puts earned profits of approximately $2.5 million. Christian Berthelsen, et al., *Suspicious Profits Sit Uncollected*, SAN FRANCISCO CHRONICLE, p. A–1, (September 29, 2001). Was Osama Bin Laden guilty of insider trading under Rule 10b–5?

7. Please make sure you understand how the notes and questions after *Dirks* and *O'Hagan* have answered all of the questions before *Dirks*.

8. Again, Rule 10b–5 is only one of many federal securities and related provisions. Mr. O'Hagan was convicted not only under Rule 10b–5, but under Rule 14e–3(a), and money laundering provisions. While most of these (other than Rule 10b–5) are the focus of other courses, there is one other major federal securities regulation we must address here. It's next.

f.   Section 16(b) and Short-Swing Trading

Read §§ 16 (a) and 16 (b) of the '34 Act.

RELIANCE ELECTRIC CO. V. EMERSON ELECTRIC CO.

United States Supreme Court, 1972
404 U.S. 418

STEWART, J. Section 16(b) of the Securities Exchange Act of 1934 provides, among other things, that a corporation may recover for itself the profits realized by an owner of more than 10% of its shares from a purchase and sale of its stock within any six-month period, provided that the owner held more than 10% "both at the time of the purchase and sale."* **[1]** In this case, the respondent, the owner of 13.2% of a corporation's shares, disposed of its entire holdings in two sales, both of them within six months of purchase. The first sale reduced the respondent's holdings to 9.96%, and the second disposed of the remainder. The question presented is whether the profits derived from the second sale are recoverable by the Corporation under § 16(b). We hold that they are not.

On June 16, 1967, the respondent, Emerson Electric Co., acquired 13.2% of the outstanding common stock of Dodge Manufacturing Co., pursuant to a tender offer made in an unsuccessful attempt to take over Dodge. The purchase price for this stock was $63 per share. Shortly thereafter, the shareholders of Dodge approved a merger with the petitioner, Reliance Electric Co. Faced with the certain failure of any further attempt to take over Dodge, and with the prospect of being forced to exchange its Dodge shares for stock in the merged corporation in the near future, Emerson, following a plan outlined by its general counsel, decided to dispose of enough shares to bring its holdings below 10%, in order to immunize the disposal of the remainder of its shares from liability under § 16(b). Pursuant to counsel's recommendation, Emerson on August 28 sold 37,000 shares of Dodge common stock to a brokerage

---

* **[1]** Section 16(b) provides:

For the purpose of preventing the unfair use of information which may have been obtained by such beneficial owner, director, or officer by reason of his relationship to the issuer, any profit realized by him from any purchase and sale, or any sale and purchase, of any equity security of such issuer (other than an exempted security) within any period of less than six months . . . shall inure to and be recoverable by the issuer, irrespective of any intention on the part of such beneficial owner, director, or officer in entering into such transaction of holding the security purchased or of not repurchasing the security sold for a period exceeding six months . . . This subsection shall not be construed to cover any transaction where such beneficial owner was not such both at the time of the purchase and sale, or the sale and purchase, of the security involved, or any transaction or transactions which the Commission by rules and regulations may exempt as not comprehended within the purpose of this subsection. 15 U.S.C. § 78p(b). The term "such beneficial owner" refers to one who owns "more than 10 per centum of any class of any equity security (other than an exempted security) which is registered pursuant to section (12) of this title." Securities Exchange Act of 1934, § 16(a), 15 U.S.C. § 78p(a).

house at $68 per share. This sale reduced Emerson's holdings in Dodge to 9.96% of the outstanding common stock. The remaining shares were then sold to Dodge at $69 per share on September 11.

After a demand on it by Reliance for the profits realized on both sales, Emerson filed this action seeking a declaratory judgment as to its liability under § 16(b). Emerson first claimed that it was not liable at all, because it was not a 10% owner at the time of the purchase of the Dodge shares. The District Court disagreed, holding that a purchase of stock falls within § 16(b) where the purchaser becomes a 10% owner by virtue of the purchase. The Court of Appeals affirmed this holding, and Emerson did not cross-petition for certiorari. Thus that question is not before us.

Emerson alternatively argued to the District Court that, assuming it was a 10% stockholder at the time of the purchase, it was liable only for the profits on the August 28 sale of 37,000 shares, because after that time it was no longer a 10% owner within the meaning of § 16(b). After trial on the issue of liability alone, the District Court held Emerson liable for the entire amount of its profits. The court found that Emerson's sales of Dodge stock were "effected pursuant to a single predetermined plan of disposition with the overall intent and purpose of avoiding Section 16(b) liability," and construed the term "time of . . . sale" to include "the entire period during which a series of related transactions take place pursuant to a plan by which a 10% beneficial owner disposes of his stock, holdings."

On an interlocutory appeal under 28 U.S.C. § 1292(b), the Court of Appeals upheld the finding that Emerson "split" its sale of Dodge stock simply in order to avoid most of its potential liability under § 16(b), but it held this fact irrelevant under the statute so long as the two sales are "not legally tied to each other and (are) made at different times to different buyers. . . ." Accordingly, the Court of Appeals reversed the District Court's judgment as to Emerson's liability for its profits on the September 11 sale, and remanded for a determination of the amount of Emerson's liability on the August 28 sale. Reliance filed a petition for certiorari, which we granted in order to consider an unresolved question under an important federal statute.

The history and purpose of § 16(b) have been exhaustively reviewed by federal courts on several occasions since its enactment in 1934. Those courts have recognized that the only method Congress deemed effective to curb the evils of insider trading was a flat rule taking the profits out of a class of transactions in which the possibility of abuse was believed to be intolerably great.

Thus Congress did not reach every transaction in which an investor actually relies on inside information. A person avoids liability if he does not meet the statutory definition of an "insider," or if he sells more than six months after purchase. Liability cannot be imposed simply because the investor structured his transaction with the intent of avoiding liability under § 16(b). The question is, rather, whether the method used to "avoid" liability is one permitted by the statute.

Among the "objective standards" contained in § 16(b) is the requirement that a 10% owner be such "both at the time of the purchase and sale . . . of the security involved." Read literally, this language clearly contemplates that a statutory insider might sell enough shares to bring his holdings below 10%, and later—but still within six months—sell additional shares free from liability under the statute. Indeed, commentators on the securities laws have recommended this exact procedure for a 10% owner who, like Emerson, wishes to dispose of his holdings within six months of their purchase.

Under the approach urged by Reliance, and adopted by the District Court, the apparent immunity of profits derived from Emerson's second sale is lost where the two sales, though independent in every other respect, are "interrelated parts of a single plan." But a "plan" to sell that is conceived within six months of purchase clearly would not fall within § 16(b) if the sale were made after the six months had expired, and we see no basis in the statute for a different result where the 10% requirement is involved rather than the six-month limitation. * * *

The judgment is affirmed.

QUESTIONS AND NOTES

1.   The seller in *Reliance Electric* was correct that the sale of stock that took it from owning 9.96 percent to zero was not covered by § 16(b). Note, however, that it abandoned the argument that its original purchase—the one that took it from zero to owning 13.2 percent—should not be covered. Bad move. In a later case, the Supreme Court held that such a purchase is not covered under the provision of § 16(b) relating to shareholders. *Foremost-McKesson, Inc. v. Provident Securities Co.*, 423 U.S. 232 (1976).

So to determine whether one qualifies as one who owns more than ten percent of the stock under § 16(b), one takes a snap shot of the level of ownership immediately *before* both the buy and the sell. To qualify, one must own more than 10% at both times.

Roberts owns no stock in Bubba's Burritos, Inc. He then purchases 15 percent of the company's stock. That purchase is not covered under § 16(b), *because* immediately before the purchase, his ownership was zero. Now Roberts buys an additional five percent of the Bubba's stock. That purchase is covered, because he was above ten percent when he made this purchase. Now Roberts sells all 20 percent of the Bubba's stock. That sale is covered, because he was above ten percent when he made the sale. The profit on the purchase and sale on 5% would be calculated in the method explored in the Problems below.

Don't get so focused on the percentage of ownership that you forget who else falls within § 16(b). If Roberts were an officer or director of Bubba's either when he bought or sold, he would be covered by the statute—regardless of how much Bubba's stock he owned. If the reason for this is not clear, look at the language of § 16(b) again. It clearly applies its (very mechanical) rule to three types of corporate big-shots: officers, directors and shareholders with more than ten percent of the corporation's stock. We will do more with this with some Problems at the end of these notes.

2.   Section 16(b) applies only to large corporations—those which are required to register under § 12 of the '34 Act. So the statute basically creates problems only for the "big machers" of publicly traded corporations. This is different from Rule 10b–5, which has no such size limitation.

3.   Compare § 16(b) and Rule 10b–5. In *Reliance*, why didn't someone bring an action under Rule 10b–5?

4.   The policy behind § 16(b) was to deter transactions that have a high potential for fraud. However, Congress determined that it was not practical to require proof of improper intent or scienter in cases of insider trading, and thus, § 16(b) was written to impose strict liability.

The statute does not require proof that the trading information was improperly obtained. It is enough to prove an insider relationship that gives rise to the potential that improper information "may have been obtained" and utilized in the trade. We find a "clear congressional intent to provide a catch-all, prophylactic remedy, not requiring proof of actual misconduct." *First Golden Bancorporation v. Weiszmann*, 942 F.2d 726, 729 (10th Cir. 1991).

5.   The *Reliance Electric* case was a declaratory judgment action by the seller of corporate stock to determine its possible liability under § 16(b). Who is usually the plaintiff in a § 16(b) action? How does that plaintiff discover that it has a § 16(b) cause of action? *See* § 16(a) of the '34 Act. Notice how § 16(a) requires disclosure that would make a § 16(b) case easy.

6.   Section 16(b) creates a claim for the corporation. Accordingly, if the corporation does not bring the suit, a shareholder may do so through the device of the shareholder derivative suit, which we studied in Chapter 6, at p. 208. Unlike other derivative suits, under § 16(b), a shareholder need not make demand on the directors to bring the suit. In addition, the shareholder-plaintiff need not have owned stock when the claim arose; owning it at the time the case is filed is sufficient. Why would § 16(b) suits be subject to these different rules?

7.   "In general, insiders may plan their transactions to avoid the literal language of the statute (§ 16(b)) and thus escape or reduce liability." Peter G. Samuels, *Liability for Short-Swing Profits and Reporting Obligations Under Section 16(b) of the Securities Exchange Act of 1934*, in PLI Securities Filing 2000, 1205 PLI/Corp 603 (October 5, 2000). Do you agree? You will be in a better position to understand § 16(b) and this statement when you take the Securities Regulation course or, if your professor insists, after you work through the following problems.

PROBLEMS

1.   The stock of Bubba's Burritos, Inc. is registered under the '34 Act with 1,000,000 shares outstanding. Roberts is not a director or an officer. Initially, he has no shares of Bubba's. He then buys 200,000 shares at $10 a share on January 20. What is his § 16(b) liability if:

    a)   On May 1, he sells all 200,000 shares for $30 a share?

    b)   On May 1, he sells 110,000 shares for $30 a share, and on May 10, he sells the other 90,000 shares for $40 a share?

2.   Same facts as Problem 1 except that Roberts was also a director of Bubba's.

3.   Freer is an officer of Bubba's Burritos, Inc. Its stock is registered under the '34 Act. Freer owns 200,000 of the 1,000,000 outstanding shares of Bubba's. He bought the stock two years ago for $70 a share. On January 15, Freer sells 100,000 shares for $30 a share. On March 1, Freer buys 110,000 shares for $20 a share. Who can sue whom for what under § 16(b)?

C. DIVIDENDS

1. WHAT IS A DIVIDEND?

We have already seen dividends in *Giannotti* and in several of the other cases we have considered. To understand dividends, we first need to understand the definition of a "distribution." A distribution is a payment by the corporation to a shareholder depending on how many shares the shareholder owns. In turn, a dividend is a "special type of distribution, a payment to shareholders by the corporation out of its current or retained earnings in proportion to the number of shares owned by the shareholder." Robert W. Hamilton, BUSINESS ORGANIZATIONS: ESSENTIAL TERMS AND CONCEPTS 434 (1996). That is, a dividend is a payment that a shareholder receives per share that she owns.

A salary that a shareholder receives to manage the corporation would not be a distribution. The salary does not depend on how many shares the shareholder owns.

There can be distributions other than dividends. For example, a corporation makes a distribution to you if it repurchases your stock.

2. WHY DO CORPORATIONS PAY DIVIDENDS?

Most don't. And for those that do, the dividends are usually small. We have already seen that most close corporations do not pay dividends. Neither do small growth companies; they usually have no money to distribute because they often have few profits and must reinvest their profits to survive and keep growing.

Of large public corporations, only about half regularly declare dividends. And the size of the dividends is only a modest fraction of their profits. For example, the companies in the S&P 500 index distribute only about a third of their profits as dividends.

Whether to pay dividends is a management decision, to be made by the board of directors. Usually, the decision is protected by the business judgment rule. How do the directors decide?

Here's the general rule about how a corporation should decide whether to pay a dividend. The corporation should not pay a dividend if the returns that it can earn with the money are higher than the returns that the shareholder could earn if the money were distributed to them. That is, a corporation might appropriately pay no dividend because it has attractive investment opportunities that might be missed if it paid dividends. If the corporation makes these investments instead of paying dividends, it increases the value of the shares by more than the amount of the lost dividends.

For example, suppose that the company has opportunities to earn 20% with the money, but the shareholders can earn only 5% if the money is distributed to them and they invest it themselves. It is in the interests of the shareholders for the company to retain the money rather than to pay it in dividends. If the funds are distributed as a dividend, the shareholders receive a return of only 5%. In contrast, if the money is retained, the company, and indirectly its shareholders, earn a 20% return on the money. The shareholders benefit from the 20% return because it causes the company's stock price to increase proportionately, so that shareholders enjoy a capital gain. Shareholders receive capital appreciation greater than the dividends that they missed. Moreover, such capital gains have historically been taxed at lower effective rates than dividends.

In contrast, a corporation might consider a dividend if the company lacks any special investment opportunities—if the corporation's investment returns are no better than the returns that the shareholders could obtain if they invested the money themselves. This helps to explain Microsoft's recent large dividends. The company has large amounts of cash, but no especially lucrative projects in which to invest it.

The company run by Warren Buffet, the famously successful investor, has never paid a dividend for exactly these reasons. As Buffet notes in the following article, he thinks he can obtain a higher return for the shareholders if he reinvests the company's profits than if he distributed the company's profits, and the shareholders invested themselves.

Even some of Warren Buffett's friends want him to pay a cash dividend, but so far he's sticking with his no-dividend policy. And he wants those friends, and all of Berkshire Hathaway Inc.'s 600,000 shareholders, to know why. So his latest letter to shareholders includes a 2,100-word essay on why some companies pay dividends but not Berkshire, the company Buffett heads as chairman and CEO.*

Shareholders by now are familiar with the fact that Buffett has never paid a dividend on Berkshire stock, preferring to keep the company's cash—now at about $47 billion—within the business so it can be invested in new stocks or used to buy whole businesses. "It puzzles them that we relish the dividends we receive from most of the stocks that Berkshire owns, but pay out nothing ourselves," Buffett wrote. Many companies pay annual or quarterly dividends to shareholders out of the profits they earn, or use profits to buy back their stock.

Because of his success at investing Berkshire's profits, he said, "our shareholders are far wealthier today than they would be if the funds we used for acquisitions had instead been devoted to share repurchases or dividends." As long as acquisitions leave shareholders wealthier, he said, dividends don't make sense. * * * Overall, he said, the sell-off option is favorable for shareholders who want cash and gives each shareholder a choice of getting cash or not.

Steve Jordon, *Buffet Makes His Case For No Dividends*, OMAHA WORLD-HERALD, March 2, 2013.†

Some companies offer high dividends because they specialize in serving investors who prefer large dividends. For example, elderly shareholders may be on fixed incomes and they need dividend income to live on. In addition, stock that pays dividends may be especially desirable to other corporations; corporations may deduct from their taxable income a large fraction, or even all, of the dividend income that they receive from their shareholdings in other corporations. This is designed to prevent the triple taxation of dividends: once when the original income is earned by the first company, a second time when included in the receiving corporation's income (if not for the deduction described), and a third time when received by the shareholders of this second company. Similarly, nonprofit entities, such as most universities, may seek out stock with dividends because nonprofits also pay no tax on the dividends.

A company that has decided to distribute cash to shareholders has two choices: pay a dividend or buy back shares. The tax implications are different. If the company pays a dividend, the investor will pay taxes on

---

*   Editor's Note: If you would like to read Mr. Buffett's explanation of his dividend policy, (which includes not only 2100 words BUT ALSO NUMBERS AND MATH), go to this link http://www.businessinsider.com/warren-buffett-on-dividends–2013–3.

†   http://www.omaha.com/apps/pbcs.dll/article?AID=/20130301/MONEY/703029927/1697.

the payments at their high personal tax rate. In contrast, in a share repurchase, the selling shareholder pays tax on the difference between her cost and the selling price. But the tax rate is the lower capital gain rates. Thus, shareholders are better off when the company distributes its cash through a stock buyback than through dividends.

QUESTIONS

1.   Are you "puzzled" that Berkshire invests in corporations that pay their shareholders dividends but does not pay dividends itself?

2.   Assume that Bubba's Burritos, Inc. is considering paying $200,000 in dividends to its shareholders. How, if at all, would paying $200,000 in cash dividends affect Bubba's Burritos' balance sheet?

3.   Name a few companies that you think of as growth companies—do they pay dividends? What kind of companies would you expect to pay dividends?

4.   Do you agree with Warren Buffett that the "sell-off option" is more favorable to shareholders than dividends? If so, why do corporations pay dividends?

3.   WHEN MUST (AND WHEN MAY) A DIVIDEND BE PAID?

Bubba's Burritos, Inc. has done well. It had positive cash flow of $200,000 last year. It now has $300,000 in cash, $400,000 in other assets, and only $500,000 in debt.

What is the amount of its equity? Can the corporation pay that amount in dividends? Can the corporation pay $300,000 in dividends? Who decides? What if they decide not to pay any dividends?

The MBCA is not much more helpful on dividend questions than it was on salary questions. Generally, the MBCA uses the term "distribution" rather than the term "dividend" and the definition of "distribution"* includes a "dividend." *See* MBCA § 1.40.

MBCA § 6.40(c) spells out when a corporation *cannot* declare a dividend and § 8.33(b) imposes liability on directors for making distributions in violation of § 6.40(c). Please read §§ 6.40(c) and 8.33 and consider the following related questions:

- Why does a state's corporate code limit directors' discretion in declaring dividends?

---

*   Distributions are payments by the corporation to a shareholder. The three most common types of distributions are dividends, repurchases (in which the corporation enters a deal with a shareholder to purchase her stock), and redemptions (in which certain shareholders have obtained a contractual right that, under specified circumstances, the corporation must repurchase their shares at a specified price). Although the payment to the shareholders in any distribution can be made in money or property, usually payments are made in money.

- Who will complain if the directors distribute too much to shareholders?

- How can directors determine if the corporation will be able to "pay its debts as they come due in the usual course of business"? Is the balance sheet helpful? The income statement?

As the cited statutes make clear, under the MBCA a distribution is proper so long as the corporation is not insolvent and as long as the distribution does not render the corporation insolvent. This approach is the modern view, but it is not the universal view.

The traditional approach to the propriety of distributions, which is still followed in several states, including important corporate states such as Delaware and New York, requires reference to different funds or accounts that the corporate codes in such states require the corporation to keep. (We introduced these funds in Chapter 4, pp. 136–138, when we discussed issuing stock.)

One account is "earned surplus" (also known as "retained earnings"), which consists of money generated by the business itself. It consists of all earnings minus all losses minus distributions previously paid. If Bubba's Burritos, Inc. has earned surplus, it is making money in the real world by selling lots of burritos and other products. Earned surplus may be used to pay a distribution; under the traditional approach, it is a proper source from which such a payment to a stockholder can be made.

The other accounts relate to raising capital not by selling burritos (or widgets or doing whatever our corporation does), but by issuing stock. Proceeds received from the corporation's sale of stock (which is the definition of issuance, you will recall) are generally divided into two accounts under the traditional approach to the propriety of distributions, "stated capital" and "capital surplus."

"Stated capital" consists of the par value of a par issuance plus the amount allocated to stated capital on a no-par issuance. At this point you might be tempted to say "huh?" Remember from Chapter 4, p. 136, that "par" means "minimum issuance price." So if Bubba's Burritos, Inc. is selling 10,000 shares of $2 par stock, it must receive at least $2 per share for each of those shares, for a total of $20,000. That $20,000 would be allocated to stated capital. Why does this matter? Because under the traditional approach, stated capital cannot be used for a distribution. Stated capital was a cushion to provide protection for the corporation's creditors. In practice, however, corporations in these states can set par at miniscule amounts, like one-tenth of one cent.

But what if Bubba's Burritos, Inc. issued the 10,000 shares of $2 par stock for $100,000? (After all, par just means minimum issuance price. The corporation is free to sell at a higher price if it can get it.) In this hypothetical, $20,000 would be allocated to stated capital (as discussed in the previous paragraph). The other $80,000 would go into another fund, called "capital surplus." Why does this matter? Because capital surplus (like earned surplus) can be used to pay a distribution. Some states impose restrictions, such as a requirement that the shareholders receiving a distribution from capital surplus must be given notice that it is coming from that source and not from earned surplus.

Under the traditional approach, then, every cent generated from the issuance of stock is allocated either to stated capital or capital surplus. We just saw how this allocation is effected in a par issuance. What about a no-par sale of stock by the corporation? Recall that "no-par" simply means that there is no minimum issuance price. The board is free to determine the appropriate amount of consideration for such an issuance. On a no-par issuance, the directors are usually free to allocate the funds received between stated capital and capital surplus. But, perhaps counter-intuitively, if the directors do nothing, the funds go into stated capital, not capital surplus, and so they are not available for a distribution.

So when it comes to whether a corporation *may* pay a distribution, such as a dividend, there are two general approaches. The traditional view requires us to know the three accounts just described. The modern approach, typified by the MBCA, does not. Instead, it simply imposes insolvency limitations: distributions cannot be paid if the corporation is insolvent or would be rendered insolvent by the distribution. (The modern approach reflects the decline in the importance of the concept of par stock.) As the dissent in *Giannotti* points out, the "general rule is * * * the board of directors in its discretion determines whether to declare dividends on the stock." Under the modern approach, the only exception is when the corporation is about to go broke.

The following case, *Zidell v. Zidell*, shows how much discretion courts afford directors on dividend questions. In reading the case, please consider the following:

1.   Is the plaintiff in *Zidell* contending that the salaries paid by the corporations to his brother and nephew are too high?

2.   Do we know the dollar amount of dividends paid by the corporations in 1973 and 1974?

3.   Do we know the dollar amount of additional dividends the trial court ordered the corporations to declare?

ZIDELL V. ZIDELL

Supreme Court of Oregon, 1977
560 P.2d 1086

HOWELL, JUSTICE. These four suits were filed by Arnold Zidell, a minority shareholder of four related, closely held corporations, seeking to compel the directors of those corporations to declare dividends. Plaintiff's complaints alleged that defendants "arbitrarily, unreasonably and in bad faith" refused to declare more than a modest dividend in 1973. The trial court ordered each of the defendant corporations to declare additional dividends out of its earnings for 1973 and 1974. * * *

Defendants have appealed, contending that the court was not justified in ordering the declaration of any additional dividends. * * *

[Arnold Zidell owned 3/8 of the issued and outstanding stock of four affiliated different corporations that bought and sold scrap metal. The other 5/8 of the stock of each of the corporations was owned by his brother Emery Zidell, and Emery Zidell's son, Jay Zidell. (Emery held 3/8 of the corporation's stock and Jay had 1/4 (or 2/8) of the stock.) Until 1973, Arnold, Emery and Jay were the directors of all four corporations. Also, until 1973, all three were employed by the four corporations. In May of 1973, the board refused Arnold's demand that his salary be raised from $30,000 to $50,000. Arnold resigned his employment with the corporations, and his salary from the corporations ended.]

* * * Prior to Arnold's resignation, the customary practice had been to retain all earnings in the business rather than to distribute profits as dividends. Arnold had agreed with this policy, since all significant stockholders were active in the business and received salaries adequate for their needs. Following his resignation, however, Arnold demanded that the corporations begin declaring reasonable dividends. Thereafter, a dividend was declared and paid on the 1973 earnings of each corporation.

Arnold contends that these dividends are unreasonably small and were not set in good faith. He notes that at about the same time, corporate salaries and bonuses were increased substantially. Arnold does not contend that these salaries are excessive in his briefs on appeal. He does argue, however, that the change in compensation policy, coinciding as it did with his departure from active involvement in the business, is evidence of a concerted effort by the other shareholders to wrongfully deprive him of his right to a fair proportion of the profits of the business. He points out that each corporation had substantial retained earnings at the end of 1973, and he argues that he was entitled to a larger return on his equity.

The trial court specifically declined to rule that defendants acted in bad faith but held that larger dividends should have been declared in order to allow plaintiff a reasonable return. The court then ordered the declaration of a much larger dividend than that which had been set by the board of directors in each case.

We have recognized that those in control of corporate affairs have fiduciary duties of good faith and fair dealing toward the minority shareholders. Insofar as dividend policy is concerned, however, that duty is discharged if the decision is made in good faith and reflects legitimate business purposes rather than the private interests of those in control. * * *

Plaintiff had the burden of proving bad faith on the part of the directors in determining the amount of corporate dividends. In the present case, plaintiff has shown that the corporations could afford to pay additional dividends, that he has left the corporate payroll, that those stockholders who are working for the corporations are receiving generous salaries and bonuses, and that there is hostility between him and the other major stockholders. We agree with plaintiff that these factors are often present in cases of oppression or attempted squeeze-out by majority shareholders. They are not, however, invariably signs of improper behavior by the majority. *See Gottfried v. Gottfried,* [73 N.Y.S. 2d 692, 695 (1947)]:

> There are no infallible distinguishing earmarks of bad faith. The following facts are relevant to the issue of bad faith and are admissible in evidence: Intense hostility of the controlling faction against the minority; exclusion of the minority from employment by the corporation; high salaries, or bonuses or corporate loans made to the officers in control; the fact that the majority group may be subject to high personal income taxes if substantial dividends are paid; the existence of a desire by the controlling directors to acquire the minority stock interests as cheaply as possible. But if they are not motivating causes they do not constitute "bad faith" as a matter of law.

Defendants introduced a considerable amount of credible evidence to explain their conservative dividend policy. There was testimony that the directors took into consideration a future need for expensive physical improvements, and possibly even the relocation of a major plant; the need for cash to pay for large inventory orders; the need for renovation of a nearly obsolescent dock; and the need for continued short-term financing through bank loans which could be "called" if the corporations' financial position became insecure. There was also evidence that earnings for 1973 and 1974 were abnormally high because of unusual economic conditions that could not be expected to continue.

In rebuttal, plaintiff contends that the directors did not really make their decisions on the basis of these factors, pointing to testimony that they did not rely on any documented financial analysis to support their dividend declarations. This is a matter for consideration, but it is certainly not determinative. All of the directors of these corporations were active in the business on a day-to-day basis and had intimate first-hand knowledge of financial conditions and present and projected business needs. In order to substantiate their testimony that the above factors were taken into consideration, it was not necessary that they provide documentary evidence or show that formal studies were conducted. Their testimony is believable, and the burden of proof on this issue is on the plaintiff, not the defendants.

Nor are we convinced by plaintiff's arguments that we should approve the forced declaration of additional dividends in order to prevent a deliberate squeeze-out. Plaintiff left his corporate employment voluntarily. He was not forced out. Although the dividends he has since received are modest when viewed as a rate of return on his investment, they are not unreasonable in light of the corporations' projected financial needs. Moreover, having considered the evidence presented by both sides, we are not persuaded that the directors are employing starvation tactics to force the sale of plaintiff's stock at an unreasonably low price.

Since we have determined that plaintiff has not carried his burden of proving a lack of good faith, we must conclude that the trial court erred in decreeing the distribution of additional dividends.

Reversed and remanded with directions to enter decrees of dismissal.

QUESTIONS AND NOTE

1. Do you agree with the court's conclusion that "Plaintiff had the burden of proving bad faith on the part of the directors in determining the amount of corporate dividends"? Would the court in the *Giannotti* case agree? Is this case distinguishable from *Giannotti*?

2. Do you agree with the Oregon court's conclusion that the plaintiff did not satisfy his burden of proof? Would the court have reached a different decision if:

     a)   the board of directors had not declared any dividend in 1973?

     b)   the plaintiff had not resigned as an employee but instead had been fired?

3. Reconsider the court's statement: "We have recognized that those in control of corporate affairs have fiduciary duties of good faith and fair dealing toward the minority shareholder." Professor Mitchell is critical of the *Zidell* approach to fiduciary duty: "The clear import is that actions of controlling interests in close corporations will not result in liability so long as those actions are not intended to harm minority shareholders. This reduces fiduciary analysis to nothing more than the avoidance of unfair treatment of the minority, rather than exclusive pursuit of the minority's interests." Lawrence E. Mitchell, *The Death of Fiduciary Duty in Close Corporations,*

138 U. PA. L. REV. 1675, 1715–16 (1990). Do you agree with Professor Mitchell's view of *Zidell*? With his view of fiduciary duty?

4. The leading (and somewhat lonely) case requiring a corporation to pay a dividend to shareholders is *Dodge v. Ford Motor Co.*, 170 N.W. 668 (Mich. 1919). At that time, Ford Motor Company had relatively few shareholders. Two of the shareholders were the brothers Dodge (who formed their own automobile manufacturing business (which became a division of Chrysler)). Ford Motor Company had paid extraordinarily high dividends, which the Dodge Boys used to get their company rolling (so to speak). Presumably, Henry Ford was not pleased with this potential competition. At any rate, Ford Motor Company then refused to pay dividends, and the Dodges sued.

Henry Ford had legitimate reasons to use earnings for purposes other than paying dividends. He wanted to expand production facilities of Ford Motor. In addition, Ford paid his workers more than twice the going wage, and wanted to use some of the money to continue that practice as well. Although some people thought paying such high wages was a mistake, in fact it was brilliant, because it gave Ford a loyal, stable workforce. Once on the Ford line, a worker was not going to give up his job, because he was making twice as much as other auto workers. Ford knew that the new plant would enable the company to build cars far less expensively and, thus, to drive the price of the cars down. Again, some people thought this was a mistake—they asked "why not make cars more expensive?" But again, Henry Ford was brilliant. He understood that his company would make far more money by making cheaper cars and selling many more of them.

In the Dodge brothers' lawsuit, Ford could simply have testified at trial that he wanted to use earnings to make cars less expensive and to pay the higher wages to improve his workforce, both of which would increase profits. Had he done so, no court would have overruled his decision to plow the money into the new plant and not into dividends. Instead, however, Ford testified at great length about how he wanted to make sure that everyone could afford a car—that the goal of his company was not so much to make money as to provide the public with cheap cars and his workers with high wages. The Michigan Supreme Court found his stated reasons so imprudent as not to be protected by the business judgment rule. In light of the huge cash surpluses and the history of declaring dividends, the court concluded that the directors had "a duty to distribute * * * a very large sum of money to stockholders." *Id.* at 685.

Professor Charles M. Elson of the Stetson University Law School has included this case in his list of "ten top cases" that "shaped the nature of discourse on corporate governance." Charles M. Elson, *Courts and Boards: the Top Ten Cases*, SD 39 ALI-ABA 743 (1998). Nonetheless, the decision is unique. We are not aware of any other reported decision in which a court required directors to pay dividends because the corporation had a large surplus.

For an interesting treatment of the success of Henry Ford, *see* Douglas Brinkley, WHEELS FOR THE WORLD: HENRY FORD, HIS COMPANY, AND A CENTURY OF PROGRESS (2003).

We are aware of at least one reported "man bites dog" case on payment of dividends, *Sinclair Oil Corporation v. Levien*. In this case, the minority shareholder is complaining that the corporation paid too much in dividends, not too little. Please consider the following questions:

1. Who is the plaintiff?

2. Who is the defendant?

3. What does the plaintiff minority shareholder claim that the defendant majority shareholder did wrong? What does the plaintiff want the defendant to do differently? If Sinven's earnings had not been paid to shareholders in the form of dividends, what would have happened to the earnings?

SINCLAIR OIL CORPORATION V. LEVIEN
Supreme Court of Delaware, 1971
280 A.2d 717

WOLCOTT, CHIEF JUSTICE. This is an appeal by the defendant, Sinclair Oil Corporation (hereafter Sinclair), from an order of the Court of Chancery, in a derivative action requiring Sinclair to account for damages sustained by its subsidiary, Sinclair Venezuelan Oil Company (hereafter Sinven), organized by Sinclair for the purpose of operating in Venezuela, as a result of dividends paid by Sinven.

Sinclair, operating primarily as a holding company, is in the business of exploring for oil and of producing and marketing crude oil and oil products. At all times relevant to this litigation, it owned about 97% of Sinven's stock. The plaintiff owns about 3000 of 120,000 publicly-held shares of Sinven. Sinven, incorporated in 1922, has been engaged in petroleum operations primarily in Venezuela and since 1959 has operated exclusively in Venezuela.

Sinclair nominates all members of Sinven's board of directors. The Chancellor found as a fact that the directors were not independent of Sinclair. Almost without exception, they were officers, directors, or employees of corporations in the Sinclair complex. By reason of Sinclair's domination, it is clear that Sinclair owed Sinven a fiduciary duty. Sinclair concedes this.

The Chancellor held that because of Sinclair's fiduciary duty and its control over Sinven, its relationship with Sinven must meet the test of intrinsic fairness. The standard of intrinsic fairness involves both a high degree of fairness and a shift in the burden of proof. Under this standard the burden is on Sinclair to prove, subject to careful judicial scrutiny, that its transactions with Sinven were objectively fair.

Sinclair argues that the transactions between it and Sinven should be tested, not by the test of intrinsic fairness with the accompanying shift of the burden of proof, but by the business judgment rule under which a court will not interfere with the judgment of a board of directors unless there is a showing of gross and palpable overreaching. * * *

A parent does indeed owe a fiduciary duty to its subsidiary when there are parent-subsidiary dealings. However, this alone will not evoke the intrinsic fairness standard. This standard will be applied only when the fiduciary duty is accompanied by self-dealing—the situation when a parent is on both sides of a transaction with its subsidiary. Self-dealing occurs when the parent, by virtue of its domination of the subsidiary, causes the subsidiary to act in such a way that the parent receives something from the subsidiary to the exclusion of, and detriment to, the minority stockholders of the subsidiary.

We turn now to the facts. The plaintiff argues that, from 1960 through 1966, Sinclair caused Sinven to pay out such excessive dividends that the industrial development of Sinven was effectively prevented, and it became in reality a corporation in dissolution.

From 1960 through 1966, Sinven paid out $108,000,000 in dividends ($38,000,000 in excess of Sinven's earnings during the same period). The Chancellor held that Sinclair caused these dividends to be paid during a period when it had a need for large amounts of cash. Although the dividends paid exceeded earnings, the plaintiff concedes that the payments were made in compliance with 8 Del.C. § 170, authorizing payment of dividends out of surplus or net profits. However, the plaintiff attacks these dividends on the ground that they resulted from an improper motive—Sinclair's need for cash. The Chancellor, applying the intrinsic fairness standard, held that Sinclair did not sustain its burden of proving that these dividends were intrinsically fair to the minority stockholders of Sinven.

Since it is admitted that the dividends were paid in strict compliance with 8 Del.C. § 170, the alleged excessiveness of the payments alone would not state a cause of action. Nevertheless, compliance with the applicable statute may not, under all circumstances, justify all dividend payments. If a plaintiff can meet his burden of proving that a dividend cannot be grounded on any reasonable business objective, then the courts can and will interfere with the board's decision to pay the dividend.

Sinclair contends that it is improper to apply the intrinsic fairness standard to dividend payments even when the board which voted for the dividends is completely dominated. * * *

We do not accept the argument that the intrinsic fairness test can never be applied to a dividend declaration by a dominated board, although a dividend declaration by a dominated board will not inevitably demand the application of the intrinsic fairness standard. If such a dividend is in essence self-dealing by the parent, then the intrinsic fairness standard is the proper standard. For example, suppose a parent dominates a subsidiary and its board of directors. The subsidiary has outstanding two classes of stock, X and Y. Class X is owned by the parent and Class Y is owned by minority stockholders of the subsidiary. If the subsidiary, at the direction of the parent, declares a dividend on its Class X stock only, this might well be self-dealing by the parent. It would be receiving something from the subsidiary to the exclusion of and detrimental to its minority stockholders. This self-dealing, coupled with the parent's fiduciary duty, would make intrinsic fairness the proper standard by which to evaluate the dividend payments.

Consequently it must be determined whether the dividend payments by Sinven were, in essence, self-dealing by Sinclair. The dividends resulted in great sums of money being transferred from Sinven to Sinclair. However, a proportionate share of this money was received by the minority shareholders of Sinven. Sinclair received nothing from Sinven to the exclusion of its minority stockholders. As such, these dividends were not self-dealing. We hold therefore that the Chancellor erred in applying the intrinsic fairness test as to these dividend payments. The business judgment standard should have been applied.

We conclude that the facts demonstrate that the dividend payments complied with the business judgment standard and with 8 Del.C. § 170. The motives for causing the declaration of dividends are immaterial unless the plaintiff can show that the dividend payments resulted from improper motives and amounted to waste. The plaintiff contends only that the dividend payments drained Sinven of cash to such an extent that it was prevented from expanding.

* * * However, the plaintiff could point to no opportunities which came to Sinven. * * *

We will therefore reverse that part of the Chancellor's order that requires Sinclair to account to Sinven for damages sustained as a result of dividends paid between 1960 and 1966. * * *

QUESTIONS

1. How could Sinven pay dividends from 1960 through 1966 "in excess of Sinven's earnings during the same period"?

2. Which party had the burden of proof? What did that party have to prove? Did that party satisfy its burden of proof?

3.   Did we put this case in the right place in the book? Other casebooks include the *Sinclair* case in the part of the book dealing with duty of loyalty.

4. TO WHOM ARE DIVIDENDS PAID?

The answer to the question of to whom a corporation pays dividends is generally found in that corporation's articles of incorporation. To understand the answer that you find in the articles, it is necessary to understand the following terms:

(1) classes of stock;

(2) common stock;

(3) preferred stock;

(4) preferred participating stock; and

(5) preferred cumulative stock.

Recall that state corporate codes authorize a corporation, in its articles of incorporation, to create different classes or types of stock. MBCA § 6.01(a) is a representative statutory provision. Please re-read (read?) MBCA § 6.01(a) and the documents that establish Silicon Gaming, Inc.'s class D stock in Chapter 4 on pages 134–136.

Although all of the shares in a particular class must have identical rights, one class can have greater rights, or "preferences," than another. A class with such a preference is generally referred to as "preferred." The class without such a preference is generally referred to as "common."

A typical preference for a class of stock is priority in the receipt of dividends. Assume, for example, that Bubba's Burritos, Inc. has two classes of stock: Class 1 and Class 2 and that Class 2 stock is preferred stock, and must receive a payment of $2 per share before the Class 1 common stock can receive any dividend. Assume further that there are 10,000 outstanding shares of Class 1 and 2,000 shares of Class 2. If the directors of Bubba's Burritos, Inc. declare a total dividend of only $4,000, only Class 2 stock would receive a dividend ($2 × 2,000); there would be nothing left for the Class 1 shares. Preferred means "pay first."

(1) What if the directors declare a $40,000 dividend instead of a $4,000 dividend? Again, the 2,000 shares of Class 2 preferred stock would first be paid the $2 a share dividend preference for a total of $4,000. The remaining $36,000 would be paid to the 10,000 shares of Class 1 common stock. In sum, each preferred share would be paid a $2 dividend while each common share would be paid a $3.60 dividend. Class 2's preference was as to priority of payment, not amount of payment.

"Preferred participating" stock not only gets paid first (because it is preferred), but also gets paid again. "Participating" thus means that these shares also get paid, along with the common shares, in what is left over after payment of the preference. So they get paid twice!

(2) For example, take the same basic facts as above. Bubba's Burritos, Inc. declares a total dividend of $40,000. As before, there are 10,000 shares of common stock. However, suppose that the 2,000 shares of preferred stock not only have a $2 preference, but they are also participating. The preferred aspect of this stock is handled the same as in (1). Thus, the 2,000 preferred shares receive their $2 preference first, meaning they get a total of $4000. That leaves $36,000, just as in (1). But here, that $36,000 does not go only to the 10,000 common shares. Instead, that stock has to share that money with the 2,000 preferred participating shares. So the $36,000 gets divided here among a total of 12,000 shares (the 10,000 common and the 2,000 preferred participating shares). This works out to $3 per share. So the common get $3 per share. The preferred participating get $5 per share—$2 because of their dividend preference and $3 because they are participating.

Recall that there is no statutory requirement that dividends be paid. Generally, there is no right to a dividend until the board of directors declares one. And, generally, dividends do not accrue from year to year. If, for example, the board of directors of Bubba's Burritos, Inc. declares a dividend in 2008, after having paid no dividends in 2007, the holders of Class 2 stock with a $2 dividend preference would still get only $2 a share, *unless* their stock was not only preferred but preferred and *cumulative*. Cumulative dividends do accrue—do carry over from year-to-year. All omitted cumulative dividends must be paid before any dividend is paid on common stock.

(3) To take another variation of the facts, suppose Bubba's Burritos, Inc. declares a total dividend of $40,000. There are 2,000 shares of class 2 cumulative preferred stock with a $2 preference (but not participating) and 10,000 shares of class 1 common stock. Now suppose the board has not declared a dividend in any of the last three years. The cumulative preferred dividend of $2 has been accruing year-to-year over that period. So when the corporation declares any dividend, it owes each preferred share $2 for each of the three previous years as well as for this year. So they get four years' worth of a $2 preference, or $8 per share. There are 2,000 such shares, so they get a total of $16,000. That sum is paid first, because it is preferred. After paying the preferred cumulative shares their total of $16,000, that leaves $24,000 to be distributed among the common shares. There are 10,000 of those, so each common share gets $2.40 per share.

CHAPTER 9

WHAT HAPPENS WHEN A CORPORATION ENDS?

■ ■ ■

A. INTRODUCTION TO FUNDAMENTAL CORPORATE CHANGES

Some changes in the life of the corporation are so fundamental that the law does not permit the board of directors to pursue them alone. These differ from ordinary management decisions, which, as we have seen, are made by the board of directors with no input from stockholders. But when an act will fundamentally alter the corporation, corporate law generally requires not only director approval, but also approval by the shareholders. So shareholders have an important, direct voice in whether a fundamental change will occur.

Which corporate changes are fundamental? In most states, they include (1) amendment of the articles of incorporation, (2) dissolution, (3) merger, and (4) sale of substantially all of the corporation's assets. The procedure for each of these is generally the same, and consists of five steps.

First, the board of directors must approve the fundamental change. This is done the same way the board takes any act, as we saw in Chapter 5.

Second, the board must notify the shareholders of its recommendation that the fundamental change be approved.

Third, a special meeting of the shareholders must be held, at which they vote on the change. If it is approved, the corporation will go through with the change. However, if the shareholders reject the proposal, the corporation will not affect the change.

Fourth, if the change is approved, shareholders who opposed the proposed change might have a right to force the corporation to buy them out. We will explore this "dissenting shareholder's right of appraisal" in Part C of this chapter.

Fifth, the corporation is usually required to inform the state of the fundamental change by filing a document with the secretary of state.

Shareholder voting in this area differs from that in others. To see this, let's review shareholder voting, which we studied in Chapter 5. For a shareholders' meeting, we always need a quorum. Unless the articles or bylaws provide otherwise, a quorum will be a majority of the shares entitled to vote. So if Bubba's Burritos, Inc. has 6,000 outstanding voting shares, at least 3,001 would have to be represented at the shareholders' meeting. Without a quorum, the shareholders cannot act. *See, e.g.,* MBCA § 7.25(a); Delaware § 216(i).

Assume we have a quorum. What vote is required now? It depends upon what the shareholders are considering. If they are electing directors, as we discussed in Chapter 5, at page 179, all that is required is for a candidate to receive a "plurality" of the votes cast for that particular seat on the board. That is, the candidate who gets more votes than anyone else is elected, even if she does not get a majority of the votes cast.* *See, e.g.,* MBCA § 7.28(a). (Remember too that in electing directors we might use cumulative voting, which we saw in Chapter 5, at page 179.)

In addition to electing directors, shareholders get to vote in three other situations. First, are fundamental changes, which we will get to in a moment.

Second, shareholders get to vote on a nonfundamental issue if the board asks them to. Boards do this rarely. Third, shareholders are entitled to vote on certain nonfundamental proposals that shareholders put forward. SEC Rule 14a–8 regulates which of these proposals a corporation must include in the proxy materials that it provides to shareholders before the annual meeting. The shareholder proposals often suggest that the corporation's directors act in accord with social causes. For example, several decades ago, a common shareholder proposal was that the corporation not do business in South Africa.

What happens if shareholders vote on an issue that is nonfundemental? The modern view is that, if a quorum exists, a measure passes if it receives a majority of the votes *cast*.† The older view—still followed in some states—is that a measure passes only if it gets a majority of the shares *present* at the meeting. *See* Delaware § 217(ii). That is, the newer view ignores abstentions, while the old view counts them as votes against the proposal.

For example, let's say the shareholders are voting on some nonfundamental substantive measure. Assume that there are 6,000 shares entitled to vote; 3,600 of them are represented at the meeting (so we have a quorum); but only 2,000 of the 3,600 of the shares present actually vote on that measure. Under the modern view, the measure would pass if at least 1,001 shares voted for it. Why? Because all we need is a majority of the shares that actually voted (2,000). Under the older

---

*   *See* MBCA § 7.28(a) (unless the articles provide otherwise, "directors are elected by a plurality of the votes cast by the shares entitled to vote. . . .").

†   *See* MBCA § 7.25(c) (unless the articles provide otherwise, action "is approved if the votes cast within the voting group favoring the action exceed the votes cast opposing the action. . . .").

view, however, at least 1,801 shares would have to vote in favor for it to pass. Why? Because under that view, we need a majority of the shares *present* at the meeting. There were 3,600 present.

That was voting on nonfundamental issues. Now let's focus on the big issue: requirements for shareholder voting on fundamental changes. States generally fall into one of three categories.

First, in many states, voting requirements for fundamental issues are the same as for nonfundamental issues. *See* MBCA §§ 7.25(c), 10.03(e). That is, a fundamental change can be approved in some states by a majority of those actually voting, and, in others, by a majority of those present.

Second, in other states, including Delaware, the fundamental change must be approved by a majority of the shares *entitled to vote.** Based upon the numbers immediately above, we would need at least 3,001 shares to vote in favor of the fundamental change. Why? Because there are 6,000 shares *entitled to vote* and we need a majority of that number. In effect, both an abstention and a no-show are treated as votes of no.

The third approach is even tougher. It is the traditional view, still followed in a few states, including Texas and Massachusetts. It requires approval by *two-thirds of the shares entitled to vote. See, e.g.,* Texas Business Organization Act § 21.455 (2006). So if there were 6,000 shares entitled to vote, at least 4,000 would have to vote yes to approve the fundamental change. So in our hypo above, where 3,600 shares were represented at the meeting, the shareholders simply could not approve the fundamental change under this view—even if all 3,600 shares at the meeting voted yes.

Let's now start looking at the various kinds of fundamental changes. Most of this chapter is devoted to fundamental changes that either end the corporation's existence or prepare the way to end that existence. In contrast, amendment of the corporation's articles of incorporation does not kill the corporation. However, it is a fundamental corporate change because it alters the charter that created the entity. There may be any number of reasons the corporation may wish to amend its articles. For instance, because a corporation has issued all of the stock it was authorized to sell in the original articles, it may amend its charter to permit the issuance of more stock. Like all fundamental corporate changes, the amendment of the articles must be approved by the board of directors and by the shareholders, in accordance with the special voting rules we just saw.

Now we turn to those fundamental changes that actually are the end—or at least the beginning of the end—of the corporation.

---

*   See, e.g., Delaware § 242(b)(1) (amending articles requires "majority of the outstanding stock entitled to vote. . . ."); § 251(c) (same for approving a merger).

B. DISSOLUTION

One obvious end for a corporation is dissolution.

The *Giannotti* case, which we studied at page 346, showed us that statutes may allow a court to order dissolution of a corporation because of an intra-corporate dispute. Most corporation statutes provide for judicial dissolution in a proceeding brought by a shareholder who establishes that "those in control of the corporation have acted . . . in a manner that is illegal, oppressive, or fraudulent." *See, e.g.,* MBCA § 14.30(2).

Corporation statutes also generally provide for voluntary dissolution, which is effected as we discussed in Part A above. That is, the board of directors approves the dissolution, and then shareholders vote on the proposal. As we noted, some states require approval merely by a majority of the votes cast. Other states require approval by a majority of the shares entitled to vote. Some still require two-thirds of the shares entitled to vote. Compare MBCA § 14.02(e) (majority of votes cast) with Delaware § 275(b) (majority of shares entitled to vote) with Texas Business Organization Act § 21.502 (2006) (two-thirds of shares entitled to vote).

In both judicial dissolution and voluntary dissolution,

- the corporation continues after dissolution for the limited purpose of "winding up," *Cf.* MBCA § 14.05;

- winding up activities include collecting and liquidating the assets of the corporation and using the proceeds from the liquidation of the corporation's assets to pay creditors, *Id*;

- these creditors must be paid in full before the shareholders get anything from their corporation's dissolution;

- creditors who are not paid during dissolution may seek to recover later from shareholders, to the extent that the shareholders have received payments from the corporation when it was dissolved. MBCA § 14.07(d);

- notice of the dissolution is to be filed in the same public records that contain the articles of incorporation, *cf.* MBCA §§ 14.03, 14.33; and

- written notice "shall" be provided to "known claimants" and notice by publication "may" be used to reach unknown claimants, *cf.* MBCA §§ 14.06, 14.07.

PROBLEMS

1. For the last 11 weeks, Bubba's Burritos, Inc.'s operating costs have exceeded its gross receipts. The corporation owes more than $100,000. A sale of the corporation's assets would yield less than $90,000. The corporation's three shareholders and directors, Agee, Propp and Capel, have agreed to close the business permanently at the end of this week. They want to know how much it will cost them to dissolve the corporation and how they benefit by spending this money to dissolve. How do you answer their questions?

2. Propp and Capel want to operate Bubba's Burritos without Agee. They come to you with the question of whether they could (i) vote for the dissolution of Bubba's Burritos and then (ii) form a two-person partnership that would buy the assets of Bubba's Burritos during the winding up of Bubba's Burritos, Inc. How do you answer their question?

C. MERGER

Another possible end for a corporation as a business structure is merger. In a merger, two or more business entities combine into one business entity. For example, Bubba's Burritos, Inc. merges into McDonald's. In this example, McDonald's would be referred to as the "surviving corporation." Bubba's Burritos, Inc. would be referred to as the "disappearing corporation" because it would in fact and in law disappear. MBCA § 11.07(a)(2) is typical of corporate codes in providing that "When a merger becomes effective * * * the separate existence of every corporation * * * that is merged into the survivor ceases."

1. EFFECTS OF A MERGER ON SHAREHOLDRES AND CREDITORS

Section 11.07 of the MBCA sets out the effects of a merger.* Please apply § 11.07 to the following problems on a merger's impacts.

PROBLEMS

1. Bubba's Burritos, Inc. merges into McDonald's. At the time of the merger, S is a secured creditor of Bubba's. Bubba's owes S $300,000 and S has a first mortgage on Bubba's real estate. U is an unsecured creditor—Bubba's owes U $40,000. Capel is a shareholder of Bubba's, and owns 51% of the outstanding stock. What effect does the merger have on the rights of S, U, and Capel?

2. What if the Bubba's and McDonald's merger is structured as a "triangular merger?" For example, McDonald's might establish a new wholly owned subsidiary, Newco, and transfer McDonald's stock to Newco in

---

* More precisely, § 11.07(a) sets out the effects of a merger that you need to know about for this course. If you do mergers and acquisition ("M & A") work in the real world, you will also need to know about a merger's tax effects and about the application of the securities laws.

exchange for all of Newco's stock. Bubba's and McDonald's could then agree to merge Bubba's into Newco. The shareholders of Bubba's would receive the McDonald's stock that had previously been transferred by McDonald's to Newco. In exchange, Newco would receive all of the Bubba's stock. Because McDonald's owned Newco, McDonalds would indirectly own all of the Bubba's stock. Why is this called a "triangular merger"? What are the possible business and legal reasons to structure a business combination as a triangular merger?

2. PROTECTING SHAREHOLDERS FROM HARMS FROM A MERGER

Because of the effect of a merger on shareholders of both the surviving and the disappearing corporations, shareholders of both corporations by case law and by statute have four potential forms of legal protection. They can (1) sue the directors who approved the merger alleging breach of common law or statutory duty of care; (2) vote against the merger; (3) assert the dissenting shareholder's right of appraisal; or (4) sue the directors who approved the merger alleging a breach of common law or statutory duty of loyalty.

a. Sue the Directors Who Approved the Merger for Breach of the Duty of Care

The MBCA, like other corporation codes, contemplates that the board of directors of each of the merging corporations will agree on a plan of merger. *See* MBCA § 11.01(a). This agreement is (of course) generally referred to as a "merger agreement" or "a plan of merger" and sets out the terms and conditions of the merger, including (i) which corporation survives and (ii) what the shareholders of the disappearing corporation receive. *Cf.* MBCA § 11.01(b). *See generally* James C. Freund, ANATOMY OF A MERGER (1975). And, as we have seen from our consideration of cases such as *Smith v. Van Gorkom* in Chapter 5, shareholders who are dissatisfied with what they receive from a merger sometimes sue the directors who approved the merger, alleging that, by approving the merger, the directors breached their duty of care.

b. Vote Against the Merger

Subject to limited exceptions, a merger requires not only approval by the board of directors of each of the merging companies, but also the approval of the shareholders. Corporation statutes vary as to what level of approval is required and what the exceptions for shareholder approval are. Apply the MBCA provisions, §§ 11.04(a), (e) and (g), and 6.21(f), to the following problem.

PROBLEM

Bubba's Burritos, Inc. is merging into McDonald's. Bubba's has 10 shareholders and 10,000 outstanding shares. McDonald's has millions of shareholders and more than a billion outstanding shares. What shareholder approval is required?

c.　Assert Dissenting Shareholders' Right of Appraisal

An individual minority shareholder's vote against a merger will not prevent the merger from happening. While state corporations statutes vary as to what level of approval is required, no state still* requires unanimous approval of a merger by all of the shareholders. Instead of providing a veto to shareholders who oppose the merger, corporations statutes today provide "appraisal rights" to shareholders who dissent from it.† *E.g.*, Delaware § 262.

The phrase "appraisal rights" is incomplete and maybe even misleading. A shareholder who opposes a merger and complies with the detailed statutory requirements in Delaware § 262 (or MBCA Chapter 13 or whatever the relevant state corporation statute is) has more than the right to have her shares appraised or valued. Rather, a shareholder who properly asserts her dissenting shareholder's right of appraisal can compel the corporation to pay her in cash the fair value of her shares as determined by a judicial appraisal process.

To illustrate, S is a 10% shareholder of T Co., which merges into A, Inc. The effect of the merger, of course, is that T Co. and its shares both cease to exist. The merger agreement values T Co. at $3,000,000 and provides that T Co. shareholders will receive consideration that has a value of $3,000,000. This consideration can be A, Inc. stock, or other stock, or other property or cash. *Cf.* MBCA § 11.02. As a 10% shareholder, S would get consideration with a value of $300,000. S instead "complies with the detailed statutory requirements" and properly asserts her dissenting shareholder's right of appraisal. What if the court decides that the fair value of T Co. was $5,000,000, and not $3,000,000? Then S, as a dissenting shareholder who seeks appraisal and "complies with the detailed statutory requirements," has a right to be paid $500,000 in cash from T Co.

Note the limiting phrase in the preceding paragraphs:

The merger must comply "with the detailed statutory requirements." As Professor Franklin Gevurtz observed, "One problem is that the statutory appraisal rights commonly require shareholders wishing to assert the rights to comply with exacting requirements which can trip up

---

*　Originally, mergers required unanimous shareholder approval.

†　Appraisal rights are not limited to mergers. MBCA § 13.02. We will consider appraisal rights again when we consider sale of all or substantially all of a corporation's property.

many persons." Franklin Gevurtz, CORPORATION LAW 648. Take a look at Delaware § 262 (or MBCA Chapter 13) to see the detailed requirements for seeking appraisal.

Although detailed statutory provisions govern how a shareholder asserts her right to be paid the fair value of her shares by her corporation, virtually no statutory provisions govern how a court is to determine that fair value. Rather, both lawyers advising clients and courts deciding cases look to reported decisions that use various standards for determining the fair value of the dissenting shares. We will study two such opinions. In reading the first, please consider the following:

1. Who merged with whom?

2. Which is the surviving corporation?

3. What did the shareholders of the disappearing corporation receive?

HMO-W INC. v. SSM HEALTH CARE SYSTEM

Wisconsin Supreme Court, 2000
611 N.W.2d 250

ANN WALSH BRADLEY, J. HMO-Wisconsin (HMO-W) seeks review of that part of a published court of appeals decision that reversed a circuit court judgment and order applying a minority discount in this dissenters' rights action. HMO-W contends that the court of appeals erred when it precluded the application of minority discounts in determining the fair value of dissenters' shares. We agree with the court of appeals and conclude that minority discounts may not be applied to determine the fair value of dissenters' shares in an appraisal proceeding. * * *

The appraisal action at the center of this review represents the culmination of a relationship between HMO-W and SSM that spanned more than a decade. In 1983, SSM and a number of other health care providers formed HMO-W as a provider-owned health care system. All shareholders assumed minority status in this closely held corporation. SSM and the Neillsville Clinic, another shareholder, together owned approximately twenty percent of HMO-W's shares.

By the early 1990's, competitive pressures from within the health care business led HMO-W to explore the possibility of merging with another health care system. SSM recommended DeanCare Health Plan (DeanCare), a company with which SSM had close connections, as a potential merger partner. HMO-W later eliminated DeanCare from consideration after having met with company representatives numerous times to discuss a partnership deal. HMO-W instead proposed a joint venture with United Wisconsin Services (United).

Before shareholder approval of the merger, HMO-W retained Valuation Research Corporation (VR) to value HMO-W's net assets both prior to and upon the merger. VR prepared a final valuation report that HMO-W accepted and which estimated the company's net value to fall within the range of $16.5 to $18 million.

Subsequently, HMO-W's board of directors voted to approve the proposed merger with United and to submit the merger to a shareholder vote. In addition to the VR report, the proxy materials sent to the shareholders informed them of their statutory right to dissent to the merger. At the shareholder meeting, both SSM and the Neillsville Clinic voted against the proposed merger. The merger was nevertheless approved.

Both SSM and the Neillsville Clinic then perfected a demand for the payment of their dissenting shares. Abandoning the VR report, HMO-W hired a new appraiser to value its assets. The appraiser arrived at a valuation of approximately $7.4 million, and based upon this valuation, HMO-W sent SSM a check for almost $1.5 million as the value of SSM's shares. Disputing HMO-W's valuation of the shares, SSM informed the company that SSM's fair value calculation of its shares yielded a figure of approximately $4.7 million. * * *

HMO-W instituted a special proceeding to determine the fair value of the dissenting shares. In response, SSM asserted that HMO-W was estopped from claiming a company value that was lower than the $16.5 to $18 million value it had represented to the shareholders prior to the merger vote.

At trial, several experts testified as to the net value of HMO-W. HMO-W's expert testified that the company's value immediately prior to the merger was $10,544,000. SSM's expert submitted the value as $19,250,000. The circuit court accepted the valuation offered by HMO-W's expert, noting various flaws in the earlier VR report that called into question the accuracy of that report.

Upon accepting HMO-W's valuation and observing the dissenters' minority status, the circuit court applied a minority discount of 30% to the value of the dissenting shares but refrained from applying a lack of marketability discount.* [3] The circuit court concluded that it was required to apply the minority discount as a matter of law. The court then ordered SSM and the Neillsville Clinic to repay with interest the amount

---

*   [3] A minority discount addresses the lack of control over a business entity on the theory that non-controlling shares of stock are not worth their proportionate share of the firm's value because they lack voting power to control corporate actions. A lack of marketability discount adjusts for a lack of liquidity in one's interests in a firm, on the theory that there is a limited supply of potential buyers in closely held corporations. The type of discount at issue in this case is the minority discount, and thus we do not address the applicability of a lack of marketability discount under the statute.

by which HMO-W's initial payment exceeded the court's fair value determination.

* * *

The court of appeals affirmed in part and reversed in part, remanding the case for a fair value determination without the application of a minority discount. It held as a matter of law that the Wisconsin statutes governing dissenters' rights do not allow minority discounts to be applied in determining the fair value of a dissenter's shares.

The court reasoned that minority discounts frustrate the purpose of dissenters' rights statutes, which protect the rights of shareholders to voice objection to corporate actions and to receive an equitable value for their minority shares. However, the court of appeals affirmed the circuit court's determination as to HMO-W's net asset value. It concluded that SSM had failed to prove harm in reliance on the VR report that initially valued HMO-W's net assets at $16.5–$18 million.

Two issues are currently presented for review, and both are issues of first impression for this court. Initially we address the issue of whether a minority discount may apply in determining the fair value of a dissenter's shares. This inquiry involves statutory interpretation and presents a question of law. Second, we address whether a court in making its fair value determination may consider evidence of unfair dealing relating to the value of the dissenter's shares. This also presents a question of law.
* * *

Tracing the evolution of dissenters' appraisal rights provides a context for the discussion of the two issues presently before this court. At common law, unanimous shareholder consent was required to achieve fundamental corporate changes. Courts and legislatures questioned the wisdom of allowing one shareholder to frustrate changes deemed desirable and profitable by the majority and thus modified tradition by authorizing majority consent.

Although permitting the majority to approve fundamental changes was viewed as a solution to the potential stalemate attendant to a requirement of corporate unanimity, majority consent nevertheless opened the door to victimization of the minority. In response, legislatures widely adopted statutes to address minority victimization by affording dissenters appraisal rights for their shares.

The appraisal remedy has its roots in equity and serves as a *quid pro quo*: minority shareholders may dissent and receive a fair value for their shares in exchange for relinquishing their veto power. Appraisal thus grants protection to the minority from forced participation in corporate actions approved by the majority.

Wisconsin law currently allows a minority shareholder to dissent from a fundamental corporate action, such as a merger, and to receive the fair value of those minority shares. Wisconsin Stat. § 180.1302(1) states that except in certain statutorily defined circumstances, "a shareholder or beneficial shareholder may dissent from, and obtain payment of the fair value of his or her shares in the event of [a merger or other enumerated corporate actions]." If the shareholder expresses dissatisfaction with the payment of shares offered by the corporate entity and complies with the appropriate procedures, a corporation may institute a special proceeding and petition the court to make a binding determination as to the fair value of the shares.

We turn now to address the first issue: whether a minority discount may apply in determining the fair value of a dissenter's shares. * * *

Appraisal rights represent a legislative response to the minority's lack of corporate veto power and the consequential vulnerability to majority oppression. To compensate for nominal control, the legislature granted minority shareholders the right to receive fair value for their shares if they objected to a particular corporate action.

Consistent with the statutory purpose in granting dissenters' rights, an involuntary corporate change approved by the majority requires as a matter of fairness that a dissenting shareholder be compensated for the loss of the shareholder's proportionate interest in the business as an entity. Otherwise, the majority may "squeeze out" minority shareholders to the economic advantage of the majority.

As the Delaware Supreme Court observed in the seminal case of *Cavalier Oil Corp. v. Harnett*, 564 A.2d 1137, 1145 (Del.1989):

> Where there is no objective market data available, the appraisal process is not intended to reconstruct a pro forma sale but to assume that the shareholder was willing to maintain his investment position, however slight, had the merger not occurred. . . . [T]o fail to accord to a minority shareholder the full proportionate value of his shares imposes a penalty for lack of control, and unfairly enriches the majority shareholders who may reap a windfall from the appraisal process by cashing out a dissenting shareholder, a clearly undesirable result.

> A minority discount based on valuing only the minority block of shares injects into the appraisal process speculation as to the myriad factors that may affect the market price of the block of shares. Examining the purpose of dissenters' rights statutes, we conclude that the application of a minority discount in determining the fair value of a dissenter's shares frustrates the equitable purpose to protect minority shareholders.

A dissenting stockholder is thus entitled to the proportionate interest of his or her minority shares in the going concern of the entire company. *Weinberger v. UOP, Inc.*, 457 A.2d 701, 713 (Del.1983). Although Wis. Stat. § 180.1301(4) defines "fair value" as "the value of the shares" immediately before the corporate action, the focus of fair valuation is not the stock as a commodity but rather the stock only as it represents a proportionate part of the enterprise as a whole. * * *

In rejecting the application of a minority discount, we join a significant number of jurisdictions that have likewise disavowed the minority discount. These courts have also concluded that a minority discount thwarts the purpose of dissenters' rights statutes to protect shareholders subjected to an involuntary corporate change.

Reasoning against a minority discount, courts have recognized that to apply such a discount inflicts a double penalty upon the minority shareholder and upsets the *quid pro quo* underlying dissenters' appraisal rights. The shareholder not only lacks control over corporate decision making, but also upon the application of a minority discount receives less than proportional value for loss of that control. * * *

Having concluded that a minority discount may not apply in determining the fair value of a dissenter's shares, we turn next to the second issue: whether a fair value determination of a dissenter's shares may include consideration of unfair dealing in the valuation of those shares. SSM contends that in this appraisal proceeding, the circuit court should have considered HMO-W's unfair dealing in initially setting the company's net value at $16.5–$18 million and subsequently representing significantly lower values. According to SSM, the court should have bound HMO-W to its initial represented value.

We note at the outset that SSM has not pled breach of fiduciary duty or sought damages based on such a breach. Rather, it states that the issue of unfair dealing is raised as an affirmative defense. SSM has relied on general principles of fiduciary duty to support its contention that HMO-W's unfair dealing should be considered in the valuation of SSM's shares. SSM has also maintained from the initial stage of this action that HMO-W should be estopped from claiming a lower value in this appraisal proceeding than the value established in the initial VR report that was submitted to the shareholders. * * *

Wisconsin law has established that in the absence of fraud or breach of fiduciary duty, appraisal represents the exclusive remedy for a shareholder objecting to the valuation of shares under a plan of corporate merger. Appraisal is a limited remedy, and the dissenter in an appraisal proceeding may assert only a right to the fair value of the dissenter's shares.

However, Wisconsin law has not shed light on whether evidence of unfair dealing and other misconduct in the valuation of a dissenter's shares may be presented in an appraisal proceeding. Furthermore, cases in this state have not addressed whether actions for fraud or breach of fiduciary duty must be brought as separate actions or may be consolidated with an appraisal proceeding.

Delaware appears to represent the jurisdiction that has most frequently addressed whether claims of misconduct and wrongdoing may be submitted in an appraisal action. Recognizing the limited scope of an appraisal proceeding, in which the only issue to be litigated remains the valuation of a dissenter's shares, Delaware has established that claims for fraud and breach of fiduciary duty must be instituted separately.

The ALI, however, observes that no apparent reason exists as to why such actions may not be consolidated with an appraisal proceeding in the discretion of the court. ALI PRINCIPLES, Comment e to § 7.22 at 326. Endorsing the position that courts should not foster a separate and unnecessary damages forum, the ALI suggests that courts entertain claims of fraud or breach of fiduciary duty in the appraisal proceeding. Because we determine that the allegation of unfair dealing in this case directly relates to the issue of fair value, we need not answer the unresolved issue of consolidation. * * *

A court determining the fair value of shares subject to appraisal must consider "all relevant factors." These factors may include evidence of unfair dealing affecting the value of a dissenter's shares. Additionally, courts may examine wrongful actions in gauging or impeaching the credibility of majority shareholders with respect to their valuation contentions.

In this case, SSM's assertion of unfair dealing concerns the value of its shares. SSM neither disputes the legitimacy of the business purpose to be served by HMO-W's merger with United nor contends that the merger should be invalidated. Rather, SSM contends that HMO-W's unfair dealing directly reduced the fair value of shares owned by SSM and that the appropriate remedy for HMO-W's unfair dealing should involve valuing the entity at the original net value advanced by HMO-W: $16.5–$18 million. Because the assertion of unfair dealing relates to the value of SSM's shares, we determine that it is a proper subject for consideration in this appraisal proceeding.

Having determined that SSM's allegation of unfair dealing may be raised in this appraisal action, we now conclude that the circuit court adequately considered the evidence of unfair dealing in rendering its fair value determination. A fair value determination is necessarily a fact-specific process. We will not upset a circuit court's findings of fact unless they are against the great weight and clear preponderance of the evidence.

SSM invokes principles of fiduciary duty and estoppel to assert that HMO-W should be bound to the initial representation of its net asset value. Because HMO-W endorsed the VR report that it submitted as part of its proxy materials to shareholders, and as a result secured shareholder approval for the United merger, SSM contends that HMO-W cannot now subvert the appraisal process by disavowing the VR report. If HMO-W had reservations about the validity of the report, SSM claims that HMO-W was under a duty to inform its shareholders of potential flaws, particularly in light of the significance of the report in influencing shareholder approval.

According to SSM, HMO-W's actions in asserting lower values in the subsequent appraisal proceedings are evidence of unfair dealing because these actions reduced the fair value of SSM's shares. SSM claims that HMO-W's unfair dealing was reflected in its decision to hire a new appraiser for the purposes of maligning the VR report and consequently offering to SSM a significantly depressed value for its dissenting shares. In remedying HMO-W's unfair dealing, SSM urges this court to bind HMO-W to the initial representation of the company's value, thereby altering the fair value of SSM's dissenting shares.

We note that the circuit court addressed SSM's arguments of unfair dealing in the valuation of HMO-W. The record reflects that the court examined all of the relevant evidence, including the allegations of corporate misconduct. The court determined that HMO-W had not made a material misrepresentation to its shareholders and that the initial VR report contained several flaws.

Upon hearing testimony from three experts and the corporate officers of HMO-W, SSM, and United, the court rendered a decision accepting the valuation of HMO-W's second appraiser. We perceive no reason for the court to have relied solely on the value and methodology of the first appraiser or to have accepted a valuation it deemed inaccurate. The circuit court is in the best position to gauge the credibility of witnesses and the relative weight to be given to their testimony. Furthermore, the court decides fair value and is not required to accept any one party's represented valuation.

As the circuit court apparently concluded, SSM has failed to establish that it relied to its detriment on the initial VR report or that but for the report, HMO-W's shareholders would not have approved the United merger that forced SSM to sell its shares. In this proceeding, the circuit court properly considered SSM's assertion of unfair dealing as it affected the fair value of the shares owned by SSM. The court then made a determination of HMO-W's net value that is not against the great weight and clear preponderance of the evidence.

In sum, we conclude that a minority discount may not be applied to determine the fair value of a dissenter's shares in an appraisal action.

This discount unfairly penalizes dissenting shareholders for exercising their legal right to dissent and does not protect them from oppression by the majority. We further conclude that in an appraisal proceeding, the court may entertain assertions of misconduct that relate to the value of a dissenter's shares. In this case, the circuit court properly considered SSM's evidence of unfair dealing and rendered a determination of HMO-W's net value that is supported by the record. Accordingly, we affirm the court of appeals.

QUESTIONS

1.   What is a "minority discount"? What is a "marketability discount"?

2.   When HMO-W sent SSM a check for $1.5 million, what did it send to its other shareholders? Where did the $1.5 million come from?

3.   Do we know how HMO-W's expert determined that the value of HMO-W was $10,544,000? Do we know how SSM's expert determined that the value was $19,250,000? Do we know why the court accepted the valuation of the HMO-W expert? Do we need to know any of this stuff?

4.   Was the claim asserted in this case direct or a derivative? Who pays the costs of litigating about the fair value of a dissenting shareholder's stock? Is it expensive litigation?

5.   Note that HMO-W is a small, closely held corporation. What if it were a large public corporation whose stock was traded on the New York Stock Exchange? Would there still be litigable issues as to value of HMO-W?

d.   Sue the Directors Who Approved the Merger for Breach of the Duty of Loyalty

Recall how corporation statutes (and this casebook) recognize a director's duty of loyalty. *See* MBCA § 8.31 and Delaware § 144 and Chapter 5, starting at page 230.

Duty-of-loyalty issues arise when a director engages in self-dealing or is in other ways on both sides of the deal. Assume, for example, that Bubba's Burritos, Inc. is discussing a potential merger with both McDonald's and Wendy's and that the Wendy's deal includes lucrative consulting contracts for Bubba's Burritos' present directors. Are there any duty-of-loyalty problems if the directors approve and recommend that the shareholders approve the Wendy's merger agreement?

Or assume that The Signal Companies, Inc., ("Signal") owns 50.5% of the outstanding stock of UOP, Inc. and that a majority of UOP's directors are also officers or directors of Signal or connected to Signal in some other way. The board of directors of UOP recommends a merger of UOP and Signal that will result in the shareholders of UOP other than Signal receiving $21 per share. The Signal-affiliated directors of UOP know that a study by two Signal officers concluded that the merger would be a good investment for Signal for as high as $24 a share. However, neither the other UOP directors nor the UOP shareholders know of the study at the time that they approve the merger. When the UOP shareholders later learn of the study, what are their rights and remedies?

The next case considered these facts and similar questions. As you read it, please consider the following:

1.   Who is the plaintiff—which corporation's shares did he own?

2.   Which corporation(s) is a defendant? What did the various defendants do wrong?

3.   When did the plaintiff file this suit? We know that the "merger became effective on May 26, 1978." Do we know when the lawsuit was commenced?

4.   What is the plaintiff asking the court to do?

WEINBERGER V. UOP, INC.

Delaware Supreme Court, 1983
457 A.2d 701

MOORE, JUSTICE. This post-trial appeal was reheard *en banc* from a decision of the Court of Chancery. It was brought by the class action plaintiff below, a former shareholder of UOP, Inc., who challenged the elimination of UOP's minority shareholders by a cash-out merger between UOP and its majority owner, The Signal Companies, Inc. Originally, the defendants in this action were Signal, UOP, certain officers and directors of those companies, and UOP's investment banker, Lehman Brothers Kuhn Loeb, Inc. The * * * Chancellor held that the terms of the merger were fair to the plaintiff and the other minority shareholders of UOP. Accordingly, he entered judgment in favor of the defendants. * * *

Signal is a diversified, technically based company operating through various subsidiaries. Its stock is publicly traded on the New York, Philadelphia and Pacific Stock Exchanges. UOP, formerly known as Universal Oil Products Company, was a diversified industrial company engaged in various lines of business, including petroleum and petro-chemical services and related products, construction, fabricated metal products, transportation equipment products, chemicals and plastics, and other products and services including land development, lumber products and waste disposal. Its stock was publicly held and listed on the New York Stock Exchange.

In 1974 Signal became interested in UOP as a possible acquisition. Friendly negotiations ensued. * * *

Signal achieved its goal of becoming a 50.5% shareholder of UOP.

Although UOP's board consisted of thirteen directors, Signal nominated and elected only six. Of these, five were either directors or employees of Signal. * * *

However, the president and chief executive officer of UOP retired during 1975, and Signal caused him to be replaced by James V. Crawford, a long-time employee and senior executive vice president of one of Signal's wholly-owned subsidiaries. Crawford succeeded his predecessor on UOP's board of directors and also was made a director of Signal. * * *

At the instigation of certain Signal management personnel, including William W. Walkup, its board chairman, and Forrest N. Shumway, its president, a feasibility study was made concerning the possible acquisition of the balance of UOP's outstanding shares. This study was performed by two Signal officers, Charles S. Arledge, vice president (director of planning), and Andrew J. Chitiea, senior vice president (chief financial officer). Messrs. Walkup, Shumway, Arledge and Chitiea were all directors of UOP in addition to their membership on the Signal board.

Arledge and Chitiea concluded that it would be a good investment for Signal to acquire the remaining 49.5% of UOP shares at any price up to $24 each. Their report was discussed between Walkup and Shumway who, along with Arledge, Chitiea and Brewster L. Arms, internal counsel for Signal, constituted Signal's senior management. In particular, they talked about the proper price to be paid if the acquisition was pursued, purportedly keeping in mind that as UOP's majority shareholder, Signal owed a fiduciary responsibility to both its own stockholders as well as to UOP's minority. It was ultimately agreed that a meeting of Signal's executive committee would be called to propose that Signal acquire the remaining outstanding stock of UOP through a cash-out merger in the range of $20 to $21 per share.

The executive committee meeting was set for February 28, 1978. As a courtesy, UOP's president, Crawford, was invited to attend, although he was not a member of Signal's executive committee. On his arrival, and prior to the meeting, Crawford was told of Signal's plan to acquire full ownership of UOP and was asked for his reaction to the proposed price range of $20 to $21 per share. Crawford said he thought such a price would be "generous," and that it was certainly one which should be submitted to UOP's minority shareholders for their ultimate consideration. * * *

Signal's executive committee authorized its management "to negotiate" with UOP "for a cash acquisition of the minority ownership in UOP, Inc., with the intention of presenting a proposal to [Signal's] board of directors . . . on March 6, 1978." Immediately after this February 28, 1978 meeting, Signal issued a press release stating:

The Signal Companies, Inc. and UOP, Inc. are conducting negotiations for the acquisition for cash by Signal of the 49.5 per cent of UOP which it does not presently own, announced Forrest N. Shumway, president and chief executive officer of Signal, and James V. Crawford, UOP president.

Price and other terms of the proposed transaction have not yet been finalized and would be subject to approval of the boards of directors of Signal and UOP, scheduled to meet early next week, the stockholders of UOP and certain federal agencies.

The announcement also referred to the fact that the closing price of UOP's common stock on that day was $14.50 per share.

Between Tuesday, February 28, 1978 and Monday, March 6, 1978, a total of four business days, Crawford spoke by telephone with all of UOP's non-Signal, i.e., outside, directors. Also during that period, Crawford retained Lehman Brothers to render a fairness opinion as to the price offered the minority for its stock. Second, James W. Glanville, a long-time director of UOP and a partner in Lehman Brothers, had acted as a financial advisor to UOP for many years. Crawford believed that Glanville's familiarity with UOP, as a member of its board, would also be of assistance in enabling Lehman Brothers to render a fairness opinion within the existing time constraints.

* * * The Lehman Brothers team concluded that "the price of either $20 or $21 would be a fair price for the remaining shares of UOP."

On * * * March 6, 1978, both the Signal and UOP boards were convened to consider the proposed merger. Telephone communications were maintained between the two meetings. Walkup, Signal's board chairman, and also a UOP director, attended UOP's meeting with Crawford in order to present Signal's position and answer any questions that UOP's non-Signal directors might have. Arledge and Chitiea, along with Signal's other designees on UOP's board, participated by conference telephone. All of UOP's outside directors attended the meeting either in person or by conference telephone.

First, Signal's board unanimously adopted a resolution authorizing Signal to propose to UOP a cash merger of $21 per share as outlined in a certain merger agreement and other supporting documents. This proposal required that the merger be approved by a majority of UOP's outstanding minority shares voting at the stockholders meeting at which the merger would be considered, and that the minority shares voting in favor of the merger, when coupled with Signal's 50.5% interest would have to comprise at least two-thirds of all UOP shares. Otherwise the proposed merger would be deemed disapproved.

UOP's board then considered the proposal. Copies of the agreement were delivered to the directors in attendance, and other copies had been forwarded earlier to the directors participating by telephone. They also had before them UOP financial data for 1974–1977, UOP's most recent financial statements, market price information, and budget projections for 1978. In addition they had Lehman Brothers' hurriedly prepared fairness opinion letter finding the price of $21 to be fair. * * *

While Signal's men on UOP's board participated in various aspects of the meeting, they abstained from voting. However, the minutes show that each of them "if voting would have voted yes." * * *

Despite the swift board action of the two companies, the merger was not submitted to UOP's shareholders until their annual meeting on May 26, 1978. In the notice of that meeting and proxy statement sent to shareholders in May, UOP's management and board urged that the merger be approved. The proxy statement also advised:

> The price was determined after discussions between James V. Crawford, a director of Signal and Chief Executive Officer of UOP, and officers of Signal which took place during meetings on February 28, 1978, and in the course of several subsequent telephone conversations.

In the original draft of the proxy statement the word "negotiations" had been used rather than "discussions." However, when the Securities and Exchange Commission sought details of the "negotiations" as part of its review of these materials, the term was deleted and the word "discussions" was substituted. The proxy statement indicated that the vote of UOP's board in approving the merger had been unanimous. It also advised the shareholders that Lehman Brothers had given its opinion that the merger price of $21 per share was fair to UOP's minority. However, it did not disclose the hurried method by which this conclusion was reached.

As of the record date of UOP's annual meeting, there were 11,488,302 shares of UOP common stock outstanding, 5,688,302 of which were owned by the minority. At the meeting only 56%, or 3,208,652, of the minority shares were voted. Of these, 2,953,812, or 51.9% of the total minority, voted for the merger, and 254,840 voted against it. When Signal's stock was added to the minority shares voting in favor, a total of 76.2% of UOP's outstanding shares approved the merger while only 2.2% opposed it.

By its terms the merger became effective on May 26, 1978, and each share of UOP's stock held by the minority was automatically converted into a right to receive $21 cash.

II.

A.

A primary issue mandating reversal is the preparation by two UOP directors, Arledge and Chitiea, of their feasibility study for the exclusive use and benefit of Signal. This document was of obvious significance to both Signal and UOP. Using UOP data, it described the advantages to Signal of ousting the minority at a price range of $21–$24 per share. * * *

The Arledge-Chitiea report speaks for itself in supporting the Chancellor's finding that a price of up to $24 was a "good investment" for Signal. It shows that a return on the investment at $21 would be 15.7% versus 15.5% at $24 per share. This was a difference of only two-tenths of one percent, while it meant over $17,000,000 to the minority. Under such circumstances, paying UOP's minority shareholders $24 would have had relatively little long-term effect on Signal, and the Chancellor's findings concerning the benefit to Signal, even at a price of $24, were obviously correct.

Certainly, this was a matter of material significance to UOP and its shareholders. Since the study was prepared by two UOP directors, using UOP information for the exclusive benefit of Signal, and nothing whatever was done to disclose it to the outside UOP directors or the minority shareholders, a question of breach of fiduciary duty arises. This problem occurs because there were common Signal-UOP directors participating, at least to some extent, in the UOP board's decision-making processes without full disclosure of the conflicts they faced.* **[7]** * * *

C.

The concept of fairness has two basic aspects: fair dealing and fair price. The former embraces questions of when the transaction was timed, how it was initiated, structured, negotiated, disclosed to the directors, and how the approvals of the directors and the stockholders were obtained. The latter aspect of fairness relates to the economic and financial considerations of the proposed merger, including all relevant factors: assets, market value, earnings, future prospects, and any other elements that affect the intrinsic or inherent value of a company's stock. * * *

The Arledge-Chitiea report is but one aspect of the element of fair dealing. How did this merger evolve? It is clear that it was entirely

---

* **[7]** Although perfection is not possible, or expected, the result here could have been entirely different if UOP had appointed an independent negotiating committee of its outside directors to deal with Signal at arm's length. Since fairness in this context can be equated to conduct by a theoretical, wholly independent, board of directors acting upon the matter before them, it is unfortunate that this course apparently was neither considered nor pursued. Particularly in a parent-subsidiary context, a showing that the action taken was as though each of the contending parties had in fact exerted its bargaining power against the other at arm's length is strong evidence that the transaction meets the test of fairness.

initiated by Signal. The serious time constraints under which the principals acted were all set by Signal. It had not found a suitable outlet for its excess cash and considered UOP a desirable investment, particularly since it was now in a position to acquire the whole company for itself. For whatever reasons, and they were only Signal's, the entire transaction was presented to and approved by UOP's board within four business days. Standing alone, this is not necessarily indicative of any lack of fairness by a majority shareholder. It was what occurred, or more properly, what did not occur, during this brief period that makes the time constraints imposed by Signal relevant to the issue of fairness.

The structure of the transaction, again, was Signal's doing. So far as negotiations were concerned, it is clear that they were modest at best. Crawford, Signal's man at UOP, never really talked price with Signal, except to accede to its management's statements on the subject, and to convey to Signal the UOP outside directors' view that as between the $20–$21 range under consideration, it would have to be $21. The latter is not a surprising outcome, but hardly arm's length negotiations. * * *

This cannot but undermine a conclusion that this merger meets any reasonable test of fairness. The outside UOP directors lacked one material piece of information generated by two of their colleagues, but shared only with Signal. True, the UOP board had the Lehman Brothers' fairness opinion, but that firm has been blamed by the plaintiff for the hurried task it performed, when more properly the responsibility for this lies with Signal. There was no disclosure of the circumstances surrounding the rather cursory preparation of the Lehman Brothers' fairness opinion. Instead, the impression was given UOP's minority that a careful study had been made, when in fact speed was the hallmark. * * *

Finally, the minority stockholders were denied the critical information that Signal considered a price of $24 to be a good investment. Since this would have meant over $17,000,000 more to the minority, we cannot conclude that the shareholder vote was an informed one. Under the circumstances, an approval by a majority of the minority was meaningless. * * *

E.

Turning to the matter of price, plaintiff also challenges its fairness. His evidence was that on the date the merger was approved the stock was worth at least $26 per share. In support, he offered the testimony of a chartered investment analyst who used two basic approaches to valuation: a comparative analysis of the premium paid over market in ten other tender offer-merger combinations, and a discounted cash flow analysis.

In this breach of fiduciary duty case, the Chancellor perceived that the approach to valuation was the same as that in an appraisal proceeding. Consistent with precedent, he rejected plaintiff's method of proof and accepted defendants' evidence of value as being in accord with practice under prior case law. This means that the so-called "Delaware block" or weighted average method was employed wherein the elements of value, i.e., assets, market price, earnings, etc., were assigned a particular weight and the resulting amounts added to determine the value per share. This procedure has been in use for decades. However, to the extent it excludes other generally accepted techniques used in the financial community and the courts, it is now clearly outmoded. It is time we recognize this in appraisal and other stock valuation proceedings and bring our law current on the subject.

While the Chancellor rejected plaintiff's discounted cash flow method of valuing UOP's stock, as not corresponding with "either logic or the existing law," it is significant that this was essentially the focus, i.e., earnings potential of UOP, of Messrs. Arledge and Chitiea in their evaluation of the merger. Accordingly, the standard "Delaware block" or weighted average method of valuation, formerly employed in appraisal and other stock valuation cases, shall no longer exclusively control such proceedings. We believe that a more liberal approach must include proof of value by any techniques or methods which are generally considered acceptable in the financial community and otherwise admissible in court, subject only to our interpretation of 8 Del.C. § 262(h), infra. This will obviate the very structured and mechanistic procedure that has heretofore governed such matters. * * *

The plaintiff has not sought an appraisal, but rescissory damages of the type contemplated by *Lynch v. Vickers Energy Corp.*, Del.Supr., 429 A.2d 497, 505–06 (1981) (*Lynch II*). In view of the approach to valuation that we announce today, we see no basis in our law for *Lynch II*'s exclusive monetary formula for relief. On remand the plaintiff will be permitted to test the fairness of the $21 price by the standards we herein establish, in conformity with the principle applicable to an appraisal— that fair value be determined by taking "into account all relevant factors." In our view this includes the elements of rescissory damages if the Chancellor considers them susceptible of proof and a remedy appropriate to all the issues of fairness before him. * * *

While a plaintiff's monetary remedy ordinarily should be confined to the more liberalized appraisal proceeding herein established, we do not intend any limitation on the historic powers of the Chancellor to grant such other relief as the facts of a particular case may dictate. The appraisal remedy we approve may not be adequate in certain cases, particularly where fraud, misrepresentation, self-dealing, deliberate waste of corporate assets, or gross and palpable overreaching are involved. Under such circumstances, the Chancellor's powers are complete to fashion any form of equitable and monetary relief as may be appropriate, including rescissory damages. Since it is apparent that this long completed transaction is too involved to undo, and in view of the Chancellor's discretion, the award, if any, should be in the form of monetary damages based upon entire fairness standards, i.e., fair dealing and fair price.

Obviously, there are other litigants, like the plaintiff, who abjured an appraisal and whose rights to challenge the element of fair value must be preserved. Accordingly, the quasi-appraisal remedy we grant the plaintiff here will apply only to: * * * (2) any case now pending. * * * Thereafter, the provisions of 8 Del.C. § 262, as herein construed, respecting the scope of an appraisal and the means for perfecting the same, shall govern the financial remedy available to minority shareholders in a cash-out merger. * * *

III.

Finally, we address the matter of business purpose. The defendants contend that the purpose of this merger was not a proper subject of inquiry by the trial court. The plaintiff says that no valid purpose existed—the entire transaction was a mere subterfuge designed to eliminate the minority. * * *

The requirement of a business purpose is new to our law of mergers and was a departure from prior case law.

In view of the fairness test which has long been applicable to parent—subsidiary mergers, the expanded appraisal remedy now available to shareholders, and the broad discretion of the Chancellor to fashion such relief as the facts of a given case may dictate, we do not believe that any additional meaningful protection is afforded minority shareholders by the business purpose requirement. * * *

The judgment of the Court of Chancery, finding both the circumstances of the merger and the price paid the minority shareholders to be fair, is reversed. The matter is remanded for further proceedings consistent herewith. Upon remand the plaintiff's post-trial motion to enlarge the class should be granted.

QUESTIONS AND NOTES

1. On remand, the Delaware Court of Chancery awarded Weinberger an additional $1 per share. *See Weinberger v. UOP, Inc.*, 1985 WL 11546 (Del. Ch. 1985).

2. The court describes the transaction by which Signal acquires the remaining UOP stock as a "cash-out merger." Why? Was the transaction a "merger"? *Cf.* MBCA § 11.06. Did the "separate existence" of UOP cease?

3.   Law professors have described the transaction by which Signal acquires the remaining UOP stock as a "freeze-out merger." Why? Is every "cash-out merger" also a "freeze-out merger"?

4.   The court noted that "[t]he plaintiff has not sought an appraisal but rescissory damages." What are "rescissory" damages? Why didn't the plaintiff assert his right to dissent and obtain payment of the fair value of his shares? Why isn't statutory appraisal the exclusive remedy of a shareholder who disagrees with a merger decision approved by the board of directors and a majority of the shareholders? Did the *HMO-W* case consider this question?

5.   The *Weinberger* case rejects the Delaware Block Method. More accurately, the court states that the Delaware Block Method shall no longer "exclusively control." A student law review note criticizes valuation methods:

> A gap exists between statutory language and legal reality in the context of appraisal rights: all fifty states give minority shareholders the right to fair value for their shares when they dissent from certain fundamental transactions, but courts' current valuation methods are incapable, at both a theoretical and a practical level, of providing fair value. This result is inequitable to minority shareholders and inefficient for the corporate takeover market overall. Capital cash flow (CCF) valuation better satisfies these equity and efficiency objectives for appraisal rights. Although CCF valuation was foreshadowed as early as 1986, its formal appearance in the corporate finance literature has been recent and somewhat oblique. Its most detailed exposition appears in a 1995 Harvard Business School Note. CCF valuation is slowly gaining acceptance on Wall Street, and as it does it will no doubt be promulgated in appraisal proceedings as well. However, the considerable lag-time from business schools to Wall Street to the Delaware courts has made it an unknown technique in appraisal proceedings to date. This delay is unfortunate because CCF valuation has desirable properties from the appraisal perspective. CCF valuation would provide more equitable terms for dissenting shareholders and would promote a more efficient market for corporate control.

Note, Using Capital Cash Flows to Value Dissenters' Shares in Appraisal Proceedings, 111 HARV. L. REV. 2099–100 (1998).

Professor Grossfield sums up the techniques that courts use for calculating the value of dissenting shareholders' stock: "the answer is left to the 'financial community,' where—probably—accountants [and not lawyers] have the upper hand." Bernhard Grossfield, *Lawyers and Accountants: A Semiotic Competition*, 36 WAKE FOREST L. REV. 167, 174 (2001).

6.   Suppose that a corporation's controlling shareholder admits that she had no business purpose for causing the corporation to eliminate its single minority shareholder through a cash-out merger. Instead, she just

found the shareholder annoying because he wore his hair in a mullet. Would this affect the outcome of a Delaware court's review of the merger?

7.   What did the defendants do wrong? What should the defendants have done differently? Assume that Signal had (i) made a full disclosure to the UOP directors and shareholders and (ii) had changed the terms of the merger so each share of UOP stock was exchanged for $24 and (iii) had provided ample time for the UOP board and shareholders to consider the deal. What would be the legal rights of P, a UOP shareholder who did not want to sell her shares? The next case provides the Massachusetts answer to this question (and an answer to Question 4 above).

COGGINS V. NEW ENGLAND PATRIOTS FOOTBALL CLUB, INC.

Massachusetts Supreme Judicial Court, 1986
492 N.E.2d 1112

LIACOS, JUSTICE. On November 18, 1959, William H. Sullivan, Jr. (Sullivan), purchased an American Football League (AFL) franchise for a professional football team. Four months later, Sullivan organized a corporation, the American League Professional Football Team of Boston, Inc. Sullivan contributed his AFL franchise; nine other persons each contributed $25,000. In return, each of the ten investors received 10,000 shares of voting common stock in the corporation. Another four months later, in July 1960, the corporation sold 120,000 shares of nonvoting common stock to the public at $5 a share.

Sullivan had effective control of the corporation from its inception until 1974. In 1974 the other voting stockholders ousted him from the presidency and from operating control of the corporation. He then began the effort to regain control of the corporation—an effort which culminated in this and other lawsuits.

In November, 1975, Sullivan succeeded in obtaining ownership or control of all 100,000 of the voting shares, at a price of approximately $102 a share (adjusted cash value), of the corporation, by that time renamed the New England Patriots Football Club, Inc. (Old Patriots). In order to finance this coup, Sullivan borrowed approximately $5,348,000 from the Rhode Island Hospital National Bank and the Lasalle National Bank of Chicago. As a condition of these loans, Sullivan was to use his best efforts to reorganize the Patriots so that the income of the corporation could be devoted to the payment of these personal loans and the assets of the corporation pledged to secure them. At this point they were secured by all of the voting shares held by Sullivan. * * *

In order to accomplish in effect the assumption by the corporation of Sullivan's personal obligations, it was necessary, as a matter of corporate law, to eliminate the interest of the nonvoting shares.

On October 20, 1976, Sullivan organized a new corporation called the New Patriots Football Club, Inc. (New Patriots). The board of directors of the Old Patriots and the board of directors of the New Patriots executed an agreement of merger of the two corporations providing that, after the merger, the voting stock of the Old Patriots would be extinguished, the nonvoting stock would be exchanged for cash at the rate of $15 a share, and the name of the New Patriots would be changed to the name formerly used by the Old Patriots.* **[6]** As part of this plan, Sullivan gave the New Patriots his 100,000 voting shares of the Old Patriots in return for 100% of the New Patriots stock.

General Laws c. 156B, § 78(c)(1)(iii), as amended through St. 1976, c. 327, required approval of the merger agreement by a majority vote of each class of affected stock. Approval by the voting class, entirely controlled by Sullivan, was assured. The merger was approved by the class of nonvoting stockholders at a special meeting on December 8, 1976.* **[7]** On January 31, 1977, the merger of the New Patriots and the Old Patriots was consummated.

David A. Coggins (Coggins) was the owner of ten shares of nonvoting stock in the Old Patriots. Coggins, a fan of the Patriots from the time of their formation, was serving in Vietnam in 1967 when he purchased the shares through his brother. Over the years, he followed the fortunes of the team, taking special pride in his status as an owner.* **[8]** When he heard of the proposed merger, Coggins was upset that he could be forced to sell. Coggins voted against the merger and commenced this suit on behalf of those stockholders, who, like himself, believed the transaction to be unfair and illegal. A judge of the Superior Court certified the class as "stockholders of New England Patriots Football Club, Inc. who have voted against the merger . . . but who have neither turned in their shares nor perfected their appraisal rights . . . [and who] desire only to void the merger."

---

* **[6]** Additional findings as to the purpose of this merger * * * as adopted by the trial judge, are: "Purported reasons for the merger [were] stated in the [proxy materials]. Three reasons are given: (1) the policy of the [National Football League] to discourage public ownership of member football teams, (2) the difficulty in reconciling management's obligations to the NFL with its obligations to public stockholders, and (3) the cost and possible revelation of confidential information resulting from the obligations of publicly owned corporations to file reports with various public bodies. . . . I find, however, that while some of the stated reasons may have been useful by-products of the merger, the true reason for the merger was to enable Sullivan to satisfy his $5,348,000 personal obligation to the banks. The merger would not have occurred for the considerations stated as reasons in the Proxy Statement. . . . The Proxy Statement is an artful attempt to minimize the future profitability of the Patriots and to put a wash of corporate respectability over Sullivan's diversion of the corporation's income for his own purposes."

* **[7]** On the date of the meeting, 139,800 shares of nonvoting stock were outstanding, held by approximately 2,400 stockholders. The Sullivan family owned 10,826 shares. Of the remaining 128,974, a total of 71,644 voted in favor of the merger, 22,795 did not vote, and 34,535 voted against. The plaintiffs in this case are stockholders of 2,291 of the 34,535 voting against the merger.

* **[8]** It was, in part, the goal of the Old Patriots, in offering stock to the public, to generate loyal fans.

The trial judge found in favor of the Coggins class but determined that the merger should not be undone. Instead, he ruled that the plaintiffs are entitled to rescissory damages, and he ordered that further hearings be held to determine the amount of damages. * * *

We conclude that the trial judge was correct in ruling that the merger was illegal and that the plaintiffs have been wronged. Ordinarily, rescission of the merger would be the appropriate remedy. This merger, however, is now nearly ten years old, and, because an effective and orderly rescission of the merger now is not feasible, we remand the case for proceedings to determine the appropriate monetary damages to compensate the plaintiffs. * * *

Scope of Judicial Review. In deciding this case, we address an important corporate law question: What approach will a Massachusetts court reviewing a cash freeze-out merger employ?

The parties have urged us to consider the views of a court with great experience in such matters, the Supreme Court of Delaware. We note that the Delaware court announced one test in 1977, but recently has changed to another.* [10] In *Singer v. Magnavox Co.*, 380 A.2d 969, 980 (Del.1977), the Delaware court established the so-called "business-purpose" test, holding that controlling stockholders violate their fiduciary duties when they "cause a merger to be made for the sole purpose of eliminating a minority on a cash-out basis." *Id.* at 978. In 1983, Delaware jettisoned the business-purpose test, satisfied that the "fairness" test "long . . . applicable to parent-subsidiary mergers, the expanded appraisal remedy now available to stockholders, and the broad discretion of the Chancellor to fashion such relief as the facts of a given case may dictate" provided sufficient protection to the frozen-out minority. *Weinberger v. UOP, Inc.*, 457 A.2d 701, 715 (Del.1983). "The requirement of fairness is unflinching in its demand that where one stands on both sides of a transaction, he has the burden of establishing its entire fairness, sufficient to pass the test of careful scrutiny by the courts. The concept of fairness has two basic aspects: fair dealing and fair price." We note that the "fairness" test to which the Delaware court now has adhered is, as we later show, closely related to the views expressed in our decisions. Unlike the Delaware court, however, we believe that the "business-purpose" test is an additional useful means under our statutes and case law for examining a transaction in which a controlling stockholder eliminates the minority interest in a corporation. *Cf. Wilkes v. Springside Nursing Home, Inc.*, 370 Mass. 842, 851, 353 N.E.2d 657 (1976). This concept of fair dealing is not limited to close corporations but applies to judicial review of cash freeze-out mergers.

---

* [10] We are not bound, of course, in our interpretation of Massachusetts law by decisions of the courts of our sister States interpreting their laws. We have said before, however, that we consider such decisions instructive.

The defendants argue that judicial review of a merger cannot be invoked by disgruntled stockholders, absent illegal or fraudulent conduct. They rely on G.L. c. 156B, § 98 (1984 ed.).* **[12]** In the defendants' view, "the Superior Court's finding of liability was premised solely on the claimed inadequacy of the offering price." Any dispute over offering price, they urge, must be resolved solely through the statutory remedy of appraisal.

We have held in regard to so called "close corporations" that the statute does not divest the courts of their equitable jurisdiction to assure that the conduct of controlling stockholders does not violate the fiduciary principles governing the relationship between majority and minority stockholders.* **[13]** "Where the director's duty of loyalty to the corporation is in conflict with his self-interest the court will vigorously scrutinize the situation." The court is justified in exercising its equitable power when a violation of fiduciary duty is claimed.

The dangers of self-dealing and abuse of fiduciary duty are greatest in freeze-out situations like the Patriots merger, where a controlling stockholder and corporate director chooses to eliminate public ownership. It is in these cases that a judge should examine with closest scrutiny the motives and the behavior of the controlling stockholder. A showing of compliance with statutory procedures is an insufficient substitute for the inquiry of the courts when a minority stockholder claims that the corporate action "will be or is illegal or fraudulent as to him."

A controlling stockholder who is also a director standing on both sides of the transaction bears the burden of showing that the transaction does not violate fiduciary obligations. Judicial inquiry into a freeze-out merger in technical compliance with the statute may be appropriate, and the dissenting stockholders are not limited to the statutory remedy of judicial appraisal where violations of fiduciary duties are found.

Factors in Judicial Review. Judicial scrutiny should begin with recognition of the basic principle that the duty of a corporate director must be to further the legitimate goals of the corporation. The result of a freeze-out merger is the elimination of public ownership in the corporation. The controlling faction increases its equity from a majority to 100%, using corporate processes and corporate assets. The corporate

---

*   **[12]** "The enforcement by a stockholder of his right to receive payment for his shares in the manner provided in this chapter shall be an exclusive remedy except that this chapter shall not exclude the right of such stockholder to bring or maintain an appropriate proceeding to obtain relief on the ground that such corporate action will be or is illegal or fraudulent as to him." G.L. c. 156B, § 98.

*   **[13]** We discussed the nature of a close corporation at some length in *Donahue v. Rodd Electrotype Co. of New England, Inc.*, 367 Mass. 578, 328 N.E.2d 505 (1975). We need not apply the stricter principle of good faith applied to a close corporation in *Donahue* to controlling stockholders in a public corporation to conclude, nevertheless, that the "less stringent standard of fiduciary duty to which directors and stockholders of all corporations must adhere" may warrant judicial scrutiny beyond the specified statutory appraisal right.

directors who benefit from this transfer of ownership must demonstrate how the legitimate goals of the corporation are furthered. A director of a corporation violates his fiduciary duty when he uses the corporation for his or his family's personal benefit in a manner detrimental to the corporation. Because the danger of abuse of fiduciary duty is especially great in a freeze-out merger, the court must be satisfied that the freeze-out was for the advancement of a legitimate corporate purpose. If satisfied that elimination of public ownership is in furtherance of a business purpose, the court should then proceed to determine if the transaction was fair by examining the totality of the circumstances. * * *

The plaintiffs here adequately alleged that the merger of the Old Patriots and New Patriots was a freeze-out merger undertaken for no legitimate business purpose, but merely for the personal benefit of Sullivan. While we have recognized the right to "selfish ownership" in a corporation, such a right must be balanced against the concept of the majority stockholder's fiduciary obligation to the minority stockholders. Consequently, the defendants bear the burden of proving, first, that the merger was for a legitimate business purpose, and, second, that, considering totality of circumstances, it was fair to the minority.

The decision of the Superior Court judge includes a finding that "the defendants have failed to demonstrate that the merger served any valid corporate objective unrelated to the personal interests of the majority shareholders. It thus appears that the sole reason for the merger was to effectuate a restructuring of the Patriots that would enable the repayment of the [personal] indebtedness incurred by Sullivan. . . ." The trial judge considered the defendants' claims that the policy of the National Football League (NFL) requiring majority ownership by a single individual or family made it necessary to eliminate public ownership. He found that "the stock ownership of the Patriots as it existed just prior to the merger fully satisfied the rationale underlying the policy as expressed by NFL Commissioner Pete Rozelle. Having acquired 100% control of the voting common stock of the Patriots, Sullivan possessed unquestionable authority to act on behalf of the franchise at League meetings and effectively foreclosed the possible recurrence of the internal management disputes that had existed in 1974. Moreover, as the proxy statement itself notes, the Old Patriots were under no legal compulsion to eliminate public ownership." Likewise, the defendants did not succeed in showing a conflict between the interests of the league owners and the Old Patriots' stockholders. We perceive no error in these findings. They are fully supported by the evidence. Under the approach we set forth above, there is no need to consider further the elements of fairness of a transaction that is not related to a valid corporate purpose.

Remedy. The plaintiffs are entitled to relief. They argue that the appropriate relief is rescission of the merger and restoration of the parties to their positions of 1976. We agree that the normally appropriate remedy for an impermissible freeze-out merger is rescission. Because Massachusetts statutes do not bar a cash freeze-out, however, numerous third parties relied in good faith on the outcome of the merger. The trial judge concluded that the expectations of those parties should not be upset, and so chose to award damages rather than rescission.

We recognize that, because rescission is an equitable remedy, the circumstances of a particular case may not favor its employment. The goals of a remedy instituted after a finding that a merger did not serve the corporate purpose should include furthering the interests of the corporation. Ordinarily, we would remand with instructions for the trial judge to determine whether rescission would be in the corporation's best interests, but such a remedy does not appear to be equitable at this time. This litigation has gone on for many years. There is yet at least another related case pending (in the Federal District Court). Furthermore, other factors weigh against rescission. The passage of time has made the 1976 position of the parties difficult, if not impossible, to restore. A substantial number of former stockholders have chosen other courses and should not be forced back into the Patriots corporation. In these circumstances the interests of the corporation and of the plaintiffs will be furthered best by limiting the plaintiffs' remedy to an assessment of damages.

We do not think it appropriate, however, to award damages based on a 1976 appraisal value. To do so would make this suit a nullity, leaving the plaintiffs with no effective remedy except appraisal, a position we have already rejected. Rescissory damages must be determined based on the present value of the Patriots, that is, what the stockholders would have if the merger were rescinded. On remand, the judge is to take further evidence on the present value of the Old Patriots on the theory that the merger had not taken place. Each share of the Coggins class is to receive, as rescissory damages, its aliquot share of the present assets. * * *

Summary. The freeze-out merger accomplished by William H. Sullivan, Jr., was designed for his own personal benefit to eliminate the interests of the Patriots' minority stockholders. The merger did not further the interests of the corporation and therefore was a violation of Sullivan's fiduciary duty to the minority stockholders, and so was impermissible. In most cases we would turn to rescission as the appropriate remedy. In the circumstances of this case, however, rescission would be an inequitable solution. Therefore, we remand for a determination of the present value of the non-voting stock, as though the merger were rescinded. The claim for waste of corporate assets brought against the individual defendants is reinstated. Those stockholders who voted against the merger, who did not turn in their shares, who did not perfect their appraisal rights, but who are part of the Coggins class, are to receive damages in the amount their stock would be worth today, plus interest at the statutory rate. * * *

The case is remanded to the Superior Court for further proceedings consistent with this opinion.

QUESTIONS

1.   What did the defendant do wrong? What should Sullivan have done differently?

2.   What if Sullivan had established that his reasons for the cash-out merger were that (i) he wanted to use all Old Patriots' earnings to acquire better players and build a winning team and (ii) the other shareholders of Old Patriots wanted all Old Patriots' earnings to be distributed to them as dividends?

3.   Was Old Patriots a public company? Was New Patriots a public company? Should that matter?

4.   Was the *Coggins* case direct or derivative? Which should it have been?

PROBLEM

S, an individual, owns approximately 20% of the outstanding stock of T. A, another corporation, owns just under 49% of the outstanding stock of T. T and A have entered into a cash-out merger agreement whereby A will acquire the remaining 51% of the outstanding stock of T for $30 a share. S believes that the $30 price is inadequate. She wants your advice as to whether she can obtain an injunction to bar completion of the cash-out merger. Does it matter whether Massachusetts law or Delaware law controls?

D. SALE OF SUBSTANTIALLY ALL THE ASSETS

Sale of substantially all the corporation's assets is another possible end for a corporation. For example, assume that Bubba's Burritos, Inc. sells all of its assets to McDonald's Inc., instead of merging into McDonald's. Such a sale is a fundamental corporate change, which (like the others) requires approval by the board of directors and by the shareholders, as we saw in Part A of this chapter. *See* MBCA §§ 12.01, 12.02.

1.   EFFECT OF SALE OF ASSETS ON THE CREDITORS OF THE SELLING CORPORATION

There are significant differences in the effect on the creditors of Bubba's Burritos, Inc. between a merger of Bubba's Burritos, Inc. into

McDonald's and sale of assets to McDonald's.* Recall that if Bubba's Burritos, Inc. merges into McDonald's, the merger provisions of the relevant state corporate law make the creditors of Bubba's Burritos creditors of McDonald's. That is, McDonald's is liable for Bubba's liabilities.

There are no comparable statutory provisions making a buyer of the assets of a corporation liable to that corporation's creditors. Instead, the general common-law rule is that the buyer of a corporation's assets is not liable for the selling corporation's debts.

Accordingly, if Bubba's Burritos sold its assets to McDonald's, creditors of Bubba's Burritos could not collect from McDonald's. Rather, Bubba's Burritos' creditors would be limited to collecting their claims from Bubba's Burritos.

After the sale, Bubba's Burritos, Inc. will still exist, and its creditors can still attempt to collect from it. They may be successful. After selling all of its assets, Bubba's Burritos may be going out of the burrito business, but it does not go out of legal existence. It still exists, but it just has different assets from before: it now has no burrito equipment, but it instead has lots of cash.

The sale of Bubba's assets does not necessarily harm Bubba's existing creditors. Sale of all of a corporation's assets is often followed by that corporation's dissolution, which does terminate its legal existence. We have already considered dissolution. Remember that any corporation that is considering dissolution and distribution to shareholders will have to pay off its creditors first. A corporation's failure to do this can make its shareholders personally liable to these creditors.

Although a sale of assets may not harm the selling company's *existing* creditors, the sale might harm those who would become creditors in the future. Examples are people who, years after the company dissolves, suffer injury from the company's defective products, or who are harmed by environmental damage that the company caused earlier. These are claims that were unknown at the time of the selling company's sale of assets and dissolution. Assume, for example, that 20 years after Bubba's sale of assets to McDonald's and Bubba's dissolution, P, who worked for Bubba's prior to the sale, has become sick because of Bubba's smoke-filled working conditions; Bubba's had saved money by turning off the ventilation fan over the stove. Can P now sue McDonald's? The next case deals with that question. In reading it, please consider the following questions:

1.   Which corporation allegedly wronged Jeanette Franklin?

---

* There are also significant accounting and tax differences, which we leave to your tax professors.

2.   Would Con Cal be liable to the creditors of WPS? Why/why not? Why didn't the plaintiff sue Con Cal?

FRANKLIN V. USX CORP.
California Court of Appeal, 2001
105 Cal.Rptr.2d 11

WALKER, J. Jeannette Franklin, now deceased, and her husband, Darrel Franklin (respondents), filed an action for personal injury, premises liability and loss of consortium against several defendants including appellant USX Corporation (USX). Respondents contended that Jeannette had contracted mesothelioma, an asbestos-caused cancer, as a result of childhood exposure to secondhand asbestos carried home by her parents, who worked at the Western Pipe & Steel Shipyard (WPS) in South San Francisco during World War II. Respondents sought to hold USX liable for their injuries on the theory that it was the successor in interest to WPS. * * * The trial court concluded that USX was the successor in interest to WPS, and was therefore liable for any damages caused by WPS. In a bifurcated proceeding, a jury decided the issues of liability and damages, and returned a verdict against USX in excess of $5 million.

USX appeals the trial court's conclusion that it was the successor in interest to WPS. It also appeals the jury verdict on several grounds. We hold that the trial court erred in finding USX liable as the successor in interest to WPS. Accordingly, we do not address the issues pertaining to the jury verdict.

Prior to the beginning of World War II, WPS owned a steel fabrication plant in South San Francisco, which had been used to build ships during World War I. When World War II broke out, WPS entered into a contract with the United States Maritime Commission to * * * build ships for use in the war. The contract required the use of ship-building materials containing asbestos.

Jeannette Franklin was a child during World War II. Both of her parents worked at WPS from 1942 to 1945. Neither of her parents worked directly with asbestos-containing materials, but they both worked in areas where asbestos was present. At times, they were exposed to airborne dust during the mixing of mud, during insulation work, and when workers swept up debris. Franklin alleged that she was exposed to this asbestos-containing dust because her parents brought it home on their clothing and in their car. In 1996, Franklin was diagnosed with peritoneal mesothelioma, which she maintained was caused by her childhood secondhand exposure to asbestos.

In December 1945, the assets of WPS were purchased by Consolidated Steel Corporation of California (Con Cal) for over $6.2

million in cash. In connection with the sale, Con Cal agreed to assume all of the liabilities, obligations and commitments of WPS.

* * *

On August 31, 1948, Con Cal sold the transfer assets to Con Del for almost $8.3 million in cash, plus additional consideration that brought the total purchase price to over $17 million. Con Del was later merged into U.S. Steel, which thereafter changed its name to USX, the appellant here. After August 31, 1948, Con Cal changed its name to Consolidated Liquidating Corporation, which dissolved on February 29, 1952. Alden G. Roach was Con Cal's president and chairman of the board at the time of the sale; after the sale he continued as president of Con Del * * *.

* * * In a statement of decision issued March 1, 2000, the trial court found * * * that the transaction between Con Cal [and Con Del] constituted a *de facto* merger * * * [so Con Del assumed the liabilities of Con Cal, which USX then took over after Con Del merged into it].

* * * It has been generally stated that "where one corporation sells or transfers all of its assets to another corporation, the latter is not liable for the debts and liabilities of the former unless (1) the purchaser expressly or impliedly agrees to such assumption, (2) the transaction amounts to a consolidation or merger of the two corporations, (3) the purchasing corporation is merely a continuation of the selling corporation, or (4) the transaction is entered into fraudulently to escape liability for debts." (*Ortiz v. South Bend Lathe* (1975) 46 Cal.App.3d 842, 846 *disapproved on other grounds in Ray v. Alad Corp.* (1977) 19 Cal.3d 22, 34.)* * *

The trial court also found that USX could be deemed to have assumed the liabilities of Con Cal/WPS under the *de facto* merger theory and under the theory that USX was a "mere continuation" of Con Cal. Although these two theories have been traditionally considered as separate bases for imposing liability on an successor corporation, we perceive the second to be merely a subset of the first. The crucial factor in determining whether a corporate acquisition constitutes either a *de facto* merger or a mere continuation is the same: whether adequate cash consideration was paid for the predecessor corporation's assets.

No California case we have found has imposed successor liability for personal injuries on a corporation that paid adequate cash consideration for the predecessor's assets. The trial court recognized this limitation to its holding, but found "no logical reason why the fact that the consideration for a purchase of corporate assets is cash (with an agreement to liquidate) rather than stock should in itself bar victims from recovering from the purchaser for the seller's tortious conduct." We, however, perceive a very sound reason for the rule of nonliability in adequate cash sales: predictability. "Predictability is vital in the corporate field. Unforeseeable alterations in successor liability principles complicate transfers and necessarily increase transaction costs. Major economic decisions, critical to society, are best made in a climate of relative certainty and reasonable predictability. The imposition of successor liability on a purchasing company long after the transfer of assets defeats the legitimate expectations the parties held during negotiation and sale. Another consequence that must be faced is that few opportunities would exist for the financially troubled company that wishes to cease business but has had its assets devalued by the extension of successor liability."

In addition, of course, a sale for adequate cash consideration ensures that at the time of sale there are adequate means to satisfy any claims made against the predecessor corporation.

In reaching its conclusion that the sale of Con Cal's assets to USX constituted a *de facto* merger, the trial court relied on *Marks v. Minnesota Mining & Manufacturing Co.* (1986) 187 Cal.App.3d 1429. In *Marks*, the court held that the corporate successor's acquisition of the predecessor's assets in exchange for stock constituted a *de facto* merger, rendering the successor liable for the plaintiff's product liability claim. The *Marks* court set forth five often-quoted factors that indicate whether a purported asset sale is the legal equivalent of a merger: "(1) was the consideration paid for the assets solely stock of the purchaser of its parent; (2) did the purchaser continue the same enterprise after the sale; (3) did the shareholders of the seller become the shareholders of the purchaser; (4) did the seller liquidate; and (5) did the buyer assume the liabilities necessary to carry on the business of the seller?" *Marks* held that the transaction before it satisfied all five factors, resulting in a *de facto* merger. In reaching its conclusion, the *Marks* court noted: "The critical fact is that while there was more than one merger or reorganization, an analysis of each transaction discloses to us that its intrinsic structure and nature, unlike a sale of assets for cash, was of a type in which the corporate entity was continued and all liability was transferred."

Marks is not alone in recognizing the overriding significance of the type and adequacy of consideration paid in a corporate asset sale. * * *

In discussing the mere continuation exception to the general rule of successor non-liability, the court in *Ray v. Alad* stated that liability has been imposed on a successor corporation "only upon a showing of one or both of the following factual elements: (1) no adequate consideration was given for the predecessor corporation's assets and made available for meeting the claims of its unsecured creditors; (2) one or more persons were officers, directors, or stockholders of both corporations." Respondents make much of the second prong enunciated by *Ray v. Alad*, asserting that the trial court properly found USX to be a mere continuation of Con Cal because Alden Roach was president and a board member of both the predecessor and the successor corporations. However, a review of the cases cited by the *Ray v. Alad* court to support its statement reveals that all of the cases involved the payment of inadequate cash consideration, and some also involved near complete identity of ownership, management or directorship after the transfer. * * * None of these cases involved a situation such as the one before us, where the consideration paid was undisputedly adequate, and only a single person with minimal ownership interest in either entity remained as an officer and director.

[A]lthough other factors are relevant to both the *de facto* merger and mere continuation exceptions, the common denominator, which must be present in order to avoid the general rule of successor non-liability, is the payment of inadequate consideration. The evidence presented showed that in 1948 Con Cal was paid in excess of $17 million for its business assets. As was the case in *Ray v. Alad*, no claim has been made that this consideration was inadequate, or that there were insufficient assets available at the time of the predecessor's dissolution to meet the claims of its creditors. Lacking the essential factor of inadequate consideration, there was no *de facto* merger [between Con Cal and Con Del], nor could USX be deemed a mere continuation of Con Cal.

QUESTIONS

1.   Would USX be legally obligated to WPS's creditors if it had merged with WPS?

2.   Why did the court mention that Alden Roach, president of the corporation that sold the assets, Con Cal, was the president of the corporation that bought the assets, Con Del, after the sale? Was that important?

3.   Would the court have decided this case differently if Con Del had purchased the assets of Con Cal with stock instead of cash?

4.   "The rationale behind the *de facto* merger exception is that when the end result of a transaction is substantially the same as a merger between two corporations * * * the court should treat the transaction as a merger for all purposes, including the automatic assumption by the purchasing corporation of all the debts of the selling corporation. An obvious problem with the *de facto* merger exception is figuring out when the sale of assets transaction looks enough like a merger to demand that the buyer assume all of the debts of the seller." Franklin Gevurtz, CORPORATION LAW 667. Does the California Court of Appeal have a problem in figuring out when a sale of assets transaction looks "enough like a merger"?

5. Suppose that you are the general counsel for McDonald's when McDonald's is considering merging with Bubba's Burritos, Inc. You have learned that Bubba's Burritos inadvertently used asbestos powder rather than flour in a substantial number of the tortillas that it served. If McDonald's still wants to proceed with joining up with Bubba's Burritos, how should the deal be structured?

2. EFFECT OF SALE OF ASSETS ON SHAREHOLDERS

The economic consequences to Bubba's shareholders and McDonald's shareholders of a sale of assets are basically the same as the economic consequences of a merger. If Bubba's merges into McDonald's, the shareholders of Bubba's will receive McDonald's stock (or cash from McDonald's if it is a cash merger). Similarly, if Bubba's sells all of its assets to McDonald's, Bubba's will receive McDonald's stock or cash from McDonald's which can be distributed to its shareholders.* Will the amount of cash or stock that shareholders receive be larger for a merger or a sale of assets?

In a state that has adopted the MBCA, Bubba's Burritos' shareholders and McDonald's shareholders in a sale of assets have the same appraisal rights as shareholders in a merger. MBCA § 13.02(a)(3). In contrast, in non-MBCA states, shareholders in a sale of assets may not have appraisal rights. Although corporation statutes generally require a corporation to obtain the approval of its shareholders to sell all or substantially all of its assets, in Delaware and some other states, the shareholders of the *buying* corporation have neither appraisal rights nor the right to vote on their corporation's buying the assets. The reason for this is that a sale of substantially all the assets is generally a fundamental change *only* for the selling corporation, and not for the buying corporation. Consequently, the shareholders of the buying corporation do not have a voice in whether the deal ought to be approved. But in addition, Delaware and some other states do not even provide appraisal rights for the shareholders of the *selling* corporation.

PROBLEM

Sellco and Buyco are corporations in the electronics business. Sellco agrees to (i) sell all of its assets to Buyco in exchange for 283,000 shares of Buyco, (ii) distribute these Buyco shares to Sellco's stockholders, and (iii) dissolve Sellco. You represent Capel, who owns 140,000 of the 280,000 outstanding shares of Buyco, and is opposed to Buyco's issuing an additional 283,000 shares and using the shares to acquire the assets of Sellco. Advise Capel. Does your advice differ depending on whether Buyco is incorporated in Delaware or in a state that has adopted the MBCA?

---

* Of course, upon dissolution, Bubba's must pay its creditors before it can distribute anything to Bubba's shareholders.

E. HOSTILE TAKEOVER

1. WHAT IS A HOSTILE TAKEOVER?

A shareholder's selling her shares is the end of the game for that shareholder, but not for the corporation. If that selling shareholder is selling a majority of the outstanding shares or a controlling block of the outstanding shares, the sale can be the end of the game not only for the selling shareholder, but also for the management of the corporation. The new controlling shareholder may install new directors who will then fire the corporation's existing managers. The new controlling shareholder hopes that the new managers will be able to run the company better, increasing its value for the new shareholder.

If an investor gains control of a corporation by buying existing shareholders' shares, the transaction did not require any agreement between the investor and the corporation's management or board of directors: the only contract was between the investor and the individual stockholders. The investor could have acquired control over the corporation even if the corporation's board and management opposed the transaction.

The term "hostile takeover" is used to describe such an acquisition: gaining control over a corporation despite the objection of that corporation's board of directors.[*] The acquiring company or individual is politely described as the "bidder" or "suitor," or more colorfully described as the "raider" or the "shark." The company whose stock is targeted for acquisition is the "target company."

If the target company is a public company, the usual process for acquiring the shares is a "tender offer." In a tender offer, the bidder makes a public offer of cash or the bidder's securities (or a package of cash and securities) to the target's stockholders who are willing to sell—or "tender"—their stock. The tender offer will typically be conditioned on a sufficient number of the target's shares being tendered to ensure that the bidder gains control of the target company.

While taking over control of a company by acquiring a majority of that target company's outstanding stock does not require action by the management of the target company's board of directors, it usually triggers such action. A target company's management often takes action to prevent a takeover.

Lawyers have been creative in developing (and naming) responses to takeover threats. Examples are "poison pills" (also known as "rights plans"), "golden parachutes," "shark repellents," and "white knights." For

---

[*]   The phrase "hostile takeover" is also used to describe a proxy or consent solicitation of the target company's shareholders. It seeks the shareholders' support of an effort to replace incumbent directors.

example, a poison pill works as follows. If an unwanted suitor—that is, an investor of whom the target's board does not approve—acquires more than a specified fraction of the target's stock, then the target automatically sells additional shares (for example, two for every share that the shareholders already own) at a big discount (for example, 50%) to all shareholders *other* than the suitor. Suppose that the threshold for activating the pill was 20% (a common threshold). Once the unwanted raider obtains 20% of the target's stock, then all the other shareholders (but not the raider) would get to buy two additional discounted shares for each of their shares. The raider would now have 8.3% of the shares, rather than 20%. The raider would be much farther from taking over the target.

When the target company's board acts to prevent a takeover, the action is often challenged in the courts. The unwanted bidder will already own some of the target's outstanding shares. Thus, the bidder can challenge the actions taken by the target's board to defend the company against a hostile takeover as violative of the board's fiduciary duties to its shareholders. The bidder argues that the defenses harm existing shareholders by preventing the bidder from offering high amounts to the shareholders for their shares. Instead, the bidder argues, the defenses are designed to save the jobs of incompetent managers, at shareholders' expense; if the bidder succeeded in taking over the company, the bidder would fire the existing managers and replace them with better ones who would increase the company's profits.

In response, the defendant officers and directors argue that their objective in imposing the defenses is not to entrench themselves, but instead to protect the shareholders from taking the first offer that comes along; instead, the managers and directors argue, they might be able to obtain even better offers from other bidders. The courts, particularly the Delaware courts, have created a body of case law on the standards to apply in reviewing challenges to these defenses. If you practice in this area, some of the famous cases that you will get to know are *Unocal Corp. v. Mesa Petroleum Co.*, 493 A.2d 946 (Del. 1985); *Revlon, Inc. v. MacAndrews & Forbes Holdings, Inc.*, 506 A.2d 173 (Del. 1986); *Paramount Communications, Inc. v. QVC Network, Inc.*, 637 A.2d 34 (Del. 1994); and *Moran v. Household International, Inc.*, 500 A.2d 1346 (Del. 1985).

With some exceptions, the decisions tend to side with managers, approving the defenses. For example, the *Moran* case approves poison pills.

State legislatures, including Delaware, have been even more aggressive in approving the defenses. See Del. § 203. For example, in almost all cases where a court has disapproved a poison pill, the state legislature has a passed a statue to approve the pill. Sometimes the state legislature passes an anti-takeover statute to protect a specific local business from being taken over. For example, Arvin Industries, an Indiana corporation with 2000 employees, was the target of a takeover attempt. Arvin responded by having the friendly Indiana legislature pass an anti-takeover bill that prevented the takeover. The Supreme Court later court upheld the legislation. *CTS Corp. v. Dynamics Corp. of American*, 481 U.S. 69 (1987). Courts have similarly tended to uphold anti-takeover statutes from other states. *Amanda Acquisition Corp. v. Universal Foods Corp.*, 877 F.2d 496 (7th Cir. 1989) (upholding Wisconsin statute passed to protect the G. Heileman Brewing Company from takeover).

F. BUSINESS PERSPECTIVES ON MERGERS AND ACQUISITIONS AND SPINOFFS

In the world of business and financial strategy, mergers and acquisitions are hotly debated. Although a merger and an acquisition are basically the same thing, the two terms are used in different contexts. "Merger" is used when two equals combine. The companies may combine into one, newly-formed entity. An example is when Daimler-Benz and Chrysler merged to form the new company DaimlerChrysler. Sometimes there are elaborate power sharing agreements between the leaders of the merged companies. Or there can be commitments that, after the current CEO retires, the successor CEO will be from the other company. Or there can be agreements to leave the acquired business as a separate, independent division. When the dust settles though, someone usually comes out on top.

In contrast, in an acquisition, this power dynamic is clear: one company—the target—is bought by the other, for stock or cash or some combination of the two. Often the acquired company is a smaller business. Some acquisitions are hostile. Such transactions are almost never referred to as mergers, even if the businesses are roughly the same size

From a business point of view, there are several common justifications for mergers and acquisitions:

- Vertical integration: If you imagine that a business consists of the production of raw materials, the manufacture of those raw materials into products, and the selling of those products, then vertical integration is the combination of two or more production steps into one company. Manufacturers can "backward" or "forward" integrate. For example, backwards integration would occur if a company with a large number of retail gas stations decides to buy a business that refines petroleum. Forward integration would occur if a company that manufactures paper decides to open a retail stationary store.

- Horizontal integration: This kind of merger or acquisition brings two similar businesses together. A good example of horizontal integration is the proposed merger of Comcast and TimeWarner Cable. Horizontal mergers lead to more highly "concentrated" industries, where fewer companies have greater market share. Horizontal mergers are the type most often challenged by antitrust authorities.

- Unrelated diversification: this includes the kinds of acquisitions that create "conglomerates"—groups of unrelated businesses. Examples of such conglomerates are ITT, Textron, and Berkshire-Hathaway.

- Related diversification: This kind of combination creates a business with more in common than a conglomerate but less in common than true horizontal or vertical integration. For example, a company that mills and sells lumber might decide to get into the pipe business because they have a good brand name in the construction-materials market as a whole.

In most mergers and acquisitions, the presumed rationale is some form of "synergy." That is, the combined business is worth more than the two individual companies. Sometimes the synergies are easy to see. For example, if Kraft buys Hellman's Mayonnaise, Kraft can presumably fire the Hellman's sales force and have their existing salespeople sell the product; they are already calling on the same customers. In addition, Kraft can fire the high-paid Hellman's executives, and perhaps even close the Hellman's plants and manufacture the product in the same facilities that make Kraft mayo.

Some synergies involve selling new products to the same customers. For example, General Motors buys a bank so it can start offering auto loans to its car buyers. Other synergies arise when a merger permits the merged company to sell the same products to new customers. For example, the European supermarket chain Ahold buys the New England supermarket chain Stop n' Shop. Others involve an attempt by one business to buy a technology that it can use to enhance its products and make them more competitive. For example, eBay's purchase of PayPal was an attempt to use PayPal's electronic payments technology to distinguish eBay's auction site.

Or consider the following, more-technical example. Company A and Company B each have $100 million of revenues and $10 million of earnings after tax, and trade at a P/E (price earnings ratio) of 15. So, each company has a market value of $150 million. Suppose the combined businesses would have earnings of $25 million, because of the $5 million in costs that could be saved by virtue of eliminating some common overhead expenses. Well, the combined entity should be worth 15 X $25 million, or $375 million, or $75 million more than the sum of the two companies individually. So, Company A can afford to pay Company's B's shareholders more than the current value of their business, and still be better off (or vice versa).

Often, a merger's supposed synergies turn out to be smaller than expected—or they may not exist at all. Corporate CEO's often desire, either consciously or subconsciously, to lead a business that is bigger than their present company; CEOs like to be Captains of Industry because leaders of larger businesses get more publicity and appear on more magazine covers. The quickest way to enlarge the business that you run is through mergers, rather than through internal growth. Thus, the CEO may engage in "empire building," where she enlarges her company through mergers and acquisitions, overoptimistically citing supposed synergies.

However, the synergies often do not really exist, and the larger company often turns out to be less profitable for shareholders than if the company had remained smaller. Researchers have shown that the true ability of mergers and acquisitions to create long-term value for shareholders is questionable, particularly in the case of mergers of companies in different lines of business—creating so-called conglomerates.

For example, suppose that Bubba's Burritos borrows a bunch of money and buys the Waffle Shack, a large national chain, so that it can start serving breakfast burritos in waffle tortillas. The Bubba's CEO is excited because his new combined company will be huge, the deal gets national press attention, and he claims that there will be many synergies. But are there really? Can Bubba's effectively make a waffle? Will customers patronize a Mexican-themed burrito joint to satisfy their breakfast craving for a waffle?

What happens if a merger doesn't work out? That is, what if there are no synergies, and the companies really were worth more apart than together? If the magic is gone in the relationship between the companies, the companies can split up—they can undo the merger. They can do this in two main ways. First, there can be a spin-off, sometimes also called a spin-out. A spin-off occurs when the combined company creates a new separate company and puts into it the assets of one of the two combined businesses. It then gives the shares in the new company to the combined company's existing shareholders. At the moment of the spin-off, the two businesses have the same owners. But the two businesses are now separate companies. For example, in late 2014, eBay decided to spin-off (or "spin-out") PayPal as a separate company.

Second, companies can choose to unwind a merger or acquisition by simply divesting—that is—by selling one of the businesses.

Columnist James Suroweicki discussed how some of these principles were playing out in a 2014 *New Yorker* article:

According to S. & P., the number of spinoffs announced so far this year is nearly thirty per cent higher than the number for the whole of 2013, and, in the past month, three big tech companies announced breakups. Hewlett-Packard and Symantec are both dividing their operations in two, while eBay is spinning off PayPal—all dramatic changes of direction. Between 2001 and 2011, Hewlett-Packard spent almost sixty-six billion dollars on acquisitions in the hope of making itself a one-stop shop for tech customers. Symantec is effectively reversing its 2005 acquisition of Veritas, which it said at the time would create great "synergies" among its products. As for eBay, as recently as January it was telling investors that "we have been successful exactly because PayPal and eBay are together." Now all these companies are saying that the parts are more valuable than the whole. . .

The success of divestitures doesn't mean that mergers are always a mistake. The acquisition of PayPal by eBay, in 2002, was the kind of deal that often works—the purchase, at a reasonable price, of a young company that truly complements the buyer's core business. (Google's acquisition of YouTube is another example.) Being bought by eBay gave PayPal credibility and access to a huge customer base. But, as PayPal got bigger and eBay became less important to its business, the ownership structure got to be a burden. It limited PayPal's ability to form partnerships with eBay's competitors, like Amazon and Google, and, many have argued, made the company less innovative than it could have been. The decision to split is a recognition that PayPal has outgrown its parent.

James Suroweicki, *Le Divorce*, THE NEW YORKER, November 3, 2014.

In addition to the over-optimism and self-interest of CEOs, there are two other reasons that companies engage in unfortunate mergers. First, when a company has many different businesses operating together, they often hope that the buzz from a successful business will rub off on the less highly-valued businesses and enhance the value of everything.

This approach usually fails. More often, investors feel they cannot properly analyze and appreciate the successful business because it is buried under a pile of other, less successful businesses. Investors tend to penalize the company as a whole, valuing the successful and unsuccessful business less when grouped together than if they were separated into different companies. In investor jargon, investors often prefer a "pure play." That is, they prefer to invest in a company that has only a single line of business, where 100% of their investment is riding on the success or failure of that business.

Second, companies can be led into unsuccessful mergers by investment banks. Investment banks have large mergers-and-acquisitions departments that are paid handsomely to advise on—and help consummate—mergers and acquisitions. Because the banks are paid a percentage of the deal value, they get paid only when a transaction occurs. If you think this could possibly influence the nature of the advice they give, then you are getting the idea!

In a 1989 cover story, Forbes magazine described the tactics of one of the top investment bankers of the era, Bruce Wasserstein. The magazine observed that he:

> . . . used a brand of rough 'psychological bullying' to get his clientèle of corporate empire builders to pay whatever price was necessary for victory. . .[and] was associated with some of the highest-profile takeovers in corporate history, like KKR's $31.4 billion offer for RJR Nabisco in 1989 and Philip Morris' $13 billion bid for Kraft Foods in 1988. . . he also commanded several reckless and costly deals, like Canadian real estate magnate Robert Campeau's takeovers of the retail chains Federated Department Stores and Allied Stores."* In recognition of his approach, Forbes christened him, "Bid 'Em Up Bruce," a nickname that stuck until his untimely death in late 2009.

———

We are now done with sole proprietorships, partnerships, and corporations. Before considering other business structures, think about how corporations and partnerships have become more similar and how they remain different. A couple of new similarities:

First, legal entity status. A corporation has always been a separate legal entity. Now a partnership is also a separate legal entity.

Second, management systems. Originally, unlike a partnership, a corporation was managed by its board of directors who did not have to be shareholders. Today, a corporation can eliminate its board of directors and have a system of shareholder management of the corporation that operates very much like partner management of a partnership.

A couple of important remaining differences:

---

* http://www.forbes.com/2009/10/14/bruce-wasserstein-dies-business-wall-street-lazard.html.

First, owner liability. Shareholders are not (generally) personally liable for the debts of a business structured as a corporation. Partners are personally liable for the debts of a business structured as a partnership.

Second, owner transferability. There are no general statutory constraints on a corporation's shareholder's selling to a third party her ownership interest, i.e., selling her rights as a shareholder. There are however significant statutory constraints on a partner's selling to a third party his partnership interest, i.e., selling his rights as a partner.

In addition, a partner is statutorily empowered to trigger the partnership's buyout of his rights as a partner through dissociation. There is no general corporate-statute counterpart to dissociation. Except for the limited situations that trigger a dissenting shareholder's right of appraisal, a shareholder is not statutorily empowered to trigger the corporation's buyout of her ownership interest.

CHAPTER 10

WHAT IS A LIMITED PARTNERSHIP AND HOW DOES IT WORK?

■ ■ ■

In considering what business structure to use for Bubba's Burritos, Propp, Agee, and Capel of course want "the best of both worlds."* They want a business structure that provides both the favorable tax treatment of a partnership and the protection from personal liability of a corporation.

For most of the 20th century, limited partnership was the business structure chosen by the Propps, Agees and Capels (and people with more common names) who wanted both the favorable tax treatment of a partnership and the protection from personal liability of a corporation. For the last twenty-five years or so, limited liability companies, ("LLCs") not limited partnerships, have been their choice. Nonetheless, we need to understand what limited partnerships are and how they work because:

- there are a lot of old businesses and old lawyers who use the limited partnership form;

- there is a lot of limited partnership law in the law of LLCs; and,

- there are still situations in which structuring a business as a limited partnership is the best way to meet your client's needs.

A. WHAT IS A LIMITED PARTNERSHIP?

A limited partnership is a form of business structure that is similar to but in some important respects different from a partnership. Like a partnership, a limited partnership does not pay income tax on its earnings. And like a partnership, a limited partnership has partners.

Unlike a partnership, a limited partnership has two kinds of partners—(1) "regular, plain old vanilla partners" and (2) "limited partners." In a limited partnership, any "regular, plain old vanilla partner" has management rights and liability exposure for the

---

* Epstein thought the phrase "best of both worlds" was too trite to use in a serious book like this until Shepherd pointed out that (1) it was the title of the theme song for the Hannah Montana television show, and (2) a Yale law professor used the phrase in an article published in the Harvard Law Review. *See* Bruce Ackerman, *The New Separation of Powers*, 113 HARV. L. REV. 633, 714 (2000).

partnership's debts that are similar to the management rights and liability exposure of "regular, plain old vanilla partners" in the "regular, plain old vanilla partnerships" we studied in Chapter 3.

[As you may recall, we did not use the adjectival* phrase "regular, plain, old vanilla" in describing partners and partnerships in Chapter 3. And courts and other law professors do not use that phrase, Instead, they, and hereafter, we, describe such partners as "general partners" and describe the kind of partnerships we studied in Chapter 3 as "general partnerships."]

In addition to one or more general partners who have the same legal rights and responsibilities as the partners in a general partnership, a limited partnership also has limited partners. Unlike general partners, a limited partner does not have personal liability for the limited partnership's debts. The most a limited partner can lose from her investment in a limited partnership is her investment.

Interestingly, limited partnerships are the form of organization used for many popular types of "alternative investment" funds, like venture capital, private equity and hedge funds, as well as real estate investments. The reasons for this highlight some of the distinguishing characteristics of limited partnerships.

First, limited partnerships offer the option for very creative allocation of economic gains—the carving up of cash flows from the investment. As you have seen, stock ownership in a corporation typically offers shareholders a claim on the economic value that is proportional to their shareholdings.

However, the limited partnership form allows investment partnerships of this kind offer their limited partners ("LPs") a very different kind of investment return than is provided to the general partners ("GPs"). In a typical deal, the LPs put up 99% of the money, and the GP, 1%. Had the entity been structured as a corporation, then, as common stockholders, the GP would be entitled to 1% of the economic benefits of ownership, and the LPs 99%. But, with the LP / GP structure, the LPs can get 99% of the investment returns until they have gotten 100% of their investment capital returned to them, after which, the GP can get 20% of the returns (or cash flow) and the LPs 80% (as an example). This is a typical structure for real estate deals. For hedge funds, venture capital and private equity firms, the GP often gets a 2% management fee (2% of the invested capital) and then, the GP also gets 20% of the gains. In some cases, it is 20% of the total gain (i.e., the amount of cash flow above the amount invested by the LPs). In other cases, the "20% of the gain" is computed using a hurdle rate for the LP's return i.e., the GP does not get its 20% until the LPs have received their capital plus a 5 or 8% return on

---

* It was Roberts, of course, who insisted we use the word "adjectival"—a new word for Freer.

their capital. You can see that this structure offers the possibility for any allocation of gains that can be described arithmetically and agreed to on paper (in the Limited Partnership Agreement).

This carving up of the economic gains in a non-proportional manner (i.e., not strictly in accordance with the proportion of capital contributed) is designed to create effective incentives for the general partner. Imagine two possible deals structures, one where the GP gets a flat 10% of the gain, and one in which she gets 20%, but only after she has returned 100% of the LP's invested capital to these LPs. In the second deal, the GP has a stronger incentive to generate a good outcome and high returns— she will get a bigger piece of the gain than under the first deal. And, in a deal that turns out poorly—where the returns are low—the LPs have a greater likelihood of getting their investment capital back, which seems only fair, given that the GP did not generate a great outcome.

Another reason the LP form of organization is popular is the tax treatment afforded the gains. As a pass-through entity, all of the gains are taxed only once, at the level of the partnership interest-holder. Since many investors in this type of fund may be tax-exempt entities, like pension funds and endowments, this is a highly efficient form of ownership. Like members of LLCs, LPs in a limited partnership pay tax on their share of income earned by the partnership, regardless of whether or not any of those gains are actually distributed to the partners. In operating companies, whether they are LLCs or partnerships, this can cause problems for the members or partners—if the members or partners are being allocated income, but not receiving distributions, then they will have to write a check to the IRS without any cash from the investment to pay the tax. For this reason, many agreements require the entity to make actual cash distributions sufficient to cover the tax. In investment partnerships, this is usually less of an issue. Most venture capital and private equity firms generate income (as capital gain) when they sell their investments in portfolio companies. This sale generates income for the partners, but also generates the cash for a distribution. And, for hedge funds, which may hold dividend or interest producing securities, these dividend and interest payments generate actual cash for distributions.

B. WHAT IS LIMITED PARTNERSHIP LAW?

Just as every state has a partnership statute based on a uniform act, every state also has a limited partnership statute, based on a uniform act. The original Uniform Limited Partnership Act (ULPA) was promulgated in 1916. In recent years, there have been important changes in limited partnership law. A Revised Uniform Limited Partnership Act (RULPA) was promulgated in 1976 and further significant amendments were made in 1985. Moreover, several states have in recent years made significant changes in their version of RULPA. As if that were not enough, in 2001, a new version of ULPA was promulgated which we will call "ULPA 2001". About 1/3 of the states have adopted "ULPA 2001."

Most states, including Delaware, still have a limited partnership statute based on the 1985 RULPA. In this book, we will look primarily to the Delaware limited partnership statute.

Because of the similarities between general partnerships and limited partnerships, limited partnerships have often been subject not only to limited partnership statutes but also to general partnership statutes. Thus, RULPA § 1105 provides "In any case not provided for in this act, the provisions of the Uniform Partnership Act govern." ULPA 2001, however, "de-links" the limited partnership from UPA and RUPA

No matter what limited partnership statute applies, it is clear universally that a limited partnership is an entity. It is also clear that a limited partnership is subject to federal securities laws such as Rule 10b–5 and state securities laws.*

C. WHAT ARE THE LEGAL PROBLEMS IN STARTING A BUSINESS AS A LIMITED PARTNERSHIP?

Unlike general partnerships (but like corporations), limited partnerships do not come into existence until there has been a public filing, usually with the secretary of state of the state of organization. That document is generally called a Certificate of Limited Partnership.

We have set out below the certificate of limited partnership available from the website of (you guessed it) the Delaware Division of Corporations.†

STATE of DELAWARE
CERTIFICATE of LIMITED PARTNERSHIP

The Undersigned, desiring to form a limited partnership pursuant to the Delaware Revised Uniform Limited Partnership Act, 6 Delaware Code, Chapter 17, does hereby certify as follows:

First: The name of the limited partnership is _____

Second: The address of its registered office in the State of Delaware is

---

* While the phrase "limited partnership interest" is not expressly included in the definition of "security" in § 2(a)(1) of the Securities Act of 1933, limited partnership interests come within the Supreme Court's interpretation of § 2(a)(1). SEC v. W.J. Howey Co., 328 U.S. 293, 299 (1946) (security exists "if a person invests his money in a common enterprise and is led to expect profits solely from the efforts of the promoter or a third party.")

† *Certificate of Limited Partnership*, STATE OF DELAWARE, http://corp.delaware.gov/lpform09.pdf.

SEC. C

WHAT ARE THE LEGAL PROBLEMS IN STARTING A
BUSINESS AS A LIMITED PARTNERSHIP?

497

STATE of DELAWARE
CERTIFICATE of LIMITED PARTNERSHIP

_____ in the city of _____. Zip code _____. The name of the Registered Agent at such address is _____.

Third: The name and mailing address of each general partner is as follows: _____

In Witness Whereof, the undersigned has executed this Certificate of Limited Partnership as of _____ day of _____, A.D. _____.

BY: _____

(General Partner)

NAME: _____

QUESTIONS

1. Why do limited partnership statutes condition the existence of a limited partnership on a public filing of a certificate of limited partnership when general partnership statutes do not condition the existence of a partnership on a public filing? Is the reason related to the fact that limited partners (like shareholders in a corporation) are not personally liable for business debts?

2. Agee, Capel and Propp want to make and sell Southern-style burritos near a college campus in a state other than Delaware. Can they structure their business as a limited partnership organized in Delaware?

3. What are the possible advantages of organizing a limited partnership in Delaware? Are the advantages of organizing in Delaware more important to Bubba's Hedge Fund, Limited Partnership than to Bubba's Burritos, L.P.? (Reconsider your answers after you consider _Kahn v. Icahn_ later in this chapter.)

4. Why do limited partnership statutes require that either "Limited Partnership" or "L.P." be a part of the limited partnership's name as shown on the filed certificate*?

———

Even if the Certificate of Limited Partnership meets the requirements of your state's limited partnership law, that document alone

---

*   In Delaware, for example: "§ 17–102 Name set forth in certificate.

The name of each limited partnership as set forth in its certificate of limited partnership:

(1) Shall contain the words 'Limited Partnership' or the abbreviation 'L.P.' or the designation 'LP'"

will not meet the requirements of your clients. The more important document to your clients is the limited partnership agreement.

Although RULPA does not require that there be a written limited partnership agreement, almost all limited partnerships have detailed written agreements. In particular, these partnership agreements define the relative roles of the limited partners and the general partner(s).

Recall that limited partnership statutes require that

- a limited partnership must have at least one general partner;

- this general partner, unlike the limited partners, is liable for the debts of the partnership; and

- the name and the address of the general partner must be set out in the Certificate of Limited Partnership, which is filed in public records.

The limited partnership statutes do not, however, require that the general partner be a natural, flesh-and-blood person.

Accordingly, Agee, Propp and Capel can set up a limited partnership in which none of them is the general partner, i.e., none of them is personally liable for the debts of the partnership.

If Agee, Propp, and Capel want to structure their burrito business as a limited partnership and want to avoid personal liability, they take two simple steps: (1) organize a corporation, Bubba's Burritos, Inc., and (2) organize a limited partnership, Bubba's Burritos Limited Partnership, with Bubba's Burritos, Inc. as the only general partner and each of them as limited partners. Then they use the limited partnership, Bubba's Burritos Limited Partnership, to own and operate the business. Although Bubba's Burritos, Inc. will now, as general partner, be personally liable for the limited partnership's liabilities, the *owners* of the corporation will not be; the corporate form protects Agee, Propp and Capel from personal liability.

D. WHAT ARE THE LEGAL PROBLEMS IN OPERATING A BUSINESS AS A LIMITED PARTNERSHIP?

1. WHO DECIDES WHAT

The answer to this question is found in the limited partnership statute and the limited partnership agreement.

a. General Partners?

As a rule of thumb, the answer to the question who makes the decisions for a limited partnership will be that the general partner makes the decisions. RULPA establishes this as the default rule. Unless the limited partnership agreement specifies otherwise, the general partner has the same management rights as a partner in a general partnership*. And recall that each partner in a general partnership has equal management rights unless the partnership agreement otherwise provides.

b. Limited Partners?

Delaware § 17–302(b) provides in pertinent part:

[T]he partnership agreement may grant to all or certain identified limited partners or a specified class or group of the limited partners the right to vote separately or with all or any class or group of the limited partners or the general partners, on any matter. (emphasis added).

What should a limited partnership agreement say about the role of limited partners in business decisions? Review the following two examples of limited partnership agreement provisions relating to the role of limited partners in making decisions:

Example 1: Voting Rights.

The business of the Partnership will be managed by the General Partners, and the Limited Partners will have no right to vote or participate in the affairs of the Partnership except as specifically provided in this Agreement.

(a) *Actions Requiring Unanimous Approval.* The unanimous vote or written consent of all Partners will be required to:

    (i)   increase the required contribution of a Partner;

---

   *   Delaware § 17–403 General powers and liabilities.

    (a) Except as provided in this chapter or in the partnership agreement, a general partner of a limited partnership has the rights and powers and is subject to the restrictions of a partner in a partnership that is governed by the Delaware Uniform Partnership Law in effect on July 11, 1999 (6 Del. C. § 1501 et seq.).

       * * * *

    (c) Unless otherwise provided in the partnership agreement, a general partner of a limited partnership has the power and authority to delegate to 1 or more other persons the general partner's rights and powers to manage and control the business and affairs of the limited partnership, including to delegate to agents, officers and employees of the general partner or the limited partnership, and to delegate by a management agreement or another agreement with, or otherwise to, other persons. Unless otherwise provided in the partnership agreement, such delegation by a general partner of a limited partnership shall not cause the general partner to cease to be a general partner of the limited partnership or cause the person to whom any such rights and powers have been delegated to be a general partner of the limited partnership.

(ii) compromise a Partner's obligation to make a required contribution or return an improper distribution;

(iii) alter the Percentage Interest of a Partner or the priority of a Partner as to distributions, except as provided in this Agreement; and

(iv) amend this Agreement so as to alter, directly or indirectly, the actions requiring unanimous approval of Partners.

(b) *Actions Requiring More than Majority Vote.* The vote or written consent of Limited Partners holding at least ___ [percentage, such as sixty percent (60%)] of the Percentage Interests then held by Limited Partners is required to ___ [list actions requiring greater than majority approval, such as:

(i)   remove a general partner; or

(ii) admit a new general partner; or

(iii) elect to continue the Partnership after a general partner ceases to be a general partner where there is no remaining or surviving general partner].

(c) *Actions Requiring Majority Vote.* The vote or written consent of Limited Partners holding at least a majority of the Percentage Interests then held by Limited Partners is required to approve:

(i)   the dissolution and winding up of the Partnership as provided in Article Eight;

(ii) the merger of the Partnership or the sale, exchange, lease, transfer, mortgage, pledge, or encumbrance of all or a substantial portion of its assets other than in the ordinary course of business;

(iii) the incurrence of indebtedness other than in the ordinary course of its business;

(iv) a change in the nature of the business of the Partnership; and

(v)   transactions in which any of the General Partners have an actual or potential conflict of interest with the Limited Partners or the Partnership.*

Example 2: The Limited Partners

The Limited Partners shall not take any part in the management of the business or the affairs of the Partnership in

---

* 4 CALIFORNIA TRANSACTIONS FORMS—BUS. ENTITIES § 18.33 (1996).

SEC. D

WHAT ARE THE LEGAL PROBLEMS IN OPERATING
A BUSINESS AS A LIMITED PARTNERSHIP?

501

dealing with third parties and shall have no right or authority to act for or bind the partnership in any way.[*]

QUESTIONS AND NOTE

1.   Did you read the examples? In Example 1, is a "Partner" a "General Partner?

2.   In Example 2, would the Limited Partners have any power or right to remove the General Partner who is making the decisions for the limited partnership?

3.   The Delaware Court of Chancery provides this summary of who decides what in a limited partnership:

> General partners of limited partnerships usually have most or all of the control of the limited partnership. Typically, the general partners are active managers. Limited partners are merely passive investors. In limited partnerships, the relationship between general and limited partners is usually financial. On the other hand, relationships between partners of general partnerships are usually part financial and personal, with a division of control between the partners.[†]

As the next part of the book explains, historically there has been a correlation between whether a limited partner is active in making decisions for the limited partnership and whether the limited partner is personally liable to the creditors of the limited partnership.

2.   WHO IS LIABLE TO WHOM FOR WHAT?

a.   Limited Partners' "Non-Liability" to Creditors of the Limited Partnership

If Agee and Propp are the limited partners of Bubba's Burritos Limited Partnership, creditors of the partnership generally cannot collect unpaid debts of the limited partnership from Agee or Propp personally. The original theoretical basis for the rule that limited partners are not personally liable for the unpaid debts of the limited partnership was that limited partners are more like shareholders than like partners and so should have the same protection from personal liability as shareholders.

The theory assumes, however, that the limited partner is essentially passive with regard to running the business. In time, a body of case law developed holding that a limited partner who exerted "control" over the

---

[*]   Lewis R. Kaster, *Limited Partnership Agreement for Ownership of Existing Commercial Real Estate*, 938 PLI/CORP 187 (May 1996).

[†]   Macklowe v. Planet Hollywood, Inc., 1994 WL 586838 (Del.Ch., 1994) (obiter dictum).

business of the limited partnership would become liable for the acts and debts of the business. The rationale for such cases was that by exercising "control," the limited partner had essentially become a general partner for liability purposes.

This control aspect of limited partnership law has been substantially changed by limited partnership statutes such as the following:

Delaware 17–303 Liability to third parties.

(a) A limited partner is not liable for the obligations of a limited partnership unless he or she is also a general partner or, in addition to the exercise of the rights and powers of a limited partner, he or she participates in the control of the business. However, if the limited partner does participate in the control of the business, he or she is liable only to persons who transact business with the limited partnership reasonably believing, based upon the limited partner's conduct, that the limited partner is a general partner.

(b) A limited partner does not participate in the control of the business within the meaning of subsection (a) of this section by virtue of possessing or, regardless of whether or not the limited partner has the rights or powers, exercising or attempting to exercise 1 or more of the following rights or powers or having or, regardless of whether or not the limited partner has the rights or powers, acting or attempting to act in 1 or more of the following capacities:

(1) To be . . . an officer, director or stockholder of a corporate general partner . . .,

(2) To consult with or advise a general partner or any other person with respect to any matter, including the business of the limited partnership, or to act or cause a general partner or any other person to take or refrain from taking any action, including by proposing, approving, consenting or disapproving, by voting or otherwise, with respect to any matter, including the business of the limited partnership; * * *

(8) To act or cause the taking or refraining from the taking of any action, including by proposing, approving, consenting or disapproving, by voting or otherwise, with respect to 1 or more of the following matters: . . .

b. The sale, exchange, lease, mortgage, assignment, pledge or other transfer of, or granting of a security interest in, any asset or assets of the limited partnership;

c.   The incurrence, renewal, refinancing or payment or other discharge of indebtedness by the limited partnership;

d.   A change in the nature of the business;

e.   The admission, removal or retention of a general partner;

f.   The admission, removal or retention of a limited partner;

QUESTIONS AND NOTE

1.   Do you understand why § 17–303(b) is described as providing "safe harbors"? Why the second sentence of § 17–303(a) is more important than any of the safe harbors enumerated in § 17–303(b)?

2.   Under § 17–303(b) if the Bubba's Burritos Limited Partnership Agreement includes a provision similar to Example 1 of the draft limited partnership provisions set out above, will limited partners Agee and Propp be personally liable for the limited partnership's debts?

3.   Compare the liability exposure of a shareholder of a close corporation under the rules for piercing the corporate veil in Chapter 5 with the liability exposure of a limited partner under § 17–303(b) Again, we see a similarity between a limited partner and a shareholder. In theory, each tends to be a passive investor risking only her investment and leaving management responsibilities to others (although shareholders in close corporations can have management responsibilities). But if either exercises too much control, she might become personally liable for the acts or debts of the business. How do the standards for piercing the corporate veil and the standards for liability of a limited partner under § 17–303(b) compare?

4.   Recall that the general partner of a partnership is quite often a corporation. Assume that (i) the limited partners of Bubba's Burritos Limited partnership are Propp, Agee, and Capel, (ii) the general partner is Bubba's Burritos Corp., and (iii) the principal shareholder and CEO of Bubba's Burritos Corp is Capel. Would Capel be personally liable to the creditors of Bubba's Burritos Limited Partnership? Would your answers to Questions 1 or 2 above change if Propp were the president and a director of Bubba's Burritos, Inc., the corporation that was the sole general partner of Bubba's Burritos Limited Partnership?

5.   Note

ULPA 2001 § 303(a) has gone even farther than RULPA in its protection of limited partners from the creditors of the limited partnership. It abandons the "control rule" altogether and provides the limited partners with complete freedom from liability for business debts.

b. General Partners' Liability to Creditors of the Limited Partnership

Each general partner of a limited partnership is personally liable for the partnership's debts to third parties as if the partnership were a general partnership. The first sentence of Delaware § 17–403(b) says:

> (b) Except as provided in this chapter, a general partner of a limited partnership has the liabilities of a partner in a partnership that is governed by the Delaware Uniform Partnership Law in effect on July 11, 1999 (6 Del. C. § 1501 et seq.) to persons other than the partnership and the other partners

QUESTIONS

1. If Capel is a general partner of Bubba's Burritos Limited Partnership, can creditors of the limited partnership collect unpaid debts of the limited partnership from Capel personally? Review RUPA §§ 306 and 307.

2. Could a provision in the limited partnership agreement limit the personal liability of the Capel to creditors of the limited partnership for the unpaid debts of the limited partnership?

c. Liability of Partners to the Limited Partnership and Limited Partners

Thus far, we have answered the question who is liable to creditors of the partnership for the debts of the limited partnership. A general partner in a limited partnership has liability exposure not only to creditors of the limited partnership for the debts of the limited partnership but also to the limited partnership itself and to the limited partners of the partnership. Please read Delaware Limited Partnership Act § 17–403(b) which refers to general partnership law:

> Except as provided in this chapter or in the partnership agreement, a general partner of a limited partnership has the liabilities of a partner in a partnership that is governed by the Delaware Uniform Partnership Law in effect on July 11, 1999 (6 Del. C. § 1501 et seq.) to the partnership and to the other partners. (emphasis added)

And then read:

> Delaware Uniform Partnership Law § 15–404 General standards of partner's conduct.
>
> (a) The only fiduciary duties a partner owes to the partnership and the other partners are the duty of loyalty and the duty of care set forth in subsections (b) and (c) of this section.

(b) A partner's duty of loyalty to the partnership and the other partners is limited to the following:

(1) To account to the partnership and hold as trustee for it any property, profit or benefit derived by the partner in the conduct or winding up of the partnership business or affairs or derived from a use by the partner of partnership property, including the appropriation of a partnership opportunity;

(2) To refrain from dealing with the partnership in the conduct or winding up of the partnership business or affairs as or on behalf of a party having an interest adverse to the partnership; and

(3) To refrain from competing with the partnership in the conduct of the partnership business or affairs before the dissolution of the partnership.

Note underlined portion of Delaware Limited Partnership Act § 17–403(b)—the language of the limited partnership agreement can alter a general partner's liabilities to the limited partnership and other partners.

The next case involves a limited partnership agreement with such language. In reading the case, consider the following questions:

1. Do you agree with Chancellor Chandler's first sentence describing what this case "concerns"?

2. Why does the opinion rely on Delaware § 17–1101(d) rather than Delaware § 17–403(b) set out above?

KAHN V. ICAHN

Delaware Chancery Court, 1998
1998 WL 832629

CHANDLER, CHANCELLOR. This case concerns how and why a limited partnership agreement can narrow, or redefine, the traditional fiduciary duties among and between limited partners under Delaware Law. Here, plaintiffs, who are limited partners and minority stakeholders of a Delaware limited partnership, allege the usurpation of a partnership opportunity. For the reasons that follow, I conclude that plaintiffs fail to state a claim and grant dismissal in favor of all the defendants.

I.   Background

Plaintiffs, Amanda Heather Kahn and Kimberly Robin Kahn ("Plaintiffs")* [1] bring this action derivatively on behalf of American Real

---

*   [1] Counsel for the API directors point out in their reply brief in support of their motion to dismiss the derivative complaint that, "[p]laintiffs and their family appear to have been singularly unlucky investors—they are named plaintiffs in at least thirteen lawsuits (including this one) challenging allegedly improper conduct." It is unclear what nefarious intent the

Estate Partners, L.P. ("AREP" or the "Partnership") against AREP's general partner American Property Investors, Inc. ("API"), the general partner's sole shareholder and chief executive officer, Carl C. Icahn ("Icahn"), and Bayswater Realty and Capital Corp. ("Bayswater"), a corporation affiliated with Icahn (collectively "Icahn Defendants"), and API's other directors (collectively "Defendants").

Carl Icahn*

Plaintiffs are holders of depository units representing limited partnership interests of AREP. AREP is a Delaware limited partnership, whose business is conducted through a subsidiary. AREP is in the business of acquiring and managing real estate and attendant activities. AREP has two classes of depository units—Depository Units and Preferred Units. AREP's general partner, API, is a Delaware corporation. Defendant Icahn is the chairman of the board and chief executive officer of API, and owns 100% of that company's stock. According to Plaintiffs, at the start of this litigation, Icahn, through another Delaware partnership, High Coast Limited Partnership, owned 54.1% of the Depository Units of AREP and over 88% of the Preferred Units. In addition, Plaintiffs allege that defendant Bayswater is a real estate and investment company owned and controlled by Icahn.

---

defendant directors would have me infer from this statistic. While the Kahns' experience might qualify them as icons of Delaware corporate jurisprudence, in my view, their wisdom in forum selection should hardly subject them to a presumption of misconduct.

* http://nypost.com/2014/07/28/icahn-pockets–200–profit-on–8–5b-family-dollar-sale/.

Plaintiffs assert a claim for the usurpation of partnership opportunities, or opportunities that rightfully belonged to the Partnership. More specifically, Plaintiffs' complaint alleges that Icahn breached his fiduciary duties to AREP and usurped, for himself, a corporate opportunity of AREP by failing to make the opportunities completely available to AREP and, instead, keeping a percentage of the profits for Bayswater and other affiliates.* **[3]** * * *

Defendants argue that the complaint fails to state a claim. Their principal contention is that § 6.11 of AREP's partnership agreement (the "Agreement") provides that API, the general partner, may "compete, directly or indirectly with the business of the Partnership."* **[4]** Arguing that a partnership is free to modify traditional default rules and duties of partners, Defendants insist that Plaintiffs cannot properly claim a breach of fiduciary duty under the facts alleged in the complaint.

Plaintiffs respond by saying that there is a legal distinction, cognizable in the present case, between competing with the partnership and usurping the partnership's opportunities. They add that the Icahn Defendants' actions fall into the latter category and as such their claim should withstand the motion to dismiss.

II. Analysis

A. Partnership Agreements under Delaware Law

Delaware law permits partners to agree on their rights and obligations to each other and to the partnership. This is so even where Delaware law might impose different rights and obligations absent such

---

*   **[3]** Among others, Plaintiffs identify two specific transactions that they claim qualify as AREP's missed opportunities. The first is an investment in another real estate limited partnership, Arvida/JMB Partners, L.P. ("Arvida"). That investment was made through a number of entities but ultimately, AREP received roughly 70% of the potential AREP share of the investment and Bayswater received approximately 30% of the investment. The second allegedly usurped opportunity involves the Stratosphere Corporation ("Stratosphere"), which owns and operates the Stratosphere Tower, Casino & Hotel in Las Vegas, Nevada. AREP invested $42.8 million to purchase certain mortgage notes of Stratosphere, with a face value of $55 million. According to Plaintiffs, an affiliate of Icahn has purchased $39 million face value of those notes. Plaintiffs have represented that Stratosphere has filed a voluntary plan of reorganization and AREP and the Icahn affiliate have submitted a proposal for the restructuring of Stratosphere that would entail additional investments.

*   **[4]** In full, § 6.11 states:

6.11   <u>Other Business Activities of Partners</u>. Any Partner, Record Holder or Affiliate thereof (including, without limitation, the General Partner and any of its Affiliates) *may have other business interests or may engage in other business ventures of any nature or description whatsoever, whether presently existing or hereafter created*, including, without limitation, the ownership, leasing, management, operation, franchising, syndication and/or development of real estate and *may compete, directly or indirectly, with the business of the Partnership*. No Partner, Record Holder or Affiliate thereof shall incur any liability to the Partnership as the result of such Partner's, Record Holder's or Affiliate's pursuit of such other business interests and competitive activity, and neither the Partnership nor any of the Partners or Record Holders shall have any right to participate in such other business interests or ventures or to receive or share in any income derived therefrom. (emphasis added).

agreement. § 17–1101(d) of the Delaware Revised Limited Partnership Act provides in relevant part that:

> To the extent that, at law or in equity, a partner or other person has duties (including fiduciary duties) and liabilities relating thereto to a limited partnership or to another partner . . . (2) the partner's or other person's duties and liabilities may be expanded or restricted by the provisions in a partnership agreement.

Thus, as a matter of statutory law, the traditional fiduciary duties among and between partners are defaults that may be modified by partnership agreements. This flexibility is precisely the reason why many choose the limited partnership form in Delaware. Our decisional law also has recognized and given illumination to this principle. The cases have gone so far as to suggest that partnership agreements act as safe harbors for actions that might otherwise qualify as breaches of fiduciary duties under the traditional default rules.

Given this legal backdrop, the question then arises whether or not the conduct complained of by Plaintiffs falls within the provisions of the Agreement. I hold that, as a matter of law, it does. [Section] 6.11 of the Agreement anticipates the type of conduct alleged. That sections' language (which includes specific references to the types of real estate investments at issue in this case)—in light of the statements that "[a]ny Partner, Record Holder or Affiliate thereof . . . may compete, directly or indirectly, with the business of the Partnership. . . . [a]nd neither the Partnership nor any of the Partners or Record Holders shall have any right to participate in such other business interests or ventures or to receive or share in any income derived therefrom"—is clear on its face.

In fact, Plaintiffs do not contend that Defendants have misinterpreted § 6.11. Plaintiffs make no claim that § 6.11 says anything other than what it seems to say. There is no claim that the contested investments were intended to fall out of the scope of that provision, the simple terms of § 6.11 notwithstanding. It seems that Plaintiffs would have me ignore that section in favor of finding a legal distinction between competition, as it is normally understood and as provided under § 6.11, and the usurpation of a partnership opportunity. Plaintiffs ask me to craft a new principle of law by recognizing that partners have separate and immutable duties of loyalty irrespective of clear and unambiguous modifications of fiduciary duties provided in a legally enforceable partnership agreement. Under the facts alleged I cannot so hold, for Defendants' actions are covered by the Agreement and as such are permissible as a matter of law.

The Defendants' duties to AREP (including their fiduciary duties) are defined by the AREP Partnership Agreement that clearly permitted the Icahn Defendants to make the investments without bringing them to the limited partners. Plaintiffs' arguments, that the partnership Agreement did not allow the Icahn Defendants to make investments for themselves, simply overlook the statute, make no reasonable attempt to distinguish cases most directly on point, and ignore the unambiguous terms of the Agreement. . . .

* * * The Partnership Agreement successfully did what it purports to do: modify the underlying fiduciary duties of the partners.* **[16]** Thus, even if absent the Agreement AREP might have had a legitimate claim to an "interest" or "expectancy" in the contested investments, § 6.11 modified the legal effect of such an interest.

QUESTIONS AND NOTES

1.   Why did the plaintiffs buy a limited partnership interest in AREP? Why are the plaintiffs suing the general partner?

2.   Are the facts of *Kahn* distinguishable from the facts of *Meinhard v. Salmon*, page 77?

3.   Are the facts of *Kahn* distinguishable from the facts of *Northeast Harbor Golf Club, Inc. v. Harris,* page 235?

4.   How would the Delaware Chancery Court have decided this case if § 6.11 had not been included in the partnership agreement?

5.   Reread Del. § 17–1101(d) as excerpted in the opinion. Note the phrase "may be expanded or restricted." In 2004, Delaware amended § 17–1101. It now provides:

> (c) It is the policy of this chapter to give maximum effect to the principle of freedom of contract and to the enforceability of partnership agreements.

> (d) To the extent that, at law or in equity, a partner or other person has duties (including fiduciary duties) to a limited partnership or to another partner or to another person that is a party to or is otherwise bound by a partnership agreement, the partner's or other person's duties may be expanded or restricted or eliminated by provisions in the partnership agreement; provided that the partnership agreement may not eliminate the implied contractual covenant of good faith and fair dealing.

A recent Delaware Court of Chancery opinion interpreting the amended provision stated: "[T]he Delaware Limited Partnership Act, like Delaware's other alternative entity statutes, authorizes limited partnership agreements to eliminate completely all common law duties, including fiduciary duties, that otherwise would exist. The public policy expressed in the Delaware

---

* **[16]** By the fact that the partnership agreement contained specific language authorizing competition "[some] of the fundamental concerns undergirding the law of corporate opportunity are not present." *Broz*, 673 A.2d at 155. In the present case, it seems to me, the language of the Agreement alone would justify dismissal.

Limited Partnership Act is 'to give maximum effect to the principle of freedom of contract and to the enforceability of partnership agreements.'. When parties establish a purely contractual relationship, they have chosen to limit themselves to pursuing contractual remedies against their contractual counter parties." *Allen v. El Paso Pipeline GP Company*, 2014 WL 2819005 (Del Ch 2014).

6. Notice that the plaintiffs, limited partners, brought this action derivatively for the limited partnership. RULPA provides for such derivative actions in Article 10. Derivative actions by limited partners have been recognized and required even in states without such provisions. For example, in *Energy Investors Fund, L.P. v. Metric Constructors, Inc.*, 525 S.E.2d 441, 443 (N.C. 2000), the North Carolina Supreme Court stated:

> Scholars have also analogized the role of a limited partner to that of a shareholder because [l]imited partnerships resemble corporations in various ways. Formalities of creation are much alike. Both forms of organization can attract investment capital by offering limited liability with roughly similar effects in limited partnerships and corporations. Limited liability necessitates some rules to protect corporate creditors. It facilitates passive ownership—a separation of ownership from control—that permits some efficiencies as well as poses some risks from delegated management. Thus, limited partners are somewhat analogous to shareholders. . . . Information rights and fiduciary duties owed to limited partners are similar to those owed to shareholders. Limited partners, like shareholders, may bring derivative suits on behalf of the business entity against errant management.

> While it is true that a partner and shareholder are treated differently for tax purposes, their duties are still analogous. As such, we conclude that the Court of Appeals properly equated the status of limited partners in a partnership to the relationship that exists between corporate shareholders and the corporation.

7. Notice also that one of the defendants was an individual, Carl Icahn, the corporate general partner's sole stockholder and chief executive officer. It seems clear that (1) the corporate general partner of a limited partnership owes a fiduciary duty to the limited partnership and (2) an officer or director of that corporation owes a fiduciary duty to the corporation. Is it also clear that a person who is an officer or director of a corporation that is the general partner of a limited partnership owes a fiduciary duty both to the corporation *and* to the limited partnership? If so, will those fiduciary duties ever conflict?

The next case provides the best-known discussion of the duties that the manager of a corporate general partner of a limited partnership owes to the limited partners. In reading it, please consider the following:

1.   Is it important that the Wylys own 100% of the stock of USACafes General Partner, Inc., the corporate general partner of the limited partnership?

2.   What does the plaintiff allege that the Wylys did wrong?

3.   Are the plaintiffs alleging that the $15,000,000 to $17,000,000 paid to the Wylys by Metsa in connection with Metsa's acquisition of the assets of the limited partnership should have been paid to USACafes General Partner, Inc., or to the limited partnership?

IN RE USACAFES, L.P.

Delaware Chancery Court, 1991
600 A.2d 43

ALLEN, CHANCELLOR. These consolidated actions arise out of the October 1989 purchase by Metsa Acquisition Corp. of substantially all of the assets of USACafes, L.P. a Delaware limited partnership (the "Partnership") at a cash price of $72.6 million or $10.25 per unit. Plaintiffs are holders of limited partnership units. They bring these cases as class actions on behalf of all limited partnership unitholders except defendants. The relief sought includes, *inter alia*, the imposition of constructive trusts on certain funds received by defendants in connection with the Metsa sale and an award of damages to the class resulting from the sale.

The Partnership was formed in the 1986 reorganization of the business of USACafes, Inc., a Nevada corporation. Also formed as part of that reorganization was USACafes General Partner, Inc. (the "General Partner"), a Delaware corporation that acts as the general partner of the Partnership. Both the Partnership and the General Partner are named as defendants in this action. A second category of defendants is composed of Sam and Charles Wyly, brothers who together own all of the stock of the General Partner, sit on its board, and who also personally, directly or indirectly, own 47% of the limited partnership units of the Partnership. Sam Wyly chairs the Board of the General Partner.

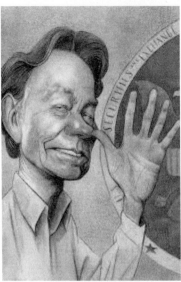

Sam Wyly*

The third category of defendants are four other individuals who sit on the board of directors of the General Partner. All of these persons are alleged to have received substantial cash payments, loan forgiveness, or other substantial personal benefits in connection with the 1989 Metsa purchase. * * *

The Theories of the Amended Complaint

* * * The first and most central theory involves an alleged breach of the duty of loyalty. In essence, it claims that the sale of the Partnership's assets was at a low price, favorable to Metsa, because the directors of the General Partner all received substantial side payments that induced them to authorize the sale of the Partnership assets for less than the price that a fair process would have yielded. Specifically, it is alleged that, in connection with the sale, (1) the Wylys received from Metsa more than $11 million in payments (or promises to pay in the future) which were disguised as consideration for personal covenants not to compete; (2) the General Partner (which the Wylys wholly own) received a $1.5 million payment right in consideration of the release of a claim that plaintiffs assert was non-existent; (3) defendant Rogers, a director of the General Partner and President of the Partnership was forgiven the payment of a $956,169 loan from the Partnership and was given an employment agreement with the Partnership that contemplated a one million dollar cash payment in the event, then imminent, of a "change in control"; (4) defendant Tuley, also a director of the General Partner, was forgiven

---

* This illustration by Steve Brodner was published in the February 2013 issue of D Magazine along with an article by Joseph Guinto entitled "Sam Wyly's $550 Million Problem" which reports that Charles Wyly died in 2011 "when an SUV T-boned his Porsche 911 Targa as he tried to cross a highway."

repayment of a $229,701 loan; and (5) the other directors were given employment agreements providing for a $60,000 payment in the event of a change in control. In sum, it is alleged that between $15 and $17 million was or will be paid to the directors and officers of the General Partner by or with the approval of Metsa; those payments are alleged to constitute financial inducements to the directors of the General Partner to refrain from searching for a higher offer to the Partnerships. Plaintiffs add that, even assuming that Metsa was the buyer willing to pay the best price, some part at least of these "side payments" should have gone to the Partnership.

The second theory of liability reflected in the amended complaint asserts that the General Partner was (or the directors of the General Partner were) not sufficiently informed to make a valid business judgment on the sale. This theory focuses upon the absence of shopping of the Partnership's assets, or of any post-agreement market check procedure, and on the alleged weakness of the investment banker's opinion. Thus, this claim is that the defendants were uninformed when they authorized the sale to Metsa. * * *

The Pending Motions

* * * [T]he Wyly defendants and the other director defendants move under Rule 12(b)(6) to dismiss the breach of fiduciary duty claims in the amended complaint asserting that, while the General Partner admittedly did owe fiduciary duties to the limited partners, they as directors of the General Partner owe no such duties to those persons. The whole remedy of the limited partners for breach of the duties of loyalty and care, it is said, is against the General Partner only and not its directors. * * *

* * * The gist of this motion is the assertion that the directors of the General Partner owed the limited partners no duty of loyalty or care. In their view their only duty of loyalty was to the General Partner itself and to its shareholders (i.e., the Wyly brothers). Thus, in alleging that the director defendants breached duties of loyalty and care running to them, the directors say the limited partners have asserted a legal nullity.

In my opinion the assertion by the directors that the independent existence of the corporate General Partner is inconsistent with their owing fiduciary duties directly to limited partners is incorrect. Moreover, even were it correct, their position on this motion would have to be rejected in any event because the amended complaint expressly alleges that they personally participated in the alleged breach by the General Partner itself, which admittedly did owe loyalty to the limited partners.

The first basis of this holding is the more significant. While I find no corporation law precedents directly addressing the question whether directors of a corporate general partner owe fiduciary duties to the partnership and its limited partners, the answer to it seems to be clearly indicated by general principles and by analogy to trust law. I understand the principle of fiduciary duty, stated most generally, to be that one who controls property of another may not, without implied or express agreement, intentionally use that property in a way that benefits the holder of the control to the detriment of the property or its beneficial owner. There are, of course, other aspects—a fiduciary may not waste property even if no self interest is involved and must exercise care even when his heart is pure—but the central aspect of the relationship is, undoubtedly, fidelity in the control of property for the benefit of another.

The law of trusts represents the earliest and fullest expression of this principle in our law, but courts of equity have extended it appropriately to achieve substantial justice in a wide array of situations. Thus, corporate directors, even though not strictly trustees, were early on regarded as fiduciaries for corporate stockholders. When control over corporate property was recognized to be in the hands of shareholders who controlled the enterprise, the fiduciary obligation was found to extend to such persons as well.

While the parties cite no case treating the specific question whether directors of a corporate general partner are fiduciaries for the limited partnership, a large number of trust cases do stand for a principle that would extend a fiduciary duty to such persons in certain circumstances. The problem comes up in trust law because modern corporations may serve as trustees of express trusts. Thus, the question has arisen whether directors of a corporate trustee may personally owe duties of loyalty to *cestui que trusts* of the corporation. A leading authority states the accepted answer:

> The directors and officers of [a corporate trustee] are certainly under a duty to the beneficiaries not to convert to their own use property of the trust administered by the corporation.... Furthermore, the directors and officers are under a duty to the beneficiaries of trusts administered by the corporation not to cause the corporation to misappropriate the property.... The breach of trust need not, however, be a misappropriation.... Any officer [director cases are cited in support here] who knowingly causes the corporation to commit a breach of trust causing loss ... is personally liable to the beneficiary of the trust....

> Moreover, a director or officer of a trust institution who improperly acquires an interest in the property of a trust administered by the institution is subject to personal liability. He is accountable for any profit.... Even where the trustee [itself] is not liable, however, because it had no knowledge that the director was making the purchase ..., the director ... is liable to the beneficiaries.... The directors and officers are in a

fiduciary relation not merely to the [corporation] . . . but to the beneficiaries of the trust administered by the [corporation]. 4 A. Scott & W. Fratcher, THE LAW OF TRUSTS § 326.3, at 304–306 (4th ed. 1989) (citing cases)

The theory underlying fiduciary duties is consistent with recognition that a director of a corporate general partner bears such a duty towards the limited partnership. That duty, of course, extends only to dealings with the partnership's property or affecting its business, but, so limited, its existence seems apparent in any number of circumstances. Consider, for example, a classic self-dealing transaction: assume that a majority of the board of the corporate general partner formed a new entity and then caused the general partner to sell partnership assets to the new entity at an unfairly small price, injuring the partnership and its limited partners. Can it be imagined that such persons have not breached a duty to the partnership itself? And does it not make perfect sense to say that the gist of the offense is a breach of the equitable duty of loyalty that is placed upon a fiduciary? * * *

While these authorities extend the fiduciary duty of the general partner to a controlling shareholder, they support as well, the recognition of such duty in directors of the General Partner who, more directly than a controlling shareholder, are in control of the partnership's property. It is not necessary here to attempt to delineate the full scope of that duty. It may well not be so broad as the duty of the director of a corporate trustee.* **[3]** But it surely entails the duty not to use control over the partnership's property to advantage the corporate director at the expense of the partnership. That is what is alleged here.

The amended complaint contains the following allegations:

16. The General Partner and its directors, the named individual defendants, are in a fiduciary relationship with the plaintiffs and the other Unitholders of USACafes. . . .

17. . . . Through their unit ownership and executive positions [the director defendants] have dominated and controlled the affairs of USACafes. Among other things, they have . . . failed to adequately solicit or consider alternative proposals for USACafes, have failed to negotiate in good faith to enhance Unitholders' values and, instead, have agreed to sell all of its assets to Metsa, which will result in the minority limited partners receiving the grossly inadequate price of $10.25 per Unit. As inducement to the individual defendants to agree to the Metsa proposal, Metsa offered to pay and the individual

---

* **[3]** For example, I imply nothing on such questions as whether a director of a corporate general partner might be held liable directly to the partnership on a "corporate" opportunity theory or for waste of partnership assets (two possible consequences of characterizing such persons as fiduciaries for the partnership).

defendants agreed to accept, certain additional payments (approximately $17 million) that were not offered to the classes. . . .

19. The individual defendants and the General Partner participated in the wrongdoing complained of in order to divert the valuable assets of USACafes for their own benefit by entering into highly favorable compensation arrangements with Metsa as part of the liquidation of USACafes.

I therefore conclude that the amended complaint does allege facts which if true establish that the director defendants have breached fiduciary obligations imposed upon them as directors of a Delaware corporation or have participated in a breach of such duties by the General Partner. The amended complaint does, in my opinion, state a claim upon which relief can be granted.

QUESTIONS

1. In this case, the plaintiffs' story was about putative "bad guys"—about the directors of the corporate general partner taking money for themselves that (plaintiffs thought) should have gone to the limited partners. Does the *USACafes* case help you in a case in which there are no "bad guys"—such as a case in which the directors of the corporate general partner make a decision that benefits the corporate general partner, and not themselves? To illustrate, assume that Hotel, Inc. is the general partner of Hotel Limited Partnership. Freer and Shepherd are two of the three directors of Hotel, Inc. They learn of a new hotel opportunity that might be of interest to either the limited partnership or the corporate general partner. Does the *USACafes* holding expose Freer and Shepherd to liability if Hotel, Inc. takes the opportunity for itself?

2. In the Hotel, Inc. problem above, would the following language in the limited partnership agreement be helpful to Freer and Shepherd: "The directors of the corporate general partner do not owe a fiduciary duty to the limited partnership or the limited partners"?

E. LEGAL ISSUES IN THE TRANSFER OF PARTNERSHIP INTERESTS

1. TRANSFER OF OWNERSHIP INTEREST TO A THIRD PARTY

Sale of an ownership interest in a limited partnership to a third party by either a general partner or a limited partner is governed by both the limited partnership agreement and the relevant limited partnership statute. For example, Delaware provides:

§ 17–701   Nature of partnership interest.

A partnership interest is personal property. A partner has no interest in specific limited partnership property.

§ 17–702   Assignment of partnership interest.

(a) Unless otherwise provided in the partnership agreement:

(1) A partnership interest is assignable in whole or in part;

(2) An assignment of a partnership interest does not dissolve a limited partnership or entitle the assignee to become or to exercise any rights or powers of a partner;

(3) An assignment of a partnership interest entitles the assignee to share in such profits and losses, to receive such distribution or distributions, and to receive such allocation of income, gain, loss, deduction, or credit or similar item to which the assignor was entitled, to the extent assigned; and

(4) A partner ceases to be a partner and to have the power to exercise any rights or powers of a partner upon assignment of all partnership interests. * * *

§ 17–704   Right of assignee to become limited partner.

(a) An assignee of a partnership interest, including an assignee of a general partner, may become a limited partner:

(1) As provided in the partnership agreement; or

(2) Unless otherwise provided in the partnership agreement, upon the affirmative vote or written consent of all partners.

(b) An assignee who has become a limited partner has, to the extent assigned, the rights and powers, and is subject to the restrictions and liabilities, of a limited partner under the partnership agreement and this chapter.

PROBLEMS AND NOTE

1.   Bubba's Burritos is a limited partnership in which Propp is one of several general partners. If Propp sells his interest in the partnership to Roberts, will Roberts have a right to participate in the management of the limited partnership? Will Propp retain his right to participate in management? What if Propp sells a fifty percent share of his partnership interest to Roberts?

2.   Suppose that BB Corp. is the only general partner of Bubba's Burritos Limited Partnership and, Roberts and Epstein are the only shareholders of BB Corp. Would the statutory provisions set out above apply if Roberts and Epstein sell all of the outstanding BB Corp stock to Freer?

3.   Our favorite student text summarizes "[P]artners in limited partnerships may have management and financial rights (although limited partners are rarely given substantial management rights.) Like general partnerships, the default rule in limited partnerships is that financial rights are unilaterally transferred by a partner but management rights are not."[*]

2.   TRANSFERS OF OWNERSHIP INTEREST TO THE LIMITED PARTNERSHIP

Recall the RUPA concept of dissociation, i.e., the statutory right of an owner of a business structured as a general partnership to force the partnership to purchase her ownership interest. Limited partnership statutes have a similar concept but use the term "withdrawal" rather than "dissociation" and distinguish between "withdrawal" by a general partner and "withdrawal" by limited partners.

Delaware § 17–602 Withdrawal of general partner and assignment of general partner's partnership interest.

(a) A general partner may withdraw from a limited partnership at the time or upon the happening of events specified in the partnership agreement and in accordance with the partnership agreement. A partnership agreement may provide that a general partner shall not have the right to withdraw as a general partner of a limited partnership. Notwithstanding that a partnership agreement provides that a general partner does not have the right to withdraw as a general partner of a limited partnership, a general partner may withdraw from a limited partnership at any time by giving written notice to the other partners. If the withdrawal of a general partner violates a partnership agreement, in addition to any remedies otherwise available under applicable law, the limited partnership may recover from the withdrawing general partner damages for breach of the partnership agreement and offset the damages against the amount otherwise distributable to the withdrawing general partner. * * *

§ 17–603   Withdrawal of limited partner.

A limited partner may withdraw from a limited partnership only at the time or upon the happening of events specified in the partnership agreement and in accordance with the partnership agreement. Notwithstanding anything to the contrary under applicable law, unless a partnership agreement provides otherwise, a limited partner may not withdraw from a limited partnership prior to the dissolution and winding up of the

---

[*]   Richard D. Freer & Douglas K. Moll, PRINCIPLES OF BUSINESS ORGANIZATIONS 530 (2013).

limited partnership. Notwithstanding anything to the contrary under applicable law, a partnership agreement may provide that a partnership interest may not be assigned prior to the dissolution and winding up of the limited partnership. * * *

§ 17–604   Distribution upon withdrawal.

Except as provided in this subchapter, upon withdrawal any withdrawing partner is entitled to receive any distribution to which such partner is entitled under a partnership agreement and, if not otherwise provided in a partnership agreement, such partner is entitled to receive, within a reasonable time after withdrawal, the fair value of such partner's partnership interest in the limited partnership as of the date of withdrawal based upon such partner's right to share in distributions from the limited partnership.

QUESTIONS

1.   What are the reasons that a limited partner would decide to withdraw from a limited partnership? Are the possible reasons that a general partner would decide to withdraw from a limited partnership different?

2.   Limited partnership statutes provide different rules for withdrawal by a general partner and withdrawal by a limited partner. Why? Do these different rules make sense?

3.   The Delaware provision for withdrawal by a limited partner is different from RULPA § 603, which provides:

"If the <u>agreement</u> does not specify <u>in writing</u> the time or the events upon the happening of which a limited partner may withdraw or a definite time for the dissolution and winding up of the limited partnership, a limited partner may withdraw upon not less than six months' prior written notice to each general partner at his [or her] address on the books of the limited partnership at its office in this State."

Why does the RULPA default rule for withdrawal by a limited partner require six months' notice? (RULPA, like Delaware, has no requirement of notice by a withdrawing general partner.)

4.   Agee, a limited partner in Bubba's Burritos Limited Partnership, wants to withdraw. The partnership agreement is silent on events permitting a limited partner to withdraw and on the consequences of such withdrawal.

    a)   Can Agee withdraw?

    b)   If so, what are the consequences of Agee's withdrawal?

5.   You are the attorney for a new limited partnership, EFRS L.P. You are meeting with L, who represents a person considering a major investment

in the limited partnership. What provisions regarding withdrawal is L likely to request?

6.   BB Corp, the only general partner in Bubba's Burritos Limited Partnership wants to withdraw. The partnership agreement is silent on events permitting a general partner to withdraw and on the consequences of such withdrawal.

a)   Can BB Corp. withdraw?

b)   If so, what are the consequences of BB Corp's withdrawal under Delaware statute set out below?

§ 17–801 Nonjudicial dissolution.

A limited partnership is dissolved and its affairs shall be wound up upon the first to occur of the following:

> (1) At the time specified in a partnership agreement, but if no such time is set forth in the partnership agreement, then the limited partnership shall have a perpetual existence; * * *

> (3) An event of withdrawal of a general partner unless at the time there is at least 1 other general partner and the partnership agreement permits the business of the limited partnership to be carried on by the remaining general partner and that partner does so, but the limited partnership is not dissolved and is not required to be wound up by reason of any event of withdrawal if

>> (i) within 90 days or such other period as is provided for in a partnership agreement after the withdrawal either

>>> (A) if provided for in the partnership agreement, the then-current percentage or other interest in the profits of the limited partnership specified in the partnership agreement owned by the remaining partners agree, in writing or vote, to continue the business of the limited partnership and to appoint, effective as of the date of withdrawal, 1 or more additional general partners if necessary or desired, or

>>> (B) if no such right to agree or vote to continue the business of the limited partnership and to appoint 1 or more additional general partners is provided for in the partnership agreement, then more than 50% of the then-current percentage or other interest in the profits of the limited partnership owned by the remaining partners or, if there is more than 1 class or group of remaining partners, then more than 50% of the then-current percentage or other interest in the profits of the limited partnership owned by each class or classes or group or groups of remaining partners

SEC. F

WHAT ARE THE LEGAL PROBLEMS IN DISSOLVING
A LIMITED PARTNERSHIP?

521

agree, in writing or vote, to continue the business of the limited partnership and to appoint, effective as of the date of withdrawal, 1 or more additional general partners if necessary or desired, or

(ii) the business of the limited partnership is continued pursuant to a right to continue stated in the partnership agreement and; the appointment, effective as of the date of withdrawal, of 1 or more additional general partners if necessary or desired;

F. WHAT ARE THE LEGAL PROBLEMS IN DISSOLVING A LIMITED PARTNERSHIP?

Most of the legal problems in dissolving a limited partnership are problems of interpretation of the language of the limited partnership agreement. The next case is not only illustrative but also (1) provides an opportunity for interesting illustrations and (2) can be edited so as to be short enough to be assigned toward the end of the semester.

IN RE DISSOLUTION OF MIDNIGHT STAR ENTERPRISES, L.P.

Supreme Court of South Dakota, 2006
724 N.W.2d 334

SABERS, JUSTICE. [1.] Petition for dissolution of a partnership was brought by the general partner. The circuit court found the fair market value of the partnership was $6.2 million and ordered the majority partners to buy the business for that price within ten days or it would be sold on the open market. The general partner sought intermediate appeal raising two issues. Since the circuit court failed to use the hypothetical transaction standard to assess the fair market value of the partnership and ordered a forced sale, we reverse and remand.

FACTS

[2.] Midnight Star Enterprises, L.P. (Midnight Star) is a limited partnership, which operates a gaming, on-sale liquor and restaurant business in Deadwood, South Dakota.*

---

* For more pictures and more than you want to know about the gaming, liquor and restaurant at Midnight Star, http://www.themidnightstar.com/.

The owners of Midnight Star consist of: Midnight Star Enterprises, Ltd. (MSEL) as the general partner, owning 22 partnership units; Kevin Costner (Costner), owning 71.50 partnership units; and Francis and Carla Caneva (Canevas), owning 3.25 partnership units each. Costner is the sole owner of MSEL and essentially owns 93.5 partnership units.

[3.] The Canevas managed the operations of Midnight Star, receiving salaries and bonuses for their employment. According to MSEL, it became concerned about the Canevas' management and voiced concerns. Communications between the Canevas and the other partners broke down and MSEL decided to terminate the Canevas' employment. MSEL inquired whether the Canevas would participate in an amicable disassociation, but the Canevas declined.

[4.] MSEL then chose to dissolve Midnight Star pursuant to Article X, Section 10.1 of the Limited Partnership Agreement and brought a Petition for Dissolution. In order to dissolve, the fair market value of Midnight Star had to be assessed. MSEL hired Paul Thorstenson (Thorstenson), an accountant, to determine the fair market value. MSEL alleged the Canevas solicited an "offer" from Ken Kellar (Kellar), a Deadwood casino, restaurant, and hotel owner, which MSEL claimed was contrary to the provisions of the partnership agreement.

[5.] At an evidentiary hearing, Thorstenson determined the fair market value was $3.1 million based on the hypothetical transaction standard of valuation. Kellar testified he offered $6.2 million for Midnight Star. MSEL argued Thorstenson used the proper valuation standard and Kellar's offer did not establish the fair market value. The circuit court disagreed and found Kellar's offer of $6.2 million to be the fair market value of Midnight Star. The circuit court ordered the majority owners to buy the business for $6.2 million within 10 days or the court would order the business to be sold on the open market.

[6.] MSEL appeals. The issues are:

1.   Whether Article 10.4 of the partnership agreement requires the Midnight Star to be sold on the open market.

2.   Whether the circuit court erred in finding the fair market value of Midnight Star was the actual offer price and not that of a hypothetical transaction.

3.   Whether the circuit court abused its discretion by ordering a forced sale of Midnight Star. * * *

Article 10.4 provides

After all of the debts of the Partnership have been paid, the General Partner or Liquidating Trustee may distribute in kind any Partnership property provided that a good faith effort is first made to sell or otherwise dispose of such property for cash or readily marketable securities at its estimated fair value to one or more third parties none of whom is an affiliate of any Partner. The General Partner or Liquidating Trustee shall value any such Partnership property at its fair market value and distribution shall then proceed as if the property had been sold for cash at such value with the resulting Net Profits and/or Net Losses allocated to the Partners as provided in Article VI and subsection 10.3.2 of this Agreement. * * *

[The court treated the first two of its three issues as issues of contract interpretation. As to the first issue, the court held that Article 10.4 did not require that the Midnight Star be sold—it merely required such a sale if the general partner chose to distribute the assets in kind, instead of a cash distribution, With respect to the second issue, the court interpreted the phrase "fair market value in Article 10.4 to the price paid in a hypothetical transaction free of "irrationalities and biases" of any real buyer. "The partnership agreement does not provide that the value of the business upon dissolution will be the highest and best offer the partnership can obtain. The circuit court should have used the hypothetical transaction standard in determining the fair market value of Midnight Star."

What follows is the court's discussion of the third issue—whether the trial court abused its discretion in ordering the sale of the Midnight Star.]

[26.]Since it was error for the circuit court to value Midnight Star at $6.2 million, it was also error to force the general partners to buy the business for $6.2 million or sell the business. However, because this issue could reappear should there be another appeal of this case after revaluation, we determine whether the circuit court can order a partnership to be sold on the open market when the majority owners want to continue to run the business.

[27.]Other jurisdictions have addressed the issue whether the business must be sold in order to liquidate after dissolution. Many of these jurisdictions allow the partnership to be sold to the willing partners even after dissolution. A withdrawing partner can be paid any contributions or profits due, but liquidation does not have to occur after dissolution. These jurisdictions have noted that forced sales typically end up in economic waste * * *

[29.]We see no reason that rationale should not be applied in this case, especially in view of our construction of the contract provisions in the partnership agreement. Instead of ordering the majority partners to purchase the whole partnership for the appraised value, the majority partners should only be required to pay any interests the withdrawing partner is due. Upon remand, the majority partners should only be required to pay the Canevas the value of their 6.5 partnership units, if any value exists after revaluation.

QUESTIONS

1.   What, if any, language, in the limited partnership agreement was relevant to the court's decision?

2.   What does the court mean by the final phrase "if any value exists after revaluation"? Is there any possibility that the Canevas' interest has no value?

3.   Why did Kevin Costner want to dissolve the limited partnership? Should that be relevant in this case?

4.   Did Mr. and Mrs. Caneva want to sell their interests in the limited partnership to Kevin Costner? Should that be relevant in this case?

5.   Should the close corporation concept of "freeze out" be relevant in this case?

G. LIMITED PARTNERSHIPS VS. LIMITED LIABILITY PARTNERSHIPS

We have been studying the limited partnership, a business entity in which

- at least one partner is a general partner;
- other partners are limited partners
- the general partner is personally liable to the limited partnership's creditors for the limited partnership's debts
- the limited partners are not generally liable to the limited partnership's creditors for the limited partnership's debt
- but there is a body of case law imposing such liability on limited partners who act too much like general partners.

Now we need to learn about the limited liability partnership (LLP), a business entity in which

- all partners are general partners and
- general partners are protected from liability to creditors of the limited liability partnership.

LLPs were invented by the Texas legislature to protect accountants and lawyers in big firms structured as general partnerships from personal liability for malpractice by their partners. Other states followed Texas' lead. All states now have some form of LLP statute, and there are LLP provisions in RUPA.

State LLP statutes vary considerably from state to state. In some states, the LLP can be used only by partnerships practicing a profession, and not for general business partnerships. In some states, partners in an LLP are protected only from liability for negligence claims, and thus remain vicariously liable in contract and for intentional torts of other partners.

Section 306(c) of RUPA is particularly broad. It provides that "[a]n obligation of a partnership while the partnership is a limited liability partnership, whether arising in contract, tort, or otherwise, is solely the obligation of the partnership. A partner is not personally liable, directly or indirectly, by way of contribution or otherwise, for such an obligation solely by reason of being or so acting as a partner."

One common feature of state LLP statutes is the LLP registration process. The Delaware provisions are illustrative:

§ 15–1001 Statement of qualification of a domestic partnership.

(a) A domestic partnership may be formed as, or may become, a limited liability partnership pursuant to this section.

(b) In order to form a limited liability partnership, the original partnership agreement of the partnership shall state that the partnership is formed as a limited liability partnership, and the partnership shall file a statement of qualification in accordance with subsection (c) of this section. In order for an existing partnership to become a limited liability partnership, the terms and conditions on which the partnership becomes a limited liability partnership must be approved by the vote necessary to amend the partnership agreement * * *

(c) The statement of qualification must contain:

(1) The name of the partnership;

[And, Delaware § 15–108(b) The name of a limited liability partnership shall contain as the last words or letters of its name the words "Limited Liability Partnership," the abbreviation "L.L.P." or the designation "LLP."]

(4) A statement that the partnership elects to be a limited liability partnership; and

(5) The future effective date or time (which shall be a date or time certain) of the statement of qualification if it is not to be effective upon the filing of the statement of qualification. * * *

(d) The status of a partnership as a limited liability partnership is effective on the later of the filing of the statement of qualification or a future effective date or time specified in the statement of qualification. * * *

(f) The filing of a statement of qualification establishes that a partnership has satisfied all conditions precedent to the qualification of the partnership as a limited liability partnership.

KUS V. IRVING

Superior Court of Connecticut, 1999
736 A.2d 946

HURLEY, JUDGE TRIAL REFEREE. The two defendants, attorneys Narcy Z. Dubicki and Garon Camassar, claim in their motion for summary judgment that there is no genuine issue of material fact as to their liability and request, as a matter of law, that the motion be granted. The law firm is a limited liability partnership.

The plaintiff, Margaret Kus, claims that a third defendant, attorney Charles J. Irving, a partner in the firm of Irving, Dubicki and Camassar, induced her to sign a fee agreement to pay him a fee of 25 percent of what he collected on the life insurance policy of the husband of the plaintiff before suit was filed and 33 percent of any proceeds after suit was brought. The policy had a death benefit of $400,000. She claims that Irving had already received the $400,000, but nevertheless filed suit to collect the larger fee of 33 percent. Irving then paid the plaintiff $270,692.26 and took a fee of $135,365.63, which the plaintiff claims was $33,841.41 too high. The plaintiff sued all three partners in the firm.

Both Dubicki and Camassar have filed affidavits stating that they had no personal knowledge of the case or the dealings between Irving and the plaintiff until November 24, 1998, which was several days after the matter between the plaintiff and Irving was concluded. They claim that under General Statutes § 34–327, they are protected from liability for any actions by their partner, Irving.

Section 34–327 provides in pertinent part: "(c) . . . a partner in a registered limited liability partnership is not liable directly or indirectly . . . for any debts, obligations and liabilities . . . chargeable to the partnership or another partner or partners . . . arising in the course of the partnership business while the partnership is a registered limited liability partnership.

"(d) The provisions of subsection (c) . . . shall not affect the liability of a partner . . . for his own negligence, wrongful acts or misconduct, or that of any person under his direct supervision or control."

In their affidavits, Dubicki and Camassar state that they had no personal knowledge of the dealings between the plaintiff and Irving, nor did they have any supervision or control of Irving. Furthermore, they state that under the partnership agreement, Irving retains all fees for his activities and does not share any of them with the other partners. * * *

[S]ince the two defendants shared no benefit, did not have direct supervision or control over Irving and did not know about the matter until nine days after the funds were distributed, the court finds that they are protected from liability by § 34–327(c).

The motion for summary judgment by defendants Dubicki and Camassar is granted.

QUESTIONS

1.   Review of first part of the course; Could Kus recover from lawyer Irving? From the law firm of Irving, Dubuclo and Camassar?

2.   Review of this part of the course: Did Kus know that the law firm is a limited liability partnership? Should that be relevant?

3.   Was it relevant that Irving took all of Kus' fee for himself?

———————

Some states have enacted limited liability limited partnerships statutes [LLLP]. Our favorite student text suggests that "In practical terms, this [limited liability limited partnership statutes] seems to reduce the importance of the control rule for limited liability. A limited partner who would be held liable for violating the control rule in a non-LLLP, in other words, has no liability in an LLLP. . . ."[*]

———————

[*]   Richard D. Freer & Douglas K, Moll, PRINCIPLES OF BUSINESS ORGANIZATIONS 552 (2013).

CHAPTER 11

WHAT IS A LIMITED LIABILITY COMPANY AND HOW DOES IT WORK?

■ ■ ■

A. WHAT IS AN LLC AND WHAT IS LLC LAW?

Another form of business structure that offers Propp, Agee, and Capel the best of both worlds is a limited liability company, which everyone calls an LLC. An LLC offers all of its owners, generally referred to as members, both (i) protection from liability for the business's debts similar to the liability protection of shareholders of a corporation and (ii) the same pass-through income tax characteristics of a partnership.

The LLC is a relatively new business structure in the United States. Its origins trace to a statute enacted in Wyoming in 1978 and a 1988 revenue ruling that Wyoming LLCs would be treated as a partnership for tax purposes.

The tax regulations in effect at that time provided that an unincorporated business entity such as an LLC would be treated as a partnership only if it had more "noncorporate" characteristics than "corporate" characteristics. More specifically, these regulations (known as the Kintner regulations) provided that a business would be taxed like a corporation if it had three or more of the following characteristics:

(1) limited liability;

(2) centralized management;

(3) free transferability of ownership interests;

(4) continued existence after an owner withdraws.

Understanding this tax history is helpful to understanding state LLC statutes—especially state LLC statutes enacted before 1997. Many such early statutes contained mandatory provisions designed to ensure that LLCs formed under the statute would obtain partnership tax treatment. Since all LLCs wanted (1) limited liability and most wanted (2) centralized management, this meant that these early state LLC statutes prohibited (3) free transferability of ownership interests and (4) owner dissociation without dissolution.

Tax law changed in 1997, and LLC statutes have been changing ever since. The IRS issued tax regulations in 1997 providing partnership tax status for all limited liability companies—even those with all 4 of the above corporate characteristics. In the years since then, the LLC business structure has become increasingly popular. Most new businesses today are LLCs.

Each state now has a statute authorizing the creation of LLCs. These statutes typically borrow both from partnership law and corporation law.

LLC statutes vary greatly from state to state. There is far more variety in state LLC laws than we find in the corporation or partnership laws of the various states. The National Conference of Commissioners on Uniform State Laws issued a Uniform Limited Liability Company Act (ULLCA) in 1996 and issued a substantially revised version (RULLCA) in 2006. Neither has been widely adopted.

As with corporations, the Delaware statute (Delaware LLCA) is important. As with corporations, more businesses operated in states other than Delaware are organized under Delaware law than under the law of any other state.

B. WHAT ARE THE LEGAL ISSUES IN STARTING A BUSINESS AS AN LLC?

1. FILING A CERTIFICATE OF FORMATION/ ARTICLES OF ORGANIZATION

Like corporations and limited partnerships, LLCs do not exist until a formal filing with the state. In Delaware, for example, a "limited liability company is formed at the time of the filing of the initial certificate of formation in the office of the Secretary of State." Delaware § 18–201.

We have set out below the Delaware Certificate of Formation.*

---

* *State of Delaware Limited Liability Company Certificate of Formation*, STATE OF DELAWARE, http://corp.delaware.gov/llcform09.pdf.

STATE *of* DELAWARE
LIMITED LIABILITY COMPANY
CERTIFICATE *of* FORMATION

- **First:** The name of the limited liability company is _____
  _____.

- **Second:** The address of its registered office in the State of Delaware is _____
  _____ in the City of _____.
  The name of its Registered agent at such address is _____
  _____.

- **Third:** *(Use this paragraph only if the company is to have a specific effective date of dissolution.)* "The latest date on which the limited liability company is to dissolve is _____."

- **Fourth:** *(Insert any other matters the members determine to include herein.)*

  _____
  _____
  _____
  _____
  _____
  _____
  _____
  _____

In Witness Whereof, the undersigned have executed this Certificate of Formation of _____this _____ day of _____, 20_____.

BY: _____
Authorized Person(s)

NAME: _____
Type or Print

_____

Other states have similar provisions although some states use the term "articles of organization" rather than "certificate of formation".

Regardless of whether relevant state law uses the term "certificate of formation" or "articles of organization" to describe the document that must be filed to create an LLC, that document typically contains very little information about the company.

2. DRAFTING AN OPERATING AGREEMENT

A limited liability company's most important document is the "Operating Agreement." The operating agreement is not a public document, i.e., it is not filed.

State limited liability company statutes do not even require that there be an operating agreement. The needs of your LLC clients, however, require that there be an operating agreement.

As the term "operating agreement"* suggests, an operating agreement governs how the limited liability company operates. In resolving disputes over the operation of a limited liability company, courts look first to the operating agreement. To quote from a New York case, "It is well-established that the court must look to the terms of the Operating Agreement to determine the rules applicable to the operation of a particular LLC. Only where the Operating Agreement is ambiguous, contrary to law or does not contain any provision for the particular matter at issue, do the statutory provisions of the Limited Liability Company Law (LLCL) control."†

And now to quote from the ULLCA, "if any provision of an operating agreement is inconsistent with the articles of organization:

(1) the operating agreement controls as to managers, members, and members' transferees; and

(2) the articles of organization control as to persons, other than managers, members and their transferees, who reasonably rely on the articles to their detriment." ULLCA § 203(c)

QUESTIONS

1. Is an operating agreement more like a partnership agreement or more like articles of incorporation?

2. Who is bound by the operating agreement?

---

* The Delaware statute uses the term "limited liability company agreement" instead of "operating agreement" but then defines the term "limited liability company agreement" as including "operating agreements." DLLCA § 101(7), Accordingly, Delaware LLC's and Delaware courts often use the term "operating agreement."

† Mizrahi v. Cohen, 2012 WL 104775 (N.Y.Sup 2012).

C. WHAT ARE THE LEGAL PROBLEMS IN OPERATING A BUSINESS AS AN LLC?

1. WHO DECIDES WHAT?

The owners of an LLC can elect the form of management. Every state's LLC statute affords the owners (members) the option of electing to manage the business themselves—"member-managed company"—or have managers—"manager-managed company"—or some combination of member-managed and manager-managed.

The decision-making authority of the members of a member-managed company is much like that of the partners in a general partnership. And the decision-making authority of the managers of a manager-managed company is much like a corporation with a board of directors, professional managers, and separation of ownership and management.

In a member-managed company, the operating agreement will answer such questions as: (1) how to determine how many votes each member has and (2) how to determine what matters require more than majority vote. In a manager-managed company, the operating agreement will answer questions such as (1) how members elect and remove managers and (2) what issues require a member vote.

PROBLEMS

1. Your client C is about to contract with a business structured as a limited liability company. How does C know whether the company is member-managed or manager-managed? Does C need to know? Does Delaware require that such information be provided in the certificate of formation? Should states require that information be included in the filed certificate of formation/articles of organization? *Cf.* ULLCA § 301.

2. E is the largest investor in and manager of Child Care of Irvine, LLC, (CCI). CCI is a limited liability company, organized in a ULLCA state. The filed articles of organization provide that CCI is to be manager-managed and that E is to be the initial manager. Although CCI retains a law firm to prepare an operating agreement, Members A, B, C, and D and E cannot agree on the terms and so there is no operating agreement. After a few months, A, B, C, and D agree that they do not want E to continue as manager. What can they do? *See* ULLCA § 404.

3. Your client has invested in the Shepherd LLC (SLLC) because SLLC owns and operates a school that teaches inner city kids how to become shepherds. SLLC is a manager-managed limited liability company in California, a RULLCA state. Your client is concerned that the new manager of SLLC, George Shepherd, will sell the school and use the proceeds to start a law school. Are the following statutory provisions helpful to you in advising your client:

§ 17701.10. Operating agreement; scope; limitations, variations, and modifications; fiduciary duty; indemnification and damages

(a) Except as otherwise provided in this section, the operating agreement governs all of the following:

(1) Relations among the members as members and between the members and the limited liability company.

(2) The rights and duties under this title of a person in the capacity of manager.

(3) The activities of the limited liability company and the conduct of those activities.

(4) The means and conditions for amending the operating agreement.

(b) To the extent the operating agreement does not otherwise provide for a matter described in subdivision (a), this title governs the matter.

§ 17704.07. Management of limited liability company; members' meetings; voting rights and limitations; officers

(c) In a manager-managed limited liability company, the following rules apply:

(1) Except as otherwise expressly provided in this title, any matter relating to the activities of the limited liability company is decided exclusively by the managers. * * *

(4) The consent of all members of the limited liability company is required to do any of the following:

(A) Sell, lease, exchange, or otherwise dispose of all, or substantially all, of the limited liability company's property, with or without the goodwill, outside the ordinary course of the limited liability company's activities. * * *

(D) Amend the operating agreement.

2. WHO IS LIABLE TO WHOM FOR WHAT?

a. LLC's Liability to Third Parties

Like a corporation, an LLC is an entity. Delaware § 18–201(b), ULLCA § 201. It can carry on "any lawful business purpose or activity." Delaware § 18–106. An LLC can incur debts from the actions and inactions of its managers or its members. ULLCA §§ 301, 302. Apply these ULLCA provisions to the following problem.

PROBLEM

Epstein, Freer, Roberts and Shepherd are the members of Bubba's Burritos, LLC. To obtain a catering contract from the Georgia Gluten-Free Group (GGG) for its annual convention, Epstein falsely represents that Bubba's burritos are gluten-free. More than a 100 GGG members who attended the GGG convention and ate the burritos that were not gluten-free became ill. Is Bubba's Burritos' liable? What, if any, additional information do you need to answer this question? Should it matter whether Bubba's Burritos is member-managed or manager-managed?

PRIMARY INVESTMENTS, LLC V. WEE TENDER
CARE III, INC.

Court of Appeals of Georgia, 2013
323 Ga.App. 196, 746 S.E.2d 823

McMILLIAN, JUDGE. This appeal arises from the multi-million dollar sale of Primary Prep Academy, a childcare facility, and subsequent attempts by the members of the seller, a limited liability company, to open another daycare center, allegedly in violation of the noncompetition clause in the sale contract. N & N Holdings, LLC ("N & N Holdings"), the purchaser of the facility, and Wee Tender Care III, Inc. ("Wee Tender Care"), the entity that is currently operating the Primary Prep Academy (collectively "Plaintiffs"), brought suit against the seller, Primary Investments, LLC, formerly known as Primary Prep Academy, LLC ("Primary, LLC"); Marguerite O'Brien, Kelli O'Brien Milz, and Erin O'Brien Fleishman (collectively the "O'Briens"), who are mother and daughters and who were members and managers of Primary, LLC; and the O'Briens' new childcare company, East Cobb Children's Academy, LLC ("East Cobb") (collectively "Defendants"). Plaintiffs filed this action for damages and equitable relief, . . . For the reasons that follow, we reverse the entry of the judgment finding Defendants liable for violation of the noncompetition clause in the parties' contract. . . .

Viewing the evidence in the light most favorable to the nonmoving parties, in 2008, Martin G. Nixon and Stephenie L. Nixon (the "Nixons") approached the O'Briens expressing an interest in purchasing Primary, LLC. After negotiations and multiple contract drafts, an asset purchase agreement ("APA") was executed on March 20, 2008 between Primary, LLC, as seller, and N & N Holdings, LLC, as buyer, for the sale and purchase of the assets of the childcare business. Marguerite O'Brien executed the APA on behalf of the seller and the Nixons each executed on behalf of N & N Holdings, LLC. The noncompetition clause of the APA provides:

> Until three years after the Closing Date (the "Noncompetition Period"), Seller agrees that neither Seller nor *its agents* will,

unless acting in accordance with Buyer's prior written consent, (i) solicit any person employed by Seller as of the Closing Date who is employed by Buyer at the Business location[,] (ii) directly contact any parent who, within a one-year period prior to the Closing has had a child enrolled at the Business Locations, for the purpose of soliciting or selling products or services to said parent in competition with Buyer, or (iii) open any child care facility within a ten-mile radius of any Business Locations being sold to the Buyer hereunder.

(Emphasis supplied).

* * * In January 2010, the O'Briens decided to open a new childcare facility and formed East Cobb, a new Georgia limited liability company through which to conduct the business. East Cobb opened its new childcare facility, which was located within a ten-mile radius of Primary Prep Academy, in September 2010. Plaintiffs subsequently filed suit seeking, inter alia, to enforce the APA's noncompetition clause. * * *

In this case, the noncompetition clause provides that the "Seller agrees that neither Seller nor its agents" will commit certain acts in competition with N & N Holdings, as the buyer. The parties do not contend, and no evidence in the record indicates, that the entity Primary, LLC was involved in opening the East Cobb childcare facility. Nor is there any evidence that the O'Briens were acting as agents for, or for any purpose related to the business and affairs of, Primary, LLC when they opened the new facility. Accordingly, Plaintiffs failed to establish any violation of the noncompetition clause by Primary, LLC. The key issue, therefore, is whether the language "neither Seller nor its agents" in the noncompetition clause barred the O'Briens, individually, from opening the East Cobb childcare facility.

It is undisputed, however, that Milz and Fleishman never signed the APA. And although Marguerite O'Brien signed the agreement, she did so only in a representative capacity. Under OCGA § 10–6–53, "if the principal's name is disclosed and the agent professes to act for him, it will be held to be the act of the principal." Consequently, Marguerite O'Brien's signature formed a contract between Primary, LLC and N & N Holdings. And "[a]n agent who, acting within the scope of his authority, enters into contractual relations for a disclosed principal does not bind himself, in the absence of an express agreement to do so." Because no such agreement appears here—the O'Briens are not even mentioned by name in the APA—the O'Briens are not parties to the APA, and "[i]t is axiomatic that a person who is not a party to a contract is not bound by its terms."

Nevertheless, Plaintiffs contend that the APA's use of the words "its agents" is unambiguous and refers specifically to the O'Briens. They assert that the Georgia Limited Liability Company Act (the "Act") defines "agent" as any manager of the limited liability company, and therefore, the term "its agents" includes the O'Briens individually. Thus, Plaintiffs argue that Primary, LLC's execution of the contract containing this language was somehow sufficient to bind the O'Briens individually to the terms of the noncompetition clause.

Plaintiffs are correct that OCGA § 14–11–301(b)(2) of the Act provides that "[i]f the articles of organization provide that management of the limited liability company is vested in a manager or managers: . . . (2) Every manager is an agent of the limited liability company for the purpose of its business and affairs. . . ." However, this statute is merely a restatement of the general principle that an agent is one who acts for another, but nothing in the language of the Act or elsewhere under Georgia law permits a principal, in this case the limited liability company, under these circumstances, to bind its agents for the limited liability company's contractual obligations. To the contrary, the O'Briens, as members and agents of Primary, LLC, are afforded protection from liability for Primary, LLC's obligations. Under the Act, "[a] person who is a member, manager, agent, or employee of a limited liability company is not liable, . . . for a debt, obligation, or liability of the limited liability company, including liabilities and obligations of the limited liability company to any member or assignee, whether arising in contract, tort, or otherwise[.]". Thus, "a member of a limited liability company . . . is considered separate from the company and is not a proper party to a proceeding by or against a limited liability company, solely by reason of being a member of the limited liability company. . . ."). Accordingly, Primary, LLC had no authority to bind the O'Briens individually to the terms of the noncompetition clause, and we find that under the Act, merely including the term "its agents" in a contract signed by a limited liability company does not bind its members or managers individually. Rather, if N & N Holdings and the Nixons wished to bind the O'Briens to the terms of the noncompetition clause, they were required to make them parties to the APA and to obtain their signatures in their individual capacities. * * *

Therefore, because Plaintiffs failed to show that Primary, LLC, the only defendant who was a party to the APA, violated the noncompetition clause and also failed to show that the O'Briens, who were not parties to the APA, were subject to the its [sic] terms, the trial court erred in granting partial summary judgment against Defendants on the liability issue.

QUESTIONS

1.   Was Seller a manager-managed LLC? Was Marguerite O'Brien the manager? Is that relevant?

2.   Who signed the APA? Is that relevant?

3.   What should the Buyer's attorney have done differently?

b.   Members' Liability to Creditors of the LLC

i.   *General Rule—No Liability*

As the *Wee Tender Care* case illustrates, generally the members of an LLC are not liable to the company's creditors. LLC statutes protect the owners from personal liability for claims against the company. Compare Delaware § 18–303 and ULLCA § 303.

Note that neither provision distinguishes the personal liability of members in member-managed LLCs from the personal liability of members in manager-managed LLCs. The members are simply not liable for the company's debts.

Well, as the following problem and next case illustrate, it is not quite that simple.

PROBLEM

Epstein, Freer, Roberts and Shepherd are the members of Bubba's Burritos, LLC, a Delaware limited liability company. To obtain a catering contract from the Georgia Gluten-Free Group (GGG) for its annual convention, Epstein falsely represents that Bubba's burritos are gluten-free. More than a 100 GGG members who attended the GGG convention and ate the Bubba's burritos that were not gluten-free became ill. Is Epstein, the wrongdoer, personally liable? Would reviewing Chapter 2 be helpful? Is the following discussion of the Delaware statute helpful?

> [W]hen a limited liability company is incorporated [sic] in another state, our statutes mandate application of the laws of that foreign state. Because Retail Relief was incorporated in Delaware, we look to Delaware law to determine the extent of the defendants' liability.

> We begin our analysis with the text of § 18–303(a) of title 6 of the Delaware Code Annotated. Section 18–303(a) provides in relevant part: "Except as otherwise provided by this chapter, the debts, obligations and liabilities of a limited liability company, whether arising in contract, tort or otherwise, shall be solely the debts, obligations and liabilities of the limited liability company, and *no member or manager of a limited liability company shall be obligated personally for any such debt, obligation or liability of the limited liability company solely by reason of being a member or acting as a manager of the limited liability company.*" (Emphasis added.) * * *

To resolve the plaintiff's claim, we must ascertain the meaning of the word "solely." . . . "[S]olely" is defined to mean "to the exclusion of alternate or competing things. . . ." Webster's Third New International Dictionary. Thus, the statute plainly provides that a limited liability company member cannot be held liable for the malfeasance of a limited liability company by virtue of his membership in the limited liability company alone; in other words, he must do more than merely be a member in order to be liable personally for an obligation of the limited liability company. The statute thus does not preclude individual liability for members of a limited liability company if that liability is not based simply on the member's affiliation with the company. * * *

Under Delaware law, a limited liability company formed under the Delaware Limited Liability Company Act is treated for liability purposes like a corporation." * * * "The default common-law rule is that corporate officials may be held individually liable for their tortious conduct, even if undertaken while acting in their official capacity. . . . [V]arious courts of [the state of Delaware] have recognized that executives, directors and officers of an entity can be held *individually* liable for the fraudulent or tortious acts which they, in their official capacities, commit, ratify or approve, despite the fact that they may have acted as an agent for or performed for the benefit of that entity at the time the fraudulent or tortious act was committed, ratified or approved." Accordingly, we conclude that although § 18–303(a) of the Delaware Code Annotated shields the defendants from personal liability based solely on their affiliation with [the limited liability company], it does not shield them from personal liability for their own tortious conduct.*

Generally, a member acquires her ownership interest in a limited liability company from the company itself by making or agreeing to make a payment or other contribution to the company. The operating agreement usually lists the amount of each member's initial contribution. And while the operating agreement commonly contains language similar to the following: "No Initial Member shall be obligated to make any Capital Contribution other than the Initial Capital Contribution on Schedule E,." the operating agreement can, as the next case illustrates, provide for additional capital contributions.

---

* Webber v. United States Sterling Securities, Inc., 924 A.2d 816. 823–825 (Conn. 2007).

RACING INVESTMENT FUND 2000, LLC v.
CLAY WARD AGENCY, INC.

Kentucky Supreme Court, 2014
320 S.W.3d 654

Opinion of the Court by *JUSTICE ABRAMSON*. Racing Investment Fund 2000, LLC is a limited liability company created in August 2000, to purchase, train and race thoroughbred horses. In May, 2004, Racing Investment entered into an agreed judgment with its former equine insurance firm, Clay Ward Agency, Inc., for past-due insurance premiums. Shortly thereafter, Racing Investment partially paid the judgment by tendering all of the remaining assets of the then-defunct limited liability company. When Racing Investment failed to pay the remainder of the amount owed, Clay Ward succeeded in having Racing Investment held in contempt of court for its failure to pay the entire judgment amount. Specifically, the trial court ruled that a provision in Racing Investment's Operating Agreement which allowed the limited liability company's Manager to call for additional capital contributions, as needed, from all members on a pro rata basis for "operating, administrative or other business expenses" provided a means of satisfying the Clay Ward judgment. The trial court ordered that Racing Investment "act accordingly to satisfy the Judgment within a reasonable period of time" or face other sanctions. After the Court of Appeals affirmed, this Court granted discretionary review to consider whether the capital call provision can be invoked by a court to obtain funds from the limited liability company's members in order to satisfy a judgment against the limited liability company. Having concluded that KRS 275.150 provides for immunity from personal liability for a limited liability company's debts unless a member agrees otherwise and, further, that members of Racing Investment did not, by signing an operating agreement allowing for periodic capital calls from the Manager, subject themselves to personal liability, we reverse. * * *

In 1994, Kentucky joined a growing national trend by recognizing limited liability companies (LLCs) through the adoption of the "Kentucky Limited Liability Company Act".... The "centerpiece" of a limited liability company is its "provision for limited liability of its members and managers in regard to the debts and obligations of the LLC...." * * *

Kentucky codified the limited liability feature of a limited liability company at KRS 275.150—"Immunity from personal liability":

(1) Except as provided in subsection (2) of this section or as otherwise specifically set forth in other sections in this chapter, no member, manager, employee, or agent of a limited liability company, including a professional limited liability company, shall be personally liable by reason of being a member, manager,

employee, or agent of the limited liability company, under a judgment, decree, or order of a court, agency, or tribunal of any type, or in any other manner, in this or any other state, or on any other basis, for a debt, obligation, or liability of the limited liability company, whether arising in contract, tort, or otherwise. The status of a person as a member, manager, employee, or agent of a limited liability company, including a professional limited liability company, shall not subject the person to personal liability for the acts or omissions, including any negligence, wrongful act, or actionable misconduct, of any other member, manager, agent, or employee of the limited liability company.

(2) Notwithstanding the provisions of subsection (1) of this section, under a written operating agreement or under another written agreement, a member or manager may agree to be obligated personally for any of the debts, obligations, and liabilities of the limited liability company.

Notably, the statute contains a strong, detailed declaration of personal immunity followed by recognition in subsection (2) that a member or members may agree in writing to be personally liable for the LLC's debts, obligations and liabilities. As one national commentator has noted, "[s]ince most LLCs are created for the purpose of obtaining limited liability, few LLCs take advantage of the opportunity to allow their members to waive limited liability under the act." Steven C. Alberty, *Limited Liability Companies: A Planning and Drafting Guide* § 3.06(b)(2) (2003).

Following the filing of articles of organization, KRS 275.020, the business of a limited liability company is typically conducted in accordance with an operating agreement, an agreement that has been analogized to a partnership agreement or even the articles of incorporation, by-laws and shareholders' agreement of a corporation. KRS 275.015(20) defines an "operating agreement" in relevant part as "any agreement, written or oral, among all of the members, as to the conduct of the business and affairs of a limited liability company." If the members of a particular LLC do not adopt a written operating agreement or adopt one which is silent on certain matters, KRS Chapter 275 contains default provisions that will govern the conduct of the entity's business and affairs.

One of the matters inevitably addressed in an operating agreement is the capitalization of the LLC. Initial capital contributions are detailed as well as any obligation for future capital infusion because "[a]n LLC may need capital in addition to that contributed at the time it is organized." Alberty at § 4.02(b)(1). Consequently, the members' commitments, if any, to make future capital contributions are also "typically set forth in the LLC's operating agreement." *Id.* * * *

Section 4.3(a) of the Racing Investment Operating Agreement, entitled "Additional Capital Contributions" provides:

> The Investor Members (*including, but not limited to,* any Investor Assignees) shall be obligated to contribute to the capital of the Company, on a prorata basis in accordance with their respective Percentage Interests, such amounts as may be reasonably deemed advisable by the Manager from time to time in order to pay operating, administrative, or other business expenses of the Company which have been incurred, or which the Manager reasonably anticipates will be incurred, by the Company. *Except* under unusual circumstances, such additional capital contributions ("Additional Capital Contributions") shall not be required more often than quarterly and shall be due and payable by each Investor Member (*including, but not limited to,* each Investor Assignee) within fifteen (15) days after such Investor Member receives written notice from the Company of the amount due (a "Quarterly Bill"), The Manager shall not be required to make any additional capital contributions.

(emphasis in original). This is the provision relied upon by Clay Ward in contending that Racing Investment was in contempt of court for not having paid the agreed judgment in full. Under Clay Ward's interpretation, Racing Investment incurred a legitimate business expense for the equine insurance premiums prior to its dissolution and the members of the LLC, by agreeing to the periodic capital contribution provision, are subject to a "last call" to satisfy the outstanding balance on the judgment. In accepting this construction, the trial court and Court of Appeals essentially concluded that, by agreeing to make periodic capital contributions pursuant to Section 4.3(a), individual members of Racing Investment are legally responsible for their pro rata share of the entity's business debt. Indeed, under this theory, any outstanding debt that remains unpaid by the LLC can be satisfied through application for a court-ordered capital call. We reject this construction as contrary to the plain terms of the Operating Agreement and the letter and spirit of the Kentucky Limited Liability Company Act.

* * * Section 4.3(a) is a provision designed to assure members will contribute additional capital, as deemed necessary by the Manager, to advance Racing Investment's thoroughbred racing venture. While Clay Ward's insurance premiums were indeed a legitimate business expense for which the Manager could have made a capital call, that premise alone does not lead *a fortiori* to the relief ordered by the trial court. Simply put, Section 4.3(a) is a not-uncommon, on-going capital infusion provision, not

a debt-collection mechanism by which a court can order a capital call and, by doing so, impose personal liability on the LLC's members for the entity's outstanding debt. Clay Ward insists that its quest to be paid is not about individual member liability, but there is no other way to construe what occurs when a court orders a capital call be made to pay for a particular LLC debt. From any viewpoint, the shield of limited liability has been lifted and the LLC's members have been held individually liable for its debt.

KRS 275.150 emphatically rejects personal liability for an LLC's debt unless the member or members, as the case may be, have agreed through the operating agreement or another written agreement to assume personal liability. Any such assumption of personal liability, which is contrary to the very business advantage reflected in the name "limited liability company", must be stated clearly in unequivocal language which leaves no room for doubt about the parties' intent. Section 4.3(a) of Racing Investment's Operating Agreement does not begin to meet this standard. A provision designed to provide on-going capital infusion as necessary, at the Manager's discretion, for the conduct of the entity's business affairs is simply not an agreement "to be obligated personally for any of the debts, obligations and liabilities of the limited liability company." KRS 275.150(2). To reiterate, assumption of personal liability by a member of an LLC is so antithetical to the purpose of a limited liability company that any such assumption must be stated in unequivocal terms leaving no doubt that the member or members intended to forego a principal advantage of this form of business entity. On this score, Section 4.3(a) simply does not qualify.

As noted by both parties, the immediately following section of the Operating Agreement, Section 4.4, provides "[e]xcept as otherwise specifically provided in the [Kentucky Limited Liability Company] Act, no Member shall have any personal liability for the obligations of the Company." This provision underscores the fundamental premise of a limited liability company. However, this provision continues by stating that, "*except.* . . . as to Additional Capital Contributions . . . no Member shall be obligated to contribute additional funds or loan money to the Company." While Clay Ward views this exception as approval of its theory regarding a last capital call, the additional capital contributions under Section 4.3(a) are, again, those periodic capital contributions which the Manager concludes are necessary to meet Racing Investment's on-going expenses. Section 4.3(a) is not a post-judgment collection device by which any legitimate business debt of the LLC can be transferred to individual members by a court-ordered capital call. A judgment creditor of a limited liability company has available all legal means for collection as against the entity itself but no means of securing relief from the LLC's individual members absent the unequivocal assumption of personal liability provided for in KRS 275.150(2).

Having concluded that Section 4.3 of the Operating Agreement does not allow the unpaid portion of the agreed judgment against Racing Investment to be satisfied through a court-ordered capital call, we reverse the opinion of the Court of Appeals. We also remand this matter to Fayette Circuit Court for additional proceedings, if any, consistent with this opinion.

QUESTIONS

1.   Who decides whether Racing Investment Fund 2000, LLC makes a capital call?

2.   Who wins and who loses in this case if the LLC's decision had been to make the capital call?

3.   To whom does the person who makes such a decision for an LLC owe a fiduciary duty? In answering this question, should it be relevant that Racing Investment Fund 2000, LLC was unable to pay its debts?

ii. Piercing the Veil

Recall that, under principles of corporation law, the limited liability of a shareholder of a corporation is limited by the concept of piercing the corporate veil. And recall that piercing the corporate veil is a common law concept. Corporation statutes do not provide for piercing the corporate veil.

In some states, such as Washington, the limited liability company act does refer to piercing the corporate veil: "members of a limited liability company shall be personally liable for any act, debt, obligation, or liability of the limited liability company to the extent that shareholders of a Washington business corporation would be liable in analogous circumstances. In this regard, the court may consider the factors and policies set forth in established case law with regard to piercing the corporate veil, except that the failure to hold meetings of members or managers or the failure to observe formalities pertaining to the calling or conduct of meetings shall not be considered a factor tending to establish that the members have personal liability for any act, debt, obligation, or liability of the limited liability company if the certificate of formation and limited liability company agreement do not expressly require the holding of meetings of members or managers." Revised Code of Washington, § 25.15.060 (2009).

As the next case illustrates, the limited liability company statute in most states and the ULLCA are not as clear.

SEC. C

WHAT ARE THE LEGAL PROBLEMS IN OPERATING A
BUSINESS AS AN LLC?

545

KUBICAN V. THE TAVERN, LLC

West Virginia Supreme Court of Appeals, 2013
752 S.E.2d 299

DAVIS, JUSTICE: This action presents this Court with a certified question from the Circuit Court of Harrison County asking whether "West Virginia's version of the Uniform Limited liability Company Act afford[s] complete protection to members of a limited liability company against a plaintiff seeking to pierce the corporate veil?" After considering the parties' briefs, their oral arguments and the relevant law, we answer this certified question in the negative.

Following an altercation that allegedly took place at Bubba's Bar and Grill in Bridgeport, West Virginia, on February 7, 2011, petitioner Joseph Kubican, who is the plaintiff below (hereinafter "Mr. Kubican"), filed a complaint, on May 27, 2011, naming as defendants Bubba's Bar and Grill and Harry Wiseman. The complaint asserted three counts against Bubba's Bar and Grill: (1) negligence; (2) negligent training and supervision of bar staff and security personnel; and (3) gross negligence, willful, wanton and reckless misconduct. Mr. Kubican subsequently learned that Bubba's Bar and Grill was a fictitious name used for business purposes by the respondent, The Tavern, LLC (hereinafter "The Tavern"). Additionally, Mr. Kubican learned that James Paugh and Lawson Mangum were the only members of The Tavern. . . . Mr. Kubican sought leave to amend his complaint . . . [to] assert a veil piercing count against Paugh and Mangum. * * *

Instead of ruling on Mr. Kubican's motion to amend his complaint, the circuit court determined that it had been presented with an issue of first impression and, therefore, certified the following question to this Court by order entered April 12, 2012:

> Does West Virginia's version of the Uniform Limited Liability Company Act afford complete protection to members of a limited liability company against a plaintiff seeking to pierce the corporate veil?

The circuit court answered this question in the affirmative based upon its conclusion that such an answer was in accord with the plain language of W. Va.Code § 31B–3–303. * * *

Mr. Kubican argues that this Court should answer the certified question in the negative and conclude that West Virginia's Uniform Limited Liability Company Act does not afford complete protection to members of an LLC against a plaintiff seeking to pierce the corporate veil. Mr. Kubican explains that West Virginia adopted its version of the act from the 1996 Uniform Limited Liability Company Act (hereinafter "ULLCA") drafted by the National Conference of Commissioners on Uniform State Laws. According to Mr. Kubican, numerous other jurisdictions that also have adopted the ULLCA have addressed the question of whether the Act precludes veil piercing. Mr. Kubican submits that "not a single court has concluded that the act prohibits" veil piercing. Finally, Mr. Kubican opines that adopting a rule that the LLC business form affords complete protection to LLC members would render West Virginia a safe haven for corporate irresponsibility and fraud.

The Tavern argues that W. Va.Code § 31B–3–303 expressly provides that members or managers of West Virginia LLCs are not personally responsible for any liability of the company. Therefore, The Tavern contends, a plain reading of the statute supports the position that piercing the veil of an LLC is not allowed. * * *

[W]e turn now to the particular language of W. Va.Code § 31B–3–303, which states in part:

> (a) Except as otherwise provided in subsection (c) of this section, the debts, obligations and liabilities of a limited liability company, whether arising in contract, tort or otherwise, are solely the debts, obligations and liabilities of the company. *A member or manager is not personally liable for a debt, obligation or liability of the company solely by reason of being or acting as a member or manager.*
>
> * * *
>
> (c) All or specified members of a limited liability company are liable in their capacity as members for all or specified debts, obligations or liabilities of the company if:
>
> > (1) A provision to that effect is contained in the articles of organization; and
> >
> > (2) A member so liable has consented in writing to the adoption of the provision or to be bound by the provision.

W.Va. Code § 31B–3–303. The language of this provision is unambiguous insofar as it declares that, with the exception noted in subsection (c), "[a] member or manager is not personally liable for a debt, obligation or liability of the company *solely by reason of being or acting as a member or manager.*" The key language relevant to the issue presented in the instant action, which is italicized in the foregoing quote, proscribes liability "*solely* by reason of being or acting as a member or manager." By proscribing liability on the *sole* basis of being a member or manager of an LLC, the Legislature implicitly has left intact the prospect of an LLC member or manager being liable on grounds that are not based solely on a person's status as a member or manager of an LLC. Our reasoning is supported by the maxim *expressio unius est exclusio alterius:* "In the interpretation of statutory provisions the familiar maxim *expressio unius est exclusio alterius,* the express mention of one thing implies the exclusion of another, applies."). . . . Accordingly, we hold that W. Va.Code § 31B–3–303 permits the equitable remedy of piercing the veil to be asserted against a West Virginia Limited Liability Company. * * *

* * * Furthermore, to pierce the veil of a limited liability company in order to impose personal liability on its member(s) or manager(s), it must be established that (1) there exists such unity of interest and ownership that the separate personalities of the business and of the individual member(s) or managers(s) no longer exist and (2) fraud, injustice or an inequitable result would occur if the veil is not pierced. This is a fact driven analysis that must be applied on a case-by-case basis, and, pursuant to W. Va.Code § 31B–3–303(b), the failure of a limited liability company to observe the usual company formalities or requirements relating to the exercise of its company powers or management of its business may not be a ground for imposing personal liability on the member(s) or manager(s) of the company.

Certified Question Answered.

QUESTIONS

1. Do you understand the *"expressio unius"* maxim? Does the West Virginia court? Do you agree with the court's statement that "Our reasoning is supported by the maxim *expressio unius est exclisio alterius*"?

2. In this case, the amended complaint's veil piercing count against the members Paugh and Magnum alleged that Paugh and Magnum (1) as the only members of The Tavern, exercised full control over the company and actively participated in its management; (2) held themselves out to others as the owners of The Tavern d/b/a Bubba's Bar and Grill; (3) held themselves out as personally responsible for the debts of the company; (4) commingled personal funds with those of the company; (5) used the company to conduct personal business; (6) used the company as a conduit to procure business and services for related entities; (7) failed to adhere to legal formalities necessary to maintain limited liability company status; (8) diverted the company's assets to their own benefit and use; (9) failed to maintain records of the company's corporate and business activities; (10) failed to insure the company and left it grossly undercapitalized for the reasonable risks of owning and operating a bar; and (11) operated the company as a mere alter ego of themselves. Which of these allegations would you omit? What does (11) add?

3. Why didn't we considering piercing the veil in the chapter on partnerships? In the chapter on limited partnerships?

c. Managers' and Members' Liability for Breach of Fiduciary Duties

i. The Basic Duties

In addition to the members' contractual obligation to make contributions to the limited liability company as in the *Racing Fund Investment* case, members of LLCs that are member-managed and managers of limited liability companies that are manager-managed also owe the company fiduciary duties. Debra Hatter and Rikiya Thomas, "BigLaw" lawyers, provide this overview of the fiduciary duties of managers and members of LLC.

> "It is well-settled within most jurisdictions that fiduciary duties are owed by managers in a manager-managed LLC and members in a member-managed LLC. However, it is often unclear what duties are actually owed. Under the Uniform Limited Liability Company Act (ULLCA), these fiduciary duties normally include duties of loyalty and care similar to those found in partnerships. In Delaware, absent a contrary provision in the operating agreement, managers owe traditional fiduciary duties of loyalty and care to the members. Similarly, in Delaware, member-managers have been held to owe the same fiduciary duties required by managers within a manager-managed entity.... [I]n ... Delaware ..., courts have applied corporate principles when addressing the issue of fiduciary duties of managers and member-managers and have held these parties to the same standards as directors and officers."[*]

As the next case—especially the footnotes in the next case—teaches us (1) the existence of a manager or member's fiduciary duties also depends on the language of the state's limited liability company act and the language of the company's operating agreement and (2) a plaintiff's success in a breach of fiduciary duty case requires that the plaintiff prove more than simply the existence of a fiduciary duty.

TOUCH OF ITALY SALUMERIA & PASTICCERIA, LLC v. BASCIO

Delaware Chancery Court, 2014
2014 WL 108895

MEMORANDUM OPINION. GLASSCOCK, VICE CHANCELLOR. A lie can be an insidious thing. It can destroy friendships and business

---

[*] Debra Hatter & Rikiya Thomas, *Swimming in Unsettled Waters: Fiduciary Duties and Limited Liability Companies*, 49 HOUSTON LAWYER 22, 24 (July–August 2011).

relationships. It can also be the basis for a successful lawsuit, where it is in aid of fraud or conceals actionable wrongdoing. But sometimes a lie, no matter how morally problematic, is just a lie. This case, as pled, involves such a lie.

In 2009, several individuals formed an LLC, Touch of Italy Salumeria & Pasticceria,* [1] LLC ("Touch of Italy") which operates a specialty Italian grocery in Rehoboth Beach. One member, Robert Ciprietti, provided cash in exchange for his membership; at least one other member, Louis Bascio a defendant here, provided business goodwill and sweat equity. The business was successful, and an additional member entered, while others left. Eventually, Louis decided to leave the business. He gave notice, as specified in the LLC agreement, and withdrew as a member on December 15, 2012.

The lie alleged is this: Louis told the other members that he was moving to Pennsylvania, perhaps to open a business there. Although he told them he would not compete with Touch of Italy after his withdrawal, ten weeks later Louis and his brother, Frank Bascio, also a defendant here, formed their own LLC, Bascio Bros. Italy, LLC ("Bascio Bros."), which then opened a competing Italian grocery, doing business as Frank and Louie's Italian Store ("Frank and Louie's"). Frank and Louie's is located on the same block in Rehoboth Beach as Touch of Italy. Louis' former partners, understandably, feel betrayed. Those partners, however, chose to associate themselves with Louis under an LLC agreement. Delaware's law with respect to LLCs, as this Court has repeatedly noted, is explicitly contrarian; it allows those associating under this business format to structure their relationship in the way they believe best suits them and their business. This particular LLC agreement was written to allow members to readily withdraw, without triggering any obligation to forgo competition thereafter. Thus, Louis faced no legal impediment to withdrawing and opening Frank and Louie's as a competing grocery. Given this fact, had his fellow members known his true intentions—that is, had the lie as alleged never occurred—they would have been contractually powerless to change the course of events. The Plaintiffs can point to no acts or omissions of their own, taken in reliance on the lie. They allege that Louis breached fiduciary duties, but fail to allege a single act undertaken before his withdrawal, other than the lie, in furtherance of his competing business or in derogation of any duty to Touch of Italy. In reality, this complaint is an attempt to achieve a result—restraint on post-withdrawal competition—that the members could have but chose not to forestall by contract. The Defendants have

---

* [1] According to the website "wiktionary," a salumeria is an Italian delicatessen; literally, a shop specializing in salami. *Salumeria*, WIKTIONARY, *http://en.wiktionary.org/wiki/ salumeria*. A *pasticceria* is an Italian cake shop. *Pasticceria*, WIKTIONARY, http://en.wiktionary. org/ wiki/pasticceria.

moved to dismiss the Plaintiffs' Verified Complaint for Permanent Mandatory Injunction (the "Complaint"). For the reasons below, the Complaint fails to state a claim, and must be dismissed. * * *

The Plaintiffs allege in Count VII of their Complaint that Louis "breached his fiduciary duties . . . by engaging in the willful, wrongful and bad faith conduct recited in [their Complaint]," including "in making arrangements for opening a competing business while he was still employed in and by Touch of Italy." The Complaint does not identify the source of the fiduciary obligations it implies that Louis owes or owed to Touch of Italy. In their Answering Brief, the Plaintiffs point to the provision in Section 11 of the Amended LLC Agreement, providing that "[a]ll the members/managers shall be faithful to the company in all transactions relating to the company." That provision goes on to limit members' unilateral rights to enter certain transactions on behalf of Touch of Italy, and is not pertinent here. I assume, for purposes of this Motion, that Louis owed fiduciary duties to Touch of Italy and its members during his membership;* **[48]** nonetheless, the Plaintiffs have failed to state a claim for the reasons that follow.

Although the Plaintiffs allege that Louis was "planning" to open a competing business while he was a member of Touch of Italy, the Complaint is devoid of any factual allegations of acts in support of that intention. Bascio Bros. was not formed until February 2013, more than ten weeks after Louis left Touch of Italy. In fact, the Complaint indicates that Louis' efforts on behalf of Touch of Italy were satisfactory, and the business successful, up to the point when he announced his withdrawal from the LLC. "[A] complaint alleging breach of fiduciary duty must plead facts supporting an inference of breach, not simply a conclusion to that effect." Further, to the extent that the Plaintiffs allege that Louis' conduct following his departure from Touch of Italy breached fiduciary duties owed to his *former* partners, this claim also fails, as, generally, no such duties exist once the fiduciary relationship has ended. As the Plaintiffs have not alleged any actionable conduct by Louis during his time of membership and employment at Touch of Italy, the Plaintiffs have not alleged facts upon which it is conceivable they could be entitled to relief. Count VII must therefore be dismissed. * * *

---

*   **[48]** The Delaware LLC Act, Chapter 18 of Title 6 of the Delaware Code (the "LLC Act"), provides, "[t]o the extent that, at law or in equity, a member . . . has duties (including fiduciary duties) to a limited liability company or to another member or manager or to another person that is a party to or is otherwise bound by a limited liability company agreement, the member's . . . duties may be expanded or restricted or eliminated by provisions in the limited liability company agreement. . . ." 6 *Del. C.* § 18–1101(c). The LLC Agreement among the parties here does not limit the fiduciary duties owed to fellow members or to the LLC. Moreover, this Agreement provides that, ". . . to the extent that this agreement is silent as to any matter to which the Delaware [LLC] Act speaks, then the provisions of the Delaware [LLC] Act shall govern this company." LLC Agmt. § 30. Pursuant to that Act, "[i]n any case not provided for in this chapter, the rules of law and equity, including the rules of law and equity relating to fiduciary duties . . . shall govern." 6 *Del. C.* § 18–1104.

There are undoubtedly sound business reasons to include—as there are to eschew—covenants not to compete in or in connection with LLC agreements. Nonetheless, the parties failed to incorporate such a covenant in the Amended LLC Agreement at issue here. For the reasons above, the Plaintiffs' attempt to replicate the effect of such a provision post hoc by alleging breaches of contract, the implied covenant of good faith and fair dealing, and fiduciary duties, must fail here. * * *

QUESTIONS

1.   Do we know whether Louis told a lie?

PICTURE OF BASCIO BROTHERS CROPPED AT THE WAIST SO THAT YOU CAN'T SEE WHETHER LOUIS'S PANTS ARE INDEED ON FIRE

2.   To recover for fraud and misrepresentation, does the plaintiff have to prove more than that the defendant told a lie?

3.   To recover for a member's breach of a fiduciary duty to a limited liability company, does the plaintiff have to prove more than that the defendant told a lie? That the defendant opened a competing business after he withdrew from the limited liability company?

4.   Do we (i.e. you) know whether a member of a Delaware limited liability company owes a fiduciary duty to the company?

ii. Role of the Operating Agreement in Creating/Limiting Fiduciary Duties

Footnote 48 of the *Touch of Italy* case contains an excerpt from Delaware § 18–1101(c). Compare Delaware § 18–1101(c), the Delaware statute on contractually limiting the fiduciary duties of managers and members—"To the extent that, at law or in equity, a member or manager or other person has duties (including fiduciary duties) to a limited liability company or to another member or manager or to another person that is a party to or is otherwise bound by a limited liability company agreement, the member's or manager's or other person's duties may be expanded or restricted or eliminated by provisions in the limited liability company agreement; provided, that the limited liability company agreement may not eliminate the implied contractual covenant of good faith and fair dealing." with Delaware § 102(b)(7), the Delaware provision on contractually limiting the fiduciary duties of directors—"A provision eliminating or limiting the personal liability of a director to the corporation or its stockholders for monetary damages for breach of fiduciary duty as a director, provided that such provision shall not eliminate or limit the liability of a director: (i) For any breach of the director's duty of loyalty to the corporation or its stockholders; (ii) for acts or omissions not in good faith or which involve intentional misconduct or a knowing violation of law; (iii) under § 174 of this title; or (iv) for any transaction from which the director derived an improper personal benefit. No such provision shall eliminate or limit the liability of a director for any act or omission occurring prior to the date when such provision becomes effective. All references in this paragraph to a director shall also be deemed to refer to such other person or persons, if any, who, pursuant to a provision of the certificate of incorporation in accordance with § 141(a) of this title, exercise or perform any of the powers or duties otherwise conferred or imposed upon the board of directors by this title."

QUESTIONS

1.   Can a Delaware LLC's operating agreement more completely limit the duties of a manager of a Delaware LLC than a Delaware corporation's certificate of incorporation can limit the duties of a director of a Delaware corporation?

2.   Consider this hypothetical posed at the beginning of an article critical of Delaware § 18–1101(c):

> Imagine that Thomas and Easton each owned 50% of T & E Boating, LLC, a limited liability company (LLC) that sold small boats on the shoreline of Connecticut. Although Thomas and Easton had intended to sign an LLC operating agreement, they never got around to it. The business was run quite informally, with Thomas as the manager and Easton involved in management matters only

occasionally. Over the next 20 years, the company acquired a small marina. Then, unbeknownst to Thomas, Easton was contacted by Christal & Krafters, Inc., which offered to buy the business for $8,000,000. Almost immediately thereafter, knowing that Thomas was planning to re-locate, Easton offered to buy out Thomas' LLC interest for $500,000. Two weeks after buying out Thomas, Easton sold the LLC to Christal and Krafters, Inc. for $8,000,000.

* * * What duty of disclosure, if any, should LLC members and investors owe, absent an LLC operating agreement? Should Thomas be able to sue Easton to effectively obtain 50% of the sales price received for the business? Should the parties have been allowed to enter into an operating agreement that eliminated all fiduciary duties?*

D. WHAT IS THE "END GAME" FOR MEMBERS OF A LIMITED LIABILITY COMPANY?

1. LLC MEMBER'S SALE OF HER INTEREST TO A THIRD PARTY

The most important limitation on an LLC member's making money by selling her interest for more than she paid for it is imposed by the market, not by the legislature, the courts or even the operating agreement. It is usually difficult to find a buyer for a minority interest in a small business or even a minority interest in large business that has relatively few owners.

Even if a member of a limited liability company is able to find a buyer for her interest, her ability to sell may be limited by statute or by the operating agreement or by both. Recall what you learned about a partner's sale of her interest. Unlike a shareholder, but like a partner, in many states, an LLC member is barred by statute from selling her full ownership interest to an outsider. For example, Delaware § 18–702 provides in part:

> (a) A limited liability company interest is assignable in whole or in part except as provided in a limited liability company agreement. The assignee of a member's limited liability company interest shall have no right to participate in the management of the business and affairs of a limited liability company except as provided in a limited liability company agreement or, unless otherwise provided in the limited liability company agreement, upon the affirmative vote or written consent of all members of the limited liability company.

---

*   Sandra K. Miller, *The Best of Both Worlds: Default Fiduciary Duties and Contractual Freedom*, 39 J. CORP.L. 295, 296–7 (2014).

(b) Unless otherwise provided in a limited liability company agreement:

> (1) An assignment of a limited liability company interest does not entitle the assignee to become or to exercise any rights or powers of a member;

> (2) An assignment of a limited liability company interest entitles the assignee to share in such profits and losses, to receive such distribution or distributions, and to receive such allocation of income, gain, loss, deduction, or credit or similar item to which the assignor was entitled, to the extent assigned.

See also ULLCA §§ 502, 503.*

Notice that these statutory restrictions are "default rules." The operating agreement can otherwise provide.

PROBLEM

Propp, Agee and Capel have decided to organize Bubba's Burritos, LLC as a Delaware limited liability company. You are drafting the operating agreement. What if anything should the operating agreement provide with respect to sales of ownership interests by members to third parties? Would your answer be different if they were organizing Bubba's Hedge Fund, LLC in Delaware?

2. MEMBER'S DISSOCIATION

Because of the market constraints and legal restrictions on a member's sale of her ownership interest in a limited liability company to an outsider, the question of whether a member of an LLC can compel the company to purchase her ownership interest is often important.

Recall a partner's power to compel the partnership to purchase her ownership interest by invoking the RUPA concept of dissociation. We hope that you don't recall a shareholder's power to compel the corporation to purchase her shares by invoking the concept of dissociation. There is no corporate law equivalent of dissociation.

---

* Remember the tax history of LLC's? If not, read on. "To appreciate the statutory provisions, it is necessary to have an historical perspective. A major reason for organizing an LLC is to avoid an entity level tax and obtain pass-through, or partnership, tax treatment as opposed to corporate tax treatment. At one point, the issue of whether the IRS would recognize that an LLC could be taxed as a partnership hinged upon the extent to which the entity exhibited certain characteristics that are common to corporations, but are usually absent from partnerships. * * *

Consequently, the first generation of LLC statutes was designed to facilitate pass-through tax treatment by having default provisions that would negate transferability . . ." Charles W. Murdock, *Limited Liability Companies in the Decade of the 1990's: Legislative and Case Law Developments and Their Implications for the Future*, 56 BUS. LAW. 499, 548–49 (2001).

SEC. D

WHAT IS THE "END GAME" FOR MEMBERS OF A
LIMITED LIABILITY COMPANY?

555

In some states, LLC members have the same dissociation rights as partners. In other states, LLC members, like shareholders, have no dissociation rights. For example, the Delaware LLC statute does not even use the term "dissociation."

Most LLC statutes use the term "dissociation," but use the term different from RUPA. Consider the California provision:

> Unless the articles of organization or written operating agreement provides otherwise, a person's dissociation does not entitle the person to a distribution, and, beginning on the date of dissociation, the dissociated person shall have only the right of a transferee of a transferable interest with respect to that person's interest in the limited liability company, and then only with respect to distributions, if any, to which a transferee is entitled under the operating agreement.[*]

The Illinois LLC statue takes a different approach to dissociation. Like RUPA, it requires the company to buy the interest of a dissociating owner but limits the right and power to dissociate to members of member-managed LLCs:

> A member of a member-managed company has the power to dissociate from a company at any time, rightfully or wrongfully, by express will under subdivision (1) of Section 35–45. If an operating agreement does not specify in writing the time or the events upon the happening of which a member of a manager-managed company may dissociate, a member does not have the power, rightfully or wrongfully, to dissociate from the company before the dissolution and winding up of the company.[†]

QUESTIONS

1.   Compare the California, Delaware and Illinois approaches to dissociation. What are the practical differences if any? Do you need to at least glance at the rest of the California, Delaware and Illinois LLC statutes to answer the question?

2.   What are the practical differences, if any, of a statutory right to compel the LLC to purchase your interest on dissociating and a contractual right to compel the LLC to purchase your interest on invoking a clause in a buy-sell agreement?

---

[*]   CALIFORNIA CORPORATIONS CODE § 17704.04(b).

[†]   805 ILCS 180/35–50.

E. WHAT ARE THE POSSIBLE END GAMES FOR THE LLC ITSELF?

1. UNHAPPY ENDINGS

LLC statutes, like partnership statutes and corporation statutes, contain dissolution provisions. Dissolution under partnership statutes and corporation statutes is more the beginning of the end than the actual end of the business. And the events triggering dissolution under the various statutes generally fit into three categories:

(1) vote of the shareholders

(2) occurrence of event stated in the operating agreement

(3) judicial order

Most of the reported cases arise under (3). The Delaware provision on judicial dissolution § 18–802. is set out below: "On application by or for a member or manager the Court of Chancery may decree dissolution of a limited liability company whenever it is not reasonably practicable to carry on the business in conformity with a limited liability company agreement."

A partner in a Delaware "Biglaw" law firm recently offered this assessment of the Delaware statute:

At first blush, the statutory exit mechanism provided in Section 18–802 of the DLLCA may appear to be a reasonable option for parties to rely upon instead of having the difficult discussion at the formation of the LLC about how members may exit the LLC. But the case law applying and interpreting Section 18–802 of the DLLCA makes clear that such reliance may not be justified. The Delaware Court of Chancery has stated that the remedy of judicial dissolution is an extreme remedy that should be used sparingly, and even if a petitioner is successful in proving the requisite elements under Section 18–802 of the DLLCA, as described by the court, it is still within the court's discretion to grant judicial dissolution.

Under Section 18–802 of the DLLCA, the case law shows that the Delaware Court of Chancery will grant judicial dissolution if either (1) the purpose for which the LLC was created no longer exists or can no longer be achieved (i.e., "frustration of purpose") or (2) a deadlock exists. With respect to a petition for judicial dissolution due to "frustration of purpose," the petitioner will need to show that it is not reasonably practicable for the LLC to carry on its business in conformity with its LLC Agreement because the defined purpose of the LLC can no longer be fulfilled. With respect to a judicial dissolution due to a deadlock, the Delaware Court of Chancery has found that the following factors are relevant (although no one factor is dispositive): (1) is there a deadlock? (2) does the governing document provide a means of navigating around the deadlock?, and (3) whether due to the LLC's financial position, is there still a business to operate? Thus, due to the difficulty of obtaining a decree of judicial dissolution, Section 18–802 of the DLLCA may offer cold comfort to a member that wants to exit an LLC. The expense of a full trial litigating judicial dissolution will not be attractive to a member, particularly when the outcome—even if the member is successful in proving the "requisite elements" required under Section 18–802 of the DLLCA—is within the Court of Chancery's broad discretion. Thus, this article recommends that counsel and his or her client consider including an appropriate exit mechanism in a multi-member LLC Agreement. A well drafted exit mechanism will save the parties money and time, should one of the parties wish to withdraw from the LLC.

Tarik J. Haskins, *Exit Stage Left: Getting Out of Your Limited Liability Company,* 2013-Jul Bus. L.Today 1.

QUESTIONS

1.   What is the statutory basis for a court's denying judicial dissolution even if the movant is successful in proving the "requisite elements required under Section 18–802 of the DLLCA"? Why would a court so decide?

2.   The Delaware lawyer's article quoted from above urges a "well drafted exit mechanism." What would be a "well drafted exit mechanism"? How about the "Shotgun mechanism" suggested in a recent article by a law professor and an economics professor?

[W]e argue that Shotgun mechanisms, where the court mandates one owner to name a single buy-sell price and compels the other owner to either buy or sell shares at that named price, should play a larger role in the judicial resolution of business deadlock. These mechanisms represent an application of the classic cake-cutting procedure: one member cuts the cake (names a price) and the other member chooses his or her piece (buys or sells shares at that price). Since the party proposing the offer may end up either buying or selling shares, the party has an incentive to identify and name a fair price. Thus, equitable outcomes are achieved without the administration costs and delays associated with external appraisers and auctions.[*]

---

[*]   Claudia M. Landeo & Kathryn E.Spier, *Shotguns and Deadlocks*, 31 YALE J. ON REG. 143, 146–7 (2014).

2.   HAPPY ENDINGS

The ending for some LLC's is a sale of its assets for a profit. The ending for other LLC's is a merger into an even more profitable LLC or corporation.

We understand that mergers of LLC's raise questions such as: should the members opposed to the merger have appraisal rights. And in the merger of and LLC and a corporation, which law governs the merger—the LLC statute or the corporation statute?* We need to leave some questions for the prof who teaches Mergers and Acquisitions at your law school.

And, we understand that not every sale of assets or merger results in a profit for the owners. It's just, like Emmy Lou Harris and countless YouTube wannabes† . . . "We believe in happy endings."‡

THE END

---

* 1 Ribstein and Keatinge on Ltd. Liab. Cos. § 11:13 provides a very helpful discussion of these questions.

† https://www.youtube.com/watch?v=ZEAsggx8etg.

‡ E.g., *Trio GaJol Synger; We Believe In Happy Endings*, YouTube, (Jun. 4, 2013), https://www.youtube.com/watch?v=62qnqkTiJTg.

INDEX

References are to Pages